Longman Annotated English Poets

GENERAL EDITORS: F. W. BATESON AND JOHN BARNARD

Pippa Passes.

New Year's Day at Asolo in the Trevisan. A large, mean, airy chamber. A girl,
Pippa, from the silk-mills, springing out of bed —

'Day!
Faster and more fast,
O'er night's brim, day boils at last;
Boils, pure gold, o'er the cloud-cup's brim
Where spurting and suppressed it lay —
For not a froth-flake touched the rim
Of yonder gap in the solid gray
Of the eastern cloud, an hour away;
But forth one wavelet, then another, curled,
Till the whole sunrise, not to be suppressed,
Rose, reddened, and its seething breast
Flickered in bounds, grew gold, then overflowed the world.

Oh, Day, if I squander a wavelet of thee,
A mite of my twelve-hours' treasure,
The least of thy gazes or glances,
(Be they grants thou art bound to, or gifts above measure)
One of thy choices, one of thy chances,
(Be they tasks God imposed thee, or freaks at thy pleasure)
— My Day, if I squander such labour or leisure,
Then shame fall on Asolo, mischief on me!

The first lines of Browning's fair copy MS of the revised Introduction to
Pippa Passes (*Poems*, 1849). Reproduced by kind permission of the Harry
Ransom Humanities Research Center, the University of Texas at Austin.

THE POEMS OF

BROWNING

EDITED BY

JOHN WOOLFORD

AND

DANIEL KARLIN

– Volume II –
1841–1846

LONGMAN
London and New York

Longman Group UK Limited
Longman House, Burnt Mill, Harlow,
Essex CM20 2JE, England
and Associated Companies throughout the world.

Published in the United States by Longman Publishing Group, New York

© Longman Group UK Limited 1991

British Library Cataloguing in Publication Data
Browning, Robert, *1812–1889*
    The poems of Browning. — (Longman annotated English poets).
    Vol. II, 1841–1846
    I. Title II. Woolford, John *1946–* III. Karlin, Daniel
    821.8
    ISBN 0–582–06399–X

Library of Congress Cataloging-in-Publication Data
Browning, Robert, 1812–1889.
    [Poems. Selections]
    The poems of Browning / edited by John Woolford and Daniel Karlin.
        p.   cm. — (Longman annotated English poets)
    Includes bibliographical references (p.   ) and index.
    Contents: v. 1. 1826–1840 — v. 2. 1841–1846.
    ISBN 0–582–48100–7 (v. 1). — ISBN 0–582–06399–X (v. 2)
    I. Woolford, John. II. Karlin, Daniel, 1953– . III. Title.
IV. Series.
PR4203.W66 1991
821'.8—dc20   90–6605
                                                                  CIP

Typeset in Linotron 202 Bembo Roman 10/10

Printed in Great Britain at The Bath Press, Avon.

Contents

Editorial Note to Volume II

Volume II contains Browning's poems from 1841 to 1846, and three dramatic works: *Pippa Passes*, *Luria*, and *A Soul's Tragedy*. We have omitted four verse plays: *King Victor and King Charles* (1842), *The Return of the Druses* (1842), *A Blot in the 'Scutcheon* (1843), and *Colombe's Birthday* (1844). Appendix C (p. 476) contains Browning's essay on Chatterton; his essay on Shelley (1852) will appear as an appendix to volume III.

We have not included three works which have been ascribed to Browning, and which would have appeared in this volume of the edition:

(a) The unfinished poem known as *Aeschylus' Soliloquy*, thought to be Browning's because an MS in the British Library is in his hand; this MS is in fact a copy of a draft by Elizabeth Barrett Browning: see *Collections* D1159, p. 353.

(b) Ten translations from Anacreon, ascribed to Browning in *Penguin* on the basis of an MS in his hand in the Houghton Library at Harvard University. But Browning himself printed a version of the seventh poem, with the title *Paraphrase on Anacreon: Ode to the Swallow*, in his edition of Elizabeth Barrett Browning's *Last Poems* (1862), and MSS in her hand exist for this and two others; the remaining seven are also hers. See *Collections* D1170-3, 1175-6, 1180-7, pp. 354-5.

(c) The unfinished poem beginning 'She was fifteen—had great eyes', an MS of which in Browning's hand is in the Pierpont Morgan Library, New York. This, too, is a copy of an MS by Elizabeth Barrett Browning: see *Collections* D845-6, p. 328.

The Pierpont Morgan Library, New York, has two copies of volume v of the *Poetical Works* of 1868, both dated 1872 (a reprint of *1870*, the first revised reissue of *1868*: see our Introduction, I xix). Both copies have corrections and revisions by B., affecting (of the works included in volume II of our edition) *Artemis Prologuizes*, *A Soul's Tragedy*, and *Luria*. The changes in the first copy (*1872 Morgan*[1]) are few in number, and seem to have been intended for *1875* (a further revised reissue of *1868*); those in the second (*1872 Morgan*[2]) are more extensive and were intended for the *Poetical Works* of 1888-9. We record only substantive readings which were not adopted in *1875* and *1888* respectively.

Acknowledgements

We have received generous assistance in the preparation of this edition from the British Academy; King's College, Cambridge; King's College, London; and the University of London (Central Research Fund).

We are grateful to the following libraries, institutions, and individuals for permission to reproduce material in their possession or for which they own copyright: the Armstrong Browning Library, Baylor University; the Beinecke Library, Yale University; the Berg Collection, New York Public Library; the Boston Public Library; Brigham Young University; the British Library; the Isabella Stewart Gardner Museum, Boston; the Houghton Library, Harvard University; the Widener Library, Harvard University; the Huntington Library; the Sterling Library, University of London; Mr John Murray; the Carl H. Pforzheimer Library; the Pierpont Morgan Library; the Robert H. Taylor Collection, Princeton University; the Pushkin Academy, Leningrad; the John Rylands Library; the George Arents Research Library, Syracuse University; the Harry Ransom Humanities Research Center, University of Texas at Austin; Texas A & M University; the Alexander Turnbull Library, National Library of New Zealand; the Victoria and Albert Museum; Wellesley College Library.

We owe an especial debt of gratitude to Anne Anninger at Wellesley College, to Betty Coley at the Armstrong Browning Library, and to Philip Kelley.

For help of various kinds we are grateful to: Sylvia Adamson, Rosemary Ashton, Janet Bately, Edmund Baxter, Roy Bolton, Roger Brooks, Penny Bullock, Janet Fairweather, Mark Farrell, Philip Ford, Wendy Gibb, Greer I. Gilman, Michael Halls, Cathy Henderson, Jack Herring, Philip Horne, Rita Humphrey, Luba Hussel, Elizabeth Jackson, David Kastan, Sheila Kay, Scott Lewis, Michael Mason, Michael Meredith, Karl Miller, Laura Morgan, Eric Mottram, John North, Leonée Ormond, Pat O'Shea, Kenneth Palmer, Richard Proudfoot, the late Philip Radcliffe, Christopher Ricks, Adam Roberts, Gill Spraggs, Guilland Sutherland, John Sutherland, Helen Weston, John Whitley, Rosemary Whitley, Neil Williams, Henry Woudhuysen, Robert Zimmerman, and Roberta Zonghi.

The first General Editor of this series, F. W. Bateson, gave valuable guidance at the outset of the project; his successor, John Barnard, has been equally shrewd and attentive. The staff at Longman have seen the first two volumes through the press with unfailing care and skill. Our copy-editor, Roger Fallon, gave invaluable assistance at a crucial stage. For their resourcefulness and technical skill, the typesetters deserve our heartfelt thanks.

Abbreviations

The place of publication is London unless otherwise specified.

I. Browning's works

Sections 1 and 2 list only those short titles which consist of dates or initials. References to all other volumes and individual poems are either complete (e.g. *Pauline*, *Waring*) or use the first word or phrase of the title (e.g. *Pippa* for *Pippa Passes*, *Artemis* for *Artemis Prologuizes*), or of the first line where no title exists. These works can be identified in full from the complete Alphabetical List of Browning's works (Appendix D, p. 505). Indefinite articles, but not definite articles, are counted in short titles (e.g. *Patriot* for *The Patriot*, *A Blot* for *A Blot in the 'Scutcheon*). The apostrophe is ignored in short titles (e.g. *Bishop Blougram* for *Bishop Blougram's Apology*).

1. Collections and Selections issued in Browning's lifetime

B & P = *Bells and Pomegranates* (see Appendix B, II 000)

B & P BYU = B.'s copy of the one-volume *Bells and Pomegranates* (Brigham Young University)

B & P Domett = Alfred Domett's copy of *Bells and Pomegranates*, with some MS corrections by B. (Harry Ransom Humanities Research Center, University of Texas, Austin)

1849 = *Poems*, 2 vols.

1863 = *Poetical Works*, 3 vols.

1863² = *Selections from the Poetical Works*

1865 = *Poetical Works*, 3 vols.

1865² = *Selection* ('Moxon's Miniature Poets')

1868 = *Poetical Works*, 6 vols.

1870 = *Poetical Works*, 6 vols.

1872 = *Selections from the Poetical Works*

1875 = *Poetical Works*, 6 vols.

1880 = *Selections from the Poetical Works, Second Series*

1884 = *Selections from the Poetical Works*, 2 vols.

1888 = *Poetical Works*, 16 vols. (1888-9)

1889 = *Poetical Works*, 16 vols.

2. Single volumes issued in Browning's lifetime

CE & ED = *Christmas-Eve and Easter-Day* (1850)
DI¹ = *Dramatic Idyls* (1879; after the publication of the next item, re-titled *Dramatic Idyls, First Series*)
DI² = *Dramatic Idyls, Second Series* (1880)
DL = Dramatic Lyrics (1842)
DL 1st Proof = Corrected proof sheets of *Dramatic Lyrics* (Widener Library, Harvard)
DL 2nd Proof = Corrected proof sheets of *Dramatic Lyrics* (Widener Library, Harvard)
DP = *Dramatis Personae* (1864)
DP² = *Dramatis Personae,* 2nd ed. (1864)
DR & L = *Dramatic Romances and Lyrics* (1845)
L & AST = *Luria* and *A Soul's Tragedy* (1846)
LS & TPC = *La Saisiaz* and *The Two Poets of Croisic* (1878)
M & W = *Men and Women* (1855)

3. Subsequent editions

1894 = Vol. xvii of *1889*, consisting of *Asolando* and notes to the poems, ed. E. Berdoe
Centenary = *The Works of Robert Browning*, ed. F. G. Kenyon, 10 vols., 1912
Florentine = *The Complete Works of Robert Browning*, ed. C. Porter and H. A. Clarke, 12 vols., New York 1898
New Poems = *New Poems by Robert Browning and Elizabeth Barrett Browning,* ed. F. G. Kenyon, 1914
Ohio = *The Complete Works of Robert Browning,* gen. ed. R. A. King Jr, Ohio University Press 1969–
Oxford = *The Poetical Works of Robert Browning,* gen. ed. I. Jack, Oxford University Press 1983–
Penguin = *Robert Browning: The Poems,* ed. T. Pettigrew and T. J. Collins, 2 vols., Harmondsworth 1981

4. Prose

Chatterton = Review of R. H. Wilde, *Conjectures and Researches Concerning the Love Madness and Imprisonment of Torquato Tasso* (2 vols., New York 1842), in the *Foreign Quarterly Review* xxxix

(July 1842) 465-83; see Appendix C, p. 476.

Shelley = Introductory Essay in *Letters of Percy Bysshe Shelley,* 1852

5. Letters (incl. Elizabeth Barrett's)

American Friends = *Browning to His American Friends: Letters Between the Brownings, the Storys and James Russell Lowell 1841-1890,* ed. G. R. Hudson, 1965

B to Fields = I. Jack, 'Browning on *Sordello* and *Men and Women*: Unpublished Letters to James T. Fields', *HLQ* xlv no. 3 (Summer 1982) 185-99

B to Ruskin = Letter from Browning to Ruskin, in W. G. Collingwood, *Life and Work of John Ruskin* (1893) i 193-202

Correspondence = *The Brownings' Correspondence,* ed. P. Kelley and R. Hudson, Winfield 1984-

Dearest Isa = *Dearest Isa: Robert Browning's Letters to Isabella Blagden,* ed. E. C. McAleer, Austin 1951

EBB to Boyd = *Elizabeth Barrett to Mr Boyd,* ed. B. P. McCarthy, New Haven 1955

EBB to Henrietta = *Elizabeth Barrett Browning: Letters to Her Sister,* ed. L. Huxley, 1929

EBB to Horne = *Letters of Elizabeth Barrett Browning Addressed to Richard Hengist Horne,* ed. S. R. Townshend Mayer, 2 vols., 1877

EBB to MRM = *The Letters of Elizabeth Barrett Browning to Mary Russell Mitford 1836-1854,* ed. M. B. Raymond and M. R. Sullivan, 3 vols., Winfield 1983

EBB to Ogilvy = *Elizabeth Barrett Browning's Letters to Mrs David Ogilvy 1849-1861,* ed. P. N. Heydon and P. Kelley, New York 1973

George Barrett = *Letters of the Brownings to George Barrett,* ed. P. Landis and R. E. Freeman, Urbana 1958

Invisible Friends = *Invisible Friends: The Correspondence of Elizabeth Barrett Barrett and Benjamin Robert Haydon 1842-1845,* ed. W. B. Pope, Cambridge (Mass.) 1972

LH = *Letters of Robert Browning Collected by Thomas J. Wise,* ed. T. L. Hood, 1933

LK = *The Letters of Robert Browning and Elizabeth Barrett Barrett 1845-1846,* ed. E. Kintner, 2 vols., Cambridge (Mass.) 1969

Learned Lady = *Learned Lady: Letters from Robert Browning to Mrs Thomas Fitzgerald 1876-1889,* ed. E. C. McAleer, Cambridge (Mass.) 1966

Letters of EBB = *The Letters of Elizabeth Barrett Browning*, ed. F. G. Kenyon, 2 vols., 1897

Letters of RB and EBB = *The Letters of Robert Browning and Elizabeth Barrett Barrett 1845-1846* [ed. R. W. B. Browning], 2 vols., 1899

More Than Friend = *More Than Friend: The Letters of Robert Browning to Katharine de Kay Bronson*, ed. M. Meredith, Waco and Winfield, 1985

New Letters = *New Letters of Robert Browning*, ed. W. C. DeVane and K. L. Knickerbocker, 1951

RB & AD = F. G. Kenyon, *Robert Browning and Alfred Domett*, 1906

RB & JW = *Robert Browning and Julia Wedgwood: A Broken Friendship as Revealed in Their Letters*, ed. R. Curle, 1937

Rossetti = A. A. Adrian, 'The Browning—Rossetti Friendship: Some Unpublished Letters', *PMLA* lxxiii (1958) 538-44

Ruskin = D. J. De Laura, 'Ruskin and the Brownings: Twenty-five Unpublished Letters', *BJRL* liv (1972) 314-56

Tennyson = *The Brownings to the Tennysons: Letters from Robert Browning and Elizabeth Barrett Browning to Alfred, Emily, and Hallam Tennyson 1852-1889*, ed. T. J. Collins, Waco 1971 (BBI)

Trumpeter = *Browning's Trumpeter: The Correspondence of Robert Browning and Frederick J. Furnivall 1872-1889*, ed. W. S. Peterson, Washington DC 1979

Twenty-two Letters = *Twenty-two Unpublished Letters of Elizabeth Barrett Browning and Robert Browning Addressed to Henrietta and Arabella Moulton Barrett*, [ed. W. R. Benet], New York 1935

II. Periodicals

BBI = Baylor University Browning Interests
BIS = Browning Institute Studies
BJRL = Bulletin of the John Rylands Library
BNL = Browning Newsletter
BNYPL = Bulletin of the New York Public Library
BSN = Browning Society Notes
EC = Essays in Criticism
ER = Edinburgh Review
Hood's = Hood's Magazine and Comic Miscellany
HLQ = Huntington Library Quarterly
MLN = Modern Language Notes
MLQ = Modern Language Quarterly
MLR = Modern Language Review

MP = Modern Philology
MR = Monthly Repository
N & Q = Notes and Queries
PMLA = Publications of the Modern Language Association of America
QR = Quarterly Review
RES = Review of English Studies
SB = Studies in Bibliography
SBC = Studies in Browning and His Circle
SP = Studies in Philology
SR = Studies in Romanticism
TLS = Times Literary Supplement
UTQ = University of Toronto Quarterly
VNL = Victorian Newsletter
VP = Victorian Poetry
VS = Victorian Studies

III. Miscellaneous

ABL = Armstrong Browning Library, Baylor University, Waco, Texas
Allingham = *William Allingham's Diary*, ed. G. Grigson, 1967
Biographie = *Biographie Universelle*, 50 vols., Paris 1811-22
Bibliography = L. N. Broughton, C. S. Northrup, and R. B. Pearsall, *Robert Browning: A Bibliography 1830-1950*, Ithaca 1953 (Cornell Studies in English xxxix)
Bibliography² = W. S. Peterson, *Robert and Elizabeth Barrett Browning: An Annotated Bibliography 1951-1970*, New York 1974
BL = British Library
Bronson¹ = K. de Kay Bronson, 'Browning in Asolo', *Century Magazine* lix (Apr. 1900) 920-31; repr. *More than Friend* 127-45
Bronson² = K. de Kay Bronson, 'Browning in Venice', *Century Magazine* lxiii (Feb. 1902); repr. *More than Friend* 147-65
BSP = *The Browning Society's Papers* (1881-91)
CH = B. Litzinger and D. Smalley (eds.), *Browning: the Critical Heritage*, 1970
Checklist = P. Kelley and R. Hudson, *The Brownings' Correspondence: A Checklist*, New York 1978
Collections = P. Kelley and B. A. Coley, *The Browning Collections: A Reconstruction with Other Memorabilia*, Winfield 1984

Concordance = L. N. Broughton and B. F. Stelter, *A Concordance to the Poems of Robert Browning*, 2 vols., New York 1924-5

Cooke = G. W. Cooke, *A Guidebook to the Poetic and Dramatic Works of Robert Browning*, Boston 1891

Cyclopaedia = E. Berdoe, *The Browning Cyclopaedia*, 1892

DeVane *Handbook* = W. C. DeVane, *A Browning Handbook*, 2nd ed., New York 1955

DeVane *Parleyings* = W. C. DeVane, *Browning's Parleyings: The Autobiography of a Mind*, New Haven 1927

Domett *Diary* = *The Diary of Alfred Domett 1872-1885*, ed. E. A. Horsman, 1953

EB = *Encyclopedia Britannica* (1911)

EBB. = Elizabeth Barrett Barrett (Browning)

Griffin and Minchin = W. H. Griffin and H. C. Minchin, *The Life of Robert Browning*, 3rd ed., 1938

J. = Samuel Johnson, *A Dictionary of the English Language,* 1755

Lemprière = J. Lemprière, *A Classical Dictionary,* 12th ed., 1823

Maynard = J. Maynard, *Browning's Youth*, Cambridge (Mass.) 1977

Melchiori = B. Melchiori, *Browning's Poetry of Reticence*, Edinburgh 1968

Miller = B. Miller, *Robert Browning: A Portrait*, 1952

Murray = Murray's *Handbook for Travellers in Northern Italy*, 1842

Murray² = Murray's *Handbook for Travellers in Central Italy*, 1843

OED = *Oxford English Dictionary*

Orr *Handbook* = A. S. Orr, *A Handbook to the Works of Robert Browning*, 7th ed., 1896

Orr *Life* = A. S. Orr, *Life and Letters of Robert Browning*, 1871

PL = Milton, *Paradise Lost*

Sismondi *Hist.* = J. C. L. Simonde de Sismondi, *Histoire des Républiques Italiennes au Moyen-Age*, 16 vols., Paris 1826 vols. i-iii

Sismondi *Lit.* = J. C. L. Simonde de Sismondi, *De la Littérature du Midi de l'Europe,* 4 vols., Paris 1813, vol. i; we quote the translation by Thomas Roscoe, *Historical View of the Literature of the South of Europe,* 1823

Texas = Harry Ransom Humanities Research Center, University of Texas at Austin

Verci = Giambattista Verci, *Storia degli Ecelini*, 3 vols., Bassano 1779

Wanley = Nathaniel Wanley, *The Wonders of the Little World*, 1667

Wellesley MS = Critical notes by EBB. on B.'s poems and plays, 1845-6, in the Special Poetry Collection, Wellesley College Library, Wellesley, Massachusetts

THE POEMS

THE POEMS

19 Incident of the French Camp

First publ. *B & P* iii (*DL*), 26 Nov. 1842, with *Soliloquy*, which followed it, under the collective title *Camp and Cloister*; the poem was called 'Camp (*French*)'. Repr. *1849* (when it was separated from *Soliloquy* and given its present title), *1863* (when it was placed in *Romances*: see Appendix A, p. 464), *1863²*, *1868*, *1872*, *1888*. Our text is *1842*. DeVane (*Handbook* 111) notes the public interest in the return of Napoleon's body from St Helena and its reinterment in the Invalides in Paris, 15 Dec. 1840; in 1841 B.'s friend R. H. Horne published a biography of Napoleon (see below). We conjecturally date the poem to early 1841. DeVane has the date of reinterment as 1841, an error repeated by both *Penguin* and *Oxford*, and hence ascribes the poem to 1842.

Mrs Orr, probably quoting B., states that 'The story is true; but its actual hero was a man' (*Handbook* 300). No written source, however, has been found; the story may have circulated orally. The French army, pursuing the Austrians under the Archduke Charles, stormed Ratisbon (Regensburg) in Bavaria, 23 Apr. 1809, under the command of one of Napoleon's most devoted marshals, Jean Lannes (1769-1809), duc de Montebello. 'A breach was quickly effected in the walls; but the Austrians, crowding to the point of danger, poured so deadly a fire upon the assailants, that they began to slacken the attack. At this moment, Lannes, seizing a ladder, rushed forward, and fixed it against the wall, exclaiming,—"I will shew you that your general is still a grenadier." The wall was surmounted in an instant; the soldiers overbore all opposition, and the combat now raged in the streets of the town' (R. H. Horne, *Life of Napoleon* [2 vols., 1841] ii 121-2). The anecdote is also found in other popular lives of Napoleon, e.g. Sir Walter Scott's (1827) and Hazlitt's (1828-30). Cp. B.'s other messenger poems, *How They Brought the Good News* and *Pheidippides*. Napoleon is mentioned (disparagingly) in *Bishop Blougram* 436ff.; see also *Apparent Failure* 37-45. French and Spanish characteristics were again juxtaposed in the pairing of *Laboratory* and *Confessional* under the title *France and Spain* in *DR & L*.

I.

You know we French stormed Ratisbon:
    A mile or so away
On a little mound, Napoléon
    Stood on our storming-day;
5 With neck out-thrust, you fancy how,
    Legs wide, arms locked behind,
As if to balance the prone brow
    Oppressive with its mind.

¶19.3. *Napoléon*] Napoleon (*1863-88*).
7-8. *the prone brow* / *Oppressive with its mind*: 'the brow bent down by the

II.

Just as perhaps he mused "My plans
10   "That soar, to earth may fall
"Let once my army-leader Lannes
"Waver at yonder wall,"
Out 'twixt the battery-smokes there flew
A rider, bound on bound
15   Full-galloping; nor bridle drew
Until he reached the mound.

III.

Then off there flung in smiling joy,
And held himself erect
By just his horse's mane, a boy:
20   You hardly could suspect—
(So tight he kept his lips compressed
Scarce any blood came thro')
You looked twice ere you saw his breast
Was all but shot in two.

IV.

25   "Well," cried he, "Emperor, by God's grace
"We've got you Ratisbon!
"The Marshal's in the market-place,
"And you'll be there anon
"To see your flag-bird flap his vans
30   "Where I, to heart's desire,
"Perched him!" The Chief's eye flashed; his plans
Soared up again like fire.

V.

The Chief's eye flashed; but presently
Softened itself, as sheathes
35   A film the mother eagle's eye
When her bruised eaglet breathes:
"You're wounded!" "Nay," his soldier's pride
Touched to the quick, he said:
"I'm killed, Sire!" And, his Chief beside,
40   Smiling the boy fell dead.

---

burden of its intellect'. Cp. the description of Hildebrand in *Sordello* v 153-7.
29. The eagle, Napoleon's emblem, was set on the top of his battle standards:
the fluttering of the flag in the breeze represents the eagle flapping his 'vans'
(wings).
34-5. as sheathes / A film: 'as a film [of tears] covers'.

20 Pippa Passes

First publ. Apr. 1841, the first number of the *B & P* series (see Appendix B, p. 471). The song 'A king lived long ago' (iii 163-224) had appeared in *MR* n.s. ix (Nov. 1835) 707-8, with the title *The King* and signed 'Z.', B.'s usual signature for contributions to this journal (see I 326). Not repr. separately; repr. *1849, 1863, 1868, 1888* (when the opening passage was formally entitled

Title.] All other eds. have the subtitle 'a drama'. For the 'Advertisement' containing the dedication of the *B & P* series to Talfourd, see Appendix B, p. 472. The 'Advertisement' was dropped in *1849*, which has: 'I dedicate my best intentions, in this poem, most admiringly to the author of "Ion,"—most affectionately to Mr. Serjeant Talfourd. R.B.' Subsequent eds. follow *1849* but delete both occurrences of the word 'most' and add 'London 1841' at the end. The dedication of *Pippa* only, instead of the whole of *B & P*, to Talfourd from *1849* may simply reflect the separation of the series' individual works from *1849*; cp. the similar change in the dedication to Landor of *B & P* viii (*Luria* and *A Soul's Tragedy*) in *1846*, which in *1849* was applied to *Luria* alone. But the further change in the wording of the dedication probably reflects a cooling in B.'s regard for Talfourd. In *1888* the opening section becomes the 'Introduction' and the following sections 'parts', and the word 'Scene.' is supplied before each opening s.d.; other eds. follow *1841*. In *1888* there is also a list of 'Persons' on the verso of the dedication, as follows:

Pippa.
Ottima.
Sebald.
Foreign Students.
Gottlieb.
Schramm.
Jules.
Phene.
Austrian Police.
Bluphocks.
Luigi and his Mother.
Poor Girls.
Monsignor and his Attendants.

The policy behind this list is not obvious. Gottlieb and Schramm, members of the 'foreign students' group, get separate billing, but not the more important Lutwyche, perhaps because his speech-prefix is always '1 Student' (though he is named several times). Nor is the Intendant distinguished from the other 'Attendants' of Monsignor, despite his major role (none of the others speaks). Possibly the list was not compiled by B. himself, but by a publisher's reader/compositor who noticed that *Pippa* was the only play lacking a *dramatis personae*; even so, B. must have passed it in proof.

Introduction, the numbered sections called 'Part I', 'Part II' etc., and the word 'scene' was supplied before each opening s.d.). The Ottima—Sebald scene (i 1-276) was repr. in *1863²*. Four songs from the play were repr. in *1865²*: 'You'll love me yet!' (iii 297-308) and 'Give her but a least excuse to love me!' (ii 195-210), both with the title *Song from Pippa Passes*; 'A king lived long ago' (iii 163-224), with the title *Romance from Pippa Passes*, and, immediately following, 'The year's at the spring' (i 215-22), with the title *Song from the Same*. Two songs were repr. in *1872*: 'The year's at the spring' and 'Give her but a least excuse to love me!' Substantive variants from all these texts are given in the notes; because of its special interest, a complete collation is given of 'The year's at the spring', incl. the available extant MSS which B. wrote as autographs. Our text is *1841*; we refer in our notes to the untitled opening section as *Intro*.

B. did not offer the play to the actor-manager William Macready, who had produced *Strafford* (1837), and indeed seems deliberately to have avoided doing so. *Pippa* had been one of three dramas announced as 'nearly ready' when *Sordello* was publ. in 1840 (see below), and Macready had already rejected the other two, *King Victor* and *Return of the Druses* (both publ. after *Pippa*: see Appendix B, p. 473). B. wrote to Macready, enclosing his presentation copy of *Pippa*: 'all things considered, I had rather publish, that is print—this play . . . than take the chance of a stage success that would in the highest degree gratify and benefit me, at the *risk of* "mettre du gêne" [putting constraint] in a friendship which I trust I know how to appreciate, by compelling you once more to say "No", where you would willingly say "Yes"' (*Correspondence* v 37). The play has never been professionally produced, though there have been numerous amateur performances and readings. For B.'s request to Eliza Flower for music for the songs, see below, p. 9; there have been many settings of the songs, notably 'The year's at the spring' (53 listed in *Bibliography*). In 1908, D. W. Griffith made a film based on the play, which is usefully discussed by E. Giuliano and R. C. Kernan in 'Browning Without Words' (*BIS* xiv [1976] 125-59) and by F. A. Hilenski in 'D. W. Griffith's Film Version of *Pippa Passes*' (*Literature/Film Quarterly* iv [Winter 1976] 76-82).

Composition and revision

'Mr. Browning was walking alone, in a wood near Dulwich, when the image flashed upon him of someone walking thus alone through life; one apparently too obscure to leave a trace of his or her passage, yet exercising a lasting though unconscious influence at every step of it; and the image shaped itself into the little silk-winder of Asolo, Felippa, or Pippa' (Orr *Life* 55). B.'s letter to Mrs Bronson describing his first visit to Asolo confirms this account; see below, pp. 10-11. The exact date cannot be fixed, but it was some time after B. returned from his 1838 trip to Italy; a likely date would be late summer 1839, when B. had recently completed *Sordello* (note the anticipation of the figure of Pippa in *Sordello* vi 849ff.). The work was described as 'nearly ready' in an advertisement at the end of *Sordello* (publ. Mar. 1840). There is no external evidence of the order of composition of the various sections. *Oxford* mistakenly suggests that pt. i must have been written before June 1839, citing a reference to the Ottima—Sebald scene in 'A Familiar Epistle to Robert Browning' by Barry Cornwall (the pseudonym of B.'s friend B. W. Procter), publ. in *English Songs and Other Small Poems* (1851). However, this reference does not occur in the portion of the poem headed 'St. John's Wood, June, 1839', which covers only ll. 1-44; the remainder, in which the reference to *Pippa* does occur (ll. 149-50), comes in a section headed 'London, 1846-1850'. In a letter of 3 May 1845, B. told EBB.: 'nobody ever sees what I do till it is printed' (*LK* 55). DeVane conjectures that pt. iii was drafted first, during or shortly after B.'s return from his travels in 1838. In a letter to Julia Wedgwood dated 17 Oct. 1864 (*RB & JW* 102), B. recalls reading the 'revise' (corrected proof) of the poem on 'Good *Saturday*', i.e. 10 Apr., since Good Friday in 1841 fell on 9 Apr. (see also headnote to *Artemis*, p. 106).

B. made a few revs. in *B & P BYU*. The poem was extensively revised for *1849*. EBB. wrote to Mrs Jameson on 4 Feb. 1847: 'Robert is very busy with his new edition, and has been throwing so much golden light into "Pippa" that everybody shall see her "pass" properly .. yes, and *surpass*' (cited in *Miller* 136-7). For B.'s own comments on the *1849* revs., see headnote to *Paracelsus*, I 102. The revs. are generally concerned with clarifying, by addition and expansion, supposed obscurities in plot and psychology. The pattern is not uniform. Revision of *Intro* was so heavy (36 new lines and numerous other changes) that B. had to write out a fair copy instead of marking up a printed text: this MS, now at *Texas*, has no substantive differences from *1849*, but a few cancelled readings. The Jules—Phene scene (ii 1-243) was even more heavily revised (*1849* adds 97 lines and deletes 13), perhaps also by means of a new fair copy, though this has not survived. In proportion to its length, the Ottima—Sebald scene (i 1-276) was least affected. Punctuation was consistently overhauled through all eds., in keeping with B.'s usual practice. There were few verbal changes after *1849*. The Ottima—Sebald scene (i 1-276) shows some points of interest in *1863*[2]. It contains many of the *1863* revs., anticipates a number of *1868* readings, but retains some from *1849* (see e.g. ll. 143^144n.), and has spellings characteristic of *1849*, suggesting that it was produced after *1863* but using *1849* as copy-text. A few readings are unique to *1863*[2]: for the only substantive one, see l. 91n. In *1863*[2] the following note, probably not B.'s but presumably approved by him, appears at the beginning of the extract: 'Pippa is a girl from a silk-factory, whose "passing" the various persons of the play, at certain critical moments, in the course of her holiday, becomes, unconsciously to herself, a determining influence on the fortune of each'.

Form

The form of *Pippa Passes*—four entirely separate one-act plays with link-passages and parallel endings—is both its most celebrated and its least documented feature. The consensus is that it is unprecedented, though we have found one particular work which challenges this assumption: see below.

A. Symons describes it as containing 'elements of the play and elements of the masque' (*An Introduction to the Study of Browning*, 2nd ed. [1906] 52). These 'elements of the masque' are presumably Pippa's songs. In Elizabethan and Jacobean masques, songs are interspersed with the action, sometimes to mark the appearance of fresh characters; such songs remain, however, subordinate to dance and spectacle. See E. Welsford, *The Court Masque* (1927). Evidence that B. envisaged a musical dimension for the work is to be found in his letter to Eliza Flower of 9 Mar. 1840: 'By the way, you speak of "Pippa"—could we not make some arrangement about it,—the lyrics *want* your music—five or six in all—how say you?' (*Correspondence* iv 256). I. Jack (*Browning's Major Poetry* [Oxford 1973] 64-5) points out that the 'dramatic scene', the form into which each section of *Pippa* falls, was very popular in the 1820s and 1830s; cp. also Lamb's *Specimens of the English Dramatic Poets* (1808). D. Hair (*Browning's Experiments with Genre* [Toronto 1972] 51) compares Landor's short dramatic pieces (e.g. *Ippolito di Este*), a comparison anticipated by EBB. (see i 4-10n.). The abrupt and discontinuous structure of Goethe's *Faust* may also have influenced B.'s approach.

The particular work, almost certainly known to B., which anticipates in detail the form of *Pippa*, is John Fletcher and Nathan Field's *Four Plays or Moral Representations in One* (?1613-15), not previously cited as a source. This consists of four separate one-act plays (or 'Triumphs'), with a prologue and epilogue, and link-passages. There is a striking thematic parallelism: the four plays are concerned successively with adultery, marriage between social unequals, the killing of a tyrant, and wealth, which are the topics, and in that order, of the sections of *Pippa*. A further parallel is that in *Four Plays* each act concludes with music: a celebratory fanfare ('The Triumph of Honour') or celebratory song ('The Triumph of Time'); or, in 'The Triumph of Love' and 'The Triumph of Death', a dramatically integrated song. The latter are of especial interest because in both the song becomes a means of dramatic reversal or conversion, as in *Pippa*; though derived from the masque (E. M. Waith, in *The Pattern of Tragi-Comedy in Beaumont and Fletcher* [Yale 1952], comments that the playlets of *Four Plays* stand 'somewhere between masques and plays'), this feature goes well beyond the masque's non-dramatic use of song. B. may have been familiar with the 1811 ed. of the Beaumont—Fletcher canon, which included *Four Plays*; the probability that he had read *Four Plays* is enhanced by the fact that it was publ. in 1840 by Moxon, B.'s publisher, in a collection of the Beaumont and Fletcher plays (ed. G. Darley): in fact, it was the format of this and other of Moxon's reissues of Elizabethan and Jacobean plays that supplied the model for *B & P* (see Appendix B, p. 471).

These reissues, assuming that B. had not already encountered the works in their original form in his father's library or in the British Museum, would also have given B. access to other experimental blends of masque and drama, such as Ford and Dekker's *The Sun's Darling*; in 1840, another publisher issued the complete works of Middleton, and B. might have read Middleton and Rowley's *The World Tost at Tennis,* where again a sequence of disparate scenes is modulated by means of songs. Equally, however, a reading of *Four Plays* might have reminded B. of the more ambitious conflations of masque and play in the works of Shakespeare and Jonson, which *Pippa* frequently echoes. However, some features of *Pippa,* such as its dramatic naturalism and integrated structure, remain unprecedented; Welsford remarks of *Four Plays*: 'there is no just cause why these four plays should be joined together' (p. 287).

Time and Place
The date of the action is contemporary, but cannot be precisely determined. The clearest indicator would be the identity of the Austrian Emperor who is the target of the assassination plot in pt. iii. But up to *1865*, the corr. reissue of *1863* (see iii 14n.), B. gave no clue to his identity, and even in *1865* it is not certain whether the mention of 'old Franz' refers to a specific individual. Francis II (1768-1835), who became Emperor in 1804, had a pathological fear of liberal or reformist opposition, personally supervised a huge police network, and was responsible, with his chief minister Metternich, for the partition of Italy after the Napoleonic Wars into separate states under Austria's rule, or subject to its influence. This partition, effected by the Treaty of Vienna in 1816, created the Austrian kingdom of Lombardy-Venetia (which included Asolo). However, Francis II died (peacefully) three years before B. went to Italy and five years before the publication of the poem. His successor Ferdinand I (1793-1875), Emperor from 1835 until his abdication in 1848, was a kindly, weak-minded, and ineffectual ruler, with far less interest than Francis in the repression of dissent. In 1830, when he bore the title of King of Hungary, an army officer with a private grudge against him attempted to shoot him. This is the only assassination attempt recorded in the period against a member of the ruling house of Hapsburg.

The action takes place at Asolo, a small village in the 'Trevisan', the district surrounding the town of Treviso in northern Italy. B. called Asolo his 'very own of all Italian cities' (*Bronson*[1] 921) and it is of crucial importance in his career. He first saw it on his 1838 journey, as he wrote to Fanny Haworth on 24 July, after his return: 'I went to Trieste, then Venice—then thro' Treviso & Bassano to the mountains, delicious Asolo' (*Correspondence* iv 68). Asolo was certainly B.'s 'discovery'; it was not a noted tourist spot (*Murray* does not mention it, though it mentions nearby Possagno). A friend later recalled: 'One day Mr. Browning related an incident of a visit to Asolo when Austria was in possession of Venetian territory. He was asked by the chief dignitary of the town, "What have you come here for?" "To see the place." "Do you intend to stay?" "Yes; I hope to remain a few days." "But you have seen the place already; how can you possibly wish to stay longer?" "Because I find it so very beautiful." The Austrian looked at him in puzzled amazement, and then, after a moment's pause, signed the "permit of sojourn" required' (*Bronson*[1] 921). In a letter dated 10 June 1889, B. remembers his first impressions of Asolo: 'When I first found out Asolo I lodged at the main Hotel in the square, an old, large Inn of the most primitive kind. The ceiling of my bedroom was traversed by a huge crack, or rather cleft; "caused by the earthquake last year; the sky was as blue as could be, and we were all praying in the fields, expecting the town to tumble in." On the morning of my arrival I walked up to the Rocca; and, on returning to breakfast, I mentioned it to the landlady, whereon a respectable, middle-aged man, sitting by, said, "You have done what I, born here, never thought of doing." . . . I took long walks every day,—and carried away a lively recollection of the general beauty,— but I did not write a word of "Pippa Passes". The idea struck me when walking in an English wood, and I made use of the Italian memories. I used to dream of seeing Asolo in the distance and making vain attempts to reach it, repeatedly dreamed this for many a year, and when I found myself once more in Italy with my sister [1878], I went there straight from Verona. We found the old inn lying in ruins, a new one about to take its place . . . People told me the number of inhabitants had greatly increased, and things seemed generally more ordinary-life-like . . . When I got my impression Italy was new to me' (*Bronson*[1] 920). With this disillusion, cp. *Prologue* (*Asolando*).

Besides personal observation, B. could have consulted, in the British Museum, an anonymous pamphlet, *Notizie Istoriche e Geografiche appartenenti alla citta' di Asolo ed al suo territorio* (Belluno 1780). Prefacing a detailed description of the four 'quarters' of the district is a general eulogy of its beauty and fertility (pp. 5-6), and there are also notes on Asolo's only claim to historical importance, the residence there of Queen Caterina Cornaro of Cyprus (see ii 200n.).

There has been some debate as to whether the day on which the action of the poem takes place, 'New Year's Day', refers to the old date, 25 Mar., rather than the modern 1 Jan. In support of the former are Pippa's song 'The year's at the spring' (i 215-22), and Luigi's mention of the cuckoo (iii 137-9); as against this, Monsignor refers to the 'winter-weather' and implies that it is 'fourteen years and a month, all but three days' since his elder brother's death on 3 Dec. (iv 6, 30-1). Furthermore, in a letter of 8 Jan. 1885 offering belated New Year greetings B. wrote: 'New Year's Day was Pippa's Day, also' (to J. Dunnachie, *ABL MS*). Pippa's itinerary has been traced in J. Korg, *Browning and Italy* (Athens, Ohio, 1983) 41-2.

Sources, and parallels in B.

(1) *The character of Pippa.* B.'s characterization of Pippa draws upon a long and varied tradition of the representation of children as figures of innocence and intuition. The Romantic idealization of childhood in e.g. Rousseau and Wordsworth (esp. *The Solitary Reaper,* which celebrates the unconscious influence of a girl's singing), emerges strongly in *Pippa*. Marguerite in Goethe's *Faust*, who stands on the borderline between childhood innocence and adult experience, complicates this figure of the child by opening it to sexual and economic exploitation, a theme which Dickens had highlighted in *Oliver Twist* (1837-8) and *The Old Curiosity Shop* (1840). It was at this period, too, that agitation about child labour began to make itself seriously felt.

Pippa's orphan state, and the discovery that she is nobly born, are stock motifs of folktale and romance. The parallel with Shakespeare's romances, esp. *Pericles* and *The Winter's Tale*, is striking, and confirmed by other echoes. The second part ('The Triumph of Love') of Fletcher and Field's *Four Plays* (see *Form*) also involves this motif; so does T. N. Talfourd's *Ion*, where Ion proves to be the son of the tyrant Adrastus. A. E. Dubois ('Robert Browning, Dramatist', *SP* xxxiii [1936] 626-55) extends the parallel, concluding that Pippa is 'a female Ion in a play dedicated to Talfourd'.

Talfourd's *Ion* (1836) concerns the cleansing of Argos from plague by Ion, a foundling, who first persuades the tyrant Adrastus to meet the priests and people, and, when that fails, joins a conspiracy to kill him, knowing that only when Adrastus' line is extinct will Argos be saved. However, during the assassination of Adrastus (not by Ion), Ion learns that he himself is Adrastus' son. He accepts the succession, and publicly kills himself in order to end the curse. Like Ion, Pippa is an orphan; she is likewise involved, though unconsciously, in the redemption of her people; and she similarly proves to be the child of a potentate. Euripides' *Ion*, on which Talfourd drew, also contributed to B.'s conception of Pippa. In Euripides' play, Ion is the secret offspring of Apollo and Creusa, brought up, without his mother's knowledge, as a slave in the temple of Apollo at Delphi. She meanwhile has married Xuthus; because they are childless they have come to Delphi to find out if they will ever have children. The oracle tells Xuthus that the first person he meets will be his son; meeting Ion, he claims him as the child of himself and a former mistress. Learning of this, Creusa conspires to kill Ion to prevent his becoming Xuthus' heir, but the plot fails and the truth is revealed. The conspiracy in *Pippa* iv, in which Pippa is to be lured to prostitution and death in order to prevent her from coming into her rightful inheritance, has strong affinities with this story.

Pippa's role, and in particular the unconscious nature of her influence through song, may owe something to the central episode of conversion in St Augustine's *Confessions*. Augustine describes how, seated in a garden, he was 'weeping in the most bitter contrition of my heart, when lo! I heard from a neighbouring house a voice, as of boy or girl, I know not, chanting, and oft repeating, "Take up and read; Take up and read." Instantly my countenance altered, I began to think most intently, whether children were wont in any kind of play to sing such words: nor could I remember ever to have heard the like. So checking the torrent of my tears, I arose; interpreting it to be no other than a command from God, to open the book, and read the first chapter I should find' (transl. 1848, pp. 169-70). B.'s letter to Fanny Haworth of [?25] Apr. 1839 has some MS music, with the comment, 'What the children were singing last year in Venice, arm over neck' (*Correspondence* iv 138-9). The figure of Pippa strikingly anticipates that of Pompilia in *Ring*.

(2) *Episode 1: Ottima and Sebald* (i 1-276). No specific source has been identified. There are echoes of various Jacobean tragedies, particularly *Macbeth* and Middleton's *The Changeling*. Ottima has some affinity with Vittoria Corrombona, and Sebald with Bracchiano, in Webster's *The White Devil*. Their situation parallels that of Alice and her lover Mosby in *Arden of*

Faversham and, more strikingly, that in Donne's *Elegy* iv.

(3) *Episode 2: Jules and Phene* (i 277 to ii 243; see also iv 39-57).

(a) *The plot of the deceptive marriage.* F. E. Faverty, 'The Source of the Jules—Phene Episode in *Pippa Passes*' (*SP* xxxviii [1941] 97-105), compares Bulwer-Lytton's successful play *The Lady of Lyons*, produced by Macready in 1838. Claude Melnotte, low-born but cultured, is married by deception to the daughter of a wealthy merchant, Pauline, whom two rejected suitors wish to humiliate. Faverty argues that B. may also have consulted Bulwer-Lytton's acknowledged source, a translation by Helen Maria Williams of a French tale (*The History of Perourou*, 1803), because there the rejected suitors are artist-engravers, and six of them (as in B.) gather to witness the dénouement. B. certainly saw Bulwer-Lytton's play, and knew both him and Macready well. Note B.'s reversal of the sex of impostor and victim. Cp. also Victor Hugo's melodrama *Ruy Blas* (1838), where a servant poses as a nobleman at the Spanish court and gains the queen's affection as part of a revenge plot by the servant's master. The theme of 'queen-worship' was a favourite of B.'s: see ii 195-210n. To Faverty's list of the literary sources may be added the Malvolio plot in *Twelfth Night* and the Beatrice—Benedick plot in *Much Ado About Nothing,* conspiracies using forged letters to deceive a man into believing that a woman is in love with him. Faverty also mentions the career of the painter Angelica Kauffmann (1741- 1807), who was tricked into marrying an impoverished adventurer. B.'s studies for *Sordello* may have informed him that the troubadour Pierre Vidal (see *Sordello* ii 714-17n.) married a Greek girl (Phene, Jules's bride, is Greek) in the mistaken belief that she was of imperial family. B. may also have known of the practical joke played by Keats's friend Charles Wells on Keats's younger brother Tom, who received love-letters purportedly from a mysterious French lady. B. could have heard the story from a number of Keats's friends, e.g. Leigh Hunt. There is an important parallel with *Ring*, where Guido forges letters between his wife and her 'lover', Caponsacchi.

(b) *The character of Jules the sculptor.* B.'s principal model was Antonio Canova (1757-1822). The action takes place at Possagno, Canova's birthplace and the site of a 'Gipsoteca' (gallery of models and casts) devoted to his work (see i 353-4). Besides direct observation during his trip to Italy in 1838 (he wrote to Fanny Haworth on 24 July 1838, after his return: 'I was disappointed in one thing, Canova' [*Correspondence* iv 67]), and personal contact with Italian intellectuals such as his tutor Angelo Cerutti, B. could have learned about Canova's work and reputation from many sources. Canova's fame was at its height in B.'s boyhood (see e.g. Byron, *Beppo* 368); his studio was an obligatory stop for connoisseurs and collectors on the Grand Tour. Of several accounts which B. might have seen in the British Museum, there are interesting parallels with the anonymous, privately printed *Journal of a Tour in Italy* (now attrib. to the Countess of Clanwilliam, and dated 1836); see e.g. ii 116-17n. The main printed source is *The Works of Antonio Canova, in Sculpture and Modelling, Engraved in Outline by Henry Moses; with Descriptions from the Italian of the Countess Albrizzi, and a Biographical Memoir by Count*

Cicognara (3 vols., 1824), whose plates and commentaries cover all the works alluded to in the poem. The following features of Canova's career and personality were major influences on B.'s conception of Jules.

i. Canova's admiration for classical Greek sculpture. This supposedly began in Venice, where he 'found an immense source of knowledge and improvement in the gallery of plaster casts of the Commendatore Farsetti, comprising all the celebrated remains of antiquity, and which, with a noble liberality, was devoted to the use of young students, and the public curiosity' (*Works of Canova* i, p. ii). Contemporaries frequently stressed the likeness of Canova's work to antique sculpture. But B. may also have noted Canova's opinion that 'The perfect and determinate models of the Greeks . . . and the just prescriptive influence of their conventional modes of art, while they assist and ennoble modern sculpture, preclude it from originality in any of its essential points' (*Works of Canova* iii 7): see below, 'Canova and painting'.

ii. Canova's technical skill. His marbles were noted for their 'softness and delicacy of contour' and 'minute accuracy of expression', while his 'susceptibility and active fancy gave great quickness and energy to his invention, prompting his imagination spontaneously, and without effort, to reach the great and excellent in his designs' (*Works of Canova* i, pp. xiii–xvii). Cp. ii 67-98 and notes.

iii. Canova's relation to his rivals. 'The influence of established practice and professional jealousy created no trifling obstacles to the progress of Canova; these, however, his modest and unpresuming conduct aided greatly to remove, while an air of triumph and superiority would, by wounding the feelings of his rivals, have created additonal opposition' (*Works of Canova* i, p. vii). The Countess of Clanwilliam commented: 'Canova was perfectly conscious of the merit of his performances, but totally unaffected and void of pretension . . . his conversation was always playful, and left a pleasing impression' (*Journal of a Tour in Italy* ii 296-7). Jules displays the exact inverse of this attitude: see i 315-17, 352-70.

iv. Canova's private life. 'More than once during his life, he experienced the passion of love, in a degree corresponding to the susceptibility of his nature . . . On two occasions he was very near to entering into the marriage state, but was, perhaps, deterred by the apprehension of its diverting him from his devotion to his art, which was always his master and engrossing passion: his heart was, however, never entangled by low attachments, but was the seat of the noblest and most elevated sentiments' (*Works of Canova* i, p. xx). Cp. i 371-8 and ii 13-24.

v. Canova and painting. This aspect of Canova's career bears principally on Jules's decision to abandon sculpture for painting, which he explains in a letter to Monsignor (see iv 45-55) as a rejection of the imitation of classical models. B. asserted in many contexts the importance of avoiding imitation in art, though in early treatments of this topic (*Pauline* 390-2, *Chatterton* 485-6) he regards a phase of imitation as a natural part of the young artist's development. Jules's letter suggests that such imitation necessarily precedes a supplantation of the models copied: see *Sordello* ii 80-4 for an example of this

process. In Jules's case the rejection of imitation is accompanied by a change
of medium, a change which takes place *after* he breaks his own statues (ii 295-
7), since at that point he still intends to continue a sculptor; some time
between 'Noon' and 'Night' he decides that his only hope of originality lies in
becoming a painter, and writes his letter to Monsignor. The motif of the
change of medium appears in *Rudel*, and most prominently in *One Word
More*, of which it is the subject. See also B.'s letter to Ripert-Monclar of 9
Aug. 1837: 'I cannot remember the time when I did not make verses [. . . but
when] subsequently real and strong feeling called for utterance, either
Drawing or Music seemed a much fitter vehicle than "verses"' (*Correspondence* iii 264) and B. to EBB., 11 Mar. 1845: 'I think you like the operation of
writing as I should that of painting or making music, do you not?' (*LK* 39).
B. was in fact an accomplished musician, and actually studied sculpture
during the 1850s. Monsignor's suggestion that Jules will however 'fail
egregiously' in his ambition perhaps reflects the fact that his original,
Canova, was a mediocre painter. His partisans claimed that he merely 'found
an agreeable relief in the occasional use of the pencil' and denied that he
'thought very highly of his pictures, and that they had withdrawn his
attention from more important subjects' (*Works of Canova* i, p. xiv); but
Thomas Moore recorded in his journal for 13 Nov. 1819: 'Called at
Canova's, and again looked over his treasures. It is strange enough (if the
world did not abound with such anomalies) that Canova prides himself more
on some wretched daubs he has perpetrated in painting, than on his best
sculpture' (*Memoirs*, ed. John Russell [5 vols., 1856] iii 71). B. himself, in a
letter of 28 Sept. 1878, noted: 'a wonder of detestability indeed is the paint-
performance of the great man!' (*Learned Lady* 93). In the same letter, B.
expressed the belief he had come to hold that an artist should aim directly at
originality: in reply to a recommendation that his son would improve as a
painter by 'imbuing himself with the works of the Great Masters', he wrote:
'Does not all mediocrity come of a beginner's determining to look at nature
through the eyes of his predecessors . . .? I should expect a genuine painter
. . . to begin by ascertaining what he likes best to see in nature generally,—
then master the means of expressing what he likes and sees,—and, *then only*,
ask himself how others have gone through the same process and with what
results' (a position which directly repudiates that of Sir Joshua Reynolds,
whose *Discourses* [1769-90] constantly insist on the importance of imitation in
a painter's development: see e.g. Discourse I, Discourse VI).

Besides Canova, B.'s presentation of Jules may owe something to
Michelangelo: Jules's Neo-Platonic philosophy and his arrogant aloofness
from social interchange recall similar features in Michelangelo's thought and
personality. See ii 67-98n. B. drew on the myth of Pygmalion and Galatea for
the actual scene between Jules and Phene (ii 1-243). In Ovid's account
(*Metamorphoses* x), Pygmalion's aversion to the debauchery of real women is
linked to his love for the beautiful statue he has made: cp. i 371-8, B. may
also have known Rousseau's 'scène lyrique' *Pygmalion* (1775), which consists
of Pygmalion's monologue in front of his statue of Galatea, before it comes

to life. In Rousseau's version, the transformation of the statue into a woman reciprocates Pygmalion's recovery of his sense of his own genius and artistic purpose; a similar reciprocation takes place when Jules discovers a new artistic 'life' as a result of 'vivifying' Phene. Pygmalion's earlier declaration that he has lost all interest in other people may have contributed to the aloofness which his enemies resent in Jules. Both scenes end in an embrace. Another poem on the subject which may have been known to B. is T. L. Beddoes' *Pygmalion*, whose hero has suggestive similarities to Jules: see i 311-14n., 373-8n., ii 67-98n. B. may also have found a ref. to the Pygmalion legend in *Works of Canova*: ' "Pity that this nymph cannot speak," said an English visitor in the studio of Canova, "and that this Hebe does not rise into the skies; if, like Pigmalion's statue, life were added to them, nothing would remain to be desired." "You are mistaken," observed the sculptor, "and would in that case have nothing to be pleased or surprised at. I do not aim in my works at deceiving the beholder; we know they are marble—mute and immobile" ' (iii 26). Cp. also the final scene of *The Winter's Tale* where the 'statue' of Hermione—supposedly the work of the 'rare Italian master, Giulio Romano; who, had he himself eternity and could put breath into his work, would beguile Nature of her custom, so perfectly he is her ape' (V ii 108-12)—comes to life. A possible source for the discussion of the relation of art to life is the first of Alciphron's *Letters of Courtesans* (Loeb ed. [1949] 251- 2), in which the courtesan Phryne writes to the sculptor Praxiteles: 'Have no fear; for you have wrought a very beautiful work of art, such as nobody, in fact, has ever seen before among all things fashioned by men's hands; you have set up a statue of your own mistress in the sacred precinct. Yes, I stand in the middle of the precinct near your Aphrodite and your Eros too. And do not begrudge me this honour. For it is Praxiteles that people praise when they have gazed at me; and it is because I am a product of your skill that the Thespians do not count me unfit to be placed between gods. One thing only is still lacking to your gift: that you come to me, so that we may lie together in the precinct. Surely we shall bring no defilement to the gods that we ourselves have created. Farewell'. Alciphron is mentioned at i 381. The most important parallels in B., among his numerous works dealing with art and artists, are *Old Pictures* and *James Lee* viii ('Beside the Drawing-Board').

(4) *Episode 3: Luigi and his mother* (ii 244 to iii 225).

   (a) Historical background for the assassination plot. See p. 10 above. B.'s detailed allusions to political conditions in Lombardy-Venetia (e.g. the presence of Austrian police, employment of spies, censorship, restriction on travel) are glossed in the notes. There was widespread sympathy for Italian nationalism in Britain, stimulated by successive waves of refugees from political repression. (B.'s Italian tutor, Angelo Cerutti, was himself such a refugee.) B.'s interest in the subject is already present in *Sordello,* where the Guelf—Ghibellin struggle parallels the modern struggle against Austria. It is the subject of *Italy,* and features prominently in *Old Pictures* and *Prince Hohenstiel*; see also *Up at a Villa* and *De Gustibus*. The attempted assassination of a reactionary Italian ruler is the subject of *A Soul's Tragedy*. Besides Italian politics, B. implies his sympathy with the English Radical cause; see iii 163–224n.

(b) Literary sources. B.'s conception of the Austrian Emperor's court, and the kind of assassination plot that Luigi outlines, seem to have been influenced by Elizabethan and Jacobean plays, notably Webster, whose work B. knew well. There are also reminiscences of *Julius Caesar* (the justice of political killing) and of *Coriolanus* (a mother persuading her son against his sense of duty). See also ii 47–9n. The major literary influence comes from Talfourd's *Ion* (see above, p. 12). Luigi's argument with his mother about the morality and expediency of assassination parallels that in *Ion* I ii between Ion and Clemanthe, his betrothed.

(5) *Episode 4: Monsignor and the Intendant* (iv 1–341). The plot to deprive Pippa of her inheritance by seducing her and forcing her into prostitution has clear affinities with *Pericles*. The confrontation between Monsignor and the Intendant is paralleled in B. by that between Ogniben and Chiappino at the end of *Soul's Tragedy,* and in another way by that between the Pope and an imaginary 'educated man' in bk. x of *Ring.*

Criticism

B. wrote to Monclar on 29 Apr. 1841: 'c'est un effort pour contenter presque tout le monde, et vous savez comme cela réussit ordinairement' [it is an attempt to please practically everybody, and you know what kind of success that normally has] (*Correspondence* v 39). His prediction was accurate: *Pippa Passes* had a mixed reception. As with *Sordello*, most critics objected to the play as obscure, esp. *Intro* and pt. ii, but its central conception was praised: 'The idea of this little drama is, in itself, we think, remarkably beautiful' (*Athenaeum*, 11 Dec. 1841, 952; repr. *Correspondence* v 399). After *1849*, the play became, as one reviewer put it, 'held as set apart and sacred in the mind of any reader' (Moncure Conway in *Victoria Magazine* ii [Feb. 1864] 309); writing in 1890, Edmund Gosse claimed that 'the public was first won to Mr. Browning by *Pippa Passes'* (*Personalia* 55). This process is mirrored in the reaction of EBB. Her first response, in a letter to Mary Russell Mitford (15 July 1841), was that '"Pippa passes" . . comprehension, I was going to say!' and, while admitting 'the presence of genius' she asked 'Was there any need for so much coarseness?' (*Correspondence* v 75); but in a letter of 20 Jan. 1842 she objected to an adverse review (*ibid.* v 221), and on 19 Oct. she praised the poem's 'unity & nobleness of conception' (*ibid.* vi 111). An early letter to B. (17 Feb. 1845) confirmed the change of heart: 'You have taken a great range—from those high faint notes of the mystics which are beyond personality . . to dramatic impersonations, gruff with nature, "Gr-r- you swine": and when these are thrown into harmony, as in a manner they are in "Pippa Passes" (which I could find it in my heart to covet the ownership of, more than any of your works,—) the combination of effects must always be striking and noble' (*LK* 22). B. told her 'I like "Pippa" better than anything else I have done yet' (26 Feb. 1845, *LK* 27). However, it seems likely that, as with *Sordello* (see headnote, I 354), she encouraged B. to remove obscurities by revision, and perhaps to mitigate the 'coarseness' of which she had complained to Miss Mitford. One of B.'s close friends, Eliza Flower, gave a strongly adverse reaction in a letter to her friend Miss Bromley: 'I send you *Bells and Pomegranates* [i.e. *Pippa*], not because you will like it any more than I do, but because you won't like it any less than I do. It is just like *his way*. This time he has got an exquisite subject, most exquisite, and it seemed so easy for a poet to handle. Yet here comes one of those fatal ifs, the egoism of the man, and the pity of it. He cannot metempsychose with his creatures, they are so many Robert Brownings. Still there are superb parts, and the very last is quite lovely. But *puppets*, what a false word to use, as if God worked by puppets as well as Robert Browning!' (quoted in Garnett, *Life of W. J. Fox* [1909] 194; for the 'puppets', see *Intro* 152).

Synopsis
In the introductory section, Pippa, an orphan girl who works in a silk factory in Asolo, decides to spend her one day's holiday of the year 'passing' by the four people whom she regards as the most fortunate in Asolo. Ottima is the wife of Pippa's employer, the old and wealthy Luca Gaddi, and has a young lover, Sebald. Jules, a young sculptor, is about to marry the beautiful Phene. Luigi is blessed by the tranquil love between himself and his mother. The holy Monsignor, visiting Asolo from Rome after the death of his brother, is happy in the love of God. In four scenes, interspersed with interludes of 'talk by the way', Pippa passes by each in turn, unconscious of the fact that their situations are the reverse of happy, and that each is facing a climactic moment of moral choice. As she passes, she sings a song which they hear, and which, unknown to her, radically affects the choices they make. The last of these episodes concerns her own fate. Still unaware of the effect of her passing, Pippa returns to her room in the final scene of the drama.

New Year's Day at Asolo in the Trevisan. A large, mean, airy Chamber. A girl, Pippa, *from the silk-mills, springing out of bed.*

Day!
Faster and more fast
O'er night's brim day boils at last;

¶20. *Intro. Opening s.d.*] *New Year's . . . Trevisan*: see headnote, pp. 10-11. *mean*: shabby. *the silk-mills*: the silk industry was one of the principal industries of the region at the time of B.'s first visit to Asolo in 1838.
1-20. Cp. *Ring* vii 1211-26, when Pompilia 'wakes' from her life of misery in Arezzo. Line 1 is the shortest whole line in B.
1-12. Cp. Talfourd's *Ion*, p. 12: 'And lo! the sun is struggling with the gloom, / Whose masses fill the eastern sky, and tints / Its edges with dull red;—but he *will* triumph; bless'd be the omen!' In Euripides' *Ion*, Ion's first

Boils, pure gold, o'er the cloud-cup's brim
5   Where spurting and supprest it lay—
For not a froth-flake touched the rim
Of yonder gap in the solid gray
Of eastern cloud an hour away—
But forth one wavelet then another curled,
10 Till the whole sunrise, not to be supprest,
Rose-reddened, and its seething breast
Flickered in bounds, grew gold, then overflowed the
     world.
Day, if I waste a wavelet of thee,
Aught of my twelve-hours' treasure—
15 One of thy gazes, one of thy glances,
(Grants thou art bound to, gifts above measure,)
One of thy choices, one of thy chances,
(Tasks God imposed thee, freaks at thy pleasure,)
Day, if I waste such labour or leisure
20 Shame betide Asolo, mischief to me!
But in turn, Day, treat me not

---

speech is similar: 'Lo, yonder the Sun-god is turning earthward his
splendour-blazing / Chariot of light; / And the stars from the firmament flee
from his fiery arrows chasing, / To the sacred night: / And the crests of
Parnassus untrodden are flaming and flushed as with yearning / Of welcome
to far-flashing wheels with the glory of daylight returning/ To mortal sight'.
8. *Of eastern*] Of the eastern (*1849-88*).
11. Rose-reddened,] Rose, reddened, (*1849-88*).
12ˆ13.] there is a space between these lines in all other eds.
13-20. Cp. *Pauline* 502-4.
13. Day, if I waste] Oh, Day, if I squander (*1849-88*).
14. Aught of] A mite of (*1849-88*).
15-20.] The least of thy gazes or glances,
        (Be they grants thou art bound to, or gifts above measure)
        One of thy choices, or one of thy chances,
        (Be they tasks God imposed thee, or freaks at thy pleasure)
        —My Day, if I squander such labour or leisure,
        Then shame fall on Asolo, mischief on me! (*1849-88*, except no
commas after 'to', 'choices', 'thee', *1868-88*).
20ˆ21.] there is a space between these lines in all other eds.
21-47.] Thy long blue solemn hours serenely flowing,
        Whence earth, we feel, gets steady help and good—
        Thy fitful sunshine minutes, coming, going,
        In which, earth turns from work in gamesome mood—
[5]   All shall be mine! But thou must treat me not
        As the prosperous are treated, those who live

At hand here, and enjoy the higher lot,
In readiness to take what thou wilt give,
And free to let alone what thou refusest;
[10]   For, Day, my holiday, if thou ill-usest
Me, who am only Pippa—old-year's sorrow,
Cast off last night, will come again to-morrow—
Whereas, if thou prove gentle, I shall borrow
Sufficient strength of thee for new-year's sorrow.
[15]   All other men and women that this earth
Belongs to, who all days alike possess,
Make general plenty cure particular dearth,
Get more joy, one way, if another, less:
Thou art my single day, God lends to leaven
[20]   What were all earth else, with a feel of heaven;
Sole light that helps me through the year, thy sun's!
Try, now! Take Asolo's Four Happiest Ones—
And let thy morning rain on that superb
Great haughty Ottima; can rain disturb
[25]   Her Sebald's homage? All the while thy rain
Beats fiercest on her shrub-house window-pane,
He will but press the closer, breathe more warm
Against her cheek; how should she mind the storm?
And, morning past, if mid-day shed a gloom
[30]   O'er Jules and Phene,—what care bride and groom
Save for their dear selves? 'Tis their marriage-day;
And while they leave church, and go home their way
Hand clasping hand,—within each breast would be
Sunbeams and pleasant weather spite of thee!
[35]   Then, for another trial, obscure thy eve
With mist,—will Luigi and his mother grieve—
The Lady and her child, unmatched, forsooth,
She in her age, as Luigi in his youth,
For true content? The cheerful town, warm, close,
[40]   And safe, the sooner that thou art morose
Receives them! And yet once again, outbreak
In storm at night on Monsignor, they make
Such stir about,—whom they expect from Rome
To visit Asolo, his brothers' home,
[45]   And say here masses proper to release
A soul from pain,—what storm dares hurt his peace?
Calm would he pray, with his own thoughts to ward
Thy thunder off, nor want the angels' guard!
But Pippa—just once such mischance would spoil
[50]   Her day that lightens the next twelvemonth's toil
At wearisome silk-winding, coil on coil! (*1849-88*, except l. [4]
'That show, earth turns', *Texas*, canc.; 'As if earth turned', *1863-88*; l. [6] 'As

As happy tribes—so happy tribes! who live
At hand—the common, other creatures' lot—
Ready to take when thou wilt give,
25   Prepared to pass what thou refusest;
Day, 'tis but Pippa thou ill-usest
If thou prove sullen, me, whose old year's sorrow
Who except thee can chase before to-morrow,
Seest thou, my day? Pippa's—who mean to borrow
30   Only of thee strength against new year's sorrow:
For let thy morning scowl on that superb
Great haughty Ottima—can scowl disturb
Her Sebald's homage? And if noon shed gloom
O'er Jules and Phene—what care bride and groom
35   Save for their dear selves? Then, obscure thy eve
With mist—will Luigi and Madonna grieve
—The mother and the child—unmatched, forsooth,
She in her age as Luigi in his youth,
For true content? And once again, outbreak
40   In storm at night on Monsignor they make
Such stir to-day about, who foregoes Rome
To visit Asolo, his brother's home,
And say there masses proper to release
The soul from pain—what storm dares hurt that
        peace?
45   But Pippa—just one such mischance would spoil,
Bethink thee, utterly next twelvemonth's toil
At wearisome silk-winding, coil on coil!

And here am I letting time slip for nought!
You fool-hardy sunbeam—caught

---

prosperous ones', *1888*: one of very few verbal changes in this ed.; l. [11]
'Pippa,—', *1863-88*; l. [12] 'to-morrow:', *1868-88*; l. [20] 'heaven,—', *1863-
88*; l. [22] 'Try', *1865-88*; l. [32] 'church', *1868-88*; l. [33] 'hand,', *1868-88*;
l. [34] 'thee.', *1868-88*; l. [37] 'Madonna and', *Texas*, canc.; The lady *1868-88*;
l. [39] 'close', *1865-88*; l. [40] 'morose,', *1863-88*; l. [41] 'them.', *1868-88*;
l. [48] 'guard.', *1868-88*).
22. 'Tribe' and its cognates are extensively used in B.'s early work, but fade
out after the 1850s: note in this connection B.'s revision of this passage.
26-7. *Day, 'tis but . . . sullen*: cp. Wordsworth, *Ode: Intimations of Immortality*
42: 'Oh, evil day! if I were sullen[!]'
48. *am I letting*] I let (*1849-88*).
49-66. Pippa fancifully imagines that a sunbeam has escaped from its pursuers
and has taken refuge in her basin, where, believing itself secure, it has fallen
asleep. When she splashes water into the basin from her jug ('ewer'), the

50 With a single splash from my ewer!
    You that mocked the best pursuer,
    Was my basin over-deep?
    One splash of water ruins you asleep
    And up, up, fleet your brilliant bits
55 Wheeling and counterwheeling,
    Reeling, crippled beyond healing—
    Grow together on the ceiling,
    That will task your wits!
    Whoever it was first quenched fire hoped to see
60 Morsel after morsel flee
    As merrily,
    As giddily . . . what lights he on—
    Where settles himself the cripple?
    Oh never surely blown, my martagon?
65 New-blown, though!—ruddy as a nipple,

---

sunbeam is 'caught': its reflections are thrown up on to the ceiling, where
they shift and flicker as the water moves. When the water settles, so does the
'cripple': the sunbeam's reflections fall on Pippa's flower (see below, l. 64n.),
which she apostrophizes, comparing its colour to a nipple's, and its fleshiness
to that of a turkey's ('Turk bird's') comb. Cp. Virgil, *Aeneid* viii 22: 'Sicut
aquae tremulum labris ubi lumen abenis / sole repercussum, aut radiantis
imagine Lunae / omnia pervolitat late loca, iamque sub auras / erigitur,
summique ferit laquearia tecti' [As water, trembling in a brass bowl, reflects
the sun's light or the form of the shining moon, and so the bright beams flit in
all directions, darting up at times to strike the lofty fretted ceilings].
Montaigne quotes this passage as an image of the mind at play in his essay 'On
Idleness' (*Essays*, bk.I, ch.viii).
49. You] Aha, you (*1849–88*).
51. mocked] would mock (*1849–88*).
56. crippled] broken (*1849–88*).
57. Grow] Now grow (*1849–88*).
59.] Whoever quenched fire first, hoped to see (*1849–65*); Whoever it was
quenched fire first, hoped to see (*1868–88*).
61–5.]   As merrily, as giddily . . .
           Meantime, what lights my sunbeam on,
           Where settles by degrees the radiant cripple?
           Oh, is it surely blown, my martagon?
           New-blown and ruddy as St. Agnes' nipple, (*1849–88*)
64. martagon: 'the Turk's cap lily, *Lilium Martagon* . . . The English name
presumably suggests the ref. to the "Turk bird" [l. 66], and to the "turban-
flowers" [l. 69]' (*Selections from the Early Poems of Robert Browning,* ed. W. H.
Griffin [1902] 170). Line 70 makes it clear that this is the scarlet martagon.

Plump as the flesh bunch on some Turk bird's poll!
Be sure if corals, branching 'neath the ripple
Of ocean, bud there,—fairies watch unroll
Such turban flowers . . I say, such lamps disperse
70   Thick red flame thro' that dusk green universe!
Queen of thee, floweret,
Each fleshy blossom
Keep I not, safer
Than leaves that embower it
75   Or shells that embosom,
From weevil and chafer?
Laugh thro' my pane then, solicit the bee,
Gibe him, be sure, and in midst of thy glee
Worship me!

80   Worship whom else? for am I not this Day
Whate'er I please? Who shall I seem to-day?
Morn, Noon, Eve, Night—how must I spend my
Day?

67-70. The details here, and more generally its underwater-world mythology, may derive from Tennyson's *Poems, Chiefly Lyrical* (1830): see *The Merman, The Mermaid, The Sea-Fairies* and *The Kraken*, where 'Unnumbered and enormous polypi / Winnow with giant arms the slumbering green' (9-10).

69. *turban flowers*: florist's name for the cultivated varieties of *Ranunculus*; more fully *Turk's Turban*. 'Turban' is also the name for certain oceanic molluscs: *OED* cites an occurrence in 1713, and records it as a common name for the genus *Turbo*, or more generally of 'all the whirls, or spires, of a Univalve' (1815). Only occurrence in B.

70. *dusk*: rare as an adj. by B.'s time, but much used by him (12 occurrences; cp. 1 in Tennyson), esp. in his early work.

71-9.] these lines are indented, *1849-65*.

71. *Queen*] I am queen (*1849-88*).

71-2. *floweret, / Each*] floweret; / And each (*1849-88*, except 'floweret!', *1865-88*).

73. *Keep*] Preserve (*1849-88*).

75. Referring to the common practice of using seashells as decorative edgings for flower-borders.

79.] Love thy queen, worship me! (*1849-88*).

81. *Who shall I seem*] What shall I please (*1849-88*).

82.] My morning, noon, eve, night—how spend my day? (*1849-65*); My morn, noon, eve and night—how spend my day? (*1868-88*).

82^83.] Tomorrow I must be Pippa who winds silk,
     The whole year round, to earn just bread and milk:
          But, this one day, I have leave to go,

Up the hill-side, thro' the morning,
Love me as I love!
85 I am Ottima, take warning,
And the gardens, and stone house above,
And other house for shrubs, all glass in front,
Are mine, and Sebald steals as he is wont
To court me, and old Luca yet reposes,
90 And therefore till the shrub-house door uncloses
I . . . what now? give abundant cause for prate
Of me (that's Ottima)—too bold of late,
By far too confident she'll still face down
The spitefullest of talkers in our town—
95 How we talk in the little town below!

But love, love, love, there's better love I know!
This love's only day's first offer—
Next love shall defy the scoffer:
For do not bride and bridegroom sally
100 Out of Possagno church at noon?
Their house looks over Orcana valley—
Why not be the bride as soon

And play out my fancy's fullest games;
I may fancy all day—and it shall be so—
That I taste of the pleasures, am named by the names
Of the Happiest Four in our Asolo! (*1849-88*, except that the last
five lines are not indented in *1868-88*; *Texas* has 'I am Pippa', canc.).
83-5.] See! Up the Hill-side yonder, through the morning,
Some one shall love me, as the world calls love:
I am no less than Ottima, take warning!
The gardens, and the great stone house above, (*1849-88*, except 'hill-
side', *1870-88*).
88. mine, and Sebald] mine; where Sebald (*1849-88*).
89. and old] while old (*1849-88*).
92.] About me—Ottima, I mean—of late, (*1849-88*).
93. By far] Too bold, (*1849-88*).
95ˆ96.] Line 95 ends a page in *1849*; in *1863* and subsequent eds. there is no
space, but l. 96 is indented as for a new paragraph.
97. This love's] This foolish love was (*1849-88*).
98.] I choose my next love to defy the scoffer: (*1849-88*).
99. bride and bridegroom] our Bride and Bridegroom (*1849-88*).
100. Possagno church: Possagno church was designed by Canova. See
headnote, p. 12ff.
102. Why not] Why should I not (*1849*); Why should not I (*1863-88*), the first
of the few verbal changes initiated in *1863*.

As Ottima? I saw, myself, beside,
Arrive last night that bride—
105   Saw, if you call it seeing her, one flash
Of the pale snow-pure cheek and blacker tresses
Than . . . not the black eyelash;
A wonder she contrives those lids no dresses
—So strict was she the veil
110   Should cover close her pale
Pure cheeks—a bride to look at and scarce touch,
Remember Jules!—for are not such
Used to be tended, flower-like, every feature,
As if one's breath would fray the lily of a creature?
115   Oh, save that brow its virgin dimness,
Keep that foot its lady primness,
Let those ancles never swerve
From their exquisite reserve,
Yet have to trip along the streets like me
120   All but naked to the knee!
How will she ever grant her Jules a bliss
So startling as her real first infant kiss?
Oh—no—not envy this!
Not envy sure, for, if you gave me
125   Leave to take or to refuse
In earnest, do you think I'd choose
That sort of new love to enslave me?
Mine should have lapped me round from the
beginning;

103. I saw, myself,] For I saw, (*1849-88*).
104. that bride] that little bride (*1849-88*).
106. blacker tresses] black bright tresses (*1849-88*).
107.] Blacker than all except the black eyelash; (*1849-88*).
108. A wonder] I wonder (*1849-88*).
112. Remember] Scarce touch, remember, (*1849-88*).
114. fray: various senses are applicable, principally 'frighten', 'assault, attack',
and (with the flower analogy) 'rub'. Cp. *Aristophanes* 655, 'Sunshine frays
torchlight', and *Magical Nature* 7: 'Time may fray the flower-face'. The
context might also favour an obsolete sense, 'deflower'.
114^115.] A soft and easy life these ladies lead! / Whiteness in us were
wonderful indeed— (*1849-88*, except 'lead:', *1865-88*, 'indeed.', *1863-88*).
115-23.] this passage is indented, *1849-65*.
117. ancles] ankles (*1863, 1870-88*; *1865* agrees, unusually, with *1841*). Both
spellings were current; cp. i 177.
123^124.] Line 123 ends a page in *1849*; in *1863-88* there is a space.
128. beginning;] emended in agreement with all other eds. from 'beginning'
in *1841*.

As little fear of losing it as winning—
130 Why look you! when at eve the pair
Commune inside our turret, what prevents
My being Luigi?—While that mossy lair
Of lizards thro’ the winter-time, is stirred
With each to each imparting sweet intents
135 For this new year, as brooding bird to bird—
I will be cared about, kept out of harm
And schemed for, safe in love as with a charm,
I will be Luigi . . . if I only knew
What was my father like . . . my mother too!

140 Nay, if you come to that, the greatest love of all
Is God’s: well then, to have God’s love befall
Oneself as in the palace by the dome
Where Monsignor to-night will bless the home
Of his dead brother! I, to-night at least,
145 Will be that holy and beloved priest.

129^130.] Lovers grow cold, men learn to hate their wives, / And only
parents’ love can last our lives: (*1849-88*, except ‘lives.’, *1863-88*).
130.] So, look you! when at eve the gentle Pair (*Texas*, canc., except ‘Pair’,
which must have been altered in proof); At eve the son and mother, gentle
pair, (*1849-88*, except ‘Son and Mother’, *1868-88*).
131. turret] Turret (*1849-65*).
135^136.] (For I observe of late, the evening walk
          Of Luigi and his mother, always ends
          Inside our ruined turret, where they talk,
          Calmer than lovers, yet more kind than friends) (*1849-88*)
136. I will] Let me (*1849*); —Let me (*1863-88*).
138-9.] Let me be Luigi! . . . If I only knew / What was my mother’s
face—my father, too! (*1849-88*, except ‘Luigi! If’, *1863-88*).
139^140.] in *1863* and *1865*, l. 139 ends a page; in *1868-88* there is no space,
but in *1888* l. 140 is indented as for a new paragraph.
140-5.] Nay, if you come to that, best love of all
          Is God’s; then why not have God’s love befall
          Myself as, in the Palace by the Dome,
          Monsignor?—who to-night will bless the home
          Of his dead brother; and God will bless in turn
          That heart which beats, those eyes which mildly burn
          With love for all men: I, to-night at least,
          Would be that holy and beloved priest! (*1849-88*, except ‘palace’,
‘God bless’, ‘men!’, *1870-88*, and ‘priest.’, *1868-88*).
142. dome: cathedral, from It. ‘Duomo’.

Now wait—even I myself already ought to share
In that—why else should new year's hymn declare

> *All service ranks the same with God:*
> *If now, as formerly he trod*
150 > *Paradise, God's presence fills*
> *Our earth, and each but as God wills*

146. even I myself] even I (*1849-88*).

147.] In God's love: what does New-year's hymn declare? / What other meaning do these verses bear? (*1849-88*; *Texas* has 'that love', canc.).

148-59. The first stanza of the hymn argues that God's control over the destiny of each individual makes all such individuals equal in relation to him. The second stanza (which parallels but does not follow from the first) suggests that, similarly, no one ought to rank their actions into hierarchies of significance; each act is equally important. It does not mean that God commands every individual 'deed' of a man's life (despite the biblical echoes of ll. 157-9). Such an interpretation would contradict all B.'s other statements on this issue, in which he invariably upholds free will (see e.g. *Prince Hohenstiel* 111-69, *Christmas-Eve* 288-95); and his own comment on ll. 152-3 (see note) suggests that the hymn is more than a dramatic statement and should therefore be reconcilable with his opinion as expressed elsewhere.

148. Cp. Milton, *Sonnets* xvi ('On his Blindness'): 'who best / Bear his mild yoke, they serve him best . . . Thousands at his bidding speed / And post o'er land and ocean without rest: / They also serve who only stand and wait' (10-11, 12-14). In a letter to EBB. of 18 Jan. 1846 (*LK* 400), B. refers to God's 'reasonable service', quoting *Romans* xii 1, a passage which continues, 'For I say . . . to every man that is among you, not to think of himself more highly than he ought to think; but to think soberly, according as God hath dealt to every man the measure of faith. For as we have many members in one body, and all members have not the same office: so we, being many, are one body in Christ, and every one members one of another' (vv. 3-5). The concept of service appears repeatedly in St Paul's epistles, and a passage in *Ephesians* (vi 5-9) expands its social aspect: 'Servants, be obedient to them that are your masters according to the flesh, with fear and trembling, in singleness of your heart, as unto Christ; not with eyeservice, as menpleasers; but as the servants of Christ, doing the will of God from the heart; with good will doing service, as to the Lord, and not to men: knowing that whatsoever good thing any man doeth, the same shall he receive of the Lord, whether he be bond or free. And, ye masters, do the same things unto them, forbearing threatening: knowing that your Master also is in heaven; neither is there respect of persons with him'. See l. 153n.

149. he] He (*1849-65*). 'When' must be understood before 'he'.

150. God's] His (*1849-65*); his (*1868-88*).

151. and each but] then each but (*Texas*, canc.); each only (*1849-88*).

> *Can work—God's puppets, best and worst,*
> *Are we; there is no last nor first.*

> Say not, a small event! Why small?
155 *Costs it more pain this thing ye call*
> *A great event should come to pass*
> *Than that? Untwine me, from the mass*
> *Of deeds that make up life, one deed*
> *Power shall fall short in or exceed!*

160 And more of it, and more of it—oh, yes!
> So that my passing, and each happiness

152-3. God's puppets . . . nor first: ABL has a scrap of paper on which is written, in B.'s early hand, 'whose puppets, best & worst, are *we*' with the comment: 'Better or worse as we may be with respect to our capabilities, & opportunities for their exercise, we are one & all, best & worst, but mere *puppets* (in our capacity of influential agents of the Divine Will—not in any other)'. Above is written, in the hand of B.'s friend R. H. Horne, 'Robt. Browning's philosophy quoad Free-will'. For Eliza Flower's comment on this passage, see headnote, p. 17. *Collections* records three examples besides this one of B. inscribing the lines for autographs (E365, E366, E367, p. 429). The last of these is dated 27 Aug. 1889.

153. there is no last nor first: cp. *Luke* xiii 29-30: 'And they shall come from the east, and from the west, and from the north, and from the south, and shall sit down in the kingdom of God. And, behold, there are last which shall be first, and there are first which shall be last'. Cp. also *Mark* ix 35: 'If any man desire to be first, the same shall be last of all, and servant of all', with *Luke* ix 46-8: 'Then there arose a reasoning among [the disciples], which of them should be greatest. And Jesus, perceiving the thought of their heart, took a child, and set him by him, and said unto them, Whosoever shall receive this child in my name receiveth me: and whosoever shall receive me receiveth him that sent me: for he that is least among you all, the same shall be great'.

154-7. Say not . . . Than that: cp. *Sordello* vi 496-502n. (I 747).

154.] Say not "a small event!" Why "small?" (*1849-88*, except '"small"?', *1888*).

155. this thing] than this, (*1849-75*); 'than' is corrected to 'that' in *1888*.

156. great event] in quotation marks, *1849-88*.

157-9. Untwine me . . . or exceed: cp. *Isaiah* xl 26: 'Lift up your eyes on high, and behold who hath created these things, that bringeth out their host by number: he calleth them all by names by the greatness of his might, for that he is strong in power; not one faileth'.

160. it: either God's love (l. 147) or his power (l. 159).

161-9.] I will pass by, and see their happiness,
> And envy none—being just as great, no doubt,
> Useful to men, and dear to God, as they! (*1849-88*)

I pass, will be alike important—prove
That true! oh yes—the brother,
The bride, the lover, and the mother,—
165 Only to pass whom will remove—
Whom a mere look at half will cure
The Past, and help me to endure
The Coming . . . I am just as great, no doubt,
As they!
170 A pretty thing to care about
So mightily—this single holiday!
Why repine?
With thee to lead me, Day of mine,
Down the grass path gray with dew,
175 'Neath the pine-wood, blind with boughs,
Where the swallow never flew
As yet, nor cicale dared carouse:
No, dared carouse!

                                [She enters the Street.

162-3. prove / That true: 'let that prove true'.

172-8.] this passage is indented, *1849-65*.

172.] But let the sun shine! Wherefore repine? (*1849-88*).

173. Day] O Day (*1849-88*).

175. 'Neath] Under (*1849-88*).

177. As yet, nor] Nor yet (*1865-88*).   *cicale*] cicala (*1863-88*). In *1863* this spelling, with the *1841* version of the rest of the line, would make the line hard to pronounce because of the change in stress. See also iii 50n. The cicale or cicada, a southern grasshopper, is noted for its shrill chirping sound. Cp. *Sordello* iii 248.

178.] Dared carouse! (*1849-63*). This line repeats the sense of the previous one: 'No' is a lyric repetition of 'nor' in the previous line, not a negation of that line's sense.

I.—*Morning. Up the Hill-side. The Shrub House.* Luca's *Wife*
Ottima, *and her Paramour the German* Sebald.

> Sebald. [*Sings*] *Let the watching lids wink!*
> *Day's a-blaze with eyes, think,—*
> *Deep into the night drink!*
> Ottima. Night? What, a Rhineland night, then?
> How these tall
5 Naked geraniums straggle! Push the lattice—
Behind that frame.—Nay, do I bid you?—Sebald,
It shakes the dust down on me! Why, of course
The slide-bolt catches—Well, are you content,
Or must I find you something else to spoil?
10 Kiss and be friends, my Sebald. Is it full morning?
Oh, don't speak then!
> Sebald.   Ay, thus it used to be!
Ever your house was, I remember, shut
Till mid-day—I observed that, as I strolled
On mornings thro' the vale here: country girls
15 Were noisy, washing garments in the brook—
Herds drove the slow white oxen up the hills—
But no, your house was mute, would ope no eye—
And wisely—you were plotting one thing there,
Nature another outside: I looked up—
20 Rough white wood shutters, rusty iron bars,

---

i *Opening s.d.*] *Up the Hill-side. The Shrub House*] Up the Hill-side, inside the
Shrub-house (*1849-88*).   *Shrub House*: conservatory.
i *1-276.* The whole of this scene was extracted for *1863²*; see headnote, p. 7.
We have included this text in our collation.
i *1-2.* Probably a ref. to the legend of Argus, who, 'as he had an hundred
eyes, of which only two were asleep at one time, Juno set him to watch Io,
whom Jupiter had changed into a heifer; but Mercury, by order of Jupiter,
slew him, by lulling all his eyes asleep with the sound of his lyre' (*Lemprière*).
i *4-10. How these tall . . . my Sebald*: in a letter to Mary Russell Mitford of 17
July 1841, EBB. says of this passage, 'Is'nt that Landor? Is'nt it his very trick
of phrase? Yet Mʳ. Browning is no imitator' (*Correspondence* v 78).
i *4.*] Night? Such may be your Rhine-land nights, perhaps;
> But this blood-red beam through the shutter's chink,
> —We call such light the morning's: let us see!
> Mind how you grope your way, though! How these tall (*1849-88*,
except 'nights perhaps', *1865-88*, 'chink', 'morning', *1868-88*).
i *10. Is it*] Is't (*1870-88*).
i *13. mid-day—I*] mid-day; I (*1863²-88*).
i *16. Herds*] Hinds (*1849-88*). 'Herd' means 'cowherd'; 'hind', 'an agricultural
labourer'.

Silent as death, blind in a flood of light,
Oh, I remember!—and the peasants laughed
And said, "The old man sleeps with the young wife!"
This house was his, this chair, this window—his.
25   *Ottima.* Ah, the clear morning! I can see St.
          Mark's:
That black streak is the belfry—stop: Vicenza
Should lie—there's Padua, plain enough, that blue.
Look o'er my shoulder—follow my finger—
          Sebald.   Morning?
It seems to me a night with a sun added:
30   Where's dew? where's freshness? That bruised plant I
          bruised
In getting thro' the lattice yestereve,
Droops as it did. See, here's my elbow's mark
In the dust on the sill.
          Ottima.   Oh shut the lattice, pray!
          Sebald. Let me lean out. I cannot scent blood here
Foul as the morn may be—
35   There, shut the world out!
How do you feel now, Ottima? There—curse
The world, and all outside! Let us throw off
This mask: how do you bear yourself? Let's out
With all of it!
          Ottima.   Best never speak of it.
40   *Sebald.* Best speak again and yet again of it,
Till words cease to be more than words. "His blood,"
For instance—let those two words mean "His blood"
And nothing more. Notice—I'll say them now,
"His blood."
          Ottima.   Assuredly if I repented
The deed—

i *24.* Cp. Donne, *Elegy i* ('Jealousy') 24-5: 'for that [his house] is / His realm,
his castle, and his diocese'. See below, ll. 70-4n.
i *25-7. I can see . . . that blue*: Ottima looks for the three principal cities of the
region, all lying about 50 km from Asolo and visible from it on a clear day. St
Mark's is San Marco, the cathedral church of Venice since 1817; its belfry
(campanile) is 'one of the boldest monuments of ancient Venice' (*Murray*).
i *28-9. Morning . . . with a sun added*: cp. *Macbeth* II iv 6-7, the morning after
the murder of Duncan: 'by the clock 'tis day, / And yet dark night strangles
the travelling lamp'. See also l. 110.
i *33. In the dust on the*] I' the dust o' the] (*1870-88*).
i *38. mask: how*] mask. How (*1863²*).
i *41-4. His blood . . . His blood*: cp. the obsession of Macbeth and Lady
Macbeth with the blood of Duncan after their murder of him. See esp. V i.

45   *Sebald.*   Repent? who should repent, or why?
    What puts that in your head? Did I once say
    That I repented?
        Ottima.   No—I said the deed—
        Sebald. "The deed" and "the event"—and just
        now it was
    "Our passion's fruit"—the devil take
        such cant!
50   Say, once and always, Luca was a wittol,
    I am his cut-throat, you are—
        Ottima.   Here is the wine—
    I brought it when we left the house above—
    And glasses too—wine of both sorts. Black? white,
        then?
        Sebald. But am not I his cut-throat? What are you?
55   *Ottima.* There trudges on his business from the
        Duomo,
    Benet the Capuchin, with his brown hood
    And bare feet—always in one place at church,
    Close under the stone wall by the south entry;
    I used to take him for a brown cold piece
60   Of the wall's self, as out of it he rose
    To let me pass—at first, I say, I used—
    Now—so has that dumb figure fastened on me—
    I rather should account the plastered wall
    A piece of him, so chilly does it strike.
    This, Sebald?

i *47-9. No—I said the deed . . . such cant*: Macbeth and Lady Macbeth habitually refer to Duncan's murder as a 'deed': see esp. II ii 72: '[Macbeth] To know my deed, 'twere best not know myself.'

i *48. and just*] just (*1849-88*).

i *50. wittol*: 'A man who knows the falsehood of his wife, and seems contented; a tame cuckold' (*J.*). A character corresponding to Luca in the first part ('The Triumph of Honour') of *Four Plays* (see headnote, p. 8) is described in the *dramatis personae* as 'a wittol sutler'.

i *51. Here is*] Here's (*1870-88*).

i *53. Black*: red wine, from It. 'vino nero'.

i *55. Duomo*: cathedral. W. H. Griffin (*Selections from the Early Poems of Robert Browning* [1902]) notes: 'the Duomo of S. Maria at Asolo is a Capuchin foundation; the road to it passes immediately below the house B. associates with this scene. The south entry to the church has a little porch with a stone seat beneath it' (p. 144).

i *56. Capuchin*: a friar of the Franciscan order, so called from the characteristic pointed hood; the order's rule stressed poverty and austerity.

i *64. so chilly does it strike*: the referent of 'it' is unclear: either 'that dumb

65   *Sebald.*   No—the white wine—the white wine!
        Well, Ottima, I promised no new year
        Should rise on us the ancient shameful way,
        Nor does it rise—pour on—To your black eyes!
        Do you remember last damned New Year's day?
70   *Ottima.* You brought those foreign prints. We
            looked at them
        Over the wine and fruit. I had to scheme
        To get him from the fire. Nothing but saying
        His own set wants the proof-mark roused him up
        To hunt them out.
            Sebald.   Faith, he is not alive
        To fondle you before my face.
75   *Ottima.*   Do you
        Fondle me then: who means to take your life
        For that, my Sebald?
            Sebald.   Hark you, Ottima,

---

figure' (l. 62) or 'the plastered wall' (l. 63), or, metonymically, both.

i *66-8. I promised no new year . . . Nor does it rise*: the suggestion here of a plan seems to contradict the apparently unpremeditated character of the murder as reported at ll. 90-1 and 141-5. There is perhaps a ref. to *Macbeth* I v 58-61: '[Macbeth] My dearest love, / Duncan comes here tonight. [Lady Macbeth] And when goes hence? / [Macbeth] Tomorrow, as he purposes. [Lady Macbeth] O! never / Shall sun that morrow see!'

i *70-4. You brought . . . To hunt them out*: this passage and l. 144 come very close to the scenario of Donne's *Elegy* I 17-24: 'We must not, as we used, flout openly, / In scoffing riddles, his deformity; / Nor at his board being together sat, / With words, nor touch, scarce looks adulterate. / Nor when he swoll'n, and pampered with great fare, / Sits down, and snorts, caged in his basket chair, / Must we usurp his own bed any more, / Nor kiss and play in his house, as before'. See above, l. 24n.

i *73. proof-mark*: a proof in engraving is either a draft or the completed print, and the various stages of production are given differential marks: as W. M. Ivins remarks, 'For many print collectors these marks play the role played by the wine label for the man who tells whether a wine is good or bad by reading in a book, not by testing in a glass' (*How Prints Look* [Boston 1958] 152). 'Proof-mark' might refer to any of these marks, and therefore any of the stages of production; the most prized specimens are either an early draft or an early copy from the first press-run of the finished print. Alternatively, B. might intend a synonym for 'plate-mark', the limit of the impress caused by the printing, whose removal lowers the value of a print.

i *77-92. Hark you, Ottima . . . forever yours*: the concept of being bound together by complicity in murder has a general resemblance to the argument

One thing's to guard against. We'll not make much
One of the other—that is, not make more
80   Parade of warmth, childish officious coil,
Than yesterday—as if, sweet, I supposed
Proof upon proof was needed now, now first,
To show I love you—still love you—love you
In spite of Luca and what's come to him.
85   —Sure sign we had him ever in our thoughts,
White sneering old reproachful face and all—
We'll even quarrel, love, at times, as if
We still could lose each other—were not tied
By this—conceive you?
     Ottima.   Love—
     Sebald.   Not tied so sure—
90   Because tho' I was wrought upon—have struck
His insolence back into him—am I
So surely yours?—therefore, forever yours?
     Ottima. Love, to be wise, (one counsel pays
       another)
Should we have—months ago—when first we loved,
95   For instance that May morning we two stole
Under the green ascent of sycamores—
If we had come upon a thing like that
Suddenly—
     Sebald.   "A thing" . . there again—"a thing!"
     Ottima. Then, Venus' body, had we come upon
100 My husband Luca Gaddi's murdered corpse

---

put forward in Middleton's *The Changeling* (1623) III iv 133-41 by De Flores
to Beatrice, at whose instigation he has murdered her betrothed Alsemero.
i *78. One thing's*] One thing (*1868-88*).
i *80. officious*: combining 'dutiful; active or zealous in doing one's duty'
and 'unduly forward in proffering services or taking business upon oneself;
meddlesome'. Cp. *My Last Duchess* 27.   *coil*: fuss, ado.
i *81. sweet*] Sweet (*1863, 1865*). Unlike the similar rev. in l. 87, this does not
appear in *1863²*.
i *82. was*] were (*1865-88*).
i *83. still love*] yes, still love (*1849-88*).
i *87. love*] Love (*1863-65*).
i *89. Love—*] Love! (*1863-88*).
i *90-1. I was wrought . . . back into him*: see ll. 66-8n.
i *91. am I*] am I, Love, (*1863²*).
i *94. ago—when*] ago, when (*1863²-88*).

Within there, at his couch-foot, covered close—
Would you have pored upon it? Why persist
In poring now upon it? For 'tis here—
As much as there in the deserted house—
105 You cannot rid your eyes of it: for me,
Now he is dead I hate him worse—I hate—
Dare you stay here? I would go back and hold
His two dead hands, and say, I hate you worse
Luca, than—
        Sebald.   Off, off; take your hands off mine!
110 'Tis the hot evening—off! oh, morning, is it?
        Ottima. There's one thing must be done—you
            know what thing.
Come in and help to carry. We may sleep
Anywhere in the whole wide house to-night.
        Sebald. What would come, think you, if we let
            him lie
115 Just as he is? Let him lie there until
The angels take him: he is turned by this
Off from his face, beside, as you will see.
        Ottima. This dusty pane might serve for looking-
            glass.
Three, four—four grey hairs! is it so you said
120 A plait of hair should wave across my neck?
No—this way!
        Sebald.   Ottima, I would give your neck,
Each splendid shoulder, both those breasts of yours,
This were undone! Killing?—Let the world die
So Luca lives again!—Ay, lives to sputter
125 His fulsome dotage on you—yes, and feign
Surprise that I returned at eve to sup,
When all the morning I was loitering here—
Bid me dispatch my business and begone.
I would—

i *105. it: for*] it. For (*1863-88*).
i *108-9. I hate you worse / Luca, than—*] in quotation marks, *1868-88.*
i *116. by this*: by this time.
i *123. This*] That this (*1849-88*).   *Let the world die*] Kill the world (*1849-88*).
i *124. sputter*: splutter. *OED* records its use as being mainly to express anger
rather than dotage. Ten occurrences in B.; typically, 'you hissed, spat and
sputtered' (*Of Pacchiarotto* 569).
i *126. returned*] return (*1868-88*).
i *128. dispatch my business*: a Shakespearean phrase; cp. *Love's Labour's Lost* II i
31 and *Antony and Cleopatra* II ii 165.

    Ottima. See!
    Sebald.   No, I'll finish. Do you think
130 I fear to speak the bare truth once for all?
    All we have talked of is at bottom fine
    To suffer—there's a recompense in that:
    One must be venturous and fortunate—
    What is one young for else? In age we'll sigh
135 O'er the wild, reckless, wicked days flown over:
    But to have eaten Luca's bread—have worn
    His clothes, have felt his money swell my purse—
    Why, I was starving when I used to call
    And teach you music—starving while you pluck'd
    Me flowers to smell!
    Ottima.   My poor lost friend!
140 *Sebald.*   He gave me
    Life—nothing less: what if he did reproach
    My perfidy, and threaten, and do more—
    Had he no right? What was to wonder at?
    Why must you lean across till our cheeks touch'd?
145 Could he do less than make pretence to strike me?
    'Tis not the crime's sake—I'd commit ten crimes
    Greater, to have this crime wiped out—undone!
    And you—O, how feel you? feel you for me?
    Ottima. Well, then—I love you better now than
      ever—
150 And best (look at me while I speak to you)—
    Best for the crime—nor do I grieve in truth
    This mask, this simulated ignorance,
    This affectation of simplicity
    Falls off our crime; this naked crime of ours
155 May not be looked over—look it down, then!
    Great? let it be great—but the joys it brought

i *132. in that*] in guilt (*1849-88*).
i *135^136.*] Still we have lived! The vice was in its place. (*1849-88*, except
'Still, we', *1863-88*, 'lived: the', *1865-88*).
i *137^138.*] Do lovers in romances sin that way? (*1849-88*).
i *139-40. you pluck'd / Me flowers*] you plucked me / These flowers (*1849-88*).
i *143^144.*] He sate by us at table quietly— (*1849-88*, except 'sat', *1863*, *1865-*
88, 'quietly:', *1865-88*).
i *144.* See ll. 70-4n.
i *145. to strike me*] to strike (*1865-88*).
i *146. not the*] not for the (*1849-63*).
i *153. simplicity:* used in the sense of 'freedom from artifice, deceit, or
duplicity; absence of affectation or artificiality'.
i *155. May not*] May not, now, (*1849-88*). *down, then!*] down! (*1870-88*).

Pay they or no its price? Come—they or it!
Speak not! The past, would you give up the past
Such as it is, pleasure and crime together?
160   Give up that noon I owned my love for you—
The garden's silence—even the single bee
Persisting in his toil, suddenly stopt
And where he hid you only could surmise
By some campanula's chalice set a-swing
As he clung there—"Yes, I love you."
165   *Sebald.*   And I drew
Back: put far back your face with both my hands
Lest you should grow too full of me—your face
So seemed athirst for my whole soul and body!
       Ottima. And when I ventured to receive you here,
Made you steal hither in the mornings—
170   *Sebald.*   When
I used to look up 'neath the shrub-house here
Till the red fire on its glazed windows spread
Into a yellow haze?
       Ottima.   Ah—my sign was, the sun
Inflamed the sere side of yon chestnut-tree
Nipt by the first frost—
175   *Sebald.*   You would always laugh
At my wet boots—I had to stride thro' grass

i *157. Pay they or no its price*: cp. *Colombe* ii 98-102.

i *158. past . . . past*] Past . . . Past (*1863-65*).

i *160. that noon*: noon was traditionally identified as the hour of the Fall of Man.

i *161-2. the single bee / Persisting in his toil*: cp. *Sordello* vi 619-28n. (I 753).

i *163-5. And where he hid . . . he clung there*: the association of the bee with sexual intercourse is common in B. Cp. *In a Gondola* 56-62, *Popularity* 46-50 and *Women and Roses* 28-32. The image may owe something to *PL* v 21-5 (Adam addressing Eve, who is waking from her dream of temptation): 'Mark . . . How nature paints her colours, how the bee / Sits on the bloom extracting liquid sweet'.

i *163. hid you*] hid, you (*1863²*). One of the few readings unique to this ed.

i *164. campanula's*] campanula (*1868-88*). Only occurrence in B; but note 'bell-flower', another name for this flower, in *A Toccata* 14.

i *164-5. a-swing / As he clung there*—] a-swing: / Who stammered— (*1863-88*).

i *167-8. your face . . . soul and body*: cp. Marlowe's *Doctor Faustus:* 'Her lips suck forth my soul: see where it flies. / Come, Helen, come, give me my soul again' (V i); and cp. *Confessional* 13-18.

i *173. Into*] To (*1849-88*).

i *174. sere*: dry, withered. Cp. *Macbeth* V ii 22-3: 'My way of life / Is fall'n into the sear, the yellow leaf'.

Over my ancles.
    Ottima.   Then our crowning night—
    Sebald. The July night?
    Ottima.   The day of it too, Sebald!
When heaven's pillars seemed o'erbowed with heat,
180   Its black-blue canopy seemed let descend
Close on us both, to weigh down each to each,
And smother up all life except our life.
So lay we till the storm came.
    Sebald.   How it came!
    Ottima. Buried in woods we lay, you recollect;
185   Swift ran the searching tempest overhead;
And ever and anon some bright white shaft
Burnt thro' the pine-tree roof—here burnt and there,
As if God's messenger thro' the close wood screen
Plunged and replunged his weapon at a venture,
190   Feeling for guilty thee and me—then broke
The thunder like a whole sea overhead—
    Sebald. Yes.
    Ottima.   While I stretched myself upon you,
    hands
To hands, my mouth to your hot mouth, and shook
All my locks loose, and covered you with them.
You, Sebald, the same you—

i *177. ancles*] ankles (*1863, 1870-88; 1865* agrees with *1841*, as at *Intro* 117).

i *179. heaven's*] the heaven's (*1849-65*).

i *180. seemed let descend*] suffered descend (*1865-88*).

i *184-91. Buried in woods . . . a whole sea overhead*: the resemblance to *King Lear* III ii has often been noted, esp. ll. 49-51: 'Let the great gods / That keep this dreadful pudder o'er our heads / Find out their enemies now'. Another source is *PL* ix 1080-90, where after his fall Adam laments: 'How shall I behold the face / Henceforth of God or angel, erst with joy / And rapture so oft beheld? Those heavenly shapes / Will dazzle now this earthly, with their blaze / Insufferably bright. O might I here / In solitude live savage, in some glade / Obscured, where highest woods impenetrable / To star or sunlight, spread their umbrage broad / And brown as evening: cover me, ye pines, / Ye cedars, with innumerable boughs / Hide me, where I may never see them more'. In a letter to EBB. about thunderstorms (13 July 1845, *LK* 121-3) B. recollected one he had seen at Possagna, the setting for pt. ii of *Pippa*. A similar storm, again associated with retribution, concludes *Caliban* (see ll. 289-91).

i *187. Burnt . . . burnt*] Burned . . . burned (*1868-88*).

195   *Sebald.*
        Ottima. And as we lay—
        Sebald.   Less vehemently—Love me—
        Forgive me—take not words—mere words—to
                heart—
        Your breath is worse than wine—breathe slow, speak
                slow—
        Do not lean on me—
            Ottima.   Sebald, as we lay,
200   Rising and falling only with our pants,
        Who said, "Let death come now—'tis right to die!
        Right to be punished—nought completes such bliss
        But woe!" Who said that?
            Sebald.   How did we ever rise?
        Was't that we slept? Why did it end?
            Ottima.   I felt
205   You tapering to a point the ruffled ends
        Of my loose locks 'twixt both your humid lips—
        (My hair is fallen now—knot it again).
            Sebald. I kiss you now, dear Ottima, now and
                now;
        This way? will you forgive me—be once more
        My great queen?
210   *Ottima.*   Bind it thrice about my brow;
        Crown me your queen, your spirit's arbitress,

---

i *201. Let death come now—'tis right to die*: cp. *Othello* II i 185-93: 'If after every
tempest come such calms, / May the winds blow till they have wakened
death . . . If it were now to die, / 'Twere now to be most happy; for I fear /
My soul hath her content so absolute / That not another comfort like to this /
Succeeds in unknown fate'.

i *202-3. nought completes such bliss / But woe*: adapting the proverbial 'No weal
without woe'. B. is fond of the 'weal—woe' doublet, replacing 'weal' with
'bliss' in only one other context (*Apollo and the Fates* 254, where, as here, a
love-relationship is involved). Cp. also Shakespeare, *Sonnets* cxxix: 'lust / Is
perjured, murderous, bloody, full of blame . . . A bliss in proof, and prov'd,
a very woe' (2-3, 11).

i *203-4. How did we . . . we slept?*: cp. Donne, *Break of Day* 3: 'Why should we
rise, because 'tis light?', and *The Good-Morrow* 1-4: 'I wonder, by my troth,
what thou and I / Did till we loved? . . . Snorted we in the seven sleepers'
den?'

i *204-5. felt / You tapering to*] felt you, / Fresh tapering to (*1849*); felt you, /
Tapering into (*1863*); felt you / Tapering into (*1863²-1865*); felt you / Taper
into (*1868-88*).

Magnificent in sin. Say that!
> *Sebald.*   I crown you
> My great white queen, my spirit's arbitress,
> Magnificent—

215   [*Without*] The year's at the spring,

i *215-76.* The dramatic structure here closely parallels that of the conclusion of 'The Triumph of Death' in *Four Plays* (see headnote, p. 8), whose protagonist, Lavall, having killed the brother of a woman he is attempting to seduce and been stabbed himself, sees a 'Spirit' which catalogues his crimes to him, and 'sings and vanishes'.

i *215-22.* For publication details, see headnote, p. 6. No single source has been suggested for Pippa's first song, but its rhythm and paratactic organization give it some resemblance to Wordsworth's *Written in March while resting at the foot of Brothers Water*, which begins: 'The Cock is crowing, / The stream is flowing, / The small birds twitter, / The lake doth glitter, / The green field sleeps in the sun'. (There is also a more general resemblance to Elizabethan spring-catalogues, e.g. Surrey's 'The soote season'.) Until recently, this song was heavily anthologized; it was also taken to 'voice the poet's belief' (W. O. Raymond, *The Infinite Moment* [2nd ed., Toronto 1965] 160). This view was attacked by E. D. H. Johnson (*The Alien Vision of Victorian Poetry* [Princeton 1952] 86) on the ground that the song is dramatically expressive of Pippa's 'naivety and child-like faith'; see also Philip Drew, *The Poetry of Browning* (1970) 19, 182-3. J. C. Ransom identifies it as an instance of 'The Concrete Universal' (*Kenyon Review* xvii [1955] 395); A. Hill describes its structure in '"Pippa's Song": Two Attempts at Structural Criticism' (*Browning's Mind and Art*, ed. C. Tracy [1968] 75-81). There is no known precedent for the song's unusual rhyme-scheme (abcd abcd), but B. may have derived it from the 'rimas dissolutas' of some troubadour lyrics, in which 'all the different verses are without a rhyme in their own stanza, but find it in the corresponding verse of another, or of all other stanzas' (F. Hueffer, *The Troubadours* [1878] 355). B.'s studies for *Sordello* would have introduced him to this device, which is very common in, for instance, the verse of Arnaut Daniel. With the context, there may be an ironic ref. to the Provençal 'Alba', sung by a watchman to warn two lovers that the day is coming and therefore danger from the jealous husband. B. frequently inscribed this song for autographs: *Collections* (E 371-6, pp. 429-30) lists six examples (1858, 1861, 1870 [called 'A Girl's Song'], 1886, 1888, 1889), the latter being possibly B.'s last autograph inscription. Variants from all of these MSS except *1888* (whose whereabouts are unknown) are recorded below.

i *215.* [*s.d.*] *From without is heard the voice of* PIPPA, *singing*— (*1849-88*, except 'PIPPA singing', *1868-75*). In *1849-88* the s.d. is placed between l. 214 and l. 215. The s.d. does not of course appear in selected eds. where the song appears as a separate item (*1865²*, *1872*), or in autographs, but does appear in *1863²*, which extracts the whole Ottima—Sebald scene.

i *215.* spring,] Spring, (*1861 MS, 1870 MS, 1889 MS*); spring (*1870-88*).

And day's at the morn:
Morning's at seven;
The hill-side's dew-pearled:
The lark's on the wing,
220   The snail's on the thorn;
God's in his heaven—
All's right with the world!

                             [Pippa *passes.*

Sebald. God's in his heaven! Do you hear that? Who
    spoke?
  You, you spoke!
    Ottima.   Oh—that little ragged girl:
225 She must have rested on the step—we give
Them but one holiday the whole year round—
Did you e'er see our silk-mills—their inside?
There are ten silk-mills now belong to you.
She stops to pick my double heartsease . . . Sh!
She does not hear—you call out louder!
230 *Sebald.*   Leave me!

---

i *216. And day's*] The Day's (*1858 MS*); And Day's (*1861 MS*).   *morn:*]
morn; (*1849-88, 1870 MS, 1889 MS*); Morn; (*1861 MS*).
i *217*. W. L. Phelps (*Browning and How to Know Him* [1915] 82-3) objects that
'at seven o'clock on the first of January in Asolo the sun is still below the
horizon'. But it is not necessary to suppose that Pippa's song describes the
actual scene on that day.
i *218. dew-pearled:*] dew-pearled; (*1861 MS, 1863-88, 1870 MS, 1889
MS; 1863²* as *1841*).
i *219. lark's*] bee's (*1858 MS*); Bee's (*1861 MS*).   *wing,*] wing; (*1849-88,
1870 MS, 1889 MS*).
i *220. snail's*] Snail's (*1861 MS*).
i *221. his*] His (*1863-68, 1872*).   *heaven—*] Heaven, (*1861 MS*); Heaven—
(*1889 MS*).
i *222. world!*] world. (*1858 MS, 1865², 1872, 1889 MS*).
i *223. his*] His (*1863-65*).
i *225-6. we give / Them but*] we give them / But this (*1849-88*).
i *227. e'er*] ever (*1849-88*).
i *229. stops*] stoops (*1849-88*).   *double heartsease*: a cultivated pansy. In 'A
Note on the Flowers in *Pippa Passes*' (*VP* xiv [Spring 1976] 59-63) W. R.
Campbell observes that in traditional flower symbolism this plant denotes
both *thought* and *willingness to love*. The word itself, as meaning 'ease of mind;
blithesomeness' is also significant. See iv 281-303n.
i *230. you call*] call you (*1863-88*).

Go, get your clothes on—dress those shoulders.
   Ottima.   Sebald?
   Sebald. Wipe off that paint. I hate you!
   Ottima.   Miserable!
   Sebald. My God! and she is emptied of it now!
Outright now!—how miraculously gone
235 All of the grace—had she not strange grace once?
Why, the blank cheek hangs listless as it likes,
No purpose holds the features up together,
Only the cloven brow and puckered chin
Stay in their places—and the very hair,
240 That seemed to have a sort of life in it,
Drops a dead web!
   Ottima.   Speak to me—not of me!
   Sebald. That round great full orbed face, where
     not an angle
Broke the delicious indolence—all broken!
   Ottima. Ungrateful—to me—not of me—perjured
     cheat—
245 A coward too—but ingrate's worse than all:
Beggar—my slave—a fawning, cringing lie!
Leave me!—betray me!—I can see your drift—
A lie that walks, and eats, and drinks!
   Sebald.   My God!
Those morbid, olive, faultless shoulder-blades—
250 I should have known there was no blood beneath!
   Ottima. You hate me, then? you hate me then?

i *232. Wipe off that paint*: drawing upon the Jacobean—Restoration obsession with cosmetics: cp. *Flight* 825-32n. This contrast between Ottima and Pippa may relate to Perdita's rejection of cultivated flowers in *The Winter's Tale* IV iv 99-103: 'I'll not put / The dibble in earth to set one slip of them; / No more than were I painted I would wish / This youth to say 'twere well'.

i *241. not*] speak not (*1849-63*).

i *244.*] To me—not of me!—ungrateful, perjured cheat— (*1849-65*); To me—not of me! Ungrateful, perjured cheat! (*1868-88*).

i *246. lie*: not normally used, as here, of a person. Out of 115 occurrences in B.'s works there is only one other instance of this sense: 'friends, a heap, / Lovers no lack—a husband in due time, / And every one of them alike a lie!' (*In a Balcony* 127-9).

i *249. morbid*: 'of the nature of, indicative of disease'; also 'productive of disease'. B. may also have had in mind, 'of flesh-tints: painted with "morbidezza"'; for 'morbidezza', *OED* cites Aglionby 1686: 'There is a thing which the Italians call Morbidezza; The meaning of which word, is to Express the Softness, and tender Liveliness of Flesh and Blood'. Only occurrence in B.

Sebald.   To think
        She would succeed in her absurd attempt
        And fascinate with sin! and show herself
        Superior—Guilt from its excess, superior
255   To Innocence. That little peasant's voice
        Has righted all again. Though I be lost,
        I know which is the better, never fear,
        Of vice or virtue, purity or lust,
        Nature, or trick—I see what I have done
260   Entirely now. Oh, I am proud to feel
        Such torments—let the world take credit that
        I, having done my deed, pay too its price!
        I hate, hate—curse you! God's in his heaven!
            Ottima.   Me!
        Me! no, no Sebald—not yourself—kill me!
265   Mine is the whole crime—do but kill me—then
        Yourself—then—presently—first hear me speak—
        I always meant to kill myself—wait you!
        Lean on my breast . . not as a breast; don't love me
        The more because you lean on me, my own
270   Heart's Sebald. There—there—both deaths presently!
            Sebald. My brain is drowned now—quite
                drowned: all I feel
        Is . . . is at swift-recurring intervals,
        A hurrying-down within me, as of waters

i 253. *with sin! and show*] by sinning; and show (*1849-75*, except 'by sinning, and show', (*1863²*, *1865-75*); by sinning, show (*1888*).

i 254-5. *Guilt from its excess, superior / To Innocence*: the thought here is Byronic; many of Byron's heroes are, like Sebald, criminals whose crime is viewed metaphysically rather than judicially. See the excellent discussion in ch. 1 ('The Dramatic Lyric and the Lyrical Drama') of R. Langbaum's *The Poetry of Experience* (2nd ed., Chicago 1985). Langbaum draws attention to the final speech of the eponymous hero of *Manfred*, which may have had some influence on this passage.   *Guilt . . . Innocence*] guilt . . . innocence (*1868-88*).

i 261. *take credit*: the usual sense, 'take responsibility', is unlikely: something like 'believe' or 'take note' is more probable.   *that*] thence— (*1849-88*).

i 263. *his*] His (*1863-65*).   *heaven!*] emended in agreement with all other eds.; *1841* has no punctuation mark.

i 271-5. A similar vision precedes the death of Lavall in pt. iii of *Four Plays* (see headnote, p. 8), and cp. the death of Hesperus in T. L. Beddoes, *The Bride's Tragedy* (1822) V iv 117-19: 'the whole earth's in motion; / I cannot stem the billows; now they roll: / And what's this deluge? Ah! Infernal flames!'

i 273. *hurrying-down*] hurry-down (*1865-88*).

Loosened to smother up some ghastly pit—
275 There they go—whirls from a black, fiery sea.
     Ottima. Not me—to him oh God be merciful!

---

*Talk by the way in the mean time. Foreign Students of Painting
and Sculpture, from Venice, assembled opposite the house of Jules,
a young French Statuary.*

1 *Student.* Attention: my own post is beneath this
     window, but the pomegranate-clump yonder will
     hide three or four of you with a little squeezing, and
280 Schramm and his pipe must lie flat in the balcony.
     Four, five—who's a defaulter? Jules must not be
     suffered to hurt his bride.
     2 *Student.* The poet's away—never having much

i *274. pit—*] pit: (*1863²-88*).

i *275. There they go*] They—they go (*1868*; possibly a mispr., since *1868* has
few unique readings and this was altered in the first corr. reissue, *1870*).

i *276.*] Not to me, God—to him be merciful! (*1849-65*); *1868-88* as *1841*,
except 'him, O God,'.

i *276ʿ277. [s.d.] Talk by the way in the mean time.*] Talk by the way, while
PIPPA is passing from the Hill-side to Orcana. (*1849-88*, except 'hill-side',
1888).   *Statuary*] Statuary, at Possagno (*1865-88*).   The '1 Student',
whose name is Lutwyche (see ll. 308-10n.), is given no nationality in *1841*,
but in *1849* is said to be English. Of the others, Schramm and Gottlieb are
clearly German, as are probably the rest (see l. 312n.). Jules's French
nationality sets him apart from them: see also ii 93-4n. The students have
come from Venice, which would be their main centre of study; Jules is living
at Possagno because of his special interest in Canova.

i *283-4. The poet's away . . . to be here*] All here! Only our poet's away—never
having much meant to be present (*1949-88*). Cp. Plato's *Phaedo*, where those
assembled to hear Socrates' dying words do not include Plato himself, a joke
repeated at the beginning of the *Timaeus*: 'One, two, three,—but where, my
dear Timaeus, is the fourth of our guests?'

i *281-2. defaulter? Jules must not . . . bride.*] defaulter? We want everybody,
for Jules must not be suffered to hurt his bride when the jest's found out.
(*1849-88*).

i *283-94. The poet's away . . . classically and intelligibly*: the *1849* revs., give the
'poet' a name, possibly in order to disguise his resemblance to B. himself.
Trieste, a city 112 km north-east of Venice across the Adriatic, was the port
B. sailed to from London on his 1838 voyage, during which he first saw
Venice and Asolo (see headnote, p. 9). B. had left 'intending to finish' *Sordello*
(*Correspondence* iv 24), whose form ('cramp couplets') and disastrous
critical reception are clearly alluded to here (see headnote to *Sordello*, I 386

meant to be here, moonstrike him! He was in love
285   with himself, and had a fair prospect of thriving in his
suit, when suddenly a woman fell in love with him
too, and out of pure jealousy, he takes himself off to
Trieste, immortal poem and all—whereto is this
prophetical epitaph appended already, as Bluphocks
290   assured me:—"*The author on the author. Here so and so,
the mammoth, lies, Fouled to death by butterflies.*" His
own fault, the simpleton! Instead of cramp couplets,
each like a knife in your entrails, he should write,
says Bluphocks, both classically and intelligibly.—
295   *Aesculapius, an epic. Catalogue of the drugs:—Hebe's*

---

and iii 924n, noting W. S. Landor's comment that B. ought to 'atticise a
little', i.e. learn from the classical Greek writers). In a letter to William
Macready of 9 Aug. 1840, B. commented: 'tomorrow will I betimes break
new ground with So & so—an epic in so many books. . .let it but do me half
the good "Sordello" has done' (*Correspondence* iv 295). It is the neo-classicism
attributed to Bluphocks (for whom see ii 243ˆ244n.) against which Jules
eventually rebels: see iv 39-57n. There may also be an allusion to the literary
controversy in Italy between the 'classicisti' and the 'romantici' which gave
rise to 'a thousand grave treatises, and lighter tracts, and satires, and
epigrams' (*European Review* i, no. 2 [July 1824] 259). This controversy had
political overtones: see iii 18n.

i *284. moonstrike him! He*] moonstrike him! The airs of that fellow, that
Giovacchino! He (*1849-88*).   *moonstrike*: not rec. as a verb in *OED*;
derived from 'moonstruck', i.e. lunatic, a traditional satirical epithet for poets
(*OED* cites Pope, *Dunciad* iv 12).   *He was in love*] He was in violent
love (*1849-88*).

i *286. suit . . . fell*] suit, so unmolested was it, when suddenly a woman falls
(*1849-88*).

i *290. assured me*] assures me (*1849-88*).

i *290-1. The author . . . the mammoth, lies,*] Here a mammoth-poem lies,—
(*1849-88*).

i *295-8. Aesculapius, an epic . . . Cures*: for Aesculapius (the Greek god of
medicine), see *Artemis*. The catalogue of drugs alludes to the catalogue of
ships at the outset of Homer's *Iliad*, and puns on the names or attributes of
other Greek divinities. Hebe was goddess of youth, and cupbearer to the
gods: the 'plaister' (*J.*: 'a glutinous or adhesive salve') is a kiss. Phoebus is
Phoebus Apollo, god of eloquence among other things: the 'emulsion' (liquid
medicine) is wine. Mercury is the Roman name for Hermes, the messenger of
the gods; here the play is on name, not function, since mercury was a
treatment for syphilis, or 'the pox'—this being the suppressed rhyme for
'box'. A bolus is a medicinal substance shaped for swallowing, larger than an
ordinary pill. All these mythological figures appear in works by Canova.

plaister—*One strip Cools your lip; Phoebus' emulsion*—
One bottle Clears your throttle; Mercury's bolus—*One box
Cures* . . .

300   3 *Student*. Subside, my fine fellow; if the marriage
was over by ten o'clock, Jules will certainly be here in
a minute with his bride.

    2 *Student*. So should the poet's muse have been
acceptable, says Bluphocks, and Delia not better
known to our dogs than the boy.

305   1 *Student*. To the point, now. Where's Gottlieb?
Oh, listen, Gottlieb—What called down this piece of
friendly vengeance on Jules, of which we now
assemble to witness the winding-up. We are all in a
tale, observe, when Jules bursts out on us by and bye:

310   I shall be spokesman, but each professes himself alike
insulted by this strutting stone-squarer, who came
singly from Paris to Munich, thence with a crowd of

i *297. throttle*: throat.
i *302-4. So should . . . the boy.*] Good!—Only, so should the poet's muse
have been universally acceptable, says Bluphocks, *et canibus nostris* . . . and
Delia not better known to our literary dogs than the boy—Giovacchino!
(*1849-88*, except 'only', *1868-88*, 'the boy Giovacchino!', *1865-88*). Cp.
Virgil, *Eclogues* iii 66-7: the shepherd Menalcas is boasting of the willingness
of his lover, the boy Amyntas, who 'comes to me unsought, so that now
Delia [i.e. the moon] is not better known to my dogs'. The *1849* rev. makes
the quotation and its application clearer.
i *305-6. Where's Gottlieb? . . . called down*] Where's Gottlieb, the new-comer?
Oh,—listen, Gottlieb, to what called down (*1849-88*). Gottlieb's name
combines the German words for 'God' and 'love'.
i *308-10. We are all . . . but each*] We are all agreed, all in a tale, observe, when
Jules shall burst out on us in a fury by and bye: I am spokesman—the verses
that are to undeceive Jules bear my name of Lutwyche—but each (*1849-88*,
except 'by-and-by:', *1863*, 'by and by:', *1865-88*).
i *311. stone-squarer*: one who shapes stone into building-blocks.
i *311-14. who came . . . indubitably*: cp. T. L. Beddoes, *Pygmalion* 39-45:
'Lonely Pygmalion: you might see him go / Along the streets where markets
thickest flow / Doubling his gown across his thinking breast / And the men
fall aside'. See also ll. 373-8n. and ii 67-98n.
i *312. singly*] alone (*1865-88*).   *Munich, thence*] Munich, and thence
(*1849-88*). Munich is the capital city of Bavaria in southern Germany. There
was a 'Glypothek' or gallery of sculpture, 'erected by von Kleuse, for the
present King [Ludwig I], who, while Crown Prince, formed the very
interesting and valuable collection deposited in it' (Murray's *Handbook for
Travellers in Southern Germany* [1837] 31-2). The collection included the
Aegina marbles and the 'Tenea kouros', a figure of Apollo, among the most

us to Venice and Possagno here, but proceeds in a day
or two alone,—oh! alone, indubitably—to Rome and
315   Florence. He take up his portion with these dissolute, brutalized, heartless bunglers! (Is Schramm
brutalized? Am I heartless?)
        Gottlieb. Why, somewhat heartless; for, coxcomb
as much as you choose, you will have brushed
320   off—what do folks style it?—the bloom of his life. Is
it too late to alter? These letters, now, you call his. I
can't laugh at them.
        4 Student. Because you never read the sham letters
of our inditing which drew forth these.
325   *Gottlieb.* His discovery of the truth will be
frightful.
        4 Student. That's the joke. But you should have
joined us at the beginning; there's no doubt he loves
the girl.
330   *Gottlieb.* See here: "He has been accustomed," he
writes, "to have Canova's women about him, in

---

famous remnants of classical sculpture. There were also works by Canova,
incl. the statue of Psyche mentioned below (l. 357). B. had visited Munich
during his 1838 travels.

i *313. Venice and Possagno*: see ll. 276^277n.

i *314. alone,—oh!*] alone again,—oh! (*1849-88*).

i *314-15. Rome and Florence*: neither was on B.'s itinerary in 1838; he first
visited them in 1844.

i *315. He take up*] He, forsooth, take up (*1849-88*).

i *315-17. dissolute, brutalized . . . Am I heartless?*] dissolute, brutalised,
heartless bunglers!—So he was heard to call us all: now, is Schramm
brutalised, I should like to know? Am I heartless? (*1849-88*, except 'so',
1865-88, 'brutalized' [both occurrences], *1863-88*).

i *318-19. for, coxcomb as much as you choose, you*] for, suppose Jules a coxcomb
as much as you choose, still, for this mere coxcombry, you (*1849-88*).

i *318. coxcomb*: 'a fop; a superficial pretender to knowledge or accomplishments' (*J.*).

i *320. the bloom of his life*: the context suggests the sense of 'bloom' given by *J.*
as 'the blue colour upon plums and grapes newly gathered', esp. taken with
'dew' in l. 335. See ll. 337-8n.

i *321. These letters, now*] These love-letters, now (*1849-88*).

i *328-9. loves the girl.*] loves the girl—loves a model he might hire by the hour!
(*1849-88*).

i *331. Canova's women*: see headnote, p. 13. Canova's sculptures of female
figures (such as the Psyche mentioned below, l. 357) were esp. celebrated. In
1817 Canova executed a series of busts intended to represent 'ideal female
beauty'.

stone, and the world's women beside him, in flesh,
these being as much below, as those above, his soul's
aspiration; but now he is to have" . . . There you
335   laugh again! You wipe off the very dew of his youth.
1 *Student*. Schramm (take the pipe out of his
mouth, somebody), will Jules lose the bloom of his
youth?
Schramm. Nothing worth keeping is ever lost in
340   this world: look at a blossom—it drops presently and

i *334. he is to have"* . . .] he is to have the real." . . . (*1849*); he is to have the
real." (*1863*); he is to have the reality." (*1865-88*).
i *335. You wipe off*] I say, you wipe off (*1849-88*).
i *337-8. will Jules lose the bloom of his youth?*: see l. 320n. The 1st student uses
the more traditional trope, where 'bloom' means 'the state of anything
improving, and ripening to a higher perfection' (*J*.). Schramm takes the
image in the literal sense of a blossom.
i *339-50. Nothing worth keeping . . . thus . . .*] Schramm and his opinions may
owe something to Thomas Carlyle, whom B. first met in 1836, and whose
work was a major influence in this period. B. spoke of his liking for Carlyle
in a letter to Fanny Haworth of 16 Dec. 1841 (*Correspondence* v 189), and was
impressed both by his talk (see his letter of 15 May 1843 to Domett,
Correspondence vii 124) and by his pipe-smoking—in a letter to EBB. of 28
June 1846 he reports Carlyle giving an opinion 'between two huge pipe-
whiffs' (*LK* 822). Schramm's German nationality may owe something to
Carlyle's position as the principal mediator of German ideas in England at
this period. Carlyle certainly advocated the kind of incessant curiosity about
life which Schramm recommends (see, for instance, his essay 'Boswell's Life
of Johnson'). Tennyson's early poem *Nothing Will Die* (1830) also has
affinities with the thought here: 'Nothing will die; / All things will change /
Through eternity. . . . The world was never made; / It will change but it will
not fade' (14-16, 30-1). Tennyson himself noted of this poem: 'All things are
evolved'. The substance of Schramm's remarks, however, combining a
hierarchy of value with an evolutionary principle, is a commonplace in B. See
Paracelsus headnote, I 000, and v 627; also *A Forest Thought*, written 1837.
Note, however, the different version which B. gives in a letter to EBB. (5
May 1846): 'Would it not be perilous in some cases,—many cases—to
contrast the present with the very early Past—the fruit time, even when there
is abundant fruit,—with the dewy springing and blossoming? One would
confess to a regret at the vanishing of that charm, at least, if it were felt to be
somehow vanished out of the present. . . . Now, hear the truth! I never, God
knows, felt the joy of being with you as I felt it YESTERDAY—the fruit of
my happiness has grown under the blossom, lifting it and keeping it as a
coronet—not one feeling is lost, and the new feelings are infinite' (*LK* 676).
i *340-1. presently, and fruits succeed; as well affirm*] presently, having done its
service and lasted its time; but fruits succeed, and where would be the

fruits succeed; as well affirm that your eye is no
longer in your body because its earliest favourite is
dead and done with, as that any affection is lost to the
soul when its first object is superseded in due course.
345 Has a man done wondering at women? There follow
men, dead and alive, to wonder at. Has he done
wondering at men? There's God to wonder at: and
the faculty of wonder may be at the same time grey
enough with respect to its last object, and yet green
350 sufficiently so far as concerns its novel one: thus . . .
    1 *Student.* Put Schramm's pipe into his mouth
again—There you see! well, this Jules .. a wretched
fribble—oh, I watched his disportings at Possagno the
other day! The Model-Gallery—you know: he
355 marches first resolvedly past great works by the
dozen without vouchsafing an eye: all at once he
stops full at the *Psiche-fanciulla*—cannot pass that old

---

blossom's place could it continue? As well affirm (*1849-88*).

i *342-3. favourite is dead*] favourite, whatever it may have first loved to look
on, is dead (*1849-88*).

i *344-5. object . . . man*] object, whatever happened first to satisfy it, is
superseded in due course. Keep but ever looking, whether with the body's
eye or the mind's, and you will soon find something to look on! Has a man
(*1849-88*).

i *348. grey*] old and tired (*1849-88*).

i *349. its last object*] its first object (*1849-88*).   *green*] young and fresh
(*1849-88*).

i *353. fribble*: a trifling, frivolous person. For the synonym 'fribbler', J. cites
Spectator 288: 'A fribbler is one who professes rapture for the woman, and
dreads her consent'.

i *353-4. Possagno . . . The Model-Gallery*: the 'Gipsoteca' at Possagno,
devoted to a permanent exhibition of Canova's plaster casts, models, etc.
Most of Canova's 'great works' were represented in this form; there were a
few marbles and bronzes.

i *354. The Model-Gallery*] Canova's gallery (*1849-88*).

i *354-5. he marches*] there he marches (*1849-88*).

i *357-60. the Psiche-fanciulla . . . at Munich*: 'Psiche-fanciulla' means
'Psyche as a young girl'—the name of a famous statue by Canova originally
executed in 1789 and repeated in 1793; the latter version was in Munich. The
'new place' is not literal, therefore, but refers to the statue's different
versions, the one at Possagno being a plaster cast (of the head only). Countess
Albrizzi gives the following description of the statue: 'Psyche is here
represented by Canova occupied in holding a butterfly, with the softest
touch, between the forefinger and thumb of her right hand, and placing it

acquaintance without a nod of encouragement—"In
your new place, beauty? Then behave yourself as well
360 here as at Munich—I see you!"—Next posts himself
deliberately before the unfinished *Pietà* for half an
hour without moving, till up he starts of a sudden
and thrusts his very nose into . . I say into—the
group—by which you are informed that precisely the
365 sole point he had not fully mastered in Canova was a
certain method of using the drill in the articulation of
the knee-joint—and that, even, has he mastered at
length! Good bye, therefore, to Canova—whose
gallery no longer contains Jules, the predestinated
370 thinker in marble!
      5 *Student.* Tell him about the women—go on to the
women.
      1 *Student.* Why, on that matter he could never be

---

gently in the palm of her left: wholly absorbed in contemplating the beautiful
insect, her features wear a smile of tranquil and celestial sweetness, expressive
of the sufficiency of the soul, of which both Psyche and the butterfly are
emblems, to its own proper and entire happiness'. She adds: 'He who long
contemplates, however, this beautiful symbol of our immaterial part, finds a
certain cheerless and inquiet feeling arising in his mind, that sufficiency to its
own enjoyment chills the heart, and his mind is led to reflect on the nature of
those unsympathising beings, who having no mutual wants or pleasures,
may enjoy solitary happiness, but never taste that of being dear to others'
(*Works of Canova* i [n.p.]).

i *360. Next posts*] Next he posts (*1849-88*).

i *361. the unfinished Pietà*: referring to the plaster cast of a 'Pietà' or
'Deposition from the Cross' (the dead Christ with the Virgin Mary and Mary
Magdalen), made in 1822 but never executed in marble.

i *364. by which you*] by which gesture you (*1849-88*).

i *365. mastered in Canova*] mastered in Canova's practice (*1849-88*).

i *367. and that, even*] and that, likewise (*1849-88*).

i *368. therefore, to Canova*] therefore, to poor Canova (*1849-88*).

i *369-70. gallery . . . thinker*] gallery no longer detain his successor Jules,
the predestinated novel thinker (*1849-88*, except 'needs', *1863-88*).

i *374-8. How should we be other . . . Psiche-fanciulla*: cp. Canova's comment: 'I
pity those young men who think to reconcile a life of amusement with the
pursuit of the arts. Art should be the ruling passion of the sculptor' (*Works of
Canova* iii 41). Cp. also (noting ll. 311-14) T. L. Beddoes, *Pygmalion* 55-63:
'Still, discontent / Over his sensual kind the sculptor went / Walking his
thoughts. Yet Cyprus' girls be fair . . . and their pleasure / Silent and deep as
midnight's starry treasure. / Lovely and young, Pygmalion yet loved none. /
His soul was bright and lonely as the sun / Like which he could create'. See
also ll. 311-14n. and ii 67-98n.

supercilious enough. How should we be other than
375   the poor devils you see, with those debasing habits
we cherish? He was not to wallow in that mire, at
least: he would love at the proper time, and
meanwhile put up with the *Psiche-fanciulla*. Now I
happened to hear of a young Greek—real Greek girl
380   at Malamocco, a true Islander, do you see, with
Alciphron hair like sea-moss—you know! White and
quiet as an apparition, and fourteen years old at
farthest; daughter, so she swears, of that hag Natalia,
who helps us to models at three *lire* an hour. So first
385   Jules received a scented letter—somebody had seen
his Tydeus at the Academy, and my picture was

i *374. other than*] other (he said) than (*1849-88*).

i *377. he would love at the proper time*] he would wait, and love only at the
proper time (*1849-88*).

i *380. Malamocco*: a village on the Lido, the littoral strip which lies between
the Lagoon of Venice and the Adriatic. *Ohio* points out that much of the
population is of Greek descent.   *a true Islander*: the Greek islands are
meant—probably the Cyclades. Venice had been trading with Greece for
centuries.

i *381. Alciphron hair like sea-moss—you know*] Alciphron's "hair like sea-
moss"—Schramm knows (*1849-88*). Alciphron was an Athenian sophist and
rhetorician of the 2nd century AD, a contemporary of Lucian. He was the
author of a collection of fictitious letters depicting four classes of society:
fishermen, farmers, parasites, and courtesans. These letters were considered
models of pure 'Attic' style. The letters concerning courtesans are a source
for the scene involving the 'poor girls' in pt. iii. The phrase 'hair like sea-
moss' occurs in a letter from Glaucippe, a fisherman's daughter, to her
mother Charope, and describes a young man: 'His hair curls more beautifully
than sea-moss' (1st Eng. transl. [1791] 146).

i *382-3. fourteen years old at farthest*: Canova's Psyche is in 'her
thirteenth or fourteenth year' according to the Countess Albrizzi
(*Works of Canova* i [n.p.]).

i *383. daughter . . . Natalia*] a daughter of Natalia, so she swears—that hag
Natalia (*1849-88*).   *so she swears*: i.e. Natalia swears.

i *384. an hour. So first*] an hour. We selected this girl for the heroine of our
jest. So, first, (*1849-88*, except 'So first,', *1865-88*).

i *386. Tydeus*: in Greek legend, one of the 'Seven against Thebes', wounded
by Menalippus, whom he killed and whose brains he tore out with his teeth
before his own death. His barbarous revenge cost him immortality, which
the goddess Athene had intended to confer on him. No statue of Tydeus by
Canova is recorded, unlike the other mythological figures—see e.g. ll. 295-8n.
See also ii 14n.   *the Academy*: the Accademia, Venice's principal art
gallery.

nothing to it—bade him persevere—would make
herself known to him ere long—(Paolina, my little
friend, transcribes divinely.) Now think of Jules
390 finding himself distinguished from the herd of us by
such a creature! In his very first answer he proposed
marrying his monitress; and fancy us over these
letters two, three times a day to receive and dispatch!
I concocted the main of it: relations were in the
395 way—secrecy must be observed—would he wed her
on trust and only speak to her when they were
indissolubly united? St—St!
    6 *Student*. Both of them! Heaven's love, speak
softly! speak within yourselves!
400   5 *Student*. Look at the Bridegroom—half his hair in
storm and half in calm—patted down over the left
temple, like a frothy cup one blows on to cool it; and
the same old blouse he murders the marble in!
    2 *Student*. Not a rich vest like yours, Hannibal

---

i *387. bade him persevere*] a profound admirer bade him persevere (*1849-88*).

i *388-9. my little friend*] my little friend of the *Fenice* (*1849-88*); 'the *Fenice*' [Phoenix] is a theatre and opera-house in Venice. It had been rebuilt in 1836, two years before B.'s visit.

i *389. divinely.) Now think*] divinely). And in due time, the mysterious correspondent gave certain hints of her peculiar charms—the pale cheeks, the black hair—whatever, in short, had struck us in our Malamocco model: we retained her name, too—Phene, which is by interpretation, sea-eagle. Now, think (*1849-88*, except 'is, by interpretation,', *1868-88*).

i *392. monitress*: 'one who warns of faults, or informs of duty; one who gives useful hints' (J.).

i *394-5. relations were in the way*: i.e. the family of the bride would object to the match.

i *395. would he wed her*] in fine, would he wed her (*1849-88*).

i *397. St—St!*] St—st—Here they come! (*1849-88*).

i *403. blouse he*] blouse that he (*1849-88*).

i *404-5. Hannibal Scratchy*: i.e. the 16th-century Bolognese painter Annibale Carracci, to whom '5 Student' (presumably, like Lutwyche, a mediocre painter) is being ironically compared. Cp. Fielding, *Joseph Andrews* III vi: 'For my own part, when I have waited behind my lady in a room hung with fine pictures, while I have been looking at them I have never once thought of their owner, nor hath any one else, as I have observed; for when it has been asked whose picture that was, it was never once answered the master's of the house; but Ammyconni, Paul Varnish, Hannibal Scratchi, or Hogarthi, which I suppose were the names of the painters'.

405   Scratchy, rich that your face may the better set it off.
        6 *Student.* And the bride—and the bride—how
      magnificently pale!
        Gottlieb. She does not also take it for earnest, I
      hope?
410   1 *Student.* Oh, Natalia's concern, that is; we settle
      with Natalia.
        6 *Student.* She does not speak—has evidently let out
      no word.
        Gottlieb. How he gazes on her!
415   1 *Student.* They go in—now, silence!

i *406-7. And the bride . . . pale!*] And the bride! Yes, sure enough, our Phene!
Should you have known her in her clothes? How magnificently pale! (*1849-
88*).
i *413. no word.*] no word. The only thing is, will she equally remember the
rest of her lesson, and repeat correctly all those verses which are to break the
secret to Jules? (*1849-88*).
i *414. gazes on her!*] gazes on her! Pity—pity! (*1849-88*).
i *415. now, silence!*] now, silence! You three,—not nearer the window, mind,
than that pomegranate—just where the little girl, who a few minutes ago
passed us singing, is seated! (*1849-88*, except 'pomegranate:', *1865-88*).

II.—*Noon. Over Orcana. The House of* Jules, *who crosses its threshold with* Phene—*she is silent, on which* Jules *begins*—

    Do not die, Phene—I am yours now—you
    Are mine now—let fate reach me how she likes
    If you'll not die—so never die! Sit here—
    My work-room's single seat—I do lean over
5 This length of hair and lustrous front—they turn
    Like an entire flower upward—eyes—lips—last
    Your chin—no, last your throat turns—'tis their scent
    Pulls down my face upon you. Nay, look ever
    That one way till I change, grow you—I could
10 Change into you, beloved!
                     Thou by me
    And I by thee—this is thy hand in mine—
    And side by side we sit—all's true. Thank God!
    I have spoken—speak thou!
                 —O, my life to come!
    My Tydeus must be carved that's there in clay,
15 And how be carved with you about the chamber?
    Where must I place you? When I think that once
    This room-full of rough block-work seemed my
        heaven
    Without you! Shall I ever work again—
    Get fairly into my old ways again—

ii *Opening s.d. Over Orcana*: overlooking the valley of Orcana from Possagno.

ii *4. I do lean over*] I over-lean (*1849-88*).

ii *5. front*: forehead.

ii *8-10. Nay, look ever . . . beloved*: a Platonic idea (see the *Symposium*), frequently echoed in love poetry: see e.g. Donne, *A Valediction Forbidding Mourning, Love's Infiniteness, The Ecstasy*. Cp. *James Lee* ix 21-5: 'Strange, if a face, when you thought of me, / Rose like your own face present now, / With eyes as dear in their due degree, / Much such a mouth, and as bright a brow, / Till you saw yourself, while you cried "'Tis She!"'

ii *9. That*] This (*1849-88*).

ii *10-13. Thou . . . thee . . . thy . . . thou*] You . . . you . . . your . . . you (*1849-88*).

ii *14.* See i 386n. Apparently Jules had exhibited this unfinished work at the Academy; Canova 'thought it very useful to let his designs be seen by the public in their unfinished state' (*Works of Canova* iii 56).

ii *15. And*] Yet (*1849-88*). *chamber*] room (*1865-88*).

ii *17. block-work*: not *OED*. Presumably unfinished work in blocks of stone, drawing on the sense of the verb 'block': 'to sketch out, mark out roughly (work to be finished afterwards)' (*OED* 9).

20   Bid each conception stand while trait by trait
      My hand transfers its lineaments to stone?
      Will they, my fancies, live near you, my truth—
      The live truth—passing and repassing me—
      Sitting beside me?
                              Now speak!
                                        Only, first,
25   Your letters to me—was't not well contrived?
      A hiding-place in Psyche's robe—there lie
      Next to her skin your letters: which comes foremost?
      Good—this that swam down like a first moonbeam
      Into my world.
                        Those? Books I told you of.
30   Let your first word to me rejoice them, too,—
      This minion of Coluthus, writ in red

ii *20-4*. The artist—model relation appears in other poems, e.g. *Andrea, James Lee* viii ('Beside the Drawing-Board'), and *Beatrice*.

ii *22. they, my*] my mere (*1849-88*).   *my truth*] their truth (*1865-88*).

ii *25. Your letters to me*—] See, all your letters! (*1849-88*).

ii *26-7*.] Their hiding-place is Psyche's robe; she keeps / Your letters next her skin: which drops out foremost? (*1849-88*). For Psyche see i *357-60*n.; a further allusion was added in *1849-88* (below, ll. *216ˆ217*n.).

ii *28-9. Good . . . my world*: perhaps alluding to the mythological love-affair between the moon-goddess Artemis and the shepherd Endymion. B. knew Keats's *Endymion*, in which the story is told, and Artemis is frequently mentioned in his work: see e.g. *Artemis* and *Pan and Luna*.

ii *28. Good*—] Ah,— (*1849-88*).

ii *29*.] Into my world!

                              Again those eyes complete
      Their melancholy survey, sweet and slow,
      Of all my room holds; to return and rest
      On me, with pity, yet some wonder too—
      As if God bade some spirit plague a world,
      And this were the one moment of surprise
      And sorrow while she took her station, pausing
      O'er what she sees, finds good, and must destroy!

What gaze you at? Those? Books I told you of; (*1849-88*, except in the fourth line 'too:', *1865-88*).   *Books I told you of*: Canova was 'very solicitous to instruct and adorn his mind in every respect that could tend to the perfect education of an artist; he read himself, but more often caused to be read to him, while at work, the classical Grecian, Roman, and Italian writers' (*Works of Canova* i xvi).

ii *31. minion of Coluthus*] minion, a Coluthus, (*1849-88*). Cp. the use of 'minion' to mean a small and delicate person in *Laboratory* 29.

ii *31-2*. 'Coluthus [or Colluthus], a native of Lycopolis in Egypt, in the time

Bistre and azure by Bessarion's scribe—
Read this line . . no, shame—Homer's be the Greek!
My Odyssey in coarse black vivid type
35 With faded yellow blossoms 'twixt page and page;
"He said, and on Antinous directed
A bitter shaft"—then blots a flower the rest!
—Ah, do not mind that—better that will look
When cast in bronze . . an Almaign Kaiser that,
40 Swart-green and gold with truncheon based on hip—

of the Emperor Anastasius, in the beginning of the 6th century, who wrote a poem on the rape of Helen, in imitation of Homer. The composition remained long unknown, till it was discovered at Lycopolis [actually at Otranto in Calabria, S. Italy] in the 15th century, by the learned Cardinal Bessarion [*c.* 1395-1472]' (*Lemprière*). The Loeb ed. (*Oppian, Colluthus, Tryphiodorus* [1963] 537) lists the MSS which probably derived from the MS found by Bessarion; they would have been very expensive by B.'s time. B.'s attention may have been drawn to Colluthus by a number of contemporary eds., incl. one of 1839. Colluthus' poem is reckoned poor stuff, so there is presumably a deliberate contrast between the beautiful MS of a bad poem and the popular ed. of a great one (Homer), mentioned at ll. 33-4. This is B.'s only ref. to Colluthus.

ii *32. Bistre*: a dark-brown pigment made by boiling soot.

ii *33.*] Read this line .. no, shame—Homer's be the Greek / First breathed me from the lips of my Greek girl! (*1849-88*, except 3-point ellipsis, *1870-88*).

ii *34. My*] This (*1865-88*).

ii *35.*] With faded yellow blossoms 'twixt page and page, / To mark great places with due gratitude; (*1849-88*).

ii *36-7.*] the quotation is italicized, *1849-88*. It translates *Odyssey* xxii 8: Odysseus is beginning the slaughter of Penelope's suitors, foremost of whom was Antinous. The passage continues: 'Now he [Antinous] was on the point of raising to his lips a fair goblet, a two-eared cup of gold, and was even now handling it, that he might drink of the wine, and death was not in his thoughts'.

ii *37. then blots a flower*] a flower blots out (*1849-88*).

ii *37ˆ38.*] Again upon your search? My statues, then! (*1849-88*).

ii *39. Almaign Kaiser*: German emperor. *Ohio* points out that B. could have seen the monument to the Emperor Maximilian I at Innsbruck on his 1838 travels. Murray's *Handbook for Travellers in Southern Germany* (1837) describes the 'row of bronze figures' around the marble sarcophagus, '28 in number, representing some of "the worthies" of Europe, but principally the most distinguished personages . . . of the house of Austria . . . they are of colossal size, skilfully executed, and the elaborate workmanship of the armour and dresses gives them an additional interest' (p. 214).

ii *40. Swart-green and gold*: dark-green (bronze) with gold-leaf ornament.   *truncheon*: 'a staff of command' (*J.*).

This rather, turn to . . but a check already—
Or you had recognized that here you sit
As I imagined you, Hippolyta
Naked upon her bright Numidian horse!
45   —Forget you this then? "carve in bold relief" . . .
So you command me—"carve against I come
A Greek, bay-filleted and thunder-free,

ii *41-2.*] This, rather, turn to! What, unrecognised? / I thought you would
have seen that here you sit (*1849-88*).

ii *43-4. Hippolyta . . . Numidian horse*: Hippolyta was queen of the Amazons,
a legendary nation of warrior-women. Numidia is the Roman name for the
region of N. Africa roughly equivalent to modern Algeria; B. follows
classical authorities (such as Diodorus Siculus) who place the Amazons in
Africa rather than Asia Minor.

ii *45.—Forget*] Recall (*1849-88*).   *in bold relief*: see ll. 50-63n.

ii *46. command me*] commanded (*1849-88*).   *against I come*: 'to be ready
when I come'.

ii *47-9.*] A Greek, in Athens, as our fashion was,
        Feasting, bay-filleted and thunder-free,
        Who rises 'neath the lifted myrtle-branch:
        '*Praise those who slew Hipparchus,*' cry the guests,
        '*While o'er thy head the singer's myrtle waves
        As erst above our champions': stand up all!*'

See, I have laboured to express your thought! (*1849-88*, except
'myrtle-branch.', *1868-88*, 'champion:', *1865-88*, 'thought.', *1868-88*; in
1868-88 the inset quotation is not in italics). In *B & P BYU* 'Praise him!' in
l. 49 is underlined. Harmodius plotted with his friend Aristogiton to kill the
Athenian tyrant Hippias, and his younger brother Hipparchus, at the
Panathenaea festival in 514 BC. 'The plot miscarried: only Hipparchus was
killed . . . After the expulsion of Hippias in 511/10 the deed of Aristogiton
and Harmodius received ample recognition, public and private. Bronze
statues of them by Antenor were set up . . . Privately, scolia [drinking-
songs] were sung claiming them as the men who gave Athens *isonomia* [equal
political rights] . . . All this fostered the popular belief that Hipparchus, not
Hippias, was the tyrant and that Aristogiton and Harmodius . . . had ended
the tyranny; and despite the deliberate refutations of this view by Herodotus
and Thucydides, it continued to influence the tradition' (*Oxford Classical
Dictionary*, 2nd ed., s.v. Aristogiton). Note the *1849* reading, and see iii 6. B.
refers specifically to a famous scolium, almost a national anthem in Athens,
which began: 'In a myrtle-branch I will carry my sword, as did Harmodius
and Aristogiton, when they slew the tyrant'. The full text is in Athenaeus,
The Deipnosophists xv 695. B.'s attention may have been drawn to it by a
parody in Aristophanes' *Wasps* (1225ff). Plutarch's account of the origin and
procedure of scolia is probably B.'s source: 'first the guests would sing the
god's song together . . . and next when to each in turn was given the myrtle

Rising beneath the lifted myrtle-branch,
Whose turn arrives to praise Harmodius."—Praise
him!
50 Quite round, a cluster of mere hands and arms
Thrust in all senses, all ways, from all sides,
Only consenting at the branch's end
They strain towards, serves for frame to a sole face—
(Place your own face)—the Praiser's, who with eyes
55 Sightless, so bend they back to light inside
His brain where visionary forms throng up,
(Gaze—I am your Harmodius dead and gone,)
Sings, minding nor the palpitating arch
Of hands and arms, nor the quick drip of wine
60 From the drenched leaves o'erhead, nor who cast off

spray . . . and too the lyre was passed around, the guest who could play the
instrument would take it and tune it and sing' (*Moralia: Table-talk* i 1 615). B.
adds the detail that the singer is 'bay-filleted', crowned with a wreath of bay-
leaves, the bay being sacred to Apollo; he is thus 'thunder-free', since the bay
was also traditionally supposed to be immune from lightning. The induction
to *Four Plays* (see headnote, p. 8) includes a ref. to the muse's 'thunder-
fearless verdant bays'.

ii *50-63*. The allusion is to a bas-relief, presumably in marble, a genre in
which Canova was renowned, though there is no record of his having
undertaken this subject. Indeed the aesthetic is quite alien to Canova's neo-
classicism, and closer to the romantic expressionism which Jules, according
to his own account, adopts only later (see iv 39-57n.).

ii *52. consenting*: 'coming together'. B. is drawing on an archaic sense of the
verb, 'to agree together'.   *branch's*] emended in agreement with all other
eds. from 'branches' in *1841*.

ii *54.*] The Praiser's—in the centre—who with eyes (*1849-88*, except
'Praiser's,', *1863-88*, 'centre:', *1865-88*).

ii *54-6. eyes . . . brain*: the contrast between eyesight and insight is traditional;
B. may also be thinking of the 'blind' appearance of 'marbled' eyes in statues.
Cp. *Aristophanes* 5264, where the statue of the blinded bard Thamyris is
described as 'Mute marble, blind the eyes and quenched the brain'. Cp. also
B.'s definition of the 'subjective poet', in *Shelley*: 'Not what man sees, but
what God sees—the *Ideas* of Plato, seeds of creation lying burningly on the
Divine Hand—it is toward these that he struggles' (p. 7).

ii *57.*] not *1849-88*.

ii *58. nor the*] not that (*1849-88*).

ii *60. the drenched leaves o'erhead*: the leaves of the 'lifted myrtle-branch' (l. 48).

ii *60-1. who cast off / Their violet crowns for him*] crowns cast off, / Violet and
parsley crowns (*1849-88*). The violet was a favourite flower in Athens; the
city itself was called 'violet-crowned'. Such wreaths (of various flowers: note
the *1849* rev.) were worn at ceremonies and festivals.

Their violet crowns for him to trample on—
Sings, pausing as the patron-ghosts approve,
Devoutly their unconquerable hymn—
But you must say a "well" to that—say "well"
65   Because you gaze—am I fantastic, sweet?
Gaze like my very life's-stuff, marble—marbly
Even to the silence—and before I found

ii *62. patron-ghosts*: the presiding spirits of Harmodius and Aristogiton.
ii *65. fantastic*: 'fanciful', 'capricious' (*OED*); 'indulgent to one's own
imagination' (*J.*).
ii *66. like . . . marble*: cp. *Sordello* i 413-15: 'just-tinged marble like Eve's lilied
flesh / Beneath her Maker's finger when the fresh / First pulse of life shot
brightening the snow'.   *marbly*: cp. *Tomb at St. Praxed's* 75: 'mistresses
with great smooth marbly limbs'. See also ll. 93-4n. below.
ii *67. silence—and*] silence! why (*1849*); silence! why, (*1863-88*).
ii *67-98. before I found . . . its track*: this complex passage blends Neo-
Platonism with alchemical speculations which recall those of Paracelsus. In
ll. 67-79 Jules combines the Neo-Platonic claim that art can forge a 'better
nature', a 'golden world' superior to the 'brazen world' of actuality, with the
Paracelsian (and Kabbalistic) claim that man (the 'Adam Kadmon' of the
Kabbala) was God's final creation, and a distillate of all other natural forms.
Jules imagines himself as, in effect, in the process of creating man from the
inferior matter of nature, re-enacting the divine creative sequence in his art.
This passage concerns the *subject-matter* of his art; in ll. 80-98 Jules considers
its *materials*, assigning to marble a similar status to that of man in the first
passage. Marble resembles the alchemists' 'prima materia', the primordial
substance out of which all material forms then emerge. As God created first
nature, then man, out of the universal 'prima materia', so Jules creates first
'baser substance' (air, diamond, metal), then human flesh, out of marble.
James Lee viii ('Beside the Drawing-Board') has many parallels: see also *A
Death* 609-22 and *Fifine* 756-870. The concept that marble *contains*, in an ideal
sense, the form which the sculptor carves from it derives from Michelangelo's famous statements to that effect, as in his sonnet *Non ha l'ottimo
artista alcun concetto*: 'The best of artists hath no thought to show / Which the
rough stone in its superfluous shell / Doth not include: to break the marble
spell / Is all the hand that serves the brain can do' (transl. J. A. Symons, *The
Sonnets of Michael Angelo Buonarrotti* [1904] 17). Cp. also T. L. Beddoes,
Pygmalion 111-27: 'The magic chisel thrust and gashed and swept / Flying and
manifold . . . And as insensibly out of a stick / Dead in the winter-time, the
dew-drops quick / And the thin sun-beams and the airy shower / Raise and
unwrap a many-leaved flower / And then a fruit . . . he, quiet as the air, /
Had shaped a lady wonderfully fair. / Dear to the eyes—a delicate delight /
For all her marble symmetry was white / As brow and bosom should be;
save some azure / Which waited for a loving lip's erasure / Upon her
shoulders to be turned to blush'. See also i 311-14n, 373-8n.

The real flesh Phene, I inured myself
To see throughout all nature varied stuff
70 For better nature's birth by means of art:
With me, each substance tended to one form
Of beauty—to the human Archetype—
And every side occurred suggestive germs
Of that—the tree, the flower—why, take the fruit,
75 Some rosy shape, continuing the peach,
Curved beewise o'er its bough, as rosy limbs
Depending nestled in the leaves—and just
From a cleft rose-peach the whole Dryad sprung!
But of the stuffs one can be master of,
80 How I divined their capabilities
From the soft-rinded smoothening facile chalk
That yields your outline to the air's embrace,
Down to the crisp imperious steel, so sure
To cut its one confided thought clean out
85 Of all the world: but marble!—'neath my tools
More pliable than jelly—as it were
Some clear primordial creature dug from deep
In the Earth's heart where itself breeds itself
And whence all baser substance may be worked;
90 Refine it off to air you may—condense it
Down to the diamond;—is not metal there
When o'er the sudden specks my chisel trips?

ii 71-2. Cp. *Paracelsus* v 666-75.

ii 73. *And*] On (*1849-88*).

ii 74. *why, take*] or take (*1849-88*).

ii 75-8. The shape of a peach and the way it hangs on its tree suggest to Jules a 'rosy shape' with 'rosy limbs', which he then identifies with the 'Dryad' (wood-nymph) of classical mythology. Dryads were typical subjects of neo-classical sculpture.

ii 80-5. The chalk is used to sketch the subject, the steel to cut it out from the marble.

ii 81. *facile*: easy to use. But B. may also have in mind J.'s sense of 'easily persuaded', since the chalk 'yields' to the persuasion of the air in l. 82.

ii 82. *your outline*: 'the outline you [the sculptor] have conceived'.

ii 82^83.] Half-softened by a halo's pearly gloom; (*1849-88*).

ii 84. *its one confided thought*: 'the one thought confided to it'.

ii 85-8. Cp. *Gerard de Lairesse* 246-50: 'Why did the chamois stand so fair a mark / Arrested by the novel shape he dreamed / Was bred of liquid marble in the dark / Depths of the mountain's womb that ever teemed / With novel births of wonder?'

ii 87. *deep*] depths (*1849-88*).

ii 92. *specks*] speck (*1865-88*).

—Not flesh—as flake off flake I scale, approach,
Lay bare those blueish veins of blood asleep?
95 Lurks flame in no strange windings where, surprised
By the swift implement sent home at once,
Flushes and glowings radiate and hover
About its track?—
      Phene? what—why is this?
Ah, you will die—I knew that you would die!

Phene *begins, on his having long remained silent.*

100 Now the end's coming—to be sure it must
Have ended sometime!—Tush—I will not speak
Their foolish speech—I cannot bring to mind
Half—so the whole were best unsaid—what care
I for Natalia now, or all of them?
105 Oh, you . . what are you?—I do not attempt
To say the words Natalia bade me learn
To please your friends, that I may keep myself
Where your voice lifted me—by letting you
Proceed . . but can you?—even you perhaps
110 Cannot take up, now you have once let fall,
The music's life, and me along with it?
No—or you would . . we'll stay then as we are

ii *93-4.* The Countess of Clanwilliam (see headnote, p. 12) records Canova's
comment on his famous statue of Pauline Borghese as Venus (Villa Borghese,
Rome): 'Ce n'est pas du marbre, mais de la chair [It is not marble, but flesh]'
(*Journal* ii 295). Note that Canova speaks in French.
ii *94.* Cp. *Tomb at St. Praxed's* 44: 'Blue as a vein o'er the Madonna's breast',
and *Statue* 183: 'the blood that blues the inside arm'.
ii *98^99.*] That whitening cheek, those still-dilating eyes! (*1849-88*, except
'still dilating', *1888*).
ii *101-2. I will not speak / Their foolish speech—*] why need I speak / Their
foolish speech? (*1849-88*).
ii *103-4.*] One half of it, besides; and do not care / For old Natalia now, nor
any of them. (*1849-88*, except 'beside', *1865-88*).
ii *105. I do not attempt*] if I do not try (*1849-88*). The alteration in the clause is
completed in l. 107.
ii *106. bade*] made (*1849-88*).
ii *107. that I may*] it is to (*1849-88*).
ii *108. your voice*: see ll. 116-17n.   *you*] it (*1849-63*); that (*1865-88*).
ii *109. can you*] can it (*1849-88*).
ii *111. it?*] that— (*1849-88*).

Above the world—
                        Now you sink—for your eyes
Are altered . . altering—stay—"I love you, love
    you,"—
115 I could prevent it if I understood
More of your words to me . . was't in the tone
Of the voice, your power?
                        Stay, stay, I will repeat
Their speech, if that affects you! only change
No more and I shall find it presently—
120 Far back here in the brain yourself filled up:
Natalia said (like Lutwyche) harm would follow
Unless I spoke their lesson to the end,
But harm to me, I thought, not you: and so

ii *113.*] —Above the world.
                        You creature with the eyes!
If I could look for ever up to them,
As now you let me,—I believe, all sin,
All memory of wrong done or suffering borne,
[5]   Would drop down, low and lower, to the earth
Whence all that's low comes, and there touch and stay
—Never to overtake the rest of me,
All that, unspotted, reaches up to you,
Drawn by those eyes! What rises is myself,
[10]   Not so the shame and suffering; but they sink,
Are left, I rise above them—Keep me so
Above the world!
                        But you sink, for your eyes (*1849-88*, except
l. [1] 'Above' *1863-88*; l. [4] 'done, suffering' and l. [10] 'Nor me', *1865-88*;
l. [11] 'them. Keep me so,', *1863-88*).
ii *114. altered . . altering*] altering—altered! (*1849-88*).   *love you,"*—] love
you" . . . (*1849-65*); love" . . . (*1868-88*).
ii *115-16. understood / More*] understood: / More (*1863-1888*).
ii *116-17. the tone / Of the voice*] the tone / Or the words (*1849-88*). The
Countess of Clanwilliam wrote of Canova: 'the tone of his voice was
particularly agreeable, and I think it would have been soothing in affliction'
(*Journal* ii 296-7).
ii *117. Stay, stay,*] Or stay— (*1849-88*).
ii *118. affects*] contents (*1849-88*).
ii *121.*] Natalia threatened me that harm would follow (*1849-88*, except
'should', *1865-88*).   *Lutwyche*: the first mention of the 1st Student's name
in *1841*; even here there is no certain indication (until l. 180) that the two are
the same. B. removed this obscurity in *1849*; see i 308-10n.
ii *123.*] But harm to me, I thought she meant, not you.
Your friends,—Natalia said they were your friends

I'll speak it,—"Do not die, Phene, I am yours" . .
125   Stop—is not that, or like that, part of what
      You spoke? 'Tis not my fault—that I should lose
      What cost such pains acquiring! is this right?
          The Bard said, do one thing I can—

      And meant you well,—because, I doubted it,
      Observing (what was very strange to see)
[5]   On every face, so different in all else,
      The same smile girls like us are used to bear,
      But never men, men cannot stoop so low;
      Yet your friends, speaking of you, used that smile,
      That hateful smirk of boundless self-conceit
[10] Which seems to take possession of this world,
      And make of God their tame confederate,
      Purveyor to their appetites . . you know!
      But no—Natalia said they were your friends,
      And they assented while they smiled the more,
[15] And all came round me,—that thin Englishman
      With light, lank hair seemed leader of the rest;
      He held a paper—"What we want," said he,
      Ending some explanation to his friends—
      "Is something slow, involved and mystical,
[20] "To hold Jules long in doubt, yet take his taste
      "And lure him on, so that, at innermost,
      "Where he seeks sweetness' soul, he may find—this!
      "—As in the apple's core, the noisome fly:
      "For insects on the rind are seen at once,
[25] "And brushed aside as soon, but this is found
      "Only when on the lips or loathing tongue."
      And so he read what I have got by heart— (*1849-88*, except l. [6]
'like me', l. [10] 'the world', l. [11] 'a tame', *1865-88*; l. [13] 'But no:', *1865*;
l. [14] 'assented though', *1868-88*; l. [16] 'light lank', *1865-88*; l. [21] 'on until,', l. [27]
'by heart:', *1865-88*.
ii *124. Phene*] love (*1849-88*).
ii *125. Stop*—] No— (*1865-88*).
ii *126-7.*] Yourself began by speaking? Strange to lose / What cost much pains
to learn! Is this more right? (*1849-88*, except 'such pains', *1863-88*).
ii *128. The Bard*: Lutwyche, the composer of the verses.
ii *128-79.*]   *I am a painter who cannot paint;*
                  In my life, a devil rather than saint,
                  In my brain, as poor a creature too—
                  No end to all I cannot do!
[5]   *Yet do one thing at least I can—*
                  Love a man, or hate a man

Supremely: thus my lore began.
Through the Valley of Love I went,
In its lovingest spot to abide,
[10] *And just on the verge where I pitched my tent,*
I found Hate dwelling beside.
(Let the Bridegroom ask what the painter meant,
Of his Bride, of the peerless Bride!)
And further, I traversed Hate's grove,
[15] *In its hatefullest nook to dwell;*
But lo, where I flung myself prone, couched Love
Where the deepest shadow fell.
(The meaning—those black bride's-eyes above,
Not the painter's lip should tell!)
[20] And here," said he, "Jules probably will ask,
"You have black eyes, love,—you are, sure enough,
"My peerless bride,—so do you tell, indeed,
"What needs some explanation—what means this?"
—And I am to go on, without a word—
[25] *So I grew wiser in Love and Hate,*
From simple, that I was of late.
For once, when I loved, I would enlace
Breast, eyelids, hands, feet, form and face
Of her I loved, in one embrace—
[30] *As if by mere love I could love immensely!*
And when I hated, I would plunge
My sword, and wipe with the first lunge
My foe's whole life out, like a sponge—
As if by mere hate I could hate intensely!
[35] *But now I am wiser, know better the fashion*
How passion seeks aid from its opposite passion,
And if I see cause to love more, or hate more
Than ever man loved, ever hated, before—
And seek in the Valley of Love,
[40] *The spot, or the spot in Hate's Grove,*
Where my soul may the sureliest reach
The essence, nought less, of each,
The Hate of all Hates, or the Love
Of all Loves, in its Valley or Grove,—
[45] *I find them the very warders*
Each of the other's borders.
I love most, when Love is disguised
In Hate; and when Hate is surprized
In Love, then I hate most: ask
[50] *How Love smiles through Hate's iron casque,*
Hate grins through Love's rose-braided mask,—
And how, having hated thee,

Love a man and hate a man
130   Supremely: thus my lore began.
Thro' the Valley of Love I went,
In its lovingest spot to abide;
And just on the verge where I pitched my tent
Dwelt Hate beside—
135   (And the bridegroom asked what the bard's smile meant
Of his bride.)
Next Hate I traversed, the Grove,
In its hatefullest nook to dwell—
And lo, where I flung myself prone,
couched Love
140   Next cell.
(For not I, said the bard, but those black bride's eyes above
Should tell!)
(Then Lutwyche said you probably would ask,
"You have black eyes, love,—you are sure enough
145   My beautiful bride—do you, as he sings, tell

I sought long and painfully
To wound thee, and not prick
[55]   *The skin, but pierce to the quick—*
Ask this, my Jules, and be answered straight
By thy bride—how the painter Lutwyche can hate! (*1849-88*,
except l. [2] 'saint;', *1888*; l. [3] 'too:', l. [6] 'man or', *1863-88*; l. [9] 'the
lovingest', l. [15] 'the hatefullest', l. [17] 'Where the shadow threefold fell.',
l. [19] 'a painter's', *1865-88*; l. [21] 'Love', *1868-88*; l. [22] 'so, do you', *1863*;
'then do you', *1865-88*; l. [23] 'explanation!', *1868-88*; l. [25] 'wise', *1865-88*;
l. [26] 'simple that', *1868-88*; l. [27] 'Once, when', l. [31] 'Once, when',
1870-88; l. [33] 'out like', *1865-88*; 'spunge—', *1863-65*; l. [36] 'passion:',
l. [37] 'love more, hate more', l. [38] 'hated', l. [40] 'The nest, or the nook in
Hate's Grove,', l. [41] 'may surely reach', l. [43] 'Hates, the Love', l. [44] 'the
Valley', l. [47] 'When I love most, Love is disguised', *1865-88*; l. [48]
'surprised', *1863-88*; l. [54] 'To reach thy heart, nor prick', l. [55] 'skin but',
1865-88. In *1868-88* single quotation marks replaced italics in ll. [21-3]. Cp.
B. to EBB. on 'the law by which opposite ideas suggest opposite, and
contrary images come together' (27 Jan. 1845, *LK* 11), an idea he repeats in a
letter of 3 Sept. 1882 to Mrs Fitzgerald (*Learned Lady* 152); and cp.
Aristophanes 2498-501: 'Love smiles "rogue" and "wretch" / When "sweet"
and "dear" seem vapid; Hate adopts / Love's "sweet" and "dear", when
"rogue" and "wretch" fall flat; / Love, Hate—are truths, then, each, in sense
not sound'.
ii *137. Next Hate*] Next of Hate (*B & P BYU*).

What needs some exposition—what is this?"
. . . And I am to go on, without a word,)
                Once when I loved I would enlace
                Breast, eyelids, hands, feet, form and face
150   Of her I loved in one embrace—
                And, when I hated, I would plunge
                My sword, and wipe with the first lunge
                My foe's whole life out like a spunge:
                —But if I would love and hate more
155   Than ever man hated or loved before—
                Would seek in the valley of Love
                The spot, or in Hatred's grove
                The spot where my soul may reach
                The essence, nought less, of each . . .
160   (Here he said, if you interrupted me
        With, "There must be some error,—who induced you
        To speak this jargon?"—I was to reply
        Simply—"Await till . . . until . ." I must say
        Last rhyme again—)
165   . . The essence, nought less, of each—
                The Hate of all Hates, or the Love
                Of all Loves in its glen or its grove,
                —I find them the very warders
                Each of the other's borders.
170   So most I love when Love's disguised
                In Hate's garb—'tis when Hate's surprised
                In Love's weed that I hate most; ask
                How Love can smile thro' Hate's barred iron
                    casque,
                Hate grin thro' Love's rose-braided mask,
175   Of thy bride, Giulio!
                            (Then you, "Oh, not mine—
        Preserve the real name of the foolish song!"

---

ii *148-50.* Cp. *Love Among the Ruins* 62-72, and *Now* 7-8: 'a moment which
gives me at last / You around me for once, you beneath me, above me'.
ii *151-3.* Cp. *Ring* v 1662-4: 'Then was I rapt away by the impulse, one /
Immeasurable everlasting wave of a need / To abolish that detested life'.
ii *172. weed*: dress; *J.* records as archaic except in the phrase 'widow's weeds'.
ii *173. casque*: 'a helmet; armour for the head: a poetical word' (*J.*, citing
Richard II I iii 81-2: 'the casque / Of thy adverse pernicious enemy').
ii *175. Giulio*: note that the lines containing this name, which strengthens the
association with the 'Giulio Romano' of *Winter's Tale* (see headnote, p. 15),
were deleted in *1849*.

But I must answer, "Giulio—Jules—'tis Jules!")
Thus I, Jules, hating thee
Sought long and painfully . . .

Jules *interposes.*

180   Lutwyche—who else? But all of them, no doubt,
Hated me—them at Venice—presently
For them, however! You I shall not meet—
If I dreamed, saying that would wake me. Keep
What's here—this too—we cannot meet again
185   Consider—and the money was but meant
For two years' travel, which is over now,
All chance, or hope, or care, or need of it!
This—and what comes from selling these—my casts
And books, and medals except . . . let them go
190   Together—so the produce keeps you safe
Out of Natalia's clutches! If by chance
(For all's chance here) I should survive the gang
At Venice, root out all fifteen of them,
We might meet somewhere since the world is wide.

1.

195   [*Without*] Give her but a least excuse to love me!
When—where—

ii *177. Jules!"*] we supply quotation-marks lacking in *1841.*
ii *181. them*] they (*1849-88*).
ii *182. For them*] Their turn (*1849-88*).
ii *183. that*] this (*1849-88*).
ii *184. this too*] this gold (*1849-63*); the gold (*1865-88*).
ii *186. now,*] emended in agreement with all other eds. from 'now' in *1841.*
ii *195-210.* For publication details, see headnote, p. 6. The opening and
closing s.d.'s are altered in *1849-88*, as with Pippa's first song, i 215-22.
Pippa's second song is based on a topic common in B., the love of a man for a
woman who is above him in rank (e.g., as here, a subject's love of his queen).
B.'s recent work on *Sordello* would have informed him that many of the
troubadours (e.g. Vidal, Folco of Marseilles) were humbly born; he may
have known of Bernard de Ventadour, the son of a scullion, who became the
troubadour and lover of Agnes of Montluçon. Cp. *Rudel* and *Cristina*, first
publ. with the collective title *Queen-Worship*; also *Colombe* and *In a Balcony*.
The idea that misfortune might give the lover his yearned-for opportunity to
serve his mistress figures in *Count Gismond, Glove* and *Daniel Bartoli*.
Collections records two examples of B. inscribing this song as an autograph
(E369, E370, p. 429). The scene is the subject of an early painting by D. G.
Rossetti, called *Hist, said Kate the queen.*

How—can this arm establish her above me
If fortune fixed my lady there—
—There already, to eternally reprove me?
200 (*Hist, said Kate the queen:*
—*Only a page who carols unseen*
Crumbling your hounds their messes!)

2.
She's wronged?—To the rescue of her honor,
My heart!
205 She's poor?—What costs it to be styled a donor?
An earth's to cleave, a sea's to part!
—But that fortune should have thrust all this
upon her!
(*Nay, list, bade Kate the queen:*
Only a page that carols unseen,
210 *Fitting your hawks their jesses!*)—

[Pippa *passes.*

ii *198. fixed my*] fixed her as my (*1849-88*).
ii *200. (Hist,*] ("Hist"— (*1849-65*); ("Hist!"— (*1868-88*).   *Kate the queen*:
Catherine Cornaro (*1454-1510*), a Venetian noblewoman who became queen
of Cyprus on the death of her husband James de Lusignan in 1473, but was
deposed by the Venetian republic in 1489. Her compensation was rule over
the town of Asolo during her lifetime, and she there created a celebrated
court, noteworthy for the presence of Cardinal Bembo, (see headnote to
Tomb at St. Praxed's, pp. 261–62, and preface to *Asolando*). The *1849* revs. give
more detail. Mrs Bronson recalls B. saying: 'People always speak of Caterina
with compassion because she lost Cyprus; but surely this is a better place, far
more beautiful than the distant island, where she was a stranger. I am sure the
happiest years of her life were those when she was queen of Asolo' (*Bronson*[1]
922).
ii *201-2.*] But "Oh—" cried the maiden, binding her tresses,
      "'Tis only a page that carols unseen"
      "Crumbling your hounds their messes!" (*1849-88*, except '"Oh"—'.
1863-75, '"Oh,"', *1872*, '"Oh!"—', *1888*, 'unseen,', *1868-88*.
ii *203. She's wronged*] Is she wronged (*1849-88*).
ii *205. She's poor*] Is she poor (*1849-88*).   *be styled*] become (*1872, 1884*).
ii *206. An*] Merely an (*1849-88*).   *earth's . . . sea's*] earth . . . sea (*1865-
88*).
ii *208. (Nay, list,*] ("Nay, list,"— (*1849-65*); ("Nay list,"— (*1865*[2]); ("Nay,
list!"— (*1868-88*).
ii *209-10.*] And still cried the maiden, binding her tresses,
      "'Tis only a page that carols unseen"
      "Fitting your hawks their jesses!") (*1849-88*, except 'unseen,',
1868-88).

Kate? Queen Cornaro doubtless, who renounced
Cyprus to live and die the lady here
At Asolo—and whosoever loves
Must be in some sort god or worshipper,
215   The blessing, or the blest one, queen or page—
I find myself queen here it seems!
                                        How strange!
Shall to produce form out of shapelessness
Be art—and, further, to evoke a soul
From form be nothing? This new soul is mine—
220   Now to kill Lutwyche what would that do?—Save

ii *211-13*.]   JULES *resumes.*
What name was that the little girl sang forth?
Kate? The Cornaro, doubtless, who renounced
The crown of Cyprus to be lady here
At Asolo, where still the peasants keep
[5]   Her memory; and songs tell how many a page
Pined for the grace of one so far above
His power of doing good to, as a queen—
"She never could be wronged, be poor," he sighed,
"For him to help her!"
                                        Yes, a bitter thing
[10]   To see our lady above all need of us;
Yet so we look ere we will love; not I,
But the world looks so. If whoever loves (*1849-88*, except
ll. [4-5] 'At Asolo, where still her memory stays, / And peasants sing how
once a certain page', *1865-88*; l. [6] 'her so far', *1868-88*; l. [7] 'good to. "She,
the queen', *1865*; 'good to. "Kate the Queen', *1868-88*; l. [9] 'Need him',
1865-88).
ii *215^216*.] Why should we always choose the page's part? / Here is a
woman with utter need of me,— (*1849-88*).
ii *216^217*.] Look at the woman here with the new soul,
Like my own Psyche's,—fresh upon her lips
Alit, the visionary butterfly,
Waiting my word to enter and make bright,
Or flutter off and leave all blank as first.
This body had no soul before, but slept
Or stirred, was beauteous or ungainly, free
From taint or foul with stain, as outward things
Fastened their image on its passiveness:
Now, it will wake, feel, live—or die again! (*1849-88*, except
'Psyche' for 'Psyche's', *1868-88*).
ii *217. shapelessness*] unshaped stuff (*1849-88*).
ii *218. art*] Art (*1863-88*).
ii *219^220*.] *1849-88* have a space between these lines.

A wretched dauber men will hoot to death
Without me.
              To Ancona—Greece—some isle!
I wanted silence only—there is clay
Every where. One may do whate'er one likes
225 In Art—the only thing is, to be sure
That one does like it—which takes pains to know.
Scatter all this, my Phene—this mad dream!
Who—what is Lutwyche—what Natalia—
What the whole world except our love—my own
230 Own Phene? But I told you, did I not,
Ere night we travel for your land—some isle
With the sea's silence on it? Stand aside—
I do but break these paltry models up
To begin art afresh. Shall I meet Lutwyche,
235 And save him from my statue's meeting him?
Some unsuspected isle in the far seas!
Like a god going thro' his world I trace

ii *222.*] Without me, from their laughter!—Oh, to hear
      God's voice plain as I heard it first, before
      They broke in with that laughter! I heard them
      Henceforth, not God!
                        To Ancona—Greece—some isle! (*1849-88*,
except 'laughter! Oh,', *1863-1865*, 'hooting. Oh,', 'with their', *1868-88*,
'God.', *1863-88*).

ii *222. Ancona*: a port with 'the best harbour on the Italian shores of the
Adriatic' (*Murray*), and thus a suitable gateway to Greece.

ii *225. be*] make (*1849-88*).

ii *228 Natalia*] Natalia's friends (*1849-88*).

ii *234-5*. On hearing an adverse criticism, Canova dissuaded his friends from
replying, 'saying, that it was for him to answer it, but only with his chisel'
(*Works of Canova* i xix).

ii *234.*] To begin Art afresh. Meet Lutwyche, I— (*1865-88*).   *meet*: for a
duel.

ii *235 statue's*] statue (*1865-88*).

ii *237. I trace*] there stands (*1849-88*). The rev., together with that in l. 240,
suggests that Jules glimpses a holy mountain rather than, as *1841* allows,
being himself the 'god'. Cp. *Return of the Druses* (1842), where 'The Cedars'
(III 164) and 'the Mountain' (V 393) represent Lebanon: Mt. Hermon, holy to
the Druses, is conflated in the Bible with Mt. Zion, the sacred mountain of
Israel. Note (in either reading) the importance of mountains in Romantic
definitions of the sublime, e.g. Wordsworth's *Simplon Pass*, Coleridge's
Hymn before Sunrise, Shelley's *Mont Blanc*.

One mountain for a moment in the dusk,
Whole brotherhoods of cedars on its brow—
240 And you are ever by me while I trace
—Are in my arms as now—as now—as now!
Some unsuspected isle in the far seas!
Some unsuspected isle in far off seas!

*Talk by the way in the mean time. Two or three of the Austrian
Police loitering with* Bluphocks, *an English vagabond, just in view
of the Turret.*

Bluphocks.* Oh! *were but every worm a maggot, Every*

* "He maketh his sun to rise on the evil and on the good, and sendeth rain on the just
and on the unjust."

ii 240. *trace*] gaze (*1849-88*).
ii 243^244. [*s.d.*] *way in the mean time*] way, while PIPPA is passing from
Orcana to the Turret (*1849-88*).   *Austrian Police*: the Austrian authorities
in the time of Francis I and his chief minister Metternich (see headnote,
p. 9, ii 285n., iii 14n.) maintained an extensive and close surveillance of
political opponents. There were secret as well as civil police; those here
appear to be a conflation, since they are engaged in undercover work but are
also the official authority issuing travel visas, etc. (see ll. 310-12n.).   *Bluphocks*: 'the name means *Blue-Fox*, and is a skit on the *Edinburgh Review*,
which is bound in a cover of blue and fox' (*Cyclopedia*). The source is
Furnivall, who may have got this explanation from B. himself; the *Edinburgh*
was notorious for its ferocious reviews of poetry.
ii 244.] *Bluphocks.** So, that is your Pippa, the little girl who passed us
singing? Well, your Bishop's Intendant's money shall be honestly earned:—
now, don't make me that sour face because I bring the Bishop's name into the
business—we know he can have nothing to do with such horrors—we know
that he is a saint and all that a Bishop should be, who is a great man besides.
Oh! were but every [etc.] (*1849-88*, except: 'business; we', 'horrors: we',
lower case for the second 'Bishop', and 'beside.' for 'besides.', *1865-88*; 'Oh
were' *1868-88*). B.'s footnote comes from Christ's sermon on the mount,
Matthew v 43-5: 'Ye have heard that it hath been said, Thou shalt love thy
neighbour, and hate thine enemy. But I say unto you, Love your enemies,
bless them that curse you, do good to them that hate you, and pray for them
which despitefully use you, and persecute you; that ye may be the children of
your Father which is in heaven: for he maketh [etc.]'.

245   *fly a grig, Every bough a christmas faggot, Every tune a*
     jig! In fact, I have abjured all religions,—but the last I
     inclined to was the Armenian—for I have travelled,
     do you see, and at Koenigsberg, Prussia Improper (so
     styled because there's a sort of bleak hungry sun
250   there,) you might remark over a venerable house-
     porch, a certain Chaldee inscription; and brief as it is,
     a mere glance at it used absolutely to change the
     mood of every bearded passenger. In they turned,
     one and all, the young and lightsome, with no
255   irreverent pause, the aged and decrepit, with a
     sensible alacrity,—'twas the Grand Rabbi's abode, in
     short. I lost no time in learning Syriac—(vowels, you
     dogs, follow my stick's end in the mud—*Celarent,*
     Darii, Ferio!) and one morning presented myself
260   spelling-book in hand, a, b, c,—what was the purport
     of this miraculous posy? Some cherished legend of
     the past, you'll say—*"How Moses hocus-pocust Egypt's*

ii *245. grig*: a grasshopper or cricket (*OED* 4; note sense 5: 'a merry grig: an extravagantly lively person, one who is full of frolic and jest').

ii *246-68. In fact . . . Stolen goods*: Bluphocks here tells a standard kind of anti-Semitic joke, using 'Armenian', 'Chaldee', and 'Syriac' as code-words for 'Jewish' or 'Hebrew'. Königsberg (l. 249) was the capital of Prussia *Proper*, the original territory before the expansion of Prussia in 1710; 'Improper' is presumably a joke, perhaps referring to the meagreness of its sunlight or, conversely, to the impropriety of its having any sun at all. B. had been in this region during his trip to Russia in 1834.

ii *257. I lost*] Struck with curiosity, I lost (*1849-88*).   (*vowels*] (these are vowels (*1849-88*).

ii *258-9. Celarent, Darii, Ferio*: alluding to the scholastic names (devised as mnemonics) of classical syllogisms. Jacob Korg ('A Reading of *Pippa Passes*', *VP* vi [1968] 5-19) points out that Bluphocks omits the first of the series, 'Barbara'; they have nothing to do with vowels. There may be an ironic echo of Christ's writing in the dust (*John* viii 3-8).

ii *260. c,—what*] c,—I picked it out letter by letter, and what (*1849-88*).

ii *261. posy*: inscription.

ii *262-6. How Moses . . . salaam*: Bluphocks refers first to two of the ten plagues called down on Egypt by Moses (*Exodus* viii 20-32, x 1-19); second, to *Jonah* i 1-3 (but he inverts the story: God commanded Jonah to prophesy to the city of Nineveh, Tarshish being the city to which Jonah fled); third, to the story of Balaam's ass, who three times saved her master's life by avoiding the angel who stood in their path to destroy him: 'And when the ass saw the angel of the Lord, she fell down under Balaam' (*Numbers* xxii 27). B. himself was fond of such grotesque rhymes, which he would often compose impromptu in reply to a challenge (see *Penguin* ii 970-1).

land with fly and locust,"—or, "How to Jonah sounded
harshish, Get thee up and go to Tarshish,"—or, "How the
265   angel meeting Balaam, Straight his ass returned a
salaam,"—in no wise! "Shackabrach—Boach—somebody
or other—Isaach, Re-cei-ver, Pur-cha-ser and Ex-chan-ger
of—Stolen goods." So talk to me of obliging a bishop! I
have renounced all bishops save Bishop Beveridge—
270   mean to live so—and die—As some Greek dog-sage,
dead and merry, Hellward bound in Charon's ferry—With
food for both worlds, under and upper, Lupine-seed and
Hecate's supper, And never an obolus . . (it might be got

ii 268. obliging a bishop] the religion of a bishop (1849-88).

ii 269. Bishop Beveridge: William Beveridge (1637-1708), scholar and divine,
became Bishop of St Asaph's in 1705. As Cyclopedia points out, Bluphocks
makes a double pun on 'bishop'—'a cant word for a mixture of wine, oranges
and sugar' (J.)—and on 'Beveridge/beverage'. Note also that Beveridge in
1658 published a treatise on oriental languages, 'especially Hebrew, Chaldee,
Syriac [etc.]' and one contemporary's attack on his style is reminiscent of
Bluphocks himself: 'He delights in jingle and quibbling, affects a tune and
rhyme in all he says, and rests arguments upon nothing but words and
sounds' (quoted DNB).

ii 270. Greek dog-sage: referring to the Cynics, Greek philosophers whose
name was popularly derived from the Greek for 'dog'; they 'received this
name . . . from their canine propensity to criticise the lives and actions of
men' (Lemprière).

ii 271. dead and merry: Bluphocks's version of Sophocles: 'Call no man happy
until he is dead'.

ii 271-5. Hellward . . . Stygian ferry: 'Charon, a god of hell, conducted the
souls of the dead in a boat over the rivers Styx and Acheron to the infernal
regions, for one obolus [see l. 273n.] . . . As all the dead were obliged to pay
a small piece of money for their admission, it was always usual, among the
ancients, to place under the tongue of the deceased, a piece of money for
Charon' (Lemprière). 'Lupine-seed' is the food of the 'upper' world (OED
cites Pliny (transl. Holland), ii 143: 'There is not a thing more light of
digestion . . . than white Lupines, if they be eaten dry'); 'Hecate's supper'
was a traditional monthly offering at the shrines of Hecate, goddess of the
underworld. Cerberus was the monstrous three-headed dog who guarded the
gates of hell. The dead were usually provided with a honey-cake as the
traditional 'sop to Cerberus'.

ii 271. Charon's ferry] Charon's wherry (B & P Domett, 1849-88). The 1841
reading is possibly, but not certainly, a mispr. in view of 'ferry' in l. 275.

ii 273. obolus: the smallest denomination of coin in classical Greece.

ii 273-9.] (it might be . . . zwanzigers.] (Though thanks to you, or this
Intendant through you, or this Bishop through his Intendant—I possess a
burning pocketful of zwanzigers) . . . To pay the Stygian ferry! (1849-

in somehow) *Tho' Cerberus should gobble us—To pay*
275 *the Stygian ferry*—or you might say, *Never an obol To*
pay for the coble . . . . Though thanks to you, or this
Intendant thro' you, or this Bishop thro' his
Intendant—I possess a burning pocket-full of
zwanzigers.
280   1 *Policeman.* I have been noticing a house yonder
this long while—not a shutter unclosed since
morning.
         2 *Policeman.* Old Luca Gaddi's, that owns the silk-
mills here: he dozes by the hour—wakes up, sighs
285 deeply, says he should like to be Prince Metternich,
and then dozes again after having bidden young
Sebald, the foreigner, set his wife to playing
draughts: never molest such a household, they mean
well.
290   *Bluphocks.* Only tell me who this little Pippa is I
must have to do with—one could make something of
that name. Pippa—that is, short for Felippa—*Panurge*
consults Hertrippa—Believ'st thou, King Agrippa?
Something might be done with that name.

---

88).   *coble*: small fishing boat.
ii *279*. *zwanzigers*: an Austrian silver coin, worth about £1 at today's values.
ii *280*. *I have been*] There is the girl, then; go and deserve them the moment
you have pointed out to us Signior Luigi and his mother. (*To the rest*) I have
been (*1849-88*).
ii *285*. *Prince Metternich*: Klemens, Prince von Metternich (1773-1859),
conservative Austrian statesman and opponent of Italian nationalism: see *Italy*
19, 121-3.
ii *290-1*. *Only . . . with—one*] Only, cannot you tell me something of this
little Pippa, I must have to do with?—one (*1849-88*, except 'with? One',
1863-88).
ii *292*. *Felippa—Panurge*] Felippa—rhyming to—*Panurge* (*1849-88*, except 'to
Panurge', *1863-88*).
ii *292-3*. *Panurge . . . Agrippa*: in Rabelais, *Gargantua and Pantagruel* (bk. III
ch. xxv) Pantagruel's companion Panurge consults 'Herr Trippa' on his
prospects for marriage, and is told he will be a cuckold. 'Herr Trippa' is a
parody of an occult philosopher, and is by association 'Agrippa' suggests
Cornelius Agrippa (see *Pauline*, epigraph, I 26). 'King Agrippa' refers,
however, to the episode in *Acts* xxvi 27-8 where the Apostle Paul confronts
King Herod Agrippa: 'King Agrippa, believest thou the prophets? I know
thou believest. Then Agrippa said unto Paul, "Almost thou persuadest me to
be a Christian"'.

295   2 *Policeman.* Your head and a ripe musk-melon
would not be dear at half a *zwanziger!* Leave this fool,
and look out—the afternoon's over or nearly so.
    3 *Policeman.* Where in this passport of Signior Luigi
does the principal instruct you to watch him so
300 narrowly? There? what's there beside a simple
signature? That English fool's busy watching.
    2 *Policeman.* Flourish all round—"put all possible
obstacles in his way;" oblong dot at the end—"Detain
him till further advices reach you;" scratch at
305 bottom—"send him back on pretence of some
informality in the above." Ink-spirt on right-hand
side, (which is the case here)—"Arrest him at once,"
why and wherefore, I don't concern myself, but my
instructions amount to this: if Signior Luigi leaves
310 home to-night for Vienna, well and good—the
passport deposed with us for our *visa* is really for his
own use, they have misinformed the Office, and he
means well; but, let him stay over to-night—there has
been the pretence we suspect—the accounts of his
315 corresponding and holding intelligence with the
Carbonari are correct—we arrest him at once—to-

ii *295. Your head*] Put into rhyme that your head (*1849-88*).   *musk-melon*:
originally denoting a particular variety of melon; then became one of the
names of the common melon, *Cucumis melo*.

ii *299. the principal*] our principal (*1849*); our Principal (*1863-88*).

ii *308-16. my instructions . . . at once*: the police suspect Luigi of belonging to
an Italian nationalist conspiracy, and of obtaining a passport for use by a
known dissident who would be prohibited from travelling. By using the
passport himself, Luigi will disarm this suspicion; by staying in Asolo he will
confirm it. The police do not realize that Luigi is about to set off on a mission
to assassinate the Austrian Emperor, and that his departure would, after all,
confirm his 'guilt' (though not as a member of a conspiracy, since he has
devised the plot himself).

ii *310-12. the passport . . . his own use*: Murray points out that in Lombardy-
Venetia, 'as in every other part of the Austrian dominions, no person can,
under any pretence, cross the frontier without a passport signed by an
Austrian minister. . . . On quitting Milan, or Venice, the passport must be
visé by the Police' (p. 125). Restrictions on travel were commonly imposed
on political dissidents.

ii *316-17. to-morrow . . . Spielberg*: many Italian patriots arrested in this period
were confined before trial in the prison of the 'Piombi' in Venice (see *Sordello*
iii 850n.) and afterwards transported to the prison of Spielberg in Moravia.
This was the case of Silvio Pellico (see iii 18n.).

ii *316. the Carbonari*: the most famous of the Italian secret societies dedicated

morrow comes Venice—and presently, Spielberg.
Bluphocks makes the signal sure enough!

to reform or revolution; they take their name from the French 'charbonniers',
a confraternity of charcoal-burners. An offshoot of freemasonry, they came
to prominence in the Napoleonic period; they were, in fact, mainly active in
southern Italy, and had lost ground, after the collapse of the 1830-1
insurrections, to movements such as Mazzini's Giovine Italia. Perhaps the
name is meant generically. The Austrians certainly had an exaggerated fear of
such societies, and repressed them ruthlessly.
ii *318. sure enough!*] sure enough! That is he, entering the turret with his
mother, no doubt. (*1849-88*).

III.—*Evening. Inside the Turret.* Luigi *and his Mother entering.*

 Mother. If there blew wind you'd hear a long sigh, easing

  The utmost heaviness of music's heart.
 Luigi. Here in the archway?
 Mother.   Oh no, no—in further.
 Where the echo is made—on the ridge.
 Luigi.   Here surely then!
5 How plain the tap of my heel as I leaped up:
 Aristogeiton! "ristogeiton"—plain
 Was't not? Lucius Junius! The very ghost of a voice—
 Whose flesh is caught and kept by those withered wall-
  flowers,
 Or by the elvish group with thin bleached hair
10 Who lean out of their topmost fortress—look

iii *Opening s.d. Inside the Turret.*] Inside the Turret on the Hill above Asolo. (*1865–88*). See ii 243ˆ244n.
iii *1–14.* Mrs Bronson records a visit by B. to la Rocca in 1889: 'He remembered an echo he had discovered within the fortress walls fifty years before . . . and so anxious was he to re-find it that he would scarcely be persuaded to wait until the fatigue of his journey from England should be dispelled before seeking to hear it again . . . Once within the Rocca fortress we could find no echo . . . "I should have thought an echo could never fade," he said rather sadly; but she was there, after all, his nymph Echo, only she proved for some reason coy on that occasion.' (*Bronson*[1] 928). Echo-scenes are fairly common in Elizabethan and Jacobean drama (e.g. Webster, *The Duchess of Malfi* V iii).
iii *6–12.*] Hark—"*Lucius Junius!*" The very ghost of a voice,
    Whose body is caught and kept by . . . what are those?
    Mere withered wall-flowers, waving overhead?
    They seem an elvish group with thin bleached hair
[5]   Who lean out of their topmost fortress—looking
    And listening, mountain men, to what we say,
    Hands under chin of each grave earthy face: (*1849–88,* except l. [1],
no italics, 'voice', *1868–88,* l. [3] 'wallflowers,', *1863–88*; l. [5] 'That lean',
ll.[5–6] 'look / and listen', l. [7], 'Hand', *1865–88,* 'face.', *1888*).
iii *6. Aristogeiton:* see ii 47–9n.
iii *7. Lucius Junius:* Lucius Junius Brutus, legendary founder of the Roman republic in the 6th century BC. He was known as 'Brutus' (stupid) because he feigned insanity during the tyrannical rule of the Tarquins, whose expulsion he instigated; Luigi's omission of the name may relate to doubts concerning his own sanity: see ll. 31–6 below. Brutus is mentioned in *Sordello* (iv 956) and *A Soul's Tragedy* (ii 39).

And listen, mountain men and women, to what
We say—chins under each grave earthy face:
Up and show faces all of you!—"All of you!"
That's the king with the scarlet comb: come down!—
"Come down."
15   *Mother.* Do not kill that Man, my Luigi—do not
Go to the City! putting crime aside,
Half of these ills of Italy are feigned—
Your Pellicos and writers for effect
Write for effect.
        Luigi.   Hush! say A writes, and B.
20   *Mother.* These A's and B's write for effect I say.
Then evil is in its nature loud, while good
Is silent—you hear each petty injury—

iii *13. "All of you!"*] in italics, *1849-65*.

iii *14.*] That's the king's dwarf with the scarlet comb; now hark— (*1849-63*);
That's the king dwarf with the scarlet comb; old Franz, (*1865-88*). The ref. to
'old Franz' in *1865-88* has generally been taken to refer to the Austrian
Emperor Francis I: see headnote, p. 9.

iii *14^15.*] Come down and meet your fate! Hark—"*meet your fate!*" (*1849-88*,
except no italics, *1868-88*; 'fate? Hark—', *1870-88*).

iii *15. Do not kill that Man*] Let him not meet it (*1849-88*).

iii *18.* Silvio Pellico (1789-1854), poet and dramatist, a major contributor to
the journal *Il Conciliatore,* and, through his friend Pietro Maroncelli, an
associate of the Carbonari (see ii 316n). He was arrested in 1820 during a
period of severe Austrian repression. Imprisoned in the 'Piombi' at Venice,
Pellico was condemned to death; the sentence was commuted to twenty
years' 'carcere duro' (harsh imprisonment). He was sent in 1822 to Spielberg
prison in Moravia (see ii 316-17n.) and released in 1830. In 1832 he published
Le mie prigioni (*My Prisons*), an account of his ordeal which made him famous,
and Spielberg infamous, thoughout Europe. B. may also have been aware of
Pellico's support for the 'romantici', and its political implications. After the
suppression of *Il Conciliatore,* Pellico commented: '*romantic* was recognised as
a symnonym for *liberal,* and nobody dared to call himself a classicist, except
for the ultras and spies' (quoted in Stuart Woolf, *A History of Italy 1700-1860*
[1979] 249). See i 283-94n. B. could have read about Pellico in *Biographie,*
where he would have found that Pellico's father was manager of a silk-mill at
Pinerolo in N. Italy, and that he had a brother called Luigi.

iii *22-4. you hear . . . stupid*: the portrait fits the age, but not the character, of
the Emperor Francis II; vice versa for his successor Ferdinand I (see headnote,
p. 9). Cp. the contrast (drawn by the Devil) between the aged George III's
domestic virtues and reactionary politics in Byron's *Vision of Judgment:* '"He
ever warr'd with freedom and the free: / Nations as men, home subjects,
foreign foes, / So that they utter'd the word 'Liberty!' / Found George the
Third their first opponent. . . . I grant his household abstinence; I grant / His

    None of his daily virtues; he is old,
    Quiet, and kind, and densely stupid—why
    Do A and B not kill him themselves?
25   *Luigi.*   They teach
    Others to kill him—me—and if I fail
    Others to succeed; now if A tried and failed
    I could not do that: mine's the *lesser* task.
    Mother, they visit night by night . . .
    Mother.   You Luigi?
30   Ah will you let me tell you what you are?
    Luigi. Why not? Oh the one thing you fear to hint
    You may assure yourself I say and say
    Often to myself; at times—nay, now—as now
    We sit, I think my mind is touched—suspect
35   All is not sound—but is not knowing that
    What constitutes one sane or otherwise?
    I know I am thus—so all is right again!
    I laugh at myself as thro' the town I walk
    And see the world merry as if no Italy
40   Were suffering—then I ponder—I am rich,
    Young, healthy, happy, why should this fact trouble
       me. . .
    More than it troubles these? But it does trouble me!
    No—trouble's a bad word—for as I walk
    There's springing and melody and giddiness,
45   And old quaint turns and passages of my youth—
    Dreams long forgotten, little in themselves—
    Return to me—whatever may recreate me,
    And earth seems in a truce with me, and heaven
    Accords with me, all things suspend their strife,
50   The very cicales laugh "There goes he and there—
    "Feast him, the time is short—he is on his way

---

neutral virtues, which most monarchs want' (ll. 353-60).

iii *23.*] None of his virtues; he is old beside, (*1865-88*).

iii *28. do*] teach (*1849-88*).   *lesser*] not italic, *1849-88*.

iii *33.*] Ever to myself; at times—nay, even now (*1849-88*, except 'myself!
At', *1868-88*).

iii *39. the world*] men (*1849-88*).

iii *41. healthy, happy,*] healthy; (*1849-88*). Unless *1841* is misprinted, a rare
case of an unmetrical line in B.

iii *42. trouble me!*] trouble! (*1863-65*); trouble. (*1868-88*); 'me!' is emended in
agreement with *1849* from 'me' in *1841*.

iii *47. recreate*] amuse (*1849-88*).

iii *50. cicales laugh*] cicalas laugh (*1849*); cicale laugh (*1863*); cicala laughs
(*1865-88*). B. had constant difficulty with this word: see *Intro.* 177n.

"For the world's sake—feast him this once, our
    friend!"
And in return for all this, I can trip
Cheerfully up the scaffold-steps: I go
This evening, mother.
55   *Mother.*   But mistrust yourself—
Mistrust the judgment you pronounce on him.
    Luigi. Oh, there I feel—am sure that I am right.
    Mother. Mistrust your judgment then of the mere
      means
Of this wild enterprise: say you are right,—
60 How should one in your state e'er bring to pass
What would require a cool head, a cold heart,
And a calm hand? you never will escape.
    Luigi. Escape—to wish that even would spoil all!
The dying is best part of it—I have
65 Enjoyed these fifteen years of mine too much
To leave myself excuse for longer life—
Was not life pressed down, running o'er with joy,
That I might finish with it ere my fellows
Who sparelier feasted make a longer stay?
70 I was put at the board head, helped to all
At first: I rise up happy and content.
God must be glad one loves his world so much—
I can give news of earth to all the dead
Who ask me:—last year's sunsets and great stars
75 That had a right to come first and see ebb
The crimson wave that drifts the sun away—
Those crescent moons with notched and burning rims
That strengthened into sharp fire and there stood
Impatient of the azure—and that day

iii *59. Of*] To (*1868-88*).
iii *63-5.*] Escape—to even wish that would spoil all!
      The dying is best part of it. Too much
      Have I enjoyed these fifteen years of mine (*1849-88*, except
'Escape? to', *1865*, 'Escape? To', *1868-88*).
iii *67.* Cp. *Luke* vi 38: 'Give, and it shall be given unto you; good measure,
pressed down, and shaken together, and running over, shall men give into
your bosom'.
iii *73-4. I can give . . . ask me*: more usually a courtesy of living visitors to the
underworld, such as Odysseus, Aeneas, Dante.
iii *74-80.* W. Sharp asserted 'it was from the Dulwich wood that, one
afternoon in March, he saw a storm glorified by a double rainbow of
extraordinary beauty' (*Life of Robert Browning* [1890] 104).
iii *75. That*] Which (*1849-88*).

80 In March a double rainbow stopped the storm—
    May's warm, slow, yellow moonlit summer nights—
    Gone are they—but I have them in my soul!
        Mother. (He will not go!)
        Luigi.   You smile at me—I know
    Voluptuousness, grotesqueness, ghastliness
85 Environ my devotedness as quaintly
    As round about some antique altar wreathe
    The rose festoons, goats' horns, and oxen's skulls.
        Mother. See now—you reach the city—you must
            cross
    His threshold—how?
        Luigi.   Oh, that's if we conspire!
90 Then come the pains in plenty you foresee
    —Who guess not how the qualities required
    For such an office—qualities I have—
    Would little stead us otherwise employed,
    Yet prove of rarest merit here—here only.
95 Every one knows for what his excellences
    Will serve, but no one ever will consider
    For what his worst defects might serve; and yet
    Have you not seen me range our coppice yonder
    In search of a distorted ash?—it happens
100 The wry spoilt branch's a natural perfect bow:
    Fancy the thrice sage, thrice precautioned man
    Arriving at the city on my errand!
    No, no—I have a handsome dress packed up—
    White satin here to set off my black hair—
105 In I shall march—for you may watch your life out
    Behind thick walls—binding friends to betray you;
    More than one man spoils every thing—March
            straight—

iii *81.* Cp. *May and Death* 7-8: 'the warm / Moon-births and the long
evening-ends'.
iii *83. I know*] 'Tis true,— (*1849-88*).
iii *90.*] Then would come pains in plenty, as you guess— (*1849-88*).
iii *91. —Who*] But (*1849-88*).   *required*] most fit (*1863-88*).
iii *93. us*] me (*1849-63*); me, (*1865-88*).
iii *94. here—here only.*] only here (*1865-88*).
iii *95-7. excellences . . . defects*] excellence . . . defect (*1849-88*).
iii *99-100. it happens / The wry spoilt branch's*] I find / The wry spoilt branch
(*1868-88*).
iii *102. city*] palace (*1849-88*).
iii *103-18.* The court here is closer to the Renaissance than to the 19th
century, esp. with the presence of a powerful 'favourite' (l. 115).
iii *106. binding friends*] make friends there (*1849-88*).

Only no clumsy knife to fumble for—
Take the great gate, and walk (not saunter) on
110 Thro' guards and guards——I have rehearsed it all
Inside the Turret here a hundred times—
Don't ask the way of whom you meet, observe,
But where they cluster thickliest is the door
Of doors: they'll let you pass . . they'll never blab
115 Each to the other, he knows not the favourite,
Whence he is bound and what's his business now—
Walk in—straight up to him—you have no knife—
Be prompt, how should he scream? Then, out with
you!
Italy, Italy, my Italy!
120 You're free, you're free—Oh mother, I believed
They got about me—Andrea from his exile,
Pier from his dungeon, Gaultier from his grave!
      Mother. Well you shall go. If patriotism were not
The easiest virtue for a selfish man
125 To acquire! he loves himself—and then, the world—
If he must love beyond, but nought between:
As a short-sighted man sees nought midway
His body and the sun above. But you
Are my adored Luigi—ever obedient
130 To my least wish, and running o'er with love—
I could not call you cruel or unkind!
Once more, your ground for killing him!—then go!
      Luigi. Now do you ask me, or make sport of me?
How first the Austrians got these provinces—
135 (If that is all, I'll satisfy you soon)
. . . Never by warfare but by treaty, for
That treaty whereby . . .
      Mother.   Well?

iii *108.* Luigi will strangle the Emperor. Cp. *Italy* 121-3:
iii *119.* Cp. *De Gustibus* 39: 'Italy, my Italy!'
iii *120. I believed*] I could dream (*1849-88*).
iii *121-2. Andrea . . . Pier . . . Gaultier*: imaginary figures, in contrast to
Pellico (l. 18).
iii *123. If patriotism were not*] Yet seems this patriotism (*1849-88*).
iii *125. then*] next (*1849-88*).
iii *133. ask*] try (*1868-88*).
iii *134-7. How first . . . whereby*: the provinces are Lombardy and Venetia,
which Austria acquired by the Treaty of Vienna (1815). But the Austrians
were already in military control of northern Italy.
iii *136.*] . . . Never by conquest but by cunning, for (*1849-88*, except
'—Never', *1863-88*).

    Luigi.   (Sure he's arrived—
  The tell-tale cuckoo—spring's his confidant,
  And he lets out her April purposes!)
140 Or . . better go at once to modern times—
  He has . . they have . . in fact I understand
  But can't re-state the matter; that's my boast;
  Others could reason it out to you, and prove
  Things they have made me feel.
    Mother.   Why go to-night?
145 Morn's for adventure. Jupiter is now
  A morning-star . . . . I cannot hear you, Luigi!
    Luigi. "I am the bright and morning-star," God
    saith—
  And, "such an one I give the morning-star!"
  The gift of the morning-star—have I God's gift
  Of the morning-star?
150 *Mother.*   Chiara will love to see
  That Jupiter an evening-star next June.
    Luigi. True, mother. Well for those who live June
    over.
  Great noontides—thunder storms—all glaring pomps
  Which triumph at the heels of June the God
155 Leading his revel thro' our leafy world.
  Yes, Chiara will be here—
    Mother.   In June—remember
  Yourself appointed that month for her coming—
    Luigi. Was that low noise the echo?
    Mother.   The night-wind.
  She must be grown—with her blue eyes upturned
160 As if life were one long and sweet surprise—

iii *140. times*] time (*1865-88*).

iii *147-8.* The first quotation is from *Revelation* xxii 16: 'I Jesus have sent mine angel to testify unto you these things in the churches. I am the root and the offspring of David, and the bright and morning star'. The second is from *Revelation* ii 26-8: 'And he that overcometh, and keepeth my works unto the end, to him will I give power over the nations . . . And I will give him the morning star.' See also iv 219n.

iii *147. God saith*] saith God (*1868-88*).

iii *148.* "*such*] "to such (*1849-88*).

iii *150. Chiara*: lit., 'bright'.

iii *152. June over*] through June (*1849-88*).

iii *154. June the God*] sovereign June (*1849*); the god June (*1863*); June the god (*1865-88*).

iii *155.*] Leading his glorious revel thro' our world. (*1849*). With the prec. line, this is a rare example of a return to the *1841* reading after *1849* or *1863*.

In June she comes.
　　Luigi.　　　　　　We are to see together
The Titian at Treviso—there again!

　　　　　[*Without*] A king lived long ago,
　　　　　In the morning of the world,
165　　　When earth was nigher heaven than now:
　　　　　And the king's locks curled
　　　　　Disparting o'er a forehead full
　　　　　As the milk-white space 'twixt horn and horn

iii *161. are*] were (*1849-88*).

iii *162. The Titian at Treviso*: a fresco of the Annunciation, in the chapel of that name in the Cathedral at Treviso; in the diary of his 1838 trip B. records visiting Treviso on 17 June (*Correspondence* iv, p. xiii).

iii *163-224.*] For publication details, see headnote, p. 5. Variants from the *MR* text are not rec. here; see I 326. The opening and closing s.d.'s are altered in *1849-88* as for Pippa's first song (i 215-22). There are no s. d.'s in *1865²*; *1863-88* have no intermediate s. d.'s at ll. 178 and 204; in *1849* these read '[From without.]'. The poem's original appearance in *MR* had signalled B.'s affiliation to the political radicalism of that journal's editor, W. J. Fox (see headnote to *Paracelsus*, I 107). In *MR* the poem comes immediately after an article by Fox 'On Organic Reforms' which attacks both conservatives and moderate reformers from a radical and republican perspective: 'The old slavish devotion to a particular family, the unquestioning loyalty which was claimed by and vowed to the Stuarts, is, I know, transferred by many to the forms of our Government, and the ancient privileges of certain classes of society. It is not much the better for the transfer. . . . Irresponsible power may be one of the "branches" of the constitution; but what then, if it bear bitter fruit, and overshadow the land pestiferously? Nay, even should "unquestionable danger to the Monarchy" be logically predicated of any arrangements which are essential to the nation's rights, security, prosperity, and improvement, then must such danger be incurred, unless we are prepared to revert to "the monstrous faith of millions made for one."' In this light B.'s poem, with its mythical setting and idealized portrait of a just monarch, suggests an ironic contrast with present-day rulers, a contrast which Luigi implicitly grasps in *1841* and explicitly states in *1849-88* (see below, ll. 224-5n.). Cp. Pope's evocation of a primitive social order in which 'each Patriarch sate, / King, priest, and parent of his growing state; / On him, their second Providence, they hung, / Their law his eye, their oracle his tongue' (*Essay on Man* iii 215-18); and note that Pope, following Locke, sees this as a state antecedent and opposed to that of absolute monarchy, 'Th' enormous faith of many made for one' (l. 242; note Fox's misquotation of this line in the passage just cited). Pope himself glossed this section of the *Essay*: 'Origin of True Religion and Government from the Principle of Love: and of Superstition and Tyranny from that of Fear'.

   Of some sacrificial bull—
170 Only calm as a babe new-born:
   For he was got to a sleepy mood,
   So safe from all decrepitude,
   Age with its bane so sure gone by,
   (The Gods so loved him while he dreamed,)
175 That, having lived thus long, there seemed
   No need the king should ever die.

  Luigi. No need that sort of king should ever die.

   [*Without*] Among the rocks his city was:
   Before his palace, in the sun,
180 He sate to see his people pass,
   And judge them every one
   From its threshold of smooth stone.
   They haled him many a valley-thief
   Caught in the sheep-pens—robber-chief,
185 Swarthy and shameless—beggar-cheat—
   Spy-prowler—or some pirate found
   On the sea-sand left aground;
   Sometimes there clung about his feet
   With bleeding lip and burning cheek
190 A woman, bitterest wrong to speak
   Of one with sullen, thickset brows:
   Sometimes from out the prison-house
   The angry priests a pale wretch brought,
   Who through some chink had pushed and
    pressed,
195 Knees and elbows, belly and breast,
   Worm-like into the temple,—caught
   He was by the very God,
   Who ever in the darkness strode
   Backward and forward, keeping watch
200 O'er his brazen bowls, such rogues to catch:
   These, all and every one,
   The king judged, sitting in the sun.

iii *173. Age*] From age (*1849-88*).
iii *186. some pirate*] rough pirate (*1849-88*).
iii *188. Sometimes*] And sometimes (*1849-88*).
iii *192. Sometimes from out*] And sometimes from (*1849-88*).
iii *195. Knees*] On knees (*1849-88*).
iii *197.*] At last there by the very God, (*1849-63; 1865-88* as *1841*, except 'god', the MR reading).
iii *201. These*] And these (*1849-63*).

Luigi. That king should still judge sitting in the
   sun.

[*Without*] His councillors, on left and right,
205   Looked anxious up,—but no surprise
         Disturbed the king's old smiling eyes,
         Where the very blue had turned to white.
         A python passed one day
         The silent streets—until he came,
210   With forky tongue and eyes on flame,
         Where the old king judged alway;
         But when he saw the sweepy hair,
         Girt with a crown of berries rare
         The God will hardly give to wear
215   To the maiden who singeth, dancing bare
         In the altar-smoke by the pine-torch lights,
         At his wondrous forest rites,—
         But which the God's self granted him
         For setting free each felon limb
220   Because of earthly murder done
         Faded till other hope was none;—
         Seeing this, he did not dare
         Approach that threshold in the sun,
         Assault the old king smiling there.
                                    [Pippa *passes.*

iii *208.*] 'Tis said, a Python scared one day (*1849-88,* except 'python', *1865²*).
iii *209.*] The breathless city, till he came (*1849-88*).
iii *213-17.* The details suggest that the God is Bacchus (Dionysus) whose
festivals were celebrated with orgiastic dancing; *Lemprière* notes that
'According to Pliny, he was the first [god] who ever wore a crown'.
iii *214. The God*] Which the God (*1849-88,* except 'god' *1865²-88*).
iii *218-21.*] not *1849-88.*
iii *222. Seeing*] Beholding (*1849-63*).
iii *224-5.*] Assault the old king smiling there.
         Such grace had kings when the world begun!
                                    (PIPPA *passes.*)
      Luigi. And such grace have they, now that the world ends!
      The Python in the city, on the throne,
[5]   And brave men, God would crown for slaying him,
      Lurk in bye-corners lest they fall his prey!
      Are crowns yet to be won, in this late trial,
      Which weakness makes me hesitate to reach?
      'Tis God's voice calls, how could I stay? Farewell! (*1849-88,*
except l. [4], 'Python at', *1865-88*; l. [7] 'won', *1865-88*, 'late time', *1863-88*,
l. [9], 'calls: how', *1865-88*).

225   *Luigi.* Farewell, farewell—how could I stay?
        Farewell!

Talk by the way in the mean time. Poor Girls sitting on the steps of
Monsignor's *brother's house, close to the Duomo S. Maria.*
        1 *Girl.* There goes a swallow to Venice—the stout
            sea-farer!
        Let us all wish; you wish first.
        2 *Girl.*   I? This sunset
        To finish.
        3 *Girl.* That old . . . somebody I know,
        To give me the same treat he gave last week—
230   Feeding me on his knee with fig-peckers,
        Lampreys, and red Breganze-wine, and mumbling
        The while some folly about how well I fare—
        Since had he not himself been late this morning
        Detained at—never mind where—had he not . .
235   Eh, baggage, had I not!—
        2 *Girl.*   How she can lie!
        3 *Girl.* Look there—by the nails—
        2 *Girl.*   What makes your fingers red?
        3 *Girl.* Dipping them into wine to write bad
            words with
        On the bright table—how he laughed!
        1 *Girl.*   My turn:
        Spring's come and summer's coming: I would wear
240   A long loose gown—down to the feet and hands—

---

iii *225^226*. [*s. d.*] Talk by the way, while Pippa is passing from the Turret to
the Bishop's brother's House, close to the Duomo S. Maria. Poor Girls
sitting on the steps. (*1849-88*, except 'Brother's', *1865-88*).
iii *226^227*.] Seeing those birds fly, makes one wish for wings. (*1849-88*).
iii *228-44*. The contrast between rich, sophisticated food (ll. 230-1) and a
simple rural diet (ll. 243-4) reappears in the *Prologue* to *Ferishtah* as a contrast
between Italy and England. See also l. 286n.
iii *228^229*.] Greyer and older than my grandfather, (*1849-88*).
iii *230. fig-peckers*: It. 'beccafico'; small migratory birds of the genus Sylvia,
eaten as dainties in the autumn, when they have fattened on figs and grapes.
iii *231. Lampreys*: eel-like fish. A citation dated 1720 in *OED* suggests an
aphrodisiac effect. Not mentioned by B. outside this poem.   *Breganze-*
wine: wine from Breganze, a town 30 km west of Asolo.
iii *232^233*.] To be let eat my supper quietly— (*1849-88*, except 'quietly:',
1863-88, 'Let sit and', *1868-88*).
iii *235. Eh, . . . not!*] in quotation marks, *1849-88*.

With plaits here, close about the throat, all day:
And all night lie, the cool long nights, in bed—
And have new milk to drink—apples to eat,
Deuzans and junetings, leather-coats . . ah, I should
    say
This is away in the fields—miles!
245   3 *Girl.*   Say at once
You'd be at home—she'd always be at home!
Now comes the story of the farm among
The cherry orchards, and how April snowed
White blossoms on her as she ran: why fool,
250   They've rubbed the chalk-mark out how tall you
    were,
Twisted your starling's neck, broken his cage,
Made a dunghill of your garden—
    1 *Girl.*   They destroy
My garden since I left them? well—perhaps!
I would have done so—so I hope they have!
255   A fig-tree curled out of our cottage wall—
They called it mine, I have forgotten why,
It must have been there long ere I was born,
Criq—criq—I think I hear the wasps o'erhead
Pricking the papers strung to flutter there
260   And keep off birds in fruit-time—coarse long papers
And the wasps eat them, prick them through and
    through.
    3 *Girl.* How her mouth twitches! where was I
    before
She broke in with her wishes and long gowns
And wasps—would I be such a fool!—Oh, here!

iii *244. Deuzans and junetings, leather-coats*: 'Three kinds of apple. *Deuzan* (fr.
deux ans) was so called as it was supposed to keep for two years. *Juneting* [is]
the earliest apple of the year[.] *Leather-coat*, the golden russet, is so named
from the leathery brown skin. Cf. *2 Henry IV* V iii 44: "There's a dish of
leather-coats for you"' (W. H. Griffin, *Selections from the Early Poems of Robert
Browning* [1902] 154-5). Only occurrences in B.
iii *248-9.* Cp. Wordsworth, *The Green Linnet* 1-2: 'Beneath these fruit-tree
boughs that shed / Their snow-white blossoms on my head', and see *Home-
Thoughts, from Abroad* 11-13.
iii *250.*] They've rubbed out the chalk-mark of how tall you were, (*1849-63*;
1865-88 as *1841*, except 'out, how').
iii *255.* The fig-tree recalls Biblical imagery of peace and plenty, as in *1
Kings* iv 25: 'And Judah and Israel dwelt safely, every man under his vine and
under his fig-tree'. Cp. *Jochanan* 263-5, where Jochanan 'sits / Under his vine
and fig-tree mid the wealth / Of garden-sights and sounds'.

265   This is my way—I answer every one
        Who asks me why I make so much of him—
        (Say, you love him—he'll not be gulled, he'll say)
        "He that seduced me when I was a girl
        Thus high—had eyes like yours, or hair like yours,
270   Brown, red, white,"—as the case may be—that
          pleases!
        (See how that beetle burnishes in the path—
        There sparkles he along the dust—and there—
        Your journey to that maize-tuft's spoilt at least!
          1 *Girl.* When I was young they said if you killed
            one
275   Of those sunshiny beetles, that his friend
        Up there would shine no more that day or next.
          3 *Girl.* When you were young? Nor are you
            young, that's true!
        How your plump arms, that were, have dropped
          away!
        Why I can span them! Cecco beats you still?
280   No matter so you keep your curious hair.
        I wish they'd find a way to dye our hair
        Your colour—any lighter tint, indeed,
        Than black—the men say they are sick of black,
        Black eyes, black hair!
          2 *Girl.*   Sick of yours, like enough,
285   Do you pretend you ever tasted lampreys
        And ortolans? Giovita, of the palace,
        Engaged (but there's no trusting him) to slice me
        Polenta with a knife that had cut up

iii *267.*] (If you say, you love him—straight "he'll not be gulled") (*1849-88*, except "'you love him"—', *1868-88*, 'gulled!'", *1863-88*).

iii *273. maize-tuft's*] maize-tuft (*1865-88*).

iii *276. or*] nor (*1849-88*).

iii *277-91.*] in *1841* the order of speakers is given as '2 Girl . . . 3 Girl . . . 2 Girl'. This makes nonsense of the dialogue, since '3 Girl' is made to contradict her claim to have been fed on dainties by her rich admirer (ll. 228-31). B. corrected the error in *B & P Domett*, and we have emended accordingly; in *1849-88* he introduced a new character, '4 Girl', to speak ll. 284-9, leaving '2 Girl to speak ll. 289-91 as she does in the unemended *1841* text.

iii *280. curious*: unusual; also perhaps 'such as interests the curioso or connoisseur' (*OED* 17).

iii *286. ortolans*: 'The Ortolan is a small singing-bird . . . common in France, Italy and other parts of Europe. It is the epicure's prime morceau' (*OED*, 1837). The *Prologue* to *Ferishtah* gives an Italian recipe for cooking the bird.

iii *288. Polenta*: 'A large flat thin cake made of the meal of maize or ground

An ortolan.
    3 Girl.   Why—there! is not that Pippa
290 We are to talk to, under the window, quick
Where the lights are?
    1 Girl.   No—or she would sing
—For the Intendant said . . .
    3 Girl.   Oh, you sing first—
Then, if she listens and comes close . . I'll tell you,
Sing that song the young English noble made,
295 Who took you for the purest of the pure
And meant to leave the world for you—what fun!
    2 Girl. [Sings]

        You'll love me yet!—and I can tarry
        Your love's protracted growing:
        June reared that bunch of flowers you carry
300   From seeds of April's sowing.

        I plant a heartfull now—some seed
        At least is sure to strike
        And yield—what you'll not care, indeed,
        To pluck, but, may be like

305   To look upon . . my whole remains,
        A grave's one violet:
        Your look?—that pays a thousand pains.
        What's death?—You'll love me yet!

    3 Girl. [To Pippa *who approaches]* Oh, you may
come closer—we shall not eat you!

---

chestnuts; it is a favourite food of the Italian peasantry' (W. H. Griffin,
Selections from the Early Poems of Robert Browning [1902], note to l. 244).
iii *291. No—or*] That she? No, or (*1868-88*).
iii *297-308.* For publication details, see headnote, p. 6. This is the only song
not sung by Pippa herself. In *1863-88* the shorter lines are indented.
iii *297-8.* Cp. Marvell, *To his Coy Mistress,* esp. ll. 11-12: 'My vegetable Love
should grow / Vaster than Empires, and more slow.'
iii *303-5.*] And yield—what you'll not pluck indeed,
    Not love, but, may be, like!

    You'll look at least on love's remains, (*1849-88*, except 'like.',
1868-88).
iii *310. eat you!*] eat you! Why, you seem the very person that the great rich
handsome Englishman has fallen so violently in love with! I'll tell you all
about it. (*1849-88*).

IV.—*Night. The Palace by the Duomo.* Monsignor, *dismissing his* Attendants.

> *Monsignor.* Thanks, friends, many thanks. I desire
> life now chiefly that I may recompense every one of
> you. Most I know something of already. *Benedicto*
> *benedicatur* . . ugh . . ugh! Where was I? Oh, as you
> 5 were remarking, Ugo, the weather is mild, very
> unlike winter-weather,—but I am a Sicilian, you
> know, and shiver in your Julys here: To be sure,
> when 'twas full summer at Messina, as we priests
> used to cross in procession the great square on
> 10 Assumption Day, you might see our thickest yellow
> tapers twist suddenly in two, each like a falling star,
> or sink down on themselves in a gore of wax. But
> go, my friends, but go! [*To the* Intendant] Not you,
> Ugo! [*The others leave the apartment, where a table with*

iv *Opening s.d.*] *The Palace*] Inside the Palace (*1865-88*). *Palace*: transl. of It. 'palazzo', a 'large, stately dwelling'. *Monsignor*: 'an ecclesiastical title attached to an office or distinction ordinarily bestowed by the Pope. It is also used in some countries . . . as a regular style for archbishops and bishops' (*Oxford Dictionary of the Christian Church*, 2nd ed.). Its use here suggests the Bishop's closeness to the Pope. *his Attendants*: i.e. his brother's servants.
iv *1-2. I desire life now chiefly*] I chiefly desire life now (*1849-88*).
iv *2. recompense*: in the (hidden) sense of 'punish, pay back'.
iv *3. already.*] already. What, a repast prepared? (*1849-88*).
iv *3-4. Benedicto benedicatur*: lit., 'it is blessed in being blessed', a standard Catholic grace before meals.
iv *4. ugh . . . ugh*: the sound of a cough, as in e.g. Jonson's *Volpone*.
iv *7-12. To be sure . . . a gore of wax*: referring to the feast celebrating the ascent of the Virgin Mary into heaven, held on 13 Aug. in Catholic countries. Cp. *England* 250ff. and *Up at a Villa* 51-2. Murray's *Handbook for Travellers in Southern Italy* says: 'The great feast of the Virgin in Messina is in August, to commemorate her Assumption [. . . It] occupies three days (from the 13th to the 15th) . . . at night the city is illuminated, and all Messina is in the streets. In the evening of the 14th the Cathedral is also lighted up with more than 8000 wax tapers, and makes a brilliant spectacle' (pp. 501-2).
iv *8. Messina*: Sicilian city, situated opposite the Italian mainland; an archiepiscopal see and capital of Messina province.
iv *9. the great square*: the Piazza del Duomo, 'the finest in Messina, having on the E. the Cathedral with its quaint facade and its modern campanile' (Murray's *Handbook for Travellers in Southern Italy* 477).
iv *11. tapers*: ecclesiastical candles.
iv *14-15. s.d.*] [The others leave the apartment.] (*1849-88*).

15   *refreshments is prepared.*] I have long wanted to
converse with you, Ugo!
     Intendant. Uguccio—
     Monsignor. . . 'guccio Stefani, man! of Ascoli,
Fermo, and Fossombruno:—what I do need instruct-
20   ing about are these accounts of your administration of
my poor brother's affairs. Ugh! I shall never get
through a third part of your accounts: take some of
these dainties before we attempt it, however: are you
bashful to that degree? For me, a crust and water
25   suffice.
     Intendant. Do you choose this especial night to
question me?
     Monsignor. This night, Ugo. You have managed
my late brother's affairs since the death of our elder
30   brother—fourteen years and a month, all but three
days. The 3rd of December, I find him . . .
     Intendant. If you have so intimate an acquaintance
with your brother's affairs, you will be tender of
turning so far back—they will hardly bear looking
35   into so far back.
     Monsignor. Ay, ay, ugh, ugh,—nothing but dis-
appointments here below! I remark a considerable
payment made to yourself on this 3rd of December.
Talk of disappointments! There was a young fellow

iv *15-19 converse with you, Ugo . . . Fossombruno*: the Intendant objects to
Monsignor's abbreviation of his name, but Monsignor affects to take him to
mean that he does not know it, or the details of his career.

iv *18-19. Ascoli, Fermo, and Fossombruno*: all the towns, here and ll. 89, 91, in
which the Intendant is said to have lived are in central Italy, in the Papal
States. All are also the seats of bishops or archbishops.

iv *23-5. these dainties . . . For me, a crust and water suffice*: Monsignor may
have in mind *Psalms* cxli 4: 'Incline not my heart to any evil thing, to practise
wicked works with men that work iniquity: and let me not eat of their
dainties'. See also *Luke* xiv 12, and cp. the self-denying frugality of the Pope
in *Ring* i 320-1.

iv *28. This night*: in the light of many echoes of the Gospels in this episode,
perhaps a ref. to *Luke* xii 19-20: 'And I will say to my soul, Soul, thou hast
much goods laid up for many years; take thine ease, eat, drink, and be merry.
But God said unto him, Thou fool, this night thy soul shall be required of
thee: then whose shall those things be, which thou hast provided?'

iv *31. The 3rd*] On the 3rd (*1849-63*); On the Third (*1865-88*).

iv *38. on this 3rd*] on this Third (*1865-88*).

iv *39-57. Talk of disappointments . . . eh, Ugo*: there is no hint in the former
episode that Jules has been patronized by Monsignor. The relationship

40   here, Jules, a foreign sculptor, I did my utmost to
      advance, that the church might be a gainer by us
      both: he was going on hopefully enough, and of a
      sudden he notifies to me some marvellous change that
      has happened in his notions of art; here's his
45   letter,—"He never had a clearly conceived Ideal
      within his brain till to-day. Yet since his hand could
      manage a chisel he has practised expressing other
      men's Ideals—and in the very perfection he has
      attained to he foresees an ultimate failure—his
50   unconscious hand will pursue its prescribed course of
      old years, and will reproduce with a fatal expertness
      the ancient types, let the novel one appear never so
      palpably to his spirit: there is but one method of
      escape—confiding the virgin type to as chaste a hand,
55   he will paint, not carve, its characteristics,"— strike

parallels that between Caponsacchi and his Bishop in *Ring*: see vi 264-331,
349-89, 463-78. Nor was there any hint that Jules intends to abandon
sculpture (see ii 233-5 for evidence to the contrary). See also headnote,
pp. 13-14.

iv 55. *he will paint*] he will turn painter instead of sculptor, and paint (*1849-
88*).

iv *55-6. strike out . . . Correggio*: Antonio Allegri (1494-1534), called
Correggio after his birthplace, was described by Vasari in terms which
support the parallel drawn by Monsignor: 'Correggio was the first in
Lombardy who commenced the execution of works in the modern manner,
and it is thought that if he had travelled beyond the limits of his native
Lombardy and visited Rome, he would have performed wonders . . . Be this
as it may, his works, being what they are, although he had never seen those
of antiquity, nor was even acquainted with the best works of the modern
masters; it necessarily follows that if he had studied these works he would
have materially improved his own' (*Lives of the Painters*, transl. Mrs J. Foster
[1850] 403-4). The painter Annibale Caracci (1560-1609) put the case less
negatively: 'the thoughts and conceptions of Correggio were his own,
evidently drawn from his own mind, and invented by himself, guided only
by the original idea. The others all rest on something not their own; some on
models, some on statues and paintings' (quoted in the anonymous *Sketches of
the Lives of Correggio and Parmigianino* [1823] pp. v-vi). By B.'s time,
however, this view was controversial: A. Mengs argued that an artist as great
as Correggio must have 'studied the works and maxims of the ancients and of
the best masters' (*Mengs on Painting* [1796] ii 57). So Monsignor is taking one
side in a controversy that centrally reflects Jules's dilemma. The sense in
which Correggio began 'a school' is equally controversial. Vasari claimed
that 'the Lombards were induced by his example to open their eyes: the result

out, I dare say, a school like Correggio: how think
you, Ugo?
 Intendant. Is Correggio a painter?
 Monsignor. Foolish Jules! and yet, after all, why
60 foolish? He may—probably will, fail egregiously: but
if there should arise a new painter, will it not be in
some such way—a poet, now, or a musician, spirits
who have conceived and perfected an Ideal through
some other channel, transferring it to this, and
65 escaping our conventional roads by pure ignorance of
them, eh, Ugo? If you have no appetite, talk at least,
Ugo!
 Intendant. Sir, I can submit no longer to this course
of yours: first, you select the group of which I
70 formed one,—next you thin it gradually,—always
retaining me with your smile,—and so do you
proceed till you have fairly got me alone with you
between four stone walls: and now then? Let this
farce, this chatter end now—what is it you want with
75 me?
 Monsignor. Ugo . . .
 Intendant. From the instant you arrived I felt your
smile on me as you questioned me about this and the
other article in those papers—why, your brother
80 should have given me this manor, that liberty,—and
your nod at the end meant,—what?
 Monsignor. Possibly that I wished for no loud talk
here—if once you set me coughing, Ugo!

---

of his painting has seen more than one fine genius belonging to that country
subsequently following his steps' (p. 410). Mengs cites the Caracci as having
'formed their style of design upon that of Correggio' (ii 47) but adds that, like
Raphael, he was 'little imitated' (ii 171). The author of *Sketches* notes that 'he
seems to have instructed few or no regular scholars' (p. 199), but also that 'he
shone forth as the founder of a new school of painting' (p. 70). Canova's
career was viewed in a similar fashion: 'The age was prepared in some
measure to hail a reformer, but seemed incapable by its own energies of
producing one. Canova at this crisis appeared, than whom, perhaps, no
illustrious name ever owed less to external circumstances, in the cultivation
of talents' (*Works of Canova* iii 5). It is also noted that Canova had no pupils as
such.
iv *62. a poet*] by a poet (*1849-88*).
iv *80. this manor, that liberty*] this villa, that *podere* (*1849-88*); replacing the
English terms, here and on subsequent occurrences, by their Italian
equivalents. A 'liberty' is a person's domain or property.

Intendant. I have your brother's hand and seal to all
85 I possess: now ask me what for! what service I did
him—ask me!

Monsignor. I had better not—I should rip up old
disgraces—let out my poor brother's weaknesses. By
the way, Maffeo of Forli, (which, I forgot to observe,
90 is your true name) was the interdict taken off you for
robbing that church at Cesena?

Intendant. No, nor needs be—for when I murdered
your brother's friend, Pasquale for him . . .

Monsignor. Ah, he employed you in that matter,
95 did he? Well, I must let you keep, as you say, this
manor and that liberty, for fear the world should find
out my relations were of so indifferent a stamp:
Maffeo, my family is the oldest in Messina, and
century after century have my progenitors gone on
100 polluting themselves with every wickedness under
Heaven: my own father . . . rest his soul!—I have, I
know, a chapel to support that it may: my dear two
dead brothers were,—what you know tolerably well:
I, the youngest, might have rivalled them in vice, if
105 not in wealth, but from my boyhood I came out from
among them, and so am not partaker of their plagues.
My glory springs from another source, or if from
this, by contrast only,—for I, the bishop, am the
brother of your employers, Ugo. I hope to repair
110 some of their wrong, however; so far as my brother's
ill-gotten treasure reverts to me, I can stop the

iv *87. I had better not*] I would better not (*1863-88*).

iv *89-91.* Forli and Cesena lie close together and about 190 km north of the
complex of towns mentioned at ll. 18-19.

iv *90. interdict*: in Catholic Church law, an instruction debarring particular
persons from taking the sacraments. Since the Intendant's crimes were
committed in the Papal States, which are under Church jurisdiction, it is
possible that his presence in Asolo is a result of flight from that jurisdiction.   *taken off*] ever taken off (*1849-88*).

iv *94. that matter*] that business (*1849-88*).

iv *95-6. this manor and that liberty*] this villa and that *podere* (*1849-88*).

iv *102. may: my dear*] may rest: my dear (*1849-88*).

iv *105-6. I came out . . . their plagues*: cp. *Revelation* xviii 4: 'And I heard
another voice from heaven, saying, Come out of her [Babylon] my people,
that ye be not partakers of her sins, and that ye receive not of her plagues'.

iv *110. so far as my brother's*] so far as my brothers' (*1870-88*; probably, as
Oxford suggests, a mispr., since 'his' in l. 112 is unchanged).

consequences of his crime, and not one *soldo* shall
escape me. Maffeo, the sword we quiet men spurn
away, you shrewd knaves pick up and commit
115 murders with; what opportunities the virtuous
forego, the villanous seize. Because, to pleasure
myself, apart from other considerations, my food
would be millet-cake, my dress sackcloth, and my
couch straw, am I therefore to let the off-scouring of
120 the earth seduce the ignorant by appropriating a
pomp these will be sure to think lessens the
abominations so unaccountably and exclusively
associated with it? Must I let manors and liberties go
to you, a murderer and thief, that you may beget by
125 means of them other murderers and thieves? No . . .
if my cough would but allow me to speak!
     Intendant. What am I to expect? you are going to
punish me?
     Monsignor. Must punish you, Maffeo. I cannot
130 afford to cast away a chance. I have whole centuries

iv *112-13. not one soldo shall escape me*: cp. *Luke* xii 58-9: 'When thou goest
with thine adversary to the magistrate, as thou art in the way, give diligence
that thou mayest be delivered from him; lest he hale thee to the judge, and the
judge deliver thee to the officer, and the officer cast thee into prison. I tell
thee, thou shalt not depart thence, till thou hast paid the very last
mite'.   *soldo*: a coin valued at one-twentieth of a lire, i.e. of very small
value.

iv *116. villanous*: the standard spelling until the late 19th century, unchanged
in all eds.

iv *118. sackcloth*: the traditional garb of repentance: cp. e.g. *Daniel* ix 3: 'And I
set my face unto the Lord God, to seek by prayer and supplications, with
fasting, and sackcloth, and ashes'.

iv *119-23. am I therefore . . . associated with it*: cp. *Luke* xvi 15: 'And he said
unto them, Ye are they which justify yourselves before men; but God
knoweth your hearts: for that which is highly esteemed among men is
abomination in the sight of God'.

iv *119-20. to let . . . ignorant*] to let you, the off-scouring of the earth, seduce
the poor and ignorant, (*1849-88*, except 'ignorant', *1865-88*).

iv *123-5. Must I let . . . murderers and thieves*: the sense is that the Intendant's
bad example will mislead others, not that he will literally father wicked
children.

iv *123. manors and liberties*] villas and *poderes* (*1849*); villas and *poderi* (*1863-88*).

iv *124. a murderer and thief*: cp. *Job* xxiv 14: 'The murderer rising with the light
killeth the poor and needy, and in the night is as a thief'.

iv *129-32. I cannot afford . . . do it in*: cp. the Pope in *Ring* x 337-45, who also
sees his condemnation of Guido as potentially his last act.

of sin to redeem, and only a month or two of life to
do it in! How should I dare to say . . .
   Intendant. "Forgive us our trespasses."
   Monsignor. My friend, it is because I avow myself a
135 very worm, sinful beyond measure, that I reject a line
of conduct you would applaud, perhaps: shall I
proceed, as it were, a-pardoning?—I?—who have no
symptom of reason to assume that aught less than my
strenuousest efforts will keep myself out of mortal
140 sin, much less, keep others out. No—I do trespass,
but will not double that by allowing you to trespass.
   Intendant. And suppose the manors are not your
brother's to give, or yours to take? Oh, you are hasty
enough just now!
145   *Monsignor.* 1, 2—No. 3!—ay, can you read the
substance of a letter, No. 3, I have received from Rome?
It is on the ground I there mention of the suspicion
I have that a certain child of my late elder brother,
who would have succeeded to his estates, was
150 murdered in infancy by you, Maffeo, at the instigation of my late brother—that the pontiff enjoins on
me not merely the bringing that Maffeo to condign
punishment, but the taking all pains, as guardian of
that infant's heritage for the church, to recover it
155 parcel by parcel, howsoever, whensoever, and where-

iv *133.* "*Forgive us our trespasses*": from the Lord's Prayer. *Matthew* has 'And
forgive us our debts, as we forgive our debtors' (vii 12); *Luke* has 'sins' (xi 4).
Matthew goes on: 'For if ye forgive men their trespasses, your heavenly father
will also forgive you: But if ye forgive not men their trespasses, neither will
your father forgive your trespasses' (vii 15). In *Matthew*, this quotation
comes, like many others in this episode, from the Sermon on the Mount.
iv *134-5. I avow . . . measure*: cp. *Psalms* xxii 6: 'But I am a worm, and no
man; a reproach of men, and despised of the people', and the Apocryphal
Prayer of Manasses: 'thou hast promised repentance to them that have sinned;
thou hast not appointed repentance to the just, which have not sinned, but to
me, for I have sinned above the number of the sands of the sea; I have sinned,
O Lord, I have sinned'.
iv *142. suppose the manors*] suppose the villas (*1849-88*).
iv *143. or yours*] nor yours (*1849-88*).
iv *147. on the ground I there mention*] precisely on the ground there mentioned,
(*1849-88*).
iv *151. my late brother*] my late younger brother (*1870-88*).
iv *152-3. condign punishment*: appropriate punishment. By B.'s time 'condign'
was used only in this phrase.
iv *154. that infant's heritage*] the infant's heritage (*1865-88*).

soever. While you are now gnawing those fingers,
the police are engaged in sealing up your papers,
Maffeo, and the mere raising my voice brings my
people from the next room to dispose of yourself.
160 But I want you to confess quietly, and save me
raising my voice. Why, man, do I not know the old
story? The heir between the succeeding heir, and that
heir's ruffianly instrument, and their complot's effect,
and the life of fear and bribes, and ominous smiling
165 silence? Did you throttle or stab my brother's infant?
Come, now!

   Intendant. So old a story, and tell it no better? When
did such an instrument ever produce such an effect?
Either the child smiles in his face, or, most likely, he
170 is not fool enough to put himself in the employer's
power so thoroughly—the child is always ready to
produce—as you say—howsoever, wheresoever, and
whensoever.

   Monsignor. Liar!

175 *Intendant.* Strike me? Ah, so might a father chastise!
I shall sleep soundly to-night at least, though the
gallows await me to-morrow; for what a life did I
lead? Carlo of Cesena reminds me of his connivance
every time I pay his annuity (which happens
180 commonly thrice a year). If I remonstrate, he will
confess all to the good bishop—you!

   Monsignor. I see thro' the trick, caitiff! I would you
spoke truth for once; all shall be sifted, however—
seven times sifted.

iv *162-3. and that heir's*] and this heir's (*1868-88*).
iv *163. complot's*: a 'complot' is a plot or conspiracy.
iv *175. so might a father chastise*: the combination of 'father' and 'chastise'
recalls *1 Kings* xii 11: 'And now whereas my father did lade you with a heavy
yoke, I will add to your yoke: my father hath chastised you with whips, but I
will chastise you with scorpions'. However, the Intendant seems to be
making an ironic comment on the Bishop's fatherly care for him, along the
lines of *Proverbs* xix 18: 'Chasten thy son while there is hope, and let not thy
soul spare for his crying'; a third possibility is suggested by *Jeremiah* xxxi 18-
20: 'I have surely heard Ephraim bemoaning himself thus; Thou hast
chastised me . . . Is Ephraim my dear son? is he a pleasant child? . . . I will
surely have mercy upon him, saith the Lord'.
iv *179. annuity*: lit., 'a yearly grant of income'; here, a euphemism for
blackmail payments.
iv *184. seven times sifted*: a biblical intensifier; cp. *Leviticus* xxvi 18: 'I shall
punish you seven times more'; cp. *Sordello* i 434: 'Gold seven times globed'.

185   *Intendant.* And how my absurd riches encumbered
        me! I dared not lay claim to above half my
        possessions. Let me but once unbosom myself,
        glorify Heaven, and die!
        Sir, you are no brutal, dastardly idiot like your
190   brother I frightened to death . . . let us understand
        one another. Sir, I will make away with her for
        you—the girl—here close at hand; not the stupid
        obvious kind of killing; do not speak—know nothing
        of her or me. I see her every day—saw her this
195   morning—of course there is no killing; but at Rome
        the courtesans perish off every three years, and I can
        entice her thither—have, indeed, begun operations
        already—there's a certain lusty, blue-eyed, florid-
        complexioned, English knave I employ occasionally.
200   —You assent, I perceive—no, that's not it—assent I
        do not say—but you will let me convert my present
        havings and holdings into cash, and give time to cross
        the Alps? 'Tis but a little black-eyed, pretty singing
        Felippa, gay silk-winding girl. I have kept her out of
205   harm's way up to this present; for I always intended
        to make your life a plague to you with her! 'Tis as
        well settled once and forever: some women I have
        procured will pass Bluphocks, my handsome
        scoundrel, off for somebody, and once Pippa
210   entangled!—you conceive?
        Monsignor. Why, if she sings, one might . . .

        [*Without*] Over-head the tree-tops meet—

iv *191-7. Sir, I will . . . entice her thither*: cp. the episode in *Pericles* IV vi in
which Marina is sold to a brothel in Mytilene by those who have rescued her
from attempted murder.

iv *194. her or me.*] her or me! (*1849-63*); her nor of me! (*1865-88*).

iv *199. I employ*] I and the Police employ (*1849-88*).

iv *202. give time*] give me time (*1849-88*).

iv *202-3. cross the Alps*: the Intendant wants to escape from Austrian
jurisdiction; his destination is either France or Switzerland.

iv *210. you conceive?*] you conceive? Through her singing? Is it a bargain?
(*1849-88*).

iv *211.*] not *1849-88*.

iv *212-25*] the s.d.'s are altered in *1849-88* as with Pippa's first song, i *215-22*.

iv *212-16.* Cp. *Round Us the Wild Creatures* 1-2: 'Round us the wild creatures,
overhead the trees, / Underfoot the moss-tracks,—life and love with these!'

Flowers and grass spring 'neath one's feet—
What are the voices of birds
215 —Ay, and beasts, too—but words—our words,
Only so much more sweet?
That knowledge with my life begun!
But I had so near made out the sun—
Could count your stars, the Seven and One!
220 Like the fingers of my hand—
Nay, could all but understand
How and wherefore the moon ranges—
And just when out of her soft fifty changes
No unfamiliar face might overlook me—
225 Suddenly God took me.

[Pippa *passes.*

Monsignor [*Springing up*] My people—one and
all—all—within there! Gag this villain—tie him hand
and foot: he dares—I know not half he dares—but

iv *213⌢214.*] There was nought above me, and nought below, / My
childhood had not learned to know! (*1849-88*, except 'know:', *1863-88*; 'me,
nought', *1865-88*).

iv *214. What*] For, what (*1849-88*).

iv *215. and beasts, too*—] and of beasts,— (*1849-88*).

iv *217. That knowledge*] The knowledge of that (*1849-88*). Cp. Wordsworth,
My heart leaps up 1-6: 'My heart leaps up when I behold / A rainbow in the
sky: / So was it when my life began; / So is it now I am a man; / So be it when
I shall grow old, / Or let me die!'

iv *219. Could count*] And counted (*1849-88*).   *the Seven and One*: lit., the
constellation of the Pleiades or Seven Sisters, and one of the other major
stars, perhaps Aldebaran or Fomalhaut (the latter is mentioned in *Sordello* iii
417); but B. probably also alludes to the 'seven stars' held in the right hand of
Christ, *Revelation* i 16, and to Christ himself as the 'bright and morning star',
Revelation xxii 16: see above, iii 147-8n. Cp. also, noting the next lines,
Psalms viii 3: 'When I consider thy heavens, the work of thy fingers, the
moon and the stars, which thou hast ordained'.

iv *221. Nay, could*] Nay, I could (*1849-88*).

iv *222.*] Wherefore through heaven the white moon ranges (*1849-88*).

iv *223. fifty*: often used by B. with the indefinite sense of 'a large number': cp.
Sordello v 182: 'For one thrust forward, fifty such fall back!' But cp. the link
between the moon as image of EBB. and the fifty poems of *M & W* in *One
Word More*.

iv *225. took me.*] took me! (*1849-88*).

remove him—quick! *Miserere mei, Domine!* quick, I
230   say!

Pippa's *Chamber again. She enters it.*

The bee with his comb,
The mouse at her dray,
The grub in its tomb
Wile winter away;
235   But the fire-fly and hedge-shrew and lobworm, I pray,
Where be they?
Ha, ha, thanks my Zanze—
"Feed on lampreys, quaff Breganze"—
The summer of life's so easy to spend!
240   But winter hastens at summer's end,
And fire-fly, hedge-shrew, lob-worm, pray,
Where be they?
No bidding you then to . . what did Zanze say?
"Pare your nails pearlwise, get your small feet shoes
245   "More like . . (what said she?)—and less like canoes—"
Pert as a sparrow . . . would I be those pert

iv 229. *Miserere mei, Domine*: 'Have mercy on me, Lord'. From *Psalms* li, a
Penitential Psalm: 'Have mercy upon me, O God, according to thy
lovingkindness: according to the multitude of thy tender mercies blot out my
transgressions'. A standard prayer in the Catholic Church. *OED* cites
Blount, 1656: '*Miserere* . . . is commonly that Psalm, which the Judge gives
to such guilty persons as have the benefit of Clergy allowed by the Law'.
iv *231-6*. Adapting Aesop's fable of the grasshopper and the ant. Croxall's
translation (known to B.) concludes: 'they who drink, sing and dance in
Summer, must starve in Winter'. Croxall's moral, like Pippa's, relates the
fable to youth, as either misspent or prudent.
iv *232. dray*: lit., a squirrel's nest; not applied to mice in any *OED* citation.
iv *233. its*] his (*1888*).
iv *236.*] How fare they? (*1849-88*).
iv *237.*] Ha, ha, best thanks for your counsel, my Zanze— (*1849-88*, except
'ha, thanks', *1865-88*; 'Zanze!', *1868-88*).
iv *238. "Feed on*] "Feast upon (*1849-88*).   *quaff Breganze"*—] quaff the
Breganze"— (*1849-75*). See iii 231n.
iv *239. life's*] life (*1865-88*).   *spend!*] spend, (*1849-88*; see next note).
iv *239^240.*] And care for to-morrow so soon put away! (*1849-88*).
iv *242.*] How fare they? (*1849-88*).
iv *246. Pert as a sparrow . . .*] How pert that girl was!— (*1849-88*). The
sparrow was Venus' bird and associated with lust.

Impudent staring wretches! it had done me,
However, surely no such mighty hurt
To learn his name who passed that jest upon me.—
250 No foreigner, that I can recollect,
Came, as she says, a month since to inspect
Our silk-mills—none with blue eyes and thick rings
Of English-coloured hair, at all events.
Well—if old Luca keeps his good intents
255 We shall do better—see what next year brings—
I may buy shoes, my Zanze, not appear
So destitute, perhaps, next year!
Bluf—something—I had caught the uncouth name
But for Monsignor's people's sudden clatter
260 Above us—bound to spoil such idle chatter,
The pious man, the man devoid of blame,
The . . . ah, but—ah, but, all the same
No mere mortal has a right
To carry that exalted air;
265 Best people are not angels quite—
While—not worst people's doings scare
The devils; so there's that regard to spare!
Mere counsel to myself, mind! for
I have just been Monsignor!

iv 247. *wretches*] women (*1849-88*).
iv 253. *English-coloured hair*] raw-silk-coloured hair (*1849-88*).
iv 256. *not appear*] nor appear (*B & P BYU*).
iv 257.] More destitute than you, perhaps, next year! (*1849-88*, except 'you perhaps', *1865-88*).
iv 260. *chatter,*] chatter (*1849-88*); see next note.
iv 260^261.] As ours; it were, indeed, a serious matter / If silly talk like ours should put to shame (*1849-88*, except 'ours:', *1868-88*; 'it were indeed', *1865-88*).
iv 261. Cp. *Ephesians* i 4: 'holy and without blame'.
iv 265. Conflating two proverbs: 'the best of men are but men at best' and 'men are not angels'. *Oxford Dictionary of Proverbs* cites T. Cooper, 1589: 'They [bishops] are men, and no Angels . . . He is an Angel that never falleth, hee is no man'; also *Henry VIII* V iii 10-14 (spoken to Archbishop Cranmer): 'we all are men, / In our own natures frail and capable / Of our flesh; few are angels; out of which frailty / And want of wisdom, you, that best should teach us, / Have misdemean'd yourself'. Cp. also *Psalms* viii 5: 'For thou hast made him [man] a little lower than the angels'.
iv 266. *not worst people's*] not the worst of people's (*1849-88*).
iv 267. *devils*] devil (*1863-88*).   *regard*] proud look (*1849-88*).
iv 268. *Mere*] Which is mere (*1849-88*). This line is indented, *1868-88*.
iv 269. *Monsignor*] the holy Monsignor (*1849-88*).

270 And I was you too, mother,
      And you too, Luigi!—how that Luigi started
      Out of the Turret—doubtlessly departed
      On some love-errand or another—
      And I was Jules the sculptor's bride,
275 And I was Ottima beside,
      And now what am I?—tired of fooling!
      Day for folly, night for schooling—
      New year's day is over—over!
      Even my lily's asleep, I vow:
280 Wake up—here's a friend I pluckt you.
      See—call this a heart's-ease now!
      Something rare, let me instruct you,
      Is this—with petals triply swollen,
      Three times spotted, thrice the pollen,
285 While the leaves and parts that witness
      The old proportions and their fitness
      Here remain, unchanged unmoved now—
      Call this pampered thing improved now!
      Suppose there's a king of the flowers
290 And a girl-show held in his bowers—
      "Look ye, buds, this growth of ours,"
      Says he, "Zanze from the Brenta,
      I have made her gorge polenta

iv *270. mother*] Luigi's gentle mother (*1849-88*).

iv *273. love-errand*] good errand (*1849-88*).   *another*—] another, (*1849-88*); see next note.

iv *273^274.*] For he past just now in a traveller's trim,
               And the sullen company that prowled
               About his path, I noticed, scowled
               As if they lost a prey in him. (*1849-88*, except 'pass'd', *1863-65*; 'passed', *1868-88*).

iv *278. over—over!*] over and spent, (*1849-88*); see next note.

iv *278^279.*] Ill or well, I must be content! (*1849-88*, except 'content.', *1865-88*). The next line is indented as for a new para., *1868-88*.

iv *280. I pluckt you.*] I've pluckt you! (*1849-88*, except 'plucked', *1868-88*).

iv *281-303.* With Pippa's criticism of the over-cultivated flower, and the parallel between flowers and girls which follows, cp. Perdita in *Winter's Tale* IV iv 79ff.

iv *281. See—call this*] See—call this flower (*1849-63*); Call this flower (*1865-88*).   *heart's-ease*: pansy. See i 229n.

iv *282. Something*] And something (*1849-63*).

iv *286. The old*] Old (*1865-88*).

iv *288. Call*] So call (*1849*); So, call (*1863*).

iv *293. polenta*: see iii 288n.

Till both cheeks are near as bouncing
295   As her . . . name there's no pronouncing!
See this heightened colour too—
For she swilled Breganze wine
Till her nose turned deep carmine—
'Twas but white when wild she grew!
300   And only by this Zanze's eyes
Of which we could not change the size,
The magnitude of what's achieved
Elsewhere may be perceived!"

Oh what a drear, dark close to my poor day!
305   How could that red sun drop in that black cloud!
Ah, Pippa, morning's rule is moved away,
Dispensed with, never more to be allowed.
Day's turn's over—now's the night's—
Oh Lark be day's apostle
310   To mavis, merle and throstle,
Bid them their betters jostle
From day and its delights!
But at night, brother Howlet, over the woods
Toll the world to thy chantry—
315   Sing to the bats' sleek sisterhoods
Full complines with gallantry—
Then, owls and bats, cowls and twats,

iv 295. *As her . . . pronouncing*: her breasts.
iv 302. *what's achieved*] all achieved (*1865-88*).
iv 303. *Elsewhere*] Otherwise (*1849-88*).
iv 308.] Day's turn is over—now arrives the night's— (*1849-88*, except 'over:', *1863-65*; 'over,', *1868-88*; 'night's.', *1863-88*).
iv 309-12. Cp. *Luke* xiv 15-24, the parable of the rich man who 'bids' many guests to his 'great supper'; when they do not come he commands his servants to 'bring in hither the poor' instead.
iv 310. The 'mavis' is the song-thrush, the 'merle' the blackbird. The 'throstle' is another name for the song-thrush.
iv 313. *brother*: monk.   *Howlet*: owl.   *over*] far over (*1849-63*).
iv 314. *chantry*: a chapel where mass is sung for the souls of the dead.
iv 316. *complines*: in the Roman Catholic liturgy, the last service of the day, completing the services of the canonical hours.   *gallantry*] emended in agreement with *1863-88* from 'galantry', *1841-49*. Although *OED* has a couple of instances of 'galantry', none is recorded after the 17th century.
iv 317.] Then, owls and bats, / Cowls and twats, (*1870-88*).   *twats*: B. wrote to Furnivall: 'In the Royalist rhymes entitled "Vanity of Vanities, or Sir Harry Vane's Picture"—wherein Vane is charged with being a Jesuit— occur these lines " 'Tis said they will give him a Cardinal's hat: / They sooner

        Monks and nuns, in a cloister's moods,
        Adjourn to the oak-stump pantry!
                 [After she has begun to undress herself.
320 Now one thing I should like to really know:
        How near I ever might approach all these
        I only fancied being this long day—
        . . . Approach, I mean, so as to touch them—so
        As to . . in some way . . move them—if you please,
325 Do good or evil to them some slight way.
        For instance, if I wind
        Silk to-morrow, silk may bind
                 [Sitting on the bedside.
        And broider Ottima's cloak's hem—
        Ah, me and my important passing them
330 This morning's hymn half promised when I rose!
        True in some sense or other, I suppose.
                 [As she lies down.
        God bless me tho' I cannot pray tonight.
        No doubt, some way or other, hymns say right.
        All service is the same with God—

---

will give him an old nun's twat!" The ballad is partly quoted in the Appendix to Forster's Life of Vane, but the above lines are left out—I remember them, however, and the word struck me as a distinctive part of a nun's attire that might fitly pair off with the cowl appropriated to a monk' (*Trumpeter* 135). B.'s surmise is famously wrong; the word means 'cunt'. B. slightly misquotes the lines, which in the original broadside ballad to which he refers read: 'They talkt of his having a Cardinalls Hat, / They'd send him as soon an Old Nuns Twat'. The ballad is undated; in two copies in the Bodleian Library, Oxford (Wood 416 [32, 91]) the date is conjectured as 1659 or 1661-2. It was also repr., as *Oxford* points out, in *Rump, or an Exact Collection of the Choycest Poems and Songs Relating to the Late Times* (2 pts., 1662) ii 108-11. Forster's version, considerably abridged, appears in Appendix C of his *Life of Sir Henry Vane* (*Lives of Eminent British Statesmen* iv [1838] 398-400).

iv *320. to really*] really to (*1849-88*).

iv *327. silk*] my silk (*1849-88*).

iv *328. broider*] border (*1868-88*).

iv *329. Ah, me*] Ah me, (*1865-88*).   *passing them*] part with them (*1849-88*).

iv *331. suppose.*] suppose, (*1849-63*); see next note.

iv *331^332.*] Though I passed by them all, and felt no sign. (*1849-63*). This is a rare example of a whole line being added in one ed. and deleted later.

iv *332.*] God bless me! I can pray no more to-night. (*1849-88*).

iv *334-6.* The last three lines echo the 'new year's hymn', *Intro* 148-59.

iv *334. is*] ranks (*1865-88*).

335 *Whose puppets, best and worst,*
     Are we . . . . . .
                                            [*She sleeps.*

21 Artemis Prologuizes

First publ. *B & P* iii (*DL*), 26 Nov. 1842; repr. *1849, 1863* (when 'Prologuizes' was changed to 'Prologizes' and it was placed in *Men, and Women*: see Appendix A, p. 464), *1865²*, *1868*, *1880*, *1888*. Our text is *1842*. The date of composition was Easter 1841. In a note appended to *DL 1st Proof* but omitted from the published text B. wrote: 'I had better say perhaps that the above is nearly all retained of a tragedy I composed, much against my endeavour, while in bed with a fever two years ago—it went further into the story of Hippolytus and Aricia; but when I got well, putting only thus much down at once, I soon forgot the remainder, which came nearer the mark, I think'. Mrs Orr, who cites the note up to 'remainder' (*Life* 131), comments: 'When Mr. Browning gave me these supplementary details for the *Handbook*, he spoke as if his illness had interrupted the work, not preceded its conception' (*ibid.* n. 1). B. retold the story to Julia Wedgwood: 'yes, I had another slight touch of something unpleasant in the head which came on, one Good *Saturday*, as I sat reading the revise of "Pippa Passes"—and my hair was cut off, but I soon got well. I wrote in bed such a quantity of that "Hippolytus", of which I wrote down the Prologue, but forgot the rest, though the resuscitation-scene which was to have followed, would have improved matters' (*RB & JW* 102). A revise is a corrected proof-sheet; since Easter Day in 1841 (the year *Pippa* was published) fell on 11 Apr., *Artemis* was presumably written around this time.

In the variant of the myth which B. follows, Hippolytus was rescued by Artemis and resuscitated by Aesculapius; after his revival he fell in love with the nymph Aricia, who gave her name to the city founded by Hippolytus in Italy. According to Mrs Orr, the first scenes of B.'s play would have included a 'chorus of nymphs, the awakening of Hippolytus, and with it the stir of the new passion within him' (*Handbook* 120). The poem's principal source is Euripides' *Hippolytus*, which concludes with the death of Hippolytus and Artemis' rebuke to Theseus. B. may have been following Euripides' own practice (in e.g. *Helen* and *Iphigenia in Tauris*) of dramatizing a secondary and reconciliatory myth, imposing a 'happy ending' on a traditionally tragic story. Euripides was B.'s favourite Greek dramatist; *Balaustion* and *Aristophanes* contain versions of his *Alcestis* and *Heracles*. Ovid, in *Metamorphoses* xv 492-546, gives an account which includes Hippolytus' resuscitation, but makes no direct reference to Aricia. See also Virgil, *Aeneid* vii 765-77. The

Title. Artemis: daughter of Zeus, king of the gods, and the nymph Leto. 'She was born at the same birth as Apollo; and the pains which she saw her mother suffer during her labour, gave her such an aversion to marriage, that she obtained of her father to live in perpetual celibacy, and to preside over the travails of women. To shun the society of men, she devoted herself to hunting' (*Lemprière*). Artemis was worshipped as the triple goddess of heaven, earth, and the underworld (see ll. 4-9).   *Prologuizes*: in origin a poem is unusual for B., in this period, for its stately, classicized idiom, mixing Greek and Latin (Miltonic) constructions; it was praised by Matthew Arnold, probably for this: 'one of the very best antique fragments I know is a fragment of a Hippolytus by him' (*Letters of Matthew Arnold 1848-88*, ed. Russell [1895] i 61). It is the first example of B.'s revision of the customary anglicization of Greek proper names, e.g. Hippolutos for Hippolytus: see also *Balaustion* and *Aristophanes*. B. defended his practice in the preface to his translation of Aeschylus' *Agamemnon* (1877), and in a note reproduced in *Cooke* 37-8.

> I am a Goddess of the ambrosial courts,
> And save by Here, Queen of Pride, surpassed
> By none whose temples whiten this the world.
> Thro' Heaven I roll its lucid moon along;
> 5 In Hades shed o'er my pale people peace;
> On Earth, I, caring for the creatures, guard
> Each pregnant yellow wolf and fox-bitch sleek,
> And every feathered mother's callow brood,
> And all that love green haunts and loneliness.
> 10 Of men, the chaste adore me, hanging crowns
> Of poppies red to blackness, bell and stem,
> Upon my image at Athenai here;
> Of such this Youth, Asclepios bends above,

Greek word; first rec. by *OED* in the 'Induction' to *Four Plays in One*, a major source for *Pippa* (see p. 8). Cp. also *Old Pictures* 265 and *Balaustion* 166.

¶21.*1. ambrosial courts*: Olympus, seat of the gods; ambrosia was their food. Cp. the 'Attendant Spirit' at the opening of Milton's *A Mask*, which has related themes of chastity and rescue: 'Before the starry threshold of Jove's court / My mansion is . . .' (ll. 1-2); at l. 16 the Spirit refers to his 'pure ambrosial weeds [garments]'.

2. Here] Heré (*1884*, a rare example of a variant unique to this corr. reissue of *1880*). Here, or Hera, was the wife (and sister) of Zeus: she was 'the goddess of all power and empire' (*Lemprière*), and her emblem was the peacock, hence 'Queen of Pride'.

4. its] my (*1849-88*).   *lucid*: poeticism for 'shining, resplendent'.

5. In Hades shed] I shed in Hell (*1849-88*).

7. fox-bitch: vixen; this kind of compound is characteristic of Greek.

8. i.e. every she-bird's immature young: a Greek construction (cp. l. 7). *Oxford* cites *PL* vii 418-20: 'brood . . . callow young, but feathered soon'.

10-11. hanging crowns / Of poppies red to blackness: the poppy was sacred to Artemis. At the opening of the *Hippolytus*, Hippolytus lays a wreath of flowers upon her altar.

12. Athenai: Athens.

13. Of such this] And this dead (*1849-88*).   *this Youth*: Hippolytus, son of Theseus (see l. 23n.) and Hippolyta, queen of the Amazons, whom Theseus

Was dearest to me, and my buskined step
15 To follow thro' the wild-wood leafy ways,
And chase the panting stag, or swift with darts
Stop the swift ounce, or lay the leopard low,
He paid not homage to another God:
Whence Aphrodite, by no midnight smoke
20 Of tapers lulled, in jealousy despatched
A noisome lust that, as the gadbee stings,
Possessed his stepdame Phaidra for the child
Of Theseus her great husband then afar.
But when Hippolutos exclaimed with rage
25 Against the miserable Queen, she judged
Intolerable life, and, pricked at heart

---

had conquered.   *Asclepios*: or Aesculapius, the son of Apollo by a mortal, Coronis. He became a great healer, and after his death the god of healing. His skill excited the anger of Zeus, who struck him with thunder (in Virgil's account, for his revival of Hippolytus).

14. me, and] me. He (*1849-88*).   *buskined step*: buskins are half-boots, traditionally worn by Artemis for hunting; also the footwear of tragic actors in Greek drama, whence 'buskined' came to mean 'tragic; dignified, elevated, lofty'.

17. ounce: snow leopard.

18. He paid not] Neglected (*1849-88*).

19. Aphrodite: Greek goddess of love, whose rivalry with Artemis causes the tragedy.

21. gadbee: a gadfly, i.e. any fly which bites and goads cattle. There may be an allusion to Hera's punishment of Io, whom she turned into a cow and tormented with a gadfly for her love-affair with Zeus.

22. his stepdame Phaidra: Phaedra, daughter of Minos and Pasiphae, whom Theseus carried off and married after the death of Hippolyta.   *the child*] himself (*1849-88*).

23.] The son of Theseus her great absent spouse. (*1849-88*).   *Theseus*: king of Athens, and one of the heroes of Greek historical myth. Usually represented, in legend and in Greek drama, as a liberal and humane ruler, as in e.g. Sophocles' *Oedipus at Colonnus* and Euripides' *Heracles*, which B. translated in *Aristophanes*.

24-30. B.'s account follows Euripides', except in the implication (see esp. l. 30) that Phaedra attempted directly to seduce Hippolytus. In the play, the Nurse approaches him, and Phaedra neither endorses nor seconds this action. B.'s account follows Ovid's, which Racine also uses in *Phèdre*.

24.] Hippolutos exclaiming in his rage (*1849-88*).

25. miserable] fury of the (*1863-88*).

25-6. she judged / Intolerable life: i.e. she judged life to be intolerable.

26. Intolerable life] Life insupportable (*1849-88*).

An Amazonian stranger's race had right
To scorn her, perished by the murderous cord:
Yet, ere she perished, blasted in a scroll
30 The fame of him her swerving made not swerve,
Which Theseus saw, returning, and believed,
So, in the blindness of his wrath, exiled
The man without a crime, who, last as first,
Loyal, divulged not to his sire the truth.
35 But Theseus from Poseidon had obtained
That of his wishes should be granted Three,
And this one imprecated now—alive
May ne'er Hippolutos reach other lands!
Poseidon heard, ai ai! And scarce the prince
40 Had stepped into the fixed boots of the car,
That give the feet a stay against the strength
Of the Henetian horses, and around
His body flung the reins, and urged their speed
Along the rocks and shingles of the shore,
45 When from the gaping wave a monster flung

27. *An Amazonian stranger's race*: the race of Hippolyta, queen of the Amazons
(see l. 13n.).   *had right*] should dare (*1849-88*).
29. *blasted in a scroll*: 'calumniated in a letter'.
30. *fame*: repute, integrity.   *swerve,*] swerve. (*1863-88*).
31. *Which Theseus saw,*] Which Theseus read, (*1849*); And Theseus, read,
(*1863-88*, except 'Theseus read', *1884*).
32.] So, exiled in the blindness of his wrath, (*1849-88*, except 'And exiled,',
(*1863-88*).
33-4. *who, last . . . the truth*: in Euripides' *Hippolytus*, Hippolytus hints at
Phaedra's guilt to his father; B. follows Racine's *Phèdre*, where Hippolytus
says nothing in his defence beyond asserting his innocence.
35. *But*] Now (*1849-88*).   *Poseidon*: god of the sea; in some accounts,
Theseus' father.
37.] And this he imprecated straight—alive (*1849-88*, except 'And one', *1863-
88*; '"Alive' *1868-88*, where the quotation is closed after 'lands!' in the next
line).   *imprecated*: prayed for, called down.
39. *ai, ai*: stylized Greek lamentation.
39-61. *And scarce . . . horror-fixed*: B. follows Euripides' *Hippolytus* (ll. 1185-
1247) very closely, with some details from Ovid. He may also have recalled a
passage from one of the sources for *Sordello* (see below, ll. 54-9n.).
42. *Henetian horses*: from Enetia, a district of Paphlagonia in Asia Minor.
43. *reins*] rein (*1865-88*).
45. *When*] Than (*DL 1st proof*, canc.).
45-6. Cp. Ovid, *Metamorphoses* xv 508-13: 'cum mare surrexit, cumulusque
inmanis aquarum / in montis speciem curvare et crescere visus / et dare
mugitus summoque cacumine findi; / corniger hinc taurus ruptis expellitur

His obscene body in the coursers' path:
These, mad with terror as the sea-bull sprawled
Wallowing about their feet, lost care of him
That reared them; and the master-chariot-pole
50 Snapping beneath their plunges like a reed,
Hippolutos, whose feet were trammeled sure,
Was yet dragged forward by the circling rein
Which either hand directed; nor they quenched
The frenzy of their flight before each trace,
55 Wheel-spoke and splinter of the woeful car,

---

undis / pectoribusque tenus molles eretus in auras / naribus et patulo partem
maris evomit ore' [the sea rose up and a huge mound of water seemed to
swell and grow to mountain size, to give forth bellowings, and to be cleft at
its highest point. Then the wave burst and a horned bull was cast forth, and,
raised from the sea breast-high into the yielding air, he spouted out great
quantities of water from his nostrils and wide mouth].
48-9. lost care of him / That reared them: in Euripides' *Hippolytus*, Hippolytus
pleads with the horses: 'Stand horses, stand! / You were fed in my stables! Do
not kill me!' (ll. 1240-1).
51. sure] fast (*1849-88*).
53. they] was (*1849*).
54. their] that (*1849*).   *trace*: leather strap.
54-9. each trace . . . morsels of his flesh: an elaboration of Euripides' *Hippolytus*,
and following Ovid, *Metamorphoses* xv 521-9, in having Hippolytus literally
dismembered: 'nec tamen has vires rabies superasset equorum, / ni rota,
perpetuum qua circumvertitur axem, / stipitis occursu fracta ac disiecta
fuisset. / excutior curru lorisque tenentibus artus / viscera viva trahi, nervos
in stipe teneri, / membra rapi partim partimque reprensa relinqui, / ossa
gravem dare fracta sonum fessamque videres. / exhalari animam nullasque in
corpore partes, / noscere quas posses: unumque erat omnia vulnus' [Still
would the horses' mad strength not have surpassed my own had not a wheel,
striking a hub against a projecting stock, been broken and wrenched from the
axle. I was thrown from my car, and while the reins held my legs fast, you
might see my living flesh dragged along, my sinews held on the sharp stake,
my limbs partly drawn on and in part caught fast and left behind, and my
bones broken with a loud snapping sound. My spent spirit was at last
breathed out and there was no part of my body which you could recognise,
but it all was one great wound]. Cp. the description of the death of Alberic in
Sordello vi 775-9: 'Alberic . . . tied on to a wild horse, was trailed / To death
through raunce and bramble-bush'. B.'s source was *Verci* ii 407: 'Finally, the
death of Alberic brought this horrible tragedy to an end. He was tied to the
tail of a horse, and dragged through the entire army, leaving the ground wet
with his blood, and pieces of his body on every stone, branch and thorn'. See
Sordello vi 774-89n. for details of B.'s lifelong interest in this episode.

And boulder-stone, sharp stub, and spiny shell,
Huge fish-bone wrecked and wreathed amid the sands
On that detested beach, was bright with blood
And morsels of his flesh: then fell the steeds
60 Head-foremost, crashing in their mooned fronts,
Shivering with sweat, each white eye horror-fixed.
His people, who had witnessed all afar,
Bore back the ruins of Hippolutos.
But when his sire, too swoln with pride, rejoiced,
65 Indomitable as a man foredoomed,
That vast Poseidon had fulfilled his prayer,
I, in a flood of glory visible,
Stood o'er my dying votary, and deed
By deed revealed, as all took place, the truth.
70 Then Theseus lay the woefullest of men,
And worthily; but ere the death-veils hid
His face, the murdered prince full pardon breathed
To his rash sire. Whence now Athenai wails.
But I, who ne'er forsake my votaries,
75 Lest in the cross-way none the honey-cake

56. *And*] Each (*1849-88*).

59-61. then fell . . . horror-fixed: in Euripides' and Ovid's versions, the horses
vanish after dragging Hippolytus to death.

60. crashing in: just possibly an uncorrected mispr. of 'crushing in', though
'crash' can mean 'smash' and thus make sense. But since the horses appear in
the next line to remain alive, the meaning is obscure.   *mooned fronts*: their
foreheads which have moon-shaped markings.

61. horror-fixed] we supply the hyphen in agreement with *1849-88*.

73. Whence now] Whereat (*1849-88*). There is a space between this line and
l. 74 (which is indented for a new paragraph) in *1868-88*.

74-83. Artemis' motive of self-glorification (or self-justification) in reviving
Hippolytus alludes to a common motif in Euripides' plays, in which gods
constantly punish and reward men for their attitudes to the gods rather than
for their behaviour towards each other. Aphrodite, in the prologue to the
Hippolytus, offers precisely this rationale for her persecution of Hippolytus.
Artemis too was traditionally jealous of her honours. With the language of
these lines, cp. Keats's *Ode to Psyche* 28-52, lamenting that Psyche remained
unworshipped in classical times, and promising her the recompense of his
worship, esp. such phrases as 'though temple hast thou none . . . No shrine,
no grove, no oracle . . . Yes, I will be thy priest, and build a fane / In some
untrodden region of my mind'.

74. But] So (*1849-88*).

75. the cross-way: B. refers here to Artemis' association with Hecate, called
Artemis of the Crossroads, whose shrines were commonly positioned in
these places.

Should tender, nor pour out the dog's hot life;
Lest at my fane disconsolate the priests
Should dress my image with some faded poor
Few crowns, made favors of, nor dare object
80 Such slackness to my worshippers who turn
Elsewhere the trusting heart and loaded hand,
As they had climbed Olumpos to report
Of Artemis and nowhere found her throne—
I interposed: and, this eventful night,
85 While round the funeral pyre the populace
Stand with fierce light on their black robes that blind
Each sobbing head, while yet their hair they clip
O'er the dead body of their withered prince,
And, in his palace, Theseus prostrated
90 On the cold hearth, his brow cold as the slab
'Tis bruised on, groans away the heavy grief—
As the pyre fell, and down the cross logs crashed,
Sending a crowd of sparkles thro' the night,
And the gay fire, elate with mastery,
95 Towered like a serpent o'er the clotted jars
Of wine, dissolving oils and frankincense,
And splendid gums like gold,—my potency
Conveyed the perished man to my retreat
In the thrice venerable forest here.
100 And this white-bearded Sage who squeezes now
The berried plant is Phoibos' son of fame,
Asclepios, whom my radiant brother taught
The doctrine of each herb and flower and root,
To know their secret'st virtue and express
105 The saving soul of all—who so has soothed

77. *disconsolate the priests*] the priests disconsolate (*1849-88*).
79. *object*: complain about.
81.] The trusting heart and loaded hand elsewhere, (*1849-88*).
82. *As*: as if.
86. *Stand*] Stood (*1849-88*).   *that blind*] to blind (*1863-65*); which bound (*1868-88*).
87. *clip*] clipped (*1849-88*).
91. *'Tis . . . groans*] 'Twas . . . groaned (*1849-88*).
97. *gums like gold*] gums, like gold (*1849*). The sense is that the gums are like gold, not that they and the 'oils' and 'frankincense' are 'dissolving' like gold, a misreading encouraged by the *1849* revision.
102. *radiant brother*: Phoebus Apollo was the sun-god.
104. *express*: squeeze out.

With lavers the torn brow and murdered cheeks,
Composed the hair and brought its gloss again,
And called the red bloom to the pale skin back,
And laid the strips and jagged ends of flesh
110 Even once more, and slacked the sinew's knot
Of every tortured limb—that now he lies
As if mere sleep possessed him underneath
These interwoven oaks and pines. Oh, cheer,
Divine presenter of the healing rod
115 Thy snake, with ardent throat and lulling eye,
Twines his lithe spires around! I say, much cheer!
Proceed thou with thy wisest pharmacies!
And ye, white crowd of woodland sister-nymphs,
Ply, as the Sage directs, these buds and leaves
120 That strew the turf around the Twain! While I
In fitting silence the event await.

106. lavers: washes of healing waters. Cp. Milton, *Samson Agonistes* 1725-8: 'Let us go find the body where it lies / Soak'd in his enemies' blood, and from the stream / With lavers pure and cleansing herbs wash off / The clotted gore'. Cp. also the sense, 'the spiritual "washing" of baptism' (*OED* 2).   *cheeks*] a proof of *1865²* (at *Texas*) has the cancelled reading 'cheek'; all other corrections to the poem are of misprs., and this is probably also one.
114-16. the healing rod . . . spires around: Aesculapius was commonly represented 'holding in his hand a staff, round which is wreathed a serpent . . . Serpents are more particularly sacred to him, as the ancient physicians used them in their prescriptions' (*Lemprière*).
121.] Await, in fitting silence, the event. (*1849-88*).

★ 22 The Cardinal and the Dog

First publ. *Asolando*, 12 Dec. 1889. B. himself, in a letter to Furnivall of 1 Oct. 1881, referred to its much earlier composition during an explanation of the identity of the dedicatee of *Pied Piper*, Charles Macready's young son Willie (see p. 130): 'He had a talent for drawing, and asked me to give him some little thing to illustrate; so, I made a bit of a poem out of an old account of the Pope's legate at the Council of Trent—which he made such clever drawings for, that I tried a more picturesque subject, the Piper' (*Trumpeter* 27). A letter from Willie Macready thanking B. for *Cardinal* is undated, but unless B.'s account is very telescoped, the poem was, as Mrs Orr suggests, sent to him just before *Pied Piper*, i.e. early May 1842 (*Life* 122); *Penguin* conjectures 1840, but gives no reason. B.'s sister Sarianna confirms B.'s account, but Kelley and Hudson have established that B. drafted the poem well before this time, and not specifically for Willie Macready's benefit: 'his draft of this poem, in the margins of his copy of Nathaniel Wanley's *The Wonders of the Little World* . . . is dated 27 February 1841, well before the illness which is supposed to have prompted composition' (*Correspondence* v 330: Willie Macready's illustrations are reproduced opposite p. 331). Our text is that of the untitled *Wanley* MS (hereafter *1841*). Sir W. Nicholl, in *The Bookman* lii (1912) 68-9, printed the facsimile of a version of the poem in the handwriting of B.'s father (hereafter *Transcript*): Kelley and Hudson note that it is close to *1841*, and it may be a copy of *1841*; alternatively, it may be a copy of the version sent to Willie Macready. In his letter to Furnivall, B. commented: 'If you care to have the legend of the Legate I am sure you are welcome to it, when I can transcribe it from the page of the old book it remains on' (*ibid.*), implying that at that stage *1841* still represented the true text. Another version (hereafter *1889a*), much closer to *1889*, was sent by B. on an 'album-leaf' to Mrs Thomas on 30 May 1889, with the comment in an accompanying letter: 'I enclose a little sort of what you may call a childish ballad, hitherto unpublished. Will you offer it for acceptance to the young lady with the best wishes of—shall I say?—hers affectionately as yours most truly' (*ABL MS*). The text of *1889* and *1889a* is in long lines, composing three stanzas of five, five and four lines (including two extra lines after ll. 8 and 26).

The source of the poem is Nathaniel Wanley's *Wonders of the Little World* (1667), which B. also used for *Pied Piper*. Wanley's account appears in bk. VI, ch. xxvii, 'Of the Apparition of Demons and Spectres, and with what courage some have endured the sight of them': '*Crescentius* the Popes Legate at the Council of *Trent* 1552. *March* 25. was busie writing of Letters to the Pope till it was far in the night, whence rising to refresh himself, he saw a black Dog of a vast bigness, flaming eyes, ears that hung down almost to the ground enter the room, which came directly towards him, and laid himself down under the table. Frighted at the sight, he called his Servants in the Antichamber, commanded them to look for the Dog, but they could find none. The Cardinal fell melancholy, thence sick, and died at *Verona*: on his death bed he cryed out to drive away the Dog that leaped upon his bed' (p. 611). In *1889a* and *1889* the date is mistakenly given as '1522', an error presumably in either B.'s or the compositor's transcription; alternatively, B. rewrote the poem from memory without reference to *1841*. The text of *1841* is written in the margins of *Wanley* around this narrative; the fact that B. redrafted st. iii on this copy (probably because its rhymes presented difficulties: see ll. 9-12n.) suggests that it was composed impromptu rather than transcribed from a separate draft. Sts. i and iii establish the pattern of indentation of the second and fourth lines, which is less clear in the more cramped inscription of the other stanzas. At the conclusion of *1841*, B. wrote: 'Done into Dog-rel, Feby. 27, 1841'.

The last line of *1889*, not in *1841*, draws attention to the context of this story in the development of the Reformation. The Council of Trent (1545-63) was originally summoned by Pope Paul III, at the insistence of the Emperor Charles V, to attempt a reconciliation between the Catholic hierarchy and the German Protestants. However, the first phase of the Council (1545-9) was dominated by reaffirmations of Catholic doctrines and condemnation of Protestant ones as heresy. After the death of Paul III, his successor Julius III reconvened the Council in 1551 under his Legate Crescenzio; a list of Protestant doctrines was considered and anathematized; Protestant envoys arrived; it was during the controversy over their role in the Council that Crescenzio died, having played an ambiguous part in the conflict. Protestant tradition viewed him as a reactionary who had fought to prevent the Protestant deputies from attending, and the story on which the poem is based clearly reflects this tradition, since a dog was, in medieval tradition, a shape frequently assumed by the devil. However, Crescenzio was persuaded to meet the deputies in private session at his own house, and a safe-conduct was granted to them by the Council; indeed, this was the final decree of session xv, and session xvi began with a reference to his being 'absent by reason of a most grievous illness'. The note with which B.'s father prefaced *Transcript* may relate to these events, and certainly implies a more benevolent view of him: 'The following is a version of the well known story that is told of a Cardinal *Crescentius*, who was said to have been haunted by the apparition of a Dog—even after his behaviour at the Council of Trent'. Unless ironic, this comment seems to mean that Crescenzio's horrible end was undeserved; however, it is enclosed in square brackets, suggesting that it is B.'s father's own note (probably for Mrs Von Müller, to whom he presented the MS), not his transcription of one by B. The story may have interested B. for its anticipation of Goethe's *Faust*, where Mephistopheles first appears to Faust in the form of a black dog. The poem is, as B. told Mrs Thomas, 'a ballad' inasmuch as it is written in ballad metre. Its grotesque supernaturalism links it to others of the same kind, of which *Pied Piper*, *Doctor* and *Jochanan Hakkadosh* are leading examples. In *Asolando* it is first in a group concerned with Catholicism, *Pope and the Net* and *Bean-Feast* being the other two.

Crescentius the Pope's Legate,
    At Council High of Trent,
Was (Fifteen Hundred fifty-two,
    March Twenty five,) intent

5 Writing of letters to the Pope
    Till far 'twas in the night:
Whence rising to refresh himself
    He saw a monstrous sight.

A black Dog of vast bigness,
10   Eyes flaming, ears that hung
Down to the very ground almost,
    Into the chamber sprung;

Which came directly towards him
    And laid himself down under
15 The table where Crescentius wrote:
    He called in fear and wonder

¶22.*1.*] Crescentius—the Pope's Legate (*Transcript*).   *Crescentius*]
Crescenzio (*1889a-1889*).
2. *Council High of*] the High Council, (*1889a-1889*).
3-4.] —Year Fifteen hundred twenty two, March twenty five—intent (*1889a-1889*, except 'twenty-two', 'Twenty-five', *1889*).
5-8.] On writing letters to the Pope till late into the night,
    Rose, weary, to refresh himself, and saw a monstrous sight.
        (I give my Author's very words: he penned, I re-indite.) (*1889a-1889*, except 'sight:', 'give mine', *1889*).
9-12.] A black Dog of vast bigness
        And flaming eyes, and ears
    That hung down almost to the ground
        Within the room appears (*1841*, canc.). B. first wrote 'appeared', which fits the past tense of the narrative but does not rhyme correctly; the reverse applies to 'appears', hence perhaps the cancellation of the stanza.
9. *black Dog*] Black dog (*Transcript*); black dog (*1889a*).   *bigness*]
magnitude (*Transcript*).
12-13. *sprung; // Which*] sprung // And (*1889a-1889*).
13. *came directly towards*] made directly for (*1889a-1889*).
14. *down*] right (*1889*).
15. *Crescentius*] in italic, *Transcript*; Crescenzio (*1889a-1889*).
15-16. *wrote: / He*] wrote—who (*1889a-1889*). The lower case of 'who' results from the change from short to long lines in *1889a-1889*.

His servants in the Antiroom—
  Commanded every one
To look for and find out the Dog;
20   But looking they found none.

The Cardinal fell melancholy,
  Thence sick, soon after died:
And at Verona as he lay
  On his death-bed he cried
25   Aloud "to drive away the Dog
    That leapt on his bed-side."

17. Antiroom] anteroom (*1889a*); ante-room (*1889*). *Wanley* has 'Anti-chamber'; the 'i' spelling is the earlier form.
19. Dog] dog (*Transcript, 1889a*); beast (*1889*).
21.] The Cardinal full melancholy (*Transcript*); see next note.
22. Thence] Fell (*Transcript*); then (*1889a-1889*). The lower case of 'then' results from the change from short to long lines in *1889a-1889*.
23. Verona] in italic, *Transcript*.
25-6.] Aloud—"take away the Dog— / That kept at his Bedside! (*Transcript*; the absence of closing inverted commas is an error); Aloud to drive away the dog that leapt on his bedside. / Heaven keep all Protestants from harm—the rest .. no ill betide (*1889a*; the absence of a closing punctuation mark may be an error, but B. may have been playing on the fact that his signature immediately follows, so that the last words would be 'no ill betide Robert Browning.'); Aloud to drive away the Dog that leapt on his bed-side. / Heaven keep us Protestants from harm: the rest . . . no ill betide! (*1889*).

23 In a Gondola

First publ. *B & P* iii (*DL*), 26 Nov. 1842; repr. *1849* (when the numbered sections were replaced by speech headings), *1863* (when it was placed in *Romances*: see Appendix A, p. 464), *1865²*, *1868*, *1872*, *1888*. Our text is *1842*. The first section (ll. 1-7) was composed impromptu, at the instigation of B.'s friend John Forster in his house in Lincoln's Inn Fields, probably in late 1841, to serve as a catalogue entry for a painting by Daniel Maclise (1806-70) called *The Serenade*, which was exhibited at the British Institution in 1842 but which B. had not seen when he wrote the lines. Dickens may also have been present when B. composed the lines (see below). 'Forster described it well', B. wrote to Fanny Haworth shortly after, '—but I could do nothing better than this wooden ware (All the "properties," as we say, were given—and the problem was how to cataloguize them in rhyme and unreason)— [quotes the lines, which have no significant variants] Singing and stars and night and Venice streets in depths of shade and space and face and joyous heart are "properties," do you please to see. And now tell me, is this below the average of Catalogue original poetry?' (*Correspondence* v 189). B. told Furnivall in a letter of Sept. 1881: 'when I did see it, I thought the serenader somewhat too jolly for the notion I got from Forster—and I took up the subject in my own way' (*Trumpeter* 24). The exhibition opened on 5 Feb. 1842; the poem was presumably finished soon afterwards. Browning's verse for the catalogue was praised 'as an example of exceedingly rich and graceful versification from the pen of a poet, kindred to Maclise in imagination and mind' in the report of the exhibition, *Art-Union* iv (1 Apr. 1842) 76. Dickens, writing to Maclise on his journey to Italy in 1844, also remembered the association: 'In a certain picture called the Serenade for which Browning wrote that verse in Lincoln's-inn-fields you, O Mac, painted a sky. If you ever have occasion to paint the Mediterranean, let it be exactly of that colour'. Maclise's picture is now in *ABL*. B. had visited Venice in 1838 (see *Sordello* iii 591ff. and notes), and the city was traditionally associated with erotic intrigue (cp. *A Toccata*). Very little in B. is directly comparable with this poem, the only other dialogue poem of any length being *Flute-Music* (1889); but perhaps *In a Balcony* (note the parallel title) may be seen as a mature reworking of some of its topics. DeVane *Handbook* 115 suggests the influence of contemporary melodrama, esp. on the ending; there may also be some influence from Italian opera, of which B. was very fond. The theme of the all-sufficiency of love and its conquest of death is commonplace in B.: cp. e.g. *Love Among the Ruins*, *Eurydice to Orpheus*, *Prospice*, *Householder*. Regarding the end of the poem, B. was asked, in Feb. 1889: 'Was *she* true, or in the conspiracy?' He replied: 'Out of it' (*New Poems* 176).

I.

I send my heart up to thee, all my heart
   In this my singing!
For the stars help me, and the sea bears part;
   The very night is clinging
5 Closer to Venice' streets to leave one space
   Above me, whence thy face
May light my joyous heart to thee its dwelling-place.

II.

Say after me, and try to say
   My words as if each word
10 Came from you of your own accord,
   In your own voice, in your own way:
   This woman's heart, and soul, and brain
   Are mine as much as this gold chain
   She bids me wear; which (say again)
15 *I choose to make by cherishing*
   A precious thing, or choose to fling
   Over the boat-side, ring by ring;
   And yet once more say . . . no word more!
   Since words are only words. Give o'er!
20 Unless you call me, all the same,
   Familiarly by my pet-name
   Which if the Three should hear you call
   And me reply to, would proclaim
   At once our secret to them all:
25 Ask of me, too, command me, blame—
   Do break down the partition-wall
   'Twixt us the daylight world beholds
   Curtained in dusk and splendid folds.

¶23.*I.*] He sings. (*1849-88*).

II.] She speaks. (*1849-88*).

9. My] Thy (*DL 1st proof*, corrected by B.); My very (*1849-88*).

19-20.] *1849-88* have a space between these lines.

22. the Three: two are named at ll. 106-7, but they are not identified; 'Siora' at l. 221 may imply that the woman is married, and that the 'Three' are her husband and his (or her) two brothers; they may however be her father and two of his sons.

26. Do break] Do, break (*1863-88*).

27. us: 'us, whom'.

28. dusk: dark (adj.). In the eyes of the 'daylight world' (ll. 27), the lovers are 'Curtained' (disguised and separated) in the 'dusk and splendid folds' of social convention, the formal manners appropriate to their high social rank. See ll. 221-6.

III.

What's left but—all of me to take?
30   I am the Three's, prevent them, slake
Your thirst! 'Tis said the Arab sage
In practising with gems can loose
Their subtle spirit in his cruce
And leave but ashes: so, sweet mage,
35   Leave them my ashes when thy use
Sucks out my soul, thy heritage!

IV.

1.

Past we glide, and past, and past!
What's that poor Agnese doing
Where they make the shutters fast?
40   Grey Zanobi's just a-wooing
To his couch the purchased bride:
Past we glide!

2.

Past we glide, and past, and past!
Why's the Pucci Palace flaring
45   Like a beacon to the blast?
Guests by hundreds—not one caring

III.] not a separate section in *1849-88*, which have no space after l. 28.

30. prevent: anticipate, pre-empt.

31-4. 'Tis said . . . but ashes: the allusion to alchemy recalls B.'s strong interest in the occult in his early work, e.g. *Paracelsus*; the Arabs were traditionally masters of the occult arts: cp. *Sordello* i 397n. and *An Epistle*. The belief that each precious stone or gem contained a 'spirit' or hidden virtue was a commonplace of alchemical philosophy. See also l. 36n.

32. practising: experimenting, performing magical or alchemical acts.

33. cruce: crucible. See *Sordello* vi 298n.

34. mage: magician, alchemist. See *Sordello* vi 98-101n.

36. Sucks out my soul: cp. Faustus on the ghost of Helen, summoned for him by Mephistophilis, in Marlowe's *Dr Faustus* V i 100: 'Her lips suck forth my soul'. See also *Confessional* 23-4.

IV.] He sings. (*1849-88*).

37-48. Imaginary portraits of conventional 'happiness' (a rich marriage, a grand party) whose corruption and hollowness contrast with the lovers' illicit but genuine pleasure; cp. *Respectability*.

39. shutters] shutter (*1865²*).

44. Pucci: B. reused this name in *Ring* xi 2342.

If the dear host's neck were wried:
  Past we glide!

V.

1.

The Moth's kiss, first!
50 Kiss me as if you made believe
You were not sure this eve,
How my face, your flower, had pursed
Its petals up; so here and there
Brush it, till I grow aware
55 Who wants me, and wide ope I burst.

2.

The Bee's kiss, now!
Kiss me as if you entered gay
My heart at some noonday,
A bud that dares not disallow
60 The claim, so all is rendered up,
And passively its shattered cup
Over your head to sleep I bow.

VI.

1.

What are we two?
I am a Jew,
65 And carry thee, farther than friends can pursue,
To a feast of our tribe,

47. *wried*: wrung. Only occurrence in B.
V.] She sings. (*1849-88*).
49-55. Cp. Shelley, *The Sensitive Plant* ii 50-3: 'soft moths that kiss / The
sweet lips of the flowers, and harm not, did she / Make her attendant angels
be'. Also cited for *Flower's Name* 12.
54. Brush it] You brush it (*1849-88*; *1865²* as *1842*).
55. wide ope I] wide open (*1849-63*).
56-62.] In an early proof of *1865²* (*Texas*), this passage is circled and marked
'out', though the change was not made. Cp. *Women and Roses* 28-36.
VI.] He sings. (*1849-88*).
63-78. The lover's two images are of the seduction, exploitation, and death of
the woman; he conjures each image as a 'vision' from which he recoils.
64-9. I am a Jew . . . Thy: drawing on one of the many legends about the
sinister exploits of the Jews; in this instance the implied act is the sacrifice of
the woman's blood to the devil who 'blasts' (blights) the tribe.

Where they need thee to bribe
The devil that blasts them unless he imbibe
Thy . . . Shatter the vision for ever! And now,
70   As of old, I am I, Thou art Thou!

2.

But again, what we are?
The sprite of a star,
I lure thee above where the Destinies bar
My plumes their full play
75   Till a ruddier ray
Than my pale one announce there is withering away
Some . . . Scatter the vision for ever! And now,
As of old, I am I, Thou art Thou!

VII.

Oh, which were best, to roam or rest?
80   The land's lap or the water's breast?
To sleep on yellow millet-sheaves,
Or swim in lucid shallows, just
Eluding water-lily leaves,
An inch from Death's black fingers, thrust
85   To lock you, whom release he must;
Which life were best on Summer eves?

69. *Shatter*] Scatter (*1863-88*). See also l. 77n.

71-7. The speaker imagines himself to be the 'sprite' or guiding intelligence of a star (a notion common in medieval cosmology, and present in e.g. Dante), who lures the woman into his sphere 'above' the earth, since the 'Destinies' forbid him from exercizing his full power unless he absorbs the life of a mortal being, whose blood will nourish his radiance. B. here combines several motifs from legends and fairy-stories, involving the love of gods for mortals, and the envious desire of supernatural beings to feed on human life. The reverse of this—the degradation of gods or godlike creatures by lower beings—is the subject of two images in *Pauline* 99-123. The theme is handled again, with important variations, in the late poem *Rephan*.

71. *But*] Say (*1849-88*).

77. *Scatter*] Shatter (*1849*).

VII.] He muses. (*1849-88*).

79-80. B. may have had in mind Tennyson's *The Lotos-Eaters*, recently republ. in *Poems*, May 1842; note 'lotus-blossoms' at l. 157. For l. 80, *Oxford* cites Shelley, *To Jane: The Recollection* 78: 'the dark water's breast'.

82. *lucid*: pellucid, clear.

VIII.

Lie back; could I improve you?
From this shoulder let there spring
A wing; from this, another wing;
90 Wings, not legs and feet, shall move you!
Snow-white must they spring, to blend
With your flesh, but I intend
They shall deepen to the end,
Broader, into burning gold,
95 Till both wings crescent-wise enfold
Your perfect self, from 'neath your feet
To o'er your head, where, lo, they meet
As if a million sword-blades hurled
Defiance from you to the world!

100 Rescue me thou, the only real!
And scare away this mad Ideal
That came, nor motions to depart!
Thanks! Now, stay ever as thou art!

IX.

1.

He and the Couple catch at last
105 Thy serenader; while there's cast
Paul's cloak about my head, and fast
Gian pinions me, Himself has past
His stylet thro' my back; I reel;
And . . . is it Thee I feel?

VIII.] He speaks, musing. (*1849-88*).
87-99.] *DL 1st proof* has B.'s doodle of an angel opposite this passage.
87. could I] could thought of mine (*1849-88*).
98-9. Cp. Burke's lament for Marie-Antoinette in *Reflections on the Revolution in France* (1792): 'I thought ten thousand swords must have leaped from their scabbards to avenge even a look that threatened her with insult'.
100-3. Cp. *Poetics*, where the beloved's 'human self' is the highest term of comparison.
IX.] Still, he muses. (*1849-88*).
104-9. See ll. 224-30; for the 'Couple' and 'Himself', see l. 22n. above.
104.] What if the Three should catch at last (*1849-88*).
105. serenader;] serenader? (*1849-88*).
106. Paul's] Gian's (*DL 1st proof*, altered by B.).
108. stylet: stiletto (in *1865²*, B. spells the word 'stilet'); *OED* 4 cites Scott, *The Abbot* (1820): 'a stylet . . . borrowed from the treacherous Italian'.
109. Thee] Thou (*1849-63*); thou (*1865²*, *1868-88*).

2.

110 They trail me, do these godless knaves,
     Past every church that sains and saves,
     Nor stop till, where the cold sea raves
     By Lido's wet accursed graves,
     They scoop mine, roll me to its brink,
115 And . . . on Thy breast I sink!

X.

     Dip your arm o'er the boat-side elbow-deep
     As I do: thus: were Death so unlike Sleep
     Caught this way? Death's to fear from flame or steel
     Or poison doubtless, but from water—feel!

120 Go find the bottom! Would you stay me? There!
     Now pluck a great blade of that ribbon-grass
     To plait in where the foolish jewel was,
     I flung away: since you have praised my hair
     'Tis proper to be choice in what I wear.

XI.

125 Must we, must we *Home?* Too surely
     Know I where its front's demurely
     Over the Giudecca piled;
     Window just with window mating,
     Door on door exactly waiting,
130 All's the set face of a child:
     But behind it, where's a trace
     Of the staidness and reserve,
     Formal lines without a curve,

110. do these] these three (*1849-88*).
111. sains] saints (*1868-88*). 'Sains' is an archaic word for 'blesses', often used in this conjunction. 'Saints' is not an equivalent, and may be a mispr.
113. Lido's wet accursed graves: the Lido is the strip of land separating Venice from the Adriatic. There was a Jewish cemetery there ('accursed' in Catholic doctrine because the Jews were responsible for the crucifixion).
X.] She replies, musing. (*1849-88*).
121. ribbon-grass: a variety of grass with long slender leaves (*OED* cites an occurrence in Clare, 1827).
XI.] He speaks. (*1849-88*).
125.] Row home? must we row home? Too surely (*1849-88*).
127. the Giudecca: the Canale della Giudecca, a waterway dividing the northern part of the city from the smaller southern part, which includes the islet of Giudecca itself. Mentioned in *Sordello* iii 673.
133. Formal] And formal (*1849-88*).

In the same child's playing-face?
135 No two windows look one way
O'er the small sea-water thread
Below them. Ah, the autumn day
I, passing, saw you overhead!
First out a cloud of curtain blew,
140 Then, a sweet cry, and last came you—
To catch your loory that must needs
Escape just then, of all times then,
To peck a tall plant's fleecy seeds,
And make me happiest of men.
145 I scarce could breathe to see you reach
So far back o'er the balcony,
To catch him ere he climbed too high
Above you in the Smyrna peach,
That quick the round smooth cord of gold,
150 This coiled hair on your head, unrolled,
Fell down you like a gorgeous snake
The Roman girls were wont, of old
When Rome there was, for coolness' sake
To place within their bosoms.
155 Dear loory, may his beak retain
Ever its delicate rose stain
As if the wounded lotus-blossoms
Marked their thief to know again!

XII.

Stay longer yet, for others' sake
160 Than mine! what should your chamber do?
—With all its rarities that ache
In silence while day lasts, but wake

141, 155. loory] lory (*1868-88*); either spelling is valid. A bird like a parrot, with brilliant plumage.
148. Smyrna peach: peach-tree from Smyrna, now Izmir, a Turkish city on the Aegean coast.
153. When Rome there was: when Rome was 'really' Rome, i.e. in the time of the Republic; cp. *Sordello* iv 927ff.
154.] To let lie curling o'er their bosoms. (*1849-88*).
155-8. Possibly a reminiscence of Marvell, *The Nymph Complaining for the Death of her Faun* 83-6: 'Upon the Roses it would feed, / Until its Lips ev'n seem'd to bleed: / And then to me 'twould boldly trip, / And print those Roses on my Lip'.
158. Marked] Had marked (*1849-88*).
XII.] not a separate section in *1849-88*; there is a space between ll. 158 and 159.

At night-time and their life renew,
Suspended just to pleasure you
165   That brought reluctantly together
These objects and, while day lasts, weave
Round them such a magic tether
That dumb they look: your harp, believe,
With all the sensitive tight strings
170   That dare not speak, now to itself
Breathes slumbrously as if some elf
Went in and out tall chords his wings
Get murmurs from whene'er they graze,
As may an angel thro' the maze
175   Of pillars on God's quest have gone
At guilty glorious Babylon.
And while such murmurs flow, the nymph
Bends o'er the harp-top from her shell,
As the dry limpet for the lymph
180   Come with a tune he knows so well.
And how the statues' hearts must swell!
And how the pictures must descend
To see each other, friend with friend!
Oh, could you take them by surprise,

165. That] Who (*1865–88*).   *reluctantly*] against their will (*1849–88*).
168–73. your harp . . . graze: cp. *Transcendentalism* 46–51.
168. dumb they look] they look dumb (*1849–65*).
170. That] Which (*1865–88*).
171. slumbrously] slumberously (*1863–88*).
172. tall] the (*1849–88*).   *chords*: strings.
173–6.] Make murmur wheresoe'er they graze,
          As an angel may, between the maze
          Of midnight palace-pillars, on
          And on, to sow God's plagues have gone
          Through guilty glorious Babylon. (*1849–88*, except 'murmur,', *1872*,
1884; 'plagues,', *1868–88*). The allusion is to no specific passage from the
Bible, but cp. e.g. *1 Chronicles* xxi 15: 'And God sent an angel unto Jerusalem
to destroy it'; the prophetic books are filled with denunciations of the corrupt
splendour of cities such as Babylon, and prophecies of their destruction. Cp.
also the lines added to *Pippa* ii 29 in *1849* (p. 54).
179. lymph: a poeticism for pure water.
181. the statues'] your statues' (*1849–88*).
182–201. Cp. Hazlitt's essay, 'Of Persons One Would Wish to Have Seen',
first publ. *New Monthly Magazine*, Jan. 1826: 'The room was hung round
with several portraits of eminent painters. While we were debating whether
we should demand speech with these masters of mute eloquence . . . it
seemed that all at once they glided from their frames, and seated themselves

185 You'd find Schidone's eager Duke
  Doing the quaintest courtesies
  To that prim Saint by Haste-thee-Luke:
  And deeper into her rock den
  Bold Castelfranco's Magdalen
190 You'd find retreated from the ken
  Of that robed counsel-keeping Ser—
  As if the Tizian thinks of her!
  As if he is not rather bent
  On trying for himself what toys
195 Are these his progeny invent,
  What litter now the board employs
  Whereon he signed a document
  That got him murdered! Each enjoys
  Its night so well, you cannot break
200 The sport up, so, for others' sake
  Than mine, your stay must longer make!

---

at some little distance from us.' Among the painters Hazlitt mentions are
Titian and Giorgione. This essay is also a source for *Old Pictures*.

182. the pictures] your pictures (*1849-88*).

185. Schidone's eager Duke: Bartolommeo Schidone of Modena (1560-1616).

187. Haste-thee-Luke: Luca Giordano of Naples (1632-1705), nicknamed
'Luca-fa-presto' because, according to legend, his needy father constantly
urged him to 'work quickly'.

189. Castelfranco's: i.e. by Giorgione (?1478-1510), whose family came from
Castelfranco, a town near Venice.

191-8. The reference is to Titian (*c*.1485-1576), the great Venetian painter,
and one of his numerous portraits of Venetian dignitaries, here a lawyer or
judge in his robes of office; 'counsel-keeping' puns on the senses of 'one who
engages in legal activities' and 'one who keeps his counsel, is discreet'. 'Ser'
(short for 'Messer') was the Venetian honorific, here used as a noun to mean
'gentleman'. The phrase 'his progeny' (l. 195) establishes that the portrait is
of an ancestor. He is fancifully supposed to be intrigued by the objects which
now litter the desk where he once engaged in an (unspecified) plot which
proved his downfall and 'got him murdered' (l. 198).

192-4.] As if the Tizian thinks of her,
  And is not, rather, gravely bent
  On seeing for himself what toys (*1849-88*).

200-1.] The sport up, so, indeed must make / More stay with me, for others'
sake. (*1849-88*, except 'up;', *1865*[2]; 'up:', *1872, 1884*).

XIII.

1.

To-morrow, if a harp-string, say,
Is used to tie the jasmine back
That overfloods my room with sweets,
205   Be sure that Zorzi somehow meets
My Zanze: if the ribbon's black
I use, they're watching; keep away.

2.

Your gondola—let Zorzi wreathe
A mesh of water-weeds about
210   Its prow, as if he unaware
Had struck some quay or bridge-foot stair;
That I may throw a paper out
As you and he go underneath.

XIV.

There's Zanze's vigilant taper; safe are we!
215   Only one minute more to-night with me?
Resume your past self of a month ago!
Be you the bashful gallant, I will be
The lady with the colder breast than snow:
Now bow you, as becomes, nor touch my hand
220   More than I touch yours when I step to land,

XIII.] She speaks. (*1849-88*).

204. sweets: sweet smells, as in Keats, *Ode to a Nightingale* 41-3: 'I cannot see what flowers are at my feet . . . But in embalmed darkness guess each sweet'.

205-7.] Contrive your Zorzi somehow meets
      My Zanze: if the ribbon's black,
      The Three are watching; keep away. (*1849-88*, except 'Zanze!', *1868-88*; 'watching:', *1865²*, *1868-88*; 'away!', *1868-88*).

205-6. Zorzi . . . Zanze: his and her servants; following theatrical (and perhaps operatic) tradition, the main characters are accompanied by faithful retainers.

208-13. The 'mesh of water-weeds' will catch the 'paper' so that it will not appear a deliberate communication.

XIV.] not a separate section in *1849-88*; there is a space between ll. 213 and 214.

And say, All thanks, Siora . . .
                              Heart to heart,
And lips to lips! Once, ere we part,
Make me thine as mine thou art!

XV.

It was to be so, Sweet, and best
225 Comes 'neath thine eyes, and on thy breast.
Still kiss me! Care not for the cowards! Care
Only to put aside thy beauteous hair
My blood will hurt. The Three I do not scorn
To death, because they never lived: but I
230 Have lived indeed, and so—(yet one more kiss)—can
     die.

221. Siora: contraction of 'Signora', usually addressed to a married woman; see l. 22n.
222-3.] And lips to lips! Yet once more, ere we part, / Clasp me, and make me thine, as mine thou art! (*1849-88*, except 'me and', *1865²*, *1868-88*).
223. Cp. the concluding lines of George Herbert, *Clasping of Hands*: 'O be mine still! still make me thine! / Or rather make no Thine and Mine!'
XV.] XV. (He is stabbed by one of the Three) (*DL 1st proof*; not in *DL 2nd proof*); He is surprised, and stabbed. (*1849-88*). 'Surprised' means 'taken by surprise, ambushed'.
224. It was to be] It was ordained to be (*1849-88*).
225. Comes 'neath] Comes now, beneath (*1849-88*).   *and on*] upon (*1865-88*).
230. Cp. *Romeo and Juliet* V iii 120: 'Thus with a kiss I die', and *Othello* V ii 357-8: 'I kiss'd thee ere I kill'd thee; no way but this, / Killing myself to die upon a kiss'.

24 The Pied Piper of Hamelin
A Child's Story
(*Written for, and inscribed to, W. M. the Younger*)

First publ. *B & P* iii (*DL*), 26 Nov. 1842; repr. *1849, 1863* (when it was placed in *Romances*: see Appendix A, p. 464), *1863²*, *1868*, *1888*. Our text is *1842*. The poem was written for Willie, the son of the actor-manager William Macready, during the period when he and B. were close friends and colleagues. The child was in bed with a bad cough in the spring of 1842. 'He had a talent for drawing, and asked me to give him some little thing to illustrate; so, I made a bit of a poem out of an old account of the Pope's legate at the Council of Trent—which he made such clever drawings for, that I tried a more picturesque subject, the Piper' (*Trumpeter* 27). For the first poem mentioned, see *Cardinal*, p. 114 above. Two letters from Willie Macready, thanking B. for his poems and offering his illustrations, can be found in *Correspondence* v 329-31, 350-1. The second letter, which refers to *The Pied Piper*, is dated 12 May 1842. B.'s sister Sarianna's account adds some detail: 'At first, there was no thought of publishing them, but I copied the Pied Piper and showed it to Alfred Domett who was so much pleased with it that he persuaded Robert to include it in the following number of Bells and Pomegranates' (*Correspondence* v 330). Kelley and Hudson argue that Domett's departure for New Zealand on 30 Apr. makes this account 'suspect', and it does imply a somewhat protracted illness for Willie Macready; however, Sarianna's account is too circumstantial to be dismissed, though B.'s decision to publish the poem was prompted by Moxon, his publisher, who needed additional copy for *DL* to fill up the pamphlet; it is not in *DL 1st proof*, appearing first in *DL 2nd proof*.

The primary source, according to B., was a story in *Wanley* from which B. also obtained the story of *Cardinal*. In B.'s copy of *Wanley*, now in *ABL*, a note on the fly-leaf cites the passage. *Wanley*'s account is as follows:

At *Hammel*, a town in the Dutchy of *Brunswick*, in the year of Christ 1284. upon the 26. day of *June*, the Town being grievously troubled with Rats and Mice, there came to them a Piper, who promised upon a certain rate to free them from them all; it was agreed, he went from street to street, and playing upon his Pipe, drew after him out of the Town all that kind of Vermine, and then demanding his wages was denied it. Whereupon he began another tune, and there followed him one hundred and thirty Boys to a Hill called *Koppen*, situate on the North by the Road, where they perished, and were never seen after. This Piper was called the pyed Piper, because his cloaths were of several colours. This story is writ and religiously kept by them in their Annals at *Hammel*, read in their Books, and painted in their Windows and Churches, of which I am a witness by my own sight. Their elder Magistrates, for the confirmation of the truth of this, are wont to write in conjunction in their publick books, such a year of Christ, and such a year of the Transmigration of the children, &c. It's also observed in the memory of it, that in the street he passed out of, no Piper be admitted to this day. The street is called *Burgelosestrasse*; if a Bride be in that street, till she is gone out of it there is no dancing to be suffered. *Wier. de praestig. Daemon.* I. 1, c. 16. p. 47. *Schot. phys. curios.* I. 3. c. 24. p. 519. *Howels Ep.* vol. i. #. 6., *epist.* 59. *p.* 241.

B. seems to have told Frederick Furnivall for his *Bibliography* (*BSP* i 159) that he used no other sources than Wanley and the sources cited there (J. Wier, *De Presdigiis Daemonum* [1564]; G. Schott, *Physica Curiosa* [1662]; J. Howell, *Epistolae Ho-Elianae* [1645]). Howell differs from Wanley in having the children, not merely 'boys', taken into the Hill rather than killed; for other details, see notes. B. denied that he at that time consulted Richard Verstegen's *Restitution of Decayed Intelligence in Antiquities* (1605), but A. Dickson ('Browning's Source for *The Pied Piper of Hamelin*', *SP* xxiii [July 1926] 327-32) convincingly argues that some details in the poem come so close to Verstegen as to make it likely that B. was mistaken. Verstegen's account is as follows:

There came into the town of *Hamel* in the countrey of *Brunswyc* an od kynd of compagnion, who for the fantastical cote which hee wore being wrought with sundry colours, was called the pyed piper; for a pyper hee was, besides his other qualities. This fellow forsooth offred the townsmen for a certain somme of money to rid the town of all the rattes that were in it (for at that tyme the burgers were with that vermin greatly annoyed)[.] The accord in fyne beeing made; the pyed piper with a shril pype went pyping through the streets, and foorthwith the rattes came all running out of the howses in great numbers after him; all which hee led vnto the riuer of *Weaser* and therein drowned them. This donne, and no one rat more perceaued to be left in the town; he afterward came to demaund his reward according to his bargain, but beeing told that the bargain was not made with him in good earnest, to wit, with an opinion that euer hee could bee able to do such a feat: they cared not what they accorded vnto, when they imagyned it could neuer bee deserued, and so neuer to bee demaunded: but neuerthelesse seeing hee had donne such an vnlykely thing in deed, they were content to giue him a good reward; & so offred him far lesse then hee lookt for: but hee therewith discontented, said he would haue his ful recompence according to his bargain, but they vtterly denying to giue it him, hee threatened them with reuenge; they bad him do his wurst, wherevpon he betakes him again to his pype, & going through the streets as before, was followed of a number of boyes out at one of the gates of the citie, and coming to a litle hil, there opened in the syde thereof a wyde hole, into the which himself and all the children beeing in number one hundreth & thirty, did enter; and beeing entred, the hil closed vp again, and became as before. A boy that beeing lame & came somwhat lagging behynd the rest, seeing this that hapned, returned presently back & told what hee had seen; foorthwith began great lamentation among the parents for their children, and men were sent out with all dilligence, both by land & by water to enquyre yf ought could bee heard of them, but with all the enquyrie they could possibly vse, nothing more then is aforesaid could of them bee vnderstood. In memorie whereof it was then ordayned, that from thence-foorth no drum, pype or other instrument, should be sounded in the street leading to the gate through which they passed; nor no osterie to bee there holden. And it was also established, that from that tyme forward in all publyke wrytings that should bee made in that town, after the date therein set down of the yeare of our Lord, the date of the yeare of the going foorth of their children should bee added, the which they haue accordingly euer since continued. And this great wonder hapned on the 22. day of Iuly, in the yeare of our Lord one thousand three hundreth seauentie, and six.

The occasion now why this matter came vnto my remembrance in speaking of *Transiluania*, was, for that some do reporte that there are diuers found among the Saxons in *Transiluania* that haue lyke surnames vnto diuers of the burgers of *Hamel*, and wil seem thereby to inferr, that this iugler or pyed pyper, might by negromancie haue transported them thether, but this carieth little apparence of truthe; because it would haue bin almost as great a wonder vnto the Saxons of *Transiluania* to haue had so many strange children brought among them, they knew not how, as it was to those of *Hamel* to lose them: & they could not but haue kept memorie of so strange a thing, yf in deed any such thing had there hapned.

DeVane (*Handbook* 127-31) notes that various intermediate sources transmit Verstegen's account, and that a portion was repr. in Chambers' *Book of Days*, a book which B.'s father 'almost certainly' owned. *Oxford* plausibly suggests a further source, in which several details coincide with Verstegen, the entry on 'Hamelen' in Jeremy Collier's *Great Historical, Geographical, Genealogical and Poetical Dictionary*, the second edition of which (2 vols., 1701) B. told Furnivall he read 'right through' as a boy, and which his father gave him 'many years after' (*Trumpeter* 101). Collier describes Hamelin as 'Watered by the River *Weser*' and states:

It is famous for the wonderful Accident said to have happened here *July* 22. 1376; for being incredibly troubled with Rats, a Musician (whom they call'd the *Py'd-Piper*) offer'd to destroy 'em for a certain Summ which was agreed upon. Then the Piper tuning his Pipes, all the Rats in the Town danced after him as he cross'd the River, and were drowned. This done, he demanded his Pay, but was denied. Whereupon striking up a new Fit of Mirth, all the children of the Town (Male and Female) were so much charmed therewith, that they followed him to a neighbouring Hill, which opening, swallowed all up but one that lagged behind, and, according to some, they were seen again in Transilvania. In memory of this Tragedy, it was Ordered, That in all publick Writings, after the date of our Saviours Nativity, this of their Childrens being swallowed up, should be added.

B.'s father wrote three versions of a poem on the Piper; the earliest of these was begun at the same time as B.'s poem, but, according to B.'s father's MS note, abandoned when he realized that his son 'had written on this subject'; there was therefore no connection between them. (Later, however, he did complete his poem, in two versions, repr. *Oxford* iii 522-42; in both, the Piper is represented as a diabolical agent, in sharp contrast to B.'s interpretation: we therefore cannot agree with Mr Philip Kelley's suggestion to us that, by analogy with B.'s father's transcript of *Cardinal* (see p. 114), these texts may be copies of B.'s own early drafts.) See also *Flight* 545-51n. A. Kincaid and P. Blayney, in 'A Book of Browning's and his *Essay on Chatterton*', *BSN* ii (Dec. 1972) 11-25, point out that B. may well have been working on *Chatterton* at the same time as he wrote *Pied Piper*, and suggest that the theme of the artist exploited and abandoned by ungrateful patrons is common to the two works. They note that in a copy of *Walpoliana* that B. annotated during his preparation of *Chatterton* (see p. 477), he marked many passages in terms which suggest that he saw the relation between Chatterton and Walpole in this way, esp. in connection with Walpole's notorious stinginess as a patron: 'an artist has pencils, and an author has pens, and the public must reward them *as it happens*' (p. 24; B.'s italics).

The poem is written in the irregular, jocular style, full of absurd rhymes, typical of Samuel Butler's *Hudibras* and the comic poetry of Southey, Hood, and Barham. An analogy between magicianship and the poet's visionary power is a common one throughout B.'s work: see e.g. the epigraph to *Pauline* (I 26), *Paracelsus*, and *Ring* i 742ff. With the Piper's success in ridding the town of its vermin, contrast the comic failure of the artist-reformer Pacchiarotto in *Of Pacchiarotto*.

I.

Hamelin Town's in Brunswick,
   By famous Hanover city;
The river Weser, deep and wide,
Washes its wall on the southern side;
5 A pleasanter spot you never spied;
   But, when begins my ditty,
Almost five hundred years ago,
To see the townsfolk suffer so
   From vermin, was a pity.

II.

10   Rats!
They fought the dogs, and killed the cats,
   And bit the babies in the cradles,

¶24.*1*. Hamelin is in Hanover, not Brunswick; Verstegen has this error.
4. southern: actually western.
7. This dates the story in the 14th century, closer to Verstegen's and Collier's 1376 than Wanley's 1284: see ll. 267-8n.
9. was] 'twas (*1849-88*).

And eat the cheeses out of the vats,
  And licked the soup from the cooks' own ladles,
15 Split open the kegs of salted sprats,
Made nests inside men's Sunday hats,
And even spoiled the women's chats,
  By drowning their speaking
  With shrieking and squeaking
20 In fifty different sharps and flats.

III.

At last the people in a body
  To the Town Hall came flocking:
'Tis clear, cried they, our Mayor's a noddy;
  And as for our Corporation—shocking
25 To think we buy gowns lined with ermine
For dolts that can't or won't determine
What's like to rid us of our vermin!
Rouse up, Sirs! Give your brains a racking
To find the remedy we're lacking,   .
30 Or, sure as fate, we'll send you packing!
At this the Mayor and Corporation
Quaked with a mighty consternation.

IV.

An hour they sate in council,
  At length the Mayor broke silence:
35 For a guilder I'd my ermine gown sell;
  I wish I were a mile hence!
It's easy to bid one rack one's brain—
I'm sure my poor head aches again,
I've scratched it so, and all in vain.
40 Oh for a trap, a trap, a trap!
Just as he said this, what should hap
At the chamber door but a gentle tap?
Bless us, cried the Mayor, what's that?

13. *eat*] ate (*1849-88*). 'Eat' is the old form of the past tense, not an error.
21-7. In Howell's account the piper 'covenanted with the chief Burgers'.
23-30.] the people's speech is in quotation marks, *1849-88*; subsequent speeches are also marked.
27. *like*] best (*1849-88*).
27^28.] You hope, because you're old and obese, / To find in the furry civic robe ease? (*1849-88*).
35. *guilder*: a small gold coin, originally in use in the Netherlands and parts of Germany; later, a Dutch silver coin.
38. *again*,] emended in agreement with *1865-88* from 'again' in *1842-63*.

(With the Corporation as he sate,
45 Looking little though wondrous fat)
Only a scraping of shoes on the mat?
Anything like the sound of a rat
Makes my heart go pit-a-pat!

V.
Come in!—the Mayor cried, looking bigger:
50 And in did come the strangest figure!
His queer long coat from heel to head
Was half of yellow and half of red;
And he himself was tall and thin,
With sharp blue eyes, each like a pin,
55 And light loose hair, yet swarthy skin,
No tuft on cheek nor beard on chin,
But lips where smiles went out and in—
There was no guessing his kith and kin!
And nobody could enough admire
60 The tall man and his quaint attire:
Quoth one: It's as my great-grandsire,
Starting up at the Trump of Doom's tone,
Had walked this way from his painted tomb-stone!

VI.
He advanced to the council-table:
65 And, Please your honours, said he, I'm able,
By means of a secret charm, to draw
All creatures living beneath the sun,
That creep, or swim, or fly, or run,
After me so as you never saw!
70 And I chiefly use my charm
On creatures that do people harm,
The mole, and toad, and newt, and viper;
And people call me the Pied Piper.
(And here they noticed round his neck
75 A scarf of red and yellow stripe,
To match with his coat of the self same cheque;
And at the scarf's end hung a pipe;
And his fingers, they noticed, were ever straying

45. *fat*)] fat; (*1849-88*); see next note.
45^46.] Nor brighter was his eye, nor moister
       Than a too-long-opened oyster,
       Save when at noon his paunch grew mutinous
       For a plate of turtle green and glutinous) (*1849-88*)
73. *Piper*.] emended in agreement with all other eds. from 'Piper' in *1842*.

As if impatient to be playing
80   Upon this pipe, as low it dangled
Over his vesture so old-fangled.)
Yet, said he, poor piper as I am,
In Tartary I freed the Cham,
Last June, from his huge swarms of gnats;
85   I eased in Asia the Nizam
Of a monstrous brood of vampyre-bats:
And, as for what your brain bewilders,
If I can rid your town of rats
Will you give me a thousand guilders?
90   One? fifty thousand!—was the exclamation
Of the astonished Mayor and Corporation.

VII.

Into the street the Piper stept,
   Smiling first a little smile,
As if he knew what magic slept
95   In his quiet pipe the while;
Then, like a musical adept,
To blow the pipe his lips he wrinkled,
And green and blue his sharp eyes twinkled
Like a candle flame where salt is sprinkled;
100   And ere three shrill notes the pipe uttered,
You heard as if an army muttered;
And the muttering grew to a grumbling;
And the grumbling grew to a mighty rumbling;
And out of the houses the rats came tumbling.
105   Great rats, small rats, lean rats, brawny rats,
Brown rats, black rats, grey rats, tawny rats,
Grave old plodders, gay young friskers,
   Fathers, mothers, uncles, cousins,
Cocking tails and pricking whiskers,
110   Families by tens and dozens,
Brothers, sisters, husbands, wives—
Followed the Piper for their lives.
From street to street he piped advancing,
And step for step they followed dancing,
115   Until they came to the river Weser
Wherein all plunged and perished
   —Save one who, stout as Julius Caesar,

116. perished] perished! (*1863-88*, except *1863²*, as *1842*).
117. When Caesar's ship was captured at Alexandria, he swam ashore
carrying the MS of his historical memoir, *De Gallico Belli*; such texts were
known as 'commentarii'. *Oxford* notes that Willie Macready probably knew

Swam across and lived to carry
(As he the manuscript he cherished)
120 To Rat-land home his commentary,
Which was, At the first shrill notes of the pipe,
I heard a sound as of scraping tripe,
And putting apples, wondrous ripe,
Into a cider-press's gripe:
125 And a moving away of pickle-tub-boards,
And a leaving ajar of conserve-cupboards,
And a drawing the corks of train-oil-flasks,
And a breaking the hoops of butter-casks;
And it seemed as if a voice
130 (Sweeter than by harp or by psaltery
Is breathed) called out, Oh rats, rejoice!
The world is grown one vast drysaltery!
So munch on, crunch on, take your nuncheon,
Breakfast, supper, dinner, luncheon!
135 And just as one bulky sugar puncheon,
Ready staved, like a great sun shone
Glorious scarce an inch before me,
Just as methought it said, Come, bore me!
—I found the Weser rolling o'er me.

VIII.

140 You should have heard the Hamelin people
Ringing the bells till they rocked the steeple;
Go, cried the Mayor, and get long poles!
Poke out the nests and block up the holes!
Consult with carpenters and builders,
145 And leave in our town not even a trace
Of the rats!—when suddenly up the face
Of the Piper perked in the market-place,

---

the story, 'since selections from Caesar are often read by beginners at Latin'.
127. train-oil: oil obtained from whale blubber.
130. Sweeter] Sweeter far (*1849-88*).   *by . . . by*] by . . . bý (*1849-65*); bý
. . . bý (*1870-1888*). Note that *1868* returns, unusually, to the first-edition
reading.   *psaltery*: an ancient and medieval stringed instrument.
132. drysaltery: a shop dealing in chemicals, oils, sauces, tinned meats, etc.
133. nuncheon: a light refreshment taken between meals. Cp. Samuel Butler's
Hudibras: 'They took their Breakfasts or their Nuncheons' (I i 344).
135. one] a (*1849-88*).   *puncheon*: a large cask for liquids, fish, etc.
136. Ready] All ready (*1849-88*).   *staved*: broken into staves.

With a, First, if you please, my thousand guilders!

IX.

A thousand guilders! The Mayor looked blue;
150   So did the Corporation too.
For council dinners made rare havock
With Claret, Moselle, Vin-de-Grave, Hock;
And half the money would replenish
Their cellar's biggest butt with Rhenish.
155   To pay this sum to a wandering fellow
With a gipsy coat of red and yellow!
Beside, quoth the Mayor with a knowing wink,
Our business was done at the river's brink;
We saw with our eyes the vermin sink,
160   And what's dead can't come to life, I think.
So, friend, we're not the folks to shrink
From the duty of giving you something for drink,
And a matter of money to put in your poke;
But, as for the guilders, what we spoke
165   Of them, as you very well know, was in joke.
Beside, our losses have made us thrifty;
A thousand guilders! Come, take fifty!

X.

The Piper's face fell, and he cried,
No trifling! I can't wait, beside!
170   I've promised to visit by dinner time
Bagdat, and accept the prime
Of the Head Cook's pottage, all he's rich in,
For having left, in the Caliph's kitchen,
Of a nest of scorpions no survivor—
175   With him I proved no bargain-driver,
With you, don't think I'll bate a stiver!
And folks who put me in a passion
May find me pipe after another fashion.

---

151. havock] havoc (*1863–88*).
152. All names of French and German wines ('Grave' in error for 'Graves').
154. Rhenish: a general term for Rhine wine.
163. poke: purse or pocket.
166. Beside] Besides (*1849–88*).
167. Howell has 'the Burgers put him off with slightings, and neglect, offring him som small matter'.
176. stiver: a small coin, worth about a twentieth of a Dutch guilder.
178. after] to (*1849–65*).

XI.

How? cried the Mayor, d'ye think I'll brook
180 Being worse treated than a Cook?
Insulted by a lazy ribald
With idle pipe and vesture piebald?
You threaten us, fellow? Do your worst,
Blow your pipe there till you burst!

XII.

185 Once more he stept into the street;
    And to his lips again
Laid his long pipe of smooth straight cane;
    And ere he blew three notes (such sweet
Soft notes as yet musician's cunning
190   Never gave th'enraptured air)
There was a rustling, that seem'd like a bustling
Of merry crowds justling at pitching and hustling,
Small feet were pattering, wooden shoes clattering,
Little hands clapping, and little tongues chattering,
195 And, like fowls in a farm-yard when barley is
      scattering,
Out came the children running.
All the little boys and girls,
With rosy cheeks and flaxen curls,
And sparkling eyes and teeth like pearls,
200 Tripping and skipping, ran merrily after
The wonderful music with shouting and laughter.

XIII.

The Mayor was dumb, and the Council stood
As if they were changed into blocks of wood,
Unable to move a step, or cry
205 To the children merrily skipping by—
Could only follow with the eye
That joyous crowd at the Piper's back.
But how the Mayor was on the rack,
And the wretched Council's bosoms beat,
210 As the Piper turned from the High Street
To where the Weser rolled its waters

---

179. I'll] I (*1865-88*).
190. th'] the (*1849-88*).
192. 'Pitch-and-hustle' is a children's game in which coins are thrown at a
mark, the player who comes closest taking the lot.
206. Could] And could (*1849-65*); —Could (*1868-88*).

Right in the way of their sons and daughters!
However he turned from South to West,
And to Coppelburg Hill his steps addressed,
215   And after him the children pressed;
Great was the joy in every breast.
He never can cross that mighty top!
He's forced to let the piping drop,
And we shall see our children stop!
When, lo, as they reached the mountain's side,
220   A wondrous portal opened wide,
As if a cavern was suddenly hollowed;
And the Piper advanced and the children follow'd,
And when all were in to the very last,
The door in the mountain side shut fast.
225   Did I say, all? No! One was lame,
And could not dance the whole of the way;
And in after years, if you would blame
His sadness, he was used to say,—
It's dull in our town since my playmates left!
230   I can't forget that I'm bereft
Of all the pleasant sights they see,
Which the Piper also promised me;
For he led us, he said, to a joyous land,
Joining the town and just at hand,
235   Where waters gushed and fruit-trees grew,
And flowers put forth a fairer hue,
And every thing was strange and new;
The sparrows were brighter than peacocks here,
And their dogs outran our fallow deer,
240   And honey-bees had lost their stings,
And horses were born with eagles' wings;
And just as I felt assured
My lame foot would be speedily cured,
The music stopped and I stood still,
245   And found myself outside the Hill,
Left alone against my will,
To go now limping as before,
And never hear of that country more!

213-14. *from South . . . addressed*: the hill is actually east of Hamelin.
219. *mountain's side*] mountain-side (*1865-88*).
224. *mountain side*] mountain-side (*1863, 1865-88*).
230-41. This vision is in none of the sources.
234. *Joining*: adjoining.
242. *felt*] became (*1849-88*).

XIV.

Alas, alas for Hamelin!
250   There came into many a burgher's pate
A text which says, that Heaven's Gate
Opes to the Rich at as easy a rate
As the needle's eye takes a camel in!
The Mayor sent East, West, North, and South
255   To offer the Piper by word of mouth,
    Wherever it was men's lot to find him,
Silver and gold to his heart's content,
If he'd only return the way he went,
    And bring the children behind him.
260   But when they saw 'twas a lost endeavour,
And Piper and dancers were gone for ever,
    They made a decree that lawyers never
    Should think their records dated duly
If, after the day of the month and year,
265   These words did not as well appear,
"And so long after what happened here
    "On the Twenty-second of July,
"Thirteen hundred and Seventy-six:"
And the better in memory to fix
270   The place of the Children's last retreat,
They called it, The Pied Piper's Street—
Where any one playing on pipe or tabor

251-3. Cp. *Matthew* xix 24: 'And I say unto you again, It is easier for a camel to go through a needle's eye, than for a rich man to enter into the kingdom of God'.

263-81. All sources append these details, though variously. For Wanley, Verstegen, and Collier, see headnote. Howell has: 'in that Town, they date their Bills and Bonds, and other Instruments in Law, to this day from the yeer of the going out of their children: Besides, ther is a great piller of stone at the foot of the said Hill, whereon this story is ingraven'.

267. July] Júly (*1849-68*). The stress on the first syllable is the older form (so in *J.*).

267-8. B. follows Verstegen and Collier; Wanley has the accepted date, 1284. In a letter of 1884 (the six hundredth anniversary of the legend) B. stuck charmingly to his guns: 'I am obliged by . . . the suggestion of the young lady that the date of my little poem should be altered. But there is equal if not superior authority for the date as I give it,—one being probably as imaginary as the other: and since no important point of doctrine is affected by letting it continue,—while there would follow (as you observe) some trouble in un-rhyming and re-rhyming, I hope you will permit me to remain "masterly inactive" in the matter' (to unidentified correspondent, 19 Nov. 1884, *ABL MS*).

Was sure for the future to lose his labour.
Nor suffered they Hostelry or Tavern
275   To shock with mirth a street so solemn;
But opposite the place of the cavern
    They wrote the story on a column,
And on the Great Church Window painted
The same, to make the world acquainted
280   How their children were stolen away;
And there it stands to this very day.
And I must not omit to say
That in Transylvania there's a tribe
Of alien people that ascribe
285   The outlandish ways and dress
On which their neighbours lay such stress
To their fathers and mothers having risen
Out of some subterraneous prison
Into which they were trepanned
290   Long time ago in a mighty band
Out of Hamelin town in Brunswick land,
But how or why they don't understand.

XV.

So, Willy, let you and me be wipers
Of scores out with all men—especially pipers:
295   And, whether they rid us from rats or from mice,
If we've promised them aught, let us keep our
    promise.

---

275. *shock*] spoil (*DL 1st proof*, canc.).

278-80. This window was not in fact introduced until 1572.

289. *trepanned*: caught in a trap, ensnared, beguiled.

293. *Willy*: i.e. Willie Macready (see headnote).

295-6. In his copy of *1863*, now in the Tennyson Centre in Lincoln, Tennyson marked up *Pied Piper* for reading aloud to his sons, rewriting these lines: 'But don't count too much on what he said or Charlie meant— / For what each means is 'Return *me* for Parliament'.

295. *from . . . from*] from . . . fróm (*1849-63*); fróm . . . fróm (*1865-88*).

296. *promise*] B. underlined 'mise' in *DL 1st proof*. In a letter of 7 Nov. 1881 (in the possession of Mr Michael Meredith; cited in *Oxford*) B. denied that he intended the moral of the poem as a 'sly hit' at Willie Macready's father. 'I certainly had a difference with him on quite another matter—but long after the "Pied Piper" was written'. For this 'difference', see headnote to *Lines to Helen Faucit* (p. 173).

25 Waring

First publ. *B & P* iii (*DL*), 26 Nov. 1842; repr. *1849*, *1863* (when it was placed in *Romances*: see Appendix A, p. 464), *1865*[2], *1868*, *1872*, *1888*. Our text is *1842*. The date of composition was probably the early summer of 1842, in the aftermath of the emigration to New Zealand at the end of April of B.'s close friend Alfred Domett. Domett (1811-87) was a member of B.'s 'set', the 'Colloquials', contributed occasional poems to periodicals, and had published two volumes: *Poems* (1833), and *Venice* (1839), a long poem which B. mentions admiringly (*Correspondence* v 328). For further details of Domett's life, and his relations with B. when he eventually returned from New Zealand in 1872, see *RB & AD*, Domett *Diary*, and *Maynard*. In a letter of May 1842 B. expressed indignation over Domett's failure to find a commercial publisher for *Venice*: 'not even his earnest handsome face . . . not his sincere voice & gentlemanly bearing, could tempt Moxon to look at a line of it' (*Correspondence* v 328). It is likely that B. telescoped this disappointment and Domett's emigration, making one the motive of the other. In *DL 2nd proof*, the words 'Alfred Domett, or' are written over the title. In the words of another 'Colloquial', Joseph Arnould (letter to Domett, *c.* May 1843), '"Waring" delighted us all very much for we recognized in it a fancy portrait of a very dear friend' (*Correspondence* vii 391). In 1875 a correspondent asked B. if he had had in mind a real person called Waring; B. wrote: 'I assure you I never heard of the Gentleman you mention: and, if you consider, I should be little likely to address the subject of such a poem publicly by his name. I had in my mind some characteristics of an old friend who, after thirty years' absence, is returned alive and well' (to Newton Bennett, 5 Dec. 1875, *ABL MS*). Several details do not fit, e.g. the date of Domett's departure, that of 'Waring' being in winter (l. 14), and in any event the poem's fanciful and burlesque elements hinder a straightforward biographical reading; J. F. McCarthy ('Browning's "Waring": The Real Subject of the "Fancy Portrait"', *VP* ix [1971] 371-82) seems nearer the mark in describing the poem as 'an ironic treatment of the early Browning's favorite theme—the dilemma of the non-communicating artist-prophet'. It has been suggested that some details of 'Waring's' character and appearance were drawn from those of R. H. Horne, author of the 'farthing epic' *Orion* and a close friend of B.'s at this period. Horne had led an adventurous life abroad before entering English literary life in the 1830s; he later emigrated to Australia. The poem accurately portrays B.'s mixed feelings about London literary society in the period; he wrote to Domett on 22 May 1842 of its 'creeping magnetic assimilating influence nothing can block out' (*Correspondence* v 355), and again on 13 July: 'There is much, everything to be done in England just now—& I have certain plans which shall either fail or succeed, but not lie dormant.—But all my heart's interest goes to your tree-planting life . . Yet I don't know' (*ibid.* vi 33). For other refs. to Domett in B.'s poetry, see *Time's Revenges* 1-30, and *Guardian Angel* 36-7, 54-5: 'Guercino drew this angel I saw

teach / (Alfred, dear friend)—that little child to pray . . . Where are you, dear
old friend? / How rolls the Wairoa at your world's far end?' The name
'Waring' itself is that of a 'king's messenger' whom B. met during his trip to
Russia in 1834 (*Griffin and Minchin* 63); see l. 109ff. A possible literary
influence is Dryden's *Ode to the Pious Memory of the Accomplisht Young Lady
Mrs Anne Killigrew, Excellent in the two Sister-Arts of Poesie and Painting* (1686);
note the allusion to painting at ll. 146-52. Dryden stresses the corruption of
the age in contrast to the purity and integrity of Killigrew's art; cp. ll. 192-
200. There is a verbal parallel at ll. 254-5. The idea of escape from social
constrictions into Romantic vagabondage is strong in Byron, notably *Childe
Harold*; it is common to many of B.'s works of the period, e.g. *Colombe,
Flight, Glove*; cp. also the ending of *Bishop Blougram*, and contrast *How It
Strikes*.

I.

i.

What's become of Waring
Since he gave us all the slip,
Chose land-travel or seafaring,
Boots and chest, or staff and scrip,
5   Rather than pace up and down
Any longer London-town?

ii.

Who'd have guessed it from his lip,
Or his brow's accustomed bearing,
On the night he thus took ship,
10   Or started landward, little caring
For us, it seems, who supped together,
(Friends of his too, I remember)
And walked home thro' the merry weather,
Snowiest in all December;
15   I left his arm that night myself
For what's-his-name's, the new prose-poet,
That wrote the book there, on the shelf—
How, forsooth, was I to know it
If Waring meant to glide away
20   Like a ghost at break of day!
Never looked he half so gay!

¶25.4. *staff and scrip*: traditional emblems of pilgrimage ('scrip' means
wallet or satchel), both literal and figurative: cp. Raleigh, *The Passionate
Man's Pilgrimage* 2-3: 'My staff of faith . . . My scrip of joy'.
14. *Snowiest*] The snowiest (*1849-88*).
17. *That*] Who (*1865-88*).

iii.

He was prouder than the Devil:
How he must have cursed our revel!
Ay, and many other meetings,
25 Indoor visits, outdoor greetings,
As up and down he paced this London,
With no work done, but great works undone,
Where scarce twenty knew his name.
Why not, then, have earlier spoken,
30 Written, bustled? Who's to blame
If your silence kept unbroken?
True, but there were sundry jottings,
Stray-leaves, fragments, blurrs and blottings,
Certain first steps were achieved
35 Already which—(is that your meaning?)
Had well borne out whoe'er believed
In more to come: but who goes gleaning
Hedge-side chance-blades, while full-sheaved
Stand cornfields by him? Pride, o'erweening
40 Pride alone, puts forth such claims
O'er the day's distinguished names.

iv.

Meantime, how much I loved him,
I find out now I've lost him:
I, who cared not if I moved him,
45 —Could so carelessly accost him,
Never shall get free
Of his ghostly company,
And eyes that just a little wink
As deep I go into the merit
50 Of this and that distinguished spirit—
His cheeks' raised colour, soon to sink,
As long I dwell on some stupendous

32-4. sundry jottings . . . first-steps: for Domett's writing in this period, see headnote.

38. chance-blades: blades of grass which have been sown by chance; the prefix 'chance-' occurs several times in B., usually attached to a verb, e.g. 'chance-sown plant' (*Paracelsus* v 686), 'chance-sown cleft-nursed seed' (*Ring* x 1036), and 'chance-rooted' (*Inapprehensiveness* 9).

44. moved: annoyed, irritated.

45. —Could] Who could (*1849-88*).

46. Never] Henceforth never (*1849-88*).

48. And] His (*1849-88*).

And tremendous (God defend us!)
Monstr'-inform'-ingens-horrend-ous
55   Demoniaco-seraphic
Penman's latest piece of graphic.
Nay, my very wrist grows warm
With his dragging weight of arm!
E'en so, swimmingly appears,
60   Thro' one's after-supper musings,
Some lost Lady of old years,
With her beauteous vain endeavour,
And goodness unrepaid as ever;
The face, accustomed to refusings,
65   We, puppies that we were . . . Oh never
Surely, nice of conscience, scrupled
Being aught like false, forsooth, to?
Telling aught but honest truth to?
What a sin had we centupled
70   Its possessor's grace and sweetness!
No! she heard in its completeness
Truth, for truth's a weighty matter,
And, truth at issue, we can't flatter!
Well, 'tis done with: she's exempt
75   From damning us thro' such a sally;
And so she glides, as down a valley,
Taking up with her contempt,

53. God] Heaven (*1849-88*).

54. A burlesque of Virgil, *Aeneid* iii 658: 'Monstrum horrendum, informe, ingens' [a horrid monster, mis-shapen, huge]. There may be a hint of self-parody of *Sordello*; see also *Pippa* i 283-94n.

55. The accent falls on the third syllable, the 'i' of 'Demoniaco', pronounced 'eye'.

59-79. The speaker feels the ghostly presence of Waring as he would that of a woman whom he and others had formerly treated with arrogant 'frankness', being proud of their forthrightness about her lack of beauty, and not valuing her real qualities; she is now dead, and 'exempt', therefore, from 'damning them' by really telling the truth about them, as they had made a show of doing about her. In the same way, Waring is now past being affected by his friend's former misprision.

59-61. Cp. *Dubiety*, in which the speaker, 'ensconce[d] / In luxury's sofa-lap of leather' (ll. 3-4), muses on the past, and remembers 'when a woman leant / To feel for my brow where her kiss might fall' (ll. 22-3).

73. And, truth] And truth (*1863-1888*, except *1872, 1884* as *1842*).

77. Either 'accepting, swallowing our contempt for her' or 'espousing, adopting her attitude of contempt for us'.

Past our reach; and in, the flowers
Shut her unregarded hours.

v.

80 Oh, could I have him back once more,
    This Waring, but one half-day more!
    Back, with the quiet face of yore,
    So hungry for acknowledgment
    Like mine! I'd fool him to his bent!
85 Feed, should not he, to heart's content?
    I'd say, "to only have conceived
    "Your great works, tho' they never progress,
    "Surpasses all we've yet achieved!"
    I'd lie so, I should be believed.
90 I'd make such havoc of the claims
    Of the day's distinguished names
    To feast him with, as feasts an ogress

78-9. *and in . . . hours*: 'the flowers [of the grave] enclose her sad history of neglect'; cp. the use of 'shut in' in the final lines of *Love Among the Ruins*.
81. *This Waring*: a typical Carlylean phrasing.
84. *I'd fool him to his bent*: from *Hamlet* III ii 408: 'They fool me to the top of my bent'. See also ll. 185-6n.
86-8. Cp., among many other expressions of this idea in B.'s work, *A Grammarian* 97ff.
86-7. *conceived / Your great works, tho' they never progress,*] conceived / Your great works, tho' they ne'er make progess, (*1849-65*); conceived, / Planned your great works, apart from progress, (*1868-88*).
88. *all we've yet*] little works (*1868-88*).
90-8. Cp. B. to Domett, 13 July 1842 (*Correspondence* vi 33): 'Sir L. Bulwer has published a set of sing-songs—I read two, or one, in a Review—& thought them abominable. Mr Taylor's affected unreal putting-together, called "Edwin the Fair," is the flattest of fallen. . . . Dickens is back, and busy in "doing" America for his next numbers—sad work'. See also ll. 199-200n.
92-3. *as feasts an ogress . . . child!*: taken, with characteristic variations, from one of Charles Perrault's fairy-stories, 'Little Thumb' ('Le Petit Poucet', originally publ. in *Histoires et contes du temps passé*, Paris 1697) in which Little Thumb and his six brothers come to an ogre's house; his wife takes pity on them and attempts to conceal them, but the ogre discovers their hiding-place: 'Here is good game, which comes very luckily to entertain three Ogres of my acquaintance, who are to pay me a visit in a day or two . . . The Ogre had seven daughters, all little children, and these young Ogresses . . . had little grey eyes quite round, hooked noses, wide mouths and very long sharp teeth, standing at a good distance from each other. They were not as yet over and above mischievous; but they promised very fair for it; for they already bit little children, that they might suck their blood. They had been put to bed

Her sharp-toothed golden-crowned child!
Or, as one feasts a creature rarely
95   Captured here, unreconciled
To capture; and completely gives
Its pettish humours licence, barely
Requiring that it lives.

vi.

Ichabod, Ichabod,
100   The glory is departed!
Travels Waring East away?
Who, of knowledge, by hearsay,
Reports a man upstarted
Somewhere as a God,
105   Hordes grown European-hearted,
Millions of the wild made tame
On a sudden at his fame?
In Vishnu-land what Avatar?
Or, North in Moscow, toward the Czar,
110   Who, with the gentlest of footfalls
Over the Kremlin's pavement, bright
With serpentine and siennite,
Steps, with five other Generals,

---

early, with every one a crown of gold upon her head' (transl. R. Samber, 1729).

93.] Her feverish sharp-toothed gold-crowned child (*1868-88*).

94-8. Cp. the description of Goito as a 'captured creature in a pound' (*Sordello* i 384ff.).

99-100. Cp. *1 Samuel* iv 21; the daughter-in-law of Eli, the high priest, gives birth at a time of calamity: 'And she named the child Ichabod, saying, The glory is departed from Israel'.

103. upstarted: 'who has sprung up'.

108. 'Vishnu-land' is India. B. refers to the cycles of creation over which the god Vishnu rules in Hindu religious myth. 'To each cycle of creation there corresponds an "avatar", literally a "descent", of the god Vishnu. These avatars theoretically number ten, but the wealth of popular imagination has greatly increased the number' ('Mythology of Hinduism', *Larousse Encyclopedia of Mythology*).

109-10.] Or who, in Moscow, toward the Czar, / With the demurest of footfalls (*1849-88*, except 'who in' *1865-88*).

112. Serpentine is an ornamental stone with markings resembling those of a serpent's skin; siennite (syenite) is a crystalline rock allied to granite.

Who simultaneously take snuff,
115   That each may have pretext enough
To kerchiefwise unfurl his sash
Which, softness' self, is yet the stuff
To hold fast where a steel chain snaps,
And leave the grand white neck no gash?
120   In Moscow, Waring, to those rough
Cold natures borne, perhaps,
Like the lambwhite maiden, (clear
Thro' the circle of mute kings,
Unable to repress the tear,
125   Each as his sceptre down he flings),
To the Dome at Taurica,
Where now a priestess, she alway
Mingles her tender grave Hellenic speech
With theirs, tuned to the hailstone-beaten beach,
130   As pours some pigeon, from the myrrhy lands

114. Who] That (*1849-88*).

115. That each may] For each to (*1849-88*).

116. To] And (*1865-88*).   *unfurl*] unfold (*1863-88*).

120-33. This sentence lacks a main verb, unless 'is' is understood before 'borne' in l. 121.

120. In Moscow, Waring] Waring, in Moscow (*1849-88*, except 'Waring in', *1865-88*).

121. Cold natures] Cold northern natures (*1849-88*).

122-33. The 'lambwhite maiden' is Iphigenia, for whose sacrifice by her father Agamemnon, at the outset of the expedition against Troy, the other Greek leaders reluctantly voted (by throwing their sceptres to the ground), in order to ensure a favourable wind; however, in one version of the legend she was spirited away by Artemis to her temple at Tauris, in Scythia (Asia Minor), where she became priestess; she was eventually rescued by her brother Orestes. In Euripides' *Iphigenia at Tauris*, which B. greatly admired, Iphigenia laments her enforced isolation among barbarians who do not speak her language. B. treats a similar legend, the rescue of Hippolytus, in a poem written in the same period, *Artemis*.

122. maiden, (clear] maiden clear (*1849-88*; the closing bracket was removed in l. 125).

123. Thro'] From (*1849-88*).

126. the Dome] Dian's fane (*1849-88*); i.e. 'temple'. 'Dian' (Diana) is the Latin name for Artemis.

127. a priestess] a captive priestess (*1849-88*).

130. the myrrhy lands: Arabia, or 'the East' generally, the source of myrrh; B.'s use is the first rec. in *OED*.

Rapt by the whirlblast to fierce Scythian strands
Where breed the swallows, her melodious cry
Amid their barbarous twitter!
In Russia? Never! Spain were fitter!
135   Ay, most likely 'tis in Spain
That we and Waring meet again—
Now, while he turns down that cool narrow lane
Into the blackness, out of grave Madrid
All fire and shine—abrupt as when there's slid
140   Its stiff gold blazing pall
From some black coffin-lid.
Or, best of all,
I love to think
The leaving us was just a feint;
145   Back here to London did he slink;
And now works on without a wink
Of sleep, and we are on the brink
Of something great in fresco-paint:
Some garret's ceiling, walls and floor,
150   Up and down and o'er and o'er
He splashes, as none splashed before
Since great Caldara Polidore:
Then down he creeps and out he steals
Only when the night conceals
155   His face—in Kent 'tis cherry-time,
Or, hops are picking; or, at prime
Of March, he steals as when, too happy,
Years ago when he was young,

131. whirlblast: a Cumbrian dialect word for a whirlwind or hurricane, popularized by Wordsworth, after whom *OED* cites Coleridge and Shelley.
134. Spain were fitter: B. had not visited Spain.
145. slink: the implication of stealth is usually, but not always, pejorative.
152. great Caldara Polidore: Polidoro Caldara da Caravaggio (*c.*1492-1543), a painter B. greatly admired (see *Pauline* 656-67n.).
152 ˆ153.] Or Music means this land of ours
          Some favour yet, to pity won
          By Purcell from his Rosy Bowers,—
          "Give me my so long promised son,
          "Let Waring end what I begun!" (*1849-88*)
Henry Purcell (1659-95) was working on a setting of 'From Rosy Bowers' at his death.
153-82. In *Sordello* i, Sordello goes through a similar formative process in which the mastery of the imagination excuses him from any practical creative work.
157. he steals as when] he wanders as (*1849-88*).

Some mild eve when woods were sappy,
160   And the early moths had sprung
To life from many a trembling sheath
Woven the warm boughs beneath,
While small birds said to themselves
What should soon be actual song,
165   And young gnats, by tens and twelves,
Made as if they were the throng
That crowd around and carry aloft
The sound they have nursed, so sweet and pure,
Out of a myriad noises soft,
170   Into a tone that can endure
Amid the noise of a July noon,
When all God's creatures crave their boon,
All at once and all in tune,
And get it, happy as Waring then,
175   Having first within his ken
What a man might do with men,
And far too glad, in the even-glow,
To mix with the world he meant to take
Into his hand, he told you, so—
180   And out of it his world to make,
To contract and to expand
As he shut or oped his hand.
Oh, Waring, what's to really be?
A clear stage and a crowd to see!
185   Some Garrick—say—out shall not he
The heart of Hamlet's mystery pluck?
Or, where most unclean beasts are rife,
Some Junius—am I right?—shall tuck

159. were sappy] grew sappy (*1849-88*).
178. the world] your world (*1849-88*).
185-6. David Garrick (1717-79), the great actor and friend of Samuel Johnson, was especially celebrated in the role of Hamlet; l. 186 is an adaptation of Hamlet's words to Guildenstern (III ii 389): 'you would pluck out the heart of my mystery'. This comes from the same portion of the play as the allusion in l. 84 above. Cp. also *Bishop Blougram* 946-7, and note that Gigadibs in that poem ends by emigrating.
187. unclean beasts: alluding to the Old Testament prohibition of the eating of certain animals; here used metaphorically to mean corrupt politicians.
188. Junius: pseudonym (borrowed from the Roman satirist) of the famous 18th-century Whig pamphleteer who castigated corruption in government, and whose real identity is still at issue. Books relating to the controversy over his identity were in the library of B.'s father, who also wrote a short essay on the subject (*Collections* J 83, p. 533).

His sleeve, and out with flaying-knife!
190   Some Chatterton shall have the luck
Of calling Rowley into life!
Some one shall somehow run a muck
With this old world, for want of strife
Sound asleep: contrive, contrive
195   To rouse us, Waring! Who's alive?
Our men scarce seem in earnest now:
Distinguished names, but 'tis, somehow,
As if they played at being names
Still more distinguished, like the games
200   Of children. Turn our sport to earnest
With a visage of the sternest!
Bring the real times back, confessed
Still better than the very best!

II.

i.
"When I last saw Waring . . ."
205   (How all turned to him who spoke—
You saw Waring? Truth or joke?
In land-travel, or sea-faring?)

ii.
"We were sailing by Triest,

190-1. Thomas Chatterton (1752-70) passed off some of his own poetry as the work of a medieval priest called Rowley. B. defended him in *Chatterton*, written in the same period as *Waring* (see Appendix C, p. 476).

192-203. Cp. Wordsworth's two sonnets *London, 1802* and *Written in London, September, 1802*, and Shelley's *Sonnet: England in 1819*.

193-4. this old world, for want of strife / Sound asleep: cp. B. to Domett, 15 May 1843 (*Correspondence* vii 124): 'What shall I tell you?—that we are dead asleep in literary things and in great want of a "rousing word" (as the old puritans phrase it) from New Zealand or any place *out* of this snoring dormitory'. This is clearly a case of the poem influencing the letter, but see also the letters of 22 May and 13 July 1842 quoted above, and next note.

199-200. like the games / Of children: cp. B. to Domett, 13 July 1842 (*Correspondence* vi 33): 'our poems &c are poor child's play'.

200-3. Turn our sport . . . the very best: Carlyle is indicated here. See headnote to *Flight*, p. 297.

203. the] our (*1849-88*).

208. Triest: the modern spelling is Trieste; B. had visited this Adriatic port on his 1838 trip.

"Where a day or two we harboured:
210 "A sunset was in the West,
"When, looking over the vessel's side,
"One of our company espied
"A sudden speck to larboard.
"And, as a sea-duck flies and swims
215 "At once, so came the light craft up,
"With its sole lateen sail that trims
"And turns (the water round its rims
"Dancing as round a sinking cup)
"And by us like a fish it curled,
220 "And drew itself up close beside,
"Its great sail on the instant furled,
"And o'er its planks, a shrill voice cried,
"(A neck as bronzed as a Lascar's)
"'Buy wine of us, you English Brig?
225 "'Or fruit, tobacco and cigars?
"'A Pilot for you to Triest?
"'Without one, look you ne'er so big,
"'They'll never let you up the bay!
"'We natives should know best.'
230 "I turned, and 'just those fellows' way,'
"Our captain said, 'The 'long-shore thieves
"'Are laughing at us in their sleeves.'

iii.

"In truth, the boy leaned laughing back;
"And one, half-hidden by his side
235 "Under the furled sail, soon I spied,

213. to larboard: to the port side.
214-15. And . . . At once: cp. Pope, *Dunciad* ii 63-4: 'As when a dabchick waddles through the copse / On feet and wings, and flies, and wades, and hops'.
214. sea-duck: the eider duck.
216. lateen sail: a triangular sail suspended by a long yard at an angle of 45 degrees to the mast; lateen-rigged boats such as feluccas were common in the Mediterranean.
222. planks] thwarts (*1868-88*); 'thwarts' are rowing-benches.
223. Lascar's: Lascars were East Indian sailors.
227. look you ne'er so big: 'no matter how important a pose you strike'.
231. 'long-shore: from 'along shore', i.e. employed or active on the shoreline; often derogatory, as here (*OED* cites Marryat, 1837: 'half-bred, long-shore chap').

"With great grass hat, and kerchief black,
"Who looked up, with his kingly throat,
"Said somewhat while the other shook
"His hair back from his eyes to look
240 "Their longest at us; and the boat,
"I know not how, turned sharply round,
"Laying her whole side on the sea
"As a leaping fish does; from the lee
"Into the weather cut somehow
245 "Her sparkling path beneath our bow;
"And so went off, as with a bound,
"Into the rose and golden half
"Of the sky, to overtake the sun,
"And reach the shore like the sea-calf
250 "Its singing cave; yet I caught one
"Glance ere away the boat quite passed,
"And neither time nor toil could mar
"Those features: so I saw the last
"Of Waring!"—You? Oh, never star
255 Was lost here, but it rose afar!
Look East, where whole new thousands are!
In Vishnu-land what Avatar?

240. *and*] then (*1849–88*).
247. *rose*] rosy (*1863–88*).
248. *Of the*] O' the (*1870–88*).
249. *sea-calf*: the common seal.
254–5. Cp. Dryden, *Ode to . . . Mrs Anne Killigrew* (see headnote): 'But look aloft, and if thou ken'st from far / Among the *Pleiads* a new-kindl'd star, / If any sparkles, than the rest, more bright, / 'Tis she that shines in that propitious light'; also Shelley, *Adonais* 494–5: 'The soul of Adonais, like a star, / Beacons from the abode where the Eternal are'.

26 Through the Metidja to Abd-el-Kadr—1842

First publ. *B & P* iii (*DL*), 26 Nov. 1842; repr. with the date below the main title in *1849, 1863* (when it was placed in *Lyrics*: see Appendix A, p. 464), *1868, 1872*; repr. without the date in *1888*. Our text is *1842*. In the contents page, but not the text, of *1872* (and its corr. reissue, *1884*), the title reads 'Abd-el-Kader', the correct spelling.

There was widespread interest in 1842 in the exploits of the Arab leader Abd-el-Kader, whose name means 'servant of God'. Born in Algeria in 1807, he became leader of the Arabs against the French in 1831. Made Emir of Mascara in a short peace in 1831, he repulsed further French attacks, and won victory in 1835. During renewed hostilities, Abd-el-Kader managed to unite the Arab tribes but suffered reverses in 1842, barely escaping from a raid on his camp; he rallied his troops again in June. He was eventually defeated and imprisoned in 1847. In a letter of 3 Dec. 1848, EBB. records B.'s indignation at the 'treatment of Abd-el-Kader' after his surrender (*Letters of EBB* i 388).

In the summer of 1842 B. was ordered to ride every day for his health; this poem celebrates the experience. See also *How They Brought the Good News* and *Last Ride*. The poem has affinities (partly reversed) with *Childe Roland*.

I.

As I ride, as I ride,
With a full heart for my guide,
So its tide rocks my side,
As I ride, as I ride,
5 That, as I were double-eyed,
He, in whom our Tribes confide,
Is descried, ways untried
As I ride, as I ride.

II.

As I ride, as I ride
10 To our Chief and his Allied,
Who dares chide my heart's pride
As I ride, as I ride?
Or are witnesses denied—
Through the desert waste and wide
15 Do I glide unespied
As I ride, as I ride?

¶26. *Title*. The Metidja is a coastal plain in Algeria, beginning on the eastern side of the Bay of Algiers.
7. *ways untried*: 'in a visionary or exceptional way'.

III.

As I ride, as I ride,
When an inner voice has cried,
The sands slide, nor abide
20 (As I ride, as I ride)
O'er each visioned Homicide
That came vaunting (has he lied?)
To reside—where he died
As I ride, as I ride.

IV.

25 As I ride, as I ride,
Ne'er has spur my swift horse plied,
Yet his hide, streaked and pied,
As I ride, as I ride,
Shows where sweat has sprung and dried,
30 —Zebra-footed, ostrich-thighed—
How has vied stride with stride
As I ride, as I ride!

V.

As I ride, as I ride,
Could I loose what Fate has tied,
35 Ere I pried, she should hide
As I ride, as I ride,
All that's meant me: satisfied
When the Prophet and the Bride
Stop veins I'd have subside
40 As I ride, as I ride!

21. visioned: 'seen in a vision' or 'visionary'. Cp. *Sordello* ii 15 (*1863* text) and *Gerard de Lairesse* 45, the latter similarly ambiguous.
23. reside] emended in agreement with all other eds. from 'abide' in *1842*. The printers ignored B.'s correction of this mispr. (carried down from l. 19) in *DL 2nd proof*; he made the correction again in *B & P Domett* and *B & P BYU*.
34-9. Even if he were able to see into the future, the speaker would refuse to know his fate; whenever death comes, he will accept it. The syntax of 'satisfied . . . subside' represents the speaker's conviction that, when his death comes by the will of 'the Prophet and the Bride', it will be seconded, even anticipated, by his own will.
36.] this line is in parentheses, *1849-88*.
38. the Prophet and his Bride: Mahomet and his wife, Ayeshah.

27 My Last Duchess
Ferrara

First publ. *B & P* iii (*DL*), 26 Nov. 1842, with *Count Gismond*, which followed it, under the collective title *Italy and France*; the title was *Italy*. Repr. *1849* (when it was separated from *Count Gismond* and given its present title and subtitle), *1863* (when it was placed in *Romances*: see Appendix A, p. 464), *1863²*, *1868*, *1872*, *1888*. Our text is *1842*. The date of composition is conjectural, but there are suggestive links with *Flight* and *Chatterton*, which would place the poem in the late summer of 1842.

The poem, like *Sordello*, is written in heroic couplets; it may have been during his researches into the history of Ferrara and the Este family for *Sordello* that B. came across the figure of Alfonso II (1533-98), fifth Duke of Ferrara and last of the Este line, whom L. S. Friedland ('Ferrara and *My Last Duchess*', *SP* xxxiii [1936] 656-84) claims as the original of B.'s Duke. Alfonso married the 14-year-old Lucrezia de' Medici in 1558; she died in 1561, and there were suspicions (almost certainly groundless) that she had been poisoned. Four years later Alfonso married Barbara, daughter of the Emperor Ferdinand I of Austria. It was the Emperor's son, Ferdinand, Count of Tyrol, who, after his father's death in 1564, negotiated the marriage through his envoy, Nikolaus Madruz, a native of Innsbruck (see ll. 49n., 54-6n.). DeVane (*Handbook* 108) succinctly describes Alfonso's character: 'he was cold and egotistical, vengeful and extremely possessive; and a patron of the arts, painting, music, and literature'. In particular, he was the patron of the poet Torquato Tasso, about whom B. would have read in the biography of Tasso which he 'reviewed' in July 1842 as a preliminary to his essay on Chatterton (see Appendix C, p. 476). It should be emphasized, however, that B. did not name the Duke, and that the location, Ferrara, was first indicated in a subtitle in *1849*: Friedland's source is convincing, but not definitive in terms of the poem's interpretation. Shakespeare's Leontes (*The Winter's Tale*) has also been proposed as a source for the Duke, though DeVane (*Handbook* 109) objects that Leontes' sexual jealousy differs from the Duke's possessive egotism. Even so, the play's final scene, in which the 'statue' of Hermione comes to life, may be an inverse source for the poem. In Feb. 1889, B. himself, when he was asked whether the Duchess '[was] in fact shallow and easily and equally well pleased with any favour: or did the Duke so describe her as a supercilious cover to real and well justified jealousy', replied: 'As an excuse—mainly to himself—for taking revenge on one who had unwittingly wounded his absurdly pretentious vanity, by failing to recognize his superiority in even the most trifling matters' (*New Poems* 175). See also l. 6n. For B.'s personal attitude to this topic, see his account to EBB., in a letter of 18 Jan. 1846, of his 'nightmare dreams' of 'the infliction of tyranny on the unresisting', and the subsequent anecdote of a former friend's ill treatment of his wife (*LK* 399). A source for the portrait of the Duchess has been suggested by C. E. Carrington (*TLS* 6 Nov. 1969, p. 1288): the portrait of a young woman, item no. 254 in the Dulwich collection with which B. was familiar from boyhood. The portrait is assigned to the school of Susterman (1506-60), a Flemish painter who worked in Florence. There are portraits of Lucrezia, though none in Ferrara. But as with the character of the Duke, the historical identification of the portrait is not a necessary feature of its presence in the poem, and it may be taken as being, to all intents and purposes, imaginary (see also l. 3n., and headnote to *Pictor*, p. 252).

The poem's setting relates it to other Renaissance character studies in B., such as *Tomb at St. Praxed's* and *Andrea*; the Duke in *Flight* seems a bathetic parody of the one here. The figure of Guido in *Ring* is the most complex and extended study of the type; the Duchess may be a prototype of Pompilia. Cp. also *A Forgiveness*. B.'s interest in the mysterious expressiveness of portraits is most fully developed in *A Likeness*. The collective title under which the poem was first published reflects B.'s interest in national characteristics and in categories generally during this period, and also his lifelong practice of pairing poems with or against each other.

> That's my last Duchess painted on the wall,
> Looking as if she were alive; I call
> That piece a wonder, now: Frà Pandolf's hands
> Worked busily a day, and there she stands.
> 5 Will't please you sit and look at her? I said
> "Frà Pandolf" by design, for never read
> Strangers like you that pictured countenance,

¶27. *1. painted on the wall*: either a framed portrait or, more likely, a fresco; this phrase, and the speed of Frà Pandolf's work (see l. 4), favour the latter, 'piece' in l. 3 the former; either might be concealed by the 'curtain' of l. 10. B. N. Pipes Jr. ('The Portrait of "My Last Duchess"', *VS* iii [1959-60] 381-6) points out that Alfonso II (see headnote) ordered a number of portrait frescoes in 1559, the year in which his bride Lucrezia came to Ferrara, though they were too decayed by B.'s day to indicate whether a portrait of Lucrezia was among them.

3. Frà Pandolf is an imaginary painter, though B. may have taken the name from that of the painter Giovanni Antonio Pandolfi, who, as Friedland points out (see headnote), was employed by the Este family to paint a portrait of Alfonso II's sister Lucrezia in 1570 (nine years after the death of Lucrezia de' Medici, Alfonso's first wife); the name occurs in Pilkington's *Dictionary of Painters* (1805), a standard reference work which B. knew well. 'Frà' means 'brother', i.e. the painter is a monk; cp. such real Italian Renaissance painters as Fra Angelico and Fra Bartolommeo, as well as B.'s own *Fra Lippo Lippi*.

6. by design: B. was asked 'By what design?' and replied 'To have some occasion for telling the story, and illustrating part of it' (*New Poems* 175). For another reply from the same letter of Feb. 1889, see headnote, and see also ll. 45-6n.

The depth and passion of its earnest glance,
But to myself they turned (since none puts by
10 The curtain I have drawn for you, but I)
And seemed as they would ask me, if they durst,
How such a glance came there; so not the first
Are you to turn and ask thus. Sir, 'twas not
Her husband's presence only, called that spot
15 Of joy into the Duchess' cheek: perhaps
Frà Pandolf chanced to say "Her mantle laps
"Over my Lady's wrist too much," or "Paint
"Must never hope to reproduce the faint
"Half-flush that dies along her throat;" such stuff
20 Was courtesy, she thought, and cause enough
For calling up that spot of joy. She had
A heart . . how shall I say? . . too soon made glad,
Too easily impressed; she liked whate'er
She looked on, and her looks went everywhere.
25 Sir, 'twas all one! My favor at her breast,
The dropping of the daylight in the West,
The bough of cherries some officious fool
Broke in the orchard for her, the white mule
She rode with round the terrace—all and each
30 Would draw from her alike the forward speech,
Or blush, at least. She thanked men,—good; but thanked
Somehow . . I know not how . . as if she ranked

17-19. "Paint . . . throat;": cp. *Ring* xi 1554-6: 'slur / The line o' the painter just where paint leaves off / And life begins'.

21-43. She had . . . Never to stoop: cp. the Duke in *Flight*, who (with his mother) tries to 'lesson' his wife in this way; see ll. 309-31.

23-4. she liked . . . everywhere: cp. *Andrea* 29-32.

25. Sir: the first indication of the envoy's identity; the Duke addresses him politely, but as an inferior.   *favor:* reversing the usual application of the term to a token (such as a scarf or ribbon) given by a lady to her chosen lover.

25-9. My favor . . . terrace: Pipes (see l. 1n.) suggests that the Duke borrows these pictorial details from the painting, where they form part of Frà Pandolf's pictorial reading of the Duchess's character; alternatively, they might spring to the Duke's mind by their evocation of a common response in the Duchess.

27. officious: the sense, still current in B.'s time, of 'attentive, obliging' is overlaid here by the contemptuous sense of 'importunate, meddling'. Cp. *Pippa* i 80.

30. forward] approving (*1849-88*). Like 'officious' (l. 27), 'forward' could have both good and bad senses in B.'s time: 'warm, earnest' or 'immodest, presumptuous'.

My gift of a nine hundred years old name
With anybody's gift. Who'd stoop to blame
35 This sort of trifling? Even had you skill
In speech—(which I have not)—could make your will
Quite clear to such an one, and say "Just this
"Or that in you disgusts me; here you miss,
"Or there exceed the mark"—and if she let
40 Herself be lessoned so, nor plainly set
Her wits to yours, forsooth, and made excuse,
—E'en then would be some stooping, and I chuse
Never to stoop. Oh, Sir, she smiled, no doubt,
Whene'er I passed her; but who passed without
45 Much the same smile? This grew; I gave commands;
Then all smiles stopped together. There she stands
As if alive. Will't please you rise? We'll meet
The company below then. I repeat,
The Count your Master's known munificence
50 Is ample warrant that no just pretence
Of mine for dowry will be disallowed;
Though his fair daughter's self, as I avowed
At starting, is my object. Nay, we'll go
Together down, Sir! Notice Neptune, tho',
55 Taming a sea-horse, thought a rarity,
Which Claus of Innsbruck cast in bronze for me.

33. a nine hundred years old name: the Este family (see headnote) traced their
ancestry even further back than this: see *Sordello* i 291ff.

45-6. I gave commands; / Then all smiles stopped together: in response to
questions about the fate of the Duchess, B. 'replied meditatively, "Yes, I
meant that the commands were that she be put to death." And then, after a
pause, he added, with a characteristic dash of expression, and as if the
thought had just started up in his mind, "Or he might have had her shut up in
a convent"' (H. Corson, *An Introduction to the Study of Robert Browning's
Poetry* [3rd ed., Boston 1903] p. viii).

49. The identification of the Duke's prospective father-in-law as a 'Count'
supports the connection of the Duke with Alfonso II (see headnote), although
Alfonso's second wife was a sister, not daughter, of the Count of Tyrol. See
also next note.

54-6. Notice . . . for me: the statue and sculptor, like the portrait and painter,
are imaginary; the classical subject is typical of the period, during which
Innsbruck (which B. visited in 1838) was a famous centre of bronze-casting.
Innsbruck was also the capital of Tyrol, and Nikolaus Madruz, the Count of
Tyrol's envoy to Alfonso II in the negotiations over his second marriage, was
a native of that city. See prec. note and headnote.

28 Count Gismond
Aix in Provence

First publ. *B & P* iii (*DL*), 26 Nov. 1842, with *My Last Duchess*, which preceded it, under the collective title *Italy and France*; the title was *France*. Repr. *1849* (when it was separated from *My Last Duchess* and given its present title and subtitle), *1863* (when it was placed in *Romances*: see Appendix A, p. 464), *1863²*, *1868*, *1872*, *1888*. Our text is *1842*. The date of composition is unknown.

There is no historical source for the poem: the subtitle added in *1849* indicates a generalized chivalric setting, Provence being the home of troubadour culture. F. Allen ('Ariosto and Browning: A Reexamination of "Count Gismond"', *VP* xi [1973] 15-25) argues convincingly that the literary source of the poem is the Genevra—Airodant episode in bk. V of Ariosto's *Orlando Furioso*, which was also the source for the episode of the Palmer and Sir Guyon in bk. II of Spenser's *Faerie Queene*, and of the plot of the false accusation of Hero in *Much Ado About Nothing* (see esp. ll. 91-102n.). The poem may also be seen as a variant of the Cinderella myth—oppressed heroine triumphing over two wicked sisters (here, cousins). Cp., in B., the court intrigue surrounding Colombe in *Colombe*, and the lady in *Glove*. B. had a lifelong preoccupation with providential rescue; see *Pauline* 656-67n. The strongest parallel is with the situation of Guido, Pompilia, and Caponsacchi in *Ring*. With the duel (ll. 67-102) cp. *Before*.

I.
Christ God, who savest man, save most
   Of men Count Gismond who saved me!
Count Gauthier, when he chose his post,
   Chose time and place and company
5 To suit it; when he struck at length
My honor's face 'twas with full strength.

II.
And doubtlessly ere he could draw
   All points to one, he must have schemed!
That miserable morning saw
10   Few half so happy as I seemed,
While being dressed in Queen's array

¶28.*1. man*] men (*1849*, *1863²*).
6.] My honor 'twas with all his strength. (*1849-88*, except 'honour,', *1863²*, *1868-88*).
11-12. She has been chosen 'Queen' for the day of the tournament, because of her beauty; she implies in the following lines that her cousins are jealous of

To give our Tourney prize away.

III.

I thought all loved me, did me grace
   To please themselves; 'twas all their deed;
15 God makes, or fair or foul, our face;
   If showing mine so caused to bleed
My Cousins' hearts, they should have dropped
A word, and all the play had stopped.

IV.

They, too, so beauteous! Each a queen
20   By virtue of her brow and breast;
Not needing to be crowned, I mean,
   As I do. E'en when I was dressed,
Had either of them spoke, instead
Of glancing sideways with still head!

V.

25 But no: they let me laugh, and sing
   My birthday song quite through; adjust
The last rose in my garland, fling
   A last look on the mirror, trust
My arms to each an arm of theirs,
30 And so descend the castle-stairs—

VI.

And come out on the morning troop
   Of merry friends who kissed my cheek,
And called me Queen, and made me stoop
   Under the canopy—(a streak
35 That pierced it, of the outside sun,
Powdered with gold its gloom's soft dun)—

---

the distinction. This detail may invert the situation in the first part of
Tennyson's *The May Queen*, where the speaker exults in her beauty and
crows over the rivals at whose expense she has been elected 'Queen'.

12. Tourney: tournament.

13. all] they (*1849-88*).

18. play: game.

24. Cp. the way Geraldine 'looked askance' at Christabel in Coleridge's
Christabel (see ll. 580-7).

34-6. Cp. *Sordello* i 393-5.

VII.

And they could let me take my state
   And foolish throne amid applause
Of all come there to celebrate
40   My Queen's day—Oh, I think the cause
Of much was, they forgot no crowd
Makes up for parents in their shroud!

VIII.

Howe'er that be, when eyes were bent
   Upon me, both my Cousins cast
45   Theirs down; 'twas time I should present
     The victor with his . . . there, 'twill last
No long time . . the old mist again
Blinds me . . but the true mist was rain.

IX.

See! Gismond's at the gate, in talk
50   With his two boys: I can proceed.
Well, at that moment, who should stalk
     Forth calmly (to my face, indeed)
But Gauthier, and he thundered "Stay!"
And all did stay. "No crowns, I say!

X.

55   "Bring torches! Wind the penance-sheet
     "About her! Let her shun the chaste,
"Or lay herself before their feet!
     "Shall she, whose body I embraced
"A night long, queen it in the day?
60   "For Honor's sake no crowns, I say!"

43. Howe'er] However (*1865-88*).   *when*] all (*1849-88*).
44. both] when (*1849-88*).
46. victor with his] victor's crown, but (*1849-88*).
47-8. the old mist . . . rain: i.e. the memory ('the old mist'), returning, brings tears, but the experience itself ('the true mist') was far more painful.
48.] Blinds me as then it did. How vain! (*1849-88*).
52. calmly] boldly (*1849-88*).
54. did stay. "No] stayed. "Bring no (*1849-88*). In a diary entry for 30 Apr. 1878, Alfred Domett recorded telling B. that this rev. was 'An inconceivably blundering correction, *possibly* made to avoid the double rhyme "stay" and "say", in one line, which could only be perceptible to a stupid, utterly unimpassioned reader' (*Diary* 214). But although B., according to Domett, accepted the criticism, no change was made.   *say!*] emended in agreement with other eds. from 'say!"' in *1842*.

XI.

I? What I answered? As I live,
   I never thought there was such thing
As answer possible to give.
   What says the body when they spring
65 Some monstrous torture-engine's whole
Strength on it? No more says the soul.

XII.

Till out strode Gismond; then I knew
   That I was saved. I never met
His face before, but, at first view,
70   I felt quite sure that God had set
Himself to Satan; who would spend
A minute's mistrust on the end?

XIII.

He strode to Gauthier, in his throat
   Gave him the lie, then struck his mouth
75 With one back-handed blow that wrote
   In blood men's verdict there. North, South,
East, West, I looked. The lie was dead,
And damned, and truth stood up instead.

XIV.

This glads me most, that I enjoyed
80   The heart of the joy, nor my content
In watching Gismond was alloyed
   By any doubt of the event:
God took that on him—me he bid
Watch Gismond for my part: I did.

XV.

85 Did I not watch him while he let
   His armourer just brace his greaves,

62.] I never fancied such a thing (*1849-88*).
64-6. EBB., applying these lines to her mental prostration after her brother
Edward's death, wrote to B.: 'you never wrote anything which *lived* with me
more than *that*. It is such a dreadful truth' (20-22 Aug. 1845, *LK* 170-1).
80. *of the*] o' the (*1872, 1884*).
80-1. *nor . . . was alloyed*] with . . . unalloyed (*1849-88*).
82. *event*: result; cp. *Artemis* 121.
83. *me he*] I was (*B & P BYU, 1849-88*).
86. *greaves*: armour for the legs.

Rivet his hauberk, on the fret
   The while! His foot . . my memory leaves
No least stamp out, nor how anon
90 He pulled his ringing gauntlets on.

XVI.

And e'en before the trumpet's sound
   Was finished there lay prone the Knight,
Prone as his lie, upon the ground:
   My Knight flew at him, used no sleight
95 Of the sword, but open-breasted drove,
Cleaving till out the truth he clove.

XVII.

Which done, he dragged him to my feet
   And said "Here die, but end thy breath
"In full confession, lest thou fleet
100   "From my first, to God's second death!
"Say, hast thou lied?" And, "I have lied
"To God and her," he said, and died.

XVIII.

Then Gismond, kneeling to me, asked
   —What safe my heart holds tho' no word
105 Could I repeat now, if I tasked
   My powers for ever, to a third
Dear even as you are. Pass the rest
Until I sank upon his breast.

87. *hauberk*: breastplate.   *on the fret*: impatient for the combat to begin.
91-102. F. Allen (see headnote) compares the combat between the false accuser Polinesso and the champion Renaldo in *Orlando Furioso* (transl. Sir John Harington, 1591): 'Their trumpets blew, they set their speares in rest, / Renaldo commeth on a mighty pace, / For at this fight he finish will the feast, / And where to strike him he designes a lace: / His very first encounter was so fierce, / Renaldos speare the tothers sides did pierce. // And having overthrowne the Duke by force, / As one unable so great strokes to bide, / And cast him cleane six paces from his horse, / Himselfe alights and th'others helme untide, / Who making no resistance like a corse, / With faint low voice for mercy now he cride, / And plaine confest with this his later breath, / The fault that brought him this deserved death. // No sooner had he made this last confession, / But that his life did faile him with his voyce'.
92. there lay prone the] prone lay the false (*1849-88*).
94. My Knight] Gismond (*1849-88*).
95. Of the sword] O' the sword (*1863²*, *1870-88*).
103-8. Cp. B. to Fanny Haworth, 20 July 1861 (three weeks after EBB.'s

XIX.

Over my head his arm he flung
110   Against the world; and scarce I felt
His sword, that dripped by me and swung,
   A little shifted in its belt,
For he began to say the while
How South our home lay many a mile.

XX.

115 So 'mid the shouting multitude
   We two walked forth to never more
Return. My Cousins have pursued
   Their life untroubled as before
I vexed them. Gauthier's dwelling-place
120   God lighten! May his soul find grace!

XXI.

Our elder boy has got the clear
   Great brow; tho' when his brother's black
Full eye shows scorn, it . . . Gismond here?
   And have you brought my tercel back?
125 I just was telling Adela
How many birds it struck since May.

---

death): 'Then came what my heart will keep till I see her and longer—the most perfect expression of her love to me within my whole knowledge of her . . . and in a few minutes she died in my arms' (*LH* 65).

113-14. Cp. Keats, *Eve of St. Agnes* 350-1: 'Awake! arise! my love, and fearless be, / For o'er the southern moors I have a home for thee'.

116. two] emended in agreement with *B & P Domett, B & P BYU* and all other texts from 'too' in *1842*.

124. tercel: the male of any kind of hawk.

125. Adela: pronounced to rhyme with 'May'; cp. 'Taurica/alway' in *Waring* 126-7, and 'pray/Africa' in *Home-Thoughts, from the Sea* 6-7. The rhyme is Shelleyan (e.g. 'gondola/way', *Julian and Maddalo* 139-40). Adela is the 'dear' friend of ll. 106-7.

29 Soliloquy of the Spanish Cloister

First publ. *B & P* iii (*DL*), 26 Nov. 1842, with *Incident*, which preceded it, under the collective title *Camp and Cloister*, with the title 'Cloister (*Spanish*)'. Repr. *1849* (when it was separated from *Incident* and given its present title), *1863* (when it was placed in *Lyrics*: see Appendix A, p. 464), *1863*², *1868*, *1880*, *1888*. In *1863* the poem was listed on the contents page as no. III of *Garden-Fancies*, but, though it immediately follows that poem in the text, it retains its separate identity. The contents page may be misprinted, or may contain the trace of a change which B. thought better of; the contents page of *1865*, the revised reissue of *1863*, lists the poem separately. The date of composition is unknown. J. U. Rundle (*N & Q* cxcvi [1951] 252) suggests a debt to Burns's *Holy Willie's Prayer*. G. Bornstein, in *Poetic Remaking: The Art of Browning, Yeats and Pound* (Pennsylvania 1988, p. 23) suggests that the poem 'may glance at the debate over religious ritual stirred by the Oxford Movement': see headnote to *Tomb at St Praxed's* (p. 260). The setting is contemporary, but articulates a traditional Protestant attack on monastic life as a breeding-ground for petty feuds and religious hypocrisy; cp. the 'old monk' in *Sordello* i 299-308. False or perverted religious feeling, whether Protestant or Catholic, is a recurring topic of B.'s work; cp., in this period, *Johannes* and *Tomb at St. Praxed's*. Spanish Catholicism in particular is further attacked in *Confessional*.

I.
Gr-r-r—there go, my heart's abhorrence!
    Water your damned flower-pots, do!
If hate killed men, Brother Lawrence,
    God's blood, would not mine kill you!
5 What? your myrtle-bush wants trimming?
    Oh, that rose has prior claims—
Needs its leaden vase filled brimming?
    Hell dry you up with its flames!

II.
At the meal we sit together:
10   *Salve tibi!* I must hear
Wise talk of the kind of weather,
    Sort of season, time of year:
Not a plenteous cork-crop: scarcely
    Dare we hope oak-galls, I doubt:

¶29.*10*. *Salve tibi*: a Latin greeting, lit. 'hail to thee'.
14. *oak-galls*: growths produced by gall-flies on various species of oak; used in the manufacture of ink. See also *Sordello* iii 42n. and *Caliban* 52.

15 *What's the Latin name for "parsley"?*
     What's the Greek name for Swine's Snout?

III.
     Phew! We'll have our platter burnished,
       Laid with care on our own shelf!
     With a fire-new spoon we're furnished,
20   And a goblet for ourself,
     Rinsed like something sacrificial
       Ere 'tis fit to touch our chaps—
     Marked with L. for our initial!
       (He, he! There his lily snaps!)

IV.
25 *Saint*, forsooth! While brown Dolores
       Squats outside the Convent bank,
     With Sanchicha, telling stories,
       Steeping tresses in the tank,
     Blue-black, lustrous, thick like horsehairs,
30   —Can't I see his dead eye grow
     Bright, as 'twere a Barbary corsair's?
       That is, if he'd let it show.

V.
     When he finishes refection,
       Knife and fork across he lays
35 Never, to my recollection,
       As do I, in Jesu's praise.
     I, the Trinity illustrate,
       Drinking watered orange-pulp;
     In three sips the Arian frustrate;

---

16. Swine's Snout: the dandelion (punningly insulting Brother Lawrence's appearance). The phrase 'swine's snout' also occurs in *Proverbs* xi 22.

17 . Phew] Whew (*1849-88*).

22. chaps: jaws or cheeks.

24. R. A. Day (*Explicator* xxiv, no. 4 [Dec. 1965] item 33) points out that the lily is a traditional emblem of chastity, and that this line is immediately followed by the erotic images of the following stanza.

30-1. grow / Bright, as] glow / Bright, as (*1849, 1863²*); glow, / Bright as (*1863, 1865-88*).

32.] (That is, if he'd let it show!) (*1849-88*).

33. refection: a light meal.

34-5. across he lays / Never,] he never lays / Cross-wise, (*1849-88*).

37-40. The speaker's 'three sips' symbolize his adherence to the doctrine of the Trinity, rejected by the 4th-century theologian Arius (the 'Arian' heresy).

40   While he drains his at one gulp!

VI.

Oh, those melons! If he's able
  We're to have a feast; so nice!
One goes to the Abbot's table,
  All of us get each a slice.
45   How go on your flowers? None double?
  Not one fruit-sort can you spy?
Strange!—And I, too, at such trouble,
  Keep 'em close-nipped on the sly!

VII.

There's a great text in Galatians,
50   Once you trip on it, entails
Twenty-nine distinct damnations,
  One sure, if another fails.
If I trip him just a-dying,
  Sure of Heaven as sure can be,
55   Spin him round and send him flying
  Off to Hell a Manichee?

42. feast;] feast! (*1870-88*, except 'feast:', *1884* , a rare example of a reading unique to this ed.).
48. Keep 'em] Keep them (*1863-88*, except *1863²*, as *1842*).
49-56. No passage in *Galatians* can be made to fit the context satisfactorily. B. later wrote admitting that the reference was inaccurate, adding that he 'was not careful to be correct' (letter of Apr. 1888 in *SBC* ii, no. 1 [1974] 62). An ingenious, but not wholly convincing, attempt has been made by R. B. Pearsall ('Browning's Texts in Galatians and Deuteronomy', *MLQ* xiii [1952] 256-8) to transfer the 'twenty-nine distinct damnations' to the litany of curses in *Deuteronomy* xxviii 16-44, a passage connected with *Galatians* iii 10. As *Oxford* remarks, the general tenor of *Galatians*, with its attack on formal religious observance, fits the poem; cp. also the contrast between flesh and spirit in v 19-23: 'Now the works of the flesh are manifest, which are these; Adultery, fornication, uncleanness, lasciviousness, idolatry, witchcraft, hatred, variance, emulations, wrath, strife, seditions, heresies, envyings, murders, drunkenness, revellings, and such like . . . But the fruit of the Spirit is love, joy, peace, longsuffering, gentleness, goodness, faith, meekness, temperance: against such there is no law'. With the speaker's fantasy of 'tripping' Brother Lawrence, cp. Hamlet's notion of killing Claudius when he is 'about some act / That has no relish of salvation in't; / Then trip him, that his heels may kick at heaven, / And that his soul may be as damn'd and black / As hell, whereto it goes' (III iii 91-5).
56. Manichee: a follower of the Manichaean heresy; a dualist, holding that good and evil are independent and equally balanced forces in the cosmos,

VIII.

Or, my scrofulous French novel,
   On grey paper with blunt type!
Simply glance at it, you grovel
60   Hand and foot in Belial's gripe.
If I double down its pages
   At the woeful sixteenth print,
When he gathers his greengages,
   Ope a sieve and slip it in't?

IX.

65 Or, the Devil!—one might venture

---

rather than, as Christian orthodoxy maintains, both being the work of God. See M. K. Starkman, 'The Manichee in the Cloister: A Reading of Browning's "Soliloquy of the Spanish Cloister"', *MLN* lxxv (1960), 399-405.
57. scrofulous: morally corrupt (from scrofula, the 'king's evil', a disease of the lymph glands).   *French novel*: French literature was associated with hedonism and immorality; cp. the 'jolly chapter of Rabelais' in *Sibrandus* 32, and the 'little edition of Rabelais' in the bachelor's apartment in *A Likeness* 24.
60. Belial's gripe: Belial is associated with lust; cp. *PL* i 490-2: 'Belial came last, than whom a Spirit more lewd / Fell not from heaven, or more gross to love / Vice for itself'.
62. the woeful sixteenth print: the illustrations to French novels were considered one of their most licentious features; Starkman (see l. 56n.) cites *Manon Lescaut*; other examples include works by the Marquis de Sade, whose illustrations were 'woeful' both in the obscenity of their content and the execrable standard of their draughtsmanship.
64. sieve: a basket, used chiefly for market produce.
65-6.] Or, there's Satan!—one might venture / Pledge one's soul to him, yet leave (*1849-88*).
65-70. Or, the Devil . . . so proud of: the speaker would trick the devil into persecuting Brother Lawrence, by pretending to pledge the devil his (the speaker's) soul, but leaving a 'flaw' in the contract which would allow him to escape damnation, a flaw which the devil would not notice until after he had fulfilled his side of the bargain. The apparent triviality of asking the devil to do no more than 'blast' (wither) a plant has led some commentators to argue that the 'rose-acacia' is a symbol of Brother Lawrence himself. See L. D. Fryxell and V. H. Adair in *Explicator* xxii, no. 4 (Dec. 1963) item 24. Adair makes the useful point that the 'rose-acacia' appears in *Flora's Dictionary* (1832) as a symbol of friendship, but her speculation about its theological application (rose = Lawrence, from Latin 'laurus' = Greek 'rhododendron', a rose-tree; acacia = Arian heretic, follower of Acacius, Bishop of Caesarea) seems far-fetched. Other commentators have defended the literal sense as both appropriate to the speaker's pettiness and indicated by the use of 'that',

Pledge one's soul yet slily leave
Such a flaw in the indenture
    As he'd miss till, past retrieve,
    Blasted lay that rose-acacia
70   We're so proud of! *Hy, Zy, Hine* . . .

---

which would suggest that the speaker has just noticed Brother Lawrence tending to this particular shrub. See e.g. R. G. Malbone in *VP* iv (1966) 218-21. By this reading, the 'we' of l. 70 would be a further example of the speaker's sarcastic identification with Lawrence, as in st. iii, rather than the collective voice of the monastery, as in st. vi. In our view, the 'rose-acacia' is both a literal plant and a symbol of everything that the speaker hates about Brother Lawrence; his asking the devil to destroy it has, therefore, a metaphorical as well as a literal force, but a sense of incongruity at the triviality for which the speaker is prepared to risk his soul remains appropriate. Cp. Burns, *Holy Willie's Prayer* 78-9: 'Curse thou his basket and his store, / Kail and potatoes', and see headnote to *Johannes* (I 333) for another ref. to this poem.

69. rose-acacia: a tree with rose-coloured flowers, *Robina hipsida*.

70. Hy, Zy, Hine: only two of the astonishingly numerous and frequently bizarre accounts of this phrase carry any conviction, those of G. Pitts ('Browning's "Soliloquy of the Spanish Cloister": *Hy, Zy, Hine*', *N & Q* xiii [1966] 339-40) and J. F. Loucks ('"Hy, Zy, Hine" and Peter of Abano', *VP* xii [1974] 165-9). Pitts argues that B. derived it from a medieval liturgical parody, the Mass of the Ass; Loucks, that B. adapted the phrase from a string of nonsense words in a medieval manual of magic formulae, the *Heptameron*, or *Elementa Magica*, ascribed to Pietro of Abano (*c.* 1250-*c.* 1316). B. was certainly familiar with Abano's work from his reading in the occult (see headnote to *Paracelsus*, I 105); cp. also his translation of a quatrain ascribed to Abano (p. 371) and the much later poem *Pietro of Abano*. S. H. Aiken ('"Hy, Zy, Hine" and Browning's Medieval Sources for "Soliloquy of the Spanish Cloister"', *VP* xvii [1979] 377-85), while admitting that B.'s spelling of the phrase may have been influenced by the Abano source, supports Pitts' argument by drawing attention to the availability of the Mass of the Ass in learned and popular writings of the period, esp. William Hone's *Ancient Mysteries Described* (1823). Hone notes that the mock-ceremony begins before vespers and parodies vesper anthems; he also mentions the survival of such customs in contemporary Spain. Aiken's argument is persuasive except that it gives the speaker no motive for uttering the phrase other than a general inclination to mock Brother Lawrence; Loucks's interpretation, that the phrase is the beginning of a magic formula which will raise the devil with whom the speaker proposes (whether in earnest or no) to make his pact, fits the context better.

St, there's Vespers! *Plena gratiâ*
Ave, Virgo! Gr-r-r—you swine!

71-2. Plena gratiâ / Ave, Virgo: 'full of grace, hail, Virgin'. Two problems arise in connection with this phrase: the first, that its Latin, besides being in an odd order, represents a hybrid of two prayers, the 'Hail Mary' and the 'Litany to the Blessed Virgin'; and second, that neither of these two was the conventional opening of vespers in the 19th century. It is unlikely either that the speaker would deliberately mock the ritual, or that he, of all people, would make a mistake; according to C. T. Phipps, SJ (*VP* vii [1969] 158-9), the error is B.'s, and 'resulted from equating the vesper bell with the evening *Angelus*. The thrice-daily *Angelus* bell is a signal for an antiphonal prayer honoring the Incarnation . . . which includes most of the words of the present-day form of the *Ave Maria*'. As for the words themselves, and their order, it is probable that B. altered them to fit the rhyme and rhythm of the stanza. Cp. *Ring* vi 438ff. for another passage in which the Latin liturgy is interjected with a speaker's profane comments.

31 The Lost Leader

First publ. *B & P* vii (*DR & L*), 6 Nov. 1845; repr. *1849, 1863* (when it was placed in *Lyrics*: see Appendix A, p. 464), *1868, 1872, 1888*. Our text is *1845*.

That the 'lost leader' was Wordsworth was confirmed by B. in later correspondence, most emphatically in a letter to Ruskin of 1 Feb. 1856: 'Don't tell that I thought of—who else but Wordsworth?' (*A Letter from Robert Browning to John Ruskin* [Waco 1958] n.p.). B. had met Wordsworth in 1835, after the publication of *Paracelsus* introduced him to the literary world, but the acquaintance did not develop. The poem may have been composed in repose to Wordsworth's first appearance at Court as Poet Laureate (25 Apr. 1845), when B. wrote sardonically to EBB. of the ridiculous figure which Wordsworth cut in Samuel Rogers' ill-fitting court costume (28 May 1845, *LK* 83); EBB. first saw the poem in proof, calling it in her letter to B. of 21-22 Oct. 1845 one of 'the new poems' (*LK* 244; her comments rec. in the notes are from *Wellesley MS*). However, B. might have withheld the poem until the last moment because EBB. did not share his hostility to Wordsworth (see below). On balance we prefer a date closer to the award of the Laureateship itself (Apr. 1843). In a fragment from an unpubl. letter to R. H. Horne (now in the Berg Collection of the New York Public Library; *Collections* E511, p. 445, though not there identified in connection with Horne), B. responds to Horne's request for a suitable epigraph for the essay on Wordsworth and Leigh Hunt in Horne's *A New Spirit of the Age* (1844) by quoting, for Wordsworth, *PL* x 441-54 (omitting l. 444), followed by a comment: 'He, thro' the midst unmarked, / In show plebeian angel militant / Of lowest order, passed: and from the door / [Of that Plutonian hall, invisible] / Ascended his high throne which, under state / Of richest texture spread, at the upper end / Was placed in regal lustre. Down awhile / He sat, and round about him saw unseen. / At last, as from a cloud, his fulgent head / And shape star-bright appeared, or brighter, *clad / With what permissive glory since his Fall / Was left him, or false glitter*. All amazed / At that so sudden blaze, the *Stygian throng / Bent their aspect*. (As Jeffrey does in the reprint of his review of the *Excursion*: this is too good a bit, I fear: take the kinder side of the matter and give him some or all of your own fine sonnet)'. Unsurprisingly, Horne did not use this passage, though he did adopt several of B.'s suggestions for other writers (see *Correspondence* viii 202-5). Since *A New Spirit of the Age* was published in March 1844, a date for the Berg letter of autumn/winter 1843 seems probable, and we date the poem to this period.

The 'handful of silver' of l. 1 may be a ref. to Wordsworth's acceptance of a government appointment in 1813, and the 'ribband' of l. 2 to the (effectively unpaid) Laureateship, though B. later denied believing that such mercenary considerations influenced Wordsworth's conduct (see below). The fact that B. did not show the poem to EBB. until *DR & L* was in proof may reflect his awareness that her opinion of Wordsworth was more sympathetic than his: in her letter of 30 May 1845, though she agreed with his ridicule of shifts the blame for the failure of *A Blot* from Macready to Forster.) The episode, along with the further disappointment over *Colombe*, probably decided B. not to write any more plays for the stage, a decision which fell in with EBB.'s hostility to the contemporary theatre: see her comment on the failure of *A Blot* in *Correspondence* vi 326-7, and her disparagement of the theatre in a letter to B. of 17 Feb. 1845 (*LK* 22-3).

> There's a sisterhood in words—
> Still along with 'flowers' go 'birds.'
> Is it but three weeks to-day
> Since they played a luckless play,
> 5 And 'the Treshams,' like a band
> Of full-fledged nestlings, left my hand
> To flutter forth, the wide world over?
> Just three weeks! yet see—each rover
> Here, with more or less unsteady
> 10 Winglets, nearly reached already,
> In the Past, so dim, so dim,
> A place where Lucy, Strafford, Pym,
> My elder brood of early years,
> Wait peacefully their new compeers.
> 15 Then, good voyage! shall it grieve me
> Vastly, that such ingrates leave me?
> Why, this March, this very morning

¶30. *1-2*. Alluding, as Lady Martin explains (op. cit. 395), to verses 'in which flowers played a prominent part' on the opposite page of the album where B. wrote his poem.

3-4. The first performance of *A Blot* took place at the Theatre Royal, Drury Lane, on 11 Feb. 1843. It was performed twice more, on 13 and 15 Feb.

5. '*the Treshams*': the name of the family at the centre of *A Blot*: Lord Tresham, his sister Mildred, his brother Austin, and their cousin, Guendolen.

5-7. like a band . . . over: cp. B.'s comment about the origin of *Flight* being a line from a song he heard as a boy: 'From so slender a twig of fact can these little singing birds start themselves for a flight to more or less distances' (*Trumpeter* 71).

8-14. The sense is that *A Blot* is already sunk in the oblivion which befell B.'s first play, *Strafford*.

12. Lucy, Strafford, Pym: characters in *Strafford*. Miss Faucit played the part of Lucy, Lady Carlisle.

17-21. A ref. to *Colombe*, which B. had indeed nearly finished by May; he wrote to Alfred Domett on 15 May: 'I want to publish a few more numbers of my "Bells"—and must also make-up my mind to finish a play I wrote lately for Charles Kean, if he will have it. (Macready has used me vilely.)'

Hatched my latest brood, take warning,
Each one worth you put together!
20 April sees them full in feather—
And how we'll welcome May's glad weather!

Helen Faucit, you have twice
Proved my Bird of Paradise!
He, who would my wits inveigle
25 Into boasting him my eagle,
Turns out very like a Raven:
Fly off, Blacky, to your haven!
But *you*, softest dove, must never
Leave me, as he does, for ever—
30 I will strain my eyes to blindness,
Ere lose sight of you and kindness.
'Genius' is a common story!
Few guess that the spirit's glory,
They hail nightly, is the sweetest,
35 Fairest, gentlest, and completest
Shakespeare's-Lady's, ever poet
Longed for! Few guess this: *I* know it.

Hatcham, Surrey, March 4, '43.

(*Correspondence* vii 125). Kean did not however produce the play, which was publ. 1844; it was first produced in 1853 with Miss Faucit in the title role.
22-3. Referring to her two roles, Lucy in *Strafford* and Mildred in *A Blot.*
24-7. A ref. to William Macready; the eagle and the raven were birds of good and ill omen in Roman augury.
32-7. The crowds who applaud the 'genius' of Miss Faucit's acting do not realize that the 'spirit's glory' which they 'hail' is also the spirit of a woman as personally attractive as Shakespeare's heroines. The difficulty arises not just from the compressed syntax but because B. uses an image drawn from drama to describe Miss Faucit's non-dramatic personality. For the contrast between public and private knowledge of a woman who is also a 'genius', cp. *One Word More.*

★ 30 Lines to Helen Faucit
('There's a sisterhood in words')

First publ. in Helena Faucit Martin, *On Some of Shakespeare's Female Characters* (5th ed., 1893) 396-7, from which our text is taken; repr. *Correspondence* vi 351-2 n.3. Composed 4 Mar. 1843 (B.'s subscription) and inscribed in an album belonging to the actress Helena (Helen) Faucit, later Lady Martin (1817-98). The album was offered for sale by Sotheby in 1936 (*Collections*, E180, p. 411) but its present location is unknown. With it was a letter from B. to Miss Faucit (*Correspondence* vi 351):

> My dear Miss Faucit,—Here is your album, with my best thanks for the honour you have done me by asking some rhymes for it: and here are the rhymes themselves—poor enough, most probably, but sincere, quite as certainly. I wish from my soul it were in my power to find some worthier way of proving the admiration and gratitude with which I remain, my dear Miss Faucit, yours ever faithfully,
> Robert Browning.

Miss Faucit was at this time an actress in William Macready's company. She had appeared first as Juliet at Richmond in 1833 (the theatre where B. saw Kean as Richard III: see headnote to *Pauline*, I 16); in 1837 she created the role of Lucy, Lady Carlisle, in B.'s *Strafford* (see l. 12); B. admired her performance, and she appeared as Mildred in *A Blot* (1843) shortly before the composition of this poem. B.'s lines refer to his disappointment at the failure of *A Blot* (the 'luckless play', l. 4) and his resentment at the behaviour of Macready, who had accepted the play reluctantly, insisted on alterations many of which B. disapproved, and quarrelled with him over who was to play the leading role of Lord Tresham. B. and Macready were not reconciled until the 1850s, and B.'s resentment lasted until he read 'with deep & painful interest' a biography of Macready which appeared in 1875 and prompted him to write: 'I wish I had divined certain things now made clear to me. The work puts him back to his old place in my heart' (to Lady Pollock, 1 Apr. 1875, *ABL MS*). In 1884 B. wrote to the same correspondent about her own memoir of Macready, praising him warmly and referring to the quarrel over *A Blot* as 'the unlucky production . . . when he seemed unjust to our friendship simply for want of the word of explanation which would have prevented a moment's estrangement between us' (13 Nov. 1884: *ABL MS*). B. offered his next play to Macready's rival Charles Kean (see ll. 17-21n.). For Macready's account of the quarrel over *A Blot* see W. Toynbee (ed.), *The Diaries of William Charles Macready 1833-1851* (2 vols., 1912); for B.'s account and that of friends, see among others *Correspondence* vii 391-3, Orr *Life* 118-22, and William Baker, 'Robert Browning on William Charles Macready' *BSN* viii (Dec. 1978), pp. 12-18. (In the document reproduced by Baker, B.

Wordsworth's conduct in going to Court, she dissociated herself from 'the sighing kept up by people about that acceptance of the Laureateship . . . Not that the Laureateship honored *him*, but that he honored it; & that, so honoring it, he preserves a symbol instructive to the masses, who are children & to be taught by symbols now as formerly . . . And wont the laurel (such as it is) be all the worthier of *you* for Wordsworth's having worn it first?' (*LK* 84). After the publication of the poem, however, B. made further savagely satirical remarks about Wordsworth's character in a letter to EBB. of 15 Feb. 1846 (*LK* 464), and the poem makes it clear that, contrary to her, he saw the Laureateship as a symbolic climax to Wordsworth's defection from the liberal cause. B. shared the opinion of the second generation of Romantic writers (Shelley, Byron, Keats, Hazlitt, Leigh Hunt) that the first (Wordsworth, Coleridge, Southey: the 'Lake School') had committed political apostasy in their conversion to conservatism; hence his remark to EBB. that 'I always retained my first feeling for Byron in many respects . . . while Heaven knows that I could not get up enthusiasm enough to cross the room if at the other end of it all Wordsworth, Coleridge & Southey were condensed into the little China bottle yonder, after the Rosicrucian fashion' (22 Aug. 1846, *LK* 986). In later life, however, B. played down his hostility. He wrote in 1875 to the Rev. A. Grosart: 'I *did* in my hasty youth presume to use the great and venerable personality of Wordsworth as a sort of painter's model; one from which this or the other particular feature may be selected and turned to account: had I intended more, above all, such a boldness as portraying the entire man, I should not have talked about "handfuls of silver and bits of ribbon". These never influenced the change of politics in the great poet; whose defection, nevertheless, accompanied as it was by a regular face-about of his special party, was to my juvenile apprehension, and even mature consideration, an event to deplore . . . so, though I dare not deny the original of my little poem, I altogether refuse to have it considered as the "very effigies" of such a moral and intellectual superiority' (*LH* 166-7).

B. was interested, esp. during this period, in political apostasy: *Strafford* and *A Soul's Tragedy* both have close parallels to *Lost Leader*; see also *Italy*, and, later, *Prince Hohenstiel* (1871); for non-political parallels, cp. *Pictor* and *Andrea*.

I.

Just for a handful of silver he left us,
    Just for a ribband to stick in his coat—
Got the one gift of which fortune bereft us,
    Lost all the others she lets us devote;
5 They, with the gold to give, doled him out silver,

¶31.*1*. A ref. to Judas's betraying Christ for thirty pieces of silver.
3. Got] Found (*1849-88*).
4. devote: 'to dedicate; to consecrate; to appropriate by vow' (*J.*). Cp. *Leviticus* xxvii 28 (quoted in *J.*): 'No devoted thing, that a man shall devote unto the

So much was their's who so little allowed:
How all our copper had gone for his service!
   Rags—were they purple his heart had been proud!
We that had loved him so, followed him, honoured
     him,
10   Lived in his mild and magnificent eye,
Learned his great language, caught his clear accents,
   Made him our pattern to live and to die!
Shakespeare was of us, Milton was for us,
   Burns, Shelley, were with us,—they watch from
     their graves!
15 He alone breaks from the van and the freemen,
   He alone sinks to the rear and the slaves!

II.

We shall march prospering,—not thro' his presence;
   Songs may excite us,—not from his lyre;
Deeds will be done,—while he boasts his quiescence,
20   Still bidding crouch whom the rest bade aspire:
Blot out his name, then,—record one lost soul more,
   One task unaccepted, one footpath untrod,
One more devils'-triumph and sorrow to angels,
   One wrong more to man, one more insult to God!

Lord of all that he hath . . . shall be sold or redeemed: every devoted thing is
most holy unto the Lord'. The context is a list of the things (including
quantities of 'silver') to be dedicated to God.

13-14. B. commented: 'Shakespeare was *of* us—not *for* us, like Him of the
Defensio [Shelley]; nor abreast with our political sympathies like the other
two: I wish he had been more than *of* us' (letter to Ruskin: see headnote).

13.] When the poem was in proof, EBB. jotted down 'Burns was with us'
without comment, perhaps to remind herself to suggest a change at a meeting
with B. on 21 Oct. 1845, when the proofs of *DR & L* were discussed. B. may
have altered this line and l. 16 from singular to plural forms. See also ll. 24n.,
32n.

18. excite] inspirit (*1849-88*).

22.] One task more declined, one more footpath untrod, (*1849-88*).

23. devils'-triumph] triumph for devils (*1849-88*, except 'devil's triumph',
1872, 1884).

24.] EBB. made a note of this line when the poem was in proof, with 'done'
canc. after 'wrong' and replaced by 'more'; it is not certain whether the canc.
reading was authorial or EBB.'s slip.

25   Life's night begins: let him never come back to us!
      There would be doubt, hesitation and pain,
    Forced praise on our part—the glimmer of twilight,
      Never glad confident morning again!
    Best fight on well, for we taught him,—come
        gallantly,
30   Strike our face hard ere we shatter his own;
    Then let him get the new knowledge and wait us,
    Pardoned in Heaven, the first by the throne!

29. come] strike (*1849-88*).

30.] Aim at our heart ere we pierce through his own; (*1849*); Menace our heart ere we master his own; (*1863-88*).

31. get] receive (*1849-88*).   *new knowledge*: cp. *Colossians* iii 9-10: 'Lie not to one another, seeing that ye have put off the old man with his deeds; and have put on the new man, which is renewed in knowledge after the image of him that created him'.

32. Pardoned in Heaven] EBB. jotted this phrase down when the poem was in proof, without comment. Cp. *Hebrews* viii 1: 'We have such an high priest [Jesus], who is set on the right hand of the throne of the Majesty in the heavens'.

32 A Soul's Tragedy

Part First, being what was called the Poetry of Chiappino's Life: and Part Second, its Prose.

Text and publication
First publ. with *Luria, B & P* viii (13 Apr. 1846); *A Soul's Tragedy* was second in order. Neither the pamphlet nor the individual plays were separately repr.; both plays repr. *1849* (in the same order but not linked, and with the dedication to the whole pamphlet affixed to *Luria* alone: see p. 374), *1863*, *1868* (in reverse order), *1888* (*A Soul's Tragedy* in vol. iii, *Luria* in vol. vi). *A Soul's Tragedy*, in contrast to *Luria*, was very lightly revised. Our text is *1846*.

Date and composition
DeVane (*Handbook* 190) convincingly ascribes the conception and first draft of the play to the early 1840s. B. wrote to Alfred Domett on 22 May 1842 that he intended to 'finish a wise metaphysical play (about a great mind and soul turning to ill)' (*Correspondence* v 357). On 10 Mar. 1844, he wrote to Christopher Dowson of 'two other productions I have by me in a state of forwardness' (*Correspondence* viii 252), one of which is almost certainly *A Soul's Tragedy* (all B.'s other plays are ruled out; the other work may have been *Flight*). The title first appears in a letter to EBB. dated 26 Feb. 1845: 'I have one [play] done here,—"A Soul's Tragedy," as it is properly enough called' (*LK* 26). On 3 Aug. 1845 he repeated that the play 'could go to press next week' (*LK* 143). On 11 Feb. 1846 B. reread it, and decided to postpone publication, for the ostensible reason, as he explained to EBB. in his letter of 13 Feb., that it was likely to be unpopular, because more difficult than *Luria*, and so unsuitable to wind up *B & P*: 'whereas, if I printed it first in order, my readers, according to custom, would make the (comparatively) little they did not see into, a full excuse for shutting their eyes at the rest' (*LK* 455). But,

Title.] in *1863* B. added '1846' below the title; in *1868* this became 'London, 1846' and was placed below the subtitle. B. presumably made the *1868* rev. in order to avoid the implication that the play was set in 1846 (see next note). *Subtitle. Part First . . . Part Second*] Act First . . . Act Second (*1868-88*). In *1865*, the corr. reissue of *1863*, which has the same pagination, a list of persons etc. is squeezed into two lines between the subtitle and 'Part I': 'Persons—Luitolfo and Eulalia, betrothed lovers: Chiappino, their friend: / Ogniben, the Legate: Citizens of Faenza. Time, 15—. Place, Faenza.' In *1868-88* the list was properly tabulated, and Ogniben is 'the Pope's Legate'.

after commenting on the play's 'moral effect' (see below, *Criticism*), B. concluded: 'perhaps the truth is, that I am tired, rather, and desirous of getting done . . . will not the best way be to reserve this unlucky play and in the event of a second edition . . . might not this be quietly inserted?—in its place, too, for it was written two or three years ago' (*ibid.*). On 25 Feb. he was more sanguine: 'I looked yesterday over the "Tragedy"—and think it will do after all. I will bring one part at least next time . . . Don't think I am going to take any extraordinary pains' (*LK* 493). But on 27 Feb. he wrote that there might be a delay: 'My sister is copying it as I give the pages, but—in fact my wise head does ache a little' (*LK* 501). He finally brought EBB. pt. i on 9 Mar. She wrote at once to express her delight (see below, *Criticism*). On 18 Mar. B. wrote: 'all the morning I have been going for once and ever thro' the Tragedy, and it is *done* (done *for*). Perhaps I may bring it to-morrow—if my sister can copy all' (*LK* 546). But he seems to have brought pt. ii only on 28 Mar.; the following day EBB. wrote redoubling her praise (*LK* 569-70). On 30 Mar., EBB. returned the complete MS and her critical notes on pt. i (*Wellesley MS*; all her comments recorded in our notes derive from this source, unless otherwise specified). She did not have time to write any on pt. ii, since the play was going to the printers. B. sent her the proofs on 4 Apr. and EBB. returned them the next day with 'ever so much improvidence, which you will glance at and decide upon finally' (*LK* 590). B. sent a corrected proof on 6 Apr. and discussed the play with EBB. on a visit the same day, a week before publication.

Sources, and parallels in B.
No specific historical source for the play has been found. It is just possible that B. saw B. Righi's *Annali della Città di Faenza* (3 vols., Faenza 1840-1); in vol. iii, ch. 9, Righi describes the events which in 1509 led to the expulsion of the Venetians, who at that time controlled the town, and its return to papal rule. That the action takes place in the early 16th century is indicated by Ogniben's allusion (ii 349) to the newly discovered 'Western lands'; in *1865* B. confirmed this by adding the date '15—' to the title-page. In B.'s play, too, Faenza returns to papal rule. Apart from these details, there is little resemblance between the two accounts. B. had not visited Faenza when he wrote the play; note, however, that it lies in the same central and north-eastern region which B. had visited in 1838, and which formed the background of both *Sordello* and *Pippa*.

EBB., not yet having seen the text of the play, commented that the title 'sounds to me like the step of a ghost of an old Drama!' (27 Feb. 1845, *LK* 29). Cp. such Elizabethan and Jacobean titles as *The Spanish Tragedy*, *The Revenger's Tragedy*, and *The Atheist's Tragedy*. B. probably knew T. L. Beddoes' *The Bride's Tragedy* (1822; see *Pippa* i 271-5n.). B. later wrote a short poem called *The Heretic's Tragedy* (1855). There is a resemblance between Angelo in *Measure for Measure* and Chiappino, who, like Angelo, is corrupted by power and publicly unmasked at the end of the play; cp. also *Coriolanus* and *Julius Caesar*, where the fickle allegiance of the citizenry, and the problem of rightful rebellion against tyranny, are central elements. The more general issue of the relations between idealism (Chiappino), compromise (Luitolfo), and quietism (Ogniben) is frequently treated in B.: cp. esp. *Sordello* and *Bishop Blougram*.

The formal division of the play into verse and prose parts is apparently unique. The closest parallel is with B.'s own *Pippa*, which also has thematic parallels (in pt. iii, Luigi's argument about the rightfulness of tyrannicide; in pt. iv, Monsignor's confrontation with the Intendant, which resembles that between Ogniben and Chiappino). Sordello, like Chiappino, is offered the chance of political power at the cost of spiritual integrity, but refuses. Political turncoats are common in B.'s work of this period: Wentworth in *Strafford*, Charles in *Italy*, the poet of *Lost Leader*, the speaker of *Patriot*; in later work, cp. the Prince in *Prince Hohenstiel*.

Criticism

B & P viii was not widely reviewed, and *Luria* received most of the attention. An unsigned review in *Douglas Jerrold's Shilling Magazine* iii (June 1846) 573-4 praised *A Soul's Tragedy* as 'one of the most intensely dramatic works ever penned', but went on: 'The theatre and Mr. Browning's works are never likely to come into contact'; five years later, a review in *Fraser's Magazine* xliii (Feb. 1851) singled it out with *Pippa Passes* as superior to B.'s other dramas because his 'characteristic personality shows itself more clearly' (p. 174). B. and EBB. discussed the play, though in less detail than *Luria* because EBB. saw it closer to publication. B. associated the play with *Luria* as work conceived before he knew EBB.: 'there is no trace of you there . . . it is all sneering and *disillusion*—and shall not be printed but burned if you say the word' (11 Feb. 1846, *LK* 451-2). B. explained his doubts about publishing the play: 'at bottom, I believe the proper objection is to the immediate, *first* effect of the whole,—its moral effect,—which is dependent on the contrary supposition of its being really understood, in the main drift of it,—yet I don't know,—for I wrote it with the intention of producing the best of all effects . . . I have lost, of late, interest in dramatic writing, as you know—and, perhaps, occasion' (13 Feb. 1846, *LK* 455). EBB., however, when she finally saw pt. i of the play, 'was quite possessed with it, & fell finally into a mute wonder how you could for a moment doubt about publishing it. It is very vivid, I think, & vital, & impressed me more than the first act of "Luria" did' (10 Mar. 1846, *LK* 525); she was equally enthusiastic about pt. ii: 'Such thoughts, you have, in this second part of the Tragedy! . . . No one *thinks* like you—other poets talk like the merest women in comparison' (29 Mar., *LK* 569). B. replied: 'How you surprize me, (what ever you may think) by liking that Tragedy! It seems as if, having got out of the present trouble, I shall never fall into its fellow—I will strike, for the future, on the glowing, malleable metal; afterward, *filing* is quite another process than hammering, and a more difficult one' (*LK* 572). He had told EBB. that he had 'cut out a huge kind of sermon from the middle [of pt. ii] and reserve it for a better time' (18 Mar., *LK* 546), and EBB. later agreed that he was right: 'It would clog the action .. & already I am half inclined to fancy it a little clogged in one or two places' (29 Mar., *LK* 570). The nature of this 'sermon' is indicated in a passage from a later letter in which B. says that he has 'put in a few phrases' in pt. ii in order to 'give a little more insight as to his [Ogniben's] character—which I meant for that of a man of wide speculation and narrow practice,—universal understanding of men & sympathy with them, yet professionally restricted claims for himself, for his own life. *There*, was the theology to have come in! He should have explained, "the belief in a future state, with me, modifies every feeling derivable from this present life—I consider *that* as dependent on foregoing *this*—consequently, I may see that your principles are perfectly right and proper to be embraced as far as concerns this world, tho' I believe there is an *eventual* gain, to be obtained elsewhere, in either opposing or disregarding them,—in not availing myself of the advantages they procure"' (*LK* 579). Later still, when the play was in proof, after discussing an unidentified passage of pt. ii with EBB. in which she suggested making one of Ogniben's remarks into an aside, B., declining the suggestion, commented: 'if I make the speech an "aside," I *commit* Ogniben to that opinion' (7 Apr., *LK* 598). Of Chiappino, EBB. remarked that he 'is highly dramatic in that first part, & speaks so finely sometimes, that it is a wrench to one's sympathies to find him overthrown' (5 Apr., *LK* 589).

Part I.

Inside Luitolfo's *house at Faenza.*

Chiappino, Eulalia.

Eulalia. What is it keeps Luitolfo? Night's fast falling,
And 'twas scarce sunset . . . had the Ave-bell
Sounded before he sought the Provost's House?
I think not: all he had to say would take
5   Few minutes, such a very few, to say!

¶32. *Part I*] Act I (*1868-88*).
i *Opening s.d.*] *Inside* Luitolfo's *house at Faenza.*] Inside Luitolfo's house. (*1865-75*); Scene.—Inside Luitolfo's house. (*1888*).   *Luitolfo's*: this name occurs in *Verci* (i 60), one of B.'s major sources for *Sordello*.   *Faenza*: a town in northern Italy, south-east of Bologna. It was an independent commune in the 12th and 13th centuries; in the 14th it was ruled by the Manfredi family; it eventually became part of the Papal States, and was so still at the time B. wrote the play.
i 2. *Ave-bell*: the bell rung for Vespers, an early-evening service in the Catholic Church.
i 3. *Provost's*: translating It. 'preposto', an archaic term for the governor of a city or province.

How do you think, Chiappino? If our lord
The Provost were less friendly to your friend
Than everybody here professes him,
I should begin to tremble—should not you?
10   Why are you silent when so many times
I turn and speak to you?
    Chiappino.   That's good!
    Eulalia.   You laugh?
    Chiappino. Yes. I had fancied nothing that bears price
In the whole world was left to call my own,
And, may be, felt a little pride thereat:
15   Up to a single man's or woman's love,
Down to the right in my own flesh and blood,
There's nothing mine, I fancied,—till you spoke!
—Counting, you see, as "nothing" the permission
To study this peculiar lot of mine
20   In silence: well, go silence with the rest
Of the world's good! What can I say shall serve?
    Eulalia. This, lest you, even more than needs, embitter
Our parting: say your wrongs have cast, for once,
A cloud across your spirit!
    Chiappino.   How a cloud?
25   *Eulalia.* No man nor woman loves you, did you say?
    Chiappino. My God, were't not for thee!
    Eulalia.   Ay, God remains,
Even did Men forsake you.
    Chiappino.   Oh, not so!
Were't not for God, I mean, what hope of truth—
Speaking truth, hearing truth, would stay with Man?
30   I, now—the homeless, friendless, penniless,
Proscribed and exiled wretch who speak to you,
Ought to speak truth, yet could not, for my death,
(The thing that tempts me most) help speaking lies
About your friendship, and Luitolfo's courage,
35   And all our townsfolk's equanimity,—
Through sheer incompetence to rid myself
Of the old miserable lying trick
Caught from the liars I have lived with,—God,
Did I not turn to thee! It is thy prompting
40   I dare to be ashamed of, and thy counsel
Would die along my coward lip, I know—
But I do turn to thee! This craven tongue,

i *30. homeless, friendless, penniless,*] homeless friendless penniless (*1868-88*).
i *38-42.* Cp. (noting ll. 45-6) *Pauline* 822-30.

These features which refuse the soul its way,
Reclaim Thou! Give me truth—truth, power to speak
45   —And after be sole present to approve
The spoken truth!—or, stay, that spoken truth,
Who knows but you, too, might approve?
    Eulalia.   Ah, well—
Keep silence, then, Chiappino!
    Chiappino.   You would hear,
And shall now,—why the thing we're pleased to style
50   My gratitude to you and all your friends
For service done me, is just gratitude
So much as yours was service—and no more.
I was born here, so was Luitolfo,—both
At one time, much with the same circumstance
55   Of rank and wealth; and both, up to this night
Of parting company, have side by side
Still fared, he in the sunshine—I, the shadow:
"Why?" asks the world: "Because," replies the world
To its complacent self, "these playfellows,
60   Who took at church the holy-water drop
One from the other's finger, and so forth,—
Were of two moods: Luitolfo was the proper
Friend-making, everywhere friend-finding soul,
Fit for the sunshine, so it followed him;
65   A happy-tempered bringer of the best
Out of the worst; who bears with what's past cure
And puts so good a face on't—wisely passive
Where action's fruitless, while he remedies
In silence what the foolish rail against;
70   A man to smooth such natures as parade
Of opposition must exasperate—

i *45. be sole present*: 'be the only one there'.
i *49.*] You shall now,—why the thing we please to style (*1868-88*).
i *52. and no more*] no whit more (*1888*).
i *60-1*. The friends have shared the holy water with which Catholics make the sign of the cross on entering church, one dipping his fingers into the basin and the other content to take the 'holy-water drop' from him.
i *61. One*] Each (*1865-88*).
i *70-1*. Cp. to EBB., 18 Jan. 1846, speaking of a man 'whom it was to be death to oppose', who bullies his wife at a dinner-party, upon which 'the biggest, stupidest of the company, began to remark "what a fortunate thing it was that Mr So-&-so had such a submissive wife—not one of the women who would resist—that is, attempt to resist,—and so exasperate our gentleman into .. Heaven only knew what!"' (*LK* 399).

No general gauntlet-gatherer for the weak
Against the strong, yet over-scrupulous
At lucky junctures; one who won't forego
75   The after-battle work of binding wounds,
Because, forsooth, he'd have to bring himself
To side with their inflictors for their leave!"
—Why do you gaze, nor help me to repeat
What comes so glibly from the common mouth
80   About Luitolfo and his so-styled friend?
        Eulalia. Because that friend's sense is obscured . . .
        Chiappino.   I thought
You would be readier with the other half
Of the world's story,—my half!—Yet, 'tis true,
For all the world does say it! say your worst!
85   True, I thank God, I ever said "you sin,"
When a man did sin: if I could not say it,
I glared it at him,—if I could not glare it,
I prayed against him,—then my part seemed over;
God's may begin yet—so it will, I trust!
        Eulalia. If the world outraged you, did we?
90   *Chiappino.*   What's "me"
That you use well or ill? It's Man, in me,
All your successes are an outrage to,
You all, whom sunshine follows, as you say!

i 72-7. Luitolfo is not the sort of reformer who, though generally outspoken
on behalf of the oppressed, refuses to compromise when the opportunity
arises of doing something for them.
i *74. one who won't forego*] EBB. quoted 'One who dont forgo', and
commented: 'Strictly speaking, is not "doesn't" the right abbreviation for
only the *third* person? I don't—he doesn't—"who *wont* go" you might say
with accuracy perhaps'.
i *77. their inflictors*] wound-inflictors (*1863-88*).
i *85-9.* Cp. B. to Domett, 23 Nov. 1845, on the Puritan revolutionary John
Lilburne, who 'when pilloried, or carted rather, "did justify himself to all
men," whereon they gagged him and tied his hands lest he should gesticulate
and explain something by that; "yet did he protest against them by a
stamping with his feet," to the no small comfort of his stout heart, I warrant'
(*RB & AD* 118-19).
i *88-9. then . . . trust:* cp. B. to Julia Wedgwood (June 1864): 'nothing is to be
overleaped, the joy no more than the sorrow, and then, your part done,
God's may follow, and will, I trust' (*RB & JW* 36).
i *90. What's "me"*] EBB. quoted 'Who's "me"—', and commented: 'It sounds
awkward—"What's I"—yet I doubt altogether. . . . Would "What's 'me'"
sound less awkward: "What's 'me'?—*Its* man in me". Yes, I think it should
be "what" .. for the relation of the "It" afterwards'.

Here's our Faenza birthplace—they send here
95 A Provost from Ravenna—how he rules,
You can at times be eloquent about—
"Then, end his rule"! ah yes, one stroke does that!
But patience under wrong works slow and sure:
Must violence still bring peace forth? He, beside,
100 Returns so blandly one's obeisance—ah—
Some latent virtue may be lingering yet,
Some human sympathy which, once excite,
And all the lump were leavened quietly—
So, no more talk of striking for this time!
105 But I, as one of those he rules, won't bear
These pretty takings-up and layings-down
Our cause, just as you think occasion suits!
Enough of earnest, is there? You'll play, will you?
Diversify your tactics,—give submission,
110 Obsequiousness and flattery a turn,
While we die in our misery patient deaths?
We all are outraged then, and I the first!
I, for Mankind, resent each shrug and smirk,
Each beck and bend, each . . all you do and are,
I hate!
115   *Eulalia.* We share a common censure, then!
'Tis well you have not poor Luitolfo's part
Or mine to point out in the wide offence.
        Chiappino. Oh, shall I let you so escape me, Lady?
Come, on your own ground, Lady,—from yourself,
120 Leaving the people's wrong, which most is mine,
What have I got to be so grateful for?
These three last fines, no doubt, one on the other
Paid by Luitolfo?
        Eulalia.   Shame, Chiappino!
        Chiappino.   Shame
Fall presently on who deserves it most!
125 Which is to see: he paid my fines—my friend,
Your prosperous smooth husband presently,

i *103.* Cp. (also in the context of political or social change) *Prince Hohenstiel*
326-9: 'not by unperceived degrees / Nor play of elements already there, /
But quite new leaven, leavening the lump, / And liker, so, the natural
process'. The phrase is from *Galatians* v 9.
i *111.* Cp. *Sordello* v 249-52.
i *114. beck*: an obeisance, a bow. Only occurrence in this sense in B.
i *126. husband*] lover (*1863-88*).
i *126-7.* As the revs. make clear, B. at first intended 'presently' to apply to the
future: 'the man who is to become your husband . . . and who is now your

Then, scarce your wooer,—now your lover: well—
I loved you!
    Eulalia.   Hold!
    Chiappino.   You knew it, years ago;
When my voice faltered and my eyes grew dim
130   Because you gave me your silk mask to hold—
My voice that greatens when there's need to curse
The people's Provost to their heart's content,
—My eyes, the Provost, who bears all men's eyes,
Banishes now because he cannot bear!
135   You knew .. but you do your parts—my part, I!
So be it! you flourish—I decay! All's well!
    Eulalia. I hear this for the first time!
    Chiappino.   Oh, the fault was there?
Then my days spoke not and my nights of fire
Were voiceless? Then the very heart may burst
140   Yet all prove nought, because no mincing speech
Tells leisurely that thus it is and thus?
Eulalia—truce with toying for this once—
A banished fool, who troubles you to-night
For the last time—Oh, what's to fear from me?
You knew I loved you!
145   *Eulalia.*   Not so, on my faith!
You were my now-affianced lover's friend—
Came in, went out with him, could speak as he;
All praise your ready parts and pregnant wit;
See how your words come from you in a crowd!
150   Luitolfo's first to place you o'er himself
In all that challenges respect and love—
Yet you were silent then, who blame me now!
I say all this by fascination, sure—
I am all but wed to one I love, yet listen—
155   It must be, you are wronged, and that the wrongs
Luitolfo pities . . .
    Chiappino.   —You too pity? Do!

---

lover'. Presumably the sequence struck him as awkward, and 'presently' now
refers to the present: 'the man who is currently your lover . . . and who is
soon to be your husband'.

i *126. husband*] lover (*1863-88*).

i *127. now your lover*] soon, your husband (*1863-88*).

i *129, 133. my eyes . . . —My eyes*] my eye . . . —My eye (*1865-88*).

i *137. Oh, the fault was there?*] The fault's there? (*1863-88*).

i *142. truce with toying*: 'no beating about the bush'.

i *144. Oh*] why (*1863-88*).

i *154. I am all but wed*] I, all but wed (*1888*).

But hear first what my wrongs are; so began
This talk and so shall end this talk. I say,
Was't not enough that I must strive, I saw,
160   To grow so far familiar with your charms
As to contrive some way to win them—which
To do, an age seemed far too little—for, see!
We all aspire to Heaven—and there is Heaven
Above us—go there! Dare we go? no, surely!
165   How dare we go without a reverent pause,
A growing less unfit for Heaven?—Even so,
I dared not speak—the greater fool, it seems!
Was't not enough to struggle with such folly,
But I must have, beside, the very man
170   Whose slight, free, loose and incapacious soul
Gave his tongue scope to say whate'er he would
—Must have him load me with his benefits
For fortune's fiercest stroke!
    Eulalia.   Justice to him
That's now entreating, at his risk perhaps,
175   Justice for you! Did he once call those acts
Of simple friendship—bounties, benefits?
    Chiappino. No—the straight course had been to call
    them so—
Then, I had flung them back, and kept myself
Unhampered, free as he to win the prize
180   We both sought—but "the gold was dross," he said,
"He loved me, and I loved him not—to spurn
"A trifle out of superfluity:
"He had forgotten he had done as much"!
So had not I!—Henceforth, try as I could
185   To take him at his word, there stood by you

i *160-1.*] EBB. quoted 'To grow so far familiar with all you / As find & take some way to get you', and commented: 'There is something obscure, as it strikes me, in the expression of this— "As *to* find" seems necessary to the construction. But *"all you"* (besides) appears to lead the thought from Eulalia—& you mean Eulalia, .. I think. The reader will doubt here, & have first & second thoughts'.

i *161. As to*] As next (*1863-88*).

i *162. little*] brief (*1888*).

i *163. there is*] there lies (*1888*).

i *166. Even so*] Just so (*1888*).

i *170. slight, free,*] slight free (*1868-88*).

i *173. stroke!*] stroke? (*1863-88*).

i *177. so*] thus (*1888*).

i *181-2. to spurn . . . superfluity:*] why spurn . . . superfluity? (*1865-88*).

My benefactor—who might speak and laugh
And urge his nothings—even banter me
Before you—but my tongue was tied. A dream!
Let's wake: your husband . . . how you shake at that!
Good—my revenge!
190   *Eulalia.*   Why should I shake? what forced,
Or forces me to be Luitolfo's bride?
        Chiappino. There's my revenge, that nothing forces
        you!
No gratitude, no liking of the eye,
Nor longing of the heart, but the poor bond
195 Of habit—here so many times he came,
So much he spoke,—all these compose the tie
That pulls you from me! Well, he paid my fines,
Nor missed a cloak from wardrobe, dish from table—
—He spoke a good word to the Provost here—
200 Held me up when my fortunes fell away
—It had not looked so well to let me drop—
Men take pains to preserve a tree-stump, even,
Whose boughs they played beneath—much more a
        friend!
But one grows tired of seeing, after the first,
205 Pains spent upon impracticable stuff
Like me: I could not change—you know the rest.
I've spoke my mind too fully out, for once,
This morning to our Provost; so ere night
I leave the city on pain of death—and now
210 On my account there's gallant intercession
Goes forward—that's so graceful!—and anon
He'll noisily come back: the intercession
Was made and fails—all's over for us both—
'Tis vain contending—I had better go:
215 And I do go—and so to you he turns
Light of a load, and ease of that permits
His visage to repair its natural bland
Oeconomy, sore broken late to suit
My discontent: so all are pleased—you, with him,

---

i *198.*] EBB. quoted 'Nor missed a cloak from wardrobe, nor a dish from table', and commented: 'Why such a dragging line just here? An oversight probably—The second "*nor a*" might drop out to advantage'.

i *207. for once*] by chance (*1868-88*).

i *215. so to*] straight to (*1868-88*).

i *217. its*] the (*1868-88*).

i *218. Oeconomy*: make-up, constitution. Cp. *Colombe* iii 62, *Prince Hohenstiel* 355, and *George Bubb Dodington* 241-3.

220　He with himself, and all of you with me
　　　—Who, say the citizens, had done far better
　　　In letting people sleep upon their woes,
　　　If not possessed with talent to relieve them
　　　When once they woke;—but then I had, they'll say,
225　Doubtless some unknown compensating pride
　　　In what I did—and as I seem content
　　　With ruining myself, why so should they be,
　　　And so they are, and so be with his prize
　　　The devil when he gets them speedily!
230　Why does not your Luitolfo come? I long
　　　To don this cloak and take the Lugo path.
　　　It seems you never loved me, then?
　　　　　Eulalia.　　　　　　　　　　Chiappino!
　　　Chiappino. Never?
　　　　　Eulalia.　　　　　Never.
　　　Chiappino.　　　　　　That's sad—say what I might,
　　　There was no helping being sure this while
235　You loved me—love like mine must have return,
　　　I thought—no river starts but to some sea!
　　　And had you loved me, I could soon devise
　　　Some specious reason why you stifled love,
　　　Some fancied self-denial on your part
240　Which made you choose Luitolfo; so excepting
　　　From the wide condemnation of all here,
　　　One woman! Well, the other dream may break!
　　　If I knew any heart, as mine loved you,

i *224. they woke*] awake (*1868-88*).

i *231. Lugo*: a town approx. 17 km north of Ferrara.

i *234. helping being*] help from being (*1865-88*).

i *235-6.* Chiappino compares his love to a river, and the state of being loved in return to the sea to which it naturally flows. Cp. *Ecclesiastes* i 7: 'All the rivers run into the sea; yet the sea is not full; unto the place from whence the rivers come, thither they return again'.

i *243-6.* Cp. B. to EBB., 30 Aug. 1845: 'Let me say now—*this only once—* that I loved you from my soul, and gave you my life . . . and all that is *done*, not to be altered now: it was, in the nature of the proceeding, wholly independent of any return on your part' (*LK* 176). On 12 Nov. 1845 EBB. wrote to B. about a conversation she remembered on the subject of love: 'I took it into my head to say that the best [attachment] was where there was no cause at all for it, & the more wholly unreasonable, the better still, .. that the motive sh^d lie in the feeling itself & not in the object of it—& that the affection which could (if it could) throw itself out on an idiot with a goitre would be more admirable than Abelard's—Whereupon everybody laughed, & some one thought it affected of me & no true opinion, & others said plainly

Loved me, tho' in the vilest breast 'twere
  lodged,
245 I should, I think, be forced to love again—
Else there's no right nor reason in the world!
  Eulalia. "If you knew," say you,—but I did not
   know—
That's where you're blind, Chiappino! a disease
Which if I may remove, I'll not repent
250 The listening to: you cannot, will not, see
How, place you but in every circumstance
Of us, you are just now indignant at,
You'd be as we.
  Chiappino. I should be? .. that again!
I, to my Friend, my Country and my Love,
255 Be as Luitolfo and these Faentines?
  Eulalia. As we.
  Chiappino. Now I'll say something to remember!
I trust in Nature for the stable laws
Of Beauty and Utility—Spring shall plant,
And Autumn garner to the end of time:
260 I trust in God—the Right shall be the Right
And other than the Wrong while He endures—
I trust in my own soul that can perceive
The outward and the inward, nature's good
And God's—So—seeing these men and myself,
265 Having a right to speak, thus do I speak:
I'll not curse . . . God bears with them—well may I—
But I—protest against their claiming me!
I simply say, if that's allowable,
I would not . . broadly . . do as they have done—
270 —God curse this townful of born slaves, bred slaves,
Branded into the blood and bone slaves! Curse
Whoever loved, above his liberty,
House, land or life! and . . .
        [*A knocking without.*

---

that it was immoral, and somebody else hoped, in a sarcasm, that I meant to
act out my theory for the advantage of the world. To which I replied quite
gravely that I had not virtue enough' (*LK* 266). Cp. the late poem *Which?*
where the winner of the 'trial of who judged best / In esteeming the love of a
man' is the woman who chooses 'a wretch, / Mere losel in body and soul, /
Thrice accurst! What care I, so he stretch / Arms to me his sole saviour, love's
ultimate goal' (ll. 2-3, 19-22).
i *245. again*: in return.
i *272. loved*] loves (*1868-88*).

                 . . . Bless my hero-friend,
Luitolfo!
  Eulalia. How he knocks!
  Chiappino.   The peril, Lady!
275 "Chiappino, I have run a risk! My God!
  "How when I prayed the Provost—(he's my friend)—
  "To grant you a week's respite of his sentence
  "That confiscates your goods, and exiles you,
  "He shrugged his shoulder .. I say, shrugged it! Yes,
280 "And fright of that drove all else from my head.
  "Here's a good purse of *scudi*—off with you!
  "Lest of that shrug come—what God only knows!
  "The *scudi*—friend, they're trash—no thanks, I beg—
  "Take the North gate,—for San Vitale's suburb
285 "Whose double taxes you appealed against,
  "In discomposure at your ill-success
  "Is apt to stone you: there, there—only go!
  "Beside, Eulalia here looks sleepily—
  "Shake . . . oh, you hurt me, so you squeeze my
        wrist!"
290 —Is it not thus you'll speak, adventurous friend?
      [*As he opens the door,* Luitolfo *rushes in, his garments*
                            disordered.
  Eulalia. Luitolfo! Blood?
  Luitolfo.   There's more—and more of it!
Eulalia—take the garment .. no .. you, friend!
You take it and the blood from me—you dare!
  Eulalia. Oh, who has hurt you? where's the wound?
  Chiappino.   "Who," say you?

i *275. risk! My God!*] risk—a risk! (*1868-88*).
i *276. How*] For (*1868-88*).
i *277. his*] the (*1868-88*).
i *278. and exiles you*] exiles yourself (*1868-88*).
i *281. scudi*: the scudo was a silver coin, first struck by Charles V in Milan, and rapidly adopted by other Italian states. It was still circulating in the 19th century. It was occasionally struck in gold. A lady's ruff costs 13 scudi in *Andrea* 240.
i *283.* Cp. (noting 'purse', l. 281) *Othello* III iii 157: ' Who steals my purse steals trash'.
i *284. San Vitale's suburb*: a church of San Vitale is shown on the west side of Faenza, near the gate opening on the Imola road, in an 18th-century plan (*Novum Italiae Theatrum* [Paris 1724] vol. iii). Chiappino already intends to leave by the north gate, for Lugo: see ll. 231, 338-41. The 'San Vital' quarter of Ferrara in *Sordello* iv 96 is associated with 'Cino': see below, ll. 382-4.

295 The man with many a touch of virtue yet!
     The Provost's friend has proved too frank of speech
     And this comes of it. Miserable hound!
     This comes of temporizing, as I said!
     Here's fruit of your smooth speeches and fair looks!
300 Now see my way! As God lives, I go straight
     To the palace and do justice, once for all!
           Luitolfo. What says he?
           Chiappino.   I'll do justice on him!
           Luitolfo.   Him?
           Chiappino. The Provost.
           Luitolfo.   I've just killed him!
           Eulalia.   Oh, my God!
           Luitolfo. My friend, they're on my trace—they'll
               have me—now!
305 They're round him, busy with him: soon they'll find
     He's past their help, and then they'll be on me!
     Chiappino! save Eulalia .. I forget ..
     Were you not bound .. for ..
           Chiappino.   Lugo!
           Luitolfo.   Ah—yes—yes—
     That was the point I prayed of him to change.
310 Well—go—be happy .. is Eulalia safe?
     They're on me!
           Chiappino.   'Tis through me they reach you,
               then!
     Friend, seem the man you are! Lock arms—that's
         right.
     Now tell me what you've done; explain how you
     That still professed forbearance, still preached peace,
     Could bring yourself . . .
315   *Luitolfo.*   What was peace for, Chiappino?
     I tried peace—did that say that when peace failed
     Strife should not follow? All my peaceful days
     Were just the prelude to a day like this.
     I cried "You call me 'friend'—save my true friend!
     "Save him, or lose me!"
320   *Chiappino.*   But you never said
     You meant to tell the Provost thus and thus!
           Luitolfo. Why should I say it? What else did I mean?

i *295.* i.e. the Provost (see l. 101).
i *299. fair*] soft (*1868-88*).
i *304. on my trace:* cp. *Italy* 5.
i *308. Lugo!*] Lugo? (*1868-88*).
i *316. say that*] promise, (*1863-88*).

Chiappino. Well? He persisted?
Luitolfo.   . . Would so order it
You should not trouble him too soon again—
325 I saw a meaning in his eye and lip—
I poured my heart's store of indignant words
Out on him—then,—I know not.—He retorted—
And I .. some staff lay there to hand—I think
He bade his servants thrust me out—I struck—
330 .. Ah, they come! Fly you, save yourselves, you two!
The dead back-weight of the beheading axe!
The glowing trip-hook, thumbscrews and the gadge!
Eulalia. They do come! Torches in the Place!
     Farewell—
Chiappino! You can work no good to us—
335 Much to yourself; believe not all the world
Must needs be cursed henceforth!
     Chiappino.   And you?
     Eulalia.   I stay.
     Chiappino. Ha, ha! now listen! I am master here!
This was my coarse disguise—this paper shows
My path of flight and place of refuge—see—
340 Lugo—Argenta—past San Nicolo—
Ferrara, then to Venice and all's safe!
Put on the cloak! His people have to fetch
A compass round about.—There's time enough

i *332. trip-hook:* OED records this as a possible error (see 'gadge'); B. may
have been thinking of heated hooks drawn across the flesh of the
victim.   *gadge:* EBB., returning the proofs to B., thought this a mispr.
for 'gag' (5 Apr. 1846, *LK* 590-1); B. replied: 'gadge is a real name (in
Johnson, too) for a torturing iron' (6 Apr. 1846, *LK* 593-4). The word is not
in Johnson's *Dictionary,* and OED cites B.'s usage as a nonce-word. B.
commented further: 'it is part of the horror of such things that they should be
mysteriously named,—indefinitely . . . Besides, am I not a rhymester? Well,
who knows but one may want to use such a word in a couplet with
"*badge*"—which, if one reject the old & obsolete "*fadge*," is rhymeless'. Cp.
Childe Roland 200-4. With the whole line, cp. *Sordello* vi 768: 'Kings of the
gag and flesh-hook, screw and whip'; cp. also *Ring* i 979-1014.
i *333. Place:* square (from 'piazza').
i *340-1.* Chiappino's route would take him to Lugo, then to Argenta, a town
approx. 25 km north of Lugo, past San Nicolo, 15 km north-west of
Argenta, which is itself about 15 km from Ferrara. It is an unobtrusive
pointer to a historical, not contemporary, setting (see headnote, p. 181): in
the 16th century Venice was the bitter enemy of the Papacy, but in B.'s day
Chiappino would have been fleeing to the Austrian province of Lombardy-
Venetia.

Ere they can reach us—so you straightway make
345   For Lugo .. Nay, he hears not! On with it—
The cloak, Luitolfo, do you hear me? See—
He obeys he knows not how.—Then, if I must . . .
Answer me! Do you know the Lugo gate?
  Eulalia. The north-west gate, over the bridge!
  Luitolfo.   I know!
350 *Chiappino.* Well, there—you are not frightened? All
  my route
Is traced in that—at Venice you'll escape
Their power! Eulalia—I am master here!
  [*Shouts from without. He pushes out* Luitolfo, *who
         complies mechanically.*
In time! nay, help me with him—So!—he's gone.
  Eulalia. What have you done? On you, perchance
  all know
355   The Provost's hater, will men's vengeance fall
As our accomplice ..
  Chiappino.   Mere accomplice? See!
      [*Putting on* Luitolfo's *vest.*
Now, Lady, am I true to my profession,
Or one of these?
  Eulalia.   You take Luitolfo's place?
  Chiappino. Die for him!
  Eulalia.   Well done!
         [*Shouts increase.*
  Chiappino.   How the people tarry!
360   I can't be silent .. I must speak .. or sing—
How natural to sing now!
  Eulalia.   Hush and pray!
We are to die—but even I perceive
'Tis not a very hard thing so to die—
My cousin of the pale-blue tearful eyes,
365   Poor Cesca, suffers more from one day's life
With the stern husband; Tisbe's heart goes forth
Each evening after that wild son of hers,
To track his thoughtless footstep thro' the streets—
How easy for them both to die like this!
370   I am not sure that I could live as they.
  Chiappino. Here they come, crowds! They pass the
  gate? Yes!—No!—
One torch is in the court-yard. Here flock all!

i *351. you'll*] you (*1868-88*).
i *357-8. Now . . . these?*: i.e. 'am I true to my professed principle of conduct,
or am I like my fellow-citizens?'

Eulalia. At least Luitolfo has escaped!—What cries!
Chiappino. If they would drag one to the market-
place
One might speak there!
Eulalia.   List, list!
375   *Chiappino.*   They mount the steps!
                                        [*Enter the* Populace.
Chiappino. I killed the Provost!
The Populace, speaking together. 'Twas Chiappino,
friends!
Our saviour.—The best man at last as first!
He who first made us see what chains we wore,
He also strikes the blow that shatters them,
380   He at last saves us—our best citizen!
—Oh, have you only courage to speak now?
My eldest son was christened a year since
"Cino" to keep Chiappino's name in mind—
Cino, for shortness merely, you observe!
385   The City's in our hands.—The guards are fled—
Do you, the cause of all, come down—come down—
Come forth to counsel us, our chief, our king,
Whate'er rewards you! Choose your own reward!
The peril over, its reward begins!
390   Come and harangue us in the market-place!
        Eulalia. Chiappino!
        Chiappino.   Yes . . I understand your eyes!
You think I should have promptlier disowned
This deed with its strange unforeseen success
In favour of Luitolfo—but the peril,
395   So far from ended, hardly seems begun!
To-morrow, rather, when a calm succeeds,
We easily shall make him full amends:
And meantime . . if we save them as they pray,
And justify the deed by its effects?
400   *Eulalia.* You would, for worlds, you had denied at
once!
        Chiappino. I know my own intention, be assured!
All's well! Precede us, fellow-citizens!

---

i *378. see*] feel (*1868–88*).
i *381.* A member of the crowd turns on another who has just spoken.
i *382–4.* See l. 284n.
i *387. forth*] out (*1868–88*).
i *390.* Cp. *Julius Caesar* III, where speeches in the 'market-place' follow the
assassination of Caesar.
i *391. Chiappino!*] Chiappino? (*1868–88*).

Part II

The Market-place. Luitolfo *in disguise mingling with the*
Populace *assembled opposite the* Provost's *Palace.*

    1st Bystander. [*To* Luitolfo] You a friend of
Luitolfo's? Then your friend is vanished,—in all
probability killed on the night that his patron the
tyrannical Provost was loyally suppressed here,
5 exactly a month ago, by our illustrious fellow-citizen,
thrice-noble saviour, and new Provost that is like to
be this very morning,—Chiappino!
    Luitolfo. He the new Provost?
    2nd Bystander. Up those steps will he go, and
10 beneath yonder pillar stand, while Ogniben, the
Pope's Legate from Ravenna, reads the new
dignitary's title to the people, according to established
usage.—For which reason there is the assemblage you
inquire about.
15   *Luitolfo.* Chiappino—the old Provost's successor?
Impossible! But tell me of that presently—What I
would know first of all is, wherefore Luitolfo must so
necessarily have been killed on that memorable night?
    3rd Bystander. You were Luitolfo's friend? So was
20 I—Never, if you will credit me, did there exist so
poor-spirited a milk-sop! He, with all the opportunities in the world, furnished by daily converse with
our oppressor, would not stir a finger to help us: so
when Chiappino rose in solitary majesty and . . . . .
25 how does one go on saying? . . dealt the godlike
blow,—this Luitolfo, not unreasonably fearing the
indignation of an aroused and liberated people, fled
precipitately: he may have got trodden to death in the
press at the south-east gate when the Provost's guards
30 fled thro' it to Ravenna with their wounded master,—
if he did not rather hang himself under some hedge.

Part II] Act II (*1868-88*).
ii *Opening s.d.*] *The Market-place.*] Scene.—The Market-place. (*1888*).
ii *2. Luitolfo's?*] Luitolfo's! (*1849*).
ii *8. He*] not italic, *1865-88*.
ii *10-11. Ogniben, the Pope's Legate from Ravenna:* see below, l. 87ff., and cp.
Legate Montelungo in *Sordello* iv 284-9.
ii *13. usage*] custom (*1868-88*).
ii *15. old*] late (*1868-88*).
ii *23. so*] and, (*1863-88*).

Luitolfo. Or why not simply have lain *perdue* in
some quiet corner,—such as San Cassiano, where his
estate was,—receiving daily intelligence from some
35 sure friend, meanwhile, as to the turn matters were
taking here . . . how, for instance, the Provost was
not dead after all, only wounded . . or, as to-day's
news would seem to prove, how Chiappino was not
Brutus the Elder, after all, only the new Provost . .
40 and thus Luitolfo be enabled to watch a favourable
opportunity for returning—might it not have been
so?
   3rd Bystander. Why, he may have taken that care of
himself, certainly, for he came of a cautious stock.—
45 I'll tell you how his uncle, just such another gingerly
treader on tiptoes with finger on lip,—how he met
his death in the great plague-year: *dico vobis!* Hearing
that the seventeenth house in a certain street was
infected, he calculates to pass it in safety by taking
50 plentiful breath, say, when he shall arrive at the
eleventh house; then scouring by, holding that
breath, till he be got so far on the other side as
number twenty-three, and thus elude the danger.—
And so did he begin—but, as he arrived at thirteen,
55 we will say,—thinking to improve on his precaution
by putting up a little prayer to St. Nepomucene of
Prague, this exhausted so much of his lungs' reserve,
that at sixteen it was clean spent,—consequently at
the fatal seventeen he inhaled with a vigour and
60 persistence enough to suck you any latent venom out
of the heart of a stone—Ha, ha!
   Luitolfo. [*Aside*] (If I had not lent that man the
money he wanted last spring, I should fear this

---

ii *32. perdue*: hidden, lying in wait; cp. *Sordello* v 31-2, *Easter-Day* 402-3: 'a
closet where might keep / His watch perdue some murderer', and *Instans
Tyrannus* 18.

ii *39. Brutus the Elder*: Lucius Junius Brutus, said to have expelled the
Tarquins from Rome and founded a Republic in the 6th century BC; as
distinct from Marcus Brutus, who took part in the assassination of Julius
Caesar in 44 BC. Cp. *Sordello* iv 959-60 and *Pippa* iii 7.

ii *47. dico vobis*: I'm telling tell you (emphatic).

ii *51. scouring by*: hurrying by.

ii *56. St. Nepomucene of Prague*: the choice of this saint for a facetious allusion
may have been influenced by Coleridge in ch. iii of *Biographia Literaria*: 'it is
said that St Nepomuc was installed the guardian of bridges because he had
fallen over one and sunk out sight'.

65 bitterness was attributable to me.) Luitolfo is dead then, one may conclude!

3rd Bystander. Why, he had a house here, and a woman to whom he was affianced; and as they both pass naturally to the new Provost, his friend and heir . . .

70 *Luitolfo.* Ah, I suspected you of imposing on me with your pleasantry—I know Chiappino better!

1st Bystander. (Our friend has the bile! after all, I do not dislike finding somebody vary a little this general gape of admiration at Chiappino's glorious

75 qualities—.) Pray how much may you know of what has taken place in Faenza since that memorable night?

Luitolfo. It is most to the purpose that I know Chiappino to have been by profession a hater of that very office of Provost, you now charge him with

80 proposing to accept.

1st Bystander. Sir, I'll tell you. That night was indeed memorable—up we rose, a mass of us, men, women, children—out fled the guards with the body of the tyrant—we were to defy the world: but, next

85 grey morning, "what will Rome say," began everybody—(you know we are governed by Ravenna, which is governed by Rome). And quietly into the town by the Ravenna road comes on muleback a portly personage, Ogniben by name,

90 with the quality of Pontifical Legate—trots briskly thro' the streets humming a "*Cur fremuêre gentes*," and makes directly for the Provost's Palace—there it faces you—"One Messer Chiappino is your leader? I have known three-and-twenty leaders of revolts!" (laugh-

ii 72-5. *(Our friend . . . qualities—.)*: the 1st Bystander addresses Luitolfo in an aside about the 3rd ('Our friend').

ii 78. *by profession*: avowedly, according to his own statements. See i 357-8n.

ii 85-7. *"what will Rome say . . . Rome*: Faenza was part of the Papal States; it lies between Bologna and Ravenna. In Righi's *Annali* (see headnote, p. 181) the Papal Legate who recovers the town from the Venetians is from Bologna.

ii 91. *Cur fremuêre gentes*: properly 'Quare fremuere gentes', the opening of *Psalms* ii: 'Why do the heathen rage, and the people imagine a vain thing?' The Authorized Version gives 'tumultuously assemble' as a variant for 'rage'. In the Psalm, it is the 'kings of the earth . . . and the rulers' who are the rebels (against God); and 'He that sitteth in the heavens shall laugh: the Lord shall have them in derision' (vv. 2, 4).

ii 94-5. *(laughing gently to himself)*: in the proofs, this was mistakenly printed in italics as a stage-direction to the 1st Bystander, whereas it was intended, B.

95   ing gently to himself)—"Give me the help of your
     arm from my mule to yonder steps under the
     pillar—So! And now, my revolters and good friends,
     what do you want? The guards burst into Ravenna
     last night bearing your wounded Provost—and,
100 having had a little talk with him, I take on myself to
     come and try appease the disorderliness, before
     Rome, hearing of it, resorts to another method; 'tis I
     come, and not another, from a certain love I confess
     to, of composing differences. So, do you understand,
105 you are about to experience this unheard-of tyranny
     from me, that there shall be no heading nor hanging,
     no confiscation nor exile,—I insist on your simply
     pleasing yourselves,—and now pray what does please
     you? To live without any government at all? Or
110 having decided for one, to see its minister murdered
     by the first of your body that chooses to find himself
     wronged, or disposed for reverting to first principles
     and a Justice anterior to all institutions,—and so will
     you carry matters, that the rest of the world must at
115 length unite and put down such a den of wild beasts?
     As for vengeance on what has just taken place,—once
     for all, the wounded man assures me he cannot
     conjecture who struck him—and this so earnestly,
     that one may be sure he knows perfectly well what
120 intimate acquaintance could find admission to speak
     with him so late that evening—I come not for
     vengeance therefore, but from pure curiosity to hear
     what you will do next."—And thus ran he on easily
     and volubly, till he seemed to arrive quite naturally at
125 the praise of Law, Order and Paternal Government
     by somebody from rather a distance: all our citizens
     were in the snare, and about to be friends with so
     congenial an adviser; but that Chiappino suddenly
     stood forth, spoke out indignantly and set things
130 right again . . .
         Luitolfo. Do you see?—I recognise him there!

---

wrote to EBB., as 'characteristic' of Ogniben's speech: 'All these opinions
should be delivered "with a gentle laughter to himself"' (7 Apr. 1846, *LK*
598).
ii *106. heading*: beheading; considered a less ignoble form of punishment than
hanging, as in *Ring* i 124: 'heading or hanging as befitted ranks'.
ii *121. so late that*] late last (*1863-88*).
ii *123. ran he on*] he ran on, (*1849-65*); ran he on, on, (*1868-88*).

3rd Bystander. Ay, but mark you, at the end of
Chiappino's longest period in praise of a pure
Republic . . "And by whom do I desire such a
135 government should be administered, perhaps, but by
one like yourself?"—returns the Legate—thereupon
speaking, for a quarter of an hour together, on the
natural and only legitimate government by the Best
and Wisest—and it should seem there was soon
140 discovered to be no such vast discrepancy at bottom
between this and Chiappino's theory, place but each
in its proper light—"Oh, are you there?" quoth
Chiappino:—"In that, I agree," returns Chiappino,
and so on.
145   *Luitolfo.* But did Chiappino cede at once to this?
1st Bystander. Why, not altogether at once—for
instance, he said that the difference between him and
all his fellows was, that they seemed all wishing to be
kings in one or another way,—whereas what right,
150 asked he, has any man to wish to be superior to
another?—whereat, "Ah Sir," answers the Legate,
"this is the death of me, so often as I expect
something is really going to be revealed to us by you
clearer-seers, deeper-thinkers—this—that your right-
155 hand, (to speak by a figure) should be found taking
up the weapon it displayed so ostentatiously, not to
destroy any dragon in our path, as was prophesied,
but simply to cut off its own fellow left-hand—
yourself set about attacking yourself—for see now!
160 Here are you who, I make sure, glory exceedingly in
knowing the noble nature of the soul, its divine
impulses, and so forth; and with such a knowledge
you stand, as it were, armed to encounter the natural

ii *143.* "*In*] "Ay, in (*1868-88*).
ii *161. the noble nature of the soul*: from Seneca, *Epistolae Morales* XLIV, sect. v:
'Animus facit nobilem' [the soul alone renders us noble]. Cp. also Malvolio
in *Twelfth Night* IV ii 60: 'I think nobly of the soul'. B.'s letter to EBB. of ?18
July 1845, cited in the headnote to *Pictor* (p. 251), has the phrase 'thinks nobly
of the soul' (*LK* 128); the phrase appears again at the head of B.'s fair copy
(undated, but probably made after EBB.'s death) of Herrick's poem *Comfort
to a Youth that had lost his Love* to indicate his rejection of Herrick's view that
the dead take no further interest in their earthly loves: '("I think nobly of the
soul, and no way incline to his opinion"—Malvolio and RB)' (*ABL MS*).
ii *163-4. armed . . . fears*: cp. *Hamlet* III i 56ff.: 'Take arms / Against a sea of
troubles . . . The heart-ache and the thousand natural shocks / That flesh is
heir to'.

doubts and fears as to that same inherent nobility,
165   that are apt to waylay us the weaker ones in the road
of Life,—and when we look eagerly to see them fall
before you, lo, round you wheel, only the left hand
gets the blow; one proof of the soul's nobility
destroys simply another proof, quite as good, of the
170   same,—you are found delivering an opinion like this!
Why, what is this perpetual yearning to exceed, to
subdue, to be better than, and a king over, one's
fellows,—all that you so disclaim,—but the very
tendency yourself are most proud of, and under
175   another form, would oppose to it,—only in a lower
stage of manifestation? You don't want to be vulgarly
superior to your fellows after their poor fashion—to
have me hold solemnly up your gown's tail, or hand
you an express of the last importance from the Pope,
180   with all these bystanders noticing how unconcerned
you look the while—but neither does our gaping
friend, the burgess yonder, want the other kind of
kingship, that consists in understanding better than
his fellows this and similar points of human nature,
185   nor to roll under the tongue this sweeter morsel still,
the feeling that, thro' immense philosophy, he does
not feel, he rather thinks, above you and me!"—And
so chatting they glided off arm in arm.
       Luitolfo. And the result is . .
190   *1st Bystander.* Why, that a month having gone by,
the indomitable Chiappino, marrying as he will
Luitolfo's love—at all events succeeding to Luitolfo's
goods,—becomes the first inhabitant of Faenza, and a
proper aspirant to the Provostship—which we
195   assemble here to see conferred on him this morning.
The Legate's Guard to clear the way! He will follow
presently!
       Luitolfo. [*Withdrawing a little*] I understand the drift
of Eulalia's communications less than ever—yet she
200   surely said, in so many words, that Chiappino was in

ii *165. that*] which (*1870-88*).

ii *170. same,—you*] same, for you (*1868-88*).

ii *177-81. to have . . . the while*: cp. the description of Taurello Salinguerra,
Sordello i 286-9.

ii *185. the tongue*] his tongue (*1863-88*).

ii *187. he rather thinks*: i.e. 'on balance', 'after considering the matter'.

ii *193. goods*] wealth (*1868-88*).

urgent danger,—wherefore, disregarding her injunctions to continue in my retreat and wait the result
of, what she called, some experiment yet in process—
I hastened here without her leave or knowledge—
205 what could I else?—Yet if what they say be true . . if
it were for such a purpose, she and Chiappino kept
me away . . . Oh, no, no! I must confront him and
her before I believe this of them—and at the word,
see!
                              [*Enter* Chiappino *and* Eulalia.
210   *Eulalia.* We part here, then? The change in your
principles would seem to be complete!
        Chiappino. Now, why refuse to see that in my
present course I change no principles, only re-adapt
them and more adroitly? I had despaired of what you
215 may call the material instrumentality of Life; of ever
being able to rightly operate on mankind thro' such a
deranged machinery as the existing modes of
government—but now, if I suddenly discover how to
inform these perverted institutions with fresh
220 purpose, bring the functionary limbs once more into
immediate communication with, and subjection to
the soul I am about to bestow on them . . . do you
see? Why should one desire to invent, so long as it
remains possible to renew and transform? When all
225 further hope of the old organization shall be extinct,
then, I grant you, it will be time to try and create
another.
        Eulalia. And there being discoverable some hope
yet in the hitherto much-abused old system of
230 absolute government by a Provost here, you mean to

ii *201-2. injunctions*] injunction (*1863-88*).
ii *205. what could I*] how could I (*1888*).   *Yet*] But (*1863-88*).   *what*]
this (*1868-88*).
ii *210-85. We part here . . . so we perform*: cp. *Pauline* 458-61: 'First went my
hopes of perfecting mankind, / And faith in them—then freedom in itself, /
And virtue in itself—and then my motives' ends, / And powers and loves;
and human love went last'. Chiappino's position resembles that of Sordello
when he is offered the leadership of the Ghibellin party, and, like Sordello, he
articulates his ideas in an extended architectural metaphor (see *Sordello* v and
vi). Chiappino's self-justification anticipates that of the Prince in *Prince
Hohenstiel*: 'I like to use the thing I find, / Rather than strive at unfound
novelty: / I make the best of the old, nor try for new . . . Our time requires
. . . No fresh force till the old have spent itself' (ll. 266-8, 352-5).
ii *226. will*] may (*1863-88*).

take your time about endeavouring to realize those
visions of a perfect State, we once heard of?

   Chiappino. Say, I would fain realize my conception
of a Palace, for instance, and that there is, ab-
235 stractedly, but a single way of erecting one perfectly;
here, in the market-place is my allotted building-
ground; here I stand without a stone to lay, or a
labourer to help me,—stand, too, during a short day
of life, close on which the night comes. On the other
240 hand, circumstances suddenly offer me . . turn and
see it . . the old Provost's House to experiment
upon—ruinous, if you please, wrongly constructed at
the beginning, and ready to tumble now—but
materials abound, a crowd of workmen offer their
245 services; here, exists yet a Hall of Audience of
originally noble proportions, there, a Guest-chamber
of symmetrical design enough; and I may restore,
enlarge, abolish or unite these to heart's content—
ought I not rather make the best of such an
250 opportunity, than continue to gaze disconsolately
with folded arms on the flat pavement here, while the
sun goes slowly down, never to rise again? But you
cannot understand this nor me: it is better we should
part as you desire.

255   *Eulalia.* So the love breaks away too!

   Chiappino. No, rather my soul's capacity for love
widens—needs more than one object to content
it,—and, being better instructed, will not persist in
seeing all the component parts of love in what is only
260 a single part,—nor in finding the so many and so
various loves, united in the love of a woman,—

---

ii *238-9. a short day . . . night comes*: from *John* ix 4 (a favourite text of B.'s): 'I
must work the works of him that sent me, while it is day: the night cometh,
when no man can work'. B. wrote to EBB. about Harriet Martineau: 'if she
realises a very ordinary scheme of literary life, planned under the eye of God
not "the public," and prosecuted under the constant sense of the Night's
coming which ends it good or bad' (15 Feb. 1846, *LK* 465). Note also the
morning-to-night structure of *Pippa*, *Colombe*, and *Luria*.
ii *249. not rather*] not (*1865-88*).
ii *250. than*] rather than (*1865-88*).
ii *252. But*] Since (*1863-88*).
ii *256-68. No, rather . . . What do I lose*: cp. Schramm's speech in *Pippa* i 339-
50.
ii *260-1. the . . . loves,*] that . . . loves are (*1868-88*).

finding all uses in one instrument, as the savage has
his sword, sceptre and idol, all in one club-stick.
Love is a very compound thing. I shall give the
265   intellectual part of my love to Men, the mighty dead,
or illustrious living; and determine to call a mere
sensual instinct by as few fine names as possible.
What do I lose?

Eulalia. Nay, I only think, what do I lose! and, one
270   more word—which shall complete my instruction—
does Friendship go too?—What of Luitolfo—the
author of your present prosperity?—

Chiappino. How the author?—

Eulalia. That blow now called yours . . .

275   *Chiappino.* Struck without principle or purpose, as
by a blind natural operation—and to which all my
thoughts and life directly and advisedly tended. I
would have struck it, and could not. He would have
done his utmost to avoid striking it, yet did so. I
280   dispute his right to that deed of mine—a final action
with him, from the first effect of which he fled
away—a mere first step with me, on which I base a
whole mighty superstructure of good to follow.
Could he get good from it?

285   *Eulalia.* So we profess, so we perform!
                    [*Enter* Ogniben. Eulalia *stands apart.*

Ogniben. I have seen three-and-twenty leaders of
revolts!—By your leave, Sir! Perform? What does the
lady say of Performing?

Chiappino. Only the trite saying, that we must not
290   trust Profession, only Performance.

Ogniben. She'll not say that, Sir, when she knows
you longer; you'll instruct her better. Ever judge of

ii *262. finding all*] manifold (*1863-88*).

ii *263. sword,*] sword, staff, (*1888*).

ii *264-6. I . . . living*] The intellectual part of my love I shall give to men, the
mighty dead or the illustrious living (*1868-88*), see *Paracelsus* i 409n.

ii *269. lose!*] emended in agreement with *1849* from 'love!' in *1846*; *1863-88*
have 'lose?'

ii *274-84.* Cp. *Return of the Druses* iv 29, where Anael, who has just killed the
Prefect, says: 'Djabal, 'tis thy deed!'

ii *276-7. and . . . thoughts*] yet . . . thought (*1863-88*).

ii *292-301. Ever judge . . . nor will be:* cp. *Saul* (*1855*) 295: "tis not what man
Does which exalts him, but what man Would do!', and *Apollo* 211-13:
'Manhood—the actual? Nay, praise the potential! . . . What *is?* No, what *may*
be—sing! that's Man's essential!' B. wrote to EBB. on the day of their

men by their professions! For tho' the bright moment
of promising is but a moment and cannot be
295 prolonged, yet, if sincere in its moment's extravagant
goodness, why, trust it and know the man by it, I
say—not by his performance—which is half the
world's work, interfere as the world needs must with
its accidents and circumstances,—the profession was
300 purely the man's own! I judge people by what they
might be,—not are, nor will be.
    Chiappino. But have there not been found, too,
performing natures, not merely promising?
    Ogniben. Plenty: little Bindo of our town, for
305 instance, promised his friend, great ugly Masaccio,
once, "I will repay you"!—for a favour done him: so
when his father came to die and Bindo succeeded to
the inheritance, he sends straightway for Masaccio
and shares all with him; gives him half the land, half
310 the money, half the kegs of wine in the cellar.
"Good," say you—and it is good: but had little Bindo
found himself possessor of all this wealth some five
years before—on the happy night when Masaccio
procured him that interview in the garden with his
315 pretty cousin Lisa—instead of being the beggar he
then was,—I am bound to believe that in the warm
moment of promise he would have given away all the
wine-kegs, and all the money, and all the land, and
only reserved to himself some hut on a hill-top hard
320 by, whence he might spend his life in looking and
seeing his friend enjoy himself: he meant fully that
much, but the world interfered!—To our business—
did I understand you just now within-doors? You are
not going to marry your old friend's love, after all?
325   *Chiappino.* I must have a woman that can

marriage (12 Sept. 1846): 'I could wish the past were to do over again, that in
it I might somewhat more,—never so little more, conform in the outward
homage to the inward feeling: what I have professed .. (for I have performed
nothing—) seems to fall short of what my first love required even' (*LK* 1062).
ii *325-54. I must have a woman . . . put your foot to her lips:* cp. B. to EBB. on
'the point I have all along been honestly earnest to set you right upon—my
real inferiority to you' (24 May 1845, *LK* 74), and EBB. to B.: 'Always I
know, my beloved, that I am unworthy of your love in a hundred ways—yet
I do hold fast my sense of advantage in one,— .. that, as far as I can see, I see
after you .. understand you, divine you .. call you by your right name' (12
Aug. 1846, *LK* 958). The topic is central to B.'s early writing about love

sympathize with and appreciate me, I told you.

    Ogniben. Oh, I remember! you, the greater nature,
needs must have a lesser one (—avowedly lesser—
contest with you on that score would never do!)—
330 such a nature must comprehend you, as the phrase is,
accompany and testify of your greatness from point
to point onward: why, that were being not merely as
great as yourself, but greater considerably! Meantime,
might not the more bounded nature as reasonably
335 count on your appreciation of it, rather?—on your
keeping close by it, so far as you both go together,
and then going on by yourself as far as you please? So
God serves us!

    Chiappino. And yet a woman that could understand
340 the whole of me, to whom I could reveal alike the
strength and the weakness—

    Ogniben. Ah, my friend, wish for nothing so
foolish! Worship your love, give her the best of you
to see; be to her like the Western Lands (they bring us
345 such strange news of) to the Spanish Court—send her
only your lumps of gold, fans of feathers, your spirit-
like birds, and fruits and gems—so shall you, what is
unseen of you, be supposed altogether a Paradise by
her,—as these Western lands by Spain—tho' I warrant
350 there is filth, red baboons, ugly reptiles and squalor
enough, which they bring Spain as few samples of as
possible. Do you want your mistress to respect your
body generally? Offer her your mouth to kiss—don't
strip off your boot and put your foot to her lips! You
355 understand my humour by this time? I help men to

---

relationships; cp. e.g. *Pippa* ii 213-15: 'whosoever loves / Must be in some
sort god or worshipper, / The blessing, or the blest one'.

ii *344. the Western Lands*: Ogniben refers to recent voyages of exploration by
Columbus (1492) and others. One of the few indications of the play's
historical setting (see headnote, p. 181).

ii *354-8. You understand . . . make ten*: in a letter to EBB. of 18 Mar. 1846, B.
wrote that he had 'cut out a huge kind of sermon' by Ogniben (*LK* 546); for
his further comments, see headnote, p. 182. It is difficult to fit the 'sermon'
into the existing text. But Ogniben's comment here (which he echoes at
ll. 466-8 and 516-17 below) may be one of the 'few phrases' which B. added
to pt. ii in order, he told EBB., to 'give a little more insight as to his
character' (1 Apr. 1846, *LK* 579).

ii *355. humour*: temperament, disposition (with a pun on 'sense of humour').

carry out their own principle: if they please to say
two and two make five, I assent, if they will but go
on and say four and four make ten!

    Chiappino. But these are my private affairs—what I
360 desire you to occupy yourself about, is my public
appearance presently: for when the people hear that I
am appointed Provost, tho' you and I may thoroughly
discern—and easily too—the right principle at bottom
of such a movement, and how my republicanism
365 remains thoroughly unaltered, only takes a form of
expression hitherto commonly judged . . and heretofore by myself . . incompatible with its existence . .
when thus I reconcile myself to an old form of
government instead of proposing a new one . . .
370   *Ogniben.* Why, you must deal with people broadly.
Begin at a distance from this matter and say,—new
truths, old truths! why there is nothing new possible
to be revealed to us in the moral world—we know all
we shall ever know, and it is for simply reminding us,
375 by their various respective expedients, how we do
know this and the other matter, that men get called
prophets, poets and the like: a philosopher's life is
spent in discovering that, of the half-dozen truths he
knew when a child, such an one is a lie, as the world
380 states it in set terms; and then, after a weary lapse of

---

ii *356. principle*] principles (*1863-88*).

ii *370-404. Why, you must deal . . . say you*: Ogniben puts forward (in ironic
'justification' of Chiappino) a number of philosophical commonplaces,
several of which are treated in earnest elsewhere in B. The notion that genius
is not original comes both from the Bible (*Ecclesiastes* i 9: 'The thing that hath
been, it is that which shall be; and that which is done is that which shall be
done: and there is no new thing under the sun') and from Plato's theory of
knowledge as recollection (*Phaedo* xviii); cp. *Mr. Sludge* 1351-3: 'Your so-
styled great men, / Do they accept one truth as truth is found, / Or try their
skill at tinkering?' With the idea that 'There is Truth in Falsehood, Falsehood
in Truth', cp. e.g. Pascal, *Pensées* I ix 63: 'Chaque chose est vrai en partie, et
fausse en partie' [Each thing is partly true, and partly false]; this forms the
starting-point for B.'s defence of Chatterton (see Appendix C, p. 476) and for
the composition of *Ring* (see bk. i); cp. also, among many other passages, *Mr.
Sludge* 1461-2: '"How many lies did it require to make / The portly truth you
here present us with?"' B. wrote to EBB. of the 'law by which opposite ideas
suggest opposite, and contrary images come together' (27 Jan. 1845, *LK* 11);
he may also have known Blake's axiom, from *The Marriage of Heaven and
Hell*, that 'Without contraries is no progression'.

ii *372. why*] sirs, (*1863-88*).

years, and plenty of hard thinking, it becomes a truth
again after all, as he happens to newly consider it and
view it in a different relation with the others—and so
he restates it, to the confusion of somebody else in
385   good time.—As for adding to the original stock of
truths,—impossible!—So you see the expression of
them is the grand business:—you have got a truth in
your head about the right way of governing people,
and you took a mode of expressing it—which now
390   you confess to be imperfect—but what then? There is
Truth in Falsehood, Falsehood in Truth.—No man
ever told one great truth, that I know, without the
help of a good dozen of lies at least, generally
unconscious ones: and as when a child comes in
395   breathlessly and relates a strange story, you try to
conjecture from the very falsities in it, what the reality
was,—do not conclude that he saw nothing in the sky,
because he assuredly did not see a flying horse there as
he says,—so, thro' the contradictory expression, do
400   you see, men should look painfully for, and trust to
arrive eventually at, what you call the true principle at
bottom. Ah, what an answer is there! to what will it
not prove applicable!—"Contradictions?"—Of course
there were, say you!
405   *Chiappino.* Still the world at large may call it
inconsistency, and what shall I say in reply?
        Ogniben. Why look you, when they tax you with
tergiversation or duplicity, you may answer—you
begin to perceive that, when all's done and said, both
410   great parties in the state, the advocators of change in
the present system of things, and the opponents of it,
patriot and anti-patriot, are found working together
for the common good, and that in the midst of their
efforts for and against its progress, the world some-
415   how or other still advances—to which result they
contribute in equal proportions, those who spent their
life in pushing it onward as those who gave theirs to
the business of pulling it back—now, if you found the
world stand still between the opposite forces, and were

ii *394-9. as when a child . . . as he says*: it seems probable that, as Kintner
suggests, B. used this image at his first meeting with EBB. to allude to the
fanciful rumours which circulated about her seclusion in Wimpole Street (see
EBB.'s letter of 29 Mar. 1846, *LK* 570 and 571 n.4).
ii *406. say in reply*] urge in reply (*1863-88*).
ii *416-17. spent . . . gave*] spend . . . give (*1868-88*).

420   glad, I should conceive you—but it steadily advances,
you rejoice to see! By the side of such a rejoicer, the
man who only winks as he keeps cunning and quiet,
and says, "Let yonder hot-headed fellow fight out my
battle; I, for one, shall win in the end by the blows he
425   gives, and which I ought to be giving"—even he seems
graceful in his avowal, when one considers that he
might say, "I shall win quite as much by the blows our
antagonist gives him, and from which he saves me—I
thank the antagonist equally!" Moreover, you must
430   enlarge on the loss of the edge of party-animosity with
age and experience—
        Chiappino. And naturally time must wear off such
asperities—the bitterest adversaries get to discover
certain points of similarity between each other,
435   common sympathies—do they not?
        Ogniben. Ay, had the young David but sate first to
dine on his cheeses with the Philistine, he had soon discovered an abundance of such common sympathies—
He of Gath, it is recorded, was born of a Father and
440   Mother, had brothers and sisters like another man,—
they, no more than the sons of Jesse, were used to eat
each other; but, for the sake of one broad antipathy that
had existed from the beginning, David slung the
stone, cut off the giant's head, made a spoil of it, and
445   after ate his cheeses alone with the better appetite for
all I can learn. My friend, as you, with a quickened
eyesight, go on discovering much good on the worse
side, remember that the same process should proportionably magnify and demonstrate to you the
450   much more good on the better side—and when I
profess no sympathy for the Goliahs of our time, and
you object that a large nature should sympathize with
every form of intelligence, and see the good in it,
however limited—I answer, so I do—but preserve the
455   proportions of my sympathy, however finelier or
widelier I may extend its action. I desire to be able,
with a quickened eyesight, to descry beauty in

---

ii *428. and from which*] blows from which (*1868-88*).

ii *429. you must*] you may (*1868-88*).

ii *436-46. Ay . . . learn*: the story of David and Goliath is told in *1 Samuel*
xvii. The cheeses were a present from David's father Jesse to the captain of
the troop in which David's brothers were serving. Goliath's four brothers,
'born to the giant in Gath', are mentioned in *2 Samuel* xxi 15-22.

ii *451. Goliahs*] Goliaths (*1875-88*). The original spelling is a common variant.

corruption where others see foulness only,—but I
hope I shall also continue to see a redoubled beauty in
460   the higher forms, where already every body sees no
foulness at all. I must retain too my old power of
selection, and choice of appropriation, to apply to such
new gifts . . else they only dazzle instead of enlighten-
ing me. God has his Archangels and consorts with
465   them—tho' he made too, and intimately sees what is
good in the worm. Observe, I speak only as you
profess to think and so ought to speak—I do justice to
your own principles, that is all.

Chiappino. But you very well know that the two
470   parties do, on occasion, assume each other's characteristics: what more disgusting, for instance, than to see
how promptly the newly emancipated slave will
adopt, in his own favour, the very measures of
precaution, which pressed soreliest on himself as
475   institutions of the tyranny he has just escaped from.—
Do the classes, hitherto without opinion, get leave to
express it? there is a confederacy immediately, from
which—exercise your individual right and dissent, and
woe be to you!

480   *Ogniben.* And a journey over the sea to you!—That
is the generous way. Say—emancipated slaves, the
first excess, and off I go! The first time a poor devil,
who has been bastinadoed steadily his whole life long,
finds himself let alone and able to legislate, so begins
485   pettishly while he rubs his soles, "Woe be to whoever
brings any thing in the shape of a stick this way,"—
you, rather than give up the very innocent pleasure of
carrying one to switch flies with,—you, go away to
every body's sorrow! Yet you were quite reconciled to
490   staying at home while the governors used to pass,
every now and then, some such edict as "Let no man
indulge in owning a stick which is not thick enough to
chastise our slaves if need require." Well—there are

---

ii *460. forms*] forms of matter (*1849-88*).

ii *464-6. God . . . worm*: cp. *Christmas-Eve* 285: 'the loving worm within its
clod', and *La Saisiaz* 316: 'the making of the worm there in yon clod its
tenement'. Cp. also *Sordello* i 543-6. For a different emphasis, cp. *Mr. Sludge*
1075-1127.

ii *477. there is a confederacy*] there follows a confederacy (*1868-88*).

ii *480. a journey over the sea*: i.e. self-imposed exile.

ii *481. Say*] Cry (*1863-88*).

ii *483. bastinadoed*: beaten on the soles of the feet.

495 pre-ordained hierarchies among us, and a profane
vulgar subjected to a different law altogether—yet I
am rather sorry you should see it so clearly—for, do
you know what is to . . all but save you at the Day of
Judgment, all you Men of Genius? It is this—that,
while you generally began by pulling down God, and
500 went on to the end of your life, in one effort at setting
up your own Genius in his place,—still, the last,
bitterest concession wrung with the utmost unwilling-
ness from the experience of the very loftiest of you,
was invariably . . would one think it? . . that the rest
505 of mankind, down to the lowest of the mass, was not,
nor ever could be, just on a level of equality with
yourselves.—That will be a point in the favour of all
such, I hope and believe!
 Chiappino. Why, men of genius are usually charged,
510 I think, with doing just the reverse, and at once
acknowledging the natural inequality of mankind by
themselves participating in the universal craving after,
and deference to the civil distinctions which represent
it. You wonder they pay such undue respect to titles
515 and badges of superior rank!
 Ogniben. Not I! (always on your own ground and
showing, be it noted!) Who doubts that, with a
weapon to brandish, a man is the more formidable?
Titles and badges are exercised as such a weapon, to
520 which you and I look up wistfully.—We could pin
lions with it moreover, while in its present owner's
hands it hardly prods rats. Nay, better than a mere
weapon of easy mastery and obvious use, it is a
mysterious divining rod that may serve you in
525 undreamed-of ways.—Beauty, Strength, Intellect—
men often have none of these and yet conceive pretty
accurately what kind of advantages they would bestow

ii *505-6. was . . . be*] stood . . . stand (*1863-88*).

ii *509-14. Why, men of genius . . . represent it*: paraphrasing this passage for
EBB., B. wrote: 'Chiappino remarks that men of genius usually do the
reverse .. of beginning by dethroning etc. and so arriving with utmost
reluctancy at the acknowledgment of a natural and unalterable *inequality* of
Mankind, instead of *that*, they begin *at once*, he says, by recognizing it in their
adulation &c &c—I have supplied the word "*at once*," and taken out
"virtually," which was unnecessary; so that the parallel possibly reads
clearlier' (6 Apr. 1846, *LK* 594). 'Virtually' presumably formed part of the
phrase 'doing just the reverse'.

ii *524. serve you*] serve us (*1863-88*).

on the possessor.—You know at least what it is you
make up your mind to forego, and so can apply the
530   fittest substitute in your power; wanting Beauty, you
cultivate Good Humour, missing Wit, you get Riches;
but the mystic unimaginable operation of that gold
collar and string of Latin names which suddenly
turned poor stupid little peevish Cecco of our own
535   town into natural Lord of the best of us—a Duke, he is
now! there indeed is a Virtue to be reverenced!

    Chiappino. Ay, by the vulgar—not by Messere
Stiatta the poet, who pays more assiduous court to
him than any body.

540   *Ogniben.* What else should Stiatta pay court to? He
has talent, not honor and riches—men naturally covet
what they have not.

    Chiappino. No—or Cecco would covet talent
which he has not, whereas he covets more riches, of
545   which he has plenty already.

    Ogniben. Because a purse added to a purse makes
the holder twice as rich—but just such another talent
as Stiatta's, added to what he now possesses, what
would that profit him? Give the talent a purse indeed,
550   to do something with! But lo, how we keep the good
people waiting. I only desired to do justice to the
noble sentiments which animate you, and which you
are too modest to duly enforce. Come, to our main
business: shall we ascend the steps? I am going to
555   propose you for Provost to the people; they know
your antecedents and will accept you with a joyful
unanimity: whereon I confirm their choice. Rouse up!
you are nerving yourself to an effort? Beware the
disaster of Messere Stiatta we were talking of—who
560   determining to keep an equal mind and constant face
on whatever might be the fortune of his last new
tragedy with our townsmen,—heard too plainly
"hiss, hiss, hiss," increase every moment, till at last
the man fell senseless—not perceiving that the
565   portentous sounds had all the while been issuing from
between his own nobly clenched teeth, and nostrils
narrowed by resolve!

    Chiappino. Do you begin to throw off the mask?
to jest with me, having got me effectually into your
570   trap?

ii *528-31. You . . . you . . . your . . . your . . . you . . . you*] We . . . we . . .
our . . . our . . . we . . . we (*1863-88*).

Ogniben. Where is the trap, my friend? You hear
what I engage to do, for my part—you, for yours,
have only to fulfil your promise made just now
within doors, of professing unlimited obedience to
575   Rome's authority in my person—and I shall authorize
no more than the simple re-establishment of the
Provostship and the conferment of its privileges upon
yourself—the only novel stipulation being a birth of
the peculiar circumstances of the time.
580   *Chiappino*. And that stipulation?
Ogniben. Oh, the obvious one—that in the event of
the discovery of the actual assailant of the late
Provost . . .
Chiappino. Ha!
585   *Ogniben*. Why, he shall suffer the proper penalty, of
course; what did you expect?
Chiappino. Who heard of this?
Ogniben. Rather who needed to hear of this?
Chiappino. Can it be, the popular rumour never
590   reached you . . .
Ogniben. Many more such rumours reach me,
friend, than I choose to receive: those which wait
longest have best chance—has the present one
sufficiently waited? Now is its time for entry with
595   effect. See the good people crowded about yonder
palace-steps which we may not have to ascend after
all!—my good friends—(nay, two or three of you will

ii *580-95. And that stipulation? . . . entry with effect*: the 'popular rumour' of
l. *589* is that Chiappino *was* the assailant. He says 'Who heard of this'—i.e.
that he was *not* the assailant. Ogniben replies that he deduced it for himself (in
line with his previous hint that he guessed the Provost to be shielding an
'intimate acquaintance', ll. 117-21 above). Chiappino thought that Ogniben
must have heard the 'popular rumour' and decided to take no action.
Ogniben had indeed heard the rumour, but had delayed acknowledging it in
order to engineer Chiappino's downfall. Ogniben knows that the Faentines
all believe Chiappino to be their liberator, and that Chiappino's change of
political allegiance, and acceptance of the Provostship, depends for its success
on his fellow-citizens continuing to believe this. When Ogniben proclaims
that Chiappino seeks justice on the assailant of his predecessor (ll. 597-602),
he destroys Chiappino's credibility, as has all along been his intention. 'Now
is its time for entry with effect' may be paraphrased: 'Now is the time when I
admit [to you] that I knew of the rumour that you were the assailant; and I
am going to use it against you, by pretending [to the citizens] that I know
nothing about it'.
ii *581. Oh,*] Just (*1863-88*).

answer every purpose)—who was it fell upon and
proved nearly the death of your late Provost?—his
600 successor desires to hear, that his day of inauguration
may be graced by the act of prompt, bare justice we
all anticipate? Who dealt the blow that night, does
anybody know?
      Luitolfo. [*Coming forward*] I!
605   *All.* Luitolfo!
      Luitolfo. I avow the deed, justify and approve it,
and stand forth now to relieve my friend of an
unearned responsibility.—Having taken thought, I
am grown stronger—I shall shrink from nothing that
610 awaits me. Nay, Chiappino—we are friends still—I
dare say there is some proof of your superior nature
in this starting aside, strange as it seems at first. So
they tell me my horse is of the right stock, because a
shadow in the path frightens him into a frenzy, makes
615 him dash my brains out. I understand only the dull
mule's way of standing stockishly, plodding soberly,
suffering on occasion a blow or two with due
patience.
      Eulalia. I was determined to justify my choice,
620 Chiappino; to let Luitolfo's nature vindicate itself.
Henceforth we are undivided, whatever be our
fortune.
      Ogniben. Now, in these last ten minutes of silence,
what have I been doing, deem you? Putting the
625 finishing stroke to a homily of mine I have long taken
thought to perfect, on the text "Let whoso thinketh
he standeth take heed lest he fall." To your house,
Luitolfo.—Still silent, my patriotic friend? Well, that
is a good sign! And you will go aside for a
630 time? That is better still. I understand—it would be
easy for you to die of remorse here on the spot, and
shock us all, but you will live and grow worthy of
coming back to us one day. There, I will tell every

---

ii *612. seems*] seemed (*1863-88*).

ii *626-7. Let . . . fall: 1 Corinthians* x 12. Note also the next verse: 'There
hath no temptation taken you but such as is common to man: but God is
faithful, who will not suffer you to be tempted above that ye are able; but will
with the temptation also make a way to escape, that ye may be able to bear
it'.

ii *627-8. To your house, Luitolfo*: i.e. he will not be punished.

ii *632. will live*] mean to live (*1863-88*).

body; and you only do right to believe you will get
635 better as you get older! All men do so,—they are
worst in childhood, improve in manhood, and get
ready in old age for another world: Youth, with its
Beauty and Grace, would really seem bestowed on us
for some such reason as to make us partly endurable
640 till we have time for really becoming so of ourselves,
without their aid, when they leave us. The sweetest
child we all smile on for his pleasant want of the
whole world to break up, or suck in his mouth,
seeing no other good in it—he would be rudely
645 handled by that world's inhabitants, if he retained
those angelic infantine desires when he got six feet
high, black and bearded: but, little by little, he sees fit
to forego claim after claim on the world, puts up
with a less and less share of its good as his proper
650 portion,—and when the octogenarian asks barely a
sup of gruel and a fire of dry sticks, and will thank
you as for his full allowance and right in the common
good of life,—hoping nobody may murder him,—he
who began by asking and expecting the whole of us
655 to bow down in worship to him,—why, I say he is
advanced, far onward, very far, nearly out of sight
like our friend Chiappino yonder! And now—(Ay,
good bye to you! He turns round the North-west
gate—going to Lugo again? Good bye)!—And now
660 give thanks to God, the keys of the Provost's Palace
to me, and yourselves to profitable meditation at
home. I have known *Four*-and-twenty leaders of
revolts!—

---

ii *634-41. you only do right . . . when they leave us:* cp. B. to Julia Wedgwood,
Sept. 1864: 'I observe nowhere in youth, except in diseased and dying youth,
the religious instinct . . . the real instinct is developed with maturer years . . .
while this life suffices, I don't see that another incentive to push on through
its insufficiency, in the shape of a conceived possibility of a life beyond, is
ever given us' (*RB & JW* 73-4). Cp. *Rabbi Ben Ezra*, contemporary with this
letter.
ii *634-5. will get better*] must get better (*1863-88*).
ii *638. really seem*] seem (*1849-88*).
ii *644. he would*] would (*1849-88*).
ii *646. when he got*] when he has grown (*1849-88*, except 'had' *1868-88*).

33 The Laboratory
Ancien Régime

First publ. *Hood's Magazine* i (June 1844) 513-14, during the crisis caused by the illness of its editor, Thomas Hood. Repr. *B & P* vii (*DR & L*), 6 Nov. 1845, paired with *Confessional* under the collective title *France and Spain*, and with the stanzas numbered; then *1849* (when the collective title was dropped, though the poem still appeared alongside *Confessional*), *1863* (when it was placed in *Lyrics*: see Appendix A, p. 464), *1863*^{2}, *1868*, *1872*, *1888*. Our text is *Hood's*.

B. knew Thomas Hood (1799-1845), the comic poet and essayist (though best known today for a serious poem, *Song of the Shirt*), and admired his work, suggesting to R. H. Horne that the entry on Hood in *A New Spirit of the Age* (1844) should have for its motto a passage from Jonson's *Cynthia's Revels*: 'Act freely, carelessly, and capriciously; as if our veins ran with quicksilver; and not utter a phrase but what shall come forth steeped in the very brine of conceit, and sparkle like salt in fire' (*Correspondence* viii 202). All Hood's friends were approached for contributions to his magazine during his last illness: see T. L. Hood, *Memorials of Thomas Hood* (1860) ii 200. B. was approached for a contribution by F. O. Ward, acting editor of *Hood's*, and responded on 22 May 1844: 'I will this minute set about transcribing the best of whatever I can find in my desk likely to suit you—and will send it in the course of the day . . . morning, I hope' (*Correspondence* viii 318). It is probable that *Laboratory* alone was initially sent: a second letter, headed 'Friday Mg.', and conjecturally dated 24 May 1844 in *Correspondence*, encloses another poem or poems (probably *Claret and Tokay*), and adds: 'Do as you like about putting in, or out, the one you have already. Take counsel with yourself, too, about the line I have noted: nor forget to send proofs & copy' (*ibid.*, p. 319). Hood died on 3 May 1845.

The date of composition is unknown; 1843-4 seems likely (see below). The speaker has been identified with Marie-Madeleine de Brinvilliers (*c.* 1630-76), a notorious poisoner during the reign of Louis XIV, an identification supported by the subtitle. She obtained poison from her lover, Sainte-Croix, and murdered her father and her two brothers; in an experimental spirit, she was also alleged to have poisoned her maid and large numbers of poor women. The death of Sainte-Croix, in his laboratory, poisoned by his own poison when his glass mask slipped, brought about her exposure, and later her trial, torture, and execution. Her story is in *Biographie*; B. may also have read it in Alexandre Dumas' *Crimes Célèbres* (London 1843). A review of *Crimes Célèbres* in the *Foreign Quarterly Review* (xxx [1842] 26-60) devoted three pages to Brinvilliers. A poem entitled *Brinvilliers*, by B.'s father, is in the Library of Northwestern University (*Collections* J 63, p. 531). No source gives Brinvilliers' motive as jealousy, but this idea but may have been partly suggested by the contrast between her small stature and delicate features, as described by Dumas and transcribed by his reviewer, and the more robust beauty of the heroine of the next case cited by the reviewer, the Marchioness de Ganges (see ll. 23-4n.), who was poisoned by her brothers-in-law. The 'old man' may have been inspired either by the Italian Exili, a famous poisoner whom Sainte-Croix met in the Bastille, and who taught him his trade, or by the apothecary Glazer, who was later Sainte-Croix's accomplice, working for him in a small secret laboratory. The detail of the laboratory in the poem corresponds to descriptions of this laboratory, and of the secret closet which, as Dumas reports, was discovered in 1814 in the castle where Brinvilliers poisoned her father. Another source, suggested to us by Mr Michael Meredith, is a chapter entitled 'The Laboratory' in Harrison Ainsworth's *Crichton* (1837), which begins with an elaborate description of the laboratory of Cosmo Ruggieri, an old astrologer: 'On the floor near to the furnaces is strewn all the heterogeneous lumber proper to the retreat of an adept; to wit, earths, metals, "vitriol, sal-tartar, argaile, alkali," gums, oils, retorts, alembics, "crosslets, crucibles and curcurbites." Nor must we omit a slab of black marble, on which are deposited certain drugs and small phials, together with a vizard of glass, a circumstance testifying to the subtle and deadly nature of the tinctures sometimes extracted by the inmates of the chamber' (ii 138-9). In the remainder of the chapter, Ruggieri and Catherine de' Medici confer over the life and possible death by poison of Crichton, who is her enemy. For another important borrowing from Ainsworth, see headnote to *How They Brought the Good News*, p. 240. The poem illustrates B.'s interest in the psychology of murder; cp. *Porphyria, My Last Duchess, A Forgiveness*, and most fully, *Ring*. EBB., who first saw the poem with B.'s other contributions to *Hood's*, commented in her letter of 21 July 1845: 'the Laboratory is hideous as you meant to make it:—only I object a little to your tendency . . which is almost a habit . . & is very observable in this poem I think, . . of making lines difficult for the reader to read . . see the opening lines of this poem. Not that music is required everywhere, nor in *them* certainly, but that the uncertainty of rhythm throws the reader's mind off the *rail* . . & interrupts his progress with you & your influence with him. Where we have not direct pleasure from rhythm, & where no peculiar impression is to be produced by the changes in it, we sh^d be encouraged by the poet to *forget it altogether*; should we not?' (*LK* 131). See also l. 1n. All EBB.'s other comments on the poem recorded in the notes derive from *Wellesley MS*, unless otherwise stated.

> Now I have tied thy glass mask on tightly,
> May gaze thro' these faint smokes curling whitely,

¶33.*1*.] Now that I, tying thy glass mask tightly, (*1845-88*). The rev., prompted by EBB. (see headnote), left at least one other reader still dissatisfied: W. L. Phelps (*Robert Browning* [1931] 200) records that 'Tennyson passed a severe judgment on the first line . . . saying that it lacked smoothness, that it was a very difficult mouthful'.

As thou pliest thy trade in this devil's-smithy,
Which is the poison to poison her, prithee?

5 He is with her; and they know that I know
Where they are—what they do: they believe my tears
flow
While they laugh—laugh at me—at me fled to the drear
Empty church to pray God in for them!—I am here.

Grind away, moisten and mash up thy paste,
10 Pound at thy powder—am I in haste?
Better sit thus, and observe thy strange things,
Then go where men wait me, and dance at the king's.

That in the mortar—call you a gum?
Ah, the brave tree whence such gold oozings come!
15 And yon soft phial, the exquisite blue,
Sure to taste sweetly—is that poison too?

Had I but all of them, thee and thy treasures—
What a wild crowd of invisible pleasures—
To carry pure death in an earring, a casket,
20 A signet, a fan-mount, a filagree-basket!

Soon, at the king's, but a lozenge to give,
And Pauline should have just thirty minutes to live!
To light a pastille, and Elise, with her head,

10. *am I in haste?*] I am not in haste! (*1849-88*).
13. *call you*] you call it (*1845-88*). EBB. queried 'call you' in proof.
15. *yon*] yonder (*1845-88*). EBB. jotted down 'yonder' in proof, either suggesting or recording this rev.
19-20. Brinvilliers's poisons were administered in food, but Sainte-Croix was a connoisseur who wished to rediscover the secret of the kind of poisons mentioned here.
19. *an*] emended in agreement with other eds. from 'a' in *Hood's*.
20. *filagree*: or filigree: jewel-work in threads and beads of gold or silver.
21. *but a*] a mere (*1849-88*).
23-4. Cp. (with ll. 29-32) a passage describing the Marchioness de Ganges quoted by the reviewer of Dumas's *Crimes Célèbres* immediately after his summary of the Brinvilliers case (see headnote): 'This brilliancy of her face was set off by the decided blackness of her hair . . . The roundness of her face, produced by an *embonpoint bien ménagé*, presented all the vigour and freshness of health. To complete her charms, the Graces seemed to direct her looks, the movement of her lips, and of her head; her figure corresponded to the beauty of her face; indeed, her arms, her hands, her carriage, and her

And her breast, and her arms, and her hands, should
   drop dead!

25 Quick—is it finished? The colour's too grim;
Why not like the phial's, enticing and dim?
Let it brighten her drink, let her turn it and stir,
And try it and taste, ere she fix and prefer!

What a drop! She's not little—no minion like me;
30 That's why she ensnared him: this never will free
The soul from those strong, great eyes: say, "No!"
To that pulse's magnificent come-and-go.

For only last night, as they whispered, I brought
My own eyes to bear on her so, that I thought,
35 Could I keep them one half minute fixed, she'd fall
Shrivelled: she fell not; yet this does it all!

Not that I bid you spare her pain!

---

deportment, left nothing to desire if we would have the most agreeable image
of a beautiful person'.
23. To] But to (*1849-88*).
26. not like] not soft like (*1849-88*).
29. minion: a small, delicate creature; hence insignificant. The context requires
this sense, which is not rec. in *OED*; the word is close to 'minim', one of
whose senses is 'a creature of the least size or importance', and which B. later
used to describe an insect in *Red Cotton* iv 169: 'Look how the marvel of a
minim crawls!' The connotations of 'minion', all originally positive
('darling', 'beloved', 'favourite'), are now all negative ('pampered creature',
'servile courtier'): the word could thus encapsulate the speaker's sense of the
loss of her lover's favour. Cp. the use of the word in *Pippa* ii 31.
31.] EBB. quoted this line and commented: 'Will you read this line with
the context, & see if the rhythm is not perplexed in it?'   *strong, great*]
masculine (*1845*, *1863-88*). It is very unusual for B. to restore his original
reading in a later text (here, *1849*) and then re-revise it.
35. she'd fall] she would fall (*1845-88*). EBB. suggested the rev. in her original
notes on the poem; she jotted down 'she would fall' in proof, either repeating
her suggestion or noting its adoption.
37-40. Lionel Stevenson (*UTQ* xxi [1952] 243-4) compares Racine, *Andro-
mache* IV iv, where the intended victim is a faithless lover: 'Quel plaisir de
venger moi-même mon injure, / De retirer mon bras teint du sang du
parjure, / Et pour rendre sa peine et mes plaisirs plus grands, / De cacher ma
rivale à ses regards mourants!' [What pleasure to take revenge myself for the
wrong done to me, to withdraw my arm stained with the perjured man's

Let death be felt and the proof remain;
Brand, burn up, bite into its grace—
40   He is sure to remember her dying face!

Is it done? Take my mask off! Be not morose!
It kills her, and this prevents seeing it close—
The delicate droplet, my whole fortune's fee—
If it hurts her, beside, can it ever hurt me?

45   Now, take all my jewels, gorge gold to your fill,
You may kiss me, old man, on my mouth, if you will!
But brush this dust off me, lest horror there springs
Ere I know it—next moment I dance at the king's.

blood, and, to increase his pain and my pleasures, to prevent him from
looking his last on my rival!]. Cp. also the final lines of Tennyson's *The Lady
of Shalott* (1842 text): 'But Lancelot mused a little space; / He said, "She has a
lovely face; / God in his mercy lend her grace, / The Lady of Shalott."'
37.] EBB. quoted the line and commented: 'And the rhythm here! Is it well
done that it should change?'   *pain*] the pain (*1845-88*).
41-2. The speaker insists, despite the old man's objection that it is dangerous,
on removing her mask for a closer view of the poison.
41. Be] Nay, be (*1845-88*).
47.] EBB. quoted this line, underlining its last three words, and commented:
'The last words are clogged, I think . . & the expression seems
forced'.   *there springs*] it brings (*1845-88*).

34 Claret and Tokay
[Nationality in Drinks i and ii]

First publ. *Hood's Magazine* i (June 1844) 525; for B.'s contributions to *Hood's*, see p. 218. Repr. *B & P* vii (*DR & L*), 6 Nov. 1845, virtually unrevised. EBB. thought it 'inferior to all' the other *Hood's* poems (21 July 1845, *LK* 131), and there are no notes on the poem in *Wellesley MS*. Omitted from *1849*, possibly at EBB.'s suggestion, but repr. *1863* as the first and second sections of *Nationality in Drinks*, with *Here's to Nelson's memory* forming the third (there were no section nos.; the poems were divided by lines across the page), and placed in *Lyrics*: see Appendix A, p. 464. *Claret* and *Tokay* were repr. as separate poems in *1865²; Nationality in Drinks* was repr. *1868, 1888*. Our text is *Hood's*. B.'s letter to F. O. Ward, conjecturally dated 24 May 1844, almost certainly refers to *Claret and Tokay*: 'How do you like these? Lilt them a little, for the music. But, of all things, print them together' (*Correspondence* viii 319). The date of composition is unknown, but there are affinities with *Laboratory, Sibrandus*, and *Flight*. Both sections are variants on traditional drinking-songs (see e.g. *Othello* II iii 64-8), but replace the customary praise of the effects of drink by fanciful characterizations of the drinks themselves. Mr Michael Meredith has suggested a debt to Harrison Ainsworth's *Crichton* ii 118-19, where a poem entitled *Ale and Sack* appears. See also E. C. McAleer, *Explicator* xx (1961) item 34.

1.

My heart sunk with our claret-flask,
   Just now, beneath the heavy sedges
That serve this pond's black face for mask;
   And still at yonder broken edges
5 Of the hole, where up the bubbles glisten,
After my heart I look and listen.

2.

Our laughing little flask, compelled
   Through depth to depth more bleak and shady;
As when, both arms beside her held,
10   Feet straightened out, some gay French lady
Is caught up from life's light and motion,

¶34.*1*. Mrs Orr (*Handbook* 292-3) suggests that the claret-flask is plunged into the pond 'for cooling', McAleer (see headnote) that it is simply thrown away.   *sunk*] sank (*1863-88*).
5. Of the] O' the (*1870-88*).
9-12. Cp. *Laboratory* 21-4.

And dropped into death's silent ocean!

Up jumped Tokay on our table,
Like a pigmy castle-warder,
15 Dwarfish to see, but stout and able,
Arms and accoutrements all in order;
And fierce he looked north; then, wheeling south,
Blew with his bugle a challenge to Drouth,
Cocked his flap-hat with the tosspot-feather,
20 Twisted his thumb in his red moustache,
Gingled his huge brass spurs together,
Tightened his waist with its Buda sash,
And then with an impudence naught could abash,
Shrugged his hump-shoulder,
25 To tell the beholder,
For twenty such knaves he should laugh but the
      bolder;
And so, with his sword-hilt gallantly jutting,
And dexter hand on his haunch abutting,
Went the little man from Ausbruch, strutting!

13-29. McAleer suggests that the figure described in the poem derives from the label on the bottle of Tokay; equally, it could relate to the bottle itself, since Tokay, an expensive aromatic dessert wine from Hungary, usually comes in small bottles.

18. Drouth: thirst.

19. flap-hat: a hat having flaps or flapping brims. See *Flight* 253 for another occurrence.   *tosspot-feather*: apparently B.'s coinage. A 'tosspot' is 'a toper, a heavy drinker' (*J.*).

21. Gingled] Jingled (*1863-88*).

22. Buda: now part of Budapest, the capital of Hungary.

24-5.] one line, *1863-88*.

28. dexter: right.

29. man from] man, Sir (*1863-88*). McAleer argues that B. originally took 'Ausbruch' to be a place, when in fact it means, like the German 'Auslese', a wine made with specially selected grapes, and on learning of his mistake 'cleverly emended the line'.

35 Garden Fancies

First publ. *Hood's Magazine* ii (July 1844) 45-8; for B.'s contributions to *Hood's*, see p. 218. A letter of July 1844 from B. to F. O. Ward, the acting editor of *Hood's* (*LH* 10), shows that Ward, and Hood himself, suggested revs. in proof, but the lines to which they refer must have been further changed, since the fragmentary phrases which B. quotes fit neither *Garden Fancies* nor any other poem of the period. Repr. *B & P* vii (*DR & L*), 6 Nov. 1845, with both sections given stanza numbers; then *1849, 1863* (when it was placed in *Lyrics*: see Appendix A, p. 464), *1868, 1880, 1888*. Our text is *Hood's. Garden Fancies* is the only one of B.'s collective titles for paired poems (e.g. *Italy and France* for *My Last Duchess* and *Count Gismond*, *Queen-Worship* for *Rudel* and *Cristina*) which survived *1849*. With his letter of ?18 July 1845 (*LK* 129), B. sent EBB. all the poems he had publ. in *DR & L*, for criticism before publication in *DR & L*; her comment on *Sibrandus* 46 (*Wellesley MS*; all her comments recorded in the notes are from this text, unless otherwise stated) makes it clear that he showed her his own MS, not the printed texts.

For B.'s love of plants and small wild creatures, see *Pauline* 716-28, *Sordello* vi 619-28n., and *Flight* 726-30n. *Miller* 155 perceptively links the poem with Shelley's *The Sensitive Plant*; cp. esp. the description of the 'ruling Grace' of the garden, 'A Lady, the wonder of her kind' in part ii, e.g. ll. 29-32: 'I doubt not the flowers of that garden sweet / Rejoiced in the sound of her gentle feet; / I doubt not they felt the spirit that came / From her glowing fingers through all their frame', and ll. 37-40: 'She lifted their heads with her tender hands, / And sustained them with rods and osier-bands; / If the flowers had been her own infants, she / Could never have nursed them more tenderly'. (For other parallels, see notes.) *Sibrandus*, by contrast, may be seen as a humorous tribute to B.'s father's large library, which contained many antiquarian volumes. In one of these, Nathaniel Wanley's *Wonders of the Little World* (1667; also a source for *Pied Piper* and *Cardinal*: see pp. 114 and 130 above), B. found the name Sibrandus of Aschaffenburg, a town in Bavaria (hence 'Schafnaburgensis'). E. Cook (*Browning's Lyrics* [Toronto 1974] 79) cites Rabelais, *Gargantua* I i: a mouldy, vermin-eaten book containing Gargantua's genealogy is found in a tomb with the inscription 'Hic bibitur' [Here be drinking]. For a further source in Rabelais, see ll. 17-72n. DeVane (*Handbook* 169) suggests that the incident is authentic, though B. told EBB.: 'I have no little insight into the feelings of furniture, and treat books and prints with a reasonable consideration' (26 Feb. 1845, *LK* 27). In a letter to Mrs Fitzgerald of 4 Dec. 1886, B. wrote that he was 'beginning to somewhat arrange my books—such a chaotic mass, in real want of a good clearing fire! For how can I part with old tomes annotated by my Father, and yet how can nine out of ten of them do other than cumber the shelves like the dead weight they *are*? Oh that *helluo librorum* [devourer of books] my father, best of men, most indefatigable of book-digesters!' (*Learned Lady* 193). Cp. the attack on pedantry in *Paracelsus*; also *Master Hugues, A Grammarian*, and *Transcendental-*

ism. The poem was 'a great favourite' with EBB.: 'it is so new, & full of a
creeping crawling grotesque life'.

I. The Flower's Name

Here's the garden she walked across,
 Arm in my arm, such a short while since:
Hark, now I push its wicket, the moss
 Hinders the hinges and makes them wince!
5 She must have reached this shrub ere she turned,
 As back with that murmur the wicket swung;
For she laid the poor snail, my chance foot spurned,
 To feed and forget it the leaves among.

Down this side of the gravel-walk
10 She went while her robe's edge brushed the box:
And here she paused in her gracious talk
 To point me a moth on the milk-white flox.
Roses, ranged in valiant row,
 Think will I never she passed you by!
15 She loves noble roses, I know;
 But this—so surely this met her eye!

This flower she stopped at, finger on lip,
 Stooped over, in doubt, settling its claim,
Till she gave me, with pride to make no slip,
20 Its soft meandering Spanish name:

¶35.i *1-3.* Cp. Shelley, *The Sensitive Plant* i 49-50: 'sinuous paths of lawn
and of moss, / Which led through the garden along and across'. The rhyme
recurs in *Sibrandus* 33-5.
i *10. box:* an evergreen shrub, used as a hedge or border.
i *12.* Cp. (noting ll. 35-6) Shelley, *The Sensitive Plant* ii 50-2: 'soft moths that
kiss / The sweet lips of the flowers, and harm not, did she / Make her
attendant angels be', cited also for *In a Gondola* 49-55.
i *14. Think will I never*] I will never think (*1849-88*).
i *15. loves*] loves you (*1849-88*).
i *16.*] But yonder, see, where the rock-plants lie! (*1845-88*). EBB. quoted the
Hood's reading and commented: 'Is it hypercritical to complain of this "eye".
I seldom like the singular "eye"—and then, when it is a Spanish eye!—The
line is not a great favorite of mine altogether—and the poem *is*—& you see
the least speck on a Venice glass: and if it is "*my fancy*", at least I speak it off
my mind & have done with it. The beauty & melody we never shall have
done with .. none of us'.
i *18. settling*] as settling (*1845-88*).
i *20.* In her letter of 21 July 1845 (*LK* 130), EBB. praised 'that beautiful &

What a name! Was it love, or praise?
    Speech half-asleep, or song half-awake?
I must learn Spanish one of these days,
    Only for that slow sweet name's sake.

25   Roses, if I live and do well,
       I may bring her, one of these days,
To fix you fast with as fine a spell,
    Fit you each with his Spanish phrase!
But do not detain me now; for she lingers
30   There, like sunshine over the ground,
And ever I see her soft white fingers
    Searching after the bud she found.

Flower, you Spaniard, look you grow not,
    Stay as you are and be loved for ever!
35   Bud, if I kiss you, 'tis that you blow not,
    Mind the pink shut mouth opens never!
For while it pouts thus, her fingers wrestle,
    Twinkling the audacious leaves between,
Till round they turn and down they nestle—
40   Is not the dear mark still to be seen?

---

musical use of the word "meandering," which I never remember having seen
used in relation to *sound* before. It does to mate with your "*simmering* quiet" in
Sordello' (referring to i 910).

i *22*. In her letter of 21-22 Oct. 1845 (*LK* 244), EBB. used this line to describe
the rhythm of *Flight*; cp. *Flight* 512 and see also *Sibrandus* 52n.

i *23-4*. In 1834 B. wrote to Amédée de Ripert-Monclar (see headnote to
Paracelsus, I 101) that he had 'learned Spanish enough [to] be able to read "the
majestic Tongue which Calderon along the desert flung!—"' (*Correspondence*
iii 111; B quotes Shelley, *Letter to Maria Gisborne* 180-1). In 1878 he wrote to
Mrs Fitzgerald: 'a few weeks since, I took it into my head to learn
Spanish,—which I have so far managed as to read ordinary prose easily
enough . . . Of the pronunciation I know nothing but what the grammar
attempts to teach . . . Of course, like everybody, I had amused myself years
ago by stumbling along a few passages, by means of Latin and Italian'
(*Learned Lady* 55-6).

i *33*. *look*] look that (*1845-88*). EBB. suggested the change.

i *35-6*. Cp. Keats, *Eve of St Agnes* 243: 'As though a rose should shut, and be a
bud again'. Cp. B.'s *A Face* 4-10.

i *36*. *Mind the pink shut*] Mind that the pink (*1845*); Mind, the shut pink (*1849-
88*). EBB. had commented: 'A clogged line—is it not? Difficult to read'.

i *37*. *it pouts thus*] thus it pouts (*1845-65*); it pouts (*1868-88*).

Where I find her not, beauties vanish;
  Whither I follow her, beauties flee;
Is there no method to tell her in Spanish
  June's twice June since she breathed it with me?
45 Come, bud, show me the least of her traces,
  Tread in my lady's lightest foot-fall
—Ah, you may flout and turn up your faces!
  Roses, are you so fair after all?

II. Sibrandus Schafnaburgensis

Plague take all pedants, say I!
  He who wrote what I hold in my hand,
Centuries back was so good as to die,
  Leaving this rubbish to bother the land;
5 This, that was a book in its time,
  Printed on paper and bound in leather,
Last month in the white of a matin-prime
  Just when the birds sang all together.

Into the garden I brought it to read;

i 46. *Tread in*] Treasure (*1845-88*).
i 47. *flout*: jeer.
i 48. *are you . . . all?*] you are not . . . all. (*1845-88*, except 'all!', *1849-88*).
EBB. quoted the line, commenting: 'And I just ask whether to put it in the
affirmative thus // "Roses, ye are not so fair after all." // does not satisfy the
ear & mind better. It is only *asking*, you know'.

ii *1.* In Richard Henry Wilde's *Conjectures and Researches concerning . . .
Tasso* (1842), the book which he was ostensibly reviewing when he wrote
Chatterton (see Appendix C, p. 474), B. could have read: 'At the time of his
departure for Modena, he [Tasso] jokes with *Scalabrino*, crying, "plague on
the pedants!"' (i 154).   *pedants*] your pedants (*1849-88*).
ii *4. bother*] cumber (*1849-88*).
ii *7-8.* In the sense intended here, 'white' means 'propitious, favourable' or
'highly prized, precious'; for its use as a noun in this construction, *OED* cites
only Keats, *Endymion* iii 402: 'I loved her to the very white of truth'. 'Matin-
prime' means, first, 'the best part of the morning' (or 'the beginning of the
morning': l. 8 could refer to the dawn chorus), but matins and prime are both
early-morning religious services, and l. 8 suggests that B. may be recalling
OED sense 2a: 'chiefly of birds . . . to sing their morning song' (as in Milton,
L'Allegro 114: 'Ere the first cock his matin rings'), and, by extension, *Job*
xxxviii 4-7, where God speaks of the time 'when I laid the foundations of the
earth' and 'the morning stars sang together'. Cp. *Fifine* 855: 'fresh morning-
prime'.

10   And under these arbutes and laurustine
      Read it, so help me grace in my need,
      From title-page to closing line.
      Chapter on chapter did I count,
      As a curious traveller counts Stonehenge;
15   Added up the mortal amount;
      And then proceeded to my revenge.

      Yonder's a plum-tree, with a crevice
      An owl would build in, were he but sage;
      For a lap of moss, like a fine pont-levis
20   In a castle of the middle age,
      Joins to a lip of gum, pure amber;
      When he'd be private, there might he spend
      Hours alone in his lady's chamber:
      Into this crevice I dropped our friend.

25   Splash, went he, as under he ducked,
      —I knew at the bottom rain-drippings stagnate:
      Next a handful of blossoms I plucked

ii *10. these arbutes*] the arbute (*1845-49*). EBB. quoted the *Hood's* reading and commented: 'Are these pluralities quite correct? You know best . . & I doubt, at worst'. She suggested the revised reading as 'a more *consistent* course . . but I do not attempt even to decide'. The 'arbutes' belong to the genus *Arbutus*, evergreen shrubs and trees; the name was commonly applied to the strawberry-tree. For the form 'arbute', *OED* cites Dryden's translation of Virgil's *Georgics* (ii 96).   *laurustine*: laurustinus, an evergreen winter-flowering shrub.

ii *17-72.* Cp., noting l. 32n., Rabelais, *Gargantua and Pantagruel* (bk. III, ch. xxi) where Panurge visits the death-bed of the 'vieil poète', Raminagrobis, who says, 'J'ay ce jourd'huy, à grande fatigue et difficulté, chassé un tas de villaines, inmondes et pestilentes bestes, noires, guarres, fauves, blanches, cendreés, grivoleés, les quelles laisser ne me vouloient à mon aise mourir; et par fraudulentes poinctures, gruppemens harpyiacques, importunitez freslonniques, toutes forgées en l'officine de ne sçay quelle insatiabilité, me evocquoient du doulx pensement au quel je acquiesçois' [Today I have, with great fatigue and difficulty, driven out a rabble of villainous, shameless and pestilent creatures, black, striped, buff, white, ashen, speckled, which would not let me die in peace; and by insidious prickings, harpylike clutchings, hornet-like importunities, all forged in the workshop of I know not what insatiable being, they drew me out of that sweet contemplation to which I was yielding] (*Oeuvres Complètes*, ed. A. Lafranc, iii [Paris 1931] 166). This chapter is also a source for *Of Pacchiarotto*.

ii *19. pont-levis*: drawbridge.

ii *26.*] At the bottom, I knew, rain-drippings stagnate; (*1870-88*).

To bury him with, my book-shelf's magnate:
Then I went in-doors, brought out a loaf,
30   Half a cheese, and a bottle of Chablis;
Lay on the grass and forgot the oaf
Over a jolly chapter of Rabelais.

Now, this morning, betwixt the moss
And gum that locked our friend in limbo,
35   A spider had spun his web across,
And sate in the midst with arms a-kimbo:
So I took pity, for learning's sake,
And, *de profundibus, accentibus laetis,*
Cantate, quoth I, as I got a rake,
40   And up I fished his delectable treatise.

Here you have it, dry in the sun,
With all the binding all of a blister,
And great blue spots where the ink has run,
And reddish streaks that wink and glister
45   O'er the page so beautifully yellow—
Oh, the droppings have played their tricks!

ii *32. Rabelais:* François Rabelais (*c.* 1483-1553), the great Renaissance physician, humanist scholar, and writer; the 'jolly chapter' is doubtless from his comic masterpiece *Gargantua and Pantagruel.* Rabelais's name in the period was synonymous with bawdy; cp. *A Likeness* where 'the little edition of Rabelais' (l. 24) figures in the description of a bachelor's lodgings. In 1879 B. was invited to join the Rabelais Club, and sent a gracious refusal: 'I have a huge love for Rabelais, and hope to die even as did his Raminagrobis,—but, what Johnson calls a "clubbable person"—I am *not,*—and why should I pretend to be one?' (to W. H. Pollock, 28 June 1879, *ABL MS*). For Raminagrobis, see ll. 17-72n. With the phrasing here, cp. H. Ainsworth, *Crichton* (1837; see headnote to *Laboratory,* p. 219) I xli: 'jolly old Rabelais'.
ii *34. limbo:* combining the senses of 'prison' and 'a condition of neglect or oblivion'. K. Allott (*Browning: Selected Poems* [Oxford 1967] 203), noting ll. 38-9 and ll. 71-2, suggests an allusion to the Christian limbo.
ii *35-6.* In a letter of *c.* June 1843 to R. H. Horne, B. wrote that he had two skulls in his writing room, 'each on its bracket by the window . . . a huge field-spider [has] woven his platform-web from the under-jaw of one of these sculls [sic] to the window-sill . . . the spider's self is on the watch, with each great *arm* wide out in a tooth-socket' (*Correspondence* vii 184).
ii *38-9.* The Latin means 'sing from the depths in joyful accents'; cp. the opening of *Psalms* cxxx, in the Vulgate *De profundis clamavi:* 'Out of the depths have I cried unto thee, O Lord'.
ii *46. the droppings have*] well have the droppings (*1845-88*). EBB. quoted the line and commented: '"Oh, well have the droppings" you had

Did he guess how toadstools grew, this fellow?
    Here's one stuck in his chapter six!

How did he like it when the live creatures
50   Tickled and toused and browsed him all over,
And worm, slug, eft, with serious features,
    Came in, each one, for his right of trover;
When the water-beetle with great blind deaf face
    Made of her eggs the stately deposit,
55 And the newt borrowed so much of the preface
    As tiled in the top of his black wife's closet.

All that life, and fun, and romping,
    All that frisking, and twisting, and coupling,
While slowly our poor friend's leaves were swamping,
60   Clasps cracking, and covers suppling!
As if you had carried sour John Knox
    To the play at Paris, Vienna, or Munich,
Fastened him into a front-row box,

---

written—& better written, I think'. This indicates that she was working from
B.'s MS, though not whether it was the printer's copy for *Hood's*.

ii *50. toused*: rumpled, pulled about. Only occurrence in B.

ii *51. eft*: newt, species of lizard. B. wrote enthusiastically to EBB. about the
'English water-eft' (4 Jan. 1846, *LK* 356), and told an anecdote in the same
letter which displayed his knowledge of newts (see l. 55).

ii *52. right of trover*: a mock-solemn form of 'finders keepers', derived from
one of the senses of 'treasure-trove'; technically, 'trover' is an action to
recover illegally-held property. EBB. commented that B. had 'right of
trover' to the 'novel effects of rhythm' in *Flight* (21-22 Oct. 1845); see
Flower's Name 22n.

ii *55. so*] just so (*1849-88*).

ii *60. Clasps*] And clasps were (*1845-88*). EBB. quoted the *Hood's* reading and
commented: 'Or query . . "While clasps were crackling & covers suppling."
A good deal is to be said for the abrupt expression of the "text" . . but the
other is safer . . & less trusting the reader. You will judge'.

ii *61-4*. After praising the poem (see headnote), EBB. added: 'Ah but . . do
you know besides, . . it is almost reproachable in you to hold up John Knox
to derision in this way!' Knox (*c.* 1514-72) was the foremost leader of the
Reformation in Scotland, and a type of stern Calvinist morality. Extreme
Protestants had a particular aversion to drama and dance as immoral
activities, and to theatres as immoral places; theatres in foreign (and Catholic)
cities would of course be even worse.

ii *62. play*] play-house (*1845-88*).

And danced off the Ballet in trowsers and tunic.

65 Come, old martyr! what, torment enough is it?
        Back to my room shall you take your sweet self!
    Good bye, mother-beetle; husband-eft, *sufficit!*
        See the snug niche I have made on my shelf.
    A's book shall prop you up, B's shall cover you,
70   Here's C to be grave with, or D to be gay,
    And with E on each side, and F right over you,
        Dry-rot at ease till the judgment-day!

ii *64. in*] with (*1845-88*).   *trowsers*] trousers (*1845-88*); the *Hood*'s spelling
is the earlier form and was still allowed, though becoming rare.
ii *67. sufficit*: enough (Latin).

36 The Boy and the Angel

First publ. *Hood's Magazine* ii (Aug. 1844) 140-2; for B.'s contributions to *Hood's*, see p. 218. Repr. *B & P* vii (*DR & L*), 6 Nov. 1845, with ten new lines, and several alterations suggested by EBB. Her main criticism was of the poem's narrative compression: 'I do ask you to think . . . whether a little dilation of the latter stanzas of this simple noble ballad, would not increase the significance & effect of the whole. Readers will not see at a glance all you have cast into it, unless you make more *surface*' (*Wellesley MS*: all her comments recorded in the notes derive from this text, unless otherwise stated). Then repr. *1849* (with two further new lines), *1863* (when it was placed in *Romances*: see Appendix A, p. 464), *1868*, *1880*, and *1888*. Our text is *Hood's*.

The date of composition is unknown; Easter may be indicated by the importance of Easter Day in the story, and 1844 is a possible year, if J. Addis (*N & Q* 3rd series, xii [6 July 1867] 6-7) is right in finding a source for the story in the 16th-century metrical romance *Robert of Cisille*, which appeared in 1844 in J. O. Halliwell-Phillips, *Nugae Poeticae*. Robert, King of Sicily, is punished for his pride by being degraded to the position of court jester by an angel who takes his identity and reigns in his stead. The substitution takes place while Robert is visiting his brother, the Pope, 'to see hys nobull and ryalle arraye / In Rome on Halowe Thursdaye'. After three years, the repentant Robert is restored to his identity and his kingdom. But Halliwell-Phillips's version did not appear until after the poem was written, and the verbal resemblances cited by Addis are unconvincing. The story exists in various other versions, such as the *Gesta Romanorum*: as *Robert the Devil* it was a familiar sensational play: Hazlitt records having seen it 'thirty times at least' ('The Free Admission', *New Monthly Magazine* [July 1830]; *Works*, ed. Waller and Glover [1904], xii 124). Assuming that B. knew the outline of the story, he followed his usual practice of making considerable changes. *Job* xxxiii 15-26 anticipates several of the poem's central motifs: 'In a dream, in a vision of the night, when deep sleep falleth upon men, in slumberings upon the bed; then he openeth the ears of men, and sealeth their instruction, that he may withdraw man from his purpose, and hide pride from man . . . He is chastened also with pain upon his bed . . . His flesh is consumed away . . . Yea, his soul draweth near unto the grave, and his life to the destroyers. If there be a messenger with him, an interpreter, one among a thousand, to shew unto man his uprightness: then he is gracious unto him, and saith, Deliver him from going down to the pit: I have found a ransom. His flesh shall be fresher than a child's; he shall return to the days of his youth: he shall pray unto God, and he will be favourable unto him'. B.'s revs. at ll. 52^53 strengthen the connection. A commentary on *Job* published in 1844 gives a lengthy note on the controversy surrounding thëinterpretation of 'messenger' in this passage, which has been rendered 'human messenger', 'divine messenger' (angel), or 'the Messiah', invoking the idea of divine substitution,

whether by an angel or by Christ, which is at the centre of the poem. B.'s use
of the concept of substitution may also owe something to Hazlitt's essay 'On
Personal Identity', which appeared in the *Monthly Magazine* in Jan. 1828.
Hazlitt argues that no one really wishes to exchange identity with anyone
else, if this involves 'getting rid . . . of all recollection that there ever was
such a [being] as himself'; he goes on: 'No man, if he had his choice, would
be the angel Gabriel tomorrow! What is the angel Gabriel to him but a
splendid vision? . . . he would rather remain a little longer in this mansion of
clay, which, with all its flaws, inconveniences, and perplexities, contains all
that he has any real knowledge of, or any affection for' (*Works* xii 199-200).
The word 'footstool' at l. 40 suggests a source in *Isaiah* lxvi 1-2 for the
contrast between Theocrite's 'cell' and 'Peter's dome': 'Thus saith the Lord,
the heaven is my throne, and the earth is my footstool: where is the house
that ye build unto me? and where is the place of my rest? For all those things
hath mine hand made, and all those things have been, saith the Lord: but to
this man will I look, even to him that is poor and of a contrite spirit, and
trembleth at my word'. The centrality of praise in human existence is a theme
of the Psalms, one of B.'s favourite sources of ideas and phrases, and is the
keynote of one of the poems he most admired, Christopher Smart's *Song to
David*, a source for B.'s *Saul*. The idea that all praise is precious to God,
whether from humble or exalted persons, recalls *Pippa Intro* 148-59 ('All
service ranks the same with God'). B.'s emphasis, like that of many Victorian
thinkers, notably Carlyle, falls upon the idea of work as the most effective
form of praise.

   The poem's chronology involves a logical impossibility if the story is
assumed to take place in 'real' time. Theocrite is given two lifetimes—one as
humble craftsman, the other as ambitious priest—with Gabriel intervening in
both; but at the same time as Theocrite is returned to his original state and
age, Gabriel is carrying on the identity which Theocrite had developed in his
career as a priest. But since Theocrite's papacy *follows* either version of his
existence (whether carried on by himself or Gabriel), it cannot take place
simultaneously, as the poem suggests at ll. 63-4. The explanation, in our
view, hinges on the distinction between divine and human time which is
explicitly stated at ll. 21-2. Theocrite's life as a priest is 'present' to God in the
same timeless moment as his craftsman's life; Gabriel's intervention, which
causes the irresolvable problem in the chronology, draws attention by this
very fact to the inadequacy of human conceptions of time. Similar time-loops
occur in *Easter-Day* and *Pietro*, and (though arguably) in *Childe Roland*.

> Morning, noon, eve, and night,
> "Praise God," sang Theocrite;

¶36.1.] Morning, evening, noon, and night, (*1845-88*, except 'noon and',
1868-88)—suggested by EBB., 'for rhythm'. Cp. *Psalms* lv 17: 'Evening, and
morning, and at noon, will I pray, and cry aloud: and he shall hear my voice'.

Then to his poor trade he turn'd,
By which the daily meal was earn'd.

5   Hard he labour'd, long and well,
O'er the work his boy's curls fell;

But ever, at each period,
He stopp'd and sang, "Praise God;"

Then back again his curls he threw,
10   And cheerful turn'd to work anew.

Said Blaise, the listening monk, "Well done;
"I doubt not thou art heard, my son;

"As if thy voice to-day
"Were praising God the Pope's great way;

15   "This Easter Day, the Pope at Rome
"Praises God from Peter's dome."

Said Theocrite, "Would God that I
"Might praise Him, that great way, and die!"

Night pass'd, day shone,
20   And Theocrite was gone.

With God a day endures alway,
A thousand years are as a day:

In Heaven God said, "Nor day nor night
"Brings one voice of my delight."

4. By which] Whereby (*1849-88*).

7. at each period: at the conclusion of each task.

13. As if] As well as if (*1845-88*). Suggested by EBB., who added: 'Not that the short lines are not good in their *place*'.

21-2.] EBB. began to copy these lines in her notes, but then changed her mind and deleted them without indicating what her comment would have been. The source is *2 Peter* iii 8 (following *Psalms* xc 4): 'be not ignorant of this one thing, that one day is with the Lord as a thousand years, and a thousand years as one day'.

22. as a day] but a day (*1845-88*).

23. In Heaven God said] God said in Heaven (*1845-88*). Suggested by EBB. as 'a simpler & rather solemner intonation'.

24. Brings one voice] Now brings the voice (*1845-88*). EBB felt that the line

25   Then Gabriel, like a rainbow's birth,
      Spread his wings and sank to earth,

      Enter'd the empty cell,
      And play'd the craftsman well,

      And morn, noon, eve, and night,
30   Prais'd God in place of Theocrite.

      And from a boy to youth he grew;
      The man put off the stripling's hue;

      The man matured, and fell away
      Into the season of decay;

35   Yet ever o'er the trade he bent,
      And ever lived content.

      God said, "A praise is in mine ear;
      "There is no doubt in it, no fear:

      "So sing old worlds, and so
40   "New worlds that from my footstool go;

      "Clearer loves sound other ways;

'might be more definite in meaning'.

27-8.] Entered in flesh the empty cell, / Lived there, and played the craftsman well (*1845-88*, except 'well;', *1863-88*. EBB. commented: 'Do you prefer to have short lines in this place . . . and why?'

29.] And morning, evening, noon, and night, (*1845-88*). Altered to conform with l. 1.

35. Yet ever] And ever (*1845-88*).

36.] And ever lived on earth content. (*1845-88*).

36^37.] (He did God's will; to him, all one / If on the earth or in the sun.) (*1849-88*).

39-40. The 'old worlds' are the spheres whose music, in Christian adaptations of Platonic cosmology (e.g. Dante), expresses the universe's praise of God; the 'New worlds' are those which God's inexhaustible creativity continually brings into being. Both (unlike the human world) are perfect. This contrast is developed in a late poem, *Rephan*.

40. footstool: cp. *Psalms* xcix 5: 'Exalt ye the Lord our God, and worship at his footstool'. See also headnote, p. 234.

41. Love of God which has no 'doubt or fear' sounds different from human love; God therefore 'sees through' Gabriel's disguise as Theo-

"I miss my little human praise."

Then forth sprang Gabriel's wings, off fell
The flesh, remain'd the cell.

45 'Twas Easter Day: he flew to Rome,
And paused above the dome.

In the tiring-room, close by
The great outer gallery,

With his holy vestments dight,
50 Stood the new Pope, Theocrite,

And all his past career
Came back upon him clear—

How rising from the sickness drear
He grew a priest and now stood here.

55 To the east with praise he turn'd,

crite.   *Clearer*: combining the senses of purity, distinctness, and brightness; also possibly of serenity, cheerfulness, as in *PL* viii 336-7: 'soon his clear aspect / Returned'.

43-4.] EBB. commented: 'Is not something wrong here? If you mean that the flesh remained in the cell (named before) you do not say it: & what else is said?' B. accordingly altered l. 44 (see next note).

44.] The flesh disguise, remained the cell. (*1845-88*).

46. the dome] Saint Peter's dome (*1845-88*).

47-62. Cp. *Bishop Blougram* 65-76: 'An unbelieving Pope won't do, you say. / It's like those eerie stories nurses tell, / Of how some actor played Death on a stage . . . Then going in the tire-room afterward . . . Got touched upon the sleeve familiarly . . . By Death himself. Thus God might touch a Pope / At unawares, ask what his baubles mean, / And whose part he presumed to play just now?'

47. tiring-room: dressing-room; esp. associated with the theatre.

49. dight: dressed (archaic). Not used elsewhere in B.'s poetry.

52ˆ53.] Since when, a boy, he plied his trade
     Till on his life the sickness weighed:

     And in his cell when death drew near
     An angel in a dream brought cheer: (*1845-88*, except 'trade,', 'weighed;', 'cell,', *1849-88*).

53. How rising] And rising (*1845-88*).

And in the Angel burn'd:—

"Vainly I left my sphere,
"Vainly hast thou lived many a year;

"Go back, and praise again
60   "The early way, while I remain;

"Be again the boy all curl'd;
"I will finish with the world."

Theocrite grew old at home,
Gabriel dwelt in Peter's dome:

65   One vanish'd as the other died;
They sought God side by side.

56.] And on his sight the angel burned. (*1845-88*). EBB. commented: 'I like & see plainly this burning in of the Angel upon Theocrite as he looks to the east: but I doubt whether it will be as clear to all readers, you suggest it so very barely. Would not a touch or two improve the revelation?'

56^57.] "I bore thee from thy craftsman's cell, / And set thee here; I did not well. (*1845-88*, except 'cell', *1888*). These lines, unlike the others added in *1845*, change the interpretation of the story rather than making it more explicit.

57. sphere] angel's sphere (*1845-49*); angel-sphere (*1863-88*).

58.] Vain was thy dream of many a year. (*1845-88*).

58^59.] Thy voice's praise seemed weak; it dropped— / Creation's chorus stopped! (*1845-88*).

60^61.] With that weak voice of our disdain, / Take up Creation's pausing strain. (*1845-88*).

61-2.] Back to the cell and poor employ: / Become the craftsman and the boy!" (*1845-88*, except 'Resume the craftsman', *1868-88*). EBB. objected strongly to l. 61: 'At any rate you will write "Be thou again" .. will you not? but I doubt about the curled boy. Anyone "*becurled*" may be right .. but a curled boy "tout rond" does strike me as of questionable correctness'.

64. Gabriel] A new Pope (*1845-88*).

37 "How They Brought the Good News from Ghent to Aix"

First publ. *B & P* vii (*DR & L*), 6 Nov. 1845, the opening poem of the pamphlet; repr. *1849*, *1863* (when it was placed in *Lyrics*: see Appendix A, p. 464), *1868*, *1872*, *1888*. Our text is *1845*. B. was often asked for details of the composition and background; the following is a conflation of his replies (see esp. *LH* 215-16; *NL* 300; *BSP* i 49; *Pall Mall Gazette*, 31 Dec. 1889). He drafted the poem in Aug. 1844, while 'on board ship off Tangiers' in transit 'from Sicily to Naples', 'after I had been at sea long enough to appreciate even the fancy of a gallop on a certain good horse "York," then in my stable at home'. 'The poem was written . . . in a gay moment on the inside of the cover of the one book I had with me,—Bartoli's "Simboli" ': i.e. his teacher Angelo Cerutti's 1830 ed. of Daniello Bartoli's *De' Simboli Trasportati al Morale* (Rome 1677). B. later carefully erased the text (the book is in the library of Balliol College, Oxford; see also headnote to *Home-Thoughts, from the Sea*, p. 246). A fair copy MS of the poem, signed and dated Paris 4 Feb. 1856, is in the Pierpont Morgan Library (no significant variants from *1849-88*), and several autographs of passages from the poem are extant; in one, of ll. 1-6, dated 1 June 1882 (now in the Huntington Library), l. 5 is incomplete and B. wrote in the margin '(forgotten!)'; see also l. 53n. In 1889 B. recorded from memory the opening lines on an Edison wax cylinder, substituting 'saddle' for 'stirrup' in l. 1, missing out l. 3 and faltering at l. 4:

> I sprang to the saddle, and Joris, and he;
> I galloped, Dirck galloped, we galloped all three;
> 'Speed!' echoed the wall to us galloping through;
> The gate shuts behind us, the lights sink to rest . . .

At this point B. stops, saying: 'I'm incredibly sorry that I can't remember me own verses' (see M. Hancher and J. Moore, 'The Sound of a Voice that is Still', *BNL* iv and v [1970]; we give our own version of B.'s words). Note that the phrase 'The gate shuts' is closer to B.'s MS, as quoted by EBB., than to the published text (see ll. 2-6n.).

There is no historical foundation for the poem, 'merely [a] general impression of the characteristic warfare and besieging which abounds in the Annals of Flanders'. Aix is besieged and about to surrender, and the 'good news' that unexpected help is on its way is brought from Ghent by a route 'hitherto impracticable' but 'discovered to be open for once'. In one place, B.

Title. The only title in B. in the form of a quotation not of literary or proverbial origin.   *Ghent*: the English form; Flemish Gent, French Gand, capital of East Flanders province in what is now Belgium.   *Aix*: short for French Aix-la-Chapelle, Flemish Aken, now Aachen in the state of North-Rhine Westphalia, Germany. All intervening places are in Belgium.

claims that he 'had no map, and wrote swiftly . . . the places mentioned were remembered or guessed at loosely enough'; but elsewhere he states that the story of the siege and the 'impracticable' route could account 'for some difficulties in the time and space occupied by the ride in one night'. B. passed through Flanders in 1834 on his way to Russia, and in 1838 and 1844 on his return from Italy. J. Platt (*N & Q* 8th series, xii [1897] 345) points out the 'medley of languages' in the place-names; but his conclusion that B. 'had never personally explored the route' is not necessarily correct; some of the forms may have been adopted for metrical reasons, and, like many Victorians, B. was cavalier about linguistic consistency. In a letter to the Rev. V. D. Davis of Dec. 1881, B. expressed vexation at the repeated inquiries. He commented that 'attention was meant to be concentrated' on the ride itself and, after giving his usual summary, concluded: 'A film or two, even so slight as the above, may sufficiently support a tolerably big spider-web of a story—where there is ability and good will enough to look most at the main fabric in the middle' (*TLS*, 8 Feb. 1952, p. 109). When she saw the poem in manuscript, EBB. wrote: 'You have finely distanced the rider in Rookwood here—not that I sh^d think of saying so, if we had not talked of him before' (*Wellesley MS*: all her comments recorded in the notes derive from this text, unless otherwise stated). The ref. is to Harrison Ainsworth's account of Dick Turpin's ride to York, in his novel *Rookwood* (1834; iii 253-355), a famous set piece in the popular genre of the 'ride'. *Rookwood* also contains an inset lyric, 'Black Bess', Turpin's tribute to his horse, in the same metre as *How They Brought the Good News*, and with some shared details. See ll. 17n., 22-30n., 47-8n., and 58n. (we are grateful to Mr Michael Meredith for drawing our attention to the importance of this source). B. may also have been influenced by Byron's *The Destruction of Sennacherib* and Scott's ballad *Lochinvar* (from *Marmion*): both are in couplets, again in the same metre as *How They Brought the Good News*, and Scott uses a six-line stanza. Other 'rides' in B. include *My Wife Gertrude* (*Cavalier Tunes* iii), *Through the Metidja*, *Last Ride*, and *Muléykeh*; cp. also *Saul* (1855) 313-18 and *Pheidippides*. EBB. further commented: 'You hear the very trampling & breathing of the horses all through—& the sentiment is left in its right place through all the physical force-display. Then the difficult management of the *three* horses, of the *three* individualities, . . & Roland carrying the interest with him triumphantly! I know you must be fond of this poem: & nobody can forget it who has looked at it once'.

I.
I sprang to the stirrup, and Joris, and He;

¶*1. Cp. Scott, Lochinvar* 40: 'So light to the saddle before her he sprung'.   *Joris*: B. may have taken the name from David Joris, the 16th-century Flemish Anabaptist leader.   *He*] he (*1849-88*). Referring to Dirck, l. 2.

I galloped, Dirck galloped, we galloped all Three;
"Good speed!" cried the watch, as the gate-bolts
    undrew;
"Speed!" echoed the wall to us galloping through;
5 Behind shut the postern, the lights sank to rest,
And into the midnight we galloped abreast.

II.

Not a word to each other; we kept the great pace
Neck by neck, stride for stride, never changing our
    place;
I turned in my saddle and made its girth tight,
10 Then shortened each stirrup, and set the pique right,
Rebuckled the cheek-strap, chained slacker the bit,
Nor galloped less steadily Roland a whit.

III.

'Twas moonset at starting; but while we drew near
Lokeren, the cocks crew and twilight dawned clear;

2-6. EBB. quoted:
    I *galloped*, Dirck *galloped*, we *galloped* all three—
    Good speed cried the watch as the eastgate undrew—
    Good speed from the wall, to us *galloping* through . .
    The gate, shut the porter, the lights sank to rest,
    And into the midnight we *galloped* abreast.
The italics are her own; she commented: 'By the way, how the word
"galloping" is a good galloping word! & how you felt it & took the effect up
& dilated it by repeating it over & over in your first stanza, . . doubling,
folding one upon another, the hoof-treads'. The changes in the published
version were presumably not suggested by her.
2. *Three*] three (*1849–88*).
5. *postern*: a back- or side-gate (i.e. the riders are not leaving by the main
gate); cp. *Flight* 800.
8. *for*] by (*1849–88*).
10. *set the pique right*: in a letter of 1884, B. wrote: 'I certainly had and have
the impression that the old-fashioned projection in front of the military
saddle on the Continent was called the "pique"—and, when of a smaller size,
the "demi-pique": I might as well have styled it simply the "peak". In a large
loose-sitting saddle, the "pique" might, by shifting it to one side, show that
the trim wanted adjustment—"setting right," opposite the withers of the
horse. Such was my impression,—how far justified I cannot immediately
say, the question never before having occurred to me' (to Messrs Blackie &
Son, 20 Feb. 1884, *ABL MS*).
14.] EBB. quoted 'Lokeren, the cocks crew & twilight seemed clear', and
commented: 'I doubt about "twilight seeming clear". Is it a happy

15   At Boom, a great yellow star came out to see;
     At Düffeld, 'twas morning as plain as could be;
     And from Mecheln church-steeple we heard the half-
        chime,
     So Joris broke silence with, "Yet there is time!"

IV.

     At Aerschot, up leaped of a sudden the sun,
20   And against him the cattle stood black every one,
     To stare thro' the mist at us galloping past,
     And I saw my stout galloper Roland at last,

---

expression? But I only *doubt*, you know'. Twilight can refer to either
morning or evening.   *Lokeren*: a town 18 km east-north-east of Ghent;
Platt (see headnote) points out that it is wrongly accented on the second
syllable instead of the first.

15. Boom: a town 25 km east of Lokeren.

16. Düffeld: now Duffel, a town 10 km east of Boom.

17. Mecheln: Flemish Mechelen, French Malines; Platt (see headnote) queries
the use of the German form. A town 7 km south-south-west of Duffel.

     church-steeple: the cathedral of St Rumboldus at Mechelen has a tall
steeple and a 49-bell carillon. Cp. *Rookwood* iii 292: 'as Turpin rode through
the deserted streets of Huntingdon, he heard the eleventh hour given from
the iron tongue of Saint Mary's spire'.

19-30. EBB. admired this passage: 'The leaping up of the sun . . . & the
cattle standing black against him, & staring through the mist at the riders, . .
all that, . . I do not call it *picture*, because it is so much better . . it is the very
sun & mist & cattle themselves. And I like the description of Roland, . . I like
him . . seeing him, . . with one sharp ear bent back & the other pricked out! it
is so livingly the horse—even to me who know nothing of horses in the
ordinary way of sitting down & trying to remember what I know, but who
recognize this for a real horse galloping'.

19. Aerschot: properly Aarschot, the second syllable pronounced 'scot' (Platt;
see headnote); a town 25 km south-east of Duffel.

20. him: the sun; cp., among several other examples, *Morning* 3.

22-30. This passage was clearly influenced by sts. iii-iv of Ainsworth's 'Black
Bess': 'Look! look! how that eyeball glows bright as a brand! / That neck
proudly arches, those nostrils expand! / Mark! that wide-flowing mane! of
which each silky tress / Might adorn prouder beauties—though none like
Black Bess. // Mark! that skin sleek as velvet, and dusky as night, / With its
jet undisfigured by one lock of white; / That throat branched with veins,
prompt to charge or caress, / Now is she not beautiful—bonny Black Bess?'
(iii 241).

22. stout: of a horse: characterized by endurance or staying power, contrasted
with 'speedy'.

With resolute shoulders, each butting away
The haze as some bluff river headland its spray.

V.

25   And his low head and crest, just one sharp ear bent
         back
     For my voice, and the other pricked out on his track;
     And one eye's black intelligence,—ever that glance
     O'er its white edge at me, his own master, askance!
     And the thick heavy spume-flakes which aye and anon
30   His fierce lips shook upwards in galloping on.

VI.

     By Hasselt, Dirck groaned; and cried Joris, "Stay spur!
     "Your Roos galloped bravely, the fault's not in her,
     "We'll remember at Aix"—for one heard the quick
         wheeze
     Of her chest, saw the stretched neck and staggering
         knees,
35   And sunk tail, and horrible heave of the flank,
     As down on her haunches she shuddered and sank.

VII.

     So left were we galloping, Joris and I,
     Past Looz and past Tongres, no cloud in the sky;
     The broad sun above laughed a pitiless laugh,
40   'Neath our feet broke the brittle bright stubble like
         chaff;
     Till over by Dalhem a dome-spire sprang white,
     And "Gallop," gasped Joris, "for Aix is in sight!

29-30. Cp. (noting l. 24) Byron, *The Destruction of Sennacherib* 15-16: 'And the foam of his gasping lay white on the turf, / And cold as the spray of the rock-beating surf'.

29. spume-flakes: cp. *Childe Roland* 114: 'bespate with flakes and spumes'.

31. Hasselt: a town 35 km east-south-east of Aarschot.

37. left were we] we were left (*1849-88*).

38. Looz: the French form; Flemish Loon, now Borgloon, 15 km south of Hasselt.   *Tongres*: again the French form; Flemish Tongeren, 7 km south-east of Borgloon.

41. Dalhem: a village so called lies 20 km south-east of Tongeren, but it is another 30 km east-north-east of Aachen, which is meant to be 'in sight'.   *dome-spire*: Charlemagne's famous Palace Chapel at Aachen has a high dome.

42. sight!] emended in agreement with *1872, 1884* from 'sight!"', all other eds. (since Joris clearly speaks the next sentence).

VIII.

"How they'll greet us"— and all in a moment his roan
Rolled neck and croup over, lay dead as a stone;
45 And there was my Roland to bear the whole weight
Of the news which alone could save Aix from her fate,
With his nostrils like pits full of blood to the brim,
And with circles of red for his eye-sockets' rim.

IX.

Then I cast loose my buffcoat, each holster let fall,
50 Shook off both my jack-boots, let go belt and all,
Stood up in the stirrup, leaned, patted his ear,
Called my Roland his pet-name, my horse without
    peer;
Clapped my hands, laughed and sang, any noise, bad
    or good,
Till at length into Aix Roland galloped and stood.

X.

55 And all I remember is, friends flocking round
As I sate with his head 'twixt my knees on the ground,
And no voice but was praising this Roland of mine,

44. *neck and croup*: cp. the expression 'neck and crop', 'bodily, completely'. The 'croup' is a horse's rump or hindquarters: cp. Scott, *Lochinvar* 39: 'So light to the croup the fair lady he swung'. B. has 'neck by croup' in *Muléykeh* 94.

47-8. Cp. *Rookwood* iii 318: 'her eyeballs were dilated, and glowed like flaming carbuncles; while her widely distended nostril seemed . . . to snort forth smoke'.

49. *buffcoat*: a stout coat of buff leather; used again, with 'jackboots' (see next line), in *Flight* 253.

53.] In an undated autograph of the last two stanzas of the poem, now in the Berg Collection of the New York Public Library, 'any' is replaced by 'every'.

55-60.] EBB. had 'One query at the last stanza'. She quoted the line 'That they saved to have drunk our Duke's health in, but grieved', and commented: 'You mean to say . . "would have grieved" . . do you not? The construction seems a little imperfect'. It is possible, though not certain, that this line came in the place of l. 59; in any case the rhyme-word for 'grieved' has been lost. In a letter to B. of 12-14 Nov. 1845 (after publication), EBB. praised 'that touch of natural feeling at the end, to prove that it was not in brutal carelessness that the poor horse was driven through all that suffering . . yes, & how that one touch of softness acts back upon the energy & resolution & exalts both, instead of weakening anything, as might have been expected by the vulgar of writers or critics' (*LK* 267).

    As I poured down his throat our last measure of wine,
    Which (the burgesses voted by common consent)
60 Was no more than his due who brought good news
      from Ghent.

---

58. Conflating two incidents from *Rookwood*, one the report of a publican: ' "I know he gave his mare more ale than he took for himself" ' (iii 276), the other describing how Turpin gave his horse a restorative potion: 'Raising her head upon his shoulder, Dick poured the contents of the bottle down the throat of his mare' (iii 333).

38 Home-Thoughts, from the Sea

First publ. *B & P* vii (*DR & L*), 6 Nov. 1845, as the last of three untitled sections with the collective title *Home-Thoughts, from Abroad*. This title was later exclusively used for the first section (see p. 283); the second section consisted of *Here's to Nelson's memory*, later incl. in *Nationality in Drinks* (see p. 248). Repr., with the title *Home-Thoughts, from the Sea*, in *1849*, *1863* (when it was placed in *Lyrics*: see Appendix A, p. 464), *1865²*, *1868*, *1888*. Our text is *1845*. The date of composition is uncertain. DeVane (*Handbook* 163-5) ascribes both it and *Here's to Nelson's memory* to B.'s sea trip to Italy in Aug. 1844. The copy of Bartoli's *De' Simboli Trasportati al Morale* in which B. is known to have drafted *How They Brought the Good News* during the 1844 voyage (see headnote, p. 239) also contains an erased draft of *Home-Thoughts, from the Sea*; however, the first four lines, according to *Griffin and Minchin*, 'are an exact transcript of the scene which [B.] beheld from the deck of the *Norham Castle* on the evening of Friday, 27 April, 1838' (p. 127), i.e. during B.'s first trip to Italy. Mrs Orr dates the poem to 1838, quoting B.'s sister Sarianna, who told her that 'the Captain supported [B.] on to the deck as they passed through the Straits of Gibraltar, that he might not lose the sight' (Orr *Life* 94). DeVane argues that, had the poems been written in 1838, B. would have included them in *B & P* iii (*DL*) in 1842, for which he was short of copy. But since he made up this deficiency with *Pied Piper*, which is nearly 300 lines long, he clearly needed more material than these poems would have supplied. Furthermore, if the poems were written on the 1844 voyage, they would have been available for publication in *Hood's Magazine* in the spring of 1845; and DeVane's explanation that they were not used because of B.'s low opinion of them would equally explain their earlier exclusion from *DL*. However, DeVane is on surer ground in pointing to the phrase 'the second time' in l. 2 of *Here's to Nelson's memory* as evidence for the 1844 date, at any rate for that poem. B. also told Fanny Haworth that he had written nothing except a few lines for *Sordello* on the 1838 trip (see headnote, I 351). It is possible that *Home-Thoughts, from the Sea* was written in 1838 and *Here's to Nelson's memory* in 1844, but on balance we agree with DeVane in dating them both to 1844.

The poem, along with *Here's to Nelson's memory*, reflects B.'s interest in Nelson, evoked here by reference to two of his greatest victories (see ll. 1-4.). The following passage from Southey's popular *Life of Nelson* (1813) is suggestive. Nelson was returning to England from India, ill and discouraged about his career: 'I felt impressed with a feeling that I should never rise in my profession. My mind was staggered with a view of the difficulties I had to surmount, and the little interest I possessed. After a long and gloomy reverie, in which I almost wished myself overboard, a sudden glow of patriotism was kindled within me, and presented my king and country as my patron. "Well then", I exclaimed, "I will be a hero! and, confiding in Providence, I will brave every danger!"' Southey adds: 'Long afterwards Nelson loved to speak of the feelings of that moment: and from that time, he often said, a radiant orb was suspended in his mind's eye which urged him onward to renown', also calling this moment of conversion 'a prophetic glory' and 'a light from heaven'. B. refers in a letter of 1884 to Nelson's famous signal before Trafalgar, 'England expects that every man will do his duty', calling it 'sublime' (*New Letters* 298).

EBB. first saw the poem in proof; in her letter of 21-22 Oct. 1845 she wrote praising 'the last "Thought" which is quite to be grudged to that place of fragments . . those grand sea-sights in the long lines' (*LK* 244).

Nobly Cape Saint Vincent to the north-west died away;
Sunset ran, one glorious blood-red, reeking into Cadiz Bay;
Bluish mid the burning water, full in face Trafalgar lay;
In the dimmest north-east distance, dawned Gibraltar grand
    and gray;
"Here and here did England help me,—how can I help
    England?"—say,
Whoso turns as I, this evening, turn to God to praise and
    pray,
Yonder where Jove's planet rises silent over Africa.

¶38.*1-4*. The scene recalls British military and naval victories: Cape St Vincent (14 Feb. 1797) and Trafalgar (1 Oct. 1805), naval battles won by the British fleet under Nelson; Cadiz, the port from which the French and Spanish fleets sailed to Trafalgar, also the scene of Sir Francis Drake's raid (29 Apr. 1587) which 'singed the King of Spain's beard'; Gibraltar, British stronghold since 1713 which resisted numerous sieges.

1. Nobly] Nobly, nobly (*1849-88*).

7.] While Jove's planet rises yonder, silent over Africa. (*1849-88*).   *Jove's planet*: Jupiter.   *Africa*: pronounced to rhyme with the other end-words; see *Count Gismond* 125n.

39 'Here's to Nelson's memory' [Nationality in Drinks iii]

First publ. *B & P* vii (*DR & L*), 6 Nov. 1845, as the second of three untitled sections with the collective title *Home-Thoughts, from Abroad*. This title was later exclusively used for the first section (see p. 283); the third section consisted of the lines later called *Home-Thoughts, from the Sea* (p. 246). Not *1849*. Repr. as the final part of *Nationality in Drinks* in *1863* (when that poem was placed in *Lyrics*: see Appendix A, p. 464, and headnote to *Claret and Tokay*, p. 223); then *1868*, *1888*. Our text is *1845*. For the date of composition, see headnote to *Home-Thoughts, from the Sea*. In 'The Dating of Browning's "Here's to Nelson's Memory"', *SBHC* iv (Fall 1976) 71-2, J. F. Loucks suggests that 'the poem may have been written as late as August 1845, and that the impetus to compose the poem—and to include it in the 1845 volume, *Dramatic Romances and Lyrics*—may have come from a current event: the recent donation, to Greenwich Hospital, of the coat in which Nelson was wounded at the Battle of Trafalgar' (71). Loucks notes that up to this time, Greenwich possessed another coat which, though not possessing tar marks, 'does have a noticeable deposit of greasy dirt across the center seam between the shoulders, where Nelson's pigtail may have rubbed'; since, however, B. could have seen this coat before Loucks's suggested date, and since the coat presented in 1845 has no marks, and is connected to the poem solely by the common link to Trafalgar, we do not regard Loucks's evidence as conclusive proof of a dating in late summer, 1845, though this is clearly possible. The 'Captain' (l. 9) may be Captain Davidson of the *Norham Castle*, 'a rough north-countryman' who liked B. so much that he 'carefully preserved, by way of remembrance, a pair of very old gloves worn by him on deck' (Orr *Life* 101). Nelson, and, more generally, patriotic declamation, vanish from B.'s work after this point, until the tribute to Pym at the end of *Charles Avison*.

> Here's to Nelson's memory!
> 'Tis the second time that I, at sea,
> Right off Cape Trafalgar here,
> Have drunk it deep in British beer:
> 5   Nelson for ever—any time
> Am I his to command in prose or rhyme!
> Give me of Nelson only a touch,

¶39.7. Cp. Nelson's letter to Lady Hamilton (1 Oct. 1805): 'when I came to explain to them the "Nelson touch", it was like an electric shock'. Cp. also the Prologue to Act IV of *Henry V*: 'A little touch of Harry in the night' (l. 47).

And I guard it, be it little or much;
Here's one the Captain gives, and so
10 Down at the word, by George, shall it go!
He says that at Greenwich they show the beholder
Nelson's coat, "still with tar on the shoulder,
"For he used to lean with one shoulder digging,
"Jigging, as it were, and zig-zag-zigging,
15 "Up against the mizen-rigging!"

8. *guard*] save (*1863-88*).
9. *the*] our (*1863-88*).
11-15. There are many relics of Nelson at Greenwich, the best-known being
the coat in which he was killed at Trafalgar; see headnote.
11. show] point (*1863-88*).
12. Nelson's] To Nelson's (*1863-88*).
15. mizen-rigging: or mizzen-rigging (B.'s spelling, unchanged in all eds., was
standard in the period); the rigging of the mizzen-mast, i.e. the aftermost
mast of a three-masted ship.

40 Earth's Immortalities

First publ. *B & P* vii (*DR & L*), 6 Nov. 1845; repr. *1849* (when the section numbers were replaced with the subtitles 'Fame' and 'Love'), *1863* (when it was placed in *Lyrics*: see Appendix A, p. 464), *1868, 1872, 1888.* Our text is *1845*. On the evidence of her letter to B. of 29 Oct. 1845 (*LK* 252), EBB. first saw the poem in proof. DeVane (*Handbook* 176) suggests that the first section was composed after Oct. 1844, when B. visited the graves of Keats and Shelley in Rome. His suggestion that the second section was composed in December (see l. 9) is less persuasive, since the form (love following the course of the seasons) is traditional. For sect. i, cp. Gray's *Elegy* and Byron, *Churchill's Grave*, esp. ll. 5-7: 'that neglected turf and quiet stone, / With name no clearer than the names unknown, / Which lay unread around it', and ll. 41-3: 'that Old Sexton's natural homily, / In which there was Obscurity and Fame— / The Glory and the Nothing of a Name'. In B., cp. *Bad Dreams* iv.

I.

See, as the prettiest graves will do in time,
Our poet's wants the freshness of its prime;
Spite of the sexton's browsing horse, the sods
Have struggled thro' its binding osier-rods;
5 Headstone and half-sunk footstone lean awry,
Wanting the brick-work promised by and by;
How the minute gray lichens, plate o'er plate,
Have softened down the crisp-cut name and date!

II.

So the year's done with!
10   (*Love me for ever!*)
All March begun with,
    April's endeavour;
May-wreaths that bound me
June needs must sever!
15 Now snows fall round me,
    Quenching June's fever—
    (*Love me for ever!*)

¶40.3. *sods*: J. cites Swift, *Elegy on the . . . Death of Mr Demar* 37: 'The sexton shall green sods on thee bestow'.
4. *osier-rods*: the grave has willow palings to prevent the grass coming through. Shelley, *The Sensitive Plant* ii 37, has 'rods and osier-bands'.
7. *plate o'er plate*: in overlapping circular formations.
10. In Feb. 1889 B. was asked whether the refrain was 'cynical, or sad, or trustful?' He replied: 'A mournful comment on the short duration of the conventional "For Ever!"' (*New Poems* 176).

41 Pictor Ignotus
Florence, 15—

First publ. *B & P* vii (*DR & L*), 6 Nov. 1845; repr. *1849, 1863* (when it was placed in *Men, and Women*: see Appendix A, p. 464), *1865²*, *1868, 1872, 1888*. The Latin title means lit. 'painter unknown', used for anonymous works; 'ignotus' can also mean 'of low birth' and (as past participle of 'ignosco') 'forgiven', 'overlooked'. The date of composition is unknown, but a time during or shortly after B.'s second trip to Italy (Aug.-Dec. 1844) is likely. DeVane (*Handbook* 155) argues that it was 'certainly conceived, and possibly written, during Browning's visit to Florence, which may have been early in November, 1844'. Rome, however, which B. visited during his 1844 trip, is also an important presence in the poem; B. would have seen there the work of Raphael, to whom Pictor contrasts himself (see ll. 1-2).

Kintner suggests that it was to this poem that B. referred in a letter to EBB. of ?18 July 1845 (*LK* 128-9) in which he describes

> a poem you are to see—written some time ago—which advises nobody who thinks nobly of the Soul, to give, if he or she can help, such a good argument to the materialist as the owning that any great choice of that Soul, which it is born to make and which—(in its determining, as it must, the whole future course and impulses of that soul)—which must endure for ever (even tho' the object that induced the choice should disappear)— owning, I say, that such a choice may be scientifically determined and produced, at any operator's pleasure, by a definite number of ingredients, so much youth, so much beauty, so much talent &c &c with the same certainty and precision that another kind of operator will construct you an artificial volcano with so much steel filings and flower of sulphur and what not. There is more in the soul than rises to the surface and meets the eye; whatever does *that*, is for the world's immediate uses; and were this world *all*, *all* in us would be producible and available for use, as it *is* with the body now—but with the soul, what is to be developed *afterward* is the main thing, and instinctively asserts its rights—so that when you hate (or love) you shall not be able to explain "why" ("You" is the ordinary enough creature of my poem—*he* might not be so able).

Pictor's 'great choice', according to this theory, would be his decision to retire to a monastery instead of pursuing the commercial career that his 'talent' might seem to warrant; and this decision results from a hatred of the world which reflects Pictor's instinctive longing to transcend it, though he himself is unable to understand his action in those terms, and represents it as misanthropy, or dislike of commercialism. The question of the value or otherwise of popularity to a poet was discussed by B. and EBB. during their early correspondence, and *Pictor* may have been written in the context of their debate: see EBB. to B., 3 Feb. 1845, and B.'s reply, 11 Feb. 1845 (*LK* 14-15, 18-19).

A historical original for the painter has been suggested by J. B. Bullen ('Browning's "Pictor Ignotus" and Vasari's "Life of Fra Bartolommeo di San Marco"', *RES* xxiii [1972] 313-19). Bullen argues that it was from Vasari's *Vite de' Pittori* (Florence 1550) and A. F. Rio's *De la Poésie Chrétienne* (Paris 1836) that B. learned of Bartolommeo (*c.* 1475-1517), who painted predominantly religious subjects, and who, under the influence of Savanarola, entered the Dominican Order in 1499 and abandoned painting altogether for four years, a decision Vasari attributes in part to personal timidity. Bullen points out that Fra Bartolommeo's surname was unknown, and that he was commonly called simply 'il Frate' (the Friar); following earlier commentators, he identifies the 'youth' of l. 1 with Raphael, and goes on to suggest a reference to the period (mentioned by Vasari and Rio) when Bartolommeo visited Rome and painted with him. Cp. Anna Jameson, *Memoirs of the Early Italian Painters* (first publ. 1843): '[Bartolommeo] might have been *the* Raphael, had not Fortune been determined in favour of the other'. See also headnote to *Lines on Correggio*, p. 454. M. H. Bright ('Browning's Celebrated Pictor Ignotus', *ELN* xiii [1976] 192-4) objects to the identification both on circumstantial grounds (Fra Bartolommeo did paint on canvas and in the houses of rich men, whereas Pictor paints frescoes in churches; Bartolommeo did sell his pictures; he was not a monotonous anti-realist but was praised for the animation of his figures, etc.), and on the interpretative ground that the poem hinges on the fact that the painter has not achieved, and will not achieve, recognition, either during his lifetime or after death, a state of affairs which emphatically did not apply to Fra Bartolommeo. For further exchanges between Bullen and Bright, see *ELN* xiii (1976) 206-15; we accept Bright's view that Bartolommeo is not the literal subject of the poem; but it is plausible to claim that B. drew on some details of his career.

Many *DR & L* poems, such as *Lost Leader*, *Lost Mistress*, *Time's Revenges*, also deal with loss, renunciation, and defection, but by placing *Pictor*, in *1863*, in *Men, and Women*, B. elected to stress its place in his theory of the development of Renaissance art. EBB. commented: 'This poem is so fine, .. so full of power, . . as to claim every possible attention to the working of it. It begins greatly, grandly, & ends so—the winding up winds up the soul in it. The versification too is noble . . & altogether it classes with your finest poems of the length—does it not, in your own mind? I cannot tell you how much it impresses mine' (*Wellesley MS*: all her comments recorded in the notes derive from this text, unless otherwise stated). William Stigand, summing up B.'s career towards the close of his review of *DP* (*ER* cxx [Oct. 1864] 537-65; repr. *CH* 230-60), suggested an analogy between B.'s own attitude to popular success, and Pictor's: 'Mr. Browning has always chosen . . . to remain apart from the beaten track of the ordinary world; and we can imagine him sharing in the feelings of his own "Pictor Ignotus" who . . . thus expresses his contempt for the vulgar crowd— [quotes ll. 46-57]. So Mr. Browning has chosen his portion, and the popularity which he has despised will in all probability never be thrust upon him.'

I could have painted pictures like that youth's
    Ye praise so. How my soul springs up! No bar
Stayed me—ah, thought which saddens while it
      soothes!
    Never did fate forbid me, star by star,
5 To outburst on your night with all my gift
    Of fires from God: nor would this flesh have shrunk
From seconding that soul, with eyes uplift
    And wide to Heaven, or, straight like thunder, sunk
To the centre of an instant, or around
10   Sent calmly and inquisitive to scan
The license and the limit, space and bound,
    Allowed to Truth made visible in Man.
And, like that youth ye praise so, all I saw,
    Over the canvass could my hand have flung,
15 Each face obedient to its passion's law,
    Each passion clear proclaimed without a tongue;
Whether Hope rose at once in all the blood,
    A-tiptoe for the blessing of embrace,
Or Rapture drooped the eyes as when her brood
20   Pull down the nesting dove's heart to its place,
Or Confidence lit swift the forehead up,
    And locked the mouth fast, like a castle braved,—
Men, women, children, hath it spilt, my cup?

¶41.6-7. *this . . . that*] my . . . my (*1849-88*).

7-10. *uplift . . . sunk . . . Sent*: these verbs are all past participles modifying 'eyes'.

8-9.] EBB. quoted: 'like a thunder sunk / To the centre of an instant', and commented: 'Is there not something obscure in the expression? And it is all so fine here, that you should let the reader stand up as straight as he can, to look round'.

10. *Sent*] Turned (*1849-88*).

15-16. Cp. *Fifine* 1719-26: 'the infinitude / Of passions, loves and hates, man pampers till his mood / Becomes himself, the whole sole face we name him by, / Nor want denotement else, if age or youth supply / The rest of him: old, young,—classed creature: in the main / A love, a hate, a hope, a fear, each soul a-strain / Some one way through the flesh—the face, the evidence / O' the soul at work inside'.

19-20. EBB. quoted these lines (with 'rapture' for 'Rapture' and 'her eyes' for 'the eyes') and commented: 'A most exquisite image, & perfect in the expression of it I think'. Cp. *A Forest Thought* 52, 'the brood-song of the cushat-dove'.

23. *Men, women, children*] O Human faces (*1849-88*, except 'human', *1863-88*).

23-4. The 'cup' is a frequent biblical image of God's bounty: the speaker's use

What did ye give me that I have not saved?
25   Nor will I say I have not dreamed (how well!)
Of going—I, in each new picture,—forth,
And making new hearts beat and bosoms swell,
As still to Pope and Kaiser, South and North,
Bound for the calmly satisfied great State,
30   Or glad aspiring little burgh, it went,
Flowers cast upon the car which bore the freight
Through old streets named afresh from its event,
—Of reaching thus my home, where Age should greet
My face, and Youth, the star as yet distinct

---

of it contrasts with *Psalms* xxiii 5: 'thou hast anointed my head with oil; my cup runneth over'.

26-35. These lines, together with ll. 57-68, suggest a contrast, not simply between secular and religious art, but between easel painting (portable and therefore saleable) and fresco (stationary: the usual medium of ecclesiastical art). *Murray²* claims: 'in the sixteenth century, it may be doubted whether any *cabinet pictures*, that is to say, moveable pictures, intended merely to hang upon the wall and be looked at as ornaments . . . ever existed' (p. 428).

27.] EBB. quoted 'Ever new hearts made beat & bosoms swell', and commented: 'The construction seems to me to be entangled a little by this line, . . & the reader pauses before he clears the meaning to himself. Why not clear it for him by writing the line thus . . for instance . . ? "New hearts being made to beat, & breasts to swell" or something better which will strike you. Will you consider?'   *And*] As, (*1849-88*).

28.] To Pope or Kaiser, East, West, South or North, (*1849-88*, except 'South, or', *1870-88*). For 'Kaiser' see *Sordello* i 78-9n., 131n.

32. DeVane (*Handbook* 156) suggests a reference to the Borgo Allegri in Rome, so named after a Madonna by Cimabue was carried along it.   *its event*] the event (*1865-88*). The *1845* reading involves an unusual sense of 'event', as meaning something like 'appearance, apparition'.

33.] Till it reached home, where learned Age should greet (*1849-88*, except 'age', *1868-88*). EBB. quoted 'And thus to reach my home, where Age sh^d greet', and commented: 'Should you not write it . . "Of reaching thus my home" &c, the construction taking you back to what he dreamed of. First he dreamed "of going"—& then "of reaching" his home &c'.   *home*: the picture's 'home', where it is to be hung (not the painter's literal home).

34. as yet] not yet (*1849-88*). With the *1845* text, cp. Wordsworth's *Ode: Intimations of Immortality*, where 'The Soul that rises with us, our life's Star' fades for 'The Youth, who daily farther from the east / Must travel' (ll. 59, 72-3); note also ll. 122-3: 'Thou little Child, yet glorious in the might / Of heaven-born freedom'. With the revised reading, cp. *A Soul's Tragedy* ii 634-41n. Cp. also *In a Balcony* 688-9: 'I am not bid create, they see no star / Transfiguring my brow'.

35   Above his hair, lie learning at my feet,—
       Oh, thus to live, I and my pictures, linked
     With love about, and praise, till life should end,
       And then not go to Heaven but linger here,
     Here on my earth, its every man my friend,—
40   Oh, that grows frightful, 'tis so wildly dear!
     But a voice changed it! Glimpses of such sights
       Have scared me, like the revels thro' a door
     Of some strange House of Idols at its rites;
       This world seemed not the world it was before!
45   Mixed with my loving ones there trooped—for what?
       Who summoned those cold faces which begun
     To press on me and judge me? As asquat
       And shrinking from the soldiery a nun,
     They drew me forth, and spite of me . . enough!
50   These buy and sell our pictures, take and give,
     Count them for garniture and household-stuff,

36. *pictures*] picture (*1849-88*).

38. EBB. quoted 'And then not go to Heaven &c', adding: 'Fine, all this!'

39. *its*] earth's (*1849-88*).

40.] The thought grew frightful, 'twas so wildly dear! (*1849-88*).

41-56. Mrs Jameson (see headnote) cites one description of Bartolommeo as 'a monk in the retirement of his cloister, shut out from the taunts and criticisms of the world'. Bullen (see headnote) argues that the 'voice' is that of Savanorola, whose preaching caused Fra Bartolommeo to destroy all his studies of nudes, and probably influenced his temporary abandonment of painting. According to Vasari, Bartolommeo was 'a man of little courage, or rather, very timid and retiring', and on the occasion of an attack upon a convent where he was staying, 'began to be in great fear, and made a vow that if he escaped he would assume the religious habit'. But the parallel cannot be pressed too far: there is no evidence that Bartolommeo's withdrawal expressed a distaste for commercialism, and B. presumably meant Pictor's 'voice' to be understood metaphorically rather than literally, since without an explicit identification with Bartolommeo the reference to Savanorola could not be appreciated.

41. *it!*] it. (*1865²*, *1868-88*).

45.] Mixed with my loving trusting ones there trooped (*1849-88*, except 'ones,' *1870-88*).

46. *which*] that (*1849-88*).

47. *As asquat*] Tho' I stooped (*1849-88*, except 'Though', *1863-88*).

48. *And shrinking*] Shrinking, as (*1849-88*).

50.] EBB. quoted 'These men may buy us, sell us, &c.', and commented: 'meaning pictures, by "*us*". But the reader cannot see it until afterwards, & gets confused. Is it not so? And moreover I do think that by a touch or two you might give a clearer effect to the previous verses about the "jibing" &c'. These 'previous verses' were altered, beyond reconstruction.

And where they live needs must our pictures live,
And see their faces, listen to their prate,
Partakers of their daily pettiness,
55   Discussed of,—"This I love or this I hate,
"This likes me more and this affects me less!"
Wherefore I chose my portion. If at whiles
My heart sinks as monotonous I paint
These endless cloisters and eternal aisles
60   With the same series, Virgin, Babe, and Saint,
With the same cold, calm, beautiful regard,
At least no merchant traffics in my heart;
The sanctuary's gloom at least shall ward
Vain tongues from where my pictures stand apart;
65   Only prayer breaks the silence of the shrine
While, blackening in the daily candle smoke,
They moulder on the damp wall's travertine,
'Mid echoes the light footstep never woke.
So die, my pictures; surely, gently die!

52. *needs must our pictures*] our pictures needs must (*1849-63*).
55-6. Contrast B. to EBB., 24 May 1845: 'I do myself justice, and dare call things by their names to myself, and say boldly, this I love, this I hate, this I would do, this I would not do, under all kinds of circumstances' (*LK 75*).
57-61. If at whiles . . . regard: Murray[2], speaking of ecclesiastical painters in fresco, comments: 'From the fixed types of sacred subjects, transmitted from the earlier ages, no artist could dare to depart' (p. 428). Speaking of Bartolommeo, Rio (see headnote) mentions that accusations of 'powerlessness to draw the nude' were perhaps intended to tempt him to 'transgress the narrow circle of religious representations to which he had scrupulously confined himself' (p. 285).
57. chose] choose (*1865*[2]).
58. paint] emended in agreement with all other eds. from 'paint,' in *1845*.
60. Virgin, Babe, and Saint: Fra Bartolommeo (see headnote), along with Raphael, 'evolved a new treatment . . . of the theme of the Madonna and Child with the Infant S. John in a Landscape' (*Oxford Companion to Art*). See however ll. 26-35n. Cp. Lippo's impatience, 'A-painting for the great man, saints and saints / And saints again' (*Fra Lippo* 48-9).
63-9. Cp. *Old Pictures* 185-93, where the 'ghosts' of the early Florentine painters 'stand . . . Watching each fresco flaked and rasped, / Blocked up, knocked out, or whitewashed o'er / —No getting again what the church has grasped! / The works on the wall must take their chance, / "Works never conceded to England's thick clime!" / (I hope they prefer their inheritance / Of a bucketful of Italian quick-lime.)'
67. travertine: a hard, white stone, used for building in Italy; cp. *Tomb at St. Praxed's* 66n.

70   Oh youth men praise so, holds their praise its
          worth?
      Blown harshly, keeps the trump its golden cry?
      Tastes sweet the water with such specks of earth?

---

71. *trump*: trumpet. Fama (fame) 'was worshipped by the ancients as a
powerful goddess, and generally represented blowing a trumpet' (*Lemprière*).
Cp. Chaucer, *House of Fame* iii, where the goddess summons her trumpeter,
Eolus, to proclaim either infamy with his 'blake trumpe of bras' (l. 545) or
honour with his 'trumpe of gold' (l. 687).

42 The Tomb at St Praxed's [The Bishop Orders His Tomb at Saint Praxed's Church]

Rome, 1 5—

Text and publication

First publ. *Hood's Magazine* iii (March 1845) 237-9; for B.'s contributions to *Hood's*, see p. 218. Repr. *B & P* vii (*DR & L*), Nov. 1845, *1849* (with the later title), *1863* (when it was placed in *Men, and Women*: see Appendix A, p. 464), *1868, 1872, 1888*.

Date and composition

K. I. D. Maslen, citing a source for ideas and images in the poem from 1840 (for details see below) suggests that 'as with many of Browning's later poems, the idea had been with him for some years'; but the composition of the poem itself probably belongs to the winter of 1844-5. B. saw the church of Santa Prassede in Rome during his second trip to Italy in the autumn of 1844. Shortly after his return, in a letter to EBB. of 27 Jan. 1845 (*LK* 11), he mentioned 'three or four half-done-with' poems; he sent the poem to F. O. Ward, acting editor of *Hood's*, on 18 Feb.: 'I send you *one* poem as long as the two I promised (about 4 pages, I think) and I pick it out as being a pet of mine, and just the thing for the time—what with the Oxford business, and Camden society and other embroilments' (*New Letters* 35-6). DeVane's assumption (*Handbook* 166) that B. conceived the poem during his 1844 visit is challenged by *Penguin*, which argues that the phrase 'I pick it out' in B.'s letter to Ward, together with the ref. to the Tractarian controversy ('the Oxford business'), which had been in progress for many years, could imply an earlier date. An error taken from *Murray*[2] (see ll. 48-9n.) could mean either that B. used this guidebook before he went to Italy in 1844, or that he used it after his return to refresh his memory. However, DeVane makes the point that B. would probably have sent the poem to *Hood's* before Feb. 1845 had he written it earlier. We concur with this view, and would add that another inaccuracy in B.'s description of the church supports the later date. Santa Prassede has a domed apse, whereas in the poem it is said to have a full dome; this would accord well with an imperfect recollection.

B. sent the poem to EBB. along with his other 'sins of commission with Hood' in a letter of ?18 July 1845 (*LK* 129). The evidence of *Wellesley MS* suggests that she gave him a batch of notes on all the *Hood's* poems at a meeting on 22 Sept. She criticized the phrasing of ll. 17-18, but suggested no other revs. in her notes or in her letter commenting on the proofs of *DR & L* (21-22 Oct. 1845, *LK* 244). She may, of course, have made suggestions verbally to B.

Sources and influences; parallels in B.

'Praxed' is the anglicized form of 'Prassede'; B. would have found 'Praxed' in *Murray²*, which says that the church was 'founded on the site of a small oratory built here by Pius I A.D. 160 as a place of security to which the early Christians might retire during the persecutions' (p. 367). As the daughter of a senator, Pudens (mentioned in *2 Timothy* iv 21), Prassede had great wealth which she used to help other Christians during the persecutions. An 18th-century painting in the church shows her having a vision of the martyrdom of her fellow-Christians. Commentators have perceived some irony in the contrast between her and the Bishop; this is supported by the presence in the church of a slab of granite on which Prassede was reputed to sleep. B.'s knowledge of Church history makes it unlikely that he committed the error which has been attributed to him (at l. 95) of mistaking Prassede's gender; his visit to the church makes such an error practically inconceivable.

B.'s choice of the church of Santa Prassede as the setting for the poem has been much misunderstood. Mrs Orr (*Handbook* 247) states, probably on B.'s authority: 'The Bishop's tomb is entirely fictitious; but something which is made to stand for it is now shown to credulous sightseers in St. Praxed's Church'. Since the Bishop's sons have obviously no intention of complying with his grandiose design, no exact model of the tomb could possibly exist; if anything, an inferior tomb should be looked for. The church in fact contains two funerary monuments of Cardinals of Santa Prassede. The first, of Cardinal Anchero Pantaleone of Troyes, dating from 1287, is small, modestly decorated, with an inscription which does not mention the Cardinal's name. The second, of Cardinal Cetti (who was also Bishop of Sabina), dating from 1474, is much larger and more lavish, decorated 'with portraits of himself, St. Peter and St. Paul, and statues of S. Prassede and S. Pudenzia' (*Murray²* 382). Murray implies that the two monuments are within sight of each other, though in fact they are not; but whether B. was relying on Murray or on his own memory, the conjunction of these two monuments could have suggested the idea of rivalry. This possibility is strengthened by the fact that there are no other similar monuments in the church. J. W. Binns ('Real Sources for the Bishop's Tomb in the Church of St. Praxed', *SBC* xii [1984] 160-66) points out that the 'statue' of S. Prassede is in fact a bas-relief and that other details such as the 'tripod' and 'vase' also appear on the tomb (see ll. 56, 58; and see also l. 60n.). Competition for the best location for one's tomb was common in the period in which the poem is set: the best position was thought to be in the choir, near the altar (see ll. 20-4, and L. M. Thompson, 'The Placement of the Bishop's Tomb in St. Praxed's Church', *SBC* xi [1983] 74-5).

The Bishop compares a detail of his projected tomb with one belonging to the monument to St Ignatius Loyola, founder of the Jesuit order and one of the chief architects of the Counter-Reformation, in the Gesù church in Rome (see ll. 48-9). Scholars have pointed out that the date of the monument (1690) is incompatible with the date of the poem. This anachronism is however presumably a deliberate mistake drawing attention to an argument in the poem, articulated through the development of funerary sculpture, about the history and contemporary state of the Roman Catholic Church. According to this argument, the poem's setting in the 16th century places it at a mid-point between the decline of the Renaissance Church into corruption and materialism, with the consequent devastation of the Reformation, and its resurgence in the 17th century, the period of the Counter-Reformation. This mid-point is represented by the Bishop's visionary tomb, which both sums up the sensuality and paganism of the High Renaissance, and anticipates the militant splendour of the Baroque. Browning's satire in the poem would therefore hit simultaneously at the old, unregenerate Catholic Church, and at its Counter-Reformation successor; the allusion to Loyola would be apt because the Jesuits were devoted to the Papacy and had helped to restore its power and prestige. But this same satire could also be applied to the Anglican Church: hence B.'s claim that it was 'just the thing for the time, what with the Oxford business'. The Tractarian (or 'Oxford') movement in England was a kind of 'Counter-Reformaton' within the Church of England, which sought to bring it closer to Catholic doctrine and practice (some of its leading figures, such as Newman and Pugin, did in fact become Catholics, Newman in 1845, the year of the poem's publication). The poem could be seen as a Dissenter's view of this controversy, in which the Anglican Church is both paralleled to the Roman Catholic Church in its internal divisions, and ideologically associated with it despite surface differences.

B.'s mention of the 'Camden society' in his letter to Ward leads to another set of possible sources. R. A. Greenberg, in an excellent article ('Ruskin, Pugin, and the Contemporary Context of *The Bishop Orders His Tomb*', *PMLA* lxxxiv [1960] 1588-94), points out that there were two Camden Societies at this time, both internally divided between Catholic and Protestant interpretations of the antiquarian and historical research in which they were engaged, and both taking part in the Tractarian controversy. He notes that these divisions were at their fiercest in both societies in late 1844. Greenberg quotes extensively from ch. i of Pugin's *Contrasts* (2nd ed., 1842) as a parallel to B.'s reflections on what Pugin calls 'the revived paganism'. Pugin's hostility, as a devout Catholic, to the mingling of Christian and pagan motifs in every aspect of ecclesiastical architecture (including 'monuments for the dead') may be gauged from the following passages: 'The inverted torch, the club of Hercules, the owl of Minerva, and the cinerary urn, are carved . . . on the tombs of popes, bishops, kings, ecclesiastics . . . frequently accompanied by pagan divinities, in pagan nudity'; 'When I see a man professedly a Christian, who, neglecting the mysteries of the faith, the saints of the Church, and the glories of religion, surrounds himself with the obscene and impious fables of mythology, and the false divinities of the heathen, I may presume, without violation of charity, that although he is nominally a son of Christian Rome, his heart and affections are devoted to that city in the days of its Paganism'.

K. I. D. Maslen ('Browning and Macaulay', *N & Q* n. s. xxvii [1980] 525-7) suggests that 'the germs, and indeed the main ingredients of the poem are to be found already gathered in a review by Macaulay in the *Edinburgh Review* for October 1840 of Leopold von Ranke's *Ecclesiastical and political history of the Popes of Rome*, translated by Sarah Austin'. Maslen quotes persuasively from Macaulay's review: 'During the generation which preceded the Reformation, that court [of Rome] had been a scandal to the Christian name. Its annals are black with treason, murder, and incest. Even its more respectable members were utterly unfit to be ministers of religion. . . . Their years glided by in a soft dream of sensual and intellectual voluptuousness. Choice cookery, delicious wines, lovely women, hounds, falcons, horses, newly-discovered manuscripts of the classics, sonnets and burlesque romances in the sweetest Tuscan . . . plate from the hand of Benvenuto, designs for palaces by Michael Angelo, frescoes by Raphael, busts, mosaics, and gems just dug up from among the ruins of ancient temples and villas;—these things were their delight and even the serious business of their lives . . . it was felt that the Church could not be safely confided to chiefs whose highest praise was, that they were good judges of Latin compositions, of paintings, of statues, whose severest studies had a Pagan character'.

G. Monteiro (*VP* viii [1970] 209-18) gives an interesting though occasionally strained account of biblical sources. P. A. Cundiff, in 'Browning's Old Bishop' (*VP* ix [1971] 452-3), suggests a verbal and structural parallel with *Job*, ch. vii; note T. Scott's translation of vv. 5-7, in *The Book of Job in English Verse* (1773): 'Behold my putrid frame; it was not cast / A substance through whole centuries to last' (p. 48), which comes close to the central motif of the poem. The iconography of the Bishop's projected tomb is usefully discussed in *Melchiori* 20-39.

There is no single original for the Bishop himself. J. D. Rea's derivation of certain details from Ireneo Affo's *Vita de Vespasiano Gonzaga* ('My Last Duchess', *SP* xxix [1932] 120-1) is disputed by L. S. Friedland ('Ferrara and *My Last Duchess*', *SP* xxxiii [1936] 657, 665), but Rea's argument retains some conviction. He finds a 'Gandolfo' who is a priest in the *Vita* (though Friedland argues it is a common Italian name); more important, he cites a passage from Gonzaga's will which describes him as 'lying in bed in a certain state chamber of the prefect's palace': cp. 'As here I lie / In this state-chamber' (ll. 10-11). In the will itself, Gonzaga orders his daughter to construct him a sumptuous tomb, and mentions 'the stones necessary to adorn the aforesaid tomb, which I have had brought from Rome'. The rare form 'elucescebat' (see l. 99) also occurs in the *Vita*. Dr M. Halls has suggested to us a resemblance between the Bishop and Cardinal Pietro Bembo (1470-1547): advocacy of Cicero's Latin style, sexual profligacy before ordination, and interest in pagan antiquity and classical scholarship are in common between them. B. may have known W. P. Greswell, *Memoirs of Politianus* (1805), which contains all these details. Greswell mentions Bembo's 'connection with a beautiful female' with whom he had three sons and a daughter, but stresses that this affair came before his ordination (cp. ll. 3-7). He notes that 'Bembo is charged with carrying his affected imitation of the style of Cicero to so ridiculous an extreme as professedly to avoid perusal of his Bible and breviary, for fear of spoiling his latinity'. Bembo founded a society no member of which might use a non-Ciceronian word, and engaged in a protracted controversy with Pico Gianfrancesco as to the value of the Ciceronian style (cp. ll. 77-9, 98-100). Bembo was also accused of denying the doctrine of a future state. B. certainly knew of Bembo. Two of Bembo's works were in his library (*Collections* A192 and A193, p. 18). In a letter to EBB. of 28 June 1846, he quotes Carlyle's opinion of Bembo as the type of Italian scholar who neglected to 'examine the new problems of the Reformation &c—trim the balance at intervals, and throw overboard the accumulation of falsehood', and instead devoted themselves to 'verse-making, painting, music-scoring' (*LK* 822). B. mentions Bembo in two later works (*Ring* vi 1666, and the preface to *Asolando*), referring both times to his literary dilettantism. B. may well have used Bembo as a model for the Bishop, but the poem is not a portrait of Bembo; cp. the use of Fra Bartolommeo in *Pictor* (headnote, p. 252). The Bishop has affinities with the Intendant in *Pippa* iv, who has also robbed a church and amassed many villas, and with the Duke of *My Last Duchess*.

Two important literary sources have been suggested by H. M. Richmond in 'Personal Identity and Literary Persona: A Study in Historical Psychology', *PMLA* xc (1975) 209-19, who describes the poem as 'a clever superimposition of the theatrical death-bed episodes from Izaak Walton's *Life of Donne*, on analogous but purely pagan and frivolous material excerpted from the role-playing of Trimalchio in the *Satyricon* of Petronius' (p. 219). The latter ref. is to *Satyricon* lxxi, part of the 'Cena Trimalchionis' (Trimalchio's Feast), in which the wealthy sensualist Trimalchio gives a lavish supper to his cronies and hangers-on: towards the end of the supper he becomes maudlin and reads out his will to the assembled company. He then turns to his friend Habinnas with some instructions concerning his tomb:

> Are you building my monument the way I told you? I particularly want you to keep a place at the foot of my statue and put a picture of my pup there, as well as paintings of wreaths, scent-bottles, and the contents of Petraites, and thanks to you I'll be able to live on after I'm dead . . . After all, it's a big mistake to have nice houses just for when you're alive and not worry about the one we have to live in for much longer. And that's why I want this written up before anything else:
> THIS MONUMENT DOES NOT GO TO THE HEIR
> But I'll make sure in my will that I don't get done down once I'm dead . . . Propped up on a lot of cushions, he stretched out along the edge of the couch and said: 'Pretend I'm dead and say something nice' (transl. J. Sullivan [Harmondsworth 1965]).

B. owned a copy of the *Satyricon* (*Collections* A1841, p. 157). Richmond's other source is the account of Donne's last days in Izaak Walton's *Life*:

> It is observed, that a desire of glory or commendation is rooted in the very nature of man; and, that those of the severest and most mortified lives . . . have not been able to kill this desire of glory . . . and, we want not sacred examples to justifie the desire of having our memory to out-live our lives:

which I mention, because Dr. *Donne* . . . easily yielded at this very time to
have a Monument made for him . . . Dr. *Donne* sent for a Carver to make
him in wood the figure of an *Urn* . . . and, to bring with it a board of the
height of his body. These being got, then without delay a choice Painter
was to be in a readiness to draw his picture, which was taken as
followeth.— Several Charcole-fires being first made in his large Study, he
brought with him into that place his winding-sheet in his hand; and,
having put off all his cloaths, had this sheet put on him . . . as dead bodies
are usually fitted to be shrowded and put into the grave. Upon this *Urn* he
thus stood with his eyes shut, and with so much of the sheet turned aside as
might shew his lean, pale, death-like face; which was purposely turned
toward the East, from whence he expected the second coming of his and
our Saviour. Thus he was drawn at his just height; and when the picture
was fully finished, he caused it to be set by his bed-side, where it
continued, and became his hourly object till his death: and, was then given
to his dearest friend and Executor Dr. *King*, who caused him to be thus
carved in one entire piece of white Marble, as it now stands in the
Cathedral Church of St. *Pauls*; and by Dr. *Donne's* own appointment,
these words were to be affixed to it as his Epitaph: [quotes Latin epitaph].
Upon Monday following, he took his last leave of his beloved Study; and,
being sensible of his hourly decay, retired himself to his bed-chamber: and,
that week sent at several times for many of his most considerable friends,
with whom he took a solemn and deliberate farewell; commending to their
considerations some sentences useful for the regulation of their lives, and
then dismist them, as good *Jacob* did his sons, with a spiritual benediction.
(*The Lives of Dr. John Donne, Sir Henry Wotton* [etc.], 1670, repr. 1969,
74-7)
The biblical allusion in Walton's last sentence is to *Genesis* xlix; in vv. 29-30
Jacob instructs his sons on his place of burial.

B. himself drew attention to the strain of anti-Catholicism in the poem (see
above), but his attitude to the Catholic Church was flexible, ranging from
uncompromising hostility (*Paracelsus, Confessional, Holy-Cross Day*) to the
interest and limited tolerance of *CE & ED. Sordello, Bishop Blougram,* and
Ring show B.'s attitude at its most complex.

Criticism
The poem was, for B., 'a pet of my own', and EBB. praised it as 'of course
the finest & most powerful' of the *Hood's* poems (21 July 1845, *LK* 130); in
her critical notes, she wrote: 'This is a wonderful poem I think—& classes
with those works of yours which show most power . . most unquestionable
genius in the high sense. You force your reader to sympathize positively in
his glory in being buried!' (*Wellesley MS*). Ruskin quoted ll. 10-81 (with a
few omissions) in *Modern Painters* iv (1856; *Works*, ed. Cook and
Wedderburn [1913] vi 448), as an example of B.'s 'unerring' historical sense,
'always vital, right, and profound', and in particular B.'s understanding of
'the kind of admiration with which a southern artist regarded the *stone* he

worked in; and the pride which populace or priest took in the possession of precious mountain substance, worked into the pavements of their cathedrals, and the shafts of their tombs'. Ruskin concluded: 'I know of no other piece of modern English, prose or poetry, in which there is so much told, as in these lines, of the Renaissance spirit,—its worldliness, inconsistency, pride, hypocrisy, ignorance of itself, love of art, of luxury, and of good Latin. It is nearly all that I have said of the central Renaissance in thirty pages of the *Stones of Venice*, put into as many lines, Browning's also being the antecedent work'. B. was vexed that Ruskin's praise was not more widely circulated by Chapman, his publisher at this period (*New Letters* 93), but it undoubtedly helped the improvement of his literary reputation in the 1860s.

> Vanity, saith the Preacher, vanity!
> Draw round my bed: is Anselm keeping back?
> Nephews—sons mine . . . ah God, I know not! Well—
> She, men would have to be your mother once,
> 5   Old Gandolf envied me, so fair she was!
> What's done is done, and she is dead beside,
> And long ago, and I am Bishop since,
> And as she died so must we die ourselves,
> And thence ye may perceive the world's a dream.
> 10   Life, how and what is it? As here I lie

¶42.*1.* From *Ecclesiastes* i 2: 'Vanity of vanities, saith the Preacher; vanity of vanities, all is vanity'. The Preacher is Solomon. 'Vanity' here means 'futility', 'worthlessness', 'emptiness'. This line is the first of several biblical tags in the poem, all of them implying that there is no life after death, and that life is therefore pointless. See ll. 51n., 101n. *Melchiori* 29 points out that the verse also recurs in the final chapter of *Ecclesiastes* (xii 8), and that the preceding verse may therefore be relevant to the poem: 'Then shall the dust return to the earth as it was: and the spirit shall return unto God who gave it'.
2-3. S. A. Brooke (*The Poetry of Robert Browning* [1902] 283) compares this scene to the deathbed of St John in *A Death*. Rabbi Ben Ezra, in his 'Song of Death' in *Holy-Cross Day*, 'Called sons and sons' sons to his side' (l. 68).
3. It was not uncommon for a powerful (and nominally celibate) Roman Catholic priest in this period to pass off his own children as nephews or nieces (hence the term 'nepotism'). B.'s library included a volume (by G. Leti) called *Il Nipotismo di Roma, or The History of the Pope's Nephews* (1669): *Collections* A1442, p. 123. Cp. *Ring* iii 1475-6 and xi 1088, 1097-98, and the 'Prior's niece' in *Fra Lippo Lippi* 170-1, 195-7, where the fiction conceals a mistress rather than a child.
6. Cp. *Macbeth* III ii 12 ('What's done is done') and Marlowe, *Jew of Malta* IV i: 'Thou hast committed— / Fornication: but that was in another country, and besides, the wench is dead'.
7. And long ago] Dead long ago (*1845-88*).
10. Life, how and what is it?: cp. Shelley, *Triumph of Life* 544: 'Then, what is

In this state-chamber, dying by degrees,
Hours and long hours in the dead night, I ask
"Do I live, am I dead?" Peace, peace seems all:
St. Praxed's ever was the church for peace;
15 And so, about this tomb of mine. I fought
With tooth and nail to save my niche, ye know:
—Old Gandolf came me in, despite my care,
For a shrewd snatch out of the corner south
To grace his carrion with, God curse the same!
20 Yet still my niche is not so cramp'd but thence
One sees the pulpit o' the epistle-side,
And somewhat of the choir, those silent seats,
And up into the aery dome where live
The angels, and a sunbeam's sure to lurk:
25 And I shall fill my slab of basalt there,

---

life? I cried', and its biblical source, *James* iv 14: 'For what is your life? It is even a vapour, that appeareth for a little time, and then vanisheth away'. Also Mrs Barbauld, *Life*, a poem known to B. (a transcription of it exists in his hand: see *Collections* E547, p. 448): 'Life! I know not what thou art, / But know that thou and I must part; / And when, or how, or where we met / I own to me's a secret yet'. A poem entitled *What is Life?* appeared in Coleridge's *Literary Remains* i 60.

15-16. Melchiori 27-8, following a suggestion in DeVane (*Parleyings* 57), cites a passage from Daniello Bartoli, *De' Simboli Trasportati al Morale*, a book B. knew well. The living who seek refuge in the Theatre of Pompey are crowded out by the profusion of statuary: 'there is no room for them because all the niches are full; how many of them, full of the statues of men: how few of men! . . . All the niches are full, and there is no room left for you: look elsewhere, and take refuge where you may'.

17-19.] —Old Gandolf cozened me, despite my care;
  Shrewd was that snatch from out the corner South
  He graced his carrion with, God curse the same! (*1845-88*)
EBB. had objected to the phrasing of l. 17: 'Is that "came me in" a correct expression . . or rather, does it *express* . . does it not make the meaning hard to get at?' (*Wellesley MS*). It is in fact a fencing term, meaning 'to make a pass or home-thrust, to get within an opponent's guard'. *OED* cites *2 Henry IV* III ii 283: 'He would about, and about, and come you in, and come you in'.
21. o' the] on the (*1872, 1884*).   *epistle-side*: the south side of the church, from which the epistle (an extract from one of the Apostles' letters) is read.
23. the aery dome: S. Prassede in fact has a domed apse: see headnote. B. may have had in mind the Gesù church (see ll. 48-9n.), which does have a dome.
25. The Bishop means that his statue will lie outstretched on the basalt lid of his tomb. Basalt is a stone like marble, whose colour can be green or brownish-black.

And 'neath my tabernacle take my rest
With those nine columns round me, two and two,
The odd one at my feet where Anselm stands:
Peachblossom-marble all, the rare, the ripe
30   As fresh-pour'd red wine of a mighty pulse
—Old Gandolf with his paltry onion-stone,
Put me where I may look at him! True peach,
Rosy and flawless: how I earn'd the prize!
Draw close: that conflagration of my church
35   —What then? So much was sav'd if aught were miss'd!
My sons, ye would not be my death? Go dig
The white-grape vineyard where the oil-press stood,
Drop water gently till the surface sinks,
And if ye find . . Ah, God I know not, I! . . .
40   Bedded in store of rotten figleaves soft,
And corded up in a tight olive-frail,
Some lump, ah God, of *lapis lazuli*,

26. *tabernacle*: here, a sculpted canopy supported by the 'columns' of l. 27. The word has strong religious associations: in Judaism it is the tent which contains the Ark of the Covenant; in Christian (esp. Catholic) tradition, it is a receptacle for the vessel containing the consecrated Host.

27. *two and two*: Melchiori 33 notes the phrase 'Pilasters of the Corinthian order, two and two together' in Gerard de Lairesse's *Art of Painting* (1778 ed.), one of B.'s favourite books.

31. *onion-stone*: an inferior kind of marble, as B. explained to Ruskin: 'the grey *cipollino*—good for pillars and the like, bad for finer work, thro' its being laid coat upon coat, onion-wise,—don't I *explain* by translating the word, and do you like it a whit more?' ('A Letter from Robert Browning to John Ruskin', *BBI* xvii [Waco 1958], n. p.). Ruskin accepted B.'s definition, glossing the word, together with 'antique-black' (l. 54), in his published comments on the poem (see headnote): '"Nero Antico" is more familiar to our ears: but Browning does right in translating it; as afterwards "cipollino" into "onion-stone". Our stupid habit of using foreign words without translation is continually losing us half the force of the foreign language. How many travellers hearing the term "cipollino" perceive the intended sense of a stone splitting into concentric rings, like an onion?'

38. *sinks*] sink (*1865-88*).

41. *olive-frail*: a frail is 'a basket made of rushes' (*J.*).

42. *lapis lazuli*: *J.* cites John Hill's *General Natural History* (1748): 'The lapis lazuli, or azure stone, is a copper ore, very compact and hard, so as to take a high polish . . . It is found in detached lumps, of an elegant blue colour, variegated with clouds of white, and veins of a shining gold colour'. See ll. 48-9n.

Big as a Jew's head cut off at the nape,
Blue as a vein o'er the Madonna's breast . . .
45   Sons, all have I bequeath'd you, villas, all,
That brave Frascati villa with its bath,
So let the blue lump poise between my knees,
Like God the Father's globe on both his hands
Ye worship in the Jesu church so gay,
50   For Gandolf shall not choose but see and burst!
Swift as a weaver's shuttle fleet our years:
Man goeth to the grave, and where is he?
Did I say basalt for my slab, sons? Black—
'Twas ever antique-black I meant! How else
55   Shall ye contrast my frieze to come beneath?
The bas-relief in bronze ye promis'd me,
Those Pans and Nymphs ye wot of, and perchance

43-4. The Bishop's imagery draws on traditional subjects of religious art: the beheading of John the Baptist, and pictures of the Virgin Mary.

46. That brave Frascati villa: the slopes above Frascati, a town 21 km south-east of Rome, were a favourite site for villas in Roman times; Cicero owned a small property in the area, and Lucullus a villa famed for its luxury. This classical association was part of the attraction when the site came to be built over again from the mid-16th century—notably by several of the great Roman cardinals. These Renaissance villas were of unparalleled architectural and decorative splendour: see C. L. Franck, *The Villas of Frascati* (1966). *brave:* fine, splendid. *bath:* this could be the bath mentioned in l. 70, but the Bishop possibly refers to an apartment for bathing, a feature of both classical and Renaissance villas. Franck (pp. 11-12) points out that 'the hills of Tusculum have no natural resources of water . . . Hence the endeavours of the cardinals eager to build again at Frascati had to be directed, almost in the first place, to the construction of pipelines . . . all but the very rich had to drop out of this contest'. This may be why the Bishop singles out Frascati from among his villas, and the bath as its principal luxury.

48-9. The Gesù church in Rome contains the tomb of St Ignatius Loyola, founder of the Jesuit order. It is to this monument that the Bishop refers—anachronistically, since it was not built till 1690. Its enormous, sumptuous and elaborate structure is topped by a lapis lazuli globe such as the Bishop describes, which, however, is held not by God but by a *putto.* This mistake occurs in *Murray²:* 'The globe held by the Almighty is to said to be the largest lump of lapis lazuli in existence' (p. 367). The 'bas-relief in bronze' (l. 56) also derives from the Loyola monument.

51-2. Cp. *Job* vii 6: 'My days were swifter than a weaver's shuttle', and xiv 10: 'But man dieth and wasteth away: yea, man giveth up the ghost, and where is he?'

54. antique-black: 'antico-nero, a black marble much more valuable than basalt' (K. Allott, *Browning: Selected Poems* [Oxford 1967] 202). See l. 31n.

Some tripod, thyrsus, with a vase or so,
The Saviour at his sermon on the mount,
60 St. Praxed in a glory, and one Pan
Ready to twitch the nymph's last garment off,
And Moses with the tables . . . but I know
Ye mark me not! What do they whisper thee,
Child of my bowels, Anselm? Ah, ye hope
65 To revel down my villas while I gasp
Brick'd o'er with beggar's mouldy travertine
Which Gandolf from his tomb-top chuckles at!
Nay, boys, ye love me—all of jasper then!
'Tis jasper ye stand pledged to, lest I grieve
70 My bath must needs be left behind, alas!
One block, pure green as a pistachio nut,
There's plenty jasper somewhere in the world—
And I shall have St. Praxed's ear to pray
Horses for ye, and brown Greek manuscripts,
75 And mistresses with great smooth marbly limbs
—That's if ye carve my epitaph aright,

58. tripod: 'a seat with three feet, such as that from which the priestess of Apollo [at Delphi] delivered oracles' (*J.*).   *thyrsus*: a staff or spear tipped with an ornament like a pine-cone, and sometimes wreathed with ivy and vine-branches; borne by Dionysus (Bacchus) and his votaries.

60. St. Praxed in a glory: a 'glory' is a halo; Binns (see headnote, p. 259) points out that 'Around the head of the statue' of St. Praxed in the bas-relief on the Cetti tomb in St. Praxed's Church 'is a shelled vault in the form of a halo' (p. 161).

64. Child of my bowels: cp. 2 *Samuel* xvi 11: 'Behold, my son, which came forth of my bowels, seeketh my life'. The speaker is David, lamenting the rebellion of Absalom, his favourite son.

66. Brick'd o'er: implying that there will be no statue on the tomb-top.   *beggar's mouldy travertine*: travertine is a hard, white stone, used for ordinary building in Italy. Cp. *Pictor* 67n, 'moulder on the damp wall's travertine'.

68. jasper: 'a hard stone of a bright beautiful green colour, sometimes clouded with white, found in masses of various sizes and shapes. It is capable of a very elegant polish' (*J.*). Like lapis lazuli (see l. 42n.), jasper is not a building material (but see next note). Both form part of the fabric of the New Jerusalem in *Revelation* xxi 11-12, 18-20.

70. bath: Melchiori 27 suggests that the Bishop's jasper bath derives from 'the great green jasper bath of the Emperor Constantine, which stands in the Baptistery of the Church of San Giovanni in Laterano, Rome'. Cp. *Bishop Blougram* 112: 'slabbed marble, what a bath it makes!'

73. I shall have] have I not (*1845-88*).

Choice Latin, picked phrase, Tully's every word,
No gaudy ware like Gandolf's second line
—Tully, my masters? Ulpian serves his need!
80 And then how I shall lie through centuries
And hear the blessed mutter of the mass,
And see God made and eaten all day long,
And feel the steady candle-flame, and taste
Good strong thick stupifying incense-smoke!
85 For as I lie here, hours of the dead night,
Dying in state and by such slow degrees,
I fold my arms as if they clasp'd a crook,
And stretch my feet forth straight as stone can point,
And let the bed-clothes for a mortcloth drop
90 Into great laps and folds of sculptors'-work:
And as yon tapers dwindle, and strange thoughts
Grow, with a certain humming in my ears,
About the life before this life I lived,
And this life too, Popes, Cardinals and Priests,
95 St. Praxed at his sermon on the mount,

77-9. 'Tully' was the common English Renaissance version of the name of
Marcus Tullius Cicero (106-43 BC), the great lawyer and orator of
Republican Rome, whom the apostles of the 'revived paganism' (see
headnote) held to be the ideal Latin stylist. 'Ulpian' refers to Domitius
Ulpianus, a lawyer and scholar who died 228 AD during the reign of the
Emperor Alexander Severus. See ll. 99-100n. F. J. Chierenza (*Explicator* xix
[1961] item 22) argues that the Bishop is remembering his instructions to the
craftsmen ('my masters') who carved Gandolf's tomb to give him an epitaph
in inferior Latin. 'My masters' certainly appears frequently in Shakespeare as
a form of address to social inferiors, or as a form of condescension. But
the connection between this line and ll. 99-100 seems to indicate that the
Bishop is expressing his contempt of Gandolf's own taste, esp. in view of
B.'s comment that the phrasing of Gandolf's epitaph was chosen 'to provoke
the bile of my Bishop'.
81-4. EBB. thought this 'a grand passage' (*Wellesley MS*). Line 82 refers to
the Catholic doctrine of the 'real presence' of the body of Christ in the
communion wafer. A. C. Dooley, in 'An Echo of Wesley in *The Bishop
Orders His Tomb*', SBC xiii (1980) 54-5, compares John Wesley, *An Earnest
Appeal to Men of Reason and Religion* (1743): 'Is it now in your power to see, or
hear, or taste, or feel God?'
87. *crook*: the Bishop's crozier, symbol of his pastoral office, which would be
carved as part of his funerary statue.
89. *mortcloth*: funeral pall.
93. *this life I liv'd*] I lived this life (*1863-88*).
95. B. commented: 'the blunder about the sermon is the result of the dying
man's haziness; he would not reveal himself as he does but for that' (*Select

Your tall pale mother with her talking eyes,
And new-found agate urns as fresh as day,
And marble's language, Latin pure, discreet,
—Aha, ELUCESCEBAT, quoth our friend?
100 No Tully, said I, Ulpian at the best!
Evil and brief hath been my pilgrimage.
All *lapis*, all, sons! Else I give the Pope
My villas: will ye ever eat my heart?
Ever your eyes were as a lizard's quick,
105 They glitter like your mother's for my soul,

Poems of Robert Browning, ed. W. J. Rolfe and H. E. Hersey [New York 1886]
195). There are actually two blunders: the confusion of St Praxed with
Christ, and the mistake about the Saint's gender. It is not certain which one
B. means, but he would have known that both were blunders: see headnote,
and cp. *Flight* 884n.
97. *new-found agate urns*: urns (normally funerary) from the classical period,
recently unearthed. Agate, a variety of chalcedony, with colours in separate
bands or blended in clouds, is an unlikely material for such urns, which were
usually of earthenware or metal. Cp. *Ring* i 2-5.
99-100. The Bishop's invocation of 'marble's language' reminds him of the
word 'elucescebat', which occurs in Gandolf's epitaph. The Bishop claims
that the word is 'No Tully', that is, not used by Cicero, but 'Ulpian at the
best', and therefore inferior Latin. The Bishop is right. Dr J. Fairweather has
pointed out to us that the *Thesaurus Linguae Latinae* (Leipzig 1953) v 2 records
the earliest use of 'elucescebat' in the sense of 'to shine, be notable' in the
writings of St. Jerome, who died AD 420, nearly two centuries *after* Ulpian,
who died in 228. Gandolf had confused the word with 'elucere', which *is* in
Cicero (*De Oratorio* 255) and would be considered the canonical form. In
1886, F. Hitchman wrote to B. asking where he had found the word, and
commenting that it occurred in the epitaph of his ancestor Humphrey
Henchman (1592-1675), Bishop of London (whereabouts of this letter
unknown; see *Checklist* 328). B. replied that this 'curious fact' was 'quite
unknown' to him: 'I wanted a word "infimae latinitatis" [in the lowest style
of Latin] to provoke the bile of my Bishop, and took the one you
know—simply because a classical writer would use "eluceo": and I charged it
upon "Ulpian" at a venture. This is one of perhaps fifty instances that have
occurred to me in the course of my literary experience—of how fancies have
already been forestalled by facts' (3 Nov. 1886, *ABL MS*).
101. Cp. *Genesis* xlvii 9: 'few and evil have been the days of the years of my
life'.
105ˆ106.] Or ye would heighten my impoverished frieze,
          Piece out its starved design, and fill my vase
          With grapes, and add a vizor and a Term, (*1845-88*)

Or to the tripod ye would tie a lynx
That in his struggle throws the thyrsus down,
To comfort me on my entablature
Whereon I am to lie till I must ask
110 "Do I live, am I dead?" There, leave me, there!
For ye have stabb'd me with ingratitude
To death—ye wish it—God, ye wish it! Stone—
Gritstone, a-crumble! Clammy squares which sweat
As if the corpse they keep were oozing through—
115 And no more *lapis* to delight the world!
Well, go! I bless ye. Fewer tapers there,
But in a row: and, going, turn your backs
—Ay, like departing altar-ministrants,
And leave me in my church, the church for peace,
120 That I may watch at leisure if he leers—
Old Gandolf, at me, from his onion-stone,
As still he envied me, so fair she was!

106-7. Melchiori 29-36 suggests that the details here derive from an emblem,
'Sweete Repose Disturbed by Lewdness', in Lairesse, *Art of Painting*, one of
B.'s favourite books (see also l. 27n.). The point is strengthened by the lines
added in *1845* (see prec. note). A group of satyrs find some 'almost naked'
nymphs asleep; they hang the nymphs' hunting equipment on the genitals of
a 'Priapus term', 'sticking their *thyrses* in the ground round about it, and
adorning them with vizors'; they scatter the nymphs' clothes in the branches
of a tree, below which they set two panthers to prevent the nymphs from
retrieving them, together with wine and grapes. The satyrs taunt the nymphs
when they awaken, until the appearance of Diana puts them to flight: 'the
term of *Priapus* fell to the ground, and the panther at the tree endeavoured to
get loose'. Melchiori points out the affinity of this scene with ll. 60-1, and
suggests a further connection with *Pan and Luna*.
106. Or] And (*1845-88*).
108. entablature: the slab, whether of 'basalt' (l. 25) or 'antique-black' (ll. 53-4)
on which the Bishop's effigy is to lie.
111. Cp. *Julius Caesar* III ii 176, 183-6: 'the well-beloved Brutus stabb'd . . .
This was the most unkindest cut of all; / For when the noble Caesar saw him
stab, / Ingratitude, more strong than traitors' arms / Quite vanquish'd him'.
There was a tradition that Brutus was Caesar's son.
113. Gritstone: coarse sandstone.
117-18. turn your backs . . . altar-ministrants: the Bishop tells his sons to back
away from him, as though he himself were the Christ above the altar, whom
the priest's acolytes, under the old rites, must always face during a service.

43 Italy in England
[The Italian in England]

First publ. *B & P* vii (*DR & L*), 6 Nov. 1845; repr. *1849* (when the title was changed in accordance with B.'s practice of removing overt refs. to national stereotypes), *1863* (when it was placed in *Romances*: see Appendix A, p. 464), *1868*, *1872*, *1888*. Our text is *1845*.

EBB. saw a draft of the poem in Aug. 1845. However, the date of composition is probably earlier; the subject of Italian politics would have been on B.'s mind during and immediately after his long tour of Italy (Aug.-Dec. 1844). The poem may have been one of the 'three or four half-done-with "Bells"' which B. mentions in a letter to EBB. of 27 Jan. 1845 (*LK* 11); we would date it to the early spring of that year.

The action is set during the Risorgimento, the period of agitation and struggle for Italian unity and independence, which concluded in 1861. Britain harboured many Italian political exiles, among them B.'s friend and teacher Angelo Cerutti. F. G. Kenyon (*Centenary* iii, p. xxxiv) first suggested as a specific source the abortive uprising of the Bandiera brothers in the summer of 1844. Attilio and Emilio Bandiera were officers in the Austrian navy who became nationalist sympathizers. In 1844 they deserted and fled to Corfu, and from there, on 12 June, they launched an ill-advised expedition into Calabria. They were betrayed by one of their comrades, captured by the Bourbon authorities, and executed on 25 July. Giuseppe Mazzini, one of the leading figures of the Risorgimento, who lived in exile in London and was a friend of the Carlyles, edited a pamphlet, *Ricordi dei Fratelli Bandiera* [etc.] (Paris 1844), a copy of which, inscribed by Mazzini, B. owned; he sent it to EBB. a few weeks after the publication of *DR & L* (20 Nov. 1845, *LK* 278). It is arguable whether the pamphlet is a source for the poem. Perhaps Mazzini, having read the poem and made the connection in his own mind, presented B. with the pamphlet as a result; Kintner thinks so, arguing that an undated letter of Mazzini referring to his admiration for the poem accompanied the gift, and that 'Mazzini's intimacy with the Carlyles would explain so early an acquaintance with the poem' (p. 278 n.1). This is possible, though it is surprising that B. should not mention Mazzini's letter to EBB. (there is indeed no mention of him in their correspondence), and it may be that he had already obtained the pamphlet independently and that Mazzini autographed it when they first met in 1852; this would make it more plausible as a direct source. B. 'was proud to remember that Mazzini informed him he had read this poem to certain of his fellow-exiles in England to show how an Englishman could sympathize with them' (Orr *Handbook* 306 n.1). The parallel with the Bandiera affair is in any case general, not specific: the scene of the poem is northern, it has a single protagonist who makes good his escape, and it does not refer to a failed uprising. B. may have been influenced by Shelley's *Marenghi*, a source also for *England* and *Luria*.

For a direct treatment of Italian nationalism in the 1840s, cp. *Pippa* iii; in
the 1850s, *Old Pictures* 249-88 and *De Gustibus* 33-8; in the aftermath of
unification (1860-1), *Prince Hohenstiel* (publ. 1871 but conceived 1859-60).
Cp. also *Sordello*, *A Soul's Tragedy* and *Luria*, where contemporary Italian
politics are alluded to by analogy with past history. *Lost Leader*, *Confessional*,
and *Patriot* are thematically parallel. The relationship between the speaker and
the peasant woman who helps him anticipates that between Pompilia and
Caponsacchi in *Ring*.

When she saw the poem, EBB. suggested only one rev. (see l. 122n.). She
commented: 'A serene, noble poem this is—an heroic repose in it—but
nothing to imagine queries out of . . . I like the simplicity of the great-
heartedness of it, (though perhaps half Saxon in character)' (*Wellesley MS*).
See also her letter to B. of 12-14 Nov. 1845 (*LK 268*).

That second time they hunted me
From hill to plain, from shore to sea,
And Austria, hounding far and wide
Her blood-hounds thro' the country-side,
5   Breathed hot and instant on my trace,
I made six days a hiding-place
Of that dry green old aqueduct
Where I and Charles, when boys, have plucked
The fire-flies from the roof above,
10 Bright creeping thro' the moss they love.
—How long it seems since Charles was lost!
Six days the soldiers crossed and crossed
The country in my very sight;
And when that peril ceased at night,
15 The sky broke out in red dismay
With signal-fires; well, there I lay
Close covered o'er in my recess,

¶43.2-5. The setting is an area between Padua and the Adriatic coast, in the
then kingdom of Lombardy-Venetia, part of the Hapsburg Empire since
1815. Cp. *Pippa* iii 134-7n.

3. hounding: here, 'to set . . . *at* a quarry; to incite or urge *on* to attack or chase
anything'.

5. instant: 'pressing', 'importunate'; also 'impending, imminent'. Cp.
Balaustion 541: 'the abrupt Fate's footstep instant now'.   *trace*,] trace,—
(*1849-88*). The revised reading allows the syntax of ll. 1-6 to be read as three
self-contained clauses ('they hunted me', 'Austria . . . Breathed', and 'I made
. . . a hiding-place'), whereas *1845* has one main clause ('I made . . . a hiding-
place') to which the others are subordinate.

11. lost: equivocating between 'dead' and 'lost to the cause' (as in *Lost Leader*);
'Charles's miserable end' (l. 20) is similarly ambivalent; l. 116 decides the
question.

Up to the neck in ferns and cress,
Thinking on Metternich our friend,
20 And Charles's miserable end,
And much beside, two days; the third,
Hunger o'ercame me when I heard
The peasants from the village go
To work among the maize; you know,
25 With us, in Lombardy, they bring
Provisions packed on mules, a string
With little bells that cheer their task,
And casks, and boughs on every cask
To keep the sun's heat from the wine;
30 These I let pass in jingling line,
And, close on them, dear noisy crew,
The peasants from the village, too;
For at the very rear would troop
Their wives and sisters in a group
35 To help, I knew; when these had passed,
I threw my glove to strike the last,
Taking the chance: she did not start,
Much less cry out, but stooped apart
One instant, rapidly glanced round,
40 And saw me beckon from the ground:
A wild bush grows and hides my crypt;
She picked my glove up while she stripped
A branch off, then rejoined the rest
With that; my glove lay in her breast:
45 Then I drew breath: they disappeared:
It was for Italy I feared.

An hour, and she returned alone
Exactly where my glove was thrown.
Meanwhile came many thoughts; on me
50 Rested the hopes of Italy;
I had devised a certain tale

19. Metternich our friend: ironic; the Austrian statesman Klemens, Prince von Metternich (1773-1859), a chief architect of the reactionary post-Napoleonic political order in Europe, opposed Italian unity as part of a wider anti-reformist policy. See *Pippa* ii 285.
41. crypt: fig., a recess or secret hiding-place; B. Brown (*VP* vi [1968] 179-83) connects the more usual sense of a burial vault with l. 7, and comments: 'Ironically, the "crypt" proved not to be a tomb, but a womb of new life; the aqueduct, which seemed to be dried up, proved to be a sort of spiritual baptismal font'. Cp. *Sordello* i 410, 438 ('font' linked to 'crypt'), and vi 630 ('that cold font-tomb').

Which, when 'twas told her, could not fail
Persuade a peasant of its truth;
This hiding was a freak of youth;
55 I meant to give her hopes of pay,
And no temptation to betray.
But when I saw that woman's face,
Its calm simplicity of grace,
Our Italy's own attitude
60 In which she walked thus far, and stood,
Planting each naked foot so firm,
To crush the snake and spare the worm—
At first sight of her eyes, I said,
"I am that person on whose head
65 "They fix the price because I hate
"The Austrians over us: the State
"Will give you gold—oh, gold so much,
"If you betray me to their clutch!
"And be your death, for aught I know,
70 "If once they find you saved their foe.
"Now, you must bring me food and drink,
"And also paper, pen, and ink,
"And carry safe what I shall write
"To Padua, which you'll reach at night
75 "Before the Duomo shuts; go in,
"And wait till Tenebrae begin;
"Walk to the Third Confessional,
"Between the pillar and the wall,
"And kneeling whisper *whence comes peace?*
80 "Say it a second time; then cease;

54-5.] I meant to call a freak of youth / This hiding, and give hopes of pay, (*1849-88*).

61-2. Brown (see l. 41n.) compares God's curse on the serpent, *Genesis* iii 15: 'I will put enmity between thee and the woman, and between thy seed and her seed; it shall bruise thy head, and thou shalt bruise his heel'. Cp. also *Ring* v 1667-8: 'I was mad, / Blind, stamped on all, the earth-worms with the asp'.

64. *person on*] man upon (*1849-88*).

75. *the Duomo*: the Cathedral.

76. *Tenebrae*: 'the office of matins and lauds for the three last days in Holy Week. Fifteen lighted candles are placed on a triangular stand, and at the conclusion of each psalm one is put out, till a single candle is left at the top of the triangle. The extinction of the other candles is said to figure the growing darkness of the world at the time of the Crucifixion. The last candle (which is not extinguished, but hidden behind the altar for a few moments) represents Christ over whom Death could not prevail' (*Cyclopaedia* 226). Brown (see l. 41n.) suggests a metaphor of rebirth in the setting of the action at Eastertide.

"And if the voice inside returns,
"*From Christ and Freedom; what concerns*
"*The cause of Peace?*—for answer, slip
"My letter where you placed your lip;
85 "Then come back happy we have done
"Our mother service—I, the son,
"As you the daughter of our land!"

Three mornings more, she took her stand
In the same place, with the same eyes:
90 I was no surer of sun-rise
Than of her coming: we conferred
Of her own prospects, and I heard
She had a lover—stout and tall,
She said—then let her eyelids fall,
95 "He could do much"—as if some doubt
Entered her heart,—then, passing out,
"She could not speak for others—who
"Had other thoughts; herself she knew:"
And so she brought me drink and food.
100 After four days the scouts pursued
Another path: at last arrived
The help my Paduan friends contrived
To furnish me: she brought the news:
For the first time I could not choose
105 But kiss her hand and lay my own
Upon her head—"This faith was shown
"To Italy, our mother;—she
"Uses my hand and blesses thee!"
She followed down to the sea-shore;
110 I left and never saw her more.

How very long since I have thought
Concerning—much less wished for—aught
Beside the good of Italy
For which I live and mean to die!
115 In love I never was; and since
Charles proved false, nothing could convince

83-4. *slip . . . lip*: i.e. slip the letter through the curtain or grate between the penitent's stall and the confessor's. Contrast the implied sympathy of the Italian priest here for the revolutionary cause with the reactionary stance of the Spanish priest in *Confessional*.
93. *stout*: strong in body; also brave, resolute.
115. *In love I never was*] I never was in love (*1849-88*).
116-17. *nothing could convince . . . had a friend;*] what shall now convince . . .

My inmost heart I had a friend;
However, if I pleased to spend
Real wishes on myself—say, Three—
120   I know at least what one should be;
I would grasp Metternich until
I felt his red wet throat distil
In blood thro' these two hands: and next,
—Nor much for that am I perplexed—
125   Charles, perjured traitor, for his part,
Should die slow of a broken heart
Under his new employers—last
—Ah, there, what should one wish? For fast
Do I grow old and out of strength;
130   If I resolved to seek at length
My father's house again, how scared
They all would look, and unprepared!
My brothers live in Austria's pay
—Disowned me long ago, men say;
135   And all my early mates who used
To praise me so—perhaps induced
More than one early step of mine—
Are turning wise; while part opine
"Freedom grows License," part suspect
140   "Haste breeds Delay," and recollect
They always said such premature
Beginnings never could endure:
So, with a sullen "All's for best,"
The land seems settling to its rest.
145   I think, then, I should wish to stand
This evening in that dear, lost land,
Over the sea the thousand miles,
And know if yet that woman smiles
With the calm smile—some little farm
150   She lives in there, no doubt—what harm
If I sate on the door-side bench,
And, while her spindle made a trench
Fantastically in the dust,
Inquired of all her fortunes—just

---

have a friend? (*1868-88*).
122.] EBB. quoted 'I felt his throat, & had my will', and commented: 'is not
"had my will" a little wrong—*I would what I would*—? There is a weakness in
the expression . . is there not?' (*Wellesley MS*)
128. one] I (*1849-88*).
138-9. part . . . part] some . . . some (*1849-88*).

155   Her children's ages and their names,
     And what may be the husband's aims
     For each of them—I'd talk this out,
     And sit there, for an hour about,
     Then kiss her hand once more, and lay
160   Mine on her head, and go my way.

     So much for idle wishing—how
     It steals the time! To business now!

44 Time's Revenges

First publ. *B & P* vii (*DR & L*), 6 Nov. 1845; repr. *1849, 1863* (when it was placed in *Romances*: see Appendix A, p. 464), *1865²*, *1868, 1872, 1888*. Our text is *1845*. EBB. first saw the poem in MS in Aug. 1845, and commented: 'It seems to me while I appreciate the conception of this poem fully, & much admire some things in it, that it requires more finishing than the other poems,—I mean particularly the first part' (*Wellesley MS*; all her comments recorded in the notes are from this source, unless otherwise stated). Lack of finish does not, however, necessarily mean that the composition was recent: the evidence rather suggests a date in Feb. 1845. The poem reflects B.'s continuing regard for Alfred Domett (see headnote to *Waring*; the two poems are juxtaposed in *1872*). Several phrases reminiscent of the poem occur in a letter to Domett of 23 Feb. 1845 (*RB & AD* 109-15): 'I cannot even write legibly' (cp. ll. 29-30); 'You will find no change . . . in this room, where I remember you so well. I turned my head, last line, to see if it was you came up with hat above the holly hedge' (cp. ll. 10-12); 'The papers will tell you of the shocking end of poor Laman Blanchard . . . Nearly the last time I saw him he talked . . . about his wife—how he was all but dead of a fever once, and she nursed him . . . "And since then," he said, "she has saved my life a dozen times"' (cp. ll. 10-14). B. also mentions Domett in a letter to EBB. of 11 Feb. 1845, again with a phrase reminiscent of the poem: 'I had rather hear from you than see anybody else—never you care, dear noble Carlyle, nor you, my own friend Alfred over the sea' (*LK* 17; cp. l. 1). In the same letter, B. goes on to talk about his indifference to the hostile critical reception of his work (*LK* 18-19; cp. ll. 39-42). The 'Lady' in the second section may represent an inverse portrait both of Blanchard's wife and of EBB. herself, who repeatedly stressed the contrast between her own seclusion and B.'s 'brilliant happy sphere' (*LK* 71). In a letter of 17 Apr. 1845 she wrote: 'As to the Polkas and Cellariuses, . . I do not covet them of course . . but what a strange world you seem to have, to me at a distance—what a strange husk of a world!' (*LK* 48). The title is from *Twelfth Night* ('And thus the whirligig of time brings in his revenges', V i 384), whose patterns of unrequited love may also have influenced the poem. Unrequited love is a common theme in B.'s work: cp. *Lost Mistress, Last Ride, Too Late*.

> I've a Friend, over the sea;
> I like him, but he loves me;
> It all grew out of the books I write;
> They find such favour in his sight
> 5   That he slaughters you with savage looks
> Because you don't admire my books:

¶44.3-6. Domett wrote *On a Critique of 'Pippa Passes'* to express his opinion of B.'s hostile critics.

He does himself though,—and if some vein
Were to snap to-night in this heavy brain,
To-morrow month, if I lived to try,
10   Round should I just turn quietly,
Or out of the bedclothes stretch my hand
Till I found him, come from his foreign land
To be my nurse in this poor place,
And make me broth, and wash my face,
15   And light my fire, and, all the while,
Bear with his old good-humoured smile
That I told him "Better have kept away
"Than come and kill me, night and day,
"With worse than fever's throbs and shoots,
20   "At the creaking of his clumsy boots."
I am as sure that this he would do
As that Saint Paul's is striking Two:
And I think I had rather . . woe is me!
—Yes, rather see him than not see,
25   If lifting a hand would seat him there
Before me in the empty chair
To-night, when my head aches indeed,
And I can neither think, nor read,
And these blue fingers will not hold

7.] EBB. quoted '*He* does though; and if some vein—', and commented: 'Will you consider, taking the context, whether "He does himself" would not be better?'

8. *this heavy brain*: B. was a lifelong sufferer from headaches; his letters to EBB. frequently refer to them, e.g. 27 Jan. 1845: 'Your books lie on my table here, at arm's length from me, in this old room where I sit all day: and when my head aches or wanders or strikes work, as it now and then will, I take my chance for either green covered volume' (*LK* 10).

9-10.] EBB. quoted 'if I lived to try / I should just turn round nor ope an eye—', and commented: 'Do you like .. "nor ope an eye"? I cannot, much. Nor do I like the "living to *try*"—'.

14. *me*] my (*1863-88*).

19. *fever's*] fever (*1870-88*).

20. *At the*] The (*1863-88*).

23. *had rather*] would rather (*1865²*); rather (*1868-88*).

24. *rather see*] rather should see (*1868-75*); rather would see (*1888*).

25. *would*] could (*1865², 1884, 1888*). A rare case of *1888* agreeing with a reading introduced in a volume of selections rather than in a previous collected edition; see also *Glove* 58n.

29.] Nor make these purple fingers hold (*1863-88*).

30   The pen; this garret's freezing cold!

      And I've a Lady—There he wakes,
      The laughing fiend and prince of snakes
      Within me, at her name, to pray
      Fate send some creature in the way
35   Of my love for her, to be down-torn
      Upthrust and onward borne
      So I might prove myself that sea
      Of passion which I needs must be!
      Call my thoughts false and my fancies quaint,
40   And my style infirm, and its figures faint,
      All the critics say, and more blame yet,
      And not one angry word you get!
      But, please you, wonder I would put
      My cheek beneath that Lady's foot
45   Rather than trample under mine
      The laurels of the Florentine,
      And you shall see how the Devil spends
      The fire God gave for other ends!
      I tell you, I stride up and down
50   This garret, crowned with Love's best crown,
      And feasted with Love's perfect feast,
      To think I kill for her, at least,
      Body and soul and peace and fame,
      Alike youth's end and manhood's aim,
55   As all my genius, all my learning
      Leave me, where there's no returning,
      —So is my spirit, as flesh with sin,
      Filled full, eaten out and in
      With the face of her, the eyes of her,
60   The lips and little chin, the stir
      Of shadow round her mouth; and she
      —I'll tell you,—calmly would decree
      That I should roast at a slow fire
      If that would compass her desire

---

36. onward borne] outward-borne (*1863-88*).

46. the Florentine: Dante, as in *Sordello* i 348.

48. The] A (*1849-88*).

55-6.] not *1849-88*. EBB. quoted the lines as they stand in *1845*,
commenting: 'Is not that . . the last line . . somewhat weak & indefinite, for
you?'

59-61. Cp. *Too Late* 121-6.

60. lips and] lips, the (*1863-88*).

65   And make her one whom they invite
     To the famous ball to-morrow night.

     There may be a Heaven; there must be a Hell;
     Meantime, there is our Earth here—well!

65.] EBB. quoted 'And purchase her the dear *invite* . .', and commented: 'I protest zealously against that word. Now isn't it a vulgarism, & out of place altogether here?'
67.] There may be Heaven; there must be Hell; (*1849-88*, except 'heaven', 'hell', *1868-88*).
68. *Earth*] earth (*1868-88*).

45 Home-Thoughts, from Abroad

First publ. *B & P* vii (*DR & L*), 6 Nov. 1845, as the first of three numbered sections with the collective title *Home-Thoughts, from Abroad*. The second section consisted of *Here's to Nelson's memory*, later incl. in *Nationality in Drinks* (see p. 248); the third consisted of the lines later called *Home-Thoughts, from the Sea* (p. 246). The title *Home-Thoughts, from Abroad* was given exclusively to the first section when it was repr. in *1849*; it was then repr. *1863* (when it was placed in *Lyrics*: see Appendix A, p. 464), *1865²*, *1868*, *1872*, *1888*. Our text is *1845*. A fair-copy MS, with some variants, is in the Pierpont Morgan Library (*Collections* E170, p. 410); it may be the one given to EBB. at a meeting on 3 Oct. 1845, in response to her request, in a letter to B. of 1 Oct., for an autograph for Mary Hunter, the daughter of the Rev. George Barrett Hunter (*LK* 219). B. responded: 'Now I will write you the verses .. some easy ones out of a paper-full meant to go between poem & poem in my next number, and break the shock of collision' (2 Oct., *LK* 221). This implies that the poem had been written some time before; a likely date on internal grounds would be the spring of 1845, supported by refs. in B.'s letters to EBB., e.g. 26 Feb. 1845, headed 'Wednesday morning—Spring!' and continuing: 'Real warm Spring, dear Miss Barrett, and the birds know it' (*LK* 25). Another topic in the letters of this period concerned England's relation to Italy (see headnote to *England*, p. 342).

When she saw the poem, EBB. wrote:

Your spring-song is full of beauty as you know very well—& "that's the wise thrush," so characteristic of you (& of the thrush too) that I was sorely tempted to ask you to write it "twice over," .. & not send the first copy to Mary Hunter notwithstanding my promise to her. And now when you come to print these fragments, would it not be well if you were to stoop to the vulgarism of prefixing some word of introduction, as other people do, you know, . . a title . . a name? You perplex your readers often by casting yourself on their intelligence in these things—and although it is true that readers in general are stupid & cant understand, it is still more true that they are lazy & wont understand . . & they dont catch your point of sight at first unless you think it worth while to push them by the shoulders & force them into the right place. Now these fragments . . you mean to print them with a line between . . & not one word at the top of it . . now dont you? And then people will read
        "Oh, to be in England"
& say to themselves ... "Why who is this? ... who's out of England?" Which is an extreme case of course,—but you will see what I mean ... & often I have observed how some of the very most beautiful of your lyrics have suffered from your disdain of the usual tactics of writers in this one respect. (4 Oct., *LK* 221-2)

Title.] no comma in *1884* (the corr. reissue of *1872* and *1880*).

B. replied: 'Thank you, thank you—I will devise titles—I quite see what you
say, now you do say it' (6 Oct., *LK* 223). In her letter of 21-22 Oct. (*LK* 244),
EBB. further suggested numbering the sections, advice which B. also took.
DeVane (*Handbook* 163) suggests that the *DR & L* title may have been
influenced by that of J. H. Newman's pamphlet *Home Thoughts Abroad*
(1836); in her letter of 1 Oct. requesting the autograph, EBB. mentioned
Shelley's *Letters from Abroad* (*LK* 218). B.'s contrast between England and
'Abroad' inverts that drawn between England and Italy in Byron's *Beppo*
321-92 ('With all its sinful doings, I must say, / That Italy's a pleasant place to
me': see headnote to *England*, p. 341), thereby echoing the preference in
Wordsworth's *I Travelled Among Unknown Men*: 'I travelled among unknown
men, / In lands beyond the sea; / Nor, England! did I know till then / What
love I bore to thee' (1-4). For another comparison in B. between Italy and
England, in which Italy is preferred, see *De Gustibus*.

> Oh, to be in England
> Now that April's there,
> And who wakes in England
> Sees, some morning, unaware,
> 5 That the lowest boughs and the brush-wood sheaf
> Round the elm-tree bole are in tiny leaf,
> While the chaffinch sings on the orchard bough
> In England—now!
>
> And after April, when May follows,
> 10 And the whitethroat builds, and all the swallows—
> Hark! where my blossomed pear-tree in the hedge
> Leans to the field and scatters on the clover
> Blossoms and dewdrops—at the bent spray's edge—
> That's the wise thrush; he sings each song twice over
> 15 Lest you should think he never could recapture
> The first fine careless rapture!
> And though the fields are rough with hoary dew,
> All will be gay when noontide wakes anew

¶45. *1-4*.] printed as two lines in *1872, 1884*.
1. In his letter of 6 Oct. 1845, referring to EBB.'s projected trip to Italy, B.
made one of his very rare self-quotations: 'Oh to be in Pisa. Now that
E. B. B. is there!' (*LK* 223).
3. who] whoever (*1849-88*).
7. orchard] fruit tree (*Pierpont MS*).
8. England—now] England now (*Pierpont MS*).
11-13. See *Pippa* iii 248-9n.
11. my] the (*Pierpont MS*).
17. are] look (*1849-88*).   *hoary*: white; lit., the colour of an old man's
hair.

The buttercups, the little children's dower,
20 —Far brighter than this gaudy melon-flower!

19. dower: gift, endowment; lit., dowry.

46 Saul

First publ. as a fragment in *B & P* vii (*DR & L*), 6 Nov. 1845, and repr., with two added lines and a few other changes, in *1849*. Our text is *1845*. B. completed the poem, changed the alternating long and short lines into a single long line (perhaps as a result of EBB.'s suggestion: see below, ll. 77–80n.), and placed it in *M & W* (1855). Our main headnote and annotation will be provided for the complete poem; the only notes to this text are those derived from EBB.'s criticisms (*Wellesley MS*; all her comments are from this source) and a record of the substantive variants between *1845* and *1849*. B. mentions the poem to EBB. in a letter of 3 May 1845 as 'one of my Dramatic Romances' which 'I should like to show you one day' (*LK* 55), implying that it was already drafted up to the point at which it breaks off in *1845*. A date in the early spring seems likely.

> Said Abner, "At last thou art come!
>   "Ere I tell, ere thou speak,—
> "Kiss my cheek, wish me well!" Then I wished it,
>   And did kiss his cheek:
> 5   And he, "Since the King, oh my friend,
>   For thy countenance sent,
> Nor drunken nor eaten have we;
>   Nor, until from his tent
> Thou return with the joyful assurance
> 10   The king liveth yet,
> Shall our lip with the honey be brightened,
>   —The water, be wet.
>
> "For out of the black mid-tent's silence,
>   A space of three days,
> 15   No sound hath escaped to thy servants,

¶46.6. *For*] emended from '"For' in *1845*, which is inconsistent in its convention for the placing of quotation marks: sometimes (e.g. ll. 2–3) they appear at the beginning of every line of a speech, but for the most part they appear only at the beginning of a verse paragraph. The quotation marks here are anomalous, since they are not continued in the following lines.

8.] EBB. quoted 'Nor till from his tent', and commented: 'Could you not rather write "until", here? to break the course of monosyllables, with another reason'.

13-14.] EBB. quoted 'For in the black mid tent silence / Three drear days—', and commented: 'A word seems omitted before silence—& the short line is too short to the ear—not to say that "drear days" conspires against "dread ways" found afterwards. And the solemn flow of these six lines sh^d be uninterrupted, I think'.

Of prayer nor of praise,
To betoken that Saul and the Spirit
    Have gone their dread ways.

"Yet now my heart leaps, O beloved!
20   God's child, with his dew
On thy gracious gold hair, and those lilies
    Still living and blue
As thou brak'st them to twine round thy harp-strings,
    As if no wild heat
25 Were raging to torture the desert!"
    Then I, as was meet,
Knelt down to the God of my fathers,
    And rose on my feet,
And ran o'er the sand burnt to powder.
30   The tent was unlooped;
I pulled up the spear that obstructed,
    And under I stooped;
Hands and knees o'er the slippery grass-patch—
    All withered and gone—
35 That leads to the second enclosure,
    I groped my way on,
Till I felt where the foldskirts fly open;
    Then once more I prayed,
And opened the foldskirts and entered,
40   And was not afraid;
And spoke, "Here is David, thy servant!"
    And no voice replied;
And first I saw nought but the blackness;
    But soon I descried
45 A something more black than the blackness
    —The vast, the upright
Main-prop which sustains the pavilion,—

18.] Have ended their strife,
    And that faint in his triumph the monarch
      Sinks back upon life. (*1849*)

30-40. EBB. commented: 'The entrance of David into the tent is very visible
& characteristic—& you see his youthfulness in the activity of it—and the
repetition of the word "foldskirts" has an Hebraic effect—'.

45.] EBB. quoted 'Something more black than the blackness—' and
commented: 'Should it not be "A something"? more definite? And the
rhythm cries aloud for it, it seems to me'.

46.] EBB. quoted 'The vast, upright—' and commented: '*quaere*—"*the*
upright" . . for rhythm?'

And slow into sight
Grew a figure, gigantic, against it,
50   And blackest of all;—
Then a sunbeam, that burst thro' the tent-roof,
Showed Saul.

He stood as erect as that tent-prop;
Both arms stretched out wide
55   On the great cross-support in the centre
That goes to each side:
So he bent not a muscle but hung there
As, caught in his pangs
And waiting his change the king-serpent
60   All heavily hangs,
Far away from his kind, in the Pine,
Till deliverance come
With the Spring-time,—so agonized Saul,
Drear and black, blind and dumb.

65   Then I tuned my harp,—took off the lilies
We twine round its chords
Lest they snap 'neath the stress of the noontide
—Those sunbeams like swords!
And I first played the tune all our sheep know,
70   As, one after one,

51-2.] EBB. quoted 'Then a sunbeam burst thro' the blind tent-roof /
Showed Saul—', and commented: 'Now, will you think whether to enforce
the admirable effect of your sudden sunbeam, this first line should not be
rendered more rapid by the removal of the clogging epithet "blind"—which
you repeat, too, I believe, farther on in the next page. What if you tried the
line thus "Then a sunbeam that burst through the tent roof— / Showed
Saul." The manifestation in the short line appears to me completer, from the
rapidity being increased in the long one. I only *ask*—It is simply an
impression—I have told you how very fine I do think all this showing of Saul
by the sunbeam—& how the more you come to see him, the finer it is'.
60. EBB. commented: 'The "All heavily hangs" as applied to the king-
serpent, you quite feel in your own muscles'.
61. *Pine*] pine (*1849*).
63.] EBB. quoted 'With springtime' in proof and suggested adding 'the'.
64. *black*] stark (*1849*).
65-71.] EBB. commented: 'The breaking of the band of lilies round the harp
is a relief & refreshment in itself after that dreadful sight—and then how
beautifully true it is that the song sh^d begin so . . with the sheep—"As one
after one / Docile they come to the pen-door—" But the rhythm sh^d not
interrupt itself where the sheep come docilely—& is not a word wanted . . a

So docile they come to the pen-door
    Till folding be done
—They are white and untorn by the bushes,
    For lo, they have fed
75 Where the long grasses stifle the water
    Within the stream's bed;
How one after one seeks its lodging,
    As star follows star
Into eve and the blue far above us,
80   —So blue and so far!

Then the tune for which quails on the cornland
    Will leave each his mate
To follow the player; then, what makes
    The crickets elate
85 Till for boldness they fight one another:
    And then, what has weight
To set the quick jerboa a-musing
    Outside his sand house
—There are none such as he for a wonder—
90   Half bird and half mouse!
—God made all the creatures and gave them
    Our love and our fear,
To show, we and they are his children,
    One family here.

95 Then I played the help-tune of our Reapers,
    Their wine-song, when hand
Grasps hand, eye lights eye in good friendship,
    And great hearts expand,
And grow one in the sense of this world's life;
100   And then, the low song
When the dead man is praised on his journey—
    "Bear, bear him along

---

syllable rather . . before that "Docile"? Will you consider?'
75.] EBB. quoted 'The long grasses stifling the water' and commented: 'how beautiful, *that* is!'
77-80.] EBB. quoted 'One after one seeks its lodging / As star follows star / Into the blue far above us / —So blue & so far!', and commented: 'It appears to me that the two long lines require a syllable each at the beginning, to keep the procession of sheep uninterrupted. The ear expects to read every long & short line in the sequences of this metre, as one long line—& where it cannot do so, a loss . . an abruption . . is felt—& there sh^d be nothing abrupt in the movement of these pastoral, starry images—do you think so?'
102.] EBB. quoted 'Bear him along' in proof and suggested the *1845* reading.

"With his few faults shut up like dead flowrets;
    "Are balm-seeds not here
105 "To console us? The land has got none such
        "As he on the bier—
    "Oh, would we might keep thee, my brother!"
        And then, the glad chaunt
    Of the marriage,—first go the young maidens—
110   Next, she whom we vaunt
    As the beauty, the pride of our dwelling:
        And then, the great march
    When man runs to man to assist him
        And buttress an arch
115 Nought can break . . who shall harm them, our
            brothers?
        Then, the chorus intoned
    As the Levites go up to the altar
        In glory enthroned—
    But I stopped here—for here, in the darkness,
120   Saul groaned:

    And I paused, held my breath in such silence!
        And listened apart—
    And the tent shook, for mighty Saul shuddered,—
        And sparkles 'gan dart
125 From the jewels that woke in his turban
        —At once with a start
    All the lordly male-sapphires, and rubies
        Courageous at heart;

105. has got] is left (*1849*).
107.] EBB. quoted 'Would we might help thee, my brother!' and
commented: 'Why not "Oh, would &c"—it throws a wail into the line, &
swells the rhythm rightly I think'.
111.] EBB. quoted 'The beauty, the pride of our dwelling—', and
commented: 'Why not "For the beauty"—or "As the beauty"—?'
115. brothers] friends (*1849*).
119.] EBB. quoted 'But I stopped—for here, in the darkness', and
commented: 'Very fine—& the preceding images full of beauty & characteristic life! but in this long line, I just ask if the rhythm would gain by
repeating here . . thus . . "But I stopped here—for here in the darkness". I
just ask, being doubtful'.
120. groaned:] groaned. (*1849*).
123-5. EBB. commented: 'And the shaking of the tent from the shudder of
the King, . . what effect it all has! and I like the jewels *waking* in his turban!'
127. All the] All its (*1849*).

So the head, but the body still moved not,—
130   Still hung there erect.
And I bent once again to my playing,
    Pursued it unchecked,
As I sang, "Oh, our manhood's prime vigour!
    —No spirit feels waste,
135 No muscle is stopped in its playing,
    No sinew unbraced,—
And the wild joys of living! The leaping
    From rock up to rock—
The rending their boughs from the palm-trees,—
140   The cool silver shock
Of a plunge in the pool's living water—
    The hunt of the bear,
And the sultriness showing the lion
    Is couched in his lair:
145 And the meal—the rich dates—yellowed over
    With gold dust divine,
And the locust's-flesh steeped in the pitcher—
    The full draught of wine,
And the sleep in the dried river channel
150   Where tall rushes tell
The water was wont to go warbling
    So softly and well,—
How good is man's life here, mere living!
    How fit to employ
155 The heart and the soul and the senses
    For ever in joy!
Hast thou loved the white locks of thy father
    Whose sword thou didst guard
When he trusted thee forth to the wolf hunt
160   For glorious reward?
Didst thou see the thin hands of thy mother
    Held up, as men sung
The song of the nearly-departed,
    And heard her faint tongue

129.] EBB. quoted 'So the head—but the body stirred not—', and commented: 'If you wrote "So the head—but the body . . *that* stirred not"—Just see the context!'
135. playing,] we supply the comma in agreement with *1849.*
142. hunt] haunt (*1849*). The *1849* reading is unique, and probably a mispr.
152.] EBB. quoted 'Softly & well—', and commented: 'Is not a syllable wanted at the beginning of the short line, to make the water warble softly . . right softly?'

165 Joining in while it could to the witness
   'Let one more attest,
  'I have lived, seen God's hand thro' that life-time,
  'And all was for best . . .'
  Then they sung thro' their tears, in strong triumph,
170 Not much,—but the rest!
  And thy brothers—the help and the contest,
   The working whence grew
  Such result, as from seething grape-bundles
   The spirit so true—
175 And the friends of thy boyhood—that boyhood
   With wonder and hope,
  And the promise and wealth in the future,—
   The eye's eagle scope,—
  Till lo, thou art grown to a monarch,
180 A people is thine!
  Oh, all, all the world offers singly,
   On one head combine,
  On one head the joy and the pride,
   Even rage like the throe
185 That opes the rock, helps its glad labour,
   And lets the gold go—
  And ambition that sees a sun lead it—
   Oh, all of these—all
  Combine to unite in one creature
190 —Saul!"

(End of Part the First.)

165.] EBB. quoted 'Join in, while it could, to the witness—', and commented: 'Would "Joining in" be better to the ear?'

177.] EBB. quoted 'And promise & wealth for the future—', and commented: 'I think you meant to write "the" before promise—'. In *1849* the line reads: 'Present promise, and wealth in the future,—'. EBB. concluded her critical notes with the comment: 'All I said about this poem in my note, I think more & more. Full of power & beauty it is,—& the conception, very striking'. The 'note' is her letter to B. of 27 Aug. 1845 (*LK* 173), which will be discussed in the headnote to the complete poem.

181. *all, all*] all gifts (*1849*).

187. *it—*] we supply the dash in agreement with *1849*.

190. *Saul!"*] emended from 'Saul!' in *1845*; David's song, beginning at l. 133, concludes here. The section of the completed poem which immediately follows is not a continuation of this song but a resumption of David's narrative.

47 The Lost Mistress

First publ. *B & P* vii (*DR & L*), 6 Nov. 1845; repr. *1849*, *1863* (when it was placed in *Lyrics*: see Appendix A, p. 464), *1865²* (which has no stanza nos.), *1868*, *1880*, *1888*. Our text is *1845*. EBB. saw the poem for the first time in proof and wrote: 'The last stanza but one of the "Lost Mistress" seemed obscure to me. Is it so really?' (21-22 Oct. 1845, *LK* 244; there is a note of the stanza on a page of jottings concerning the proofs in *Wellesley MS*). When she saw the published text, she remarked: 'One verse indeed in that expressive lyric of the "Lost Mistress," does still seem questionable to me, though you have changed a word since I saw it; and still I fancy that I rather leap at the meaning than reach it' (6 Nov. 1845, *LK* 260). She repeated her objection twice more (12-14 Nov. 1845 and 18 Jan. 1846, *LK* 267, 401), implying that her difficulty was with ll. 15-16 in particular. B. further altered the stanza in *B & P BYU* and *1849*, and *1880* (and its corrected reissue, *1884*) has one unique variant. DeVane (*Handbook* 162) connects the subject of the poem with the courtship: on 22 May 1845, after their first meeting, B. wrote a premature love-letter to EBB. which nearly caused her to end their friendship (the letter was subsequently returned and destroyed: see the letters of 23, 24, and 25 May, *LK* 72-80). There is some support for this view: vine-leaves come late, in May (ll. 5-8); EBB. had black eyes (l. 13); she mentions the snowdrop (l. 15) in an early letter (27 Feb. 1845, *LK* 29); B. was anxious after his abortive declaration to carry on with their meetings as before (l. 9), and there was some discussion as to the timing: 'And in the meantime I shall see you tomorrow perhaps?' wrote EBB. (30 May 1845, *LK* 84).

I.

All's over, then—does truth sound bitter
    As one at first believes?
Hark, 'tis the sparrows' good-night twitter
    About your cottage eaves.

II.

5 And the leaf-buds on the vine are woolly,
    I noticed that to-day;
One day more bursts them open fully
    —You know the red turns gray.

III.

  To-morrow we meet the same then, dearest?
10   May I take your hand in mine?
Mere friends are we,—well, friends the merest
    Keep much that I'll resign:

IV.

For tho' no glance of the eyes so black
But I keep with heart's endeavour,—
15   If you only wish the snowdrops back,
That shall stay in my soul for ever!—

V.

—Yet I will but say what mere friends say,
Or only a thought stronger;
I will hold your hand but so long as all may,
20   Or so very little longer!

¶47.*13-20.* The sense is that *though* the lover treasures his mistress's slightest gesture or word, *yet* his own words and gestures will barely express more feeling than a mere friend should. See following notes.

13-16.] For tho' no glance of the eyes so black
        But I'll keep with heart's endeavour,—
    Tho' you only wished the snowdrops back
        That should stay in my soul for ever,— (*B & P BYU*)

    For each glance of that eye so bright and black,
        Though I keep with heart's endeavour,—
    Your voice, when you wish the snowdrops back,
        Though it stays in my heart for ever!— (*1849-88*, except 'Each glance', *1880, 1884*; 'stay', *1863-88*; 'ever,—', *1880, 1884*).

15. back,] emended from 'back' in *1845*, a correction made by B. in *B & P Domett*; B. also underlined 'That' in the next line, making it doubly clear that it is a demonstrative referring to the mistress's imagined wish, not a relative pronoun referring to the snowdrops.

48 The Flight of the Duchess

Text and Publication

Lines 1-215 first publ. *Hood's Magazine* iii (Apr. 1845) 313-18, headed 'Part the First', and without section numbers. (For B.'s contributions to *Hood's*, see p. 218.) B. told EBB. that it was 'only the beginning of a story written some time ago, and given to poor Hood in his emergency at a day's notice,—the true stuff and story is all to come . . . what you allude to is the mere introduction—but the Magazine has passed into other hands and I must put the rest in some "Bell" or other—it is one of my Dramatic Romances' (3 May 1845, *LK* 55). The complete poem first publ. *B & P* vii (*DR & L*), 6 Nov. 1845, when the section numbers were added; repr. *1849* (when a new section number, XVII, was added after l. 832), *1863* (when it was placed in *Romances*: see Appendix A, p. 464), *1863²*, *1868* (when all the occurrences of 'Lady' were changed to 'lady'), *1872* (in *1884*, the corrected re-issue of this volume, the poem received unusual attention, with several dozen unique variants, mostly changes in punctuation but some verbal revs.; the reason may be that B.'s attention had been drawn to the poem in 1883 by Furnivall: see below), *1888* (when a good deal of functional indentation was added to guide the reader through the poem's changing metrical pattern). Our text is that of the first complete ed., *1845*.

Date and composition

In a letter of 15 Apr. 1883, B. wrote to Furnivall: 'There was an odd circumstance that either mended or marred the poem in the writing—I fancied the latter at the time. As I finished the line—which ends what was printed in Hood's Magazine as the First Part—"and the old one—you shall hear!" [l. 215] I saw from the window where I sat a friend opening the gate to our house—one Captain Lloyd—whom I jumped up to meet, judging from the time of day that something especially interesting had brought him—as proved to be the case, for he was in a strange difficulty. This took a deal of discussing,—next day, other interruptions occurred, and the end was I lost altogether the thing as it was in my head at the beginning . . . some time afterwards, I was staying at Bettisfield Park in Wales, and a guest, speaking of early winter, said "the deer had already begun to break the ice in the pond"—and a fancy struck me, which, on returning home, I worked up into what concludes the story' (*Trumpeter* 70-1). B. recorded a visit to Bettisfield Park, the Flintshire estate of the politician and minor poet Sir John Hanmer, in Sept. 1842 (*Correspondence* vi 88; see ll. 216-22n., 663-8n.); if this is the date at which he resumed work on the poem, the composition of ll. 1-215 probably dates to the spring or early summer of 1842. The poem was well advanced, or even finished in draft, when ll. 1-215 were given to *Hood's*. B. completed it during the summer of 1845. He showed the MS of ll. 216-915 to EBB., and revised them in response to her comments (*Wellesley MS*; all comments recorded in the notes derive from this source unless otherwise stated). EBB. made no notes on the *Hood's* fragment, although she did comment on the other *Hood's* poems. Her notes on *Flight* are the most detailed of the ones she made on the poems of *DR & L*, even in proportion to its greater length; this was probably because it was the first poem of B.'s which she saw after agreeing to comment on his forthcoming collection. B. wrote to her after receiving the last instalment of her notes on the poem: 'For the criticism itself, it is all true, except the overrating—all the suggestions are to be adopted, the improvements accepted . . . I shall let it lie . . . till just before I print it; and then go over it, alter at the places, and do something for the places where I (really) wrote anyhow, almost, to get done' (25 July 1845, *LK* 135). For discussion of the poem's place in B.'s courtship of EBB., see D. Karlin, *The Courtship of Robert Browning and Elizabeth Barrett* (Oxford 1985) 89-93.

Form and metre; sources and influences
The poem is written in four-stress lines, with extreme variation in the number and placing of unstressed syllables, showing in this the influence of Romantic experiments with stressed metre, e.g. Wordsworth's *The Waggoner* and Shelley's *The Sensitive Plant*. The major literary source, both metrically and in other respects, is Coleridge's *Christabel*. The resemblance (noted by EBB.—see ll. 734-7n.) concerns story as well as form. In both, a lady living in a castle is bewitched by an ambiguous outsider, and alienated from her husband/father. But B. characteristically inverts the elements: the outsider in *Flight* (the Gypsy) is younger than she appears, whereas Geraldine in *Christabel* is older; the Gypsy's spell is beneficent, Geraldine's wicked; the Gypsy and the Duchess fly from the castle to the wood, whereas Geraldine and Christabel fly from the wood to the castle. In addition to *Christabel*, B. seems to have drawn on other poems by Coleridge: the Gypsy's visionary speech, and the impossibility of fully retrieving it, recalls *Kubla Khan* (as does B.'s account of the way the composition of the poem was interrupted by a visitor); the narrator's compulsion to tell his story may owe something to *The Rime of the Ancient Mariner*. Keats's *Eve of St Agnes* (itself indebted to *Christabel*) may also have influenced the conception of *Flight*.

In his letter to Furnivall (see above) B. also stated that the poem 'originally all grew out of this one intelligible line of a song that I heard a woman singing at a bonfire on Guy Faux night when I was a boy—"Following the Queen of the Gypsies, O!"'; but he implicitly denied the connection between this song and the closest analogy in recorded ballad literature, *Johnnie Faa* or *The Gypsy Laddie*. His claim is supported by a reference in a letter to EBB. (6 Feb. 1846, *LK* 440) to the 'strange coincidence' of the resemblance between his own poem and a ballad he had only just read, though his memory may have been at fault. The poem also draws on folktale and Gothic motifs, such as escape with the Queen of the Fairies.

B. could have encountered Gypsies at the annual Camberwell Fair near his childhood home, and in the nearby Dulwich woods (*Maynard* 66, 83). The detailed account of their way of life may be indebted to George Borrow's

Zincali (1841), which stimulated an interest in Gypsy lore in the 1840s. Borrow states that Gypsies are native to Russia, Hungary, Wallachia and Moldavia (see ll. 350-6). His comments on the Hungarian Gypsies are closest to B.'s account: 'two classes are free in Hungary to do almost what they please—the nobility and—the Gypsies; the former are above the law—the latter below it'; they also make 'foreign excursions', which 'frequently endure for three or four years', during which 'they wander in bands of twelve or fourteen through France, even to Rome' (p. 10). B.'s description of Gypsy industry (ll. 361-86) also shares details with Borrow's, especially in its emphasis on smith-work (p. 53). The Gypsy Queen who draws the Duchess away to Gypsy life reflects Borrow's comment that it is the old women who, among the Gypsies, cultivate supernatural skills; her (apparently) hideous appearance echoes Borrow's remark that 'their ugliness at an advanced age is . . . loathesome, and even appalling' (p. 5). Borrow also describes 'the gypsy glance' as a 'strange stare, like nothing else in the world': cp. ll. 529-31. Finally, the emphasis in the old Gypsy's speech on the importance of the racial bond is also present in Borrow, who cites as 'their most distinguishing characteristic' the 'love of "the blood"'. According to Borrow, Gypsy race may be transmitted by metempsychosis to those not genetically of Gypsy descent, which may explain how the Gypsy Queen can claim the Duchess as a Gypsy.

The poem's satire on pseudo-medievalism relates to the contemporary cult of the age of chivalry, exemplified in the Eglinton tournament (1842). Carlyle, whose *Past and Present* (1841) did much to stimulate this cult, was strongly opposed to its excesses, for example Disraeli's Young England movement, which advocated a return to traditional social values and relationships. B. and Carlyle were friends in this period, and B. shared Carlyle's hostility to Young England: 'The cant is,' he wrote to EBB., 'that "an age of transition" is the melancholy thing to contemplate and delineate—whereas the worst thing of all to look back on are times of comparative standing still, rounded in their impotent completeness. So the Young England imbeciles hold that "belief" is the admirable point,—*in what*, they judge comparatively immaterial!' (17 May 1846, *LK* 710). The period of the poem is accordingly post-medieval and probably contemporary; the setting is specified as a duchy in the independent principality of Moldavia, a region on the shores of the Black Sea. For the physical character of the landscape, B. may be drawing on memories of his travels in Europe in 1834 and 1838.

Parallels in B.
Flight belongs to a group of works written in the 1840s concerned with rescue or escape from physical or mental oppression (*Count Gismond, Colombe*); with enchanted visions of potential happiness (*Pied Piper*); and with the power of love to transcend moral and social limits (*Glove*). *My Last Duchess* takes to its extreme the interest in the aristocratic temperament; the master—servant relationship is emphasized in the plays, esp. *A Blot*. Cp. also the supernatural

element in *Childe Roland*, and the parallel with the ethic of *Statue*. All these themes are found in *Ring*; the attraction of Gypsy life as a subversion of conventional values is strongly argued by Don Juan in *Fifine*.

Criticism

EBB. concluded her critical notes with the comment: 'It is a very singular & striking poem, full of power . . remarkable for it even among your average works, & quite wonderful for the mechanism & rhyming power of it—Also what strikes me in it is the purely beautiful manner in which the beauty reveals itself from the grotesqueness . . taking & giving effect . . & keeping such true measure with nature' (see also her letter to B. of 25 July 1845, *LK* 132-3). The most important comment on the poem is B.'s own, in a letter to EBB.: 'It is an odd fact, yet characteristic of my accomplishings one and all in this kind, that of *the poem*, the real conception of an evening (two years ago; fully)—of *that*, not a line is written—tho' perhaps, after all, what I am going to call the accessories in the story are real though indirect reflexes of the original idea, and so supersede properly enough the necessity of its personal appearance,—so to speak: but, as I conceived the poem, it consisted entirely of the Gipsy's description of the life the Lady was to lead with her future Gipsy lover—a *real* life, not an unreal one like that with the Duke—and as I meant to write it, all their wild adventures would have come out and the insignificance of the former vegetation have been deducible only—as the main subject has become now—of course it comes to the same thing, for one would never show half by half like a cut orange—' (25 July 1845, *LK* 135).

I.

You're my friend:
I was the man the Duke spoke to;
I helped the Duchess to cast off his yoke, too;
So here's the tale from beginning to end,
5   My friend!

II.

Ours is a great wild country:
If you climb to our castle's top,
I don't see where your eye can stop;
For when you've pass'd the corn-field country,
10   Where vineyards leave off, flocks are pack'd,
And sheep-range leads to cattle-tract,

¶48.2. Cp. l. 440.
9-17. Cp. *A Grammarian* 1-20.
11-12.] in *1872* l. 12 has the mispr. 'cattle-track'. In *1884* (which was set from *1872*) either B. or the compositor changed 'cattle-tract' in l. 11 to 'cattle-track', restoring the consistency but creating a defective rhyme with 'pack'd' in l. 10.

And cattle-tract to open-chase,
And open-chase to the very base
Of the mountain where, at a funeral pace,
15 Round about, solemn and slow,
One by one, row after row,
Up and up the pine-trees go,
So, like black priests up, and so
Down the other side again
20 To another greater, wilder country,
That's one vast red drear burnt-up plain,
Branch'd thro' and thro' with many a vein
Whence iron's dug, and copper's dealt;
Look right, look left, look straight before,
25 Beneath they mine, above they smelt,
Copper-ore and iron-ore,
And forge and furnace mould and melt,
And so on, more and ever more,
Till, at the last, for a bounding belt,
30 Comes the salt sand hoar of the great sea shore,
—And the whole is our Duke's country!

III.

I was born the day this present Duke was—
(And O, says the song, ere I was old!)
In the castle where the other Duke was—
35 (When I was happy and young, not old!)
I in the Kennel, he in the Bower:
We are of like age to an hour.
My father was Huntsman in that day;
Who has not heard my father say
40 That, when a boar was brought to bay,
Three, four times out of five,
With his huntspear he'd contrive

12. *open-chase*: 'a tract of unenclosed land reserved for breeding and hunting wild animals'.
16.] One after one, row upon row, (*Hood's*).
23. *dealt*: traded.
30. hoar: hoary, white (usually with age).
32. With the 'twinning' motif here, cp. the allusions to Jacob and Esau (l. 907) and Valentine and Orson (l. 910).
33. Cp. Coleridge, *Youth and Age* 20-22: 'O! the joys that came down shower-like, / Of Friendship, Love, and Liberty, / Ere I was old!'
35. *happy*] hopeful (*1849*).
36. *Kennel*: here, 'a small and mean dwelling or hut'.
41. *Three, four times*] Three times, four times (*1849-88*).

To get the killing-place transfixed,
And pin him true both eyes betwixt?
45 That's why the old Duke had rather
Lost a salt-pit than my father,
And loved to have him ever in call;
That's why my father stood in the Hall
When the old Duke brought his infant out
50 To show the people, and while they pass'd
The wondrous bantling round about,
Was first to start at the outside blast
As the Kaiser's courier blew his horn,
Just a month after the babe was born:
55 "And" quoth the Kaiser's courier, "since
"The Duke has got an Heir, our Prince
"Needs the Duke's self at his side:"
The Duke look'd down and seemed to wince,
But he thought of wars o'er the world wide,
60 Castles a-fire, men on their march,
The toppling tower, the crashing arch;
And up he looked, and awhile he eyed
The row of crests and shields and banners,
Of all achievements after all manners,
65 And "ay," said the Duke with a surly pride:
The more was his comfort when he died
At next year's end, in a velvet suit,
With a gilt glove on his hand, and his foot
In a silk shoe for a leather boot,
70 Petticoated like a herald,
In a chamber next to an ante-room,

45. *That's*] And that's (*1849-88*).
45-6. *had rather / Lost*] Would rather / Have lost (*1849*); Would rather / He lost (*1863-88*).
49-51. Cp., in *Protus*, the exhibiting of the baby heir who, as here, turns out to be feeble; and cp. *Ecclesiastes* x 16: 'Woe to thee, O land, when thy king is a child'.
51. *bantling*: a young child; but often used depreciatively, and formerly as a synonym of 'bastard'. B. uses the word pejoratively in *Ring* v 1481.
55-6. 'Kaiser' normally means 'Emperor', as in *Sordello*; here it is equivalent to 'Prince'.
64. *achievements*: combining the senses of '[real] accomplishments' and 'heraldic ensigns'.
68. *hand, and his foot*] hand, his foot (*1872, 1884, 1888*). A rare example of *1888* agreeing with a reading introduced in a volume of selections, not a previous collected ed.
69. *silk*] silken (*1849-88*).

Where he breathed the breath of page and groom,
What he called stink and they, perfume:
—They should have set him on red Berold,
75 Mad with pride, like fire to manage!
They should have got his cheek fresh tannage
Such a day as to-day in the merry sunshine!
Had they stuck on his fist a rough-foot merlin!
—Hark, the wind's on the heath at its game!
80 Oh for a noble falcon-lanner
To flap each broad wing like a banner,
And turn in the wind, and dance like flame!
Had they broach'd a cask of white beer from Berlin!
—Or if you incline to prescribe mere wine
85 Put to his lips when they saw him pine,
A cup of our own Moldavia fine,
Cotnar, for instance, green as May sorrel,
And ropy with sweet,—we shall not quarrel.

IV.

So at home the sick tall yellow Duchess
90 Was left with the infant in her clutches,
She being the daughter of God knows who:
And now was the time to revisit her tribe,
So abroad and afar they went, the two,
And let our people curse and gibe
95 At the empty Hall and extinguished fire,
Loud as we liked, but ever in vain,
Till after long years we had our desire,
And back came the Duke and his mother again.

76. *tannage*: tanning (in the sun).
78. *rough-foot*: having feathered feet.   *merlin*: a falcon, 'one of the smallest, but one of the boldest, of European birds of prey'. Not used elsewhere by B.
80. *falcon-lanner*: *Falco lanarius*, a Mediterranean species. The only other occurrence in B. is at l. 269 below.
83. a *cask of white beer*] a white-beer cask (*1888*). 'White beer' means a strong lager.
87. *Cotnar*: wine from Cotnari in Moldavia.
88. *ropy*: sticky and stringy. Not (as normally) pejorative; cp. 'streaky syrup', l. 838 below.
91-3. Contrast the Gypsy's 'tribe', l. 567, and the narrator's account of the Gypsies, l. 350ff.
93. *So abroad*] Abroad (*1865-88*).
94. *curse*] rail (*1849-88*).
96. *Loud*] As loud (*1849-88*).

V.

And he came back the pertest ape
100 That ever affronted human shape;
Full of his travel, struck at himself—
You'd say, he despised our bluff old ways
—Not he! For in Paris they told the elf
That our rough North land was the Land of Lays,
105 The one good thing left in evil days;
For the Mid-Age was the Heroic Time,
And only in wild nooks like ours
Could you taste of it yet as in its prime,
True Castles, with proper Towers,
110 Young-hearted women, old-minded men,
And manners now as manners were then.
So, all the old Dukes had been, without knowing it,
This Duke would fain know he was, without being it;
'Twas not for the joy's self, but the joy of his showing
it,
115 Nor for the pride's self, but the pride of our seeing it.
He revived all usages thoroughly worn-out,
The souls of them fumed-forth, the hearts of them
torn-out:
And chief in the chase his neck he perill'd,
On a lathy horse, all legs and length,
120 With blood for bone, all speed, no strength;
—They should have set him on red Berold,
With the red eye slow consuming in fire,
And the thin stiff ear like an abbey spire!

VI.

Well, such as he was, he must marry, we heard:
125 And out of a convent, at the word,
Came the Lady, in time of spring.
—Oh, old thoughts they cling, they cling!
That day, I know, with a dozen oaths

99. *pertest ape*] pertest little ape (*1849-88*).
104. *That our*] Our (*1888*).   *North land*: B., following Carlyle, normally uses 'North' in very general terms, to signify the non-Mediterranean countries of Europe, as well as Scandinavia; cp. his comment in a letter to EBB. of 30 Apr. 1845 that 'Italy is stuff for the use of the North, and no more' (*LK* 50).   *Lays*: songs, ballads (archaic). See *Pauline* 524n.
106. *For*] Since (*1849-88*).
109. *True Castles*] And see true castles (*1849-88*).
112. *So, all the*] So, all that the (*1849-88*).
119. *lathy*: thin like a lath (sliver of wood). Only occurrence in B.

I clad myself in thick hunting-clothes
130   Fit for the chase of urox or buffle
In winter-time when you need to muffle;
But the Duke had a mind we should cut a figure,
And so we saw the Lady arrive:
My friend, I have seen a white crane bigger!
135   She was the smallest Lady alive,
Made, in a piece of Nature's madness,
Too small, almost, for the life and gladness
That over-filled her, as some hive
Out of the bears' reach on the high trees
140   Is crowded with its safe merry bees—
In truth she was not hard to please!
Up she look'd, down she look'd, round at the mead,
Straight at the Castle, that's best indeed
To look at from outside the walls:
145   As for us, styled the "serfs and thralls,"
She as much thanked me as if she had said it,
(With her eye, do you understand?)
Because I patted her horse while I led it;
And Max, who rode on her other hand,
150   Said, no bird flew past but she enquired
What its true name was, nor ever seemed tired—
If that was an eagle she saw hover,
And the green and gray bird on the field was the
    plover?
When suddenly appeared the Duke,
155   And as down she sprung, the small foot pointed
On to my hand,—as with a rebuke,
And as if his backbone were not jointed,
The Duke stepped rather aside than forward,
And welcomed her with his grandest smile;
160   And, mind you, his mother all the while
Chilled in the rear, like a wind to Nor'ward;
And up, like a weary yawn, with its pullies
Went, in a shriek, the rusty portcullis,
And, like a glad sky the north-wind sullies,
165   The Lady's face stopped its play,
As if her first hair had grown grey—

---

130. urox] urochs (*1888*); a species of bison, cited in contemporary accounts as found in Lithuania and Germany. Only occurrence in B.   *buffle*: buffalo. Only occurrence in B.
147. eye] eyes (*1849-88*).
149. rode] went (*Hood's*).
153. And] If (*1849*).

For such things must begin some one day!

VII.

In a day or two she was well again;
As who should say, "You labour in vain!
170 "This is all a jest against God, who meant
"I should ever be, as I am, content
"And glad in his sight; therefore, glad I will be!"
So smiling as at first went she.

VIII.

She was active, stirring, all fire—
175 Could not rest, could not tire—
To a stone she had given life!
(I myself loved once, in my day,)
—For a Shepherd's, Miner's, Huntsman's wife,
(I had a wife, I know what I say,)
180 Never in all the world such an one!
And here was plenty to be done,
And she that could do it, great or small,
She was to do nothing at all.
There was already this man in his post,
185 This in his station, and that in his office,
And the Duke's plan admitted a wife, at most,
To meet his eye, with the other trophies,
Now outside the Hall, now in it,
To sit thus, stand thus, see and be seen,
190 At the proper place in the proper minute,
And die away the life between:
And it was amusing enough, each infraction
Of rule—(but for after-sadness that came)—
To hear the consummate self-satisfaction
195 With which the young Duke and the old Dame
Would let her advise, and criticise,
And, being a fool, instruct the wise,

176. had] she might have (*1863-88*).
192. each infraction: i.e. 'at each infraction'.
197. The opposition of 'fool' and 'wise' occurs throughout *Proverbs* and *Ecclesiastes* (e.g. *Proverbs* xv 2: 'The tongue of the wise useth knowledge aright: but the mouth of fools poureth out foolishness'); the irony of the application here may also refer to passages from *Romans* and *Corinthians* (e.g. *Romans* i 22: 'Professing themselves to be wise, they became fools', and *1 Corinthians* iii 18-19: 'If any man among you seemeth to be wise in this world, let him become a fool, that he may be wise. For the wisdom of this world is foolishness with God'). The Duke and his mother, however, could

And, child-like, parcel out praise or blame:
They bore it all in complacent guise,
200 As tho' an artificer, after contriving
A wheel-work image as if it were living,
Should find with delight it could motion to strike him!
So found the Duke, and his mother like him,—
The Lady hardly got a rebuff—
205 That had not been contemptuous enough,
With his cursed smirk, as he nodded applause,
And kept off the old mother-cat's claws.

IX.

So the little Lady grew silent and thin,
    Paling and ever paling,
210 As the way is with a hid chagrin;
    And the Duke perceived that she was ailing,
And said in his heart, " 'Tis done to spite me,
"But I shall find in my power to right me!"
Don't swear, friend—the Old One, many a year,
215 Is in Hell, and the Duke's self . . . you shall hear.

X.

Well, early in autumn, at first winter-warning,

also cite *2 Corinthians* xi 19: 'ye suffer fools gladly, seeing ye yourselves are wise'.

200. after contriving] having contriv'd (*Hood's*).

201. wheel-work: i.e. mechanical.   *were living*] liv'd (*Hood's*).

207. mother-cat's claws: cp. the description of Guido's mother (*Ring* x 916-24) as a 'she-pard'.

212. said in his heart: a biblical tag to express private or covert intention; cp. (noting l. 907n. below) *Genesis* xxvii 41: 'And Esau hated Jacob because of the blessing wherewith his father blessed him: and Esau said in his heart, The days of mourning for my father are at hand; then will I slay my brother Jacob'.

214. Old One] old one (*Hood's, 1865-88*); i.e. the old Duchess, but the phrase is also a traditional name for the devil.

215.] this line ends the section of the poem which B. sent to *Hood's*: see headnote. In *Hood's* it was followed by 'End of Part the First'.

216-22. EBB. commented: 'The stag—& sun melting the water—beautiful description like the morning itself'. For the importance of the image in B.'s resumption of the poem, see headnote. Cp. the opening of *Pippa*, and B. to Domett, 19 Dec. 1841: 'Our little hills are stiff & springy underfoot with the frozen grass—and you crunch the thin-white ice on the holes the cattle have made' (*Correspondence* v 190).

When the stag had to break with his foot, of a
   morning,
A drinking-hole out of the fresh tender ice
That covered the pond till the sun, in a trice,
220   Loosening it, let out a ripple of gold,
And another and another, and faster and faster,
Till, dimpling to blindness, the wide water rolled:
Then it so chanced that the Duke our master
Asked himself what were the pleasures in season,
225   And found, since the calendar bade him be hearty,
He should do the Middle Age no treason
In resolving on a hunting-party.
Always provided, old books showed the way of it!
What meant old poets by their strictures?
230   And when old poets had said their say of it,
How taught old painters in their pictures?
We must revert to the proper channels,
Workings in tapestry, paintings on pannels,
And gather up Woodcraft's authentic traditions:
235   Here was food for our various ambitions,
As on each case, exactly stated,
—To encourage your dog, now, the properest
   chirrup,

225-7.] EBB. quoted 'Finding the calendar bade him be hearty, / Did resolve
on a hunting party—' and commented: 'Does not that first line seem as if it
were meditating a rhyme for the second? I suppose the meaning is that the
time of year reminded him of the need of festivity; but there is something
forced in the expression, or appears to *me* to be so. And then the second
line . . is it not too short to the ear?—'.
228.] EBB. quoted 'Oh, and old books they knew the way of it—&c.' and
commented: 'All this is quite clear to *me*—& I like the abruptness. Still people
are sure to say, from the break in the narrative, that it's obscure—& *so* little a
change (of a word or two) would allow them to read on without
thinking!!—You had written "they *taught* the way of it"—which is clearer as
far as the word goes,—only "taught", I see, comes afterwards. Would
"showed" do? But then the next line "What meant old poets by their
strictures?" makes the meaning questionable till the reader can take the
context of before & *after* . . which is too long to wait, for readers in general'.
229. *strictures*: remarks; used here without the modern sense of rebuke.
233. *pannels*] variant spelling of 'panels', archaic by B.'s day; altered to the
modern form, *1849-88*.
234. Early uses of the term 'woodcraft' are esp. associated with hunting, as
here; *OED* cites Chaucer, *General Prologue* 110 (the Yeoman): 'Of wodecraft
wel koude he al the usage'.

Or best prayer to St. Hubert on mounting your
    stirrup—
We of the household took thought and debated.
240 Blessed was he whose back ached with the jerkin
His sire was wont to do forest-work in;
Blesseder he who nobly sunk "ohs"
And "ahs" while he tugged on his grandsire's trunk-
    hose;
What signified hats if they had no rims on,
245 Each slouching before and behind like the scallop,
And able to serve at sea for a shallop,
Loaded with lacquer and looped with crimson?
So that the deer now, to make a short rhyme on't,
What with our Venerers, Prickers, and Verderers,
250 Might hope for real hunters at length, and not
    murderers,
And oh the Duke's tailor—he had a hot time on't!

XI.

Now you must know, that when the first dizziness
Of flap-hats and buff coats and jackboots subsided,

---

238. St. Hubert: patron saint of hunting.

242. sunk: suppressed (by 'sinking' his voice).

243. trunkhose: full bag-like breeches, worn in the 16th and early 17th centuries.

244.] EBB. quoted 'What meant a hat if it had no rims on', and commented: 'Do you like "*what meant*"? I do not quite—& the connection is broken. And then, "the rims"—a hat has only one rim ever—except for the rhyme of "crimson". So why not write .. "a hat where never a rim's on". *That* w^{d} do—wouldn't it? You are not to think that I have not a proper respect & admiration for all these new live rhymes & that I would not make every sacrifice in reason for them'.

246. shallop: dinghy; *OED* cites Spenser, Waller, and Tennyson's *Lady of Shallot* (1832). Only occurrence in B.

249. Venerers: huntsmen (first citation in *OED*).   *Prickers*: mounted attendants at a hunt.   *Verderers*: judicial officers of the king's forest.

251.] EBB. quoted 'And the Duke's tailor to have &c', and commented: 'A slip of the pen for "might have" or "should have"? Otherwise "the deer" are made to hope this of the tailor. *Quaere*, if . . "And *so*, the Duke's tailor might have" &c would not assist the rhythm. I am doubtful though'.

252.] EBB. quoted 'Now you must know *that* when the first dizziness', and commented: 'Why erase "that"? Is not the rhythm better with it?'

253. flap-hats: hats with flapping brims.   *buff coats*: 'stout coats of buff leather'. Cp. *How They Brought the Good News* 49-50.

The Duke put this question, "The Duke's part
          provided,
255   "Had not the Duchess some share in the business?"
       For out of the mouth of two or three witnesses,
       Did he establish all fit-or-unfitnesses:
       And, after much laying of heads together,
       Somebody's cap got a notable feather
260   By the announcement with proper unction
       That he had discovered the lady's function;
       Since ancient authors held this tenet,
       "When horns wind a mort and the deer is at siege,
       "Let the dame of the Castle prick forth on her jennet,
265   "And with water to wash the hands of her liege
       "In a clean ewer with a fair toweling,
       "Let her superintend the disemboweling."
       Now, my friend, if you had so little religion
       As to catch a hawk, some falcon-lanner,
270   And thrust her broad wings like a banner
       Into a coop for a vulgar pigeon;
       And if day by day, and week by week,
       You cut her claws, and sealed her eyes,
       And clipped her wings, and tied her beak,
275   Would it cause you any great surprise
       If when you decided to give her an airing
       You found she needed a little preparing?
       —I say, should you be such a curmudgeon,

257-8.] EBB. quoted 'He established all fit & unfitnesses', and commented
that the line 'seems *short* too—& also the next line'.
262. held] gave (*1863-88*).
263. *wind a mort*: sound the note signalling the death of the deer.   *at
siege*: at bay (though a 'mort' would not normally be sounded until the
death).
264.] EBB. commented: 'does the Lady "pace" forth or "*prick*" forth on her
jennet?'   *prick forth*: ride out.   *jennet*: small Spanish horse.
265. *liege*: husband, with the feudal sense of 'lord and master'.
266. *ewer*: pitcher with a wide spout.
267. *superintend*] preside at (*1849-88*).
268-79. Only the female lanner was used in falconry.
268-9. EBB. commented: 'This is a beautiful image, this hawk's—& so new,
& so true!' For the reason for the stress on the ampersands, see ll. 272-4n.
269. *As to catch*] EBB. quoted 'As catch' and suggested the addition of 'to'.
272-4. *day, and week . . . claws, and sealed . . . wings, and tied*] EBB. suggested
the addition of the first 'and', and the restoration of the two others which B.
had erased, commenting: 'Your ear's first impulse led you to them, & rightly
according to mine'.

If she clung to the perch, as to take it in dudgeon?
280 Yet when the Duke to his lady signified,
Just a day before, as he judged most dignified,
In what a pleasure she was to participate,—
And, instead of leaping wide in flashes,
Her eyes just lifted their long lashes,
285 As if pressed by fatigue even he could not dissipate,
And duly acknowledged the Duke's forethought,
But spoke of her health, if her health were worth
        aught,
Of the weight by day and the watch by night,
And much wrong now that used to be right,
290 So, thanking him, declined the hunting,—
Was conduct ever more affronting?
With all the ceremony settled—
With the towel ready, and the sewer
Polishing up his oldest ewer,
295 And the jennet pitched upon, a piebald,
Black-barred, cream-coated and pink eye-ball'd,—
No wonder if the Duke was nettled!
And when she persisted nevertheless,—
Well, I suppose here's the time to confess
300 That there ran half round our Lady's chamber
A balcony none of the hardest to clamber,
And that Jacynth the tire-woman, ready in waiting,

284. EBB. thought this 'beautiful', but pointed out that in the passage as a whole 'you make your Duchess's eyes acknowledge the Duke's forethought & speak of her health &c—as if such a Duke could be likely to understand that sort of speaking. The personal pronoun has been forgotten somehow. Just see if it has not'. B., unusually, did not take her advice; the Duchess does not speak directly at any point in the poem.

287.] EBB. quoted 'if that were worth aught' and commented: ' "were worth aught"—there is something clogged in the sound'.

288.] EBB. suggested this reading, but did not record B.'s original version.

291-2.] EBB. quoted 'Could conduct be more affronting? / All the ceremony settled—', and commented: 'I like these short lines sometimes . . when anything is to be expressed by abruptness—but not here, I think. Not in the second, at least'.

293. sewer: a butler or steward.

300.] EBB. advocated a return to this, the original reading, but does not quote the MS rev.

302.] as with l. 300, EBB. recommended returning to this reading, without quoting the revised version; she added: 'Only I should be inclined to write "But" for "And". He "confesses" that the balcony went round the chamber,—the rest . . the listening . . was all matter of course . . "what need

Stayed in call outside, what need of relating?
And since Jacynth was like a June rose, why, a fervent
305   Adorer of Jacynth, of course, was your servant;
And if she had the habit to peep through the casement,
How could I keep at any vast distance?
And so, as I say, on the Lady's persistence,
The Duke, dumb stricken with amazement,
310   Stood for a while in a sultry smother,
And then, with a smile that partook of the awful,
Turned her over to his yellow mother
To learn what was decorous and lawful;
And the mother smelt blood with a cat-like instinct,
315   As her cheek quick whitened thro' all its quince-
tinct—
Oh, but the Lady heard the whole truth at once!
What meant she?—Who was she?—Her duty and
station,
The wisdom of age and the folly of youth, at once,
Its decent regard and its fitting relation—
320   In brief, my friend, set all the devils in hell free

---

of relating?"'.   *tire-woman*: lady's maid.

303.] EBB. quoted 'Would stay in call outside' and commented: 'might not
"stayed in call outside" do better, & with less clogging?'

307-8.] EBB. quoted 'How could I be &c / So as I say &c', and commented:
'Is there not a sameness in the fall of the accents which you w^d choose to
avoid. Suppose it were written "*And so*" (in the true idiom of storytellers) in
the latter line?'

310. in a sultry smother: in a state of smouldering anger.

313. was decorous] was held decorous (*1875-88*). A rare example of a
substantive rev. originating in *1875*, the second corr. reissue of *1868*.

316.] EBB. quoted 'for once', which B. altered to 'at once' in response to her
suggestion about l. *318* (see below).

317.] EBB. quoted 'duty & station', and suggested 'her duty & station'.

318.] EBB. quoted 'The wisdom of age & the folly of youth for once', and
commented: '*Would* the Dowager Duchess talk of the folly of youth *for
once*—& not always? Yet the *rhymes*! Which sh^d not be hurt for the
world!—Then why not save rhyme & reason by writing "at once" in both
places? Wouldn't it answer every purpose?' EBB. had evidently missed the
sarcasm in the original reading.

320. friend] friends (*1870-88*). If this is a mispr., it is curious that it should
appear in both collected and selected eds. between these dates. But the
narrator is clearly speaking to one 'friend' only elsewhere in the poem (ll. 1,
214, 833), though B.'s speakers do occasionally address people other than
their immediate interlocutors.

> And turn them out to carouse in a belfry,
> And treat the priests to a fifty-part canon,
> And then you may guess how that tongue of hers ran
>   on!
> Well, somehow or other it ended at last
> 325 And, licking her whiskers, out she passed;
> And after her,—making (he hoped) a face
> Like Emperor Nero or Sultan Saladin,
> Stalked the Duke's self with all the grace
> Of ancient hero or modern paladin,—
> 330 From door to staircase—oh, such a solemn
> Unbending of the vertebral column!

XII.

> However, at sunrise our company mustered,
> And here was the huntsman bidding unkennel,

321.] EBB. quoted 'And turn them to carouse', and commented: 'Did you not miss "*out*" in the transcribing?'

322. fifty-part canon: B. glossed this: 'a canon, in music, is a piece wherein the subject is repeated in various keys, and, being strictly obeyed in the repetition, becomes the "canon"—the imperative law to what follows. Fifty of such parts would be indeed a notable peal; to manage three is enough of an achievement for a good musician' (*Cyclopaedia* 180). Strictly, however, a canon consists of a melody whose harmony is supplied by repetitions of itself at the same or different pitches, but in a single key: the phrase 'in various keys' might suggest a fugue, unless 'key' is taken to mean 'pitch'. Though continental (not English) church bells are tuned melodically, and could therefore produce a simple canon, a 'fifty-part' one is, as B.'s note suggests, hyperbolic.

323.] EBB. quoted 'And for my fancy how her tongue ran on', and commented: 'I do *not* like the rhythm—though harmony is not required,—to be sure. You felt a need, by that erasure'. She does not cite the 'erasure'.

324.] B. had deleted 'Well', but restored it at EBB.'s suggestion.

326.] EBB. quoted 'And after her, making a face', and commented: 'Couldn't it be made a little longer? And I am not sure that I like the fall down the staircase, & what follows about the towel. Perhaps I do not clearly understand what Jacynth means—I *promised to tell all my impressions*'. The 'promise' refers to EBB.'s assurance to B. that she would give him critical as well as appreciative comments: see his letter of 13 July 1845 and her reply of 16-17 July (*LK* 123-6), and see l. 577n. below. The 'fall down the staircase' does not appear in the extant text; either B. deleted a passage, or EBB. misread 'From door to staircase' (l. 330). The refs. to the 'towel' and to Jacynth clearly relate to a deleted passage.

328. all the grace] the austere grace (*1849-88*).

329. paladin: see *Sordello* i 68-71n.

And there 'neath his bonnet the pricker blustered,
335   With feather dank as a bough of wet fennel;
For the court-yard's four walls were filled with fog
You might cut as an axe chops a log,
Like so much wool for colour and bulkiness;
And out rode the Duke in a perfect sulkiness,
340   Since before breakfast, a man feels but queasily,
And a sinking of the lower abdomen
Begins the day with indifferent omen:
And lo, as he looked around, uneasily,
The sun ploughed the fog up and drove it asunder
345   This way and that from the valley under;
And, looking thro' the court-yard arch,
Down in the valley what should meet him
But a troop of Gypsies on their march,
No doubt with the annual gifts to greet him.

XIII.

350   Now in this land, Gypsies reach you only
After reaching all lands beside;
North they go, south they go, trooping or lonely,
And still, as they travel far and wide,
Catch they and keep now a trace here, a trace there,
355   That puts you in mind of a place here, a place there:
But with us I believe they rise out of the ground,
And nowhere else, I take it, are found
With the earth-tint yet so freshly embrowned;
Born, no doubt, like insects which breed on
360   The very fruit they are meant to feed on:
For the earth—not a use to which they don't turn it,
The ore that grows in the mountains' womb,
Or the sand in the pits like a honeycomb,
They sift and soften it, bake it and burn it—

334. pricker: see l. 249n.
335. EBB. admired this image: 'I like it very much—see it, through the fog, close to my eyes'.
336. court-yard's four walls] court-yard walls (*1868-88*).
350. this] your (*1849-88*). The narrator is still in the Duke's service (see ll. 854-5 below), but not necessarily in his territory; the rev. makes his 'friend' a stranger, but still leaves the location unclear. EBB. quoted 'In *this* land, gypsies reach you only', and commented: 'I am not sure—but is not a word wanted? such as "can" before reach. Do read the line in connection with the following ones & see'.
353.] EBB. quoted 'Still as they travel the world wide', and commented: 'I miss something . . . perhaps "the world *so* wide". Left out by slip of the pen?'

365   Whether they weld you, for instance, a snaffle
      With side-bars never a brute can baffle;
      Or a lock that's a puzzle of wards within wards;
      Or, if your colt's fore-foot inclines to curve inwards,
      Horseshoes they'll hammer which turn on a swivel
370   And won't allow the hoof to shrivel;
      Then they cast bells like the shell of the winkle,
      That keep a stout heart in the ram with their tinkle:
      But the sand—they pinch and pound it like otters;
      Commend me to Gypsy glass-makers and potters!
375   Glasses they'll blow you, crystal-clear,
      Where just a faint cloud of rose shall appear,
      As if in water one dropped and let die
      A bruised black-blooded mulberry;
      And that other sort, their crowning pride,
380   With long white threads distinct inside,
      Like the lake-flower's fibrous roots which dangle
      Loose such a length and never tangle,
      Where the bold sword-lily cuts the clear waters,
      And the cup-lily couches with all the white daughters:
385   Such are the works they put their hand to,
      And the uses they turn and twist iron and sand to.
      And these made the troop which our Duke saw sally
      Towards his castle from out of the valley,
      Men and women, like new-hatched spiders,
390   Come out with the morning to greet our riders;
      And up they wound till they reached the ditch,
      Whereat all stopped save one, a witch,
      That I knew, as she hobbled from the group,
      By her gait, directly, and her stoop,
395   I, whom Jacynth was used to importune
      To let that same witch tell us our fortune,
      The oldest Gypsy then above ground;

365. snaffle: a simple form of bridle-bit. Only occurrence in B.
366. never a brute: i.e. 'which no horse'.
369. they'll] they (*1868-88*).
374-8.] EBB. quoted, for l. 374, 'Commend me to them for glass potters',
and commented: 'Rather short line, which, here again, I cant quite like—but
all this is so characteristic & strong & fresh—& the glass with the mulberry
tinge is so beautiful that it is shameful to talk of "not liking" in any relation'.
377. in water one] in pure water you (*1849-88*).
381-4. See ll. 663-8n.
384. the white] her white (*B & P BYU*).
386. And the uses] The uses (*1865-88*).

And, so sure as the autumn season came round,
She paid us a visit for profit or pastime,
400   And every time, as she swore, for the last time.
And presently she was seen to sidle
Up to the Duke till she touched his bridle,
So that the horse of a sudden reared up
As under its nose the old witch peered up
405   With her worn-out eyes, or rather eye-holes
Of no use now but to gather brine,
And began a kind of level whine
Such as they use to sing to their viols
When their ditties they go grinding
410   Up and down with nobody minding:
And, then as of old, at the end of the humming
Her usual presents were forthcoming
—A dog-whistle blowing the fiercest of trebles,
(Just a sea-shore stone holding a dozen fine pebbles,)
415   Or a porcelain mouthpiece to screw on a pipe-end,—
And so she awaited her annual stipend.
But this time, the Duke would scarcely vouchsafe
A word in reply; and in vain she felt
With twitching fingers at her belt
420   For the purse of sleek pine-martin pelt,
Ready to put what he gave in her pouch safe,—
Till, either to quicken his apprehension,
Or possibly with an after-intention,
She was come, she said, to pay her duty
425   To the new Duchess, the youthful beauty:
No sooner had she named his Lady,
Than a shine lit up the face so shady
And its smirk returned with a novel meaning—
For it struck him, the babe just wanted weaning;
430   If one gave her a taste of what life is and sorrow,
She, foolish to-day, would be wiser to-morrow;

398. And, so sure] And, sure (*1865-88*).
403.] EBB. quoted 'So that his *foolish* horse well nigh reared up', and commented: 'Foolish, put in afterward—& do you like that clogging rhythm?'
408. use] used (*1849-88*, except *1868, 1884*, as *1845*).   *viols*: the viol is a
stringed chamber instrument played with a bow by a seated player. Since B.
obviously refers to a 'street' instrument, he probably has in mind the hurdy-
gurdy, a stringed instrument played by means of a rosined wheel turned by
the performer (hence 'grinding' in l. 409).
430. life is] life was (*1849-88*). EBB. quoted 'give her a taste of what &c', and
commented: 'Does this connect itself aright with what precedes it? Or is
something missed? I dont see the connection'.

And who so fit a teacher of trouble
As this sordid crone bent well nigh double?
So, glancing at her wolf-skin vesture,
435 (If such it was, for they grow so hirsute
That their own fleece serves for natural fur suit)
He contrasted, 'twas plain from his gesture,
The life of the lady so flower-like and delicate
With the loathsome squalor of this helicat.
440 I, in brief, was the man the Duke beckoned
From out of the throng, and while I drew near
He told the crone, as I since have reckoned
By the way he bent and spoke into her ear
With circumspection and mystery,
445 The main of the Lady's history,
Her frowardness and ingratitude;
And for all the crone's submissive attitude
I could see round her mouth the loose plaits
tightening,
And her brow with assenting intelligence brightening
450 As tho' she engaged with hearty good will
Whatever he now might enjoin to fulfil,
And promised the Lady a thorough frightening.
And so just giving her a glimpse
Of a purse, with the air of a man who imps
455 The wing of the hawk that shall fetch the hernshaw,
He bade me take the gypsy mother
And set her telling some story or other
Of hill or dale, oak-wood or fernshaw,
To wile away a weary hour

437. He contrasted] He was contrasting (*1849-88*).

439. helicat: normally 'hellicat': a Scottish variant of 'hellcat'. *OED* cites
Scott, *The Black Dwarf* ix: 'Let us but get puir Grace out o' that auld hellicat's
clutches'.

440. Cp. l. 2.

446. frowardness: perversity, refractoriness: often applied to children.

448. plaits: folds or creases.

451.] EBB. quoted 'All he now enjoined to fulfil', and commented: 'does not
the meaning & rhythm enjoin rather "To all he engaged her to fulfil"—You
are so fond of elisions—are you not?'

454-5. imps / The wing: 'improves the flight'; in falconry, to 'imp' is to graft
feathers into the wing of a bird.

455. hernshaw: a young heron; cp. the phrase 'to know a hawk from a
heronshaw', deriving from an 18th-century emendation of *Hamlet* II ii 405: 'I
know a hawk from a handsaw'. Only occurrence in B.

458. fernshaw: a thicket of fern. Only occurrence in B.

460　For the Lady left alone in her bower,
　　　Whose mind and body craved exertion
　　　And yet shrank from all better diversion.

XIV.

　　　Then clapping heel to his horse, the mere curvetter,
　　　Out rode the Duke, and after his hollo
465　Horses and hounds swept, huntsman and servitor,
　　　And back I turned and bade the crone follow.
　　　And what makes me confident what's to be told you
　　　Had all along been of this crone's devising
　　　Is, that, on looking round sharply, behold you,
470　There was a novelty quick as surprising:
　　　For first, she had shot up a full head in stature,
　　　And her step kept pace with mine nor faultered,
　　　As if age had foregone its usurpature,
　　　And the ignoble mien was wholly altered,
475　And the face looked of quite another nature,
　　　And the change reached too, whatever the change
　　　　　meant,
　　　Her shaggy wolf-skin cloak's arrangement,
　　　For where its tatters hung loose like sedges,
　　　Gold coins were glittering on the edges,
480　Like the band-roll strung with tomans
　　　Which proves the veil a Persian woman's:
　　　And under her brow, like a snail's horns newly
　　　Come out as after the rain he paces,

463. mere curvetter: the 'curvet' is a technical manoeuvre in dressage; the implication here is that the Duke's horse is showy rather than strong. The spelling 'curvetter' was retained in *1849*, and revised to 'curveter' in *1863-88*; see also ll. 850n. and 891n.

468.] EBB. quoted 'Had all along been of her devising' and commented, 'Why not "her own devising"—for the rhythm?'

473.] EBB. quoted 'As if age forewent its usurpature', and suggested the present reading 'for rhythm & meaning'.

474-5.] EBB. commented that 'there seems to me an effort necessary on the part of the reader to keep the tune .. on account of a want of a word here & there'; but she did not quote the original readings.

475. of quite] quite of (*1849-88*).

480. band-roll: banderole, a small ornamental streamer.　　*tomans:* Persian gold coins.

482-3. Cp. *Flower's Name* 7-8 and *England* 90-1.

483.] EBB. quoted 'Come out after the rain *he traces*', and commented: 'What is quite the significance here of "traces"? You want it for "places" afterwards,—but for nothing else I fancy. It seems forced. But all this

Two unmistakeable eye-points duly
485 Live and aware looked out of their places.
So we went and found Jacynth at the entry
Of the Lady's chamber standing sentry;
I told the command and produced my companion,
And Jacynth rejoiced to admit any one,
490 For since last night, by the same token,
Not a single word had the Lady spoken:
So they went in both to the presence together,
While I in the balcony watched the weather.

XV.

And now, what took place at the very first of all,
495 I cannot tell as I never could learn it:
Jacynth constantly wished a curse to fall
On that little head of hers and burn it
If she knew how she came to drop so soundly
Asleep of a sudden and there continue
500 The whole time sleeping as profoundly
As one of the boars my father would pin you
'Twixt the eyes where the life holds garrison,
—Jacynth forgive me the comparison!
But where I begin my own relation
505 Is a little after I took my station
To breathe the fresh air from the balcony,

---

description is very vivid, & I delight in this snail-figure'.
486.] EBB. quoted 'So we went up the steps where our master', and
commented: 'Another short line'. B. dropped the line altogether, or
substituted 'and found Jacynth at the entry' for 'up the steps where our
master'; there is no indication of the presumed rhyme for 'master' in the
original, but it came perhaps in l. 489.
488.] EBB. quoted 'Told the Duke's command', and commented: 'Should it
not be "And told his command" .. for the clearness'.
489.] EBB. quoted the phrase 'Jacynth said' as part of this line (the 'next line'
after what became l. 488), which she said was 'difficult to read in time'. The
whole line may have contained the rhyme to 'master' in the original
l. 486.   rejoiced] rejoiced, she said (*1884*).
492. *So they*] They (*1863-88*). EBB. quoted 'So they went in', and
commented on the rhythm: 'I sh^d be inclined to write "So they went along",
or "And so they went in"'.   *the presence*: see *Sordello* vi 406.
502. *where the life*] where life (*1865-88*).
503. *—Jacynth forgive*] —Jacynth, forgive (*1884*).
504. *relation*] narration (*1849-88*).

And, having in those days a falcon eye,
To follow the hunt thro' the open country,
From where the bushes thinlier crested
510   The hillocks, to a plain where's not one tree:—
When, in a moment, my ear was arrested
By—was it singing, or was it saying,
Or a strange musical instrument playing
In the chamber?—and to be certain
515   I pushed the lattice, pulled the curtain,
And there lay Jacynth asleep,
Yet as if a watch she tried to keep,
In a rosy sleep on the floor
With her against the door;
520   And in the midst, on the seat of state,
Like a queen the gypsy woman sate,
With head and face downbent

508.] EBB. quoted 'Follow the hunt' and suggested adding 'To', 'for clearness'.

512.] EBB. quoted 'was it singing, was it saying ..', and commented: 'I doubt rather . . just doubt . . whether an "*or*" might not with advantage precede the "was it saying"—but this *is* very musical . . . & a worthy beginning to a passage of extreme beauty, & power too . . the whole expression & picture of it, quite exquisite, & one of the worthiest things you have done, I think'. In a letter of 26-27 July 1845, written two days after the meeting at which she gave him the notes on *Flight* which included this comment, EBB. wrote: 'I am delighted to have met your wishes in writing as I wrote; only . . . you are surely wrong in refusing to see a single wrongness in all that heap of weedy thoughts, & . . . when you look again, you must come to the admission of it. One of the thistles is the suggestion about the line "Was it singing, was it saying," which you wrote so, & which I proposed to emend by an intermediate "or". Thinking of it at a distance, it grows clear to me that you were right, & that there should be and must be no "or" to disturb the listening pause' (*LK* 136-7). B. did not restore his original reading, but note that he left l. 535, on which EBB. did not comment, and which echoes l. 512, unaltered. Cp. also *Flower's Name* 22.

518. *on the floor*] along the floor (*1849-88*). The later reading was B.'s original version; EBB. suggested 'on the floor' to 'improve the general rhythm', and because '"along" in one line is echoed too closely by "against" in the following'. This is a rare example of B.'s restoring a reading revised on EBB.'s advice.

520-54.] EBB. commented, 'I doubt whether the "hers" in some following lines do not by their distribution confuse the image a little'. Since there is little difficulty in distinguishing the Lady from the Gypsy in the lines as we have them, it seems probable that B. revised them.

520. *And*] While (*1849-88*).

On the Lady's head and face intent,
For, coiled at her feet like a child at ease,
525 The Lady sate between her knees
And o'er them the Lady's clasped hands met,
And on those hands her chin was set,
And her upturned face met the face of the crone
Wherein the eyes had grown and grown
530 As if she could double and quadruple
At pleasure the play of either pupil
—Very like by her hands slow fanning,
As up and down like a gor-crow's flappers
They moved to measure like bell clappers
535 —I said, is it blessing, is it banning,
Do they applaud you or burlesque you—
Those hands and fingers with no flesh on?
When, just as I thought to spring in to the rescue,
At once I was stopped by the Lady's expression:
540 For it was life her eyes were drinking
From the crone's wide pair unwinking,
Life's pure fire received without shrinking,
Into the heart and breast whose heaving
Told you no single drop they were leaving—

525. Lady] emended in agreement with *1849-63*, and in view of 'Lady's' in the
following line and elsewhere in the poem, from 'lady' in *1845*.

532-7. The Gypsy enchants the Duchess with her eyes, but the gestures of her
hands here may owe something to Shelley's poem *The Magnetic Lady to Her
Patient* (publ. 1832); see also ll. 540-1n. below. Cp. EBB. to B., 2-3 July 1845:
'[There is] something ghastly & repelling to me in the thought of Dr.
Elliotson's great boney fingers seeming to "touch the stops" of a whole soul's
harmonies—as in phreno-magnetism' (*LK* 114). In her critical notes EBB.
commented: 'The description of the eyes growing larger with the fanning of
the hands, is wonderful—I admire it all very much'. Cp. also B.'s *Mesmerism*.

532. hands] hands' (*1865-88*).

533. gor-crow's flappers: 'carrion-crow's wings'.

534. like] or (*1863-88*, except 'or like', *1884*).

535. OED cites Scott, *Rob Roy* xxxix, 'Ower bad for blessing, and ower gude
for banning [cursing]'. See also l. 512n.

536. burlesque you—] emended in agreement with *1863-88* from 'burlesque
you?' in *1845-49*.

538. When] But (*1863-88*).

540-1. Cp. Shelley, *The Magnetic Lady to Her Patient* 5-6: 'And from my
fingers flow / The powers of life'.

541. crone's] emended in agreement with all other eds. from 'crones" in
1845.   *pair*] pair above (*1849-88*).

545 Life, that filling her, past redundant
Into her very hair, back swerving
Over each shoulder, loose and abundant,
As her head thrown back showed the white throat
        curving,
And the very tresses shared in the pleasure,
550 Moving to the mystic measure,
Bounding as the bosom bounded.
I stopped, more and more confounded,
As still her cheeks burned and eyes glistened,
As she listened and she listened,—
555 When all at once a hand detained me,
And the selfsame contagion gained me,
And I kept time to the wondrous chime,
Making out words and prose and rhyme,
Till it seemed that the music furled
560 Its wings like a task fulfilled, and dropped
From under the words it first had propped,
And left them midway in the world,
And word took word as hand takes hand,
I could hear at last, and understand,
565 And when I held the unbroken thread,
The Gypsy said:—

And so at last we find my tribe,

545-51. Melchiori 216 notes the influence of Coleridge's *Kubla Khan* in this passage. The rhyme 'pleasure/measure' occurs in ll. 31-3, and cp. Coleridge's inspired poet, with his 'flashing eyes' and 'floating hair' (l. 50). Two of B.'s father's poems on the Pied Piper (see p. 132) have the 'pleasure/measure' rhyme; one speaks of the children whom the Piper has enchanted 'Dancing to the lively measure, / Following the sound with pleasure'.

545.] EBB. quoted 'For filling her it past redundant', and commented: 'I sh[d] be half inclined to repeat, "Life, that filling her, passed redundant["], something for rhythm, something for clearness. It is full of beauty & expression—& when the narrator says that the "contagion" gained him, the hearer feels something of the same. And when the music furled its wings . . with all that follows—it's very beautiful, & mystical in effect'.

556. And the] The (*1868-88*).

561.] EBB. quoted 'From under the words it propped', and suggested the rev. 'for the meaning's sake'.

563. And word] Word (*1868-88*). EBB. commented: 'I like *so* much . . the "word took word as hand took hand"—*all*, in fact! You have wrought the charm with power'.

567-689.] EBB. commented: 'In the incantation . . a little attention to the

And so I set thee in the midst,
And to one and all of them describe
570 What thou saidst and what thou didst,
Our long and terrible journey thro',
And all thou art ready to say and do
In the trials that remain:
I trace them the vein and the other vein
575 That meet on thy brow and part again,
Making our rapid mystic mark;
And I bid my people prove and probe
Each eye's profound and glorious globe
Till they detect the kindred spark
580 In those depths so dear and dark,
Like the spots that snap, and burst, and flee,
Circling over the midnight sea.
And on that young round cheek of thine
I make them recognise the tinge,
585 As when of the costly scarlet wine
They drip so much as will impinge
And spread in a thinnest scale afloat

---

rhythm seems necessary—and another word here & there, especially in the
early part of it. It ought to be musical—ought it not?' Another general
comment follows later: 'How I like it all . . and that grand "fronting" of the
soul [l. 683] . . to the end'.
572.] EBB. quoted 'And art ready to say & do', and suggested the present
reading.
577.] EBB. quoted 'And I bid my people probe', and commented: 'Is not *that*
more broken than, in this place, should be? Perhaps I sh^d like better "And I
speak to my people & bid them probe"—but this & ever so much before, is
such impertinence that I am quite & really ashamed of it—& should be still
more, if it did not come of obedience rather than want of reverence'. The
'obedience' refers to the promise she had made him to speak her mind on his
work: see l. 326n.   *prove*: test, examine.
581-2. The Northern Lights (aurora borealis).
581.] EBB. quoted 'Like the spots that snap burst & flee' in proof and
suggested 'and burst'.
583. *young round*] round young (*1863-88*).
585-90. Wine is poured into a dish in which there is a drop of olive oil; the
wine surrounds the drop of oil, 'impinges' on it, causing it to *rise* and *float* on
the wine (because oil has a lower density than wine) and to *spread* (because the
surface tension of oil to liquid is less than that of oil to metal). 'Impinge' (with
'on' understood) and 'spread' are both active verbs. We are grateful to
Dr N. R. Williams, of the Department of Energy, for this explanation.

One thick gold drop from the olive's coat
Over a silver plate whose sheen
590   Still thro' the mixture shall be seen.
For, so I prove thee, to one and all,
Fit, when my people ope their breast,
To see the sign, and hear the call,
And take the vow, and stand the test
595   Which adds one more child to the rest—
When the breast is bare and the arms are wide,
And the world is left outside.
For there is probation to decree,
And many and long must the trials be
600   Thou shalt victoriously endure,
If that brow is true and those eyes are sure;
Like a jewel-finder's fierce assay
Of the prize he dug from its mountain tomb,—
Let once the vindicating ray
605   Leap out amid the anxious gloom,
And steel and fire have done their part

595. Cp. *By the Fire-Side* 261: 'So the earth has gained by one man more'.

596.] EBB. quoted 'When the breast is bare & the arms ope wide' in proof and commented: 'Why not "*are* wide"? You have "ope their breast" just before [l. 592]'.

598. probation: a period of testing or trial; in religious usage it often refers to earthly life, as a trial on which salvation depends; here, the salvation is not in the afterlife, but in earthly life itself.

599-601.] EBB. quoted, in proof, 'And many & long must the trials be / All of which thou shalt endure / If that brow is true &c', and commented: 'but the "true brow" &c are not necessary for the trial so much as for the successful issue of it. Might it be "And many and long must the trials be / Thou shalt victoriously endure["] . . but you will set it right'. She had misread 'endure', which meant 'survive', not 'be subject to'.

600-2.] EBB. quoted, for l. 601, 'With the fortitude those eyes assure', and commented: 'The meaning is apparent—but "eyes assuring fortitude" is forced in the mode of expression perhaps, & looks as if the rhyme were troubling you. And then, if it is not hypercriticism, there is a rather objectionable sameness in the form of ending these three lines . . with the words "endure" . . ["]assure" . . & "assay" . . to my ear—all dissyllables & similarly accented'.

602. assay: technically, a 'trial of metals by touch, fire, etc.'; *OED* cites *Measure for Measure* III i 162: 'he hath made an assay of her virtue'.

604. vindicating ray: the jewel proves its authenticity by refracting the light of the fire of the 'assay', instead of being consumed by it.

606.] EBB. quoted 'Steel & fire have done their best', and commented: 'You had written "And steel & fire &[c"] and why not?' The change from 'best' to

And the prize falls on its finder's heart;
So, trial after trial past,
Wilt thou fall at the very last
610 Breathless, half in trance
With the thrill of the great deliverance,
Into our arms for evermore;
And thou shalt know, those arms once curled
About thee, what we knew before,
615 How love is the only good in the world.
Henceforth be loved as heart can love,
Or brain devise, or hand approve!
Stand up, look below,
It is our life at thy feet we throw
620 To step with into light and joy;
Not a power of life but we'll employ
To satisfy thy nature's want;
Art thou the tree that props the plant,
Or the climbing plant that takes the tree—
625 Canst thou help us, must we help thee?
If any two creatures grew into one,
They would do more than the world has done;
Tho' each apart were never so weak,
Yet vainly thro' the world should ye seek
630 For the knowledge and the might
Which in such union grew their right:
So, to approach, at least, that end,
And blend,—as much as may be, blend
Thee with us or us with thee,
635 As climbing-plant or propping-tree,
Shall some one deck thee, over and down,

'part' (assuming EBB. transcribed correctly) was not suggested by her.
608-89. EBB. commented: 'all this passage is quite exquisite . . I mean . . . . to
the end of the prophecy'.
610-11. EBB. quoted these lines 'Just to prove how I can like the short lines
sometimes . . . the effect is so good & startling'.
615.] EBB. quoted 'in this world' in proof, and suggested the present reading
'because "this" catches the voice'.
624. takes] seeks (*1849-88*).
629.] Ye vainly through the world should seek (*1868-88*, except 'Yet through
the world should we vainly seek', *1884*).
630. the knowledge] the sum of knowledge (*1884*).
636-41. EBB. praised this 'figure' as 'a most beautiful, infinitely beautiful
revivification of what is old in the seed of it'. Referring to the proverb, 'the
vine embraces the elm'; cp. *Comedy of Errors* II ii 173-5: 'Thou art an elm, my

Up and about, with blossoms and leaves?
Fix his heart's fruit for thy garland crown,
Cling with his soul as the gourd-vine cleaves,
640   Die on thy boughs and disappear
While not a leaf of thine is sere?
Or is the other fate in store,
And art thou fitted to adore,
To give thy wondrous self away,
645   And take a stronger nature's sway?
I foresee and I could foretell
Thy future portion, sure and well—
But those passionate eyes speak true, speak true,
And let them say what thou shalt do!
650   Only, be sure thy daily life,
In its peace, or in its strife,
Never shall be unobserved;
We pursue thy whole career,
And hope for it, or doubt, or fear,—
655   Lo, hast thou kept thy path or swerved,
We are beside thee, in all thy ways,
With our blame, with our praise,
Our shame to feel, our pride to show,
Glad, sorry—but indifferent, no!

---

husband, I a vine, / Whose weakness, married to thy stronger state, / Makes me with thy strength to communicate'.

639. gourd-vine: the bottle-gourd, a trailing or climbing plant.

641. sere: dry, withered.

644.] EBB. recommended 'To give' instead of 'Give': 'you sometimes make a dust, a dusk dust, by sweeping away your little words'.

646. and I could] and could (*1868-88*).

648. speak true, speak true,] speak true, (*1865*). A rare example of a reading unique to *1865*; it may be a mispr.

649. And let] Let (*1865-88*). 'Let' was the original reading; EBB. had suggested the *1845* reading in proof.

652.] after her note on l. 658 (see below), EBB. wrote: 'And I go back to ask if what you have written "Never shall be unobserved" w^d not be better written, for the general rhythm "Shall never be unobserved". It is just a doubt'.

654. fear,—] emended in agreement with *1849-88* from 'fear,' in *1845*.

658.] EBB. quoted 'Shame to feel & pride to show', and commented: 'Why not write "With our shame to feel—" for rhythm & clearness'.

659. sorry] angry (*1863-88*).

660   Whether it is thy lot to go,
     For the good of us all, where the haters meet
     In the crowded city's horrible street;
     Or thou step alone thro' the morass
     Where never sound yet was
665   Save the dry clap of the stork's quick bill,
     For the air is still, and the water still,
     When the blue breast of the dipping coot
     Dives under, and all is mute.
     So at the last shall come old age,
670   Decrepit as befits that stage;
     How else wouldst thou retire apart
     With the hoarded memories of thy heart,
     And gather all to the very least

660. is] be (*1868-88*).

663-8. As with ll. 381-4, perhaps recalling the great Fens Moss, an expanse of marshland near Bettisfield Park in Flintshire, where B. was staying when he restarted the poem after its interruption at l. 215 (see headnote). The owner of Bettisfield Park, Lord (formerly Sir John) Hanmer, in *A Memorial of the Parish and Family of Hanmer* (1877), wrote: 'I must breathe a word with the wind as I pass on, in favour of its wild spaces, where the grey-hen and the fern-owl and the curlew may be seen among the turf-stacks . . . Foxes prowl about the turbary and may grow old upon it if they will, for no huntsman can follow there . . . These [boundaries of the Moss] are full of wild fowl in the winter'. Hanmer also mentions red deer, otters, herons, and the water-lily whose 'broad green leaves and beautiful blossoms cover every summer many acres of Hanmer Mere'. All these feature in *Flight*. In the same book, Hanmer collected some poetry written during the period of his acquaintance with B. (who recommended his work to Alfred Domett and EBB.). Cp. a passage in his poem *Silence*: 'Oh changeful Silence, on the sedgy crown / Of a blue mere as lights a wild bird down, / Watching the air's vibration thou dost dwell'. There is also a poem about Gypsies, associating their arrival with that of winter, and describing them as looking 'wild and poor'.

663. the morass] the lone morass (*1884*).

665.] Save the dry quick clap of the stork's bill (*1849-88*). EBB. commented: 'The "dry clap of the stork's bill" I like very very much, with all the silence of the morass around it'. In proof, however, she thought the line 'wanting a syllable'.

667. dipping] dripping (*1884*); probably, but not certainly, a mispr.

668. all is] all again is (*1849*).

672.] EBB. quoted 'With the memories of thy heart', and commented that '[it] seems to me a too short line for the place'.

673.] EBB. commented: 'I am fastidious enough . . . to wish your "pick up" changed to "gather" or perhaps "gathering". "Pick up" seems a little too mean for the association, altogether'.

Of the fragments of life's earlier feast,
675 Let fall through eagerness to find
The crowning dainties yet behind?
Ponder on the entire past
Laid together thus at last,
When the twilight helps to fuse
680 The first fresh, with the faded hues,
And the outline of the whole,
As round eve-shades their framework roll,
Grandly fronts for once thy soul:
And then as, 'mid the dark, a gleam
685 Of yet another morning breaks,
And like the hand which ends a dream,
Death, with the might of his sunbeam
Touches the flesh and the soul awakes,
Then—
        Ay, then, indeed, something would happen!
690 But what? For here her voice changed like a bird's;
There grew more of the music and less of the words;
Had Jacynth only been by me to clap pen
To paper and put you down every syllable,
With those clever clerkly fingers,
695 What I've forgotten as well as what lingers
In this old brain of mine that's but ill able
To give you even this poor version
Of the speech I spoil, as it were, with stammering
—More fault of those who had the hammering
700 Of prosody into me and syntax,
And did it, not with hobnails but tintacks!
But to return from this excursion,—
Just, do you mark, when the song was sweetest,
The peace most deep and the charm completest,
705 There came, shall I say, a snap—
And the charm vanished!

677-88. Cp. *Sordello* vi 26-32 and 464-5.

694. *clerkly*: 'skilled in penmanship', with the archaic connotation 'scholarly, learned'.

695. *What*] All that (*1849-63*); All (*1865-88*).

697. *this*] the (*1884*).

702-4.] EBB. quoted 'To return from this excursion', and commented: 'Really I could almost make a general & unexcepting remark of it, that whenever you erase a word, you should immediately put it back again. Now see how short this line is—& how one just below it "Peace most deep & the charm completest" *requires* for every reason, a "The" (erased) before Peace'.

706.] EBB. quoted 'And sudden the charm vanished' and recommended

And my sense returned, so strangely banished,
And, starting as from a nap,
I knew the crone was bewitching my lady,
710 With Jacynth asleep; and but one spring made I
Down from the casement round to the portal,
Another minute and I had entered,
When the door opened, and more than mortal
Stood, with a face where to my mind centred
715 All beauties I ever saw or shall see,
The Duchess—I stopped as if struck by palsy.
She was so different, happy and beautiful,
I felt at once that all was best,
And that I had nothing to do, for the rest,
720 But wait her commands, obey and be dutiful:
Not that, in fact, there was any commanding,
—I saw the glory of her eye,
And the brow's height and the breast's expanding,
And I was hers to live or to die:
725 As for finding what she wanted,
You know God Almighty granted
Such little signs should serve his wild creatures
To tell one another all their desires,
So that each knows what its friend requires,
730 And does its bidding without teachers.
I preceded her; the crone
Followed silent and alone;

'dismissing this word *sudden*, which hinders to my mind & ear the effect of suddenness'.

715.] EBB. quoted 'All the beauties I ever saw or sháll see', and commented: 'would it not be better, if "the" were left out before "beauties". The omission helps the reader to the right accentuation of the line, I fancy—taken with [the] context'. The accent on 'shall' may be hers, or B.'s.

726-30. Cp. B. to EBB. (4 Jan. 1846): 'I always loved all those wild creatures God "sets up for themselves" so independently of us, so successfully, with their strange happy minute inch of a candle, as it were, to light them; while we run about and against each other with our great cressets and fire-pots' (*LK* 356-7). See *Sordello* vi 619-28n. (I 753) for another passage from this letter. EBB. commented: 'I like the "little sign" given to the "wild creatures"— though that line does appear rather clogged, to be sure'.

727. serve his wild] serve wild (*1868-88*).

729. its] his (*1870-88*).

731-87. EBB. commented: 'And where the lady prepares for her flight & flies, I like it all much—the very irregularity & looseness of the measure having a charm of music—falling like a golden chain, with links fastened

I spoke to her, but she merely jabbered
In the old style; both her eyes had slunk
735 Back to their pits; her stature shrunk;
In short, the soul in its body sunk
Like a blade sent home to its scabbard;
We descended, I preceding,
Crossed the court with nobody heeding,
740 All the world was at the chase,
The court-yard like a desert-place,
The stable emptied of its small fry;
I saddled myself the very palfrey
I remember patting while it carried her,
745 The day she arrived and the Duke married her;
And, do you know, though it's easy deceiving
Oneself in such matters, I can't help believing
The lady had not forgotten it either,
And knew the poor devil so much beneath her
750 Would have been only too glad for her service
To dance on hot ploughshares like a Turk dervise,
But unable to pay proper duty where owing it
Was reduced to that pitiful method of showing it:
For tho' the moment I began setting
755 His saddle on my own nag of Berold's begetting,
(Not that I meant to be obtrusive)
She stopped me, while his rug was shifting,
By a single rapid finger's lifting,
And, with a gesture kind but conclusive,
760 And a little shake of the head, refused me,—
I say, although she never used me,
Yet when she was mounted, the gypsy behind her,
And I ventured to remind her,
I suppose with a voice of less steadiness

---

though loose. And the nature, the beauty altogether!'
734-7. EBB. commented: 'And the description of the crone with her eyes
slinking back to their pits . . & the soul sinking in the body like a sword sent
home to its scabbard!—it is very striking & powerful: & does not remind me
of parts of Christabel to its own disadvantage as to originality—which you
always have, you know, by the right divine'. EBB. presumably refers to
Christabel 583-5: 'A snake's small eye blinks dull and shy; / And the lady's
eyes they shrunk in her head, / Each shrunk up to a serpent's eye'. For the
more general resemblance to *Christabel*, see headnote.
743. palfrey: a small horse for ladies. The word was revived by the Romantic
poets and appears frequently in *Christabel*.
751. dervise: dervish (B.'s spelling is found in Byron, *Don Juan* III xxix).

765 Than usual, for my feeling exceeded me,
—Something to the effect that I was in readiness
Whenever God should please she needed me,—
Then, do you know, her face looked down on me
With a look that placed a crown on me,
770 And she felt in her bosom,—mark, her bosom—
And, as a flower-tree drops its blossom,
Dropped me—ah, had it been a purse
Of silver, my friend, or gold that's worse,
Why, you see, as soon as I found myself
775 So understood,—that a true heart so may gain
Such a reward,—I should have gone home again,
Kissed Jacynth, and soberly drowned myself!
It was a little plait of hair
Such as friends in a convent make
780 To wear, each for the other's sake,—
This, see, which at my breast I wear,
Ever did (rather to Jacynth's grudgment),
And ever shall, till the Day of Judgment.
And then,—and then,—to cut short,—this is idle,
785 These are feelings it is not good to foster,—
I pushed the gate wide, she shook the bridle,
And the palfrey bounded,—and so we lost her!

XVI.

When the liquor's out, why clink the cannakin?
I did think to describe you the panic in
790 The redoubtable breast of our master the mannikin,
And what was the pitch of his mother's yellowness,
How she turned as a shark to snap the spare-rib
Clean off, sailors say, from a pearl-diving Carib,
When she heard what she called the flight of the
        feloness—
795 But it seems such child's play
What they said and did with the lady away,
And to dance on, when we've lost the music,

776.] B. had interpolated 'straight' before 'home' in this line; EBB. objected.
780.] EBB. quoted 'And wear each' and suggested '[W]earing each'.
785.] EBB. quoted ''tis no good' in proof, and suggested the change 'for the
rhythm & to escape the jingle of "no" . . "so" [l. 787]'.
788-96. Cp. Sordello vi 631-7.
788. clink the cannakin: cp. Othello II iii 72: 'And let me the canakin clink,
clink'.   cannakin] cannikin (1868-88); a small can or drinking vessel.
790. mannikin: little man (pejorative).
793. Carib: native of the Caribbean.

Always made me—and no doubt makes you—sick.
And, to my mind, the world's face looked so stern
800 As that sweet form disappeared thro' the postern,
She that kept it in constant good humour,
It ought to have stopped; there seemed nothing to do
    more.
But the world thought otherwise and went on,
And my head's one that its spite was spent on:
805 Thirty years are fled since that morning,
And with them all my head's adorning.
Nor did the old Duchess die outright,
As you expect, of suppressed spite,
The natural end of every adder
810 Not suffered to empty its poison-bladder:
But she and her son agreed, I take it,
That no one should touch on the story to wake it,
For the wound in the Duke's pride rankled fiery,
So they made no search and small inquiry—
815 And when fresh gypsies have paid us a visit, I've
Noticed the couple were never inquisitive,
But told them they're folks the Duke don't want here,
And bade them make haste and cross the frontier.
The Duchess was gone and the Duke was glad of it,
820 And the old one was in the young one's stead,
And took, in her place, the household's head,
And a blessed time the household had of it!
And were I not, as a man may say, cautious
How I trench, more than needs, on the nauseous,
825 I could favour you with sundry touches

799. *And*] Nay (*1849-88*).

800. *postern*: a back- or side-gate (i.e. not the main entrance); the word can also mean a way of escape. Cp. *How They Brought the Good News* 5.

819. *The*] Brief, the (*1849-88*).

825-32. This passage in general recalls Jacobean and Restoration attacks on women's 'painting'; the closest in vocabulary is Jonson's *Sejanus* II i 59-64: '[Livia.] How do I look today? [Eudemus.] Excellent clear, believe it. This same fucus / Was well laid on. [Livia.] Me thinks, 'tis here not white. / [Eudemus.] Lend me your scarlet, lady. 'Tis the sun / Hath given some little taint unto the ceruse, / You should have used of the white oil I gave you'. EBB. commented: 'Does he trench a little more than is needful "on the nauseous" in the description of the yellow Duchess? I *doubt*, I confess . . but you can judge better'. EBB. went on to quote l. 843: 'Whether to run on or stop short and', commenting: 'Where's the rhyme to *that*? I have looked in vain for it'. She next quoted 'Of middle-age manners, I hereby vaticinate / . . . that is innate', commenting: 'The rhyme does seem to me, & persist in

Of the paint-smutches with which the Duchess
Heightened the mellowness of her cheek's yellowness
(To get on faster) until at last her
Cheek grew to be one master-plaster
830 Of mucus and fucus from mere use of ceruse
Till in short she grew from scalp to udder
Just the object to make you shudder!
You're my friend—
What a thing friendship is, world without end!
835 How it gives the heart and soul a stir-up,
As if somebody broached you a glorious runlet,
And poured out all lovelily, sparkling, and sunlit,
Our green Moldavia, the streaky syrup,
Cotnar as old as the time of the Druids—
840 Friendship's as good as that monarch of fluids
To supple a dry brain, fill you its ins-and-outs,—
Gives your Life's hour-glass a shake when the thin
    sand doubts
Whether to run on or stop short, and guarantees

---

seeming to me, to be overstrained'. This couplet was cut; it may have come
after l. 861 below. 'Vaticinate' means 'prophesy'.
830. fucus: paint or cosmetic for the skin.   *ceruse*: a cosmetic made of
white lead.
830-1. ceruse / Till in short] ceruse: / In short (*1863-88*).
832.] *1849-88* have a new section (XVII) after this line.
834. world without end: an exclamation (here expressing enthusiasm) from the
Prayer Book tag 'world without end, amen'.
835-44. Cp. Falstaff's praise of 'sherris', *2 Henry IV* IV iii 86ff.: 'A good
sherris-sack hath a twofold operation in it. It ascends me into the brain; dries
me there all the foolish and dull and crudy vapours which environ it; makes
it apprehensive, quick, forgetive, full of nimble, fiery, and delectable shapes;
which delivered o'er to the voice, the tongue, which is the birth, becomes
excellent wit. The second property of your excellent sherris is the warming
of the blood; which before, cold and settled, left the liver white and pale . . .
but the sherris warms it, and makes it course from the inwards to the parts
extreme'. Cp. also Sancho's praise of wine in *Don Quixote* II xii-xiii, which
B. alludes to and elaborates in a letter to EBB. of 31 Mar. 1845 (*LK* 44).
837. sparkling, and sunlit] sparklingly, sunlit (*1863-88*).
840-1.] Friendship may match with that monarch of fluids! / Each supples a
dry brain, fills you its ins-and-outs, (*1863-88*).
842.] EBB. quoted 'Give Life's' in proof and suggested 'And give', 'to throw
the accent in the right place for securing the rhyme without an effort to the
reader'.

Age is not all made of stark sloth and arrant ease!
845 I have seen my Lady once more,
Jacynth, the Gypsy, Berold, and the rest of it,
For to me spoke the Duke, as I told you before;
I always wanted to make a clean breast of it,
And now it is made—why the heart's-blood, that went trickle,
850 Trickle, but anon, in such muddy dribblets,
Is pumped up brisk now, thro' the main ventricle,
And genially floats me about the giblets!
I'll tell you what I shall do:
I must see this fellow his sad life thro'
855 —He is our Duke after all,
And I, as he says, but a serf and thrall;
My father was born here and I inherit
His fame, a chain he bound his son with,—
Could I pay in a lump I should prefer it,
860 But there's no mine to blow up and get done with,
So I must stay till the end of the chapter:
For, as to our middle-age manners adapter,
Be it a thing to be glad on or sorry on,
One day or other, his head in a morion,
865 And breast in a hauberk, his heels he'll kick up,
Slain by some onslaught fierce of hiccup:
And then, when red doth the sword of our Duke rust,
And its leathern sheath is o'ergrown with a blue crust,
Then I shall scrape together my earnings;
870 For, you see, in the Churchyard Jacynth reposes,
And our children all went the way of the roses—
It's a long lane that knows no turnings—
One needs but little tackle to travel in,

845. *Lady*] little Lady (*1849-88*, except 'lady', *1868-88*).
849. *why the*] why, my (*1849-88*).
850. *but anon*] suggested by EBB. in proof, instead of 'but now', because of 'now' in l. 851.　　　*dribblets*] not revised to the usual spelling 'driblets' until *1870*. See also ll. 463n. and 891n.
852. *floats me about the giblets*: 'puts me in good heart'; *OED* records the conjectural sense of 'to levy one's giblets' as 'to summon up one's courage'.
853. *shall do*] intend to do (*1849-88*).
864. *One*] Some (*1863-88*).　　　*morion*: a helmet without a visor, worn in the 16th and 17th centuries.
865. *hauberk*: a long coat of mail.　　　*up,*] emended in agreement with *1863-88* from 'up' in *1845-49*.
866. *some*] an (*1863-88*).
868. *is*] lies (*1849*); lie (*1863-88*).

So, just one cloak shall I indue,
875 And for a staff, what beats the javelin
With which his boars my father pinned you?
And then, for a purpose you shall hear presently,
Taking some Cotnar, a tight plump skinfull,
I shall go journeying, who but I, pleasantly?
880 Sorrow is vain and despondency sinful:
What's a man's age? He must hurry more, that's all;
Cram in a day, what youth takes a year to hold;
When we mind labour, then only, we're too old—
What age had Methusalem when he begat Saul?
885 And at last, as its haven some buffeted ship sees,
(Come all the way from the north parts with sperm
     oil)
I shall get safely out of the turmoil
And arrive one day at the land of the gypsies
And find my lady or hear the last news of her
890 From some old thief and son of Lucifer,
His forehead chapletted green with wreathy hop,
Sunburned all over like an Aethiop:
And when my Cotnar begins to operate
And the tongue of the rogue to run at a proper rate,

---

874. one cloak] one stout cloak (*1849-88*).   *indue*: put on.
882. what youth takes] what his youth took (*1849-88*).
883.] EBB. quoted, in proof, 'When we mind labour then, only then, we're
too old' and suggested the present reading.
884. Methusaleh [sic] did not father Saul, who was the son of Kish (*1 Samuel*
ix 1-2); the Bible does not record how old Methusaleh was when he fathered
his last child; he was 187 years old when he fathered Lamech, his last named
child, lived for a further 782 years, 'and begat sons and daughters' (*Genesis* v
25-7). The error is meant to be the uneducated narrator's, not B.'s; for an
analogous case, see *Tomb at St. Praxed's* 95n.
887. shall] hope to (*1863-88*).
889. last news: either news of her death, or the latest news of her.
891.] EBB. quoted 'With his forehead chapletted with wreathy hop', and
suggested the present reading 'for the two "withs", & other reasons'. She
then quoted 'Jove, if in spirit thy want a cow shares', and commented: 'Do
you like that? *I* do not I confess. And I fancy that some of the next lines
might be clarified & *raised* a little to advantage'. The line (which presumably
refers to Io, who was transformed by Jupiter into a cow to escape the anger of
Juno, but was then forced to wander over the earth) was cut from the poem;
'ploughshares', a possible rhyme, appears (though not as a rhyme-word) at
l. 751 above. Like 'curvetter' in l. 463, 'chapletted' was retained in *1849*,
'chapleted' appearing first in *1863*. See also l. 850n.

895   And our wine skin, tight once, shows each flaccid
         dent,
       I shall drop in with—as if by accident—
       "You never knew then how it all ended,
       "What fortunes good or bad attended
       "The little lady your Queen befriended?"
900   —And when that's told me, what's remaining?
       This world's too hard for my explaining—
       The same wise judge of matters equine
       Who still preferred some hot four-year-old
       To the big-boned stock of mighty Berold,
905   And for strong Cotnar drank French weak wine,
       He also must be such a Lady's scorner!
       Smooth Jacob still robs homely Esau,
       Now up now down, the world's one see-saw!
       —So I shall find out some snug corner
910   Under a hedge, like Orson the wood knight,
       Turn myself round and bid the world good night,
       And sleep a sound sleep till the trumpet's blowing
       Wakes me (unless priests cheat us laymen)
       To a world where's to be no further throwing
915   Pearls before swine that can't value them: Amen.

898. *fortunes*] fortune (*1865-88*).

903. *hot*] slim (*1849-88*).

907. Cp. Jacob in *Genesis* xxvii 11: 'Behold, Esau my brother is a hairy man, and I am a smooth man'. In *Genesis* xxv and xxvii, Jacob twice robs his brother Esau, first of his birthright and then of his father's blessing. The application to the poem is complex. The Duke and the narrator are 'brothers' (see l. 32n. above), and the Duke, an effeminate man, is contrasted to the more virile huntsman. But it is the Duke who has been robbed, and by a Gypsy who, like Esau, is 'hirsute' (see ll. 435-6); and the biblical moral ('thus Esau despised his birthright', *Genesis* xxv 34) invites comparison with the narrator's moral for his story ('no further throwing / Pearls before swine that can't value them'). Perhaps the point is that whereas usually Jacob robs Esau (the effeminate overcomes the manly), this story illustrates the opposite outcome, which, however, remains exceptional.

910. *Orson the wood knight*: referring to the medieval French romance of *Valentine and Orson*, in which Orson is raised by a bear, while his twin brother is raised as a knight; continuing the Jacob—Esau contrast of l. 907.

912. *trumpet's blowing*: for the Last Judgment.   *blowing*] emended in agreement with *1849-88* from 'blowing,' in *1845*.

914. *where's to be*: where will be (*1863-88*).

914-15. *throwing / Pearls before swine that can't value them*: from *Matthew* vii 6: 'Give not that which is holy unto the dogs, neither cast ye your pearls before swine, lest they trample them under their feet, and turn again and rend you'.

49 Song

First publ. *B & P* vii (*DR & L*), 6 Nov. 1845; repr. *1849, 1863* (when it was placed in *Lyrics*: see Appendix A, p. 464), *1865²*, *1868, 1872, 1888*. Our text is *1845*. A fair-copy MS, the text of which is intermediate between *1849* and *1863*, is in *ABL*, dated 'Farnham, Aug. 23 '52'; EBB. wrote to her friend Julia Martin on 2 Sept. 1852: 'Once we went to Farnham, and spent two days with Mr. and Mrs. Paine there in that lovely heathy country, and met Mr. Kingsley, the "Christian Socialist"' (*Letters of EBB* ii 83).

The first mention of the poem comes in EBB.'s letter of 29 Oct. 1845 (*LK* 252), when she saw the proofs of *DR & L*. If, as seems likely, the poem reflects B.'s feelings for EBB., a date of composition in Aug.-Sept. 1845, when B. and EBB. acknowledged their love for each other, is indicated. B. constantly laments his inability to express his love for EBB., e.g. in a letter of 9 Nov. 1845: 'there is nothing in you that does not draw out all of me:—you possess me, dearest . . and there is no help for the expressing it all, no voice nor hand, but these of mine which shrink and turn away from the attempt' (*LK* 261). On 23 Nov. B. requested a lock of EBB.'s hair: 'give me so much of you—all precious that you are—as may be given in a lock of your hair—I will live and die with it, and with the memory of you' (*LK* 288). EBB. complied on 28 Nov., and B. wrote: 'I was happy, so happy before! But I am happier and richer now . . . I will live and die with your beautiful ring, your beloved hair—comforting me, blessing me—' (2 Dec. 1845, *LK* 300). The motif of hair, esp. gold hair, is recurrent in B.'s work: see *Porphyria* 18-20n. and esp. the 'Elys' song in *Sordello* ii 151-60; also *Gold Hair*.

I.
Nay but you, who do not love her,
   Is she not pure gold, my mistress?
Holds earth aught—speak truth—above her?
   Aught like this tress, see, and this tress,
5   And this one last tress of all,
So fair, see, ere I let it fall!

¶49.*1. Nay*] Nay, (*ABL MS*).
2. mistress] Mistress (*ABL MS*).
3.] brackets replace dashes here and in l. 10 in *ABL MS*.
5. one last] last fairest (*1849-88, ABL MS*).
6. fall!] fall? (*1863-88*).

II.
Because you spend your lives in praising;
    To praise, you search the wide world over;
So why not witness, calmly gazing,
10   If earth holds aught—speak truth—above her?
Above this tress, and this I touch
But cannot praise, I love so much!

7. *Because*] Because, (*1849-88, ABL MS*). The comma suggests that the line
responds to a question from the speaker's hearers, such as 'Why is your
mistress worth this attention?' 'Because,' occurs in six other contexts in B.,
and invariably introduces an answer to an earlier question, as in e.g. *Ring* xii
837-8: 'Why take the artistic way to prove so much? Because, it is the glory
and the good of Art'.
9. *So*] Then (*1868-88*).
11. *this I touch*] this, I touch (*1865-88*).

50 The Confessional

First publ. *B & P* vii (*DR & L*), 6 Nov. 1845, with *Laboratory* (which preceded it), under the collective title *France and Spain*, it being called 'II.—Spain—The Confessional'. Repr. *1849* (without the collective title, though still alongside *Laboratory*), *1863* (when it was placed in *Lyrics*: see Appendix A, p. 464), *1863²*, *1868*, *1888*. B. did not include it in any volume of selections chosen by himself (*1863²* was compiled by J. Forster and B. W. Procter). Our text is *1845*. DeVane (*Handbook* 171), noting the inverse parallel in *Italy* 75-87, dates the poem to the summer of 1845. The fact that B. did not offer the poem to *Hood's* may support this. It was among the poems shown to EBB.; all her comments recorded in the notes derive from *Wellesley MS*, unless otherwise stated. In contrast to other *DR & L* poems, e.g. *How They Brought the Good News*, *Pictor*, and the poem's companion *Laboratory*, there is no indication of historical period, and DeVane suggests that the setting might be contemporary. B. had not visited Spain, but was presumably aware of the current struggle between conservative and reformist factions, and the generally reactionary role of the Church. Cp. Thomas Campbell's *Stanzas to the Memory of the Spanish Patriots*, which inveighs against 'Cowled demons in Inquisitorial cells'. The Catholic Church provided a standard image in Gothic fiction of torture, espionage, and repression. For anti-Catholic feeling in B.'s poetry during this period, see headnote to *Tomb at St. Praxed's*, p. 260. B. had satirized another aspect of Spanish Catholicism in *Soliloquy*; and cp. *A Forgiveness*. The story resembles that of Samson and Delilah (*Judges* xvi 4-21); but B. makes the 'temptress' figure unaware of the use to which she is put by her lover's enemies. In Milton's *Samson Agonistes*, Delilah claims to have been influenced by religious motives: 'The priest / Was not behind, but ever at my ear, / Preaching how meritorious with the gods / It would be to ensare an irreligious / Dishonourer of Dagon' (ll. 857-61).

I.

It is a lie—their Priests, their Pope,
Their Saints, their . . . all they fear or hope
Are lies, and lies—there! thro' my door
And ceiling, there! and walls and floor,
5   There, lies, they lie, shall still be hurled,
Till spite of them I reach the world!

II.

You think Priests just and holy men!
Before they put me in this den
I was a human creature too,

¶50.5. i.e. her cry, 'lies, they lie', shall be hurled etc.

10   With flesh and blood like one of you,
     A girl that laughed in beauty's pride
     Like lilies in your world outside.

III.

     I had a lover—shame avaunt!
     This poor wrenched body, grim and gaunt,
15   Was kissed all over till it burned,
     By lips the truest love e'er turned
     His heart's own tint: one night they kissed
     My soul out in a burning mist.

IV.

     So next day when the accustomed train
20   Of things grew round my sense again,
     "That is a sin," I said—and slow
     With downcast eyes to church I go,
     And pass to the confession-chair,
     And tell the old mild father there.

V.

25   But when I faulter Beltran's name,
     Ha? quoth the father; much I blame
     The sin; yet wherefore idly grieve?
     Despair not,—strenuously retrieve!
     Nay, I will turn this love of thine
30   To lawful love, almost divine.

11-12. Cp. *Song of Solomon* ii 1-2: 'I am the rose of Sharon, and the lily of the valleys. As the lily among thorns, so is my love among the daughters', and *Matthew* vi 28-9: 'Consider the lilies of the field, how they grow . . . even Solomon in all his glory was not arrayed like one of these'.
16-17. 'By the truest lips that love ever turned to the colour of his [love's] heart [i.e. red]'.
17-18. one night . . . mist: cp. Marlowe, *Doctor Faustus* V i 100: 'Her lips suck forth my soul: see where it flies', and Tennyson, *Fatima* (1842) 19-21: 'O Love, O fire! once he drew / With one long kiss my whole soul through / My lips, as sunlight drinketh dew'. Here, the sense is 'seduced me into sexual intercourse'.
25. Beltran: an anglicization of the Spanish surname Beltrano. B. may have read about several Spanish Beltranos, e.g. Bernardino, a 16th-century explorer and missionary, and Luis, a South American revolutionary soldier (both priests). The name Beltrano is also current in southern Italy, which B. visited in 1844. B. puts the accent on the first syllable, as in Bertram.

VI.

For he is young, and led astray,
This Beltran, and he schemes, men say,
To change the laws of church and state;
So thine shall be an angel's fate,
35   Who, ere the thunder breaks, should roll
Its cloud away and save his soul.

VII.

For when he lies upon thy breast
Thou mayst demand and be possessed
Of all his plans, and next day steal
40   To me and all those plans reveal,
That I and every priest, to purge
His soul, may fast and use the scourge.

VIII.

That father's beard was long and white,
With love and truth his brow seemed bright;
45   I went back, all on fire with joy,
And, that same evening, bade the boy,
Tell me, as lovers should, heart-free,
Something to prove his love of me.

IX.

He told me what he would not tell
50   For hope of Heaven or fear of Hell;
And I lay listening in such pride,
And, soon as he had left my side,
Tripped to the church by morning-light
To save his soul in his despite.

X.

55   I told the father all his schemes,
Who were his comrades, what their dreams;

37-40. Cp. Delilah and Samson in *Judges* xvi 19: 'And she made him sleep upon her knees; and she called for a man, and she caused him to shave off the seven locks of his head . . . and his strength went from him'.
44.] EBB. quoted 'With love & truth his brow was bright', and commented: '*Looked* bright .. *seemed* so . . should it not be, for the meaning?'
46-8. Cp. *Judges* xvi 15: 'And [Delilah] said unto [Samson], How canst thou say, I love thee, when thine heart is not with me? thou hast mocked me these three times, and hast not told me wherein thy great strength lieth'.

"And now make haste," I said, "to pray
"The one spot from his soul away;
"To-night he comes, but not the same
60   "Will look!" At night he never came.

XI.

Nor next night: on the after-morn
I went forth with a strength new-born:
The church was empty: something drew
My steps into the street: I knew
65   It led me to the market-place—
And, lo,—on high—the father's face!

XII.

That horrible black scaffold drest—
The stapled block . . God sink the rest!
That head strapped back, that blinding vest,
70   Those knotted hands and naked breast—
Till near one busy hangman pressed—
And—on the neck these arms caressed . . . .

XIII.

No part in aught they hope or fear!
No Heaven with them, no Hell,—and here
75   No Earth, not so much space as pens
My body in their worst of dens
But shall bear God and Man my cry—
Lies—lies, again—and still, they lie!

---

66. And] Where (*1849-88*). EBB. quoted 'And lo!—there smiled the father's
face', and commented: 'You know the best of course—but to me, it seems
strange that she sh^d have seen "the father's face" at all—in the shadow of that
scaffold—'.

67-72. The instrument is the garrotte, the traditional method of capital
punishment in Spain; the victim is fastened to a chair, hooded, and strangled
by the compression of an iron collar.

68. The] That (*1863-88*).

73-8. EBB. quoted 'No part in aught they hope or fear! No Heaven with
them &c', and commented: 'You think at first that she means to abjure
having any part with them: but afterwards the construction seems to swing
round to another side. Does not this stanza require clearing by a moment's
attention[?] It is a striking, thrilling poem too, to make it quite worth while'.
Since EBB. does not quote the entire stanza, it is impossible to determine
whether B. responded to her objection; the ambiguity which she mentions
persists in the published text.

51 England in Italy
[The Englishman in Italy]

Piano di Sorrento

First publ. *B & P* vii (*DR & L*), 6 Nov. 1845; repr. *1849* with changed title, *1863* (when it was placed in *Romances*: see Appendix A, p. 464), *1865²*, *1868*, *1872* (with a change in line-length—see below), *1888*. Our text is *1845*. EBB. saw an unfinished draft in the summer of 1845, when the subtitle was 'Autumn at Sorrento'; all her comments recorded in the notes derive from *Wellesley MS*, unless otherwise stated. The poem is written in the same five-stress metre, divided into long and short lines, as the unfinished *Saul* (see p. 286). In the completed *Saul* (1855), B. amalgamated the long and short lines into single long lines, and in *1872* (and its corrected reissue, *1884*) he did the same with *England*, adjusting the punctuation and capitalization accordingly. Cp. the similar experiment with a long line in *Cristina* (see headnote, I 774). The first six lines read:

> Fortù, Fortù, my beloved one, sit here by my side,
> On my knees put up both little feet! I was sure, if I tried,
> I could make you laugh spite of Scirocco. Now, open your eyes,
> Let me keep you amused, till he vanish in black from the skies,
> With telling my memories over, as you tell your beads;
> All the Plain saw me gather, I garland—the flowers or the weeds.

The poem was written after B.'s return from his second trip to Italy (Aug.-Dec. 1844). There is an allusion to the 'isles of the syren' (see l. 199n.) in a letter to EBB. dated 15 Apr. 1845 (*LK* 46-7); the bulk of the source material in the letters to EBB. comes at the end of Apr. and the beginning of May (see below), and the poem was probably begun then. EBB. first saw it on 6 Aug., and gave B. her criticisms on 12 Aug.; he replied the same day that she was 'too indulgent by far' to 'treat these roughnesses as if they were advanced so many a stage' (*LK* 154); EBB. replied on 13 Aug. that she understood 'that it is *unfinished*, & in a rough state round the edges' (*LK* 155). In her letter of 21-22 Oct., when she had seen the poem in proof, EBB. remarked on B.'s additions: 'The end you have put to "England in Italy" gives unity to the whole . . just what the poem wanted. Also you have given some nobler lines to the middle than met me there before' (*LK* 244). The ending refers to debates in Parliament about the Corn-Laws; it was probably written in Sept. 1845, when these debates were at their height. The added lines in the 'middle' of the poem cannot be distinguished.

Subtitle. Piano di Sorrento: the Plain of Sorrento.

B. visited the Sorrento peninsula in 1844; the 'Piano' (Plain) extends
eastward across the peninsula from the town of Sorrento itself, which lies on
the north coast, 25 km south of Naples. Sorrento is said to derive its name
from the sirens (see ll. 200-8n.). The speaker of the poem is lodging, as B.
may have done, with a local peasant family; probably on the south-eastern
coast, as there is regular contact with towns on the Gulf of Salerno (see ll. 53,
69). Orr (*Handbook* 287 n.1) states, probably on B.'s authority, that every
detail is 'given from personal observation'. However, B. may also have
consulted a guidebook, *Notes on Naples . . . by a Traveller* (1838), which he
owned and later lent to EBB. (see *LK* 721 n.4). This describes the Piano di
Sorrento as 'one sea of ever-living leaf and fruit . . . *such* flowers and *such*
plants . . . you are enabled to see from any part of its slope, as from a theatre,
the whole of the marvellous scenery of the gulf spread out before you' (p.
99). *Notes on Naples* has B.'s spelling of 'scirocco' (see l. 5n.), and an account
of a climbing excursion similar to that described in ll. 133-228: 'Among
vineyards and olive-grounds, the fruit shaken by the wind dropping on us as
we passed, and orchards, where grows the sorbo, the most beautiful fruit-
tree in the world, and where the red pomegranate bends to the ground with
its own richness; among these we wound our tortuous way, through rocky
gully and up green ravine, mounting to surmount the mountain chain that
crowns the siren shore' (pp. 125-6). There is also a description of the
Piedigrotta fête, which mocks Catholic ritual in the same way that B. does
both in the poem (see ll. 246-85) and in an important letter to EBB. which
forms part of the background to the composition of the poem. This
background may be traced in a series of letters between B. and EBB. from
late Mar. to early May 1845 (*LK* 40-60) centred upon Hans Christian
Andersen's novel *The Improvisatore*, recently translated by Mary Howitt (2
vols., 1845). EBB. recommended it warmly (17 Apr.), and B. spoke of
seeing journal extracts 'full of truth & beauty' (30 Apr.). Their discussion of
Andersen's book became linked to exchanges about the artistic advantages
of travel, and the alleged incapacity of Italian writers to describe Italian
landscape. A review of *The Improvisatore* in the *Athenaeum* (8 Mar., p. 236),
which B. almost certainly saw, quoted lengthy passages and commented: 'It
is strange that we know of no descriptions of Italy equal to those which
travellers have given us . . . To these must Andersen's pages henceforth be
added'. On 30 Apr., B. wrote to EBB.: 'That a Dane should write so,
confirms me in an old belief—that Italy is stuff for the use of the North, and
no more . . . strange that those great wide black eyes should stare nothing
out of the earth that lies before them!' (*LK* 50). On 3 May, in the course of
elaborating this argument, he gives descriptions of his own, closely paralleled
in the poem (see ll. 133-71n.), and cites lines from Shelley's *Marenghi* which
are a specific source for ll. 138-40. He also criticizes Catholic ritual and
superstition in a manner close to ll. 246-85 in the poem: 'does not all Naples-
bay and half Sicily, shore and inland, come flocking once a year to the
Piedigrotta fête only to see the blessed King's Volanti, or livery servants all in
their best, as tho' heaven opened? and would not I engage to bring the whole

of the Piano (of Sorrento) in likeness to a red dressing gown properly spangled over, before the priest that spread it out on a pole had even begun his story of how Noah's son Shem, the founder of Sorrento, threw it off to swim thither, as the world knows he did? Oh, it makes one's soul angry, so enough of it' (*LK* 54-5). For a detailed discussion, see D. Karlin, 'The Sources of *The Englishman in Italy*', *BSN* xiv, no. 3 (Winter 1984-5) 23-43. In a letter to Isa Blagden of 19 May 1866 (when he had left Italy after EBB.'s death but was writing *Ring*, set in Italy) B. again comments on the Italians, and his own relation to them: 'I agree with you, & always did, as to the uninterestingness of the Italians individually, as thinking, originating souls: I never read a line in a modern Italian book that was of use to me,—never saw a flash of poetry come out of an Italian *word*: in art, in action, *yes*,—not in the region of ideas: I always said, they *are* poetry, don't and can't *make* poetry—& you know what I mean by *that*,—nothing relating to rhymes and melody and *lo stile* [style]: but as a nation, politically, they are most interesting to me . . . my liking for Italy was always a selfish one,—I felt alone with my own soul there: here, there are fifties and hundreds, even of my acquaintance, who do habitually walk up & down in the lands of thought I live in,—never mind whether they go up to the ends of it, or even look over them,—*in* that territory, they are,—and I never saw footprint of an Italian there yet' (*Dearest Isa* 238-9).

DeVane (*Handbook* 159) suggests Shelley's *Stanzas written in Dejection, near Naples* as an inverse source, but a likelier one is *Lines written among the Euganean Hills*, and cp. also *Ode to the West Wind*. The Romantic period saw the development of what may be called the versified travelogue (as distinct from the 18th-century 'loco-descriptive' poem), most notably Byron's *Childe Harold*; Samuel Rogers' *Italy* (1822-34), a uniformly solemn production, may have stimulated the very different tone of *England*. The climb up a mountain which leads to a revelatory vision is a familiar Romantic (esp. Words-worthian) topic, with strong biblical connotations: Moses at Pisgah (*Deuteronomy* xxxiv 1-4), Christ's transfiguration (*Mark* ix 2-10); B. reworked it in a later poem, *La Saisiaz*, and cp. *A Grammarian*. For the contrast between the (warm, sensual) life of Italy and the (cold, pettifogging) life of England, B. was indebted to Byron, and in particular to *Beppo* 321-92. In B.'s work, *Saul* (1845) is closest to the poem in tone, outlook, and structure. Among major treatments of Italian scenery and contemporary life, cp. *Pippa*, *De Gustibus*, *By the Fire-Side*, *Up at a Villa*, *Love Among the Ruins*, *Two in the Campagna*, and *Prologue* (*Asolando*). For B.'s reaction to the contemporary Catholic Church, cp. esp. *Christmas-Eve*, *Bishop Blougram*, and *Red Cotton*. Some details of the storm in ll. 117-28 reappear in *Caliban*.

EBB. responded enthusiastically to the specific descriptions in the poem (see e.g. ll. 54-64n.); in her concluding comments, she (perhaps only half-seriously) objected to the narrative frame: 'I think it will strike you when you come to finish this unfinished poem, that all the rushing & hurrying life of the descriptions of it, tossed in one upon another like the grape-bunches in the early part, & not "kept under" by ever so much breathless effort on the

poet's part [ll. 73-80], . . can be very little adapted to send anybody to sleep
. . even if there were no regular dinner in the middle of it all [ll. 101-15]. Do
consider. For giving the *sense of Italy*, it is worth a whole library of travel-
books'. W. S. Landor echoed the passage about the sirens (ll. 197-228) in his
poem *To Robert Browning*, written after receiving a presentation copy of *DR
& L*, and published in the *Morning Chronicle*, 22 Nov. 1845. The poem ends:
'warmer climes / Give brighter plumage, stronger wing: the breeze / Of
Alpine heights thou playest with, borne on / Beyond Sorrento and Amalfi,
where / The Siren waits thee, singing song for song'. This poem profoundly
affected both B. and EBB., and, as Kintner says, 'came to sound like
prophecy to the two poets when they were planning their marriage and
escape to Italy . . . the Siren became a recurrent image in these letters from
here on' (*LK* 273 n.7).

> Fortù, Fortù, my loved one,
>   Sit by my side,
> On my knees put up both little feet!
>   I was sure, if I tried,
> 5 I could make you laugh spite of Scirocco:
>   Now, open your eyes—
> Let me keep you amused till he vanish
>   In black from the skies,
> With telling my memories over
> 10   As you tell your beads;
> All the Plain saw me gather, I garland

¶ 51.1. *Fortù:* a diminutive of Fortuna or Fortunata.   *loved one*] beloved
one (*1849-88*).
2. *Sit by*] Sit here by (*1849-88*).
4. *was*] am (*1884*). A very rare example of a reading unique to this ed.
5. *Scirocco*: more usually 'sirocco': 'a warm wind which blows most
frequently in the spring and autumn when depressions in the Sahara and
western Mediterranean move eastward . . . It can blow for days or weeks on
end and is always dry . . . it often precedes a fresh cyclonic storm in the
western Mediterranean' (*Oxford Illustrated Encyclopedia*). B. conflates the
sirocco itself with its stormy aftermath. *Notes on Naples* 89 has B.'s spelling.
In the diary of his 1838 trip to Italy, B. recorded 'Fresh wind. Scirocco' on 26
May in the Adriatic (*Correspondence* iv, p. xii).
7-8.] EBB. quoted 'While I talk you asleep till he's o'er / With his black in the
skies', and commented: 'I don't like "he's o'er" much, or at all perhaps. There
is something to me weak & un-scirocco-like in the two contractions. Would
"till he carries / His black from the skies—" be more *active*'.
9-10. Cp. *By the Fireside* 148-50: 'Let us now forget and then recall, / Break
the rosary in a pearly rain, / And gather what we let fall!'
11-12. 'I put together all the experiences, good or bad, that I had in the Plain'.
11.] All the memories plucked at Sorrento (*1849*).

—Flowers prove they, or weeds.

'Twas time, for your long hot dry Autumn
    Had net-worked with brown
15 The white skin of each grape on the bunches,
    Marked like a quail's crown,
Those creatures you make such account of,
    Whose heads,—specked with white
Over brown like a great spider's back,
20   As I told you last night,—
Your mother bites off for her supper;
    Red-ripe as could be,
Pomegranates were chapping and splitting
    In halves on the tree:
25 And 'twixt the loose walls of great flintstone,
    Or in the thick dust
On the path, or straight out of the rock side,
    Wherever could thrust
Some starved sprig of bold hardy rock-flower
30   Its yellow face up,
For the prize were great butterflies fighting,
    Some five for one cup:
So I guessed, ere I got up this morning,
    What change was in store,
35 By the quick rustle-down of the quail-nets
    Which woke me before

12.] —The flowers, or the weeds. (*1849-88*).

13. 'Twas time,] Time for rain! (*1849-88*). EBB. quoted 'Twas time, for your long dry autumn', and commented: 'I just doubt if "and dry" might not improve the rhythm—doubt. Only if the emphasis is properly administered to "long", nothing of course is wanted—only, again, it is trusting to the reader!'

18. specked with white] speckled with white (*1870*); speckled white (*1875-88*). B. may have adapted a mispr. in *1870*, the first corr. reissue of *1868*; *1870* provided the copy-text for *1875*.

25. 'twixt] betwixt (*1849-88*).

29. starved] burnt (*1849-88*).

32. Some five] Five foes (*1865²*). Cp. *Two in the Campagna* 16-18.

34.] EBB. quoted 'What was in store', and commented: 'Surely "what change" or "what fate" or some additional word sh^d assist the rhythm in this place. The line is brokenly short'.

35. quail-nets: 'nets spread to catch quails as they fly to or from the other side of the Mediterranean. They are slung by rings on to poles, and stand sufficiently high for the quails to fly into them' (Orr *Handbook* 287 n.1).

I could open my shutter, made fast
   With a bough and a stone,
And look thro' the twisted dead vine-twigs,
40   Sole lattice that's known;
Sharp rang the rings down the bird-poles
   While, busy beneath,
Your priest and his brother were working,
   The rain in their teeth.
45 And out upon all the flat house-roofs
   Where split figs lay drying,
The girls took the frails under cover:
   Nor use seemed in trying
To get out the boats and go fishing,
50   For under the cliff
Fierce the black water frothed o'er the blind-rock—
   No seeing our skiff
Arrive about noon from Amalfi,
   —Our fisher arrive,
55 And pitch down his basket before us,
   All trembling alive
With pink and grey jellies, your sea-fruit,

40. i.e. the only form of lattice known to the peasants with whom the speaker is lodging.

41.] Quick and sharp rang the rings down the net-poles, (*1849-88*).

43. *were working*] tugged at them (*1849-88*).

47. *frails*: large baskets made of rushes. Cp. *Tomb at St. Praxed's* 41.

51. *blind-rock*: a concealed rock, lying just below the surface (see ll. 214-16).

52-4. i.e. 'there is no chance of seeing the fisherman arrive about noon [as usual] from Amalfi in his skiff'. 'No seeing' governs both 'our skiff / Arrive' and 'Our fisher arrive'.

53. *Amalfi*: a town on the north coast of the Gulf of Salerno, about 19km west-south-west of Salerno itself (see l. 69n.).

54-64. EBB. quoted l. 58 and commented: 'I do like all this living description . . living description which never lived before in poetry . . & now will live always. These fishes have suffered no earth-change, though they lie here so grotesquely plain between rhyme & rhyme. And the grave fisher too! & the children "brown as his shrimps"!' In a letter to John Kenyon (undated, but before July 1845 and probably before B. began corresponding with EBB.), B. wrote of an unidentified 'novel' which he was sending to Kenyon: 'Let it figure among your books (at the house-top) as one sees from time to time in the shop of a Bondstreet Fishmonger some thorny queer lump-fish suspended as a show over all the good quiet ordinary turbots and salmon—not that such a prodigy is to be eaten by any means, but to show *what* the "vast sea's entrail" can produce on occasion' (*ABL MS*).

57. *sea-fruit*: seafood; translating It. 'frutti di mare'. Not *OED*.

—Touch the strange lumps,
And mouths gape there, eyes open, all manner
60   Of horns and of humps,
Which only the fisher looks grave at,
    While round him like imps
Cling screaming the children as naked
    And brown as his shrimps,
65 Himself too as bare to the middle
    —You see round his neck
The string and its brass coin suspended,
    That saves him from wreck.
But to-day not a boat reached Salerno,
70   So back to a man
Came our friends, with whose help in the vineyards
    Grape-harvest began:
In the vat half-way up in our house-side
    Like blood the juice spins
75 While your brother all bare-legged is dancing
    Till breathless he grins
Dead-beaten, in effort on effort
    To keep the grapes under,
For still when he seems all but master
80   In pours the fresh plunder
From girls who keep coming and going
    With basket on shoulder,
And eyes shut against the rain's driving,
    Your girls that are older,—
85 For under the hedges of aloe,

58. —*Touch*] You touch (*1849-88*).

66.] EBB. suggested 'And you see round his neck', 'for rhythm. The line stops you: & you need not stop, when you are looking at him, to "see round his neck"'. This was one of the rare occasions on which B. did not follow her advice.

69. *Salerno*: a major port lying west of the mouth of the Irno river in the Gulf of Salerno, 54 km east-south-east of Naples.

73-8. EBB. commented: 'The treading of the grapes is admirable painting— that "breathless he grins", so true to life—& the effort to "keep the grapes under"!—all, admirable'.

74. *spins*: gushes or spirts (*OED* 8).

77. *Dead-beaten*: usually 'dead-beat': *OED* does not record B.'s form, which was perhaps adopted to allow a secondary sense, 'completely defeated' (by the grapes).

79. *For still*] Since still (*1849-88*).

<blockquote>
And where, on its bed
Of the orchard's black mould, the love-apple
Lies pulpy and red,
All the young ones are kneeling and filling
90   Their laps with the snails
Tempted out by the first rainy weather,—
Your best of regales,
As to-night will be proved to my sorrow,
When, supping in state,
95   We shall feast our grape-gleaners—two dozen,
Three over one plate,—
Maccaroni so tempting to swallow
In slippery strings,
And gourds fried in great purple slices,
100   That colour of kings,—
Meantime, see the grape-bunch they've brought
    you,—
The rain-water slips
O'er the heavy blue bloom on each globe
Which the wasp to your lips
105   Still follows with fretful persistence—
Nay, taste while awake,
This half of a curd-white smooth cheese-ball,
That peels, flake by flake,
Like an onion's, each smoother and whiter—
110   Next sip this weak wine
From the thin green glass flask, with its stopper,
A leaf of the vine,—
And end with the prickly-pear's red flesh
That leaves thro' its juice
115   The stony black seeds on your pearl-teeth
</blockquote>

86-7. on its bed / Of the orchard's black mould, the love-apple: i.e. the tomato on its bed of richly manured earth ('orchard' is a transferred sense from 'love-apple'). The cultivation of the 'love-apple' by 'lavishing manure' recurs in a complex figure in *Fifine* 1325ff.

91. the] this (*1863-88*).

92. regales: choice articles of food, dainties.

97-100. Maccaroni . . . strings . . . kings] With lasagne . . . ropes . . . popes (*1849-88*).

103. heavy] leaden (*B & P BYU*).

109. onion's] onion (*1863-88*).

113-15. Cp. Andersen's *Improvisatore* (see headnote) i 114: 'delicious green water-melons which . . . shewed the purple-red flesh with the black seeds', quoted in both the *Athenaeum* and the *Spectator*.

>   . . . Scirocco is loose!
>   Hark! the quick pelt of the olives
>   Which, thick in one's track,
>   Tempt the stranger to pick up and bite them
> 120   Tho' not yet half black!
>   And how their old twisted trunks shudder!
>   The medlars let fall
>   Their hard fruit—the brittle great fig-trees
>   Snap off, figs and all,
> 125 For here comes the whole of the tempest!
>   No refuge but creep
>   Back again to my side and my shoulder,
>   And listen or sleep.
>
>   O how will your country show next week,
> 130   When all the vine-boughs
>   Have been stripped of their foliage to pasture
>   The mules and the cows?
>   Last eve I rode over the mountains—
>   Your brother, my guide,
> 135 Soon left me to feast on the myrtles
>   That offered, each side,
>   Their fruit-balls, black, glossy and luscious,
>   Or strip from the sorbs

116-125. With this passage, cp. B.'s description of 'la bora' in a letter to EBB. of 13 July 1845, esp. (with ll. 123-4): 'you see the acacia heads snap off, now one, then another' (*LK* 122-3). Cp. the storm which ends *Caliban* (l. 290).

117. the quick pelt] the quick, whistling pelt (*1849-88*, except 'quick whistling', *1868-88*).

121.] How the old twisted olive trunks shudder! (*1849-88*, except 'shudder,', *1865²*, *1868-88*).

123. fruit—the] fruit, and the (*1849-88*).

126-8. Cp. *Sordello* iii 758.

127.] EBB. quoted 'Back to my side', and commented: 'Is not some word, some dissyllable, (as if you were to write "Back again" &c,) wanted for rhythm,—reading it with the preceding line?'

128 ˄ 129.] there is no division at this point in *1865²*.

133-71. Cp. B. to EBB., 3 May 1845: 'And which of you eternal triflers was it called yourself "Shelley" and so told me years ago that in the mountains it was a feast "when one should find those globes of deep red gold—Which in the woods the strawberry-tree doth bear, Suspended in their emerald atmosphere," so that when my Mule walked into a sorb-tree, not to tumble sheer over Monte Calvano, and I felt the fruit against my face, the little ragged bare-legged guide fairly laughed at my knowing them so well' (*LK* 54). The quotation is from Shelley's *Marenghi* 72-5. But B. had mistaken the 'strawberry-tree' for the sorb; it is actually the arbutus (see next note).

A treasure, so rosy and wondrous,
140   Of hairy gold orbs!
But my mule picked his sure, sober path out,
    Just stopping to neigh
When he recognised down in the valley
    His mates on their way
145 With the faggots, and barrels of water;
    And soon we emerged
From the plain where the woods could scarce follow,
    And still as we urged
Our way, the woods wondered, and left us,
150   As up still we trudged
Though the wild path grew wilder each instant,
    And place was e'en grudged
'Mid the rock-chasms, and piles of loose stones
    Like the loose broken teeth
155 Of some monster, which climbed there to die
    From the ocean beneath—
Place was grudged to the silver-grey fume-weed
    That clung to the path,
And dark rosemary, ever a-dying,
160   Which, 'spite the wind's wrath,
So loves the salt rock's face to seaward,—
    And lentisks as staunch
To the stone where they root and bear berries,
    And—what shows a branch
165 Coral-coloured, transparent, with circlets
    Of pale seagreen leaves—
Over all trod my mule with the caution
    Of gleaners o'er sheaves:

139-40.] A treasure, or, rosy and wondrous, / Those hairy gold orbs! (*1868-88*). Presumably B. made the rev. after realizing that his description of the sorb, derived from Shelley's 'strawberry-tree' (see prec. note), actually applied to the arbutus. But the original description is not inaccurate, since the sorb does have reddish-yellow fruits.

149-50. left us, / As up] left us. / Up, up (*1872, 1884*).

152. place was e'en grudged: to the 'fume-weed' of l. 157, where the phrase is repeated because of the intervening image.

157. fume-weed: fumitory (*Fumaria officinalis*), a weed which grows close to the ground; apparently B.'s coinage (not *OED*), from the Latin derivation of fumitory, 'fumus terrae' (smoke of the earth).

160. Which] That (*1849-88*).

161. rock's face] rock-face (*1865²*).

162-3. The lentisk is the mastic tree, an evergreen shrub. Cp. *Sordello* iv 798-807.

Foot after foot like a lady—
170   So round after round,
He climbed to the top of Calvano,
     And God's own profound
Was above me, and round me the mountains,
     And under, the sea,
175   And with me, my heart to bear witness
     What was and shall be!
Oh heaven, and the terrible crystal!
     No rampart excludes
The eye from the life to be lived
180   In the blue solitudes!
Oh, those mountains, their infinite movement!
     Still moving with you—
For ever some new head and breast of them
     Thrusts into view
185   To observe the intruder—you see it
     If quickly you turn
And, before they escape you, surprise them—
     They grudge you should learn
How the soft plains they look on, lean over,

169. *Foot*] Still, foot (*1849-88*).   *Foot after foot*: cp. Wordsworth, *Strange fits of passion* 21-2: 'My horse moved on; hoof after hoof / He raised, and never stopped'.
170. *So*] Still (*1872, 1884*); Till (*1888*).
171. *Calvano*: a contraction of Vico Alvano, in the southern part of the Piano. It is 642 metres high and commands a sweeping view, north across the plain and south over the Mediterranean, including the Galli islets (see l. 199n.). B. told Furnivall he was unsure of the name, which he had 'heard . . . in Sorrento . . . but the names are greatly changed in the dialect there' (*BSP* i [*1881*] 170).
172-4. Cp. Shelley, *The Triumph of Life* 27-8: 'the deep / Was at my feet, and Heaven above my head'.
172. *profound*: used in the same sense of 'sky, firmament' in *La Saisiaz* 19.
175. *with me*] within me (*1849-88*).
177. *Oh heaven,*] Oh, heaven (*1863-65, 1868-88*); Oh heaven (*1865²*).   *terrible crystal*: cp. *Ezekiel* i 22: 'And the likeness of the firmament . . . was as the colour of the terrible crystal'. Cp. *Saul* (*1855*) 99-101, *Sordello* iii 440, *Prince Hohenstiel* 1334, and *Aristophanes* 45: 'Above all crowding, crystal silentness'.
179. *The*] Your (*1849-88*).
181-7. EBB. admired this passage as 'finely true'.
183.] EBB. quoted 'For some', and suggested 'With ever some'.
189-91.] EBB. quoted 'How the soft plains they look on & love so / As they would pretend / Lower beneath them', and commented: 'I do not see the construction. The "lower" put here as a verb? & if correctly, is it clearly, so,

190   And love, they pretend,
          —Cower beneath them—the flat sea-pine crouches,
          The wild fruit-trees bend,
          E'en the myrtle-leaves curl, shrink and shut—
          All is silent and grave—
195   'Tis a sensual and timorous beauty—
          How fair, but a slave!
          So I turned to the sea,— and there slumbered
          As greenly as ever
          Those isles of the syren, your Galli;
200   No ages can sever

---

put?' In the margin B. wrote 'Cower', and explained in his letter of 12 Aug.
1845: 'So you can decypher my *utterest* hieroglyphic? Now droop the eyes
while I triumph: the plains *Cower, Cower* beneath the mountains their
masters' (*LK* 153). The changes were presumably not suggested by her. See
also l. 272n.
191. flat] black (*1872, 1884*).
194.] EBB. quoted 'All's silent & grave', and suggested the present reading:
'The rhythm gains by it, I think'.
196.] How fair! but a slave. (*1865-88*).
198.] EBB. quoted 'Greenly as ever', and commented: 'Would not "*As*
greenly as ever" take the rhythm on better?'
199. Li Galli (The Cocks) are three rocky little islets (la Castelluccia, la
Rotonda, and il Gallo Lungo), off the south-eastern coast of the Sorrento
peninsula. They are known also as the Syrenusae, from their association with
the Homeric sirens, though this title is not unique to them (see next note). In
his letter to EBB. of 15 Apr. 1845, B. made a little sketch of 'the green little
Syrenusae where I have sate and heard the quails sing' (*LK* 46-7). See ll. 223-
4n.
200.] EBB. quoted 'Years cannot sever', and suggested 'And years' or 'For
years'.
200-8. In a letter of 12 May 1846, B. told EBB., 'there are three siren's isles,
you know' (*LK* 698), but despite this he refers to five islets here. The furthest
from the coastline of the Sorrento peninsula are the Galli, the 'Three' of
l. 201, which form a distinct group. 'Their sister' is the islet of Vetara, roughly
midway between the Galli and the coast; and the 'small one' of l. 205 is the
islet of Isca, close inshore—'just launched in the wave'. All these are 'isles of
the syren': see N. Douglas, *Siren Land* (1957) 29. Vetara, swimming to join
the Galli, had got half-way there when she 'looked at Ulysses', and has got
no further; though this still seems impressive to Isca watching from the safety
of the shallows. It is not clear what variant of the myth of Ulysses and the
sirens B. is alluding to. The sirens are said to have thrown themselves into the
sea after failing to lure Ulysses from his ship with their singing, either out of
shame and vexation or in order to follow him; and to have been

The Three—nor enable their sister
    To join them,—half way
On the voyage, she looked at Ulysses—
    No farther to-day,
205 Tho' the small one, just launched in the wave,
    Watches breast-high and steady
From under the rock, her bold sister
    Swum half-way already.
O when shall we sail there together
210   And see from the sides
Quite new rocks show their faces—new haunts
    Where the syren abides?
Oh, to sail round and round them, close over
    The rocks, tho' unseen,
215 That ruffle the grey glassy water
    To glorious green,—
Then scramble from splinter to splinter,
    Reach land and explore
On the largest, the strange square black turret
220   With never a door—

---

metamorphosed into islets, their original home being a headland on the peninsula, where they later had a famous sanctuary (Strabo, *Geography* I ii 12). Possibly B. refers to their respective positions when the metamorphosis occurred. But he goes on to combine the idea of the islets being the sirens themselves with that of their being the sirens' home (ll. 209-12), and further on he interprets their song as the 'birds' quiet singing' (ll. 222-8).

205.] EBB. quoted 'Though the one breast-high in the water' and suggested 'bosom-high', 'for rhythm'. In proof she jotted down 'in the water / Watches' without comment. B. transferred 'breast-high' to l. 206 (whose original version cannot be recovered) and altered the rhythm of l. 205 in accordance with EBB.'s suggestion.

209. O when] Fortù, (*1849-88*). EBB. quoted 'When' and suggested that B. restore 'O', which he had erased, 'for rhythm & expression'.

213. Oh, to sail] Shall we sail (*1849-88*). EBB. quoted 'Oh to sail round them, close over', and commented: 'The line is broken I think. Should it not either be "And oh, to sail round them", or "Oh, to sail round & round them"'.

215.] EBB. quoted 'That ruffle the grey sea-water', and suggested 'ocean-water', 'for rhythm'. She added: 'All beautiful description'.

219-20. A cistern remains of a tower built on il Gallo Lungo (see l. 199n.) in 1330 by King Robert of Naples. See *Sordello* vi 779-85n. (I 763)

219.] EBB. quoted 'The square black tower on the largest', and commented: 'Did you write "*built* on the largest"—because [of] the eternal rhythm!' In proof, she jotted down 'The strange square black turret on the largest / Built with never a door', without comment.

Just a loop that admits the quick lizards;
　—To stand there and hear
The birds' quiet singing, that tells us
　What life is, so clear;
225　The secret they sang to Ulysses,
　　When ages ago
He heard and he knew this life's secret
　I hear and I know!

Ah see! O'er Calvano the sun breaks:
230　He strikes the great gloom
And flutters it over his summit
　In airy gold fume!
All is over. Look out, see the gypsy,
　Our tinker and smith,
235　Has arrived, set up bellows and forge,
　And down-squatted forthwith
To his hammering under the wall there;
　One eye keeps aloof
The urchins that itch to be putting
240　His jews'-harps to proof,

221. *that admits*] to admit (*1849–88*).

222. *—To*] Then, (*1849–88*).

223-4. B. may refer to the singing of quails (see l. 199n.). N. Douglas (*Siren Land* 30) says that on one of the Galli 'the laminated strata are broken to form a melodious sea-cave . . . the haunt of countless . . . swifts who raise their families in the shelving rock'. The sirens were winged or bird-bodied women; the Muses plucked their wings after defeating them in a singing contest.

225-8. Cp. Sir Thomas Browne, *Hydriotaphia, or Urne Buriall* (1658), whose final chapter opens: 'What song the Syrens sang, or what name Achilles assumed when he hid himself among women, though puzzling questions, are not beyond all conjecture'; B. quotes this in his letter to EBB. of 8 Apr. 1846 (*LK* 606). In fact Ulysses recounts the song at the court of Alcinous (*Odyssey* xii). The sirens wooed him in flattering terms, promising him knowledge of all that happened on earth, in heaven, and in the underworld. For the speaker's visionary assertion in l. 228, cp. *Saul* (1855) 312.

229.] Ah, see! The sun breaks o'er Calvano— (*1849–88*, except 'Calvano;', *1863–70, 1875, 1888*; 'Calvano.', *1872, 1884*).

230.] EBB. quoted 'Strikes the great gloom', and commented: 'For clearness, the personal pronoun is wanted, I fancy. What "strikes?"'

231. *over his*] o'er the mount's (*1849–88*).

233-44. Cp. the description of the Gypsies in *Flight* 350-89.

240. *jews'-harps*] jews'-harp (*1872, 1884*).

While the other thro' locks of curled wire
  Is watching how sleek
Shines the hog, come to share in the windfalls
  —An abbot's own cheek!
245 All is over! wake up and come out now,
  And down let us go,
And see all the fine things set in order
  At church for the show
Of the Sacrament, set forth this evening;
250 To-morrow's the Feast
Of the Rosary's virgin, by no means
  Of virgins the least—
As we'll hear in the off-hand discourse
  Which (all nature, no art)
255 The Dominican brother these three weeks
  Was getting by heart.
Not a post nor a pillar but's dizened
  With red and blue papers;
All the roof waves with ribbons, each altar's
260 A-blaze with long tapers;
But the great masterpiece is the scaffold
  Rigged glorious to hold
All the fiddlers and fifers and drummers,

241. locks of curled wire: the Gypsy's wiry hair.
243. windfalls] windfall (*1863–88*).
244.] Chew, abbot's own cheek! (*1872, 1884, 1888*; a rare example of *1888* agreeing with a rev. introduced in a vol. of selections, not a collected ed.). Cp. *Holy-Cross Day* 19–24.
245.] EBB. quoted 'And now come out, you best one' and suggested: 'And now come out, come out, you best one'.
247.] And see the fine things got in order (*1849–88*).
248–9. the show / Of the Sacrament: the ceremonial display of the Host.
250–1. the Feast / Of the Rosary's virgin: the Feast of Our Lady of the Rosary, initially commemorating the Christian victory over the Turks at Lepanto, 7 Oct. 1571. In 1716, after another victory over the Turks in Hungary, Pope Clement XI directed its observance throughout Christendom every 7 Oct.
253–6. Cp. (noting the context of anti-Catholic satire) Marvell, *Upon Appleton House* 93–6: 'And oft she spent the summer suns / Discoursing with the subtle nuns. / Whence in these words one to her weaved / (As 'twere by chance) thoughts long conceived'.
253. we'll] you'll (*1849–88*).
255. Dominican brother: members of the Dominican order were chiefly responsible for spreading the use of the rosary as a devotional exercise.
257.] Not a pillar nor post but is dizened (*1863–88*).   *dizened*: adorned.
259. altar's] altar (*1849–88*).

And trumpeters bold,
265   Not afraid of Bellini nor Auber,
       Who, when the priest's hoarse,
       Will strike us up something that's brisk
       For the feast's second course.
       And then will the flaxen-wigged Image
270   Be carried in pomp
       Thro' the plain, while in gallant procession
       The priests mean to stomp.
       And all round the glad church stand old bottles
       With gunpowder stopped,
275   Which will be, when the Image re-enters,
       Religiously popped.
       And at night from the crest of Calvano
       Great bonfires will hang,
       On the plain will the trumpets join chorus,
280   And more poppers bang!
       At all events, come—to the garden,
       As far as the wall,
       See me tap with a hoe on the plaster
       Till out there shall fall
285   A scorpion with wide angry nippers!

       . . . "Such trifles" you say?
       Fortù, in my England at home,

265. *Bellini*: Vincenzo Bellini (1801-35), Italian composer, best known for the operas *Norma* and *I Puritani*.   *Auber*: Daniel-François-Esprit Auber (1782-1871), French composer of light operas, including *Fra Diavolo* (1830).
272. EBB. quoted 'The priests mean to stamp', and commented: 'But is this word "stamp", & is it the rhyme to "pomp". I object to that rhyme—*I!!*' B. wrote 'stomp' in the margin, and explained to EBB. in his letter of 12 Aug. 1845: 'the Priests stomp over the clay ridges, (a palpable plagiarism from two lines of a legend that delighted my infancy, and now instruct my maturer years in pretty nearly all they boast of the semi-mythologic era referred to—"In London town, when reigned King Lud, His lords went stomping thro' the mud"—would all historic records were half as picturesque!)' (*LK* 153-4). *OED* records B.'s use as being only 'to obtain a rime'.
273. *And all*] All (*1868-88*).   *stand*] lie (*1849-88*).
286-92. B. alludes to the bitter debates in Parliament over the repeal of the Corn-Laws, which imposed heavy duty on the import of foreign grain. The controversy was at a peak of intensity in Sept. 1845, after the renewed failure of the potato crop in Ireland, and the consequent famine. B.'s refs. to the Corn-Laws in his letters are uniformly hostile. Cp. Byron, *Beppo* 375-7: 'I like a parliamentary debate, / Particularly when 'tis not too late; // I like the taxes, when they're not too many'.

> Men meet gravely to-day
> And debate, if abolishing Corn-laws
> 290   Be righteous and wise
> —If 'tis proper Scirocco should vanish
> In black from the skies!

290. Be] Is (*1849*).

291-2. 'It would be as absurd to debate gravely the obvious benefit of the storm ending, as it is to debate the repeal of the Corn-Laws.' Some reviewers misconstrued the passage into the opposite sense, based on the reading, 'if [abolishing Corn-laws] were proper, then Scirocco would vanish [i.e. an event against the natural order, the permanent extinction of the sirocco, would occur]'; B.'s revisions if anything progressively encouraged this error (see l. 291n.), but 'should' confirms the overall syntax.

291. *'tis*] 'twere (*1863-88*).   *proper Scirocco*] proper, Scirocco (*1849-88*).

52 Night and Morning
[Meeting at Night *and* Parting at Morning]

First publ. *B & P* vii (*DR & L*), 6 Nov. 1845; repr. *1849* (with the two sections as separate poems, *Meeting at Night* and *Parting at Morning*), and then, always together, *1863* (when they were placed in *Lyrics*: see Appendix A, p. 464), *1868, 1872, 1888*. Our text is *1845*. EBB. first saw the poem in proof, and thought it 'beautiful' (29 Oct. 1845, *LK* 252). The date of composition is unknown. The stanza-form of *Morning* is unique in B. The speaker in both poems is the man, as B. explained (see *Morning* 3-4n.).

I.—Night.

i.

The grey sea and the long black land;
And the yellow half-moon large and low;
And the startled little waves that leap
In fiery ringlets from their sleep,
5 As I gain the cove with pushing prow,
And quench its speed in the slushy sand.

ii.

Then a mile of warm sea-scented beach;
Three fields to cross till a farm appears;
A tap at the pane, the quick sharp scratch
10 And blue spurt of a lighted match,
And a voice less loud, thro' its joys and fears,
Than the two hearts beating each to each!

¶53.i *2*. Cp. Tennyson, *The Palace of Art* (1842) 65-8: 'a tract of sand . . .
Lit with a low large moon'.
i *6. in the*] i' the (*1870-88*).
i *11. thro' its joys*] through joys (*1872, 1884*).
i *12*. Cp. *Love Among the Ruins* 71-2: 'Ere we rush, ere we extinguish sight
and speech / Each on each'.

II.—Morning.

Round the cape of a sudden came the sea,
And the sun looked over the mountain's rim—
And straight was a path of gold for him,
And the need of a world of men for me.

ii *3-4*. In Feb. 1889, B. was asked about l. 4: 'Is this an expression by her of her sense of loss of him, or the despairing cry of a ruined woman?' He replied: 'Neither: it is *his* confession of how fleeting is the belief (implied in the first part) that such raptures are self-sufficient and enduring—as for the time they appear' (*New Poems* 176). In l. 3, 'him' therefore refers to the sun; cp., among other examples, *How They Brought the Good News* 20. B.'s account suggests a link to *Love Among the Ruins*: see prec. note.

53 The Glove
Peter Ronsard *loquitur*

First publ. *B & P* vii (*DR & L*), 6 Nov. 1845, the last poem in the pamphlet. EBB. first saw the poem in proof, and suggested a number of minor changes (*Wellesley MS*; all her comments recorded in the notes are from this source). Repr. *1849, 1863* (when it was placed in *Romances*: see Appendix A, p. 464), *1868, 1872, 1888*. Our text is *1845*. The date of composition is not known; the late summer of 1845 seems likely, because of the topic of courtship, and the fact that EBB. first saw the poem in proof. Cp. two passages from consecutive letters written by B. and EBB. in July 1845. In the first (13 July) B. writes: 'I have been looking thro' a poem-book just now, and was told, under the head of Album-verses alone, that for A. the writer would die, & for B. die too but a crueller death, and for C. too, & D. and so on. I wonder if they have since wanted to borrow money from him on the strength of his professions' (*LK* 121). In her reply (16-17 July) EBB. speaks of a 'letter, I had yesterday, which calls me .. let me see how many hard names .. "unbending," .. "disdainful," .. "cold hearted," .. "arrogant," .. yes, "arrogant, as women always are when men grow humble"' (*LK* 124). The letter was from the Rev. George Barrett Hunter, another suitor of EBB., who was unknown to B.

The story originates in Brantôme's *Vies des Dames Galantes*, repr. *Oeuvres Complètes du Seigneur de Brantôme* [Paris 1822-3] vii 460-1. A knight at the court of Francis I is courting a beautiful lady. She challenges him to live up to his vows of devotion by fetching her glove from a lion's den. He does so, but flings the glove in her face, to the applause of the king and court. Literary treatments before B.'s follow the original in approving of the knight's action. Two are of importance: Schiller's ballad *Der Handschuh* [The Glove] (1797), which B. could have seen either in the original or in several contemporary translations; and *The Glove and the Lions* (1836), by Leigh Hunt, whom B. knew well in the period after *Paracelsus* (1835). These poems agree in broad outline, and in their condemnation (not explicit in Schiller, however) of the lady. They differ substantially in detail. Hunt has several lions; Schiller has a single lion, which subdues a tiger and two leopards. B. follows Schiller, developing the picture of the lion and eliminating the extra animals; he may have been influenced by some details of a 'version' of Schiller's poem which appeared in *Blackwood's Magazine* IX li (1821) (hereafter *Blackwood's*). B.'s interpretation of the lady's challenge and the knight's response reverses that of all previous treatments—deliberately, as his direct quotation from Hunt's poem at ll. 100-2 makes clear. In addition, whereas Schiller and Hunt conclude with the lady's humiliation, B. continues the story by having his

Subtitle. *loquitur*: Lat., 'speaks'. Cp. 'Bow bell loquitur' in *Cockney Anthology* (I 94).

narrator question the lady about her motive, and by providing her with a lover and a happy ending. DeVane (*Handbook* 182 and n.51) suggests a source for these added elements in the memoirs of the Marquis de Lassay (*Receuil de Différentes Choses* [1756]); B. later used them, in a more direct form, in *Daniel Bartoli*.

The poem is set in the early part of the reign of Francis (François) I (1494–1547); the mention of 'peace' in l. 2 probably refers to the treaties which followed the French triumphs in Italy in 1515, the year Francis came to the throne, including the battle of Marignano mentioned in l. 82. (Francis also figures in *Andrea* 149–61.) B.'s choice of Peter (Pierre de) Ronsard (1524–1585) as narrator is anachronistic; Ronsard's first extant published poem dates from the year of Francis' death, and he did not occupy the position of court poet until a decade later. He was however a page at Francis' court, and served in the retinue of two French queens of Scotland, Madeleine de France and Marie de Guise (see ll. 157–70). Ronsard was a central figure in the 'Pléiade', a group whose aim was to create a native literature to match the classical achievement (cp. *Paracelsus* and *Sordello*, whose protagonists both consciously adopt the vernacular in furtherance of a campaign of political/cultural reform); but the interest in character and motive which B. attributes to him (ll. 121–2) is closer to B.'s than to Ronsard's aesthetics.

Count Gismond and *Flight* both have aristocratic settings whose values are exposed as shallow and false, and heroines who leave after wrongful and public disgrace; *Flight* is esp. close, with its sympathetic narrator and comic-grotesque rhymes. The theme of devoted service as the test of love is constant in B.: cp., in this period, *Pippa* ii (esp. Pippa's song, ii 195–210) and *Colombe*.

In her letter of 29 Oct. 1845 EBB. commented: 'And for your "Glove", all women should be grateful,—& Ronsard, honoured, in this fresh shower of music on his old grave . . though the chivalry of the interpretation, as well as much beside, is so plainly yours, . . could only be yours, perhaps. And even *you* are forced to let in a third person . . close to the doorway . . before you can do any good. What a noble lion you give us too . . . And then, with what a "curious felicity" you turn the subject glove to another use & strike De Lorge's blow back on him with it, in the last paragraph of your story!—And the versification! And the lady's speech—(to return) so calm, & proud—yet a little bitter!' (*LK* 252).

> "Heigho," yawned one day King Francis,
> "Distance all value enhances!
> "When a man's busy, why leisure
> "Strikes him as wonderful pleasure,—
> 5   " 'Faith, and at leisure once is he—
> "Straightway he wants to be busy.

¶53.2. Cp. Campbell, *Pleasures of Hope* i 7: 'Distance lends enchantment to the view', and Hickeringill, *Jamaica* (1661): 'Distance and absence usually enhanceth the affections of near friends'.

"Here we've got peace; and aghast I'm
"Caught thinking war the true pastime!
"Is there a reason in metre?
10   "Give us your speech, master Peter!"
I who, if mortal dare say so,
Ne'er am at a loss with my Naso,
"Sire," I replied, "joys prove cloudlets:
"Men are the merest Ixions"—
15   Here the King whistled aloud, "Let's
". . Heigho . . go look at our lions!"
Such are the sorrowful chances
If you talk fine to King Francis.

And so, to the courtyard proceeding,
20   Our company Francis was leading
Increased by new followers tenfold
Before he arrived at the penfold;
Lords, ladies, like clouds which bedizen
At sunset the western horizon,
25   And Sir De Lorge pressed 'mid the foremost
With the Dame he professed to adore most—
Oh, what a face! One by fits eyed

12. Naso: Publius Ovidius Naso, or Ovid, whose work (esp. the *Metamor-phoses*) was a major influence on Ronsard and the Pléiade. B. makes one of his rare self-quotations of this line in a letter to EBB. of 9 Nov. 1845: 'I have not had *every* love-luxury, I now find out . . where is the proper, rationally to-be-expected—"*lovers' quarrel?*" *Here*, as you will find! "Irae amantium" . . I am no more "at a loss with my Naso," than Peter Ronsard' (*LK* 262). But the tag 'Amantium irae amoris integratio est' [A lover's quarrel is a renewal of love] is not from Ovid but from Terence (*ibid.*, n.2).

13-14. 'Pleasure is illusory, as the fate of Ixion illustrates'. Ixion enjoyed the protection of Zeus until he became enamoured of Hera; Zeus created a false Hera which dissolved into a cloud when Ixion embraced her, and he was then bound on a wheel in Hades. Ovid tells the story in *Metamorphoses* xii. B. himself later treated the story, though not with this moral, in *Ixion*.

20. Francis was leading: i.e. 'which Francis was leading'.

22. penfold: a fold for penning sheep or cattle.

23. bedizen: to dress out, esp. in a vulgar and gaudy fashion. Only occurrence in B., but 'dizened' appears twice.

25-6. Cp. Leigh Hunt's *The Glove and the Lions* 4: 'And 'mongst them [the 'nobles' and 'ladies'] sat the Count de Lorge, with one for whom he sigh'd'. B. could have read about Jacques de Montgommery, seigneur de Lorges (sic) in *Biographie*, which however makes no mention of the story recorded here, but describes his career as that of 'one of the most valiant warriors of the sixteenth century'.

Her, and the horrible pitside;
For the penfold surrounded a hollow
30   Which led where the eye scarce dared follow,
And shelved to the chamber secluded
Where Bluebeard the great lion brooded.
The King hailed his keeper, an Arab
As glossy and black as a scarab,
35   And bade him make sport and at once stir
Up and out of his den the old monster.
They opened a hole in the wire-work
Across it, and dropped there a firework,
And fled; one's heart's beating redoubled;
40   A pause, while the pit's mouth was troubled,
The blackness and silence so utter,
By the firework's slow sparkling and sputter;
Then earth in a sudden contortion
Gave out to our gaze her abortion!
45   . . Such a brute! were I friend Clement Marot
(Whose experience of nature's but narrow,
And whose faculties move in no small mist
When he versifies David the Psalmist)
I should study that brute to describe you
50   *Illum Juda Leonem de Tribu!*
One's whole blood grew curdling and creepy

33-6. Schiller has the king's gesture; explicit mention of the 'keeper' is supplied by *Blackwood's* alone among the sources: 'King Francis waves his silver wand— / And straight, / The Beast-ward's ready hand / Unbars the grate'.

45-50. The sense is that if, like Marot, Ronsard were translating the Psalms, he would take this lion as a model for the phrase 'leo de Juda tribu' (see next note). Marot's verse translations of the Psalms began appearing in 1539. Ronsard, a staunch Catholic, supported the Sorbonne's condemnation of Marot's *Trente Pseaumes de David* (1542) for its reformist tendences (Marot was later encouraged by Calvin and his work became a Huguenot textbook); B.'s dating, and his linking of the controversy to aesthetics as well as theology, are however unhistorical. In general, while conceding the merit of Marot's work and calling him 'sole light in these years of vernacular poetry', Ronsard, in *La Victoire de Francis de Bourbon*, claims that he himself, 'being born in a better age, and more learned than he', will 'perfect the accomplishment of a more studied art'.

50. 'That lion of the tribe of Juda' (adapted to the accusative case and rearranged to fit the metre from 'leo de Juda tribu' [*Revelation* v 5]). The phrase does not in fact appear in *Psalms*, but derives from *Genesis* lxix 9.

51. creepy: sluggish, with associations from 'a creeping of the flesh . . . caused by horror or repugnance' (*OED* 2).

To see the black mane, vast and heapy,
The tail in the air stiff and straining,
The wide eyes, nor waxing nor waning,
55   As over the barrier which bounded
His platform, and us who surrounded
The barrier, they reached and they rested
On the space that might stand him in best stead:
For who knew, he thought, what the amazement,
60   The eruption of clatter and blaze meant,
And if, in this minute of wonder,
No outlet, 'mid lightning and thunder,
Lay broad, and, his shackles all shivered,
The lion at last was delivered?
65   Ay, that was the open sky o'erhead;
And you saw by the flash on his forehead,
By the hope in those eyes wide and steady,
He was leagues in the desert already,
Driving the flocks up the mountain,
70   Or catlike couched hard by the fountain
To waylay the date-gathering negress:
So guarded he entrance or egress.
"How he stands!" quoth the King: "we may well
swear,

52. heapy: heaped up, massive: a Miltonism.

58. On the space] O' the space (*1870, 1875*); On space (*1872, 1884, 1888*). A rare example of *1888* agreeing with a reading introduced in a volume of selections rather than in a previous collected edition; cp. *Time's Revenges* 25n.

66-7. This emphasis on the lion's eyes (see also ll. 54, 94) may reflect a similar one in *Blackwood's*. Note esp. such phrases as 'The monster views, with sullen glare'; 'Once more he glares around'; 'His huge round eyes'; 'with stern composure ey'd him'. None of them is found in Schiller.

69.] EBB. suggested 'Or driving', then retracted the suggestion.

70. Cp. *Bernard de Mandeville* 260.   *crouched*] couched (*1849-88*).

73-7. Cp. *The Glove and the Lions* 12: 'Said Francis then, "Faith, gentlemen, we're better here than there'.

73. How he stands!: B. often uses 'stand' in an active sense: cp. Johnson's *Plan of A Dictionary* (1747): 'the verb *stand* has one sense, as opposed to *fall*, and another as opposed to *fly*'. For B. the second sense is intensified into an assertion of existence, often with the connotation of resistance (again following *J.*, two of whose definitions of 'stand' are 'to be in any posture of resistance' and 'to succeed, to persist or persevere'). Cp. esp. *Saul* (1855) 312 ('See the Christ stand!'), where the word approaches the extreme sense 'to come into existence, be discovered existing'. There is a distinct change in later usage, where it is often pejoratively contrasted to motion and progress, e.g. *Rabbi Ben Ezra* 33: 'Each sting that bids nor sit nor stand but go!'

"No novice, we've won our spurs elsewhere,
75 "And so can afford the confession
"We exercise wholesome discretion
"In keeping aloof from his threshold;
"Once hold you, those jaws want no fresh hold,
"Their first would too pleasantly purloin
80 "The visitor's brisket or surloin:
"But who's he would prove so fool-hardy?
"Not the best man of Marignan, pardie!"

The sentence no sooner was uttered,
Than over the rails a glove fluttered,
85 Fell close to the lion, and rested:
The dame 'twas, who flung it and jested
With life so, De Lorge had been wooing
For months past; he sate there pursuing
His suit, weighing out with nonchalance
90 Fine speeches like gold from a balance.

Sound the trumpet, no true knight's a tarrier!
De Lorge made one spring at the barrier,

74. *we've won our spurs*: Francis I invaded Italy in the year he came to the throne, 1515, and himself fought at Marignano (see l. 82n.). He continued to lead his forces until his defeat at Pavia (1536).
80. *surloin*] sirloin (*1884*). The original is the older spelling and was still current in the 19th century; since it occurs in all other eds. (incl. *1872*, the volume of selections of which *1884* was a reissue), the *1884* reading may have been introduced by the compositor.
82. *Marignan*: the French, led by Francis I (see l. 74n.) defeated an army of Swiss mercenaries at Marignano (now Melegnano), a village near Milan, in 1515; both sides suffered heavy casualties. *pardie*: from 'par dieu', 'by God'. For a similar anglicized French usage see l. 169.
86.] EBB. suggested 'The Lady who', then retracted the suggestion.
91-102. This passage draws on all the sources. De Lorge's retrieval of the glove from beside the immobile lion is close to Schiller's version, in which the beasts also remain motionless, and contrasts with Hunt's 'lions wild'; his own 'calm' may owe something to the *Blackwood's* description of him moving 'Slow, and with tranquil mien', and contrasts with the galvanic 'leaps' performed by Hunt's de Lorge. Lines 100-2 derive solely from Hunt: '"By God! cried Francis, "rightly done!" and rose from where he sat; / "No love," quoth he, "but vanity, set love a task like that"' (23-4).
92. *spring*] leap (*1849-88*).

Walked straight to the glove,—while the lion
Ne'er moved, kept his far-reaching eye on
95 The palm-tree-edged desert-spring's sapphire,
And the musky oiled skin of the Caffre,—
Picked it up, and as calmly retreated,
Sprang back where the lady was seated,
And full in the face of its owner
Flung the glove—

100   "Your heart's queen, you dethrone her?
"So should I"—cried the King—"'twas mere vanity,
"Not love, set the task to humanity!"
Lords and ladies alike turned with loathing
From such a proved wolf in sheep's clothing.

105 Not so, I; for I caught an expression
In her brow's undisturbed self-possession
Amid the Court's scoffing and merriment,
As if from no pleasing experiment
She rose, yet of pain not much heedful
110 So long as the process was needful—
As if she had tried in a crucible
To what "speeches like gold" were reducible,
And, finding the finest prove copper,
Felt the smoke in her face was but proper;
115 To know what she had *not* to trust to,
Was worth all the ashes, and dust too.
She went out 'mid hooting and laughter;
Clement Marot stayed; I followed after,
And asked, as a grace, what it all meant—

---

96. Caffre] Kaffir (*1849-88*). The *1845* spelling is the older form. The term is used here as a synonym of 'negress' (l. 71), rather than in any of its more precise senses.
98. Sprang] Leaped (*1849-88*).
111-14. The Lady's 'experiment' (l. 108) proves De Lorge's fine words to be insincere, as a chemist's test proves base metal not to be gold (since it vaporizes at a lower temperature).
111-12. With ll. 147-52, perhaps influenced by *Blackwood's*, which has the lady tell her lover, 'Sir Knight, I would fain put your vows to the test', developing Schiller: 'Sir knight, if your love is as hot as you swear to me at every hour, well, pick my glove up!'
114. the smoke] smoke (*1872, 1884*).
119. a grace: a favour.

120   If she wished not the rash deed's recalment?
      "For I"—so I spoke—"am a Poet:
      "Human nature,—behoves that I know it!"

      She told me, "Too long had I heard
      "Of the deed proved alone by the word:
125   "For my love,—what De Lorge would not dare!
      "With my scorn—what De Lorge could compare!
      "And the endless descriptions of death
      "He would brave when my lip formed a breath,
      "I must reckon as braved, or, of course,
130   "Doubt his word—and moreover, perforce,
      "For such gifts as no lady could spurn,
      "Must offer my love in return.
      "When I looked on the lion, it brought
      "All the dangers at once to my thought,
135   "Encountered by all sorts of men
      "Before he was lodged in his den,—
      "From the poor slave whose club or bare hands
      "Dug the trap, set the snare on the sands,
      "With no King and no Court to applaud,
140   "By no shame, should he shrink, overawed,
      "Yet to capture the creature made shift
      "That his rude boys might laugh at the gift,—
      "To the page who last leaped o'er the fence
      "Of the pit, on no greater pretence
145   "Than recover the bonnet he dropped
      "Lest his pay for a week should be stopped—
      "So, wiser I judged it to make
      "One trial what 'death for my sake'
      "Really meant, while the power was yet mine,
150   "Than defer it till time should define
      "Such a phrase not so simply as I,
      "Who took it to mean just 'to die.'

120. the rash deed's recalment: 'the rash deed to be recalled, undone'.
124.] EBB. quoted 'only proved' and suggested 'proved alone', 'Because she did not mean "only proved" but "not proved at all"'.
126.] EBB. quoted 'With my scorn found he woe to compare' and objected to the 'doubtful sense'.
133-46. The construction is faulty: it requires the 'page' to be involved in the process of bringing the lion to 'his den', which his action clearly post-dates.
133. the lion] your lion (*1849-88*).
149.] EBB. quoted 'yet power was' and suggested 'the power yet was': 'it seems less strained in the rhythm'.

"The blow a glove gives is but weak—
"Does the mark yet discolour my cheek?
155   "But when the heart suffers a blow,
"Will the pain pass so soon, do you know?"

I looked, as away she was sweeping,
And saw a youth eagerly keeping
As close as he dared to the doorway:
160   No doubt that a noble should more weigh
His life than befits a plebeian;
And yet, had our brute been Nemean—
(I judge by a certain calm fervor
The youth stepped with, forward to serve her)
165   —He'd have scarce thought you did him the worst
turn
If you whispered "Friend, what you'd get, first earn!"
And when, shortly after, she carried
Her shame from the Court, and they married,
To that marriage some happiness, maugre
170   The voice of the Court, I dared augur.

For De Lorge, he made women with men vie,
These in wonder and praise, those in envy;
And in short stood so plain a head taller
That he wooed and won . . How do you call her?
175   The beauty, that rose in the sequel
To the King's love, who loved her a week well;
And 'twas noticed he never would honour
De Lorge (who looked daggers upon her)

156.] EBB. suggested 'pain' instead of 'hurt', to avoid a clash with 'heart' in the next line.
160. a noble: i.e. the 'youth', not de Lorge.
162. Nemean: Nemea was 'a town of Argolis . . . with a wood, where Hercules, in the 16th year of his age, killed the celebrated Nemaean lion. . . . It was the first labor of Hercules to destroy it; and the hero, when he found that his arrows and his club were useless against an animal whose skin was hard and impenetrable, seized him in his arms and squeezed him to death' (*Lemprière*).
167.] EBB. quoted 'speedily after' and suggested either 'quickly' or 'shortly': 'the reason being the rhythm *in reference to the previous line*'.
169. maugre: despite; only occurrence in B. Cp. l. 82n.
171-6. This part of De Lorge's career appears to be fictitious.
171-2. This rhyme appears in Butler's *Hudibras* I ii 835-6: 'Until Magnano, who did envy / That two should with so many men vye'.
175. in the sequel: after her marriage to De Lorge.

With the easy commission of stretching
180 His legs in the service and fetching
His wife from her chamber those straying
Sad gloves she was always mislaying,
While the King took the closet to chat in,—
But of course this adventure came pat in;
185 And never he finished the story,
How bringing the glove brought such glory,
But the wife smiled—"His nerves are grown firmer—
"Mine he brings now and utters no murmur!"

Venienti occurrite morbo!
190 With which moral I drop my theorbo.

185. he finished] the King told (*1849-88*).
186. the glove] a glove (*1849-88*).
189. Lit., 'meet the disease in its first stage', glossed by ll. 111-16 and 147-52
to mean, 'make your test before it's too late'. An epigram of the Roman
satirical poet Persius (AD 34-62).
190. theorbo: a large lute, having long bass strings. Perhaps alluding to the
great importance of musical instruments, the lute esp., in Ronsard's poetry
and in his definition of the poet: see B. Jeffrey, 'The Idea of Music in
Ronsard's Poetry', in T. Cave (ed.), *Ronsard the Poet* (1973). The theorbo is
not a common representative of poetic expression or inspiration, but cp.
Quarles, *Divine Emblems* (a favourite book of B.'s), Bk. I, *Invocation* 1-3:
'Rouse thee, my soul! and drain thee from the dregs / Of vulgar thoughts;
screw up the heighten'd pegs / Of thy sublime theorbo'.

★ 54 Translation of lines by Dante ('And sinners were we to the extreme hour')

First publ. in *Letters of RB and EBB* i 348; repr. *LK* 336 (which notes the first draft of l. 1: 'And sinners to the extreme hour were we;') and *Penguin* ii 951. Our text is that of the MS (now at Wellesley College) of B.'s letter of 21 Dec. 1845, the date of composition. The lines come from *Purgatorio* v 53-7. For details, including the passage in Italian, see headnote to *Sordello*, I 363.

> And sinners were we to the extreme hour;
> *Then*, light from heaven fell, making us aware,
> So that, repenting us and pardoned, out
> Of life we passed to God, at peace with Him
> 5   Who fills the heart with yearning Him to see.

★ 55 Translation of Quatrain Attributed to Pietro of Abano ('Studying my ciphers, with the compass')

First publ. *Letters of RB and EBB* i 462; repr. *LK* 444. B.'s transcript, and his account of the poem's composition, are in his letter of 8 Feb. 1846, from the MS of which (now at Wellesley College) our text is taken. It follows his extempore translation from Lorenzo de Medici (p. 373), which he did to rival that of Leigh Hunt:

> Now Ba thinks nothing can be worse than that? Then read *this* which I really told Hunt and got his praise for. Poor dear wonderful persecuted Pietro d'Abano wrote this quatrain on the people's plaguing him about his mathematical studies and wanting to burn him—he helped to build Padua Cathedral, wrote a Treatise on Magic still extant, and passes for a conjuror in his country to this day—when there is a storm the mothers tell the children that he is in the air; his pact with the evil one obliged him to drink no *milk*; no natural human food! You know Tieck's novel about him? Well, this quatrain, I believe truly, to have been discovered in a well near Padua some fifty years ago:
>
> > Studiando le mie cifre, col compasso
> > Rilevo, che presto sarò sotterra—
> > Perchè del mio saper si fa gran chiasso,
> > E gl'ignoranti m'hanno mosso guerra.
>
> Affecting, is it not, in its simple child like plaining? Now so, if I remember, I turned it—word for word—[quotes translation].

The date of this impromptu translation cannot be determined. B. had known Hunt since 1836. B. quoted a slightly different version of his translation many years later in a note to *Pietro of Abano* (1880) 39-40. Writing to F. J. Furnivall, he quoted the lines again and gave a quite different account of his impromptu composition of them (letter of 21 Oct. 1881; *Trumpeter* 36-7): he ascribes them to a meeting in Florence with 'Father Prout' (the writer F. H. Mahony). This meeting may have taken place during B.'s visit to Florence in 1844, but is more likely to date from a period in 1848 during which the two men were constantly together (see *Letters of EBB* i 385-6); B. presumably forgot, either at the time of his meeting with Mahony or when he wrote to Furnivall, that he had previously extemporized and written the translation down. In *Final Reliques of Father Prout* (1860) p. iv, Mahony gave the following account:

> From Florence the poet Browning has sent for this edition some lines lately found in the Eugenian Hills, traced on a marble slab that covered the bones of Pietro d'Abano, held in his old age to be an astrologer . . . Of which epitaph the poet has supplied this vernacular rendering *verbatim*:
>
> > "Studying my cyphers with the compass,
> > I find I shall soon be under the daisy;

Because of my lore folks make such a rumpus,
That every dull dog is thereat *unaisy*."

The last word, mocking Irish pronunciation, might suggest that Mahony himself had altered B.'s wording; alternatively, that B. adapted his translation for Mahony. Variants from *1880* and *Furnivall* are recorded in the notes.

EBB. added her own translation of the lines to the letter containing B.'s:

With my compass I take up my ciphers, poor scholar, . .
Who myself shall be taken down soon under the ground . .
Since the world at my learning roars out in its choler,
And the blockheads have fought me all round.

In her letter of 10 Feb. 1846 (*LK* 448) she expressed her approval of B.'s translation. B.'s interest in Abano reflects his general preoccupation with figures of occult learning: see *Pauline*, epigraph (I 26) and *Paracelsus*; this particular quatrain presumably appealed to him as an analogy of his own plight after the publication of *Sordello*: cp. his translation of a Goethe epigram (p. 453).

Studying my ciphers, with the compass
I reckon—who soon shall be below ground,
Because of my lore they make great "rumpus,"
And against me war makes each dull rogue round.

¶ 55. *1-2*.] Studying my ciphers with the compass, / I reckon—I soon shall be below-ground; (*1880*); Studying my cyphers with the compass, / I gather I soon shall be below ground, (*1881*).

3. Because of] Because, of (*1880*).   *they*] folks (*1880*); men (*1881*).   "rumpus,"] rumpus, (*1880, 1881*).

4. *against me war*] war on myself (*1880, 1881*).

★ 56 Translation of Lines by Lorenzo de' Medici ('Where's Luigi Pulci, that one don't the man see?')

First publ. *Letters of RB and EBB* i 461; repr. *LK* 443. Not previously publ. in a collection of B.'s poems. Composed impromptu in a postscript to B.'s letter of 8 Feb. 1846, from the MS of which (now at Wellesley College) our text is taken: 'See those lines in the Athenaeum on Pulci with Hunt's translation—all wrong—"*che non si sente*," being—"that one does not *hear* him" i.e. the ordinarily noisy fellow—and the rest, male, pessime! Sic verte, meo periculo, mî ocelle!' The Latin means 'bad, very bad! Translate it thus, at my peril, my beloved'; B. then quotes the text. He refers to a review of Leigh Hunt's *Stories from the Italian Poets: with Lives of the Writers* in the *Athenaeum* of 7 Feb. 1846 which quotes both the Italian original of these lines, from a poem entitled *La Caccia col Falcone* ('The Falcon-Hunt') by Lorenzo de' Medici, 'the Magnificent' (*c.*1449-92), and Hunt's translation of them:

Luigi Pulci ov'è, che non si sente?
Egli se n'ando dianzi in qual boschetto,
Che qualche fantasia ha per la mente;
Vorr a fantasticar forse un sonnetto.

"And where's Luigi Pulci? I saw *him*."
"Oh, in the wood there. Gone, depend upon it,
To vent some fancy in his brain—some whim,
That will not let him rest till it's a sonnet."

B. follows his translation with his version of the quatrain attributed to Pietro of Abano: see p. 371.

Where's Luigi Pulci, that one don't the man see?
He just now yonder in the copse has '*gone it*'
Because across his mind there came a fancy;
He'll wish to fancify, perhaps, a sonnet!

¶56.2. '*gone it*': opposite this phrase B. wrote '(*n*'andô)', meaning that he was translating the Italian idiom by this slang phrase in contrast to Hunt's more genteel version.

57 Luria:
A Tragedy in Five Acts

Text and publication
First publ. with *A Soul's Tragedy*, *B & P* viii (13 Apr. 1846); *Luria* was first in order. Neither the pamphlet nor the individual plays were separately repr.; both plays repr. *1849* (in the same order but not linked, and with the dedication to the whole pamphlet affixed to *Luria* alone: see below), *1863*, *1868* (in reverse order), *1888* (*A Soul's Tragedy* in vol. iii, *Luria* in vol. vi). Four passages from the play were extracted for *1863*[2]: i 133-61 (headed 'Braccio, Commissary of the Republic, speaks of Florence and her Generals'); i 290-331 (headed 'The Moorish General in service of the Florentines anticipates peace'); iii 157-226 (headed 'A country's right to individual service and sacrifice'); and iv 164 (from 'Take revenge!') to the end of the act (headed 'Luria, with Florence in his power, takes his revenge'). The text is intermediate between *1849* and *1863* and has a number of unique readings. *Luria* was heavily revised, esp. in *1849* (19 lines added, 4 deleted), *1865* (the revised reissue of *1863*), and *1868* (the last two together have over 240 verbal revs.). The extent of revision is unusual for B., and contrasts with the light revision of *A Soul's Tragedy*. Our text is *1846*. The 'Secretary' is so called in Act I; in Acts III-V he is 'Jacopo'. We have left this minor inconsistency unaltered.

Composition and revision
Luria is unusual in B.'s work in that a detailed account of its composition can be compiled from his correspondence with EBB. He probably conceived the plot and jotted down notes about the characters on his return from Italy in Dec. 1844 (he had visited Florence during the trip). On 11 Feb. 1845 he wrote to EBB. of 'this darling "Luria"—so safe in my head, and a tiny slip of paper I cover with my thumb!' (*LK* 18). On 26 Feb. he gave a general sketch of the

Title.] in *1846* there was a dedication to the whole of *B & P* viii: 'I dedicate these last attempts for the present at dramatic poetry to a great dramatic poet; "wishing what I write may be read by his light:"—if a phrase originally addressed, by not the least worthy of his contemporaries, to Shakespeare, may be applied here, by one whose sole privilege is in a grateful admiration, to Walter Savage Landor. March 29, 1846.' In *1849-88*, where *Luria* and *A Soul's Tragedy* are separated, the dedication is to *Luria* alone, and has 'this last attempt' for 'these last attempts'; *1863-88* have 'in grateful admiration' for 'in a grateful admiration'. There is no date in *1849*; in *1863-88* the date is given as 'London, 1846'. The allusion is to Webster's preface to *The White Devil* (1612), in which Shakespeare is mentioned amongst other writers; B. alters 'their light' to 'his light'. For B.'s friendship with Landor, see headnote to *Sordello* (I 368).

subject in which the names of all the characters appear, except Husain and the Secretary (*LK* 26). On 3 May he wrote that he had been ill and had not been working on the play (*LK* 55). On 14 June he envisaged a 'grand clearance' of the material which eventually made up *B & P* vii (*DR & L*) and viii, by the autumn of 1845 (*LK* 95). EBB. was doubtful: on 9 Sept. she advised B. 'against printing the tragedies now' (*LK* 185). In fact much of *Luria* was not yet written. On 6 Oct., busy with *DR & L*, B. commented 'to press they shall go, and then the plays can follow gently' (*LK* 223). It seems he had done very little to *Luria* over the summer. On 27 Oct. he wrote: 'Yesterday I took out "Luria" & read it thro', the skeleton. I shall hope to finish it soon now. . . . Would you . . no, Act by Act, as I was about to propose that you read it,— that process would affect the oneness I most wish to preserve' (*LK* 251). However, he yielded to EBB.'s entreaty (6 Nov., *LK* 260) and brought Act I on 13 Nov. EBB. responded enthusiastically but advised B. not to overwork (12-14 Nov., *LK* 266-7), advice she reiterated throughout the period of composition. B. declared himself encouraged (16 Nov., *LK* 273) and brought Act II on 1 Dec.; again EBB. praised it warmly (2 Dec., *LK* 304). On 15 Dec. B. wrote that Act III 'is just done; that is, *being* done—but . . . I cannot bring it, copied, by Wednesday, as my sister went this morning on a visit for the week' (*LK* 321). (The inference that Sarianna Browning copied the play from the MS as B. gave it to her is confirmed by an allusion to *A Soul's Tragedy* in B.'s letter of 27 Feb. 1846; see headnote to that play, p. 181.) B. brought Act III on 23 Dec.; EBB. praised it even more highly than the first two (21-24 Dec., *LK* 341-2). On 10 Jan. 1846 he reported that Act IV 'is done—but too roughly this time!' (*LK* 377). On 17 Jan. it was 'done, and copied' (*LK* 397), and he brought it on 20 Jan. EBB. commented at length, praising the style but objecting to Luria's projected suicide (21 Jan., *LK* 406-7). On 31 Jan. B. wrote that, inspired by EBB.'s gift of a penholder, he had written 'about half my last act' the day before (*LK* 429). Allowing for the humorous exaggeration, this is not implausible; though EBB. urged him not to hurry (31 Jan.-1 Feb., *LK* 433), he brought Act V on 9 Feb. On 11 Feb. B. wrote: 'And now, Luria, so long as the parts cohere and the whole is discernible, all will be well yet. I shall not look at it, nor think of it, for a week or two, and then see what I have forgotten' (*LK* 451). B. was unwell during the next fortnight, and on 26 Feb. EBB. demurred at returning the fair copy of the MS for him to revise (*LK* 495); she finally did so on 19 Mar., giving B. her critical notes on the same day (see below, *Criticism*). On 22 Mar. B. was 'unwell and entirely irritated with this sad Luria . . . I have corrected it, cut it down, and it may stand & pledge me to doing better hereafter' (*LK* 551). EBB. wrote reassuringly, but though the MS was ready for the printers on 25 Mar., B. was still despondent (*LK* 558-9). He was less so when he sent EBB. the proofs on 29 Mar. (*LK* 568). Judging from EBB.'s comments in her letter of 30 Mar. (*LK* 573), revision between MS and proof seems to have been most extensive for Act V. On 1 Apr. B. wrote acknowledging EBB.'s influence: 'I corrected everything,— altered, improved—Did you notice the alterations (curtailments) in Luria?' (*LK* 579). On 7 Apr. he sent her the proofs of the whole *B & P* pamphlet; it was published on 13 Apr.

Sources and influences

(i) *Historical*. The historical background to *Luria* is slight. Florence fought and conquered Pisa in 1406, for political and mercantile reasons. From his researches for *Sordello*, e.g. in Sismondi *Hist.*, B. could have gathered various accounts of the Florence—Pisa struggle; of the details which these accounts may have suggested, the most important are a rivalry between two of the Florentine commanders, a secret visit by the ruler of Pisa to the Florentine camp, and civilian supervision of the conduct of the war.

(ii) *Literary*. B. told EBB.: 'Luria is a Moor, of Othello's country' (26 Feb. 1845, *LK* 26); the comparison with *Othello* has frequently been made (e.g. DeVane *Handbook* 188). Like Othello, Luria is a mercenary in command of the army of an Italian city-state, in love with one of its noblewomen (Domizia), and kills himself on discovering a plot against him. The role of Iago is divided between Braccio, the author of the plot against Luria, and Puccio, the old lieutenant who resents a younger man's promotion. Contrasts are equally significant. As DeVane suggests, Luria's devotion is more to Florence than to Domizia. Where Othello gives way to Iago's insinuations, Luria refuses to believe that Florence could betray him; where Iago plots Othello's downfall ruthlessly, but without obvious motive, Braccio repents his unjust suspicion of Luria, but has been guided throughout by clear (and defensible) motives; where Desdemona loves Othello devotedly, Domizia never reciprocates Luria's love (see *Criticism*). Cp. also *Coriolanus*, which concerns a military commander who does turn against his city when it treats him ungratefully; B.'s Tiburzio, the Pisan general who tries to make Luria change sides, may owe something to the character of Aufidius. Shelley's *Marenghi* (a source for *England*) is based on an incident in the Florence—Pisa war in which a Florentine exhibits heroic devotion to his city despite having been exiled; contrast Byron's *Marino Faliero*, where the Doge of Venice plots against the city to avenge an insult. The general concept of Florence's ingratitude to its most patriotic citizens may owe something to the exile of Dante, treated in Byron's *The Prophecy of Dante*. L. Poston ('Browning's Political Skepticism: *Sordello* and the Plays', *PMLA* lxxxviii [1973] 260-70) suggests the influence of Henry Taylor's admired historical verse drama, *Philip van Artevelde* (1834): 'Luria resembles Philip perhaps more closely than any other Browning character; both are capable and energetic military leaders whose characters are displayed against a background of factionalism, civil war, and treachery' (p. 261).

Parallels in B.

The encounter of individual idealism (artistic, political, etc.) with the pressures of state and community is a recurrent theme in B.'s early work, e.g. *Paracelsus, Strafford, Sordello*; the latter is most important for *Luria*. B. wrote to EBB. that Luria 'devotes himself to something he thinks Florence, and the old fortune follows' (26 Feb. 1845, *LK* 26); cp. the subtitle of *Patriot*, 'An Old

Story' (i.e. of betrayal and disillusion). D'Ormea in *King Victor* anticipates Braccio, and Djabal in *Return of the Druses* resembles Luria, particularly as embodying a clash between reason and passion. With Luria's desert mysticism, cp. *Through the Metidja*. B. himself drew attention to the contrast between *Luria* and its companion-piece, *A Soul's Tragedy*, in their treatment of political idealism (see headnote to *A Soul's Tragedy*, p. 182).

Criticism

B & P viii was not widely reviewed. The main notice was by John Forster in the *Examiner* (25 Apr. 1846, p. 260), who was judiciously complimentary about *Luria*: 'if Mr. Browning's *tone* of treatment were simpler, less remote, less abstrusely metaphysical, the stage would find in him its noblest supporter in these latter days'. Landor responded warmly to B.'s dedication of the pamphlet to him: 'And now accept my thanks for the richest of Easter offerings made to anyone for many years. I staid at home last evening on purpose to read *Luria*, and if I lost any good music (as I certainly did) I was well compensated in mind' (*LK* 637n.2). B. and EBB., however, discussed the play in great detail. As with *A Soul's Tragedy*, B. stressed to EBB. that *Luria* was begun before he knew her, and so formed part of the work he wanted to put behind him (1 Apr. 1846, *LK* 580); his poor opinion of the play ('a pure exercise of *cleverness*, even where most successful,—clever attempted reproduction of what was conceived by another faculty, and foolishly let pass away'—22 Mar. 1846, *LK* 551) should be seen in this light. In his preliminary sketch of the play to EBB., B. set 'dear foolish (ravishing must his folly be)—golden-hearted Luria' against the Florentine characters 'with their worldly wisdom, and Tuscan shrewd ways,—and, as for me, the misfortune is, I sympathize just as much with these as with him' (26 Feb. 1845, *LK* 26). The 'misfortune' relates to the fact that *Luria* was a play, whereas B. had declared to EBB. his intention of writing 'what I hope I was born to begin and end,—"R.B. a poem"', i.e. a poem of self-expression rather than one involving 'a dramatic sympathy with certain modifications of passion' (11 Feb. 1845, *LK* 17). B. also made it clear that *Luria* was written 'for a purely imaginary Stage' (27 Oct. 1845, *LK* 251), and commented further: 'It is all in long speeches—the *action*, *proper*, is in them—they are no descriptions, or amplifications—but here . . in a drama of this kind, all the *events*, (and interest,) take place in the *minds* of the actors . . somewhat like Paracelsus in that respect' (11 Jan. 1846, *LK* 381; see preface to *Paracelsus*, I 113). Some of B.'s most notable comments were in response to EBB.'s criticism, e.g. his defence of Luria's suicide (see iv 281–329n.), and his admission of failure in the characterization of Domizia. In the latter case B. gave a rare glimpse of his method of composition: in his letter of 11 Feb. 1846, when the play was written and revised (but not yet in proof), he wrote: 'Domizia is all wrong—I told you I knew that her special colour had faded,—it was but a bright line, and the more distinctly deep that it was so narrow—One of my half-dozen words on my scrap of paper "pro memoria" was, under the "Act V," "*she loves*"—to which I could not bring it, you see! Yet the play requires it still,—something may yet be effected, though: I meant that she should propose to go to Pisa with him, and begin a new life. But there is no hurry—I suppose it is no use publishing much before Easter—I will try and remember what my whole character *did* mean—it was, in two words, understood at the time by "panther's-beauty"—on which hint I ought to have spoken! But the work grew cold, and you came between, and the sun put out the fire on the hearth' (*LK* 451; note the allusion to *Othello* I iii 166, Othello's declaration of love to Desdemona: 'Upon this hint I spake'). B.'s attempt to rework Domizia's part failed: he wrote to EBB. on 1 Apr. 1846, shortly before receiving the proofs: 'I *could not* bring her to my purpose. I left the neck stiff that was to have bowed of its own accord—for nothing graceful could be accomplished by pressing with both hands on the head above! I meant to make her leave off her own projects thro' love of Luria: as it is, they in a manner fulfil themselves, so far as she has any power over them, and then, she being left unemployed, sees Luria, begins to see him,—having hitherto seen only her own ends which he was to further' (*LK* 579-80).

EBB.'s critical notes on the play are recorded in the notes (*Wellesley MS*; her comments come from this source unless otherwise specified). Almost all concern clarity or plainness; she particularly opposed syntactical inversions. In her letters to B. she commented several times that the style of the play was too smooth and diffuse (12 Nov. and 2-3 Dec. 1845, 21 Jan. and 10 Feb. 1846, *LK* 267, 304, 407, 445). She praised the play, act by act and as a whole (though she rather overworked the adjective 'noble'), making at the same time three objections to the conduct of the action: the over-subtlety of some of the speeches (e.g. Husain's: see iv 169-83n.), Luria's suicide, and the character of Domizia, whose eventual retraction she thought insufficiently motivated (30 Mar. 1846, *LK* 573). EBB. found herself in an awkward position when, after B. showed her *A Soul's Tragedy* with warnings of its inferior quality, she realized that she preferred it to *Luria* (10 and 29 Mar. 1846, *LK* 525, 569, and see headnote to *A Soul's Tragedy*, p. 182).

Persons

LURIA, a Moor, Commander of the Florentine Forces.
HUSAIN, a Moor, his friend.
PUCCIO, the old Florentine Commander, now Luria's Chief Officer.
BRACCIO, Commissary of the Republic of Florence.

Persons. Luria: B. may have derived the name from two sources which evoke respectively Luria's military prowess and oriental birth: the famous Italian seaman Roger de Loria (also Lauria or Luria, 1250-1305), who commanded the navies of Aragon and Sicily; and the Jewish mystic Luria (Isaac ben Solomon, 1534-74), who was born in Jerusalem and later lived in Cairo.

Braccio: *Ohio* cites a celebrated Italian mercenary, Braccio de Montone, mentioned in *Biographie*, but B.'s Braccio is not a soldier, and a far likelier source is Alexandra Braccio, who according to *Biographie* was a 'Florentine

Jacopo (Lapo), his Secretary.
Tiburzio, Commander of the Pisans.
Domizia, a noble Florentine Lady.

Time, 14—.

Scene, Luria's Camp between Florence and Pisa.

Act I

Morning.

Braccio, *as dictating to his* Secretary; Puccio *standing by*.

> Braccio. [*To* Puccio] Then you join battle in an
>   hour?
> Puccio.   Not I;
> Luria, the Captain.
>   Braccio. [*To the* Secretary] "In an hour, the battle."
>   [*To* Puccio] Sir, let your eye run o'er this
>   loose digest,
> And see if very much of your report
> 5 Have slipped away through my civilian phrase.
> Does this instruct the Signory aright
> How army stands with army?
>   Puccio. [*Taking the paper*] All seems here:
> —That Luria, seizing with our City's force
> The several points of vantage, hill and plain,
> 10 Shuts Pisa safe from help on every side,
> And baffling the Lucchese arrived too late,

---

poet and litterateur of the 15th century who distinguished himself by his
aptitude for politics and his literary talents. He was, for some time, secretary
of the Republic of Florence and died in 1503'. For 'Commissary', see l. 27n.

  Domizia: *Ohio* cites Domitia, wife of the Roman Emperor Domitian.
i *Morning*: cp. *Pippa*, which is divided into four parts, Morning, Noon,
Evening, Night; and *Colombe*, which has the same structure as *Luria*, viz.
Morning, Noon, Afternoon, Evening, Night.
i 6. *Signory*: the ruling council of Florence. B. uses the term loosely, making
no distinction between the various civic and political institutions which
operated during the medieval period (see l. 27n.). Cp. (noting l. 79) *Othello* I
iii 76-7: 'Most potent, grave, and reverend signiors, / My very noble and
approved good masters'.
i *11. Lucchese*: from Lucca, a town 20 km north of Pisa, and one of its bitterest
enemies for much of the period. But Lucca was also concerned about the

Must, in the battle he delivers now,
Beat her best troops and first of chiefs.
        Braccio.   So sure?
Tiburzio's a consummate captain too!
15   *Puccio.* Luria holds Pisa's fortune in his hand.
        Braccio. [*To the* Secretary] "The Signory hold Pisa
            in their hand:"
Your own proved soldiership's our warrant, sir.
You, while my secretary ends his task,
Have out two horsemen, by the open roads,
To post with it to Florence!
20   *Puccio.* [*Returning the paper*] All seems here;
Unless . . . Ser Braccio, 'tis my last report!
Since Pisa's outbreak and my overthrow,
And Luria's hastening at the city's call
To save her as he only could, no doubt;
25   Till now that she is saved or sure to be,—
Whatever you tell Florence, I tell you:
Each day's note you, her Commissary, make
Of Luria's movements, I myself supply.

---

expansion of Florence in Tuscany. The help it gave Pisa in the 1405-6 war
was minimal; but see v 36n.
18. You] So (*1849-88*). EBB. had quoted 'And' at the proof stage, and
suggested the present reading as 'directer & more animated'.
i *21. Ser*: short for 'Messere', Master.
i *22-5.* Cp. *Othello* I iii 221-6: '[Duke.] The Turk with a most mighty
preparation makes for Cyprus. Othello, the fortitude of the place is best
known to you; and though we have there a substitute of most allowed
sufficiency, yet opinion, a most sovereign mistress of effects, throws a more
safer voice on you'.
i *22. outbreak*: eruption or rebellion. Historically, Florence had bought Pisa
from its former ruler; the Pisans refused to recognize the transaction. At
v 46-7 Puccio implies that Florence's rivals (Pisa, Siena, Lucca) had gone to
war in an effort to forestall her political and military expansion.   *overthrow*: demotion.
i *27. Commissary*: Braccio is probably a member of the Dieci di Balia, a
committee of ten appointed in wartime to manage the conduct of the war.
Representatives of the Dieci often accompanied commanders, especially
mercenaries, in the field.
i *28.*] at the proof stage, EBB. quoted 'Myself supply', and commented: 'Is
that quite correct? I *myself supply*— .. myself supplies .. I doubt a little. Then a
slight shadow seems to fall over the meaning—one thinks twice. Why not
"Of Luria's movements, I myself supply" . . It is better perhaps than the
"move"'. The original reading cannot be reconstructed with certainty: it was

No youngster am I longer, to my cost;
30 Therefore while Florence gloried in her choice
And vaunted Luria, whom but Luria still,
As courage, prudence, conduct, zeal and faith
Had never met in any man before,
I saw no pressing need to swell the cry:
35 But now, this last report and I have done—
So, ere to-night comes with its roar of praise,
'Twere not amiss if someone old i' the trade
Subscribed with, "True, for once rash counsel's best;
"This Moor of the bad faith and doubtful race,
40 "This boy to whose untried sagacity,
"Raw valour, Florence trusts without reserve
"The charge to save her, justifies her choice;
"In no point has this stranger failed his friends;
"Now praise"! I say this, and it is not here.
45 *Braccio.* [*To the* Secretary] Write, "Puccio,
      superseded in the charge
"By Luria, bears full witness to his worth,
"And no reward our Signory can give
"Their champion but he'll back it cheerfully."
Aught more? Five minutes hence, both messengers!
                              [*Exit* Puccio.
50 *Braccio.* [*After a pause, and while he slowly tears the
      paper into shreds*] I think . . . pray God I hold
      in fit contempt
This warfare's noble art and ordering,
And,—once the brace of prizers fairly matched,
Poleaxe with poleaxe, knife with knife as good,—

perhaps 'Of Luria's every move, myself supply'.
i *31.*] EBB. quoted 'And vaunted Luria Luria, who but he?', and commented:
'"—*whom* but *him*"—is it not?'
i *32.*] As if zeal, courage, prudence, conduct, faith (*1849–88*).
i *38. Subscribed:* lit., 'wrote below', suggesting also 'to attest by signing', 'to
sign one's name as a witness' (see l. 46), and 'to give one's assent to a
statement, opinion' (*OED* 3, 6, 7).
i *39–43.*] EBB. quoted 'This Moor of the bad faith &c', and commented:
'You say afterwards "The boy" & "the stranger" . . Why not "This boy" &
"this stranger" to carry forward the emphasis?'
i *39. bad faith:* referring to Luria's religion, suggesting also untrustworthi-
ness.   *doubtful race:* meaning not uncertainty about Luria's origins, but
mistrust of his character. Cp. *Othello* I iii 52–3: '[Iago.] These Moors are
changeable in their wills'. See also ll. 387–90n.
i *52. brace of prizers:* pair of prize-fighters.

Spit properly at what men term their skill . . .
55 Yet here I think our fighter has the odds;
With Pisa's strength diminished thus and thus,
Such points of vantage in our hands and such,
With Lucca off the stage, too,—all's assured:
Luria must win this battle. Write the Court
60 That Luria's trial end and sentence pass!
    Secretary. Patron,—
    Braccio.   Aye, Lapo?
    Secretary.   If you trip, I fall;
'Tis in self-interest I speak—
    Braccio.   Nay, nay,
You overshoot the mark, my Lapo! Nay!
When did I say pure love's impossible?
65 I make you daily write those red cheeks thin,
Load your young brow with what concerns it least,
And, when we visit Florence, let you pace
The Piazza by my side as if we talked,
Where all your old acquaintances may see:
70 You'd die for me, I should not be surprised!
Now then!
    Secretary. Sir, look about and love yourself!
Step after step the Signory and you
Tread gay till this tremendous point's to pass;
Which, pass not, pass not ere you ask yourself
75 Bears the brain steadily such draughts of fire,
Or too delicious may not prove the pride
Of this long secret Trial you dared plan,
Dare execute, you solitary here,
With the grey-headed toothless fools at home,
80 Who think themselves your lords, they are such
    slaves?

i *58. With Lucca*] Lucca still (*1849-88*).

i *67-9*. The implication is that Lapo will be shunned by his former
acquaintances for being thought to be in Braccio's confidence (because
Braccio is feared as an official concerned with public security).

i *68. Piazza*: perhaps the Piazza della Signoria, site of the traditional seat of
Florentine government, the Palazzo Vecchio.

i *74.*] EBB. quoted 'Which pass not, to yourself no question put—', and
commented: 'You are fond of that *absolute* construction—but I think that
sometimes it makes the meaning a little doubtful, & here there is some
weakness from the inversion. You simply mean to say . . "Which, do not
pass without consideration". Then, the "*put*" is a bad word at all times to my
ear'.

i *80. they are such slaves*] such slaves are they (*1868-88*). EBB. had quoted

If they pronounce this sentence as you bid,
Declare the treason, claim its penalty,—
And sudden out of all the blaze of life,
On the best minute of his brightest day,
85   From that adoring army at his back,
Thro' Florence' joyous crowds before his face,
Into the dark you beckon Luria . . .
            Braccio.   Then—
Why, Lapo, when the fighting-people vaunt,
We of the other craft and mystery,
90   May we not smile demure, the danger past?
            Secretary. Sir, no, no, no,—the danger, and your
                spirit
At watch and ward? Where's danger on your part
With that thin flitting instantaneous steel
'Gainst the blind bull-front of a brute-force world?
95   If Luria, that's to perish sure as fate,
Should have been really guiltless after all?
            Braccio. Ah, you have thought that?
            Secretary.   Here I sit, your scribe,
And in and out goes Luria, days and nights;
This Puccio comes; the Moor his other friend,

'such slaves are they?', and commented: 'Do you gain anything by the
inversion? If you write "they are such slaves", do you not on the contrary
gain, in force of opposition propriety of accent & directness—?'
i *81.*] EBB. quoted 'If as you bid this sentence they pronounce', and
commented: 'I have to protest against the frequent inversions. Why not
simply "If they pronounce this sentence, as you bid,"? Is there an objection?
And it gives the effect, I think, of more impulse, to these noble lines'.
i *84.* Cp., among many other such 'minutes' in B., *Two in the Campagna* 50:
'Then the good minute goes'; *One Word More* 73-4: 'Even he, the minute
makes immortal, / Proves, perchance, his mortal in the minute'; and *Ring* i
588: 'Saved for a splendid minute and no more'. Cp. also *Sordello* iv
446^447n.: 'hung a minute at the height / Then fell back to oblivion infinite'.
i *85.*] EBB. quoted 'the adoring army', and suggested the present reading.
i *89. the other craft and mystery*: politics, statecraft.   *mystery*: in the archaic
sense of 'trade, profession', though the more modern sense, as with 'craft', is
also suggested.
i *91-2. the danger, and your spirit / At watch and ward?*: i.e. 'how can there be
danger when *you* are on the alert?'
i *93-4.* EBB. found in these lines 'a noble, expressive figure'.
i *98-109.* EBB. found the description of Luria 'admirable', esp. ll. 104-6.

100   Husain; they talk—all that's feigned easily;
       He speaks (I would not listen if I could),
       Reads, orders, counsels;—but he rests sometimes,—
       I see him stand and eat, sleep stretched an hour
       On the lynx-skins, yonder; hold his bared black arms
105   Into the sun from the tent-opening; laugh
       When his horse drops the forage from his teeth
       And neighs to hear him hum his Moorish songs:
       That man believes in Florence as the Saint
       Tied to the wheel believes in God!
           Braccio.   How strange—
       You too have thought that!
110   *Secretary.*   Do but you think too,
       And all is saved! I only have to write,
       The man seemed false awhile, proves true at last;
       Bury it . . . so I write to the Signory . . .
       Bury this Trial in your breasts for ever,
115   Blot it from things or done or dreamed about,
       So Luria shall receive his meed to-day
       With no suspicion what reverse was near,—
       As if no meteoric finger hushed

i *100. all that's*] that's all (*1889*). The only verbal revision B. made to *Luria*
after the first printing of *1888*.
i *101. could*),] emended from 'could)' in *1846-65*; the comma is required by
the syntax.   *if I could*: 'if I could avoid it'.
i *106*. Cp. the description of a horse in Anne Finch, Countess of Winchilsea's
A Nocturnal Reverie (1713) 32: 'Till torn-up forage in his teeth we hear'.
i *108-9. the Saint / Tied to the wheel*: St Catherine of Alexandria, martyred,
according to legend, by being broken on a wheel, during the persecution of
the Christians by the Emperor Maxentius (early 4th century).
i *110. You too have thought that*: EBB. thought this 'finely characteristic'.
i *112-13. The man . . . it*] in quotation marks, *1863-88*.
i *113*.] EBB. quoted 'Bury it . . so I write the Signory', and commented: 'I
think you ought to have the preposition, either by . . "Bury it . . write I to
the Signory . ." or by putting the "to" into the text as it is, which would not
ruffle the line too much'.   *write to the*] write the (*1868-88*).
i *114-20. Bury . . . straight.*] in quotation marks, *1863-88*.
i *114. Trial in your breasts*] trial in your breast (*1868-88*).
i *115. or . . . or*: either . . . or (Elizabethan archaism).
i *116. meed*: reward.
i *118-20*. The image compares Luria's present happiness to a sunny day: a
storm-cloud threatens destruction, but a divine portent in the form of a
meteor averts this, and lets the sunshine continue. The thunder ('doom-
word') contained in the storm-cloud is Luria's prospective condemnation by
the Signory; the 'meteoric finger' represents the letter which Lapo hopes that

The doom-word just on the destroyer's lip,
120   Motioned him off, and let life's sun fall straight.
          Braccio. [Looks to the wall of the tent] Did he draw
              that?
          Secretary. With charcoal, when the watch
      Made the report at midnight; Lady Domizia
      Spoke of the unfinished Duomo, you remember;
      That is his fancy how a Moorish front
125   Might join to, and complete, the body,—a sketch,—
      And again where the cloak hangs, yonder in the
              shadow.
          Braccio. He loves that woman.
          Secretary.   She is sent the spy
      Of Florence,—spies on you as you on him:
      Florence, if only for Domizia's sake,
      Were surely safe. What shall I write?
130   *Braccio.*   I see—
      A Moorish front, nor of such ill design!
      Lapo, there's one thing plain and positive;
      Man seeks his own good at the whole world's cost.
      What? If to lead our troops, stand forth our chief,
135   And hold our fate, and see us at their beck,
      Yet render up the charge when peace returned,

Braccio will instruct him to write, withdrawing the charges against Luria and
asking the Signory to suppress the whole process of investigation and trial.
i *119. doom-word*: B. uses 'doom-words' to describe EBB.'s power to destroy
him by ending their relationship (6 Jan. 1846, *LK* 364).
i *121.*] at the proof stage, EBB. quoted 'Did he draw that?' and commented:
'It struck me before & does now again—why not . . for the sake of the
myopic readers, (the majority) . . put a <stage> direction here "*Looks to the
wall of the tent*"—?' EBB. presumably crossed out 'stage' because she
remembered that the play was not written for the theatre: see headnote,
p. 377.
i *123-5.* The Cathedral (Duomo) of Santa Maria del Fiore was begun in 1294,
but only consecrated in 1436. Its facade ('front') underwent much modifica-
tion: the original by Arnolfo di Cambio was continued by Francesco Talenti
and others, but was still unfinished when it was pulled down in 1588. Cp.
Old Pictures 278-80, where the completion of the bell-tower designed by
Giotto symbolizes political and social regeneration: 'The Campanile, the
Duomo's fit ally, / Soars up in gold its full fifty braccia, / Completing
Florence, as Florence, Italy'.
i *132-61.* This passage was extracted for *1863²*: see headnote, p. 374.
i *134. chief*] chiefs (*1849-88*).
i *136.*] EBB. quoted 'And yet renounce the same, its hour gone by', and

Have ever proved too much for Florentines,
Even for the best and bravest of ourselves—
If in the struggle when the soldier's sword
140 Before the statist's pen should sink its point,
And to the calm head yield the violent hand,
Virtue on virtue still have fallen away
Before ambition with unvarying fortune,
Till Florence' self at last in bitterness
145 Be forced to own defeat the natural end,
And, sparing further to expose her sons
To a vain strife and profitless disgrace,
Have said "The Foreigner, no child of mine,
"Shall henceforth lead my troops, reach height by
height
150 "The glory, then descend into the shame;

commented: 'This eloquence of Braccio should be quite uninvolved . . , now
should it not?—the connection of the different sentences, seen clearly—? Why
not without the inversion?' It seems that the prec. lines contained a referent
for 'the same', which has not survived B.'s revision.   *returned*] return
(*1868-88*).

i *137-43*.] EBB. quoted

Have ever proved too much for Florentines
Even for the best & bravest of ourselves—
If in the struggle when the soldier's sword
Before the statist's pen should sink its point,
And to the calm head, *yield*, the violent hand,
Virtue on virtue still have fallen away
Before ambition ..

and commented: 'By shifting a few of the unimportant words so, you make it
clear to run & read. And then by this shifting, you escape a rather
questionable-looking opposition of "after" & "before", in "If virtue *after*
virtue still have fallen *before* ambition"'. The italics make it clear that the
version EBB. quotes is one already altered by her. Note the further rev. of
ll. 140-1 in *1849-88*.

i *139. the struggle*: in the conscience of the military commander when the war
ends and he is tempted not to surrender power.

i *140-1*.] Should sink its point before the statist's pen, / And the calm head
replace the violent hand, (*1849-88*). A 'statist' is a politician or statesman. B.
may have recalled the word from *Hamlet* V ii 33-4: 'I once did hold it, as our
statists do, / A baseness to write fair'.

i *143. fortune*] fate (*1849-88*).

i *145. defeat*] such falls (*1849-88*).

i *148*.] Declare "The Foreigner, one not my child, (*1849-88*, except 'Declare,'
1863-88; 'foreigner', *1868-88*; *1863²* as *1849*).

"So shall rebellion be less guilt in him,
"And punishment the easier task for me"
—If on the best of us this brand she sets,
Can I suppose an utter alien here,
155 This Luria, our inevitable foe,
Confessed a mercenary and a Moor,
Born free from any ties that bind the rest
Of common faith in Heaven or hope on Earth,
No Past with us, no Future,—such a Spirit
160 Shall hold the path from which our staunchest broke,
Stand firm where every famed precursor fell?
My Lapo, I will frankly say these proofs
So duly noted of the man's intent,
Are for the doting fools at home, not me;
165 The charges here, they may be true or false,
—What is set down? Errors and oversights,
This dallying interchange of courtesies
With Pisa's General, all that hour by hour
Puccio's pale discontent has furnished us
170 Of petulant speeches, inconsiderate acts,
Now overhazard, overcaution now;
Even that he loves this Lady who believes
She outwits Florence, and whom Florence posted
By my procurement here, to spy on me,
175 Lest I one minute lose her from my sight—
She who remembering her whole House's fall,
That nest of traitors strangled in the birth,
Now labours to make Luria . . . poor device
As plain . . . the instrument of her revenge!
180 —That she is ever at his ear to prompt
Inordinate conceptions of his worth,

i *151-2.*] EBB. quoted 'So shall in him rebellion be less guilt, / And punishment for me the easier task', and commented: 'I propose still without the inversion . . "So shall rebellion be less guilt in *him*, / And punishment the easier task for *me*—" Is not the emphasis marked better so?'
i *153. this brand*] such brand (*1863-88; 1863²* as *1846*).   sets] set (*1863-88; 1863²* as *1846*).
i *154-5. here, / This*] here / Like (*1863²*).
i *157-9. Born free . . . Future*: cp. *Confessional* 73-4: 'No part in aught they hope or fear! / No Heaven with them, no Hell'.
i *157. from any*] from many (*1868-88*).
i *167. This*] A (*1863-88*).
i *169. Puccio's pale discontent*: in his sketch of the play for EBB. (26 Feb. 1845, *LK* 26) B. calls Puccio 'a pale discontented man'.
i *178-9. poor device / As plain*: 'as poor a stratagem as it is obvious'.

Exorbitant belief in its reward,
And after, when sure disappointment follows,
Proportionable rage at such a wrong—
185 Why, all these reasons, while I urge them most,
Weigh with me less than least; as nothing weigh!
Upon that broad Man's heart of his, I go!
On what I know must be, yet while I live
Will never be, because I live and know!
190 Brute-force shall not rule Florence! Intellect
May rule her, bad or good as chance supplies,—
But Intellect it shall be, pure if bad,
And Intellect's tradition so kept up
Till the good comes—'twas Intellect that ruled,
195 Not Brute-force bringing from the battle-field
The attributes of wisdom, foresight's graces
We lent it there to lure its grossness on;
All which it took for earnest and kept safe
To show against us in our market-place,
200 Just as the plumes and tags and swordsman's-gear
(Fetched from the camp where at their foolish best
When all was done they frightened nobody)
Perk in our faces in the street, forsooth,

i *182. its reward*] worth's reward (*1870-88*).
i *185.*] EBB. quoted 'Even these reasons while I urge them most—' and commented: 'This sounds to my ear *numerically* a weak line—this setting of "Even" as a dissyllable to open a line. "Why, even these reasons while I urge them most" would seem to give more freedom—will you ring it, & listen?'
i *187. Man's heart*] Man's-heart (*1863-65*); man's-heart (*1868-88*).
i *189. Will*] Shall (*1863-88*).
i *192, 194. Intellect . . . Intellect*] intellect . . . intellect (*1868-88*).
190-1. Cp. Bulwer Lytton's novel *Rienzi* (1835), set in 14th century Italy: 'the rival Spirits of Force and Intellect' (IX iv). Earlier Lytton had referred to 'knowledge' and 'brute force' (I v). See headnote to *Sordello*, I 362.
i *193-4. up / Till*] up! / Till (*1868-75*); up. / Till (*1888*, probably a mispr.; *1872 Morgan*[2] [see Editorial Note, p. vii] has 'up').
i *194. 'twas*] not italic, *1868-88*.
i *195. Brute-force*] brute-force (*1868-88*).
i *198.*] EBB. quoted 'And which it took for earnest &c' and commented: 'Did you mean to write "All which"? a slip of the pen perhaps?'   *took for earnest*: 'took to be a pledge [of future privilege]'.
i *200-4.* Cp. *Fifine* 1770-4: 'Why, those are helps thereto, which late we eyed askance, / And nicknamed unaware! Just so, a sword we call / Superfluous, and cry out against, at festival: / Wear it in time of war, its clink and clatter grate / O' the ear to purpose then!'

With our own warrant and allowance. No!
205 The whole procedure's overcharged,—its end
In too strict keeping with the bad first step.
To conquer Pisa was sheer inspiration!
Well then, to perish for a single fault,
Let that be simple justice!—There, my Lapo!
210 The Moorish front ill suits our Duomo's body—
Blot it out—and bid Luria's sentence come!
      *Luria. [Who, with Domizia, has entered unobserved at
the close of the last phrase, now advancing]* And Luria,
      Luria, what of Luria now?
      Braccio. Ah, you so close, Sir? Lady Domizia too?
I said it needs must be a busy moment
215 For one like you—that you were now i' the thick
Of your duties, doubtless, while we idlers sate . . .
      Luria. No—in that paper,—it was in that paper
What you were saying!
      Braccio.   Oh—my day's dispatch!
I censure you to Florence: will you see?
220   *Luria.* See your dispatch, the last, for the first
      time?
Why, if I should now? For in truth, Domizia,
He would be forced to set about another
In his sly cool way, the true Florentine,
To mention that important circumstance;
225 So while he wrote I should gain time, such time!
Do not send this!
      Braccio.   And wherefore?
      Luria.   These Lucchese
Are not arrived—they never will arrive!
And I must fight to-day, arrived or not,
And I shall beat Tiburzio, that is sure,
230 And then will be arriving my Lucchese,
But slowly, oh so slowly, just in time

i *205-9. The whole . . . justice*: the process whereby 'Brute-force' challenges
'Intellect' is, according to Braccio, clearly discernible in Luria's career. Just as
the 'sheer inspiration' of Luria's military victory belongs to the 'Brute-force'
of his nature, so the 'simple justice' of condemning him for the 'single fault'
of intending to seize power is appropriate to Braccio's 'Intellect'.
i *205. overcharged*: overloaded (with its ulterior, sinister motive).
i *207. inspiration!*] inspiration? (*1849-88*).
i *210. The*] A (*1849-88*).
i *211. s. d. advancing*] advances (*1888*).
i *221. Why*] Well (*1849-88*).
i *230. my*] his (*1863-88*).

To look upon my battle from the hills,
Like a late moon, of use to nobody,—
And I must break my battle up, send forth,
235 Surround on this side, hold in check on that!
Then comes to-morrow, we negotiate,
You make me send for fresh instructions home,
—Incompleteness, incompleteness!
    Braccio.   Ah, we scribes!
Why, I had registered that very point,
240 The non-appearance of our foes' ally,
As a most happy fortune; both at once
Were formidable—singly faced, each falls.
    Luria. And so no battle for my Florentines!
No crowning deed, decisive and complete,
245 For all of them, the simple as the wise,
Old, young, alike, that do not understand
Our wearisome pedantic art of war,
By which we prove retreat may be success,
Delay—best speed,—half loss, at times,—whole
    gain—
250 They want results . . . as if it were their fault!
And you, with warmest wish to be my friend,
Will not be able now to simply say
"Your servant has performed his task—enough!
"You ordered, he has executed: good!
255 "Now walk the streets in holiday attire,
"Congratulate your friends, till noon strikes fierce,
"Then form bright groups beneath the Duomo's
    shade!"
No! you will have to argue and explain,
Persuade them all is not so ill in the end,
260 Tease, tire them out! Arrive, arrive, Lucchese!
    Domizia. Well, you will triumph for the Past
    enough
Whatever be the Present's chance—no service
Falls to the ground with Florence; she awaits
Her saviour, will receive him fittingly.
265   *Luria.* Ah Braccio, you know Florence .. will she,
    think you,
Receive one . . . what means "fittingly receive?"
—Receive compatriots, doubtless—I am none:
And yet Domizia promises so much!

i *243. And so no*] So no great (*1849-88*, except 'So,', *1863-88*).
i *262. Present's*] present (*1868-88*).

Braccio. Kind women still give men a woman's
    prize.
270   I know not o'er which gate most boughs will arch,
    Nor if the Square will wave red flags or blue—
    I should have judged, the fullest of rewards
    Our State gave Luria, when she made him chief
    Of her whole force, in her best Captain's place.
275   *Luria*. That my reward? Florence on my account
    Relieved Ser Puccio?—mark you, my reward!
    And Puccio's having all the fight's true joy—
    Goes here and there, directs, may fight himself,
    While I must order, stand aloof, o'ersee!
280   That was my calling—there was my true place!
    I should have felt, in some one over me,
    Florence impersonate, my visible Head,
    As I am over Puccio,—taking life
    Directly from her eye!—They give me you!
285   But do you cross me, set me half to work?
    I enjoy nothing—but I will, for once!
    Decide, shall we join battle? may I wait?
       Braccio. Let us compound the matter; wait till
      noon;
    Then, no arrival,—
      Luria.   Ah, noon comes too fast!
290   I wonder, do you guess why I delay
    Involuntarily the final blow
    As long as possible? Peace follows it!
    Florence at peace, and the calm studious heads
    Come out again, the penetrating eyes;
295   As if a spell broke, all's resumed, each art
    You boast, more vivid that it slept awhile!
    'Gainst the glad heaven, o'er the white palace-front
    The interrupted scaffold climbs anew;

i *271*. Cp. *England* 257-8: 'Not a post nor a pillar but's dizened / With red and
blue papers'.
i *278*. *directs*] gets close (*1863-88*).
i *281-2*.] EBB. quoted 'Florence, to feel—in some one over me', and
commented: 'I quite understand . . but the construction is not clear
notwithstanding. A word will do it'.
i *282*. *impersonate*: embodied. Cp. Keats, *Isabella* 398: 'Love impersonate',
referring to Lorenzo's head.   *Head*] head (*1868-88*).
i *284*. *They*: the Signory.
i *286*. *but*] though (*1868-88*).
i *290-331*. This passage was extracted for *1863*[2]: see headnote, p. 374.
i *295*. *all's*] all (*1865-75*).

The walls are peopled by the Painter's brush;
300   The Statue to its niche ascends to dwell;
The Present's noise and trouble have retired
And left the eternal Past to rule once more.—
You speak its speech and read its records plain,
Greece lives with you, each Roman breathes your
    friend,
305   —But Luria,—where will then be Luria's place?
    Domizia. Highest in honour, for that Past's own
    sake,
Of which his actions, sealing up the sum
By saving all that went before from wreck,
Will range as part, with which be worshipped too.
310   *Luria*. Then I may walk and watch you in your
    streets
Leading the life my rough life helps no more,
So different, so new, so beautiful—
Nor fear that you will tire to see parade
The club that slew the lion, now that crooks
315   And shepherd-pipes come into use again?
For very lone and silent seems my East
In its drear vastness—still it spreads, and still
No Braccios, no Domizias anywhere—
Not ever more!—Well, well, to-day is ours!
    Domizia. [*To* Braccio] Should he not have been
    one of us?
320   *Luria*.   Oh, no!
Not one of you, and so escape the thrill
Of coming into you, and changing thus,—

i *301. Present's*] present (*1868-88*).
i *306-9*. Luria will be honoured for the sake of the past, because his actions, which preserved the heritage of that past, will be ranked as part of that heritage.
i *307. sealing up the sum*: cp. *Ezekiel* xxviii 12: 'Thou sealest up the sum, full of wisdom, and perfect in beauty'. B. uses the phrase again in *Any Wife* 94 and *Francis Furini* 435.
i *309. range*] rank (*1863²*).
i *311. Leading the life*] Lead the smooth life (*1868-88*).
i *314. The club that slew the lion*: alluding to one of the labours of Hercules, the killing of the Nemean lion; cp. *Glove* 162.
i *316. my East*: geographically, Arabia; symbolically, the home of mystical, intuitive knowledge, the antithesis of the rationalist 'North' (see v 225ff.). Cp. *Paracelsus* i 391: 'the wide east, where old Wisdom sprung'; also *Through the Metidja, Rudel*, and *Return of the Druses*.
i *322. and*] of (*1863-88; 1863²* as *1846*).

Feeling a soul grow on me that restricts
The boundless unrest of the savage heart!
325   The sea heaves up, hangs loaded o'er the land,
Breaks there and buries its tumultuous strength;
Horror, and silence, and a pause awhile;
Lo, inland glides the gulf-stream, miles away,
In rapture of assent, subdued and still,
330   'Neath those strange banks, those unimagined skies!
Well, 'tis not sure the quiet lasts for ever!
Your placid heads still find our hands new work;
Some minute's chance—there comes the need of
         mine—
And, all resolved on, I too hear at last.
335   Oh, you must find some use for me, Ser Braccio!
You hold my strength; 'twere best dispose of it!
What you created, see that you find food for—
I shall be dangerous else!
         Braccio.   How dangerous, Sir?
         Luria. Oh, there are many ways, Domizia warns me,
340   And one with half the power that I possess,
Grows very formidable! Do you doubt?
Why, first, who holds the army . . .
         Domizia.   While we talk
Morn wears, we keep you from your proper place
In the field!—
         Luria.   Nay, to the field I move no more!—
345   My part is done, and Puccio's may begin!
I cannot trench upon his province longer
With any face.—You think yourselves so safe?
Why see—in concert with Tiburzio, now—
One could . . .
         Domizia.   A trumpet!
         Luria.   My Lucchese at last!

---

i *328. gulf-stream:* i.e. an inlet of the sea, produced by a natural catastrophe
such as that described in the prec. lines; not the current of the same name.
i *332. our]* rough (*1863-88*).
i *333. minute's]* emended in agreement with *1888* from 'minutes", *1846-75:*
the correction is in *1872 Morgan²* (see Editorial Note, p. vii). See also l. 84n.
i *339. Oh, there are]* There are so (*1865-88*).
i *343-4. place / In the]* place, / The (*1868-88*).
i *346-7. I cannot trench . . . With any face:* 'I cannot interfere in Puccio's area
of responsibility (the conduct of the actual fighting) without being
embarrassed (at seeming to tell a veteran soldier his business)'.

350   Arrived, as sure as Florence stands! your leave!
                                              [*Springs out.*
            Domizia. How plainly is true greatness
                charactered
            By such unconsciousness as Luria's here,
            And sharing least the secret of itself!
            Be it with head that schemes or hand that acts,
355   Such save the world which none but they could save,
            Yet think whate'er they did, that world could do.
            Braccio. Yes: and how worthy note, that those
                same great ones
            In hand or head, with such unconsciousness
            And all its due entailed humility,
360   Should never shrink, so far as I perceive,
            From taking up whatever offices
            Involve the whole world's safety or mishap,
            Into their mild hands as a thing of course!
            The Statist finds it natural to lead
365   The mob who might as easily lead him—
            The Soldier marshals men who know as much—
            Statist and Soldier verily believe!
            While we poor scribes . . . you catch me thinking,
                now,
            That I shall in this very letter write
370   What none of you are able! To it, Lapo!
                                              [*Exit* Domizia.
            This last, worst, all affected childish fit

350-1. Cp. Carlyle's essay *Characteristics* (1829), which affirms that 'the sign
of health is Unconsciousness': 'The memory of that first state of Freedom and
paradisiac Unconsciousness has faded away into an ideal poetic dream. We
stand here too conscious of many things'.
i *352. unconsciousness*] unconscious sport (*1865-88*). At the proof stage, EBB.
had quoted '*inc*onsciousness', and commented: 'You always write incon-
sciousness. The word in general use is "*un*consciousness"—*English* use?'.
i *353. And*] Strength (*1863-88*).
i *357.*] EBB. quoted 'Yes, and how worthy note, the truly great ones', and
commented: 'If you put "*that* those same great ones", you make it clearer &
to apprehend the construction at once, the reader seeks a "that[", it] seems to
me. The thought is excellent'.   *those*] these (*1863-88*).
i *361-2. offices / Involve*] tool there be / Effects (*1865-88*).
i *366.*] The soldier marshals troops who know as much— (*1863-65*, except
'The captain', *1865*); The captain marshals troops born skilled in war—
(*1868-88*).
i *371 ˆ372.*] Of Luria's, this be-praised unconsciousness, (*1849-88*).

Convinces me: the Past was no child's play;
It was a man beat Pisa,—not a child.
'Tis mere dissimulation—to remove
375 The fear, he best knows we should entertain.
The utmost danger was at hand. 'Tis written?
Now make the duplicate, lest this should fail,
And speak your fullest on the other side.
    Secretary. I noticed he was busily repairing
380 My half-effacement of his Duomo sketch
And to it, while he spoke of Florence, turned
As the Mage Negro King to Christ the Babe.—
I judge his childishness the true relapse
To boyhood of a man who has worked lately,
385 And presently will work, so, meantime, plays:
Whence more than ever I believe in him.
    Braccio. [*After a pause*] The sword! At best, the
        soldier, as he says,
In Florence—the black face, the barbarous name,
For Italy to boast her show of the age,
390 Her man of men!—To Florence with each letter!

i *372.*] EBB. quoted 'Convinces me . . no child's play was the Past—' and commented: 'Now if you wrote straightforwardly "Convinces me the past w[as] no child's play . ." is there an objection[?] Because there is a "most say" in the next line which occupies the precisely corresponding place to "child's play" &, so, jingles . . or is it a mere fancy of mine? And then, where nothing is gained by an inversion, the simpler form seems better'. The 'next line' which contained 'most say' appears to have been cut or completely rewritten.

i *374.* 'Tis] All's (*1849-88*).

i *376.* 'Tis] Is't (*1849-88*).

i *377.*] EBB. quoted 'Now make the duplicate, if this should fail.', and commented: 'Quy. . . *lest* this should fail?'   *the*] a (*1849-88*).

i *381.*] And, while he spoke of Florence, turned to it, (*1849-88*).

i *382.* *Negro King*] Negro turns (*1863*). In pictures of the Adoration of the Magi, one of the three Magi was sometimes depicted as a Negro, according to the tradition that the Magi represented the descendants of Noah's three sons, of whom Ham was the father of the African peoples.

i *383.* *true*] mere (*1863-88*).

i *385.*] EBB. quoted 'so plays', and commented: 'Is the connection clear?—or the meaning even? For you mean "so in plays" . . "it is so in plays". But then you set your readers thinking . . or rather looking to the dictionary'. EBB.'s misreading looks odd if the contrast between 'work' and 'play' was as strongly marked in MS as in *1846*; B. may have substantially rewritten both this line and the one above.

i *390.* *man of men*: cp. *Charles Avison* 423: 'Marching say "Pym, the man of men!"' Cleopatra applies the phrase to Antony in *Antony and Cleopatra* I v 72.

Act II

Noon.

Domizia. Well, Florence, shall I reach thee, pierce
    thy heart
Thro' all its safeguards? Hate is said to help—
Quicken the eye, invigorate the arm,
And this my hate, made of so many hates,
5   Might stand in scorn of visible instrument,
And will thee dead . . . yet do I trust it not;
Nor Man's devices, nor Heaven's memory
Of wickedness forgot on Earth so soon,
But thy own nature,—Hell and thee I trust,
10   To keep thee constant in that wickedness,

ii *1-2. Well . . . safeguards?*] EBB. quoted
    Well, Florence, shall I reach thee, pierce <thy> thine heart
    Thro' all its safeguards, pass 'twixt all the play
    Of arrowy wiles
and commented: 'Does it not look, at least, like a confusion of metaphor—
though a person may be defended from a dagger for instance, by a shower of
arrows preventing the approach of an assassin. Still it would simplify it, if
you made the means of defence the seven folds of a shield, or the subtle
linkings of a mail'.
ii *4-6.* Cp. *Laboratory* 33-5.
ii *4. of so*] up of (*1849-88*).
ii *7-10.*] EBB. quoted 'Nor man's device, nor Heaven to keep in mind / The
wickedness forgot on earth too soon,' and commented: 'Might it be written
    Nor man's devic<e>es, nor Heaven's <fair> pure memory
    Of wickedness forgot on earth too soon,
    But thy own heart,—'tis Hell, I trust, & thee
    That firm thou keep &c.
I do not understand exactly . . "tis Hell & thee" if you wrote "it is for Hell &
thee / To keep thy first course firmly to its end" *that* would be clear,—but
would it be as you desire?' At the proof stage, she quoted l. 7 again as 'Nor
man's device nor Heaven's memory', and commented: 'Do you like "Heaven"
as a dissyllable? It always seems to make a weak line. <Is there an objection
to "Heaven's sure memory"?> Would not an "s" to "device" remedy it
unobjectionably?' EBB. crossed out her suggestion for 'Heaven's sure
memory' presumably because B. had not acted on her previous suggestion of
'pure memory', and clearly did not want to attach any epithet to 'memory'.
The sense is that in pursuing her revenge on Florence, Domizia will look for
aid neither to those who might plot against Florence nor to divine retribution
but to Florence's own inveterate wickedness.

Where my revenge may meet thee: turn aside
For gratitude a single step, or shame,—
Grace thou this Luria, this wild mass of rage
That I prepare to launch against thee now,
15   With other payment than thy noblest found,—
Give his desert for once its due reward,—
And past thee would my sure destruction roll.
But thou who mad'st our House thy sacrifice,
It cannot be thou dost except this Moor
20   From the accustomed fate of zeal and truth;
Thou wilt deny his looked-for recompense,
And then—I reach thee! Old and trained, my sire
Could bow down on his quiet broken heart,
Die awe-struck and submissive, when at last
25   The strange blow came for the expected wreath;
And Porzio passed in blind bewilderment
To exile, never to return,—they say,
Perplexed in his frank simple honest soul
As if some natural law had changed,—how else

ii *11-15.*] EBB. quoted 'And this wild mass of rage that I prepare / Luria, to launch against thee', and commented: 'Do observe that this line and a half seem to have fallen down from the height of the argument into a strange place. It is a distracted construction .. a little. Would it be straighter—lie more coherently, if you wrote it somehow thus ..

      turn aside
For gratitude a single step, or shame ..
Grace thou this Luria, . . this wild mass of rage
I now prepare to launch against thyself, . . .
With other payment.'
Note B.'s further revs.
ii *12.*] A single step, for gratitude, or shame,— (*1849-88*, except 'gratitude or', *1863-88*).
ii *13. thou*] but (*1849-88*).
ii *14. That I prepare*] I have prepared (*1865-88*).
ii *18-37.* Domizia further explains herself at iii 285ff.; contrast Braccio at i 176ff. It appears that Domizia's father was executed; her brother Porzio died in exile; her brother Berto committed suicide. B. takes a common feature of political conflict in medieval Italian city-states, the extermination of whole families, but ascribes it here (in contrast to *Sordello*) to the ingratitude of the state rather than to private vendetta or factional strife. B. may have been influenced by Byron's *The Two Foscari*, in which the son of the Doge is exiled, then returns to die, as the result of a family vendetta.
ii *19. dost*] wilt (*1849-88*).
ii *25.*] EBB. quoted 'For the expected wreath the strange blow came', and suggested the present reading.

30   Could Florence, on plain fact pronouncing thus,
      Judge Porzio's actions worthy such an end?
      But Berto, with the ever-passionate pulse,
      —Oh that long night, its dreadful hour on hour,
      In which no way of getting his fair fame
35   From their inexplicable charges free,
      Was found save to pour forth the impatient blood
      And show its colour whether false or no!
      My brothers never had a friend like me
      Close in their need to watch the time, then speak,
40   —Burst with a wakening laughter on their dream,
      Say, Florence was one falsehood, so false here,—
      And show them what a simple task remained—
      To leave dreams, rise, and punish in God's name
      The City wedded to its wickedness—
45   None stood by them as I by Luria stand!
      So, when the stranger cheated of his due
      Turns on thee as his rapid nature bids,
      Then, Florence, think, a hireling at thy throat
      For the first outrage, think who bore thy last,
50   Yet mutely in forlorn obedience died!
      He comes . . his friend . . black faces in the camp

ii *30-1.*] EBB. quoted 'When Florence on plain fact pronouncing so / Could to such actions such an end decree—' and commented: 'You invert & invert! Tell me if an air of stiffness is not given by such unnecessary inversions. You throw important words too at arm's length from their emphasis by it in this instance . . quy. "Could judge such actions worthy of such an end—"'.

ii *31. an end*] reward (*1868-88*).

ii *33-4.*] EBB. quoted 'not one / Possible way of getting his fair fame', and commented: 'If you repeat "one", "not one / *One* possible way of getting his fair fame" you strengthen the line, do you not. It seems a willowy line otherwise'.

ii *36-7. to pour . . . And*] pouring . . . To (*1849-88*).

ii *41.*] Say, Florence was all falseness, so false here,— (*1849-65*, except 'Cry', *1863-65*); Cry, "Florence was all falseness, so, false here!" (*1868-88*).

ii *44. to its*] to the (*1868-88*).

ii *48-50.* i.e. 'when a mercenary [Luria] attacks you at the first sign of ingratitude, then, Florence, think of those who experienced the extreme of your ingratitude, yet died without protest'.

ii *50-2.*] at the proof stage, EBB. commented: 'Observe the three concluding lines of Domizia's soliloquy. There is a rhyme between the last & the third from bottom . . "died" . . "pride"'. The exact original wording of the last line is uncertain.

Where moved those peerless brows and eyes of old!
                    [*Enter* Luria *and* Husain.
Well, and the movement—is it as you hope?
'Tis Lucca?
    Luria.   Ah, the Pisan trumpet merely!
55 Tiburzio's envoy I must needs receive—
    Domizia. Whom I withdraw before; yet if I
        lingered
You could not wonder, for my time fleets fast;
The overtaking night brings Florence' praise
And where will then be room for mine? Yet still
60 Remember who was first to promise it,
And envies those who also can perform!
                                    [*Exit.*
    Luria. This trumpet from the Pisans?—
    Husain.   In the camp;
A very noble presence—Braccio's visage
On Puccio's body—calm and fixed and good;
65 A man I seem as I had seen before—
Most like it was some statue had the face.
    Luria. Admit him! This will prove the last delay!
    Husain. Ay, friend, go on, and die thou going on!
Thou heard'st what the grave woman said but now:
70 To-night rewards thee! That is well to hear!
But stop not therefore; hear it, and go on!
    Luria. Oh, their reward and triumph and the rest
They round me in the ears with, all day long?
But that, I never took for earnest, friend!
75 Well would it suit us,—their triumphal arch
Or storied pillar, thee and me, the Moors!

ii *54. trumpet*: the bearer of a formal challenge or proposal for negotiation
(Elizabethan archaism: cp. *Troilus and Cressida* IV v 6).

ii *56. yet*] tho' (*1863-88*).

ii *58. Florence' praise*] such reward!— (*1849-88*, except 'reward!', *1863-88*).

ii *59. mine? Yet still*] me? yet still (*1849-65*); me? Yet, praised, (*1868-88*).

ii *60-1. promise . . . perform*: cp. *A Soul's Tragedy* ii 292ff.

ii *60. it*] praise (*1868-88*).

ii *61. envies*] envied (*1863-65*); envy (*1868-88*).

ii *74. But . . . took*] All . . . take (*1849-88*). EBB. quoted two MS lines which
have dropped out, but must have come between l. 34 and l. 133, and were
probably placed here: 'Devoted brows are to be crowned no longer / Whom
the smile paid, or word of praise, so well—'. She commented: 'It is not clear
. . will not be to the reader, I think—& a word or two more will ensure the
desired purpose'.

ii *76. storied*: ornamented with scenes from history or legend (*OED* cites

Just gratitude in those Italian eyes—
That, we shall get?
    Husain.   It is too cold an air—
Our sun rose out of yonder mound of mist—
80 Where is he now? So I trust none of them!
    Luria. Truly?
    Husain.   I doubt and fear. There stands a wall
'Twixt our expansive and explosive race
And those absorbing, concentrating men!
They use thee!
    Luria.   And I feel it, Husain; yes,
85 And care not—yes, an alien force like mine
Is only called to play its part outside
Their different nature; where its sole use seems
To fight with and keep off an adverse force
As alien,—which repelled, ours too withdraws;
90 Inside, they know not what to do with me;
So I have told them laughingly and oft,
But long since I prepared to learn the worst.
    Husain. What is the worst?
    Luria.   I will forestall them, Husain,
And speak my destiny they dare not speak—
95 Banish myself before they find the heart!
I will be first to say, "the work rewards!
"I know, for all your praise, my use is over,
"So may it be!—meanwhile 'tis best I go,
"And carry safe my memories of you all
100 "To other scenes of action, newer lands,"—
Thus leaving them confirmed in their belief
They would not easily have tired of me!
You think this hard to say?
    Husain.   Say it or not,

Gray, *Elegy* 41: 'storied urn'); cp. *Ring* x 468: 'storied portal, statued spire'.
ii *77. Just*] But (*1849-88*).
ii *79-80.* Husain compares the murkiness of the Italian climate to the ambiguous nature of its inhabitants. For 'our sun', cp. iv 301ff.
ii *89. ours*] mine (*1849-88*).
ii *91. So*] Thus (*1863-88*).
ii *92. I*] was (*1863-65*); am (*1868-88*).
ii *94. And speak my*] Will speak the (*1868-88*).
ii *98. be*] prove (*1863-88*).
ii *99. And*] Go (*1868-88*).
ii *103. Say it or not*] Say or not say (*1863-88*).

So thou but go, so they but let thee go!
105　This hating people, that hate each the other,
　　And in one blandness to us Moors unite—
　　Locked each to each like slippery snakes, I say,
　　Which still in all their tangles, hissing tongue
　　At threatening tail, ne'er do each other harm;
110　While any creature of a better blood,
　　They seem to fight for, while they circle safe
　　And never touch it,—pines without a wound,
　　Withers away before their eyes and breath.
　　See thou if Puccio come not safely out
115　Of Braccio's grasp, the Braccio sworn his foe,
　　And Braccio safely from Domizia's toils
　　Who hates him most!—But thou, the friend of all,
　　. . Come out of them!
　　　Luria.　　　　　The Pisan trumpet now!
　　　Husain. Breathe free—it is an enemy, no friend!
　　　　　　　　　　　　　　　　　　　　　[*Exit.*
120　　*Luria.* He keeps his instincts, no new culture mars
　　Their perfect use in him; and so the brutes
　　Rest not, are anxious without visible cause,
　　When change is in the elements at work
　　Which man's trained senses fail to apprehend.
125　But here . . he takes the distant chariot-wheels
　　For thunder, festal fire for lightning's flash, . .
　　The finer traits of cultivated life
　　For treachery and malevolence: I see.
　　　　　　　　　　　　　　　　[*Enter* Tiburzio.
　　Quick, sir, your message. I but wait your message
130　To sound the charge. You bring not overtures
　　For truce?—I would not, for your General's sake,

ii *109. At*] And (*1849–88*).
ii *113. before*] beside (*1863–88*).
ii *114–15.* The enmity between Puccio and Braccio is not explained in the
play; perhaps Braccio was responsible for Luria being promoted over
Puccio's head.
ii *115. the*] this (*1849–88*).
ii *116. And*] As (*1849–88*).
ii *121. and*] just (*1849–88*).
ii *125. chariot-wheels*] chariot-wheel (*1865–88*).
ii *126. fire*] flame (*1865–88*).
ii *129–259.* EBB. commented: 'I infinitely admire the whole interview
between Luria & Tiburzio. Nothing can be nobler. And the suppressed
emotion *tells*'. She singled out ll. 253–4.
ii *130. not overtures*] no overture (*1865–88*).

You spoke of truce—a time to fight is come,
And whatsoe'er the fight's event, he keeps
His honest soldier's name to beat me with,
135   Or leaves me all himself to beat, I trust!
      Tiburzio. I am Tiburzio.
          Luria.   You? Ah, yes . . Tiburzio!
You were the last to keep the ford i' the valley
From Puccio, when I threw in succours there!
Why, I was on the heights—thro' the defile
140   Ten minutes after, when the prey was lost!
You wore an open scull-cap with a twist
Of water-reeds—the plume being hewn away;
While I drove down my battle from the heights,
—I saw with my own eyes!
      Tiburzio.   And you are Luria
145   Who sent my cohort, that laid down its arms
In error of the battle-signal's sense,
Back safely to me at the critical time—
One of a hundred deeds—I know you! Therefore
To none but you could I . . .
      Luria.   No truce, Tiburzio!
150   *Tiburzio.* Luria, you know the peril's imminent
On Pisa,—that you have us in the toils,
Us her last safeguard, all that intercepts
The rage of her implacablest of foes
From Pisa,—if we fall to-day, she falls.

ii *133-5.* i.e. if Tiburzio wins, he will have won honourably; if he loses, Luria will have gained a victory over a worthy opponent.

ii *133.*] EBB. quoted 'And either way the fight's event, he keeps', and commented: 'It would be clearer & more unquestionable if you wrote it, perhaps, "And, let the fight end either way, he keeps" . . This is the pettiest, paltriest criticism of straws! but just these straws hide the path, with you, sometimes'.

ii *136. Ah,*] 'Tis— (*1849-88*).

ii *138. succours*: reinforcements.

ii *143. battle*: a body of troops, here probably the main division of the army; only such use in B. One of several archaisms which give the work its neo-Elizabethan flavour; OED cites *1 Henry IV* IV i 129 and *Richard III* V iii 299.

ii *150. peril's*] peril (*1863-88*).

ii *152-4.*] EBB. quoted
      Pisa's last safeguard, all to intercept
      The rage of her implacablest of foes
      From Pisa . .
and commented: 'Does the construction seem clear to yourself? Give us a little light'.

155 Tho' Lucca will arrive, yet, 'tis too late.
You have so plainly here the best of it
That you must feel, brave soldier that you are,
How dangerous we grow in this extreme,
How truly formidable by despair:
160 Still probabilities should have their weight—
The extremest chance is ours; but that chance failing,
You win this battle: wherefore say I this?
To be well apprehended when I add
This danger absolutely comes from you.
165 Were you, who threaten thus, a Florentine . . .
    Luria. Sir, I am nearer Florence than her sons.
I can, and have perhaps obliged the State,
Nor paid a mere son's duty.
    Tiburzio.   Even so!
Were you the son of Florence, yet endued
170 With all your present nobleness of soul,
No question, what I must communicate
Would not detach you from her.
    Luria.   Me detach?
    Tiburzio. Time urges: you will ruin presently
Pisa, you never knew, for Florence' sake
175 You think you know. I have from time to time
Made prize of certain secret missives sent
From Braccio here, the Commissary, home—
And knowing Florence otherwise, can piece
The entire chain out from these scattered links.
180 Your Trial occupies the Signory;
They sit in judgment on your conduct now!
When men at home enquire into the acts

ii *157. that*] as (*1849-88*).
ii *161. extremest*] extreme (*1868-88*).
ii *167.* Cp. *Othello* v ii 338: 'I have done the state some service, and they know't'.
ii *174-5. for Florence' sake / You think you know*: i.e. 'for the sake of Florence, whose character you mistakenly believe to be honourable'. Cp. B. to EBB.: 'Luria . . . devotes himself to something he thinks Florence' (26 Feb. 1845, *LK* 26).
ii *178. can*] I (*1849-88*).
ii *179.*] at the proof stage, EBB. quoted 'The entire chain out from these scattered links', and commented: 'Why not so—instead of the "my" or proposed "its"? The meaning is clear'. It is not certain whether 'these' was meant to replace 'my' or 'its', or whether the original reading was 'these my' or 'these its', and EBB. was suggesting that 'these' made sufficient sense on its own.

Which in the field e'en foes appreciate . . .
Brief, they are Florentines! You, saving them,
185   Will seek the sure destruction saviours find.
      Luria. Tiburzio—
          Tiburzio.   All the wonder is of course!
      I am not here to teach you, or direct,
      Only to loyally apprise—scarce that.
      This is the latest letter, sealed and safe,
190   As it left here an hour ago. One way
      Of two thought free to Florence, I command.
      The duplicate is on its road: but this,—
      Read it, and then I shall have more to say.
      Luria. Florence!
          Tiburzio.   Now, were yourself a Florentine,
195   This letter, let it hold the worst it can,
      Would be no reason you should fall away—
      The Mother city is the mother still,
      And recognition of the children's service
      Her own affair; reward . . there's no reward!
200   But you are bound by quite another tie;
      Nor Nature shows, nor Reason, why at first
      A foreigner, born friend to all alike,
      Should give himself to any special State
      More than another, stand by Florence' side
205   Rather than Pisa's—'tis as fair a city
      You war against, as that you fight for—famed
      As well as she in story, graced no less
      With noble heads and patriotic hearts,—
      Nor to a stranger's eye would either cause,
210   Stripped of the cumulative loves and hates
      Which take importance from familiar view,
      Stand as the Right, and Sole to be upheld.
      Therefore, should the preponderating gift
      Of love and trust Florence was first to throw,
215   Which made you hers not Pisa's, void the scale,—
      Old ties dissolving, things resume their place
      And all begins again. Break seal and read!
      At least let Pisa offer for you now!

ii *185. Will seek*] Seek but (*1868-88*).
ii *187. or*] nor (*1849-88*).
ii *197. Mother city:* cp. iv 272-4.
ii *205. Pisa's*] Pisa (*1868-88*).
ii *214. first to throw:* into the 'scale' of the next line.
ii *215.*] EBB. quoted 'Made you her own', and suggested ' "Which made you her own" ' . . . because without it, the thread of meaning gets entangled'.

And I, as a good Pisan, shall rejoice—
220 Tho' for myself I lose, in gaining you,
This last fight and its opportunity;
The chance it brings of saving Pisa yet,
Or in the turn of battle dying so
That shame should want its extreme bitterness.
225   *Luria.* Tiburzio, you that fight for Pisa now
As I for Florence . . say my chance were yours!
You read this letter, and you find . . no, no!
Too mad!
    Tiburzio. I read the letter, find they purpose
When I have crushed their foe, to crush me: well?
230   *Luria.* And you, their captain, what is it you do?
    Tiburzio. Why as it is, all cities are alike—
I shall be as belied, whate'er the event,
As you, or more: my weak head, they will say,
Prompted this last expedient, my faint heart
235 Entailed on them indelible disgrace,
Both which defects ask proper punishment.
Another tenure of obedience, mine!
You are no son of Pisa's: break and read!
    Luria. And act on what I read? what act were fit?
240 If the firm-fixed foundation of my faith
In Florence, who to me stands for Mankind,
—If that breaks up and, disemprisoning
From the abyss . . . Ah friend, it cannot be!
You may be very sage, yet . . all the world
245 Having to fail, or your sagacity,
You do not wish to find yourself alone!
What would the world be worth? Whose love be sure?
The world remains—you are deceived!
    Tiburzio.   Your hand!
I lead the vanguard.—If you fall, beside,
250 The better—I am left to speak! For me,
This was my duty, nor would I rejoice
If I could help, it misses its effect:
And after all you will look gallantly
Found dead here with that letter in your breast!

ii *230. And you,*] You, being (*1849-88*).
ii *231^232.*] Pisa will pay me much as Florence you; (*1849-63*); As Florence
pays you, Pisa will pay me. (*1865-88*).
ii *241. who*] which (*1849-63*).
ii *242. breaks*] break (*1865-88*).
ii *249-50. If you fall . . . speak*: i.e. Tiburzio would vindicate Luria's
honourable conduct.

255   *Luria.* Tiburzio—I would see these people once
        And test them ere I answer finally!
        At your arrival let the trumpet sound:
        If mine returns not then the wonted cry,
        It means that I believe—am Pisa's!
        Tiburzio.   Well!
                                                            [*Exit.*
260   *Luria.* My heart will have it he speaks true! My
            blood
        Beats close to this Tiburzio as a friend;
        If he had stept into my watch-tent, night
        And the wide desert full of foes around,
        I should have broke the bread and given the salt
265   Secure, and when my hour of watch was done
        Taken my turn to sleep between his knees
        Safe in the unclouded brow and honest cheek.
        Oh, world where all things pass and nought abides,
        Oh, life the long mutation—is it so?
270   Is it with life as with the body's change?
        —Where, e'en tho' better follow, good must pass,
        Nor manhood's strength can mate with boyhood's
            grace,
        Nor age's wisdom in its turn find strength,
        But silently the first gift dies away,
275   And tho' the new stays—never both at once!
        Life's time of savage instinct's o'er with me,
        It fades and dies away, past trusting more,
        As if to punish the ingratitude
        With which I turned to grow in these new lights
280   And learned to look with European eyes.
        Yet it is better, this cold certain way,
        Where Braccio's brow tells nothing,—Puccio's
            mouth,
        Domizia's eyes reject the searcher .. yes . .
        For on their calm sagacity I lean,

ii *258. returns*] return (*1868-88*).

ii *263. wide*] wild (*1849-88*).

ii *264.* According to Arab custom, a guest who partakes of bread and salt is
sacred to the host, whether they are enemies or not. (But Luria implies that
he, as host, would feel secure in giving Tiburzio shelter.)

ii *267. unclouded*] untroubled (*1849-88*).

ii *276. instinct's*] instinct (*1863-88*).

ii *277. past trusting more*: 'no longer trustworthy'.

285   Their sense of right, deliberate choice of good,
That as they know my deeds they deal with me.
Yes, that is better . . that is best of all!
Such faith stays when the wild belief would go!
Yes—when the desert creature's heart, at fault
290   Amid the scattering tempest and its sands,
Betrays its steps into the pathless drift—
The calm instructed eye of man holds fast
By the sole bearing of the visible star,
Sure that when slow the whirling wreck subsides,
295   The boundaries, lost now, shall be found again,—
The palm-trees and the pyramid over all!
Yes: I trust Florence—Pisa is deceived.
                    [*Enter* Braccio, Puccio, *and* Domizia.
    Braccio. Noon's at an end: no Lucca! You must
      fight.
    Luria. Do you remember ever, gentle friends,
I am no Florentine?
300   *Domizia.*   It is yourself
Who still are forcing us importunately,
To bear in mind what else we should forget.
    Luria. For loss!—For what I lose in being none!
No shrewd man, such as you yourselves respect,
305   But would remind you of the stranger's loss
In natural friends and advocates at home,
Hereditary loves, or rivalships,
With precedents for honor and reward.

---

ii *286. That*] Sure, (*1849-88*).   *they deal with me*] EBB. quoted 'with me they deal', and suggested the present reading. She added: 'Oh this Luria! how great he is'.

ii *288. the*] mere (*1849-88*).

ii *289-96.* Cp. Luria's comment on Husain, ll. 120-8.

ii *290. tempest and its*] tempest's pillared (*1849-88*). With the later reading, cp. *Caliban* 287-8: 'The wind / Shoulders the pillared dust'.

ii *291. steps*] step (*1865-88*).

ii *294. subsides*] subside (*1865-88*).

ii *296.*] EBB. quoted 'o'er all', and commented: 'Don't coop up such a wide desert-line by the contracted "o'er", jangling with "all" too. There is room for "over all" surely, said out broadly'.

ii *298 Lucca!*] Lucca? (*1849-88*).

ii *299. gentle friends*: the phrase occurs several times in Shakespeare; cp. *2 Henry IV* IV v 1: 'Let there be no noise made, my gentle friends'.

ii *307. or*] even (*1849-88*).

ii *308. precedents*] precedent (*1865-88*).

Still, there's a gain, too! If you recollect,
310   The stranger's lot has special gain as well!
Do you forget there was my own far East
I might have given away myself to, once,
As now to Florence, and for such a gift,
Stood there like a descended Deity?
315   There, worship greets us! what do I get here?
                                    [*Shows the letter.*
See! Chance has put into my hand the means
Of knowing what I earn, before I work!
Should I fight better, should I fight the worse,
With the crown palpably before me? see!
320   Here lies my whole reward! Best know it now?
Or keep it for the end's entire delight?
        Braccio. If you serve Florence as the vulgar serve,
For swordsman's pay alone,—break seal and read!
In that case you will find your full desert!
325   *Luria.* Give me my one last happy moment,
                friends!
You need me now, and all the gratitude
This letter may contain would never balance
The after-feeling that your need's at end!
This moment . . Oh the East has use with you!
330   Its sword still flashes . . is not flung aside
With the past praise in a dark corner yet!
How say you? 'Tis not so with Florentines—
Captains of yours—for them, the ended war
Is but a first step to the peace begun
335   —He who did well in war just earns the right
To begin doing well in peace, you know!
Now, certain my precursors,—would not such
Look to themselves in such a chance as this,
Secure the ground they trod upon, perhaps?

ii *309. recollect*] take it so (*1849-88*).

ii *311-14.* Cp. *Return of the Druses*, where Djabal, the Druses' leader, is taken by his people to be the incarnation of their god.

ii *315.*] There, worship waits us! what is it waits here? (*1865-88*, except 'waits us:', *1868-88*).

ii *319. the crown*] your crown (*1849-63*); payment (*1865-88*).

ii *320. know*] learn (*1865-88*).

ii *326. gratitude*] graciousness (*1865-88*).

ii *327. may . . . would*] can . . . will (*1849-88*).   *never*] hardly (*1865-88*).

ii *328. your need's at end!*] you need no more. (*1868-88*).

ii *337. Now,*] And (*1849-88*).

ii *338. this*] mine (*1865-88*).

340   For I have heard, by fits, or seemed to hear,
      Of strange occurrences, ingratitude,
      Treachery even,—say that one of you
      Surmised this letter carried what might turn
      To harm hereafter, cause him prejudice—
      What would he do?
345   *Domizia.* [*Hastily*] Thank God and take revenge!
      Turn her own force against the city straight,
      And even at the moment when the foe
      Sounded defiance . . .
               [*Tiburzio's trumpet sounds in the distance.*
      Luria.   Ah, you Florentines!
      So would you do? Wisely for you, no doubt!
350   My simple Moorish instinct leads to sink
      The obligation you relieved me from,
      Still deeper! [*To* Puccio] Sound our answer, I should say!
      And thus!—[*Tearing the paper*]—The battle! That solves every doubt!

          [*As the Trumpet answers, the scene shuts.*

ii *341. occurrences,*] mishap, mistake, (*1865-88*).
ii *342.*] EBB. quoted 'Treachery even—say that such an one', and commented: 'The line seems to want strengthening by another syllable—"Of treachery even"—? I only ask'.
ii *346. Turn*] Hurl (*1865-88*).   *straight,*] straight! (*1868-88*).
ii *350. leads to sink*] bids me sink (*1849-63*); bids me clench (*1865-88*).
ii *351. relieved*] relieve (*1849-88*).
ii *352. say!*] say, (*1868-88*).
ii *Closing s.d.*] not *1849-88*.

Act III

Afternoon.

Puccio, *as making a report to* Jacopo.

> Puccio. And here, your Captain must report the rest;
> For, as I say, the main engagement over,
> And Luria's special part in it performed,
> How could subalterns like myself expect
> 5 Leisure or leave to occupy the field
> And glean what dropped from his wide harvesting?
> I thought when Lucca at the battle's end
> Came up, just as the Pisan centre broke,
> That Luria would detach me and prevent
> 10 The flying Pisans seeking what they found,
> Friends in the rear, a point to rally by:
> But no—more honourable proved my post!
> I had the august captive to escort
> Safe to our camp—some other could pursue,
> 15 Fight, and be famous; gentler chance was mine—
> Tiburzio's wounded spirit must be soothed!
> He's in the tent there.
>   Jacopo.   Is the substance down?
> I write—"The vanguard beaten, and both wings
> In full retreat—Tiburzio prisoner"—
> 20 And now,—"That they fall back and form again
> On Lucca's coming."—Why then, after all,
> 'Tis half a victory, no conclusive one?
>   Puccio. Two operations where a sole had served.
>   Jacopo. And Luria's fault was—?
>   Puccio.   Oh, for fault . . . not much!
> 25 He led the attack a thought impetuously,
> —There's commonly more prudence; now, he seemed
> To hurry measures, otherwise well-judged;
> By over concentrating strength, at first,
> Against the enemy's van, both sides escaped:
> 30 That's reparable—yet it is a fault.
>   [*Enter* Braccio.
>   Jacopo. As good as a full victory to Florence,

---

iii 4. *subalterns like myself*] subaltern like myself (*1865-75*); a subaltern like me (*1888*).
iii 20. *fall . . . form*] fell . . . formed (*1849-88*).
iii 29. *sides*] wings (*1865-88*).

With the advantage of a fault beside—
What is it, Puccio?—that by pressing forward
With too impetuous . . .
    Braccio.   The report anon!
35 Thanks, Sir—you have elsewhere a charge, I know.
                              [*Exit* Puccio.
There's nothing done but I would do again;
Yet, Lapo, it may be the Past proves nothing,
And Luria has kept faithful to the end!
    Jacopo. I was for waiting.
    Braccio.   Yes: so was not I!
40 He could not choose but tear that letter—true!
Still, certain of his tones, I mind, and looks—
You saw, too, with a fresher soul than I.
So Porzio seemed an injured man, they say!
Well, I have gone upon the broad, sure ground.
                   [*Enter* Luria, Puccio, *and* Domizia.
45   *Luria.* [*To* Puccio] Say, at his pleasure I will see
    Tiburzio:
All's at his pleasure.
    Domizia. [*To* Luria] Were I not so sure
You would reject, as you do constantly,
Praise,—I might tell you what you have deserved
Of Florence by this last and crowning feat:
But words are vain!
50   *Luria.*   Nay, you may praise me now!
I want instruction every hour, I find,
On points where once I saw least need of it;
And praise, I have been used to do without,
Seems not so easy to dispense with now:
55 After a battle half one's strength is gone—
All justice, power and beauty scarce appear
Monopolized by Florence, as of late,
To me, the stranger; you, no doubt, may know
Why Pisa needs must give her rival place;

iii *38. end*] close (*1865-88*).
iii *44.* Cp. *Matthew* vii 13: 'Broad is the way that leadeth to destruction'.
iii *46. so sure*] forewarned (*1865-88*).
iii *48. what*] how (*1865-88*).
iii *50. are vain*] offend (*1868-88*).
iii *53. do without*] slight perhaps (*1868-88*).
iii *54. not so easy to dispense*] scarce so easily dispensed (*1865-88*).
iii *55^56.*] And glorious passion in us once appeased, / Our reason's calm cold dreadful voice begins. (*1849-88*, except 'The glorious', *1868-88*).
iii *59. give her rival place*] bear her rival's yoke (*1865-88*).

60   And I am growing nearer you, perhaps,
      For I, too, want to know and be assured:
      So, when a cause does not reward itself,
      Its friend needs fresh sustainments; praise is one,
      And here stand you—you, Lady, praise me well!
65   But yours—your pardon—is unlearned praise:
      To the motive, the endeavour,—the heart's self—
      Your quick sense looks; you crown and call aright
      The soul of the purpose, ere 'tis shaped as act,
      Takes flesh i' the world, and clothes itself a king;
70   But when the act comes, stands for what 'tis worth,
      —Here's Puccio, the skilled soldier; he's my judge!
      Was all well, Puccio?
            Puccio.   All was . . must be well:
      If we beat Lucca presently, as doubtless . . .
      —No, there's no doubt we must—All was well done.
75   *Luria.* In truth? But you are of the trade, my
            Puccio!
      You have the fellow-craftsman's sympathy!
      There's none knows like a fellow of the craft
      The all unestimated sum of pains
      That go to a success the world can see;
80   They praise then, but the best they never know:
      —But you know!—Oh, if envy mix with it,

iii *60.*] And peradventure I grow nearer you, (*1865-88*).
iii *62.*] When a cause ceases to reward itself, (*1849-88*).
iii *63. needs*] seeks (*1865-88*).
iii *68. of the*] o' the (*1870-88*).
iii *75. But*] Still, (*1865-88*).
iii *76-9.* Cp. B.'s first letter to EBB. (10 Jan. 1845), which treats of different
kinds of praise: 'I thought I would this once get out of my habit of purely
passive enjoyment, when I do really enjoy, and thoroughly justify my
admiration—perhaps even, as a loyal fellow-craftsman should, try and find
fault and do you some little good to be proud of hereafter!' (*LK* 3). In his
second letter (13 Jan.), B. speaks of 'true, peculiar artists-pleasure . . for an
instructed eye loves to see where the brush has dipped twice in a lustrous
colour, has lain insistingly along a favourite outline, dwelt lovingly in a
grand shadow—for these "too muches" for the everybody's picture are so
many helps to the making out the real painter's-picture as he had it in his
brain' (*LK* 7). In a letter written after publication of *Luria*, B. wrote to EBB.:
'I *know* that when you were only the great Poet and not my Ba, I would have
preferred your *praise*,—as competent to praise . . to that of the whole world'
(15 July 1846, *LK* 877).
iii *77-8. knows* . . . *The*] cares . . . For the (*1865-88*).
iii *81. But*] While (*1863-88*).   *Oh*] So (*1868-88*).

Hate even, still the bottom praise of all,
Whatever be the dregs, that drop's pure gold!
—For nothing's like it; nothing else records
85 Those daily, nightly drippings in the dark
Of the heart's blood the world lets drop away
For ever . . So, pure gold that praise must be!
And I have yours, my soldier; yet the best
Is still to come—there's one looks on apart
90 Whom all refers to, failure or success;
What's done might be our best, our utmost work,
And yet inadequate to serve his need:
Here's Braccio now, for Florence—here's our
          service—
Well done for us, is it well done for him?
95 The chosen engine, tasked to its full strength,
Answers the end?—Should he have chosen higher?
Do we help Florence, now our best is done?
          Braccio. This battle, with the foregone services,
Saves Florence.
          Luria.   Why then, all is very well!
100 Here am I in the middle of my friends,
Who know me and who love me, one and all!
And yet . . 'tis like . . this instant while I speak
Is like the turning moment of a dream
When . . . Ah, you are not foreigners like me!
105 Well then, one always dreams of friends at home,
And always comes, I say, the turning point
When something changes in the friendly eyes
That love and look on you . . so slight, so slight . .
And yet it tells you they are dead and gone,
110 Or changed and enemies for all their words,
And all is mockery, and a maddening show!
You, now, so kind here, all you Florentines,
What is it in your eyes . . those lips, those brows . .
Nobody spoke it . . yet I know it well!—
115 Come now—this battle saves you, all's at end,
Your use of me is o'er, for good, for evil,—

iii *94. is*] seems (*1865-88*).
iii *95. The*] His (*1849-88*).
iii *96. the*] his (*1849-63*).
iii *97. done*] wrought (*1865-88*).
iii *103, 106. turning moment . . . turning point*] turning-moment . . . turning-point (*1863-88*).
iii *105. friends at home*: i.e. friends who are at home.
iii *116. evil*] ill (*1865-88*).

Come now, what's done against me, while I speak,
In Florence? Come! I feel it in my blood,
My eyes, my hair, a voice is in my ear
120 That spite of all this smiling and kind speech
You are betraying me! What is it you do?
Have it your way, and think my use is over;
That you are saved and may throw off the mask—
Have it my way, and think more work remains
125 Which I could do,—so show you fear me not!
Or prudent be, or generous, as you choose,
But tell me—tell what I refused to know
At noon lest heart might fail me! Well? That letter?
My fate is known at Florence! What is it?
130   *Braccio.* Sir, I shall not conceal what you divine;
It is no novelty for innocence
To be suspected, but a privilege:
The after certain compensation comes.
Charges, I say not whether false or true,
135 Have been preferred against you some time since,
Which Florence was bound plainly to receive,
And which are therefore undergoing now
The due investigation. That is all.
I doubt not but your innocence will shine

iii *119. ear*] ears (*1868-88*).
iii *120. kind*] soft (*1865-88*).
iii *123. That*] Think (*1865-88*).
iii *126. generous*] daring (*1868-88*).
iii *128. might*] should (*1849-88*).
iii *129. known*] sealed (*1868-88*).
iii *130. conceal*] deny (*1868-88*).
iii *133.*] *Ohio* emends 'The after' (all eds.) to 'Then after', arguing that 'the sense requires a word other than an article'. But 'after' in the sense of 'subsequent' (*OED*: 'his after sins', 'an after compliance') appears, among many other instances, in *Sordello* iv 475: 'The after indignation'. The sense here is: 'The compensation comes that was sure to follow'. Cp. *Colombe* v 314-15: 'Who thought upon reward? And yet how much / Comes after—Oh what amplest recompense!'
iii *138^139.*] EBB. quoted a line which must come before l. 165: 'Nor did this urge me, that if judge I must', and commented 'You will wonder when I complain of darkness here—but certainly it is doubtfully worded'. There are two possible placings for this line: here, or as a version of l. 153. The latter begins with 'Nor', but the past tense of 'did' fits better with the passage here: the sense would have been: 'Nor was I influenced by the fact that, in my own opinion, I believe you to be innocent'. Whether B. rewrote the line or cut it entirely, he must have revised the surrounding lines.
iii *139. shine*] prove (*1863-88*).

140 Apparent and illustrious, as to me,
    To them this evening when the trial ends.
        Luria. My trial?
        Domizia.   Florence, Florence to the end,
    My whole heart thanks thee!
        Puccio. [*To* Braccio]   What is "Trial," Sir?
    It was not for a Trial—surely no—
145 I furnished you those notes from time to time?
    I hold myself aggrieved—I am a man—
    And I might speak,—ay, and the mere truth, too,
    And yet not mean at bottom of my heart
    What should assist a—Trial, do you say?
    You should have told me!
150   *Domizia.*   Nay, go on, go on!
    His sentence! Do they sentence? What is it?
    The block? The wheel?
        Braccio.   Sentence there is none as yet,
    Nor shall I give my own opinion here
    Of what it should be, or is like to be:
155 When it is passed, applaud or disapprove!
    Up to that point what is there to impugn?
        Luria. They are right, then, to try me?
        Braccio.   I assert,
    Maintain and justify the absolute right
    Of Florence to do all she can have done
160 In this procedure,—standing on her guard,
    Receiving even services like yours
    With utmost fit suspicious wariness.
    In other matters—keep the mummery up!
    Take all the experiences of the whole world,
165 Each knowledge that broke thro' a heart to life,
    Each reasoning which to work out cost a brain,

iii *146. hold*] held (*1863-88*).

iii *147. the*] speak (*1849-88*).

iii *151. sentence?*] sentence him? (*1849-88*).

iii *153. here*] now (*1865-88*). See also ll. 138^139n.

iii *157-226*. This passage was extracted for *1863²*: see headnote, p. 374. EBB. commented: 'Braccio's justification of Florence is . . . very subtle & noble—one half forgives Braccio in it'. With Braccio's theory of the development of the city-state, cp. *Sordello* v 95ff., which (in part) argues that 'collective man / Outstrips the individual'.

iii *157. assert,*] emended from 'assert' in *1846*; the comma is required by the syntax.

iii *164.*] at the proof stage, EBB. quoted 'Let' for 'Take', and commented: 'Let all the experiences of the whole world . . *do what? . . be what?* How is the construction here? Know these—warrant these—. Still I think that you miss a

—In other cases, know these, warrant these,
And then dispense with them—'tis very well!
Let friend trust friend, and love demand its like,
170 And gratitude be claimed for benefits,—
There's grace in that—and when the fresh heart
     breaks,
The new brain proves a martyr, what of it?
Where is the matter of one moth the more
Singed in the candle at a summer's end?
175 But Florence is no simple John or James
To have his toy, his fancy, his conceit,
That he's the one excepted man by fate,
And, when fate shows him he's mistaken there,
Die with all good men's praise, and yield his place
180 To Paul and George intent to try their chance:
Florence exists because these pass away;
She's a contrivance to supply a type
Of Man which men's deficiencies refuse;
She binds so many, she grows out of them—
185 Stands steady o'er their numbers tho' they change
And pass away . . there's always what upholds,
Always enough to fashion the great show!
As, see, yon hanging city in the sun
Of shapely cloud substantially the same!
190 A thousand vapours rise and sink again,
Are interfused, and live their life and die,—
Yet ever hangs the steady show i' the air

---

word [to] make it clearer. The noble passage deserves all possible lights along it'.   *the whole*] all the (*1865-88*).

iii *166*.] Each reasoning which, to reach, burnt out a brain, (*1865-88*). EBB. had quoted l. 165, then 'Each reasoning it cost a brain to yield', and commented: 'A noble first line & thought! and should you not interpose a word in the second . . "each reasoning *that* it cost" &c or if you wrote . . Each reasoning which to work out cost a brain. Oh . . it is only that the second line appears to sound feebly in comparison with the great thing it has to say, & also with the great line preceding it in utterance'.

iii *168. them*] these (*1865-88*).

iii *169. its*] love's (*1865-88*).

iii *171. breaks,*] emended from 'breaks' in *1846*; the comma is required by the syntax.

iii *172. martyr*] ruin (*1865-88*).   *it*] them (*1863-88*).

iii *184. many, she*] many, that she (*1849-88*).

iii *188-98*. Cp. Wordsworth, *The Excursion* ii 834ff., in which clouds form 'a mighty city', elaborately described.

Under the sun's straight influence: that is well!
That is worth Heaven to hold, and God to bless!
195　And so is Florence,—the unseen sun above,
That draws and holds suspended all of us—
Binds transient mists and vapours into one
Differing from each and better than they all.
And shall she dare to stake this permanence
200　On any one man's faith? Man's heart is weak,
And its temptations many: let her prove
Each servant to the very uttermost
Before she grant him her reward, I say!
　　　Domizia. And as for hearts she chances to
　　　　　mistake,
205　That are not destined to receive reward,
What should she do for these?
　　　Braccio.　　　　　What does she not?
Say that she gives them but herself to serve!
Here's Luria—what had profited his strength,
When half an hour of sober fancying
210　Had shown him step by step the uselessness
Of strength exerted for its proper sake?
But the truth is she did create that strength,
Drew to the end the corresponding means.
The world is wide . . are we the only men?
215　Oh, for the time, the social purpose' sake,
Use words agreed on, bandy epithets,
Call any man, sole Great and Wise and Good!
But shall we, therefore, standing by ourselves,
Insult our souls and God with the same speech?
220　There, swarm the ignoble thousands under Him—
What marks us from the hundreds and the tens?
Florence took up, turned all one way the soul

iii *194. to . . . to*] should . . . should (*1875-88*).
iii *196. That*] Which (*1849-88*).
iii *197.*] Binds transient vapours into a single cloud, (*1865-88*).
iii *205. That are*] Wronged hearts, (*1863-88*).
iii *205^206.*] Tho' they deserve it, did she only know! (*1849-88*, except
'Though', *1863-88*; 'know,', *1888*).
iii *211. its*] strength's (*1868-88*).
iii *213. Drew*] Draw (*1868-88*)　　　*the end*] their end (*1863²*).
iii *217.*] Call any man the sole great wise and good! (*1865-88*).
iii *220-1.* Cp. *Exodus* xviii 21: 'Moreover thou shalt provide out of all the
people able men, such as fear God, men of truth, hating covetousness; and
place such over them, to be rulers of thousands, and rulers of hundreds,
rulers of fifties, and rulers of tens'.
iii *222-6.* Cp. B. to EBB.: 'To be grand in a simile, for every poor speck of a

Of Luria with its fires, and here he stands!
She takes me out of all the world as him,
225   Fixing my coldness till like ice it stays
The fire! So, Braccio, Luria, which is best?
      Luria. Ah, brave me? And is this indeed the way
To gain your good word and sincere esteem?
Am I the baited tiger that must turn
230   And fight his baiters to deserve their praise?
Obedience has no fruit then?—Be it so!
Do you indeed remember I stand here
The Captain of the conquering army,—mine—
With all your tokens, praise and promise, ready
235   To show for what their names were when you gave,
Not what you style them now you take away?
If I call in my troops to arbitrate,
And in their first enthusiastic thrill
Of victory, tell them how you menace me—
240   Commending to their plain instinctive sense,
My story first, your comment afterward,—
Will they take, think you, part with you or me?
When I say simply, I, the man they know,
Ending my work, ask payment and find Florence

Vesuvius or a Stromboli in my microcosm there are huge layers of ice and
pits of black cold water—and I make the most of my two or three fire-eyes,
because I know by experience, alas, how these tend to extinction—and the ice
grows & grows' (24 May 1845, *LK* 74). With Braccio's self-description here,
contrast l. 251.

iii *223. stands*] glows (*1865-88*). See *Glove* 73n.

iii *225. stays*] checks (*1863-88*).

iii *229. tiger*] animal (*1868-88*).

iii *231. has no fruit*] is mistake (*1868-88*).

iii *233^234.*] EBB. quoted 'Who did the several acts yourselves gave names',
and commented: 'you mean "gave names to". Then why not say "yourselves
have named"—for clearness'. The line must have come between l. 166 and
l. 359, and there are two likely placings for it: here, or at ll. 243^244.

iii *235. were*] meant (*1868-88*).

iii *238. in their*] dash the (*1868-88*).

iii *239.*] Of victory, tell them how you menace now— (*1865*); Of victory
with this you menace now— (*1868-88*).

iii *240.*] Commend to the instinctive popular sense, (*1868-88*).

iii *243.*] When I say I, the labourer they know, (*1865*); If I say I, the labourer
they saw work, (*1868-88*, except 'say—I', *1888*).

iii *243^244.* See ll. 233^234n.

iii *244-9.*] Ending my work, ask pay, and find my lords

245   Has all this while provided silently
     Against the day of pay and proving words,
     By what you call my sentence that's to come—
     Will they sit waiting it complacently?
     When I resist that sentence at their head
250   What will you do, my mild antagonist?
        Braccio. Then I will rise like fire, proud and
           triumphant
     That Florence knew you thoroughly and by me,
     And so was saved: "See, Italy," I'll say,
     "The need of our precautions—here's a man
255   "Was far advanced, just touched on the reward
     "Less subtle cities had accorded him—
     "But we were wiser; at the end comes this!"
     And from that minute all your strength will go—
     The very stones of Florence cry against
260   The all-exacting, unenduring Luria,
     Resenting her first slight probation thus
     As if he only shone and cast no shade,
     He only walked the earth with privilege
     Against suspicion, free from causing fear—
265   So, for the first inquisitive mother's-word,
     Turned round and stood on his defence, forsooth!
     And you will sink into the savage back.
     Reward? you will not be worth punishment!

     Have all this while provided silently
     Against the day of pay and proving faith,
     By what you call my sentence that's to come—
     Will friends advise I wait complacently?
     If I meet Florence half way at their head, (*1868-88*)

iii *251. Then I will rise*] I will rise up (*1849-88*).

iii *254. need*] crown (*1868-88*).

iii *255. reward*] belief (*1868-88*).

iii *256. him*] long (*1868-88*).

iii *258.*] And from that minute all your strength expires. (*1865*); And from that minute, where is Luria? Lost! (*1868-88*).

iii *260. unenduring Luria*] unenduring fool (*1865*); nought-enduring fool (*1868-88*).

iii *261.*] Who thus resents her first probation, flouts (*1868-88*).

iii *264. from causing fear*] where angels fear (*1868-88*).

iii *265. So*] He (*1868-88*).

iii *266. Turned round and stood*] He turned, and stood (*1849-65*); Must turn, and stand (*1868-88*).

iii *267.*] not *1849-88*.

Luria. And Florence knew me thus! Thus I have
   lived,—
270 And thus you, with the clear fine intellect,
Braccio, the cold acute instructed mind
Out of the stir, so calm and unconfused,
Reported me—how could you otherwise!
Ay?—and what dropped from *you*, just now,
   moreover?
275 Your information, Puccio?—Did your skill
And understanding sympathy approve
Such a report of me? Was this the end?
Or is this the end even? Can I stop?
You, Lady, with the woman's stand apart,
280 The heart to see with, not those learned eyes,
. . I cannot fathom why you would destroy me,—
It is but natural, therefore, I should ask
Had you a further end in all you spoke,
All I remember now for the first time?
285   *Domizia.* I am a daughter of the Traversari,
Sister of Porzio and of Berto both.
I have foreseen all that has come to pass:
I knew the Florence that could doubt their faith,

---

iii *275-6. skill / And*] skill, / Your (*1868-88*).
iii *278.*] Or is even this the end? Can I stop here— (*1849-88*, except 'here?',
1868-88).
iii *280. not those learned eyes*] not man's learned eyes (*1863*); past man's brain
and eyes (*1865-88*).
iii *281-2.*] . . I cannot fathom why you should destroy
     The unoffending man, you call your friend—
     So, looking at the good examples here
     Of friendship, 'tis but natural I ask (*1849-88*, except 'unoffending
one', *1863-88*; 'Still, lessoned by the', *1868-88*). *1872 Morgan*[2] (see Editorial
Note, p. vii) has 'inoffensive man', an unadopted reading.
     Than profit to me, in those instances
     Of perfidy from Florence to her chiefs— (*1849-63*)
     Had you a further aim, in all you spoke,
     Than profit to me,—all those instances
     Of perfidy, all Florence wrought of wrong— (*1865*)
     Had you a further aim, in aught you urged,
     Than your friend's profit—in all those instances
     Of perfidy, all Florence wrought of wrong— (*1868-88*)
iii *285. Traversari*: B. could have come across the name (of a family of
Ravenna, not Florence) in *Biographie*, as *Ohio* suggests.
iii *286-7. both. / I*] both: / So, (*1865-70*); both, / So, (*1875-88*).

Must needs mistrust a stranger's—holding back
290 Reward from them, must hold back his reward.
And I believed, that shame they bore and died,
He would not bear, but live and fight against—
Seeing he was of other stuff than they.
    Luria. Hear them! All these against one Foreigner!
295 And all this while where is in the whole world
To his good faith a single witness?
    Tiburzio. [*Who has entered during the preceding
        dialogue*] Here!
Thus I bear witness to it, not in word
But deed. I live for Pisa; she's not lost
By many chances,—much prevents from that!
300 Her army has been beaten, I am here,
But Lucca comes at last, one chance exists.
I rather had see Pisa three times lost
Than saved by any traitor, even you.
The example of a traitor's happy fortune
305 Would bring more evil in the end than good.
Pisa rejects such: save yourself and her!
I, in her name, resign forthwith to you
My charge,—the highest of her offices.
You shall not, by my counsel, turn on Florence
310 Her army, give her calumny that ground—
Nor bring it with you: you are all we gain—
And all she'll lose, a head to deck some bridge,
And save the crown's cost that should deck the head.
Leave her to perish in her perfidy,
315 Plague-stricken and stripped naked to all eyes,

iii *289. holding back*] dealing them (*1868-88*).
iii *290.*] Punishment, would deny him his reward. (*1868-88*).
iii *291. that*] the (*1849-88*).
iii *296. s.d.*] *entered*] entered unseen (*1868-88*).
iii *297-8.*] Thus I bear witness, not in word but deed. / I live for Pisa; she's
not lost to-day (*1868-88*).
iii *301. chance exists*] happy chance (*1868-88*).
iii *302. had*] would (*1863-88*).
iii *303. even you*] even by you (*1849-88*).
iii *306.*] Pisa rejects the traitor, craves yourself! (*1868-88*).
iii *308. of her offices*] office, sword and shield (*1868-88*).
iii *310. Her*] Your (*1868-88*).
iii *311. it with you*] one soldier (*1868-88*).   *you are all we gain*] be you all
we gain (*1849-88*).
iii *313. crown's cost that*] cost o' the crown (*1865-88*).

A proverb and a bye word in men's mouths!
Go you to Pisa—Florence is my place—
Leave me to tell her of the rectitude
I from the first told Pisa, knowing it.
To Pisa!

320   *Domizia.* Ah, my Braccio, are you caught?
         Braccio. Puccio, good soldier and selected man,
Whom I have ever kept beneath my eye
Ready as fit to serve in this event
Florence who clear foretold it from the first—

325 Thro' me she gives you the command and charge
She takes, thro' me, from him who held it late!
A painful trial, very sore, was yours:
All that could draw out, marshal in array
The selfish passions 'gainst the public good—

330 Slights, scorns, neglects, were heaped on you to bear:
And ever you did bear and bow the head!
It had been sorry trial to precede
Your feet, hold up the promise of reward
For luring gleam; your footsteps kept the track

335 Thro' dark and doubt: take all the light at once!
Trial is over, consummation shines;
Well you have served, as well henceforth command!
         Puccio. No, no . . I dare not . . I am grateful, glad;
But Luria—you shall understand he's wronged—

340 And he's my Captain—this is not the way
We soldiers climb to fortune: think again!
The sentence is not even passed, beside!
I dare not . . where's the soldier could?
         Luria.   Now, Florence—
Is it to be?—You will know all the strength

345 Of the savage—to your neck the proof must go?
You will prove the brute nature? Ah, I see!
The savage plainly is impassible—
He keeps his calm way thro' insulting words,
Cold looks, sharp gestures—any one of which

350 Would stop you and offend your finer sense:

---

iii *316.* a *bye word in men's*] a bye-word in all (*1849-75*); by-word in all (*1888*).

iii *321. selected man*] good citizen (*1868-88*).

iii *337. you have*] have you (*1849-88*).

iii *345. Of the*] O' the (*1870-88*).

iii *347. impassible*: insensible (to pain or insult).

iii *349.*] Sarcastic looks, sharp gestures—one of which (*1849-88*).

iii *350. you and offend*] you, fatal to (*1849-88*).

But if he steadily pursues the path
Without a mark upon his callous hide
Thro' the mere brushwood you grow angry with,
And leave the tatters of your flesh upon,
355 —You have to learn that when the true bar comes,
The thick mid forest, the real obstacle,
Which when you reach, you give the labour up,
Nor dash on, but lie down composed before,
—He goes against it, like the brute he is!
360 It falls before him, or he dies in his course!
I kept my course thro' past ingratitude—
I saw . . it does seem now as if I saw,
Could not but see, those insults as they fell,
—Ay, let them glance from off me, very like,
365 Laughing perhaps to think the quality
You grew so bold on while you so despised,
The Moor's dull mute inapprehensive mood,
Was saving you; I bore and kept my course:
Now real wrong fronts me—see if I succumb!
370 Florence withstands me?—I will punish her!

At night my sentence will arrive, you say!
Till then I cannot, if I would, rebel—
Retaining my full power to will and do:
After—it is to see. Tiburzio, thanks!
375 Go—you are free—join Lucca. I suspend
All further operations till the night.
Thank you, and for the silence most of all!
[*To* Braccio] Let my self-justified accuser go
Safe thro' the army which would trample him
380 Dead in a moment at my word or sign!

iii *351. steadily pursues the path*] steadily advances, still (*1849-63*); steadily advance, still march (*1865*); stolidly advance, march mute (*1868-88*).
iii *356. thick*] murk (*1868-88*).   *real*] grand (*1865-88*).
iii *359-60.*] EBB. quoted 'He goes on like the brute he is *against* / It falls before him, or he dies in his course—', and commented: 'Did you mean to write "against", & not rather "until"?' 'Against' is an Elizabethan archaism for 'until': cp. *Midsummer Night's Dream* III ii 99: 'I'll charm his eyes against she do appear'. See also *Pippa* ii 4-6.
iii *366. on . . . despised,*] on, . . . despised (*1849-88*).
iii *372^373.*] —Unauthorized to lay my office down, (*1849-88*).
iii *376. the night*] to-night (*1849-88*).
iii *378. self-justified*] complacent bland (*1849-88*).
iii *378^379.*] And carry his self-approving head and heart (*1849-88*, except 'Carry', *1868-88*).

Go, Sir, to Florence; tell friends what I say—
That while I wait their sentence, theirs waits them.
[*To* Domizia] You . . Lady, you have dark Italian eyes!
I would be generous if I might . . Oh, yes
385 When I remember how so oft it seemed
You were inclined to break the barrier down
And lift me to you . . all that praise of old!
Alas for generosity—this hour
Demands strict justice—bear it as you may!
390 I must—the Moor,—the Savage,—pardon you!
[*To* Puccio] Puccio, my trusty soldier, see them
forth!—

iii *382. their*] my (*1868-88*).
iii *383. dark*] black (*1849-88*).
iii *385-6.*] For I remember how so oft you seemed / Inclined at heart to break
the barrier down (*1849-88*).
iii *387.*] Which Florence makes God build between us both. (*1849*); Which
Florence finds God built between us both. (*1863-88*).
iii *389. Demands strict justice*] Asks retribution (*1865-88*).
iii *389-90. may! / I*] may, / I (*1868-88*).
iii *391. s.d.*] not *1865-88*.
iii *391. see them forth*: see iv 53n.

Act IV

Evening.

Enter Puccio *and* Jacopo.

 Puccio. What Luria will do? Ah, 'tis yours, fair Sir,
Your and your subtle-witted master's part,
To tell me that; I tell you what he can.
 Jacopo. Friend, you mistake my station! I observe
5 The game, watch how my betters play, no more.
 Puccio. But mankind are not pieces . . there's your
  fault!
You cannot push them and, the first move made,
Lean back to study what the next should be,
In confidence that when 'tis fixed at length,
10 You'll find just where you left them, blacks and
  whites:
Men go on moving when your hand's away.
You build, I notice, firm on Luria's faith
This whole time,—firmlier than I choose to build,
Who never doubted it—of old, that is—
15 With Luria in his ordinary mind:
But now, oppression makes the wise man mad—
How do I know he will not turn and stand
And hold his own against you, as he may?
But say that he withdraws to Pisa—well,—
20 Then, even if all happens to your wish,
Which is a chance . . .
 Jacopo.   Nay—'twas an oversight
Not waiting till the proper warrant came:
You could not take what was not ours to give.

iv *1*.] the word 'will' is italicized, *1849-65*, presumably to clarify the scansion.
iv *2*. *Your*] You (*1865-75*).
iv *8*. *to . . . should*] and . . . shall (*1868-88*).
iv *9*. *at length*] upon (*1849-88*).
iv *10*.] EBB. quoted 'Just where you left them blacks & whites you'll find', and commented: 'Why not, o you inverter "You'll find just where you left them, blacks & whites." I like the thought very much'. *You'll*] You (*1868-88*).
iv *16*. Cp. *Ecclesiastes* vii 7-8: 'Surely oppression maketh a wise man mad; and a gift destroyeth the heart. Better is the end of a thing than the beginning thereof: and the patient in spirit is better than the proud in spirit'. See also l. 50.
iv *19*. *But say that he*] Suppose that he (*1849*); Suppose he but (*1863-88*). *withdraws*] withdraw (*1868-88*).

But when at night the sentence really comes,
25   And Florence authorizes past dispute
Luria's removal and your own advance,
You will perceive your duty and accept?
    Puccio.   Accept   what?   muster-rolls   of   soldiers'
    names?
An army upon paper?—I want men,
30   Their hearts as well as hands—and where's a heart
That's not with Luria in the multitude
I come from walking thro' by Luria's side?
You gave him to them, set him on to grow
A head upon their trunk, one blood feeds both,
35   They feel him there and live and well know why
—For they do know, if you are ignorant,
Who kept his own place and kept theirs alike,—
Managed their ease yet never spared his own:
All was your deed: another might have served—
40   There's peradventure no such dearth of men—
But you chose Luria—so they grew to him:
And now, for nothing they can understand,
Luria's removed, off is to roll the head—
The body's mine—much I shall do with it!
    Jacopo. That's at the worst!
45   *Puccio.*   No—at the best it is!
Best, do you hear? I saw them by his side:
Only we two with Luria in the camp
Are left that know the secret? That you think?
Hear what I saw: from rear to van no heart
50   But felt the quiet patient hero there
Was wronged, nor in the moveless ranks an eye

iv *25. And Florence*] Our city (*1868-88*).
iv *26. your own advance*] transfers the charge (*1868-88*).
iv *30. Their*] The (*1868-88*).
iv *31. That's not*] But beats (*1865-88*).
iv *33. him to them*] them Luria (*1863-88*).   *on to*] thus to (*1868-88*).
iv *34. A head*] Head-like (*1849-88*).   *one blood*] one heart (*1865-88*).
iv *35. and live*] live twice, (*1868-88*).
iv *37. kept theirs alike*] respected theirs (*1849-88*).
iv *38.*] Managed their sweat, yet never spared his blood. (*1865-88*).
iv *39. deed*] act (*1865-88*).
iv *40. men*] heads (*1868-88*).
iv *41. chose*] choose (*1865-75*).   *to him*] one flesh (*1868-88*).
iv *43. Luria's removed*] Luria removed (*1865-88*).
iv *48. know*] keep (*1868-88*).   *That you think*] You think that (*1849-88*).
iv *49. saw*] know (*1868-88*).

But glancing told its fellow the whole story
Of that convicted silent knot of spies
Who passed thro' them to Florence—they might
      pass—
55 No breast but gladlier beat when free of them!
Our troops will catch up Luria, close him round,
Lead him to Florence as their natural lord,
Partake his fortunes, live or die with him!
      Jacopo. And by mistake catch up along with him
60 Puccio, no doubt, compelled in self-despite
To still continue Second in Command!
      Puccio. No, Sir, no second nor so fortunate!
Your tricks succeed with me too well for that!
I am as you have made me, and shall die
65 A mere trained fighting hack to serve your end;
With words, you laugh at while they leave your
      mouth,
For my life's rules and ordinance of God!
Duty have I to do, and faith to keep,

iv *53.* See iii 391. Since both Domizia and the Secretary are still present in this act, it is not clear who other than Braccio has been expelled from the camp. See also l. 107n.

iv *55. them*] such (*1863-88*).

iv *57. Lead*] Bear (*1868-88*).

iv *58. fortunes*] fortune (*1868-88*).

iv *60. self-despite*: combining 'in spite of himself' and 'against his own interests'.

iv *63.*] EBB. quoted 'Your tricks with me too well succeed for that', and commented: 'Query—"Your tricks succeed with me too well for that." Is there an objection[?]'.

iv *64. and shall*] live and (*1868-88*).

iv *65.*] To serve your end; a mere trained fighting-hack (*1868-88*, except 'end! a', *1870-75*; 'end—a', 'fighting-hack,', *1888*).

iv *67. rules*] rule (*1865-88*).

iv *68-9.*] I have to do my duty, keep my faith, / And earn my praise, and guard against my blame, (*1849-88*). EBB. quoted 'Duty to do have I, & faith to keep', and commented: 'Query. "Duty have I to do,"[.] Puccio speaks admirably yet like a soldier—'.

iv *68^171.*] EBB. quoted a single line, and a line and a few words, which must come in this section, but which are hard to place. The first was 'Set you your heart on stoutness ne'er so firm', on which she commented: 'Which line I do *not* very much like. I don't like a firm stoutness, or a heart set firmly on stoutness . . read it anyway, & I set about objecting'. B. dropped the line entirely, and it is impossible to determine its location; it appears to belong to Puccio, since Husain addresses Luria as 'thou'. EBB. next quoted 'Far too

And praise to earn, and blame to guard against,
70   As I was trained. I shall accept your charge,
And fight against one better than myself,
And my own heart's conviction of his wrongs—
That you may count on!—just as hitherto
Have I gone on, persuaded I was slighted,
75   Degraded, all the terms we learn by rote,—
Because the better nature, fresh-inspired,
Mounted above me to its proper place:
What mattered all the kindly graciousness
And cordial brother's bearing? This was clear—
80   I was once captain, am subaltern now,
And so must keep complaining like a fool!
So take the curse of a lost man, I say!
You neither play your puppets to the end,
Nor treat the real man,—for his realness' sake
85   Thrust rudely in their place,—with such regard
As might console them for their altered rank.
Me, the mere steady soldier, you depose
For Luria, and here's all that he deserves!

---

plain / Souls show themselves for men to choose & read', and commented: 'It
seems to me too that the whole of this passage is somewhat diffusely given, &
not distinctly. If this soul-reading is so easy & achievable by boys, is it a
consequence that Luria should be read wrong? Will you look & wave your
wand once?' This seems to have come in one of Husain's speeches, but B.
altered the passage beyond recovery.

iv 72. *And my own*] Spite of my (*1863-88*).   *wrongs*] worth (*1849-88*).

iv 74. *Have I . . . slighted*] I have . . . wronged (*1849-88*).

iv 75. *Degraded, all the*] Slighted, and all the (*1849*); Slighted, and moody
(*1863-65*); Slighted, insulted, (*1868-88*).

iv 75ˆ76.] All because Luria superseded me— (*1849-88*).

iv 79. *And*] The (*1868-88*).

iv 80.] I, once the captain, was subaltern now, (*1849-75*); I, once the captain,
now was subaltern, (*1888*).

iv 82. *So*] Go (*1849-88*).   *man*] soul (*1865-88*).

iv 83-6. Puccio accuses the Florentine government of inconsistency: it
demotes officers of ordinary quality such as himself in favour of genuinely
talented men such as Luria, but does not then give the latter the trust they
deserve. Giving such trust would go some way towards consoling those who
have been demoted, since they would at least feel that the government had
decided to reward real merit.

iv 87. *depose*] deposed (*1865*); probably but not certainly a mispr.

iv 88. *that he*] your pet (*1863-88*).

Of what account, then, are my services?
90 One word for all: whatever Luria does,
—If backed by his indignant troops he turns
In self-defence and Florence goes to ground,—
Or for a signal, everlasting shame
He pardons you, and simply seeks his friends
95 And heads the Pisan and Lucchese troops
—And if I, for you ingrates past belief,
Resolve to fight against one false to us,
Who, inasmuch as he is true, fights there—
Whichever way he wins, he wins for me,
100 For every soldier, for the common good!
Sir, chronicling the rest, omit not this!
                    [*Exeunt. Enter* Luria *and* Husain.
     Husain. Saw'st thou?—For they are gone! The
          world lies bare
Before thee, to be tasted, felt and seen
Like what it is, now Florence goes away!
105 Thou livest now, with men art man again!
Those Florentines were eyes to thee of old;
But Braccio, but Domizia, gone is each—
There lie beneath thee thine own multitudes—

iv *89. are my services*] is your laughing-stock (*1868-88*).
iv *91. he turns*] he turn (*1865*); he turn, (*1868-88*).
iv *92. In self-defence*] Revenge himself (*1868-88*).   *goes to ground*] go to
ground (*1865-88*).
iv *94. pardons*] pardon (*1865-88*).   *and simply seeks his friends*] simply seeks
better friends (*1863-88*).
iv *95.*] And head the Pisan and the Lucchese troops (*1865*); Side with the
Pisans and Lucchese for change (*1868-88*).
iv *96. for you*] pledged to (*1868-88*).
iv *97.*] Resolve to fight against a man called false, (*1849-65*); Dare fight
against a man such fools call false, (*1868-88*).
iv *98. is true*] was true (*1863-88*).   *there*] me (*1868-88*).
iv *99. way he wins*] way he win (*1863-88*, except 'way we win', *1868-70*,
almost certainly a mispr.).   *for me*] for worth (*1868-88*).
iv *100. the common*] the true and (*1863-65*); all true and (*1868-88*).
iv *101. s.d.*] Exeunt. Enter] As they go, enter (*1849-88*).
iv *102-3. The world . . . Before thee:* cp. *PL* xii 646-7: 'The world was all
before them, where to choose / Their place of rest'.
iv *106. eyes*] all (*1868-88*).
iv *107.* But Domizia has not gone: she enters at l. 187. See l. 53n.

Sawest thou?
   Luria.   I saw.
   Husain.   So hold thy course, my King!
110 The years return—Let thy heart have its way!
Ah, they would play with thee as with all else?
Turn thee to use, and fashion thee anew,
Find out God's fault in thee as in the rest?
Oh, watch but, listen only to these men
115 Once at their occupation! Ere ye know,
The free great heaven is shut, their stifling pall
Drops till it frets the very tingling hair—
So weighs it on our head,—and, for the earth,
The common earth is tethered up and down,
120 Over and across—here shalt thou move, they say!
   Luria. Ay, Husain?
   Husain.   So have they spoiled all beside!
So stands a man girt round with Florentines,
Priests, greybeards, Braccios, women, boys and spies,
All in one tale, each singing the same song,
125 How thou must house, and live at bed and board,
Take pledge and give it, go their every way,
Breathe to their measure, make thy blood beat time
With theirs—or—all is nothing—thou art lost—
A savage . . how should such perceive as they?
130 Feel glad to stand 'neath God's close naked hand!
Look up to it! Why down they pull thy neck
Lest it crush thee who feel it and would kiss,
Without their priests that needs must glove it first
In mercy to thy lip it else will wound!
135 Love Woman—why a very beast thou art!
Thou must . . .
   Luria.   Peace, Husain!
   Husain.   Ay, but, spoiling all,
For all else true things substituting false,

iv *109. So*] Then, (*1849-88*).
iv *114. watch but*] watch, oh (*1888*).   *men*] fiends (*1868-88*).
iv *115. ye*] we (*1888*).
iv *119. The*] Our (*1849-88*).
iv *120. say*] cry (*1865-88*).
iv *124. each*] all (*1865-88*).
iv *129. should such*] shouldst thou (*1849-88*).
iv *131-4.* Cp. *Respectability* 17-20.
iv *132. feel . . . would*] feel'st . . . would'st (*1849-88*).
iv *134.*] Lest peradventure it should wound thy lip! (*1849*); Lest peradventure it offend thy lip! (*1863-65*); Lest peradventure flesh offend thy lip. (*1868-88*).

That they should dare spoil, of all instincts, thine!
Should dare to take thee with thine instincts up,
140 Thy battle-ardours, like a ball of fire,
And class them and allow them place and play
So far, no farther—unabashed the while!
Thou with the soul that never can take rest—
Thou born to do, undo, and do again,
145 But never to be still,—thou wouldst make war?
Oh, that is commendable, just and right!
Come over, say they, have the honour due
In living out thy nature! Fight thy best—
It is to be for Florence not thyself!
150 For thee it were a horror and a plague—
For us, when war is made for Florence, see,
How all is changed . . the fire that fed on earth
Now towers to heaven!—
    Luria.   And what sealed up so long
My Husain's mouth?
    Husain.   Oh, friend, oh, lord—for me,
155 What am I?—I was silent at thy side
That am a part of thee—It is thy hand,
Thy foot that glows when in the heart fresh blood
Boils up as thine does! Thou wilt live again,
Again love as thou likest, hate as freely,
160 Turn to no Braccios nor Domizias now
To ask, before thy very limbs may move,
If Florence' welfare be not touched therein!
    Luria. So clear what Florence must expect of me?
    Husain. Both armies against Florence! Take
      revenge!
165 Wide, deep—to live upon, in feeling now,—
And after, in remembrance, year by year—
And, in the dear conviction, die at last!
She lies now at thy pleasure—pleasure have!

iv *145. But*] And (*1863–88*).   *thou wouldst*] wouldst thou (*1849–88*).
iv *156. That*] Who (*1863–88*).
iv *158.*] Boils up, thou heart of me! Now live again! (*1849–88*, except 'Now,',
1863–88; 'again,', *1870–88*).
iv *159. freely,*] free! (*1849–88*).
iv *161. may*] dare (*1849–88*).
iv *162. not touched therein*] concerned thereby (*1849–88*).
iv *164–329.* This passage (from 'Take revenge!') was extracted for *1863²*: see
headnote, p. 374.
iv *166.*] And after live, in memory, year by year— (*1865–88*).
iv *167. And, in*] And, with (*1849–88*).

Their vaunted intellect that gilds our sense,
170   They blend with life to show it better by,
       —How think'st thou?—I have turned that light on
         them!
       They called our thirst of war a transient thing;
       The battle element must pass away
       From life, they said, and leave a tranquil world:
175   —Master, I took their light and turned it full
       On that dull turgid vein they said would burst
       And pass away; and as I looked on Life,
       Still everywhere I tracked this, though it hid
       And shifted, lay so silent as it thought,
180   Changed oft the hue yet ever was the same:
       Why 'twas all fighting, all their nobler life!
       All work was fighting, every harm—defeat,
       And every joy obtained—a victory!
       Be not their dupe!
                            —Their dupe? That hour is past!
185   Here stand'st thou in the glory and the calm!
       All is determined! Silence for me now!
                                                  [*Exit.*

       Luria. Have I heard all?
       Domizia. [*Advancing from the background*] No,
         Luria, I am here.
       Not from the motives these have urged on thee,

iv *169-83*. In her letter to B. of 21 Jan. 1846, EBB. commented: '*that* passage
perhaps is over-subtle for a Husain—but too nobly right in the abstract to be
altered, if it is so or not' (*LK* 407).

iv *170*. *They blend*] And blends (*1849-88*).

iv *171-2*.] EBB. quoted 'How think'st thou? I have turned on them their
arm', and commented: 'Is there an objection to making this clear by repeating
the word "light" . . "I have turned their light on *them*". Then in the next
line // A transient thing was this our thirst of war // if you wrote "They
called our thirst of war a transient thing" you allow the reader to see at a
glance what otherwise he will seek studiously. And so worthy of all
admiration it is, this discourse of Husain's, with his true doctrine that "all
work is fighting"'.

iv *180*. *oft the*] shape and (*1868-88*).

iv *187-249*. EBB. commented: 'Domizia speaks her speech . . . eloquently &
well—she has her side of truth like the rest—& one feels for poor Luria so
much the more'.

iv *187*. *I am here*] I remain (*1863-88*; *1863*[2] as *1846*).

iv *188*. *these*: since Luria has heard only one argument in this act, Domizia
presumably refers to all the motives which have previously been ascribed to
or urged on Luria, by (for example) Braccio and Tiburzio.

      Ignoble, insufficient, incomplete,
190   And pregnant each with sure seeds of decay
      As failing of sustainment from thyself,
      —Neither from low revenge, nor selfishness,
      Nor savage lust of power, nor one, nor all,
      Shalt thou abolish Florence! I proclaim
195   The angel in thee and reject the spirits
      Which ineffectual crowd about his strength
      And mingle with his work and claim a share!
      —Inconsciously to the augustest end
      Thou hast arisen: second not to him
200   In rank so much as time, who first ordained
      The Florence thou art to destroy, should be—
      Yet him a star, too, guided, who broke first
      The pride of lonely power, the life apart,
      And made the eminences, each to each,
205   Lean o'er the level world and let it lie
      Safe from the thunder henceforth 'neath their arms—

iv *192. low revenge*] hate, revenge (*1863²*).
iv *193. savage*] pride nor (*1863²*).
iv *194-5.*] EBB. quoted 'I proclaim / The angel in thee & reject the sprites',
and commented: 'A fine expression—the first—but why not write "spirits"
at length?' She argued the same point in a letter to B.: 'But why not "spirits"
rather than "sprites," which has a different association by custom? "Spirits" is
quite short enough, it seems to me, for a last word—it sounds like a
monosyllable that trembles . . or thrills, rather' (21 Jan. 1846, *LK* 407). But
in *1863-88* B. restored 'sprites'.
iv *198-249.*] EBB. quoted a line and some fragments which are hard to place.
She quoted 'Above them which still safelier bids them live', and commented:
'Not a very favorite line perhaps of mine—but the "*weaklier*" must not stand
so near it anywise. See below. The word "break" too ends two several lines.
My belief is that the whole passage will strike you as diffuse, & that you will
teach it to coil up gathering strength'. The likeliest position is ll. 221-5.
iv *198. Inconsciously*: see i 352n.
iv *199-200. to him / In rank so much as time*] in rank / So much as time, to him
(*1849-88*).
iv *199-201. him . . . should be*: i.e. Julius Caesar, who founded Florence
according to tradition.
iv *201. The*] That (*1849-88*).
iv *202-10. Ohio* takes these lines as continuing the allusion to Caesar, but this
takes no account of the antithesis which Domizia, following Braccio at iii
157ff., develops between 'lonely power' and the 'combined' strength of the
Florentine republic.
iv *204-9.* Cp. *Sordello* i 205ff., and *England* 181ff.
iv *206. arms*] tops (*1863-88; 1863²* as *1846*).

So the few famous men of old combined
And let the multitude rise underneath
And reach them and unite—so Florence grew:
210   Braccio speaks well, it was well worth the price.
But when the sheltered Many grew in pride
And grudged their station to the glorious ones,
Who, greater than their kind, are truly great
Only in voluntary servitude—
215   Which they who, being less, would fain be more,
And so accept not, then are least of all—
Time was for thee to rise, and thou art here.
Such plague possessed this Florence—who can tell
The mighty girth and greatness at the heart
220   Of those so noble pillars of the grove
She pulled down in her envy? Who as I
The light weak parasite born but to twine
Round each of them and, measuring them, so live?
My light love keeps the matchless circle safe,
225   My slender life proves what has past away!
I lived when they departed; lived to cling
To thee, the mighty stranger; thou would'st rise
And burst the thraldom, and avenge, I knew.
I have done nothing—all was thy strong heart—
230   But as a bird's weight breaks the infant tree
Which after holds an aery in its arms,
So did I care that nought should warp thy spire
From rising to the height; the roof is reached—
Break through and there is all the sky above!

iv *210. speaks well*] speaks true (*1863-88; 1863²* as *1846*).
iv *212.*] And grudged the station of the glorious ones, (*1849-88*, except
'elected ones', *1863-88; 1863²* as *1849*).
iv *213. truly*] truliest (*1863²*).
iv *215-16.*] not *1849-88*.
iv *220. noble*] perfect (*1863-88; 1863²* as *1846*).
iv *223. so live*] live (*1863-88*). At the proof stage, EBB. had quoted
'measuring them, live', and commented: 'or—"and measuring them, so
live". Is there an objection? Because the trisyllabic "measuring" weakens the
line'.
iv *229. heart*] bole (*1868-88*).
iv *230. as a bird's weight breaks*] a bird's weight can break (*1849-88*).
iv *231. aery*: eyrie.
iv *232. So did I*] And 'twas my (*1849-88*).
iv *233. reached—*] reached (*1868-88*). See next line.
iv *234.*] Break through and there extends the sky above! (*1863; 1863²* as
1846); Break through and see extend the sky above! (*1865*); O' the forest,

235 Go on to Florence, Luria! 'Tis man's cause!
But fail thou, and thy fall is least to dread!
Thou keepest Florence in her evil way,
Encouragest her sin so much the more—
And while the bloody past is justified,
240 The murder of those gone before approved,
Thou all the surelier dost work against
The men to come, the Lurias yet unborn,
That, greater than thyself, are reached o'er thee
Who giv'st the vantage-ground their foes require,
245 As o'er my prostrate House thyself wast reached!
Man calls thee—God shall judge thee: all is said!
The mission of my House fulfilled at last!
And the mere woman, speaking for herself,
Reserves speech; it is now no woman's time.
                                                [*Exit.*
250   *Luria.* [*Solus*] So at the last must figure Luria then!
Doing the various work of all his friends
And answering every purpose save his own.
No doubt, 'tis well for them to see; but him—
After the exploit what remains? Perchance
255 A little pride upon the swarthy brow
At having brought successfully to bear
'Gainst Florence' self her own especial arms,
Her craftiness impelled by fiercer strength
From Moorish blood than feeds the northern wit—

---

break through, see extend the sky! (*1868-88*). Cp. *Pauline* 781-2.

iv *236.*] Fail thou, and thine own fall is least to dread! (*1849-88*, except 'were least', *1865-88* and 'dread:', *1868-88*).

iv *239. bloody*] ignoble (*1868-88*).

iv *240.*] not *1849-88*.

iv *241. dost work against*] dost the Future wrong, (*1863-65*; *1863²* as *1846*); warp'st the future growth (*1868-88*).

iv *242. men*] chiefs (*1863-88*; *1863²* as *1846*).

iv *243-4. That . . . Who*] Who . . . That (*1849-88*).

iv *244.*] at the proof stage, EBB. quoted 'Who give the vantage ground', and commented: 'Who *giv'st*'.

iv *246. shall judge*] requites (*1863-88*; *1863²* as *1846*).

iv *250. s.d.*] not *1849-88*.   *So*] Thus (*1863-88*; *1863²* as *1846*).

iv *253. see; but*] wish; for (*1849*); wish; but (*1863-88*). EBB. had quoted ''Tis well for them to see—but him!' and commented: 'Poor Luria, how great & benignant he is in circumstances which make misanthropes of other men. It is very fine . . all to the end [of the act]'.

iv *254. remains*] is left (*1849*); were left (*1863-88*; *1863²* as *1849*).

260   But after!—once the easy vengeance willed,
       Beautiful Florence at a word laid low
       —(Not in her Domes and Towers and Palaces,
       Not in a dream that outrage!)—but laid low
       As shamed in her own eyes henceforth for ever,
265   And for the rival cities round to see,
       Conquered and pardoned by a hireling Moor!
       —For him who did the irreparable wrong
       What would be left, the life's illusion fled,—
       What hope or trust in the forlorn wide world?

270   How strange that Florence should mistake me so!
       How grew this? What withdrew her faith from me?
       Some cause! These fretful-blooded children talk
       Against their mother,—they are wronged, they say—
       Notable wrongs a smile makes up again!
275   So, taking fire at each supposed offence,
       These may speak rashly, suffer for rash speech—
       But what could it have been in word or deed
       That injured me? Some one word spoken more
       Out of my heart, and all had changed perhaps!
280   My fault it must have been,—for what gain they?
       Why risk the danger? See what I could do!

iv 263.] Not even in a dream that outrage!)—low, (*1849-88*).
iv 265. *And*] Low (*1849-88*).   *see*] laugh (*1865-88*).
iv 268. *the*] his (*1849-88*).
iv 269ˆ270.] no space here in *1849-88*; but note that in *1849*, l. 269 ends a
page.
iv 271. *How*] Whence (*1863-88*).
iv 274. *a*] her (*1863-88*).
iv 276. *These*] They (*1849-88*).   *rash*] their (*1863-88*).
iv 278. *That*] Thus (*1868-88*).
iv 281-329. When she first saw Act IV, EBB. objected to Luria's suicide: in
her letter to B. of 21 Jan. 1846, she wrote: 'is he to die *so?* can you mean it?
Oh—indeed I foresaw *that*—not a guess of mine ever touched such an
end—and I can scarcely resign myself to it as a necessity even now . . I mean,
to the act, as Luria's act, whether it is final or not—the act of suicide being so
unheroical. But you are a dramatic poet & right perhaps, where, as a didactic
poet, you would have been wrong' (*LK* 406). B. replied: 'If you have gone so
far with Luria, I fancy myself nearly or altogether safe: I must not tell
you,—but I wished just these feelings to be in your mind . . . the last act
throws light back on all, I hope. Observe only, that Luria *would* stand, if I
have plied him effectually with adverse influences, in such a position as to
render any other end impossible without the hurt to Florence which his
religion is, to avoid inflicting—passively awaiting, for instance, the sentence

And my fault wherefore visit upon them,
My Florentines? The generous revenge
I meditate! To stay here passively,
285 Go at their summons, be as they dispose—
Why, if my very soldiers stop not that,
And if I moderate my chiefs, what then?
I ruin Florence—teach her friends mistrust—
Confirm her enemies in harsh belief—
290 And when she finds one day, as she must find,
The strange mistake, and how my heart was hers,
This shall console me, that my Florentines
Walk with a sadder step, a graver face,
Who took me with such frankness, praised me so,
295 At the glad outset! Had they been less sure
They had less feared what seemed a change in me.
And is it they who will have done the harm?
How could they interpose with those old fools
In the council? Suffer for those old fools' sakes—
300 They, who made pictures of me, turned the songs
About my battles? Ah, we Moors get blind
Out of our proper world where we are right!
The sun that guides is closer to us! See—
See, my own orb! He sinks from out the sky!
305 Why there! a whole day has he blessed the land,

---

and punishment to come at night, would as surely inflict it as taking part with
her foes: his aim is to prevent the harm she will do herself by striking
him—so he moves aside from the blow' (22 Jan. 1846, *LK* 411).

iv *283. generous*] notable (*1863-88*; *1863²* as *1846*).

iv *284. meditate! To stay here*] meditated! To stay (*1868-88*).

iv *285. Go at*] Attend (*1868-88*).

iv *286. stop not that*] keep their ranks (*1849-65*); keep the rank (*1868-88*).

iv *287. I moderate my chiefs*] I pacify my chiefs (*1849-63*); my chieftains
acquiesce (*1865-88*).

iv *290. she must find*] find she must (*1868-88*).

iv *292. This shall*] Shall it (*1849-88*).

iv *293. a graver face*] in graver guise (*1865-88*).

iv *295. outset!*] outset? (*1863-88*; *1863²* as *1846*).   *been less sure*] loved me
less (*1849-88*).

iv *297.*] And after all, who did the harm? Not they! (*1849-88*).

iv *299. In the . . . sakes—*] I' the . . . sake— (*1870-88*).

iv *300. turned*] sang (*1849-88*).

iv *302. are right*] can see (*1849-88*).

iv *303. is*] was (*1863²*).

iv *303-4. See . . . See*] There . . . There (*1849-88*).

My land, our Florence all about the hills,
The fields and gardens, vineyards, olive-grounds,
All have been blest—and yet we Florentines
With minds intent upon our battle here,
310   Found that he rose too soon, or rose too late,
Gave us no vantage, or gave Pisa more—
And so we wronged him! does he turn in ire
To burn the earth that cannot understand?
Or drop out quietly, and leave the sky,
315   His task once ended? Night wipes blame away:
Another morning from my East shall rise
And find all eyes at leisure, all disposed
To watch it and approve its every work.
So, praise the new sun, the successor praise!
320   Praise the new Luria, and forget the old!
                    [*Taking a phial from his breast.*
—Strange! This is all I brought from my own Land
To help me—Europe would supply the rest,
All needs beside, all other helps save this!
I thought of adverse fortune, battles lost,
325   The natural upbraidings of the loser,
And then this quiet remedy to seek
At end of the disastrous day—

                                    [*He drinks.*
                        'Tis sought!
This was my happy triumph-morning: Florence
Is saved: I drink this, and ere night,—die!—Strange!

iv *309. minds*] souls (*1865-88*).

iv *310. or rose*] or else (*1849-63*); or set (*1865-88*).

iv *311. more*] much (*1868-88*).

iv *312. And so*] Therefore (*1865-88*).

iv *316. rise*] spring (*1863-88*).

iv *317. all disposed*] more disposed (*1849-63*).

iv *318.*] To watch it and approve its work, no doubt. (*1849*); To watch and understand its work, no doubt. (*1863-88*).

iv *323. this*] one (*1865-88*).

iv *324. battles*] battle (*1888*).

iv *325. upbraidings*] upbraiding (*1865-88*).

Act V

Night.

Luria. Puccio.

Luria. I thought to do this, not to talk this: well!
Such were my projects for the City's good,
To save her in attack or by defence.
Time, here as elsewhere, soon or late may take
5   With chance and change our foresight by surprise;
But not a little we provide against
—If you see clear on every point.
    Puccio.   Most clear.
    Luria. Then all is said—not much, to count the
        words,
Yet for an understanding ear enough,
10   And all that my brief stay permits, beside.
Nor must you blame me as I sought to teach
My elder in command or threw a doubt
Upon the very skill it comforts me
To know I leave,—that steady soldiership
15   Which never failed me: yet, because it seemed
A stranger's eye might haply note defect
Which skill thro' use and custom overlooks,
I have gone into the old cares once more,
As if I had to come and save again
20   Florence . . that May . . that morning! 'Tis night
       now—
Well—I broke off with? . .
    Puccio.   Of the past campaign
You spoke—of measures to be kept in mind
For future use.
    Luria.   True, so . . . but time—no time!
As well end here: remember this, and me!
Farewell now!
    Puccio.   Dare I speak?

v *3. save her in*] save her from (*1849*); help her in (*1863-88*).
v *5.*] Our foresight by surprise with chance and change; (*1849-88*, except
'thro' chance', *1863-88*).
v *8. to count the*] if you count (*1849-88*).
v *9. for*] to (*1865-88*).
v *14. that*] your (*1849-88*).
v *15. Which*] That (*1849-88*).
v *17. Which*] That (*1863-88*).

25   *Luria.*
        How is the second stream called . . no,—the third?
        Puccio. Pesa.
        Luria.   And a stone's cast from the fording place,
        To the East,—the little mount's name?
        Puccio.   Lupo.
        Luria.   Ay!
        Ay—there the tower and all that side is safe!
30   With San Romano, west of Evola,
        San Miniato, Scala, Empoli,
        Five towers in all,—forget not!
        Puccio.   Fear not me!
        Luria. —Nor to memorialize the Council now,
        I' the easy hour, on those battalions' claim
35   On the other side, by Staggia on the hills,
        That kept the Siennese at check!
        Puccio.   One word—
        Sir, I must speak! That you submit yourself
        To Florence' bidding howsoe'er it prove,
        And give up the command to me—is much,
40   Too much, perhaps: but what you tell me now
        Even affects the other course to choose—

v *25. The south*] South (*1868-88*).   *the river*: the Arno.

v *27. Pesa*: the third tributary on the south bank of the Arno as it flows
westwards out of Florence (towards Pisa and the sea).

v *28. Lupo*: Montelupo Fiorentino, now a small town near the junction of the
Pesa with the Arno.

v *30-1.* San Romano lies to the west of the river Egola (probably B.'s 'Evola',
as *Ohio* suggests), a tributary of the Arno about 50km from Florence. Luria
moves from the westernmost point eastwards and inland towards Florence:
San Miniato is about 10km from San Romano, Scala (or La Scala) about 3km
from San Miniato and a little to the north, and Empoli about 7km from Scala.
Fortifying these places would principally contribute to the security of
territory in the immediate neighbourhood of Florence. Cp. *Sordello* v 836-9.

v *35. On the other side,*] Who forced a pass (*1888*).   *Staggia*: a town at the
foot of the Chianti hills, about 7km south of Poggibonsi, a major junction of
roads leading northwards from Siena (see next line).

v *36. That*] Who (*1863-75*); And (*1888*).   *Siennese*: Siena, together with
Pisa and Lucca, was a rival of Florence among the Tuscan cities. It took no
part in the Pisan war, but helped Lucca (effectively) when Florence attacked
that city in 1429.

v *41. affects . . . to*] will affect . . . you (*1849-88*). EBB. had quoted the line
and commented: 'I do not like the lines which begin "Even" making a
dissyllable of it: they sound weak to me. But there is an objection here besides,

Poor as it may be, perils even that!
Refuge you seek at Pisa—yet these plans
All militate for Florence, all conclude
45 The formidable work to make her queen
Of the country,—which her rivals rose against
When you began it,—which to interrupt,
Pisa would buy you off in any case!
You cannot mean to sue for Pisa's help
With this made perfect and on record?
50   *Luria.*   I—
At Pisa, and for refuge, do you say?
   Puccio. Where are you going? Then you must
     decide
To leave the camp a silent fugitive,
Alone, at night—you stealing thro' our lines
55 Who were this morning's Luria,—you, escaped
To painfully begin the world once more,
With such a Past, as it had never been!
Where are you going?
   Luria.   Not so far, my Puccio,
But I shall get to hear and know and praise
60 (If you mind praise from your old captain yet)
Each happy blow you strike for Florence!
   Puccio.   —Ay,
But ere you gain your shelter, what may come!
For see—tho' nothing's surely known as yet,
Still . . truth must out . . I apprehend the worst.

---

because . . observe the meaning . . you do not mean to say "it even *affects* the other course" &c but that "it affects even the other *course*" &c. Do you see? I am always making that mistake myself, & everybody else makes it . . but there is a right & a wrong way after all. If you wrote "Affects the other course even, left to choose" or "Affects even the other course we have to choose"— . . see!' This is one of the rare occasions on which B. did not take EBB.'s advice in *1846*, though he did subsequently revise the line. EBB. added after this note: 'I admire the dialogue here—it is suggestive & full besides'.

v *42. perils*] peril (*1849-88*).

v *45. The*] Your (*1849-88*).

v *46. Of the*] O' the (*1870-88*).

v *48. in any case*] at any price (*1849-88*).

v *52. going? Then you*] going, then? You (*1849-88*).

v *53. To leave the camp*] On leaving us (*1849-88*).

v *55. you, escaped*] you escape (*1849-88*).

v *59.*] But that I hope to hear, and know, and praise (*1849*); But that I hope to hear, enjoy and praise (*1863-88*).

65   If mere suspicion stood for certainty
     Before, there's nothing can arrest the steps
     Of Florence toward your ruin, once on foot.
     Forgive her fifty times, it matters not!
     And having disbelieved your innocence,
70   How can she trust your magnanimity?
     You may do harm to her—why then, you will!
     And Florence is sagacious in pursuit.
     Have you a friend to count on?
          Luria.   One sure friend.
          Puccio. Potent?
          Luria.   All potent.
          Puccio.   And he is apprised?
          Luria. He waits me.
75   *Puccio.*   So!—Then I, put in your place
     Making my profit of all done by you,
     Calling your labours mine, reaping their fruit,
     To this the State's gift now add this from you—
     That I may take to my peculiar store
80   All these instructions to do Florence good,
     And if by putting some few happily
     In practice I should both advantage her
     And draw down honour on myself,—what then?
          Luria. Do it, my Puccio! I shall know and praise!
85   *Puccio.* Though so men say, "mark what we gain
               by change
     —A Puccio for a Luria!"
          Luria.   Even so.
          Puccio. Then not for fifty hundred Florences

                                    ◦

v 66. *steps*] step (*1865-88*).

v *69-70.*] EBB. quoted these lines, and commented: 'True & overcoming . .
& put so excellently well. The suggested pathos of this situation . . how deep
it is. Poor great Luria!' EBB. then added: 'I feel that I ought not to be able to
count the trefoil, when lifted to the summit of a mountain . . but I do not like
that little ending word to Puccio's speech . . "you 'bid!'" the accent on "bid".
Wont you say "you bid me" at least?' It is not certain to which of Puccio's
speeches EBB. refers; the one which ends at l. 83 is the likeliest.

v 78. *To this*] To these (*1849-65*).   *this from you*] this of yours (*1849-63*);
this beside (*1865*); yours beside (*1868-88*).

v 79. *to*] as (*1865-88*).

v 80. *All these*] All your (*1849-63*); These your (*1868-88*).   *do*] work
(*1865-88*).

Would I accept one office save my own,
Fill any other than my rightful post
90   Here at your feet, my Captain and my Lord!
That such a cloud should break, such trouble be,
Ere a man settles soul and body down
Into his true place and takes rest for ever!
There were my wise eyes fixed on your right hand,
95   And so the bad thoughts came and the worse words,
And all went wrong and painfully enough,—
No wonder, till, the right spot stumbled on,
All the jar stops and there is peace at once!
I am yours now,—a tool your right hand wields.
100   God's love, that I should live, the man I am,
On orders, warrants, patents and the like,
As if there were no glowing eye i' the world
To glance straight inspiration to my brain,
No glorious heart to give mine twice the beats!
105   For see,—the doubt where is it?—Fear? 'tis flown!
And Florence and her anger are a tale
To scare a child—Why, half a dozen words
Will tell her, spoken as I now can speak,
Her error, my past folly—and all's right,
110   And you are Luria, the great chief again!
Or at the worst—which worst were best of all—
To exile or to death I follow you.
    Luria. Thanks, Puccio! Let me use the privilege
You grant me: if I still command you,—stay!
115   Remain here—my viceregent, it shall be,
And not successor: let me, as of old,
Still serve the State, my spirit prompting yours;
Still triumph, one for both—There! Leave me now!
You cannot disobey my first command?
120   Remember what I spoke of Jacopo
And what you promised to observe with him:
Send him to speak with me—nay, no farewell—

v *92. settles soul and body*] settle soul and body (*1849*); settle, soul and body,
(*1863-88*).
v *93. takes*] take (*1849-88*).
v *94. There*] Here (*1849-88*).
v *105. the*] my (*1849-88*).
v *110. the*] our (*1849-88*).
v *111. which worst were best of all*: i.e. as proving Puccio's devotion beyond
doubt. Cp. Tiburzio at ii 249-50.
v *121. observe*] concert (*1863-88*).

You will be by me when the sentence comes.
                                         [*Exit* Puccio.
So there's one Florentine returns again!
125 Out of the genial morning company
One face is left to take into the night.
                                       [*Enter* Jacopo.
  Jacopo. I wait for your commands, Sir.
   Luria.   What, so soon?
I thank your ready presence and fair word.
I used to notice you in early days
130 As of the other species, so to speak,
The watchers of the lives of us who act—
That weigh our motives, scrutinize our thoughts;
So I propound this to your faculty
As you would tell me were a town to take
135 . . That is, of old. I am departing hence
Under these imputations: that is nought—
I leave no friend on whom they may rebound,
Hardly a name behind me in the land,
Being a stranger; all the more behoves
140 That I regard how altered were the case
With natives of the country, Florentines
On whom the like mischance should fall; the roots
O' the tree survive the ruin of the trunk—
No root of mine will throb . . you understand:
145 But I had predecessors, Florentines,
Accused as I am now and punished so—
The Traversari—you know more than I
How stigmatized they are and lost in shame.
Now, Puccio who succeeds me in command
150 Both served them and succeeded in due time;
He knows the way, and holds the documents,
And has the power to lay the simple truth
Before an active spirit, as I know yours:
And also there's Tiburzio, my new friend,
155 Will at a word confirm such evidence,
He being the chivalric soul we know.

v *123. will*] shall (*1849-88*).
v *127. commands*] command (*1865-88*).
v *131. The*] Those (*1849-88*).
v *151. and holds the*] holds proper (*1849-88*).
v *153. know*] count (*1868-88*).
v *156. the chivalric*] the great chivalric (*1865-88*). EBB. had quoted 'Being the thrice chivalric soul we know', and commented: 'Is there an objection to saying . . "He being the &c" . . because there seems a weakness otherwise . .

I put it to your instinct—were't not well,
—A grace, though but for contrast's sake, no more,
If you who witness and have borne a share
160 Involuntarily in my mischance,
Should, of your proper motion, set your skill
To indicate . . that is, investigate
The reason or the wrong of what befel
Those famous citizens your countrymen?
165 Nay—you shall promise nothing—but reflect,
And if your sense of justice prompt you—good!
    Jacopo. And if, the trial past, their fame stands
      white
To all men's eyes, as yours, my lord, to mine—
Their ghosts may sleep in quiet satisfied!
170 For me, a straw thrown up into the air,
My testimony goes for a straw's worth:
I used to hold by the instructed brain,
And move with Braccio as the master-wind;
The heart leads surelier: I must move with you—
175 As greatest now, who ever were the best.
So let the last and humblest of your servants
Accept your charge, as Braccio's heretofore.
                       [*Exit* Jacopo.
    Luria. Another!—Luria goes not poorly forth!
If one could wait! The only fault's with Time:
180 All men become good creatures . . . but so slow!
                       [*Enter* Domizia.
Ah, you once more?
    Domizia.   Domizia, that you knew,
Performed her task and died with it—'Tis I!

---

to *the ear* I mean'.

v *157. instinct*] tact, sir (*1865-88*).

v *163.*] The right or wrong of what mischance befell (*1865-88*).

v *167. white*] clear (*1849-88*).

v *173. the*] my (*1865-88*).   *master-wind*] master-mind (*B & P BYU*).

v *175.*] EBB. quoted 'As greater now who better still have been', and commented: 'Why not . . "As greater now who have been better still"—[it] is more natural, more clear, less stiff perhaps'.

v *177ˆ178.*] And offer homage, by obeying you!   (*1849-88*, with a comma after 'heretofore' in l. 177, and the s.d. 'Jacopo goes'; except 'And tender', *1865-88*).

v *179. one*] we (*1849-88*).

v *181. that*] whom (*1865-88*).

v *182ˆ183.*] Another woman, you have never known. (*1849-88*, except 'known,', *1868-75*).

Let the Past sleep now.
    Luria.   I have done with it.
    Domizia. How inexhaustibly the spirit grows!
185 One object she seemed erewhile born to reach
With her whole energies and die content,
So like a wall at the world's end it stood,
With nought beyond to live for—is it reached, . .
Already are new undreamed energies
190 Outgrowing under and extending further
To a new object;—there's another world!
See: I have told the purpose of my life,—
'Tis gained—you are decided, well or ill—
My work is done with you, your brow declares:
195 But—leave you? More of you seems yet to reach!
I stay for what I just begin to see.
    Luria. So that you turn not to the Past!
    Domizia.   You trace
Nothing but ill in it—my selfish impulse
Which sought its ends and disregarded yours?
200   *Luria.* Speak not against your nature: best each
      keep
His own—you yours—most now when I keep mine,
At least fall by it, having weakly stood.
God's finger marks distinctions all so fine
We would confound—the Lesser has its use
205 Which when it apes the Greater, is foregone.
I, born a Moor, lived half a Florentine;
But, punished properly, can die a Moor.
Beside there is what makes me understand

v *187. end*] edge (*1868-88*).

v *188. it*] that (*1865-88*).

v *193ˆ194.*] You march on Florence, or submit to her— (*1849-88*).

v *199. ends*] end (*1868-88*).

v *201. when*] that (*1868-88*).

v *202. weakly*] too weakly (*1849-88*).

v *203-5*. EBB. commented: 'I admire this excellent true thought, which cannot be said better—no, nor clearer'.

v *206-7*. Cp. (noting the brain/heart opposition in ll. 172-5 above) Djabal in *Return of the Druses* v 263-5: 'I, with an Arab instinct thwarted ever / By my Frank policy,—and, in its turn, / A Frank brain, thwarted by my Arab heart'. Djabal's words are linked to his decision to commit suicide.

v *207. die*] end (*1863-88*).

v *208. there is what*] there's something (*1868-88*).

Your nature . . I have seen it—
   Domizia.   One like mine?
210   *Luria.* In my own East . . if you would stoop and
      help
    My barbarous illustration . . it sounds ill
    Yet there's no wrong at bottom—rather praise—
    Domizia. Well?
    Luria.   We have creatures there which if you saw
    The first time, you would doubtless marvel at,
215   For their surpassing beauty, craft and strength.
    And tho' it were a lively moment's shock
    Wherein you found the purpose of their tongues
    That seemed innocuous in their lambent play,
    Yet, once made know such grace required such guard,
220   Your reason soon would acquiesce, I think,
    In the Wisdom which made all things for the best,
    So take them, good with ill, contentedly—
    The prominent beauty with the secret sting.
    I am glad to have seen you wondrous Florentines,
    Yet ..
    Domizia. I am here to listen.
225   *Luria.*   My own East!
    How nearer God we were! He glows above
    With scarce an intervention, presses close
    And palpitatingly, His soul o'er ours!
    We feel Him, nor by painful reason know!
230   The everlasting minute of creation

v *209. One*] Aught (*1863–88*).

v *213–19.* Cp. *Mr. Sludge* 539–43: 'His trade was, throwing thus / His sense out, like an anteater's long tongue, / Soft, innocent, warm, moist, impassible, / And when 't was crusted o'er with creatures—slick, / Their juice enriched his palate'.

v *217. Wherein you*] When you first (*1888*).   *of their*] of those (*1849–63*); out of (*1865*); of forked (*1868–88*).

v *218. seemed*] seem (*1865–88*). EBB. had quoted 'Whose lambent play so all innocuous seemed', and commented: 'Or . . "Whose lambent play seemed so innocuous" . . why object to natural sequency of the words'.

v *219. required*] requires (*1863–88*).

v *221. In the*] In (*1868–88*).

v *223. secret*] latent (*1865–88*).

v *224. Florentines,*] we supply the comma in agreement with *1849–88*.

v *230.*] EBB. quoted 'The everlasting minute of creation / Arrested', and commented: 'Fine, that is—but I do not see what business that word "arrested" has—it *darkens*, I fancy. "Suspended" might convey the thought . . might it not? . . but perhaps neither word is needed'. B. later quoted this line

Is felt there; *Now* it is, as it was Then;
All changes at His instantaneous will,
Not by the operation of a law
Whose maker is elsewhere at other work!
235   His soul is still engaged upon his world—
Man's praise can forward it, Man's prayer suspend,
For is not God all-mighty?—To recast
The world, erase old things and make them new,
What costs it Him? So man breathes nobly there!
240   And inasmuch as Feeling, the East's gift,
Is quick and transient—comes, and lo, is gone—
While Northern Thought is slow and durable,
Oh, what a mission was reserved for me,
Who, born with a perception of the power
245   And use of the North's thought for us of the East,
Should have stayed there and turned it to account,
Giving Thought's character and permanence
To the too-transitory Feelings there—
Writing God's messages in mortal words!
250   Instead of which, I leave my fated field
For this where such a task is needed least,
Where all are born consummate in the art
I just perceive a chance of making mine,—
And then, deserting thus my early post,
255   I wonder that the men I come among
Mistake me! There, how all had understood,
Still brought fresh stuff for me to stamp and keep,
Fresh instinct to translate them into law!
Me who . . .
       Domizia.   Who here the greater task achieve,
260   More needful even: who have brought fresh stuff
For us to mould, interpret and prove right,—
New feeling fresh from God, which, could we know
O' the instant, where had been our need of it?

---

in a letter to Furnivall about his views on Darwin (*Trumpeter* 34).
v *235. soul*] hand (*1863-88*).
v *243. Oh, what*] Surely (*1863-88*).
v *245.*] In *1872 Morgan*[2] (see Editorial Note, p. vii) 'North's' becomes 'North'
and 'thought' is replaced by an illegible reading; the rev. was not adopted.
v *246. stayed there and turned it*] remained and turned it (*1865-75*); remained,
turned knowledge to (*1888*).
v *248. Feelings*] Feeling (*1863-65*); feeling (*1868-88*).
v *249. messages*] message plain (*1865-88*).
v *262-3. feeling . . . it*] feelings . . . them (*1849-65*).

—Whose life re-teaches us what life should be,
265 What faith is, loyalty and simpleness,
All their revealment, taught us so long since
That, having mere tradition of the fact,
Truth copied falteringly from copies faint,
The early traits all dropped away,—we said
270 On sight of faith of yours, so looks not faith
We understand, described and taught before.
But still the truth was shown; and tho' at first
It suffer from our haste, yet trace by trace
Old memories reappear, the likeness grows,
275 Our slow Thought does its work, and all is known.
Oh, noble Luria! what you have decreed
I see not, but no animal revenge, . . .
It cannot be the gross and vulgar way
Traced for me by convention and mistake
280 Has gained that calm approving eye and brow.
Spare Florence after all! Let Luria trust
To his own soul, and I will trust to him!
    Luria. In time!
    Domizia.   How, Luria?
    Luria.   It is midnight now—
And they arrive from Florence with my fate.
    Domizia. I hear no step . .
285   *Luria.*   I feel it, as you say.
                   [*Enter* Husain.
    Husain. The man returned from Florence!
    Luria.   As I knew.
    Husain. He seeks thee.

v *264-71.* With the idea of successive deterioration in historical and moral truth, cp. *Ring*, esp. bks. i and x.

v *265.*] What is faith, loyalty, simpleness, (*1872 Morgan*[2]); presumably, since unmetrical, an incomplete re-drafting of the line, and not adopted.

v *266. All their revealment, taught*] All, their revealment taught (*1849-63*); All, once revealed but taught (*1865-88*).

v *270. of yours*] like yours (*1863-88*).

v *271. taught*] praised (*1865-88*).

v *272. truth was shown*] feat was dared (*1865-88*).

v *273. suffer*] suffered (*1868-88*).

v *274. the likeness grows*] old truth returns (*1865-88*).

v *275. all is known*] all's re-known (*1849-88*).

v *277ˆ278.*] No brute-like punishment of bad by worse— (*1849-88*).

v *282. and I will trust to him*] and I will trust him mine (*1868-75*); he whom I trust with mine (*1888*).

v *285. it*] one (*1865-88*).

      Luria.   And I only wait for him.
      Aught else?
      Husain. A movement of the Lucchese troops
      Southward—
        Luria.   . . . Toward Florence? Have out
        instantly . . .
290 Ah, old use clings! Puccio must care henceforth!
      In—quick—'tis nearly midnight! Bid him come!
               [*Enter* Tiburzio, Braccio, *and* Puccio.
      Tiburzio,—not at Pisa?
        Tiburzio.   I return
      From Florence: I serve Pisa, and must think
      By such procedure I have served her best.
295 A people is but the attempt of many
      To rise to the completer life of one—
      And those who live as models for the mass
      Are singly of more value than they all.
      Such man are you, and such a time is this
300 That your sole fate concerns a nation more
      Than its immediate welfare; and to prove
      Your rectitude, and duly crown the same,
      Of consequence beyond the day's event.
      Keep but the model safe, new men will rise
305 To study it, and many another day.
      I might go try my fortune as you bade,
      And joining Lucca, helped by your disgrace,

---

v *295-8.* Cp. Braccio at iii 175-98 and Domizia at iv 198-210. Cp. also *Sordello* iv 206ff., and *Prince Hohenstiel* 727-32: 'I saw that, in the ordinary life, / Many of the little makes a mass of men / Important beyond greatness here and there; / As certainly as, in life exceptional, / When old things terminate and new commence, / A solitary great man's worth the world'. Carlyle's lectures *On Heroes and Hero-Worship* (1840) influenced all these works.

v *301. its immediate . . . and*] its apparent . . . and (*1849-75*); much apparent . . . that (*1888*).

v *303.*] Imports it far beyond the day's event, (*1849-88*, except 'Imports us', *1865-88*, and 'beyond to-day's', *1888*).

v *303^304.*] Its battle's loss or gain—the mass remains, (*1849-88*, except 'A battle's' and 'gain:', *1865-88*; 'man's mass', *1888*).

v *304. the*] God's (*1888*).

v *305. study it*] take its mould (*1865-88*).   *many another day*] other days to prove (*1849-88*).

v *305^306.*] How great a good was Luria's having lived. (*1849-88*, except 'Luria's glory. True—', *1888*).

v *306. bade*] urged (*1888*).

Repair our harm—so were to-day's work done:
But I look farther. I have testified
310 (Declaring my submission to your arms)
Your full success to Florence, making clear
Your probity as none else could: I spoke—
And it shone clearly!
    Luria.   Ah—till Braccio spoke!
    Braccio. Till Braccio told in just a word the
        whole—
315 His old great error, and return to knowledge—
Which told . . Nay, Luria, *I* should droop the head,
Whom all shame rests with, yet I dare look up,
Sure of your pardon now I sue for it,
Knowing you wholly—so let midnight end!
320 Sunrise will come next! Still you answer not?
The shadow of the night is past away:
The circling faces here 'mid which it rose
Are all that felt it,—they close round you now
To witness its completest vanishing.
325 Speak, Luria! Here begins your true career—

v *308^309.*] But where were Luria for our sons to see? (*1849-88*, except 'find
Luria', *1863-75*; 'leave Luria', *1888*).

v *309. But*] No, (*1849-88*).

v *311. Your*] Her (*1863-88*).

v *313. it shone clearly . . . till*] out it shone . . . until (*1865-88*).

v *315. old great*] lapse to (*1865-88*).

v *317. Whom all*] I, whom (*1849-88*).

v *318. now*] when (*1863-75*). The only substantive rev. where *1888* alone
reverts to *1846*.

v *319. wholly—so let*] wholly. Let the (*1865-88*).

v *320. Sunrise will come next*] Sunrise approaches (*1863*); Morning approaches
(*1865*); 'T is morn approaches (*1868-88*).

v *321.*] Sunshine succeeds the shadow past away; (*1865-88*).

v *322.*] Our circling faces here 'mid which it rose (*1849-63*, except 'it grew',
1863); Our faces which phantasmal grew and false, (*1865-88*). When he sent
EBB. the proofs of *B & P* viii, B. remarked: 'All your corrections are golden.
In Luria, I alter "little circle" to "circling faces"—which is more like what I
meant' (7 Apr. 1846, *LK* 598). EBB. presumably suggested a change in the
wording of this line, but there is no written record of it.

v *323. close*] change (*1888*); *1872 Morgan*[2] (see Editorial Note, p. vii) has
'changed'.   *you now*] you, turn (*1868-88*).

v *324.*] Themselves in its completest vanishing (*1865*); Themselves now in its
complete vanishing. (*1868-75*); Truly themselves now in its vanishing.
(*1888*).

Look up to it!—All now is possible—
The glory and the grandeur of each dream—
And every prophecy shall be fulfilled
Save one . . (nay, now your word must come at last)
330   —That you would punish Florence!
       Husain. [*Pointing to* Luria's *dead body*] That is
       done!—

Curtain falls.

---

v *326. up to it*] up, advance (*1888*).

v *327.*] Fact's grandeur, no false dreaming! Dare and do! (*1888; 1872 Morgan²* [see Editorial Note, p. vii] has 'no more dreaming!'). At the time he was preparing *1888* for the press, B. was also working on *Asolando*, whose subtitle is 'Fancies and Facts', and one of whose poems, *Development*, has the line 'But then—"No dream's worth waking"—Browning says' (l. 88). 'Dare and do' derives from Christopher Smart's *Song to David*, a poem B. greatly admired; he quotes or adapts its last line, 'DETERMIN'D, DAR'D, AND DONE!!!' many times in his writings. See *Sordello* v 757n. (I 705).

v *330*. EBB. commented: 'The play ends nobly, bearing itself up to its own height to the last . . & leaving an impression which must be an emotion with all readers'.

v *Final s.d.*] not *1849-88*.

★ 58 Translation of Epigram by Goethe ('Be it your unerring rule')

First publ. *Letters of RB and EBB* ii 52; repr. *LK* 605. Composed on or before 8 Apr. 1846, when B. quoted the lines in a letter to EBB. of that date; our text is taken from the MS of this letter (now at Wellesley College). Not previously publ. in a collection of B.'s poems and not rec. in *Collections* or any other reference work as B.'s; it appears to have escaped notice because it was not written out as verse, but with commas marking the line-breaks, and no initial capitals after the first; we have supplied these capitals and removed the comma from l. 1.

The poem is a complete epigram from section vi (*Buch der Sprüche* [Book of Proverbs]) of Goethe's *West-Oestlischer Divan* (first publ. 1819). The original reads:

Laß dich nur in keiner Zeit
Zum Widerspruch verleiten!
Weise fallen in unwissheit,
Wenn sie Unwissenden streiten.

B. may have translated it directly from the German (for his knowledge of the language see headnote to *Sordello*, I 000), or with some help from friends such as Carlyle (whom he saw often in this period). The first complete translation of the *West-Oestlicher Divan* was by J. Weiss (Boston 1877).

B. quotes the poem in the context of a disagreement with EBB. about the morality of duelling; he maintained the necessity, on occasion, of standing up to 'evil', but, in response to her concern, also stressed that he was not likely to pick fights: 'I *often seriously reproach* myself with conduct quite the reverse of what you would guard against: I have too much *indifferentism* to the opinions of Mr Smith & Mr Brown—by no means am anxious to have his notions agree with mine. Smith thinks Cromwell a canting villain,—Brown believes no dissenter can be saved,—and I repeat Goethe's [quotes lines]' (*LK* 605). For B.'s interest in Goethe, see headnote to *Paracelsus*, I 103.

Be it your unerring rule
Ne'er to contradict a fool,
For if folly choose to brave you,
All your wisdom cannot save you!

★ 59 Lines on Correggio

('Could I, heart-broken, reach his place of birth')

First publ., with an extract from the letter in which it appears (see below), in Sotheby's Catalogue, 10 Dec. 1913, lot 26; repr. W. Whitla, first in his privately printed *Six Stray Verses by Robert Browning* (Oxford 1966), then in 'Four More Fugitives by Robert Browning', *N & Q* n.s. xxi (1974) 449-50; *Penguin* ii 952; *Correspondence* v 258. The title is ours (*Whitla*: 'Quatrain on Correggio'; *Penguin*: 'On Correggio'). Our text is that of the MS, now in the R. H. Taylor Collection at Princeton University.

The poem appears in a brief note (headed 'New Cross, Hatcham', and dated 'Tuesday') to Anna Brownell Jameson (1794-1860), the writer and art historian, in which B. writes: 'I shall try hard for the great pleasure of seeing you on Thursday Morning.—I am glad indeed that my play interests you in any degree', adding, in a postscript:

> A thing, by the way, I have longed to ask you— At which of the Colnaghis [print-sellers, father and son] can one see the Correggio you spoke of one evening at Carlyle's? I am just now hungry for his pictures, and mean whenever I am sore at heart to go and get well before the great cupola at——but why not versify, since that, or something like it, is my trade?— [poem follows].

Previous editors date the letter, and hence the poem, to 1851 (Whitla, *Penguin*) or mid-March 1842 (*Correspondence*). The first date is ruled out by the heading: B. moved to New Cross in Dec. 1840 and left for Italy with EBB., 19 Sept. 1846. On return visits to England they did not stay at New Cross. *Correspondence* relies on 'handwriting and form of signature': the date 'mid-March' is then fixed by the publication of *King Victor,* assumed to be the 'play' alluded to, 12 Mar. 1842. To this might be added B.'s recent admiring mention of Correggio in *Pippa* (see iv 55-6n., p. 92). However, we believe a date later in the 1840s is likelier, when B.'s friendship with both Carlyle and Mrs Jameson was closer and more informal, and when Mrs Jameson had published her *Memoirs of the Early Italian Painters.* This work first appeared in instalments in the *Penny Magazine* in 1843, and in book form in 1845; in it Mrs Jameson praises Correggio's *Assumption of the Virgin* in the cupola of the Duomo in Parma, the work B. alludes to in both letter and poem. A still more precise date may be deducible from B.'s correspondence with EBB. (in which Mrs Jameson is frequently mentioned). On 13 Apr. 1846 B. published *B & P* viii, consisting of *Luria* and *A Soul's Tragedy.* He sent Mrs Jameson a copy, and received a letter of thanks (18 Apr., *LK* 636). In the same period he saw Carlyle at least once and probably several times (21 Apr., *LK* 641). EBB. anticipated hearing from Mrs Jameson of her admiration for *Luria* (28 Apr., *LK* 664; note the ref. to the single play). B. asked EBB. how he should respond if, when he met Mrs Jameson, she relayed news of EBB.'s admiration of his work, not knowing that he and EBB. corresponded (3 May, *LK* 674). Three days later—Wednesday 6 May—B. wrote to EBB.: 'I met Mrs. Jameson last evening and she began just as I prophesied ... "but" said she "I will tell you all when you come and breakfast with me on Thursday—which a note of mine now on its way to you, desires may happen"!' (*LK* 681). This Thursday breakfast may well be the 'Thursday Morning' of B.'s letter to Mrs Jameson, the date of which would then be Tuesday 5 May (written on B.'s return from the evening party). B. did *not* in fact breakfast with Mrs Jameson on Thursday; as he told EBB., 'I got Mrs. Jameson's leave to put the breakfast off' (7 May, *LK* 685). But he would have had an opportunity to change his mind about going, and make the request in person to Mrs Jameson, because they met at yet another party on the Wednesday evening (6 May, *LK* 682). We conjecturally date letter and poem to Tuesday 5 May 1846.

Antonio Allegri (*c.* 1489-1534) was born in the town of Correggio, near Parma, after which he is named. Of two dome paintings by him in Parma, Kelley and Hudson identify his Assumption of the Virgin (1530) in the cathedral as the likely source of B.'s 'great cupola' (*Correspondence* v 259). There is no record of B. visiting Parma on his Italian journeys of 1838 or 1844. The quotation in ll. 3-4 puns on *1 Henry IV* I iii 57-8: 'telling me the sovereignest thing on earth / Was parmaceti for an inward bruise'. 'Parmaceti' is 'spermaceti', a substance derived from the sperm whale but associated with Parma by folk etymology; it was believed to dissolve coagulated blood. For other instances of B.'s fondness for grotesque rhymes and wordplay, esp. impromptu, see *Cockney Anthology* (I 93).

Could I, heart-broken, reach his Place of birth
And stand before his Pictures—could I chuse
But own at once "the sovereign'st thing on earth
"Is Parma-city for an inward bruise?"

60 Before

First publ. *M & W*, 17 Nov. 1855, with its companion-poem *After*, with which it was repr. *1863* (when they were placed in *Lyrics*: see Appendix A, p. 464), *1868*, *1880*, *1888*. The MS is not extant; a proof of *M & W* is in the Huntington Library, with some corrections by B., but none for either of these poems; a copy of *M & W*, also in the Huntington, has notes (not by B.) of numerous changes between the proofs and the first edition, but records only one minor variant in *Before* 17. The date of composition of the two poems is unknown, but we suggest the period following B.'s disagreement with EBB. on the subject of duelling in Apr. 1846. In a letter of 4 Apr., B. mentioned seeing a report in the *Athenaeum* of a trial in France arising out of a duel (see ll. 5-28n.), and commented: 'Being fired at by a Duellist is a little better, I think also, than being struck on the face by some ruffian' (*LK* 588). At their meeting on 6 Apr. he defended the practice of duelling; EBB. wrote on 7 Apr.: 'Indeed I thought you as wrong as possible .. wonderfully wrong on such a subject, for YOU .. who, only a day or two before, seemed so free from conventional fallacies' (*LK* 595). Several phrases in this letter are echoed in the poem. B. replied in a long letter of 8 Apr. (*LK* 601-6), reiterating his defence and taking a position partly reflected in that of the speaker of *Before*. EBB. replied on the same day, maintaining her view that duelling was unacceptable under any circumstances; B. wrote on 9 Apr.: 'all in MY letter was meant to be "read by your light." I submit, unfeignedly, to you, there as elsewhere. And,—as I said, I think,—I wrote *so*, precisely because it was never likely to be my own case' (*LK* 608). There were further exchanges in EBB.'s letter of 9 Apr. and B.'s of 10 Apr. (*LK* 609, 611-12), and the matter was probably resolved at their meeting on 11 Apr. A phrase in EBB.'s letter of 12 Apr. may be echoed at l. 23 of *Before*.

Duelling was a topical and controversial issue in the early 1840s. The practice had never been distinguished in English law from murder; juries, however, were reluctant to convict duellists on this charge. An Act of Parliament early in Queen Victoria's reign (1838) attempted to change this situation; but the farcical acquittal by the House of Lords of the Earl of Cardigan for wounding a fellow-officer led to a widespread campaign, supported by the *Times*, for further legislation. Following another notorious duel in 1843, between Colonel Fawcett and his brother-in-law Lieutenant Monroe, in which Fawcett was killed, legislation was introduced in Parliament, but its supporters succeeded only in securing an addition to the Articles of War, forbidding duelling between officers. Despite this, with public opinion decisively opposed to duelling, the practice seems to have died out soon after: in Trollope's *Phineas Finn* (1869), for example, Phineas and his adversary Lord Chiltern are obliged to travel to Belgium to fight their duel. B. may have read Millingan's hostile *History of Duelling* (1841), which concludes with a detailed account of the Cardigan duel; the controversy surrounding the Fawcett-Munro duel and its aftermath certainly contributed to his exchange of views with EBB., who had previously mentioned it with indignation in letters of 3 and 7 Dec. 1843 to Mary Russell Mitford (*Correspondence* viii 73, 78-9). B.'s defence of the practice in his letters is at odds with the more usual view of duelling as archaic and immoral, expressed for example by the *Times* of 11 Feb. 1841: 'The shackles of ages are falling off, and the human intellect is rising up . . . If society is to be preserved, it must be Christianised'. The speaker of *Before* articulates B.'s mistrust of the claim of law to control individual conduct in extreme circumstances (see esp. ll. 29-32).

One further indication of the date of composition may be that the metre of *After* (though not the rhyme-scheme) is that of *England* and the unfinished *Saul*, both recently publ. in *DR & L*. The metre of *Before* is unusual, and unique in B.'s work. It is based on a six-stressed line (with variation: l. 22, for example, is a 'fourteener'); the opening lines of each stanza end on a full stress, while the last two lines have feminine endings.

The duellists are old friends; one of them has committed an 'offence' or 'outrage' which has brought 'disgrace' on the other (*After* 12-15). The speaker of *Before* is either the second of the innocent man or, as P. Drew suggests, 'a neutral spectator or referee' (*The Poetry of Browning: A Critical Introduction* [1970] 82). Much of what the speaker says is premised on the assumption that the innocent man may be killed; but this does not happen. The speaker of *After* is the innocent man, who has killed his opponent.

The duellist as 'God's champion' (*Before* 33) appears in *Count Gismond*; cp. also the figure of Caponsacchi in *Ring*. In both cases, however, the champion is defending not his own honour, but another person's. A duel in very different moral circumstances is the subject of *Clive*.

1.

Let them fight it out, friend! things have gone too far.
God must judge the couple! leave them as they are
—Whichever one's the guiltless, to his glory,
And whichever one the guilt's with, to my story.

2.

5 Why, you would not bid men, sunk in such a slough,

¶60.1. Cp. 'The Duellist's Vow', *New Monthly Magazine* lxxii (Dec. 1844): 'A feeble attempt was made to patch up the quarrel, but things had gone too far'.
5-28. The speaker's position here reverses that of the writer in the *Atheneaum* article which B. mentioned to EBB. (see headnote), who argues: 'the retribution for a wrong inflicted which puts the wrong-doer and the wronged on equal ground, and leaves accident to decide by which of the two it shall be paid, is a stupid blunder' (no. 962 [4 Apr. 1846] 350). EBB. agreed: 'A man calls you "a liar" in an assembly of other men. Because he is a calumniator, & on that very account, a worse man than you, .. you ask him to go down with

Strike no arm out further, stick and stink as now,
Leaving right and wrong to settle the embroilment,
Heaven with snaky Hell, in torture and entoilment?

3.

Which of them's the culprit, how must he conceive
10   God's the queen he caps to, laughing in his sleeve!
'Tis but decent to profess oneself beneath her.
Still, one must not be too much in earnest either.

4.

Better sin the whole sin, sure that God observes,
Then go live his life out! life will try his nerves,

---

you on the only ground on which you two are equals .. the duelling-ground'
(5 Apr. 1846, *LK* 596). The speaker here implies that the outcome will not be
accidental or arbitrary, but part of a providential design. See also B.'s reply to
EBB.'s letter, accepting the possibility that the innocent party in a duel might
be killed: 'Have I to be told that in this world men, foolish or wicked, do
inflict tremendous injuries on their unoffending fellows? Let God look to it, I
say with reverence' (8 Apr. 1846, *LK* 603).
8. B. may have had in mind the celebrated classical sculpture depicting the
Trojan priest Laocoon and his two sons caught in the toils of serpents.
entoilment: B.'s is the only use of this word cited in *OED*; it may be his
coinage.
9-12. The sense is that the 'culprit' thinks of God as a hypocritical courtier
thinks of a queen, to whom he gives lip-service only. For the topic of a man's
love for a woman who is above him in rank, see headnote to *Rudel* (I 771); cp.
esp. *Pippa* ii 195-210. B. and EBB. both claimed to be the other's inferior in
their letters; B. wrote to EBB.: 'What you choose to assert of yourself, *I* feel
of myself every hour. But there must be this disproportionateness in a
beloved object . . . There is no love but from beneath, far beneath,—that is
the law of its nature' (10 Aug. 1846, *LK* 950). See also l. 23n.
9.] Who's the culprit of them? How must he conceive (*1863-88*).
10. God's the] God—the (*1863-88*).   *caps to*: takes off his cap to (as a mark
of respect).   *sleeve!*] sleeve, (*1863-88*): see next note.
11-12.] in quotation marks, *1863-88*.
13. Cp. Luther's maxim, in a letter to Melancthon (*Epistolae* [1556] i 345):
'Este peccator et pecca fortiter, sed fortius fide et gaude in Christo' [Be a
sinner and sin strongly, but more strongly have faith and rejoice in Christ],
and, in B., *Statue* 242-8: 'Let a man contend to the uttermost / For his life's set
prize, be it what it will! . . . the sin I impute to each frustrate ghost / Was, the
unlit lamp and the ungirt loin, / Though the end in sight was a crime, I say'.
See also l. 29n.
14. Then] Than (*1863*); almost certainly a mispr.

15 When the sky which noticed all, makes no disclosure,
    And the earth keeps up her terrible composure.

                        5.

Let him pace at pleasure, past the walls of rose,
Pluck their fruits when grape-trees graze him as he
    goes.
For he 'gins to guess the purpose of the garden,
20 With the sly mute thing beside there for a warden.

                        6.

What's the leopard-dog-thing, constant to his side,
A leer and lie in every eye on its obsequious hide?
When will come an end of all the mock obeisance,
And the price appear that pays for the misfeasance?

                        7.
25 So much for the culprit. Who's the martyred man?
    Let him bear one stroke more, for be sure he can.

15-16. Cp. Guido, speaking of Pompilia's stoicism in *Ring* xi 1374-8: 'Who is the friend i' the background that notes all? / Who may come presently and close accounts? / This self-possession to the uttermost, / How does it differ in aught, save degree, / From the terrible patience of God?' See also *After* 15.

20. thing beside there] thing beside, there, (*1863*); thing, beside there, (*1865-88*).

21. leopard-dog-thing: cp. the leopard in Dante, *Inferno* i 31ff., the first of the three beasts (the others are a lion and a wolf) which symbolize sin and block the narrator's path to redemption. The mention of the 'dog' also evokes Mephistophilis, who first appears to Goethe's Faust in the guise of a dog; this association is strengthened by the 'mock-obeisance' offered by the creature to its master/victim.   *to*] at (*1863-88*).

22. eye: eye-shaped spot (on the leopard's 'hide' or coat); the speaker imagines these 'eyes' to be 'leering'. Cp. the 'hoary cripple, with malicious eye / Askance to watch the working of his lie / On mine', *Childe Roland* 2-4.   *obsequious*: the primitive sense of 'obedient, dutiful' was still current in the mid-19th century, but was giving way to the modern, pejorative sense: 'servilely compliant, fawning, cringing' (*OED*).

23. mock-obeisance: cp. EBB. to B., 12 Apr. 1846: 'After all, too, you, .. with that praeternatural submissiveness of yours, . . you know your power upon the whole, & understand, in the midst of the obeisances, that you can do very much what you please, with your High priest' (*LK* 311).

24. Cp. the last lines of *Mesmerism*: 'I admonish me while I may, / Not to squander guilt, / Since require Thou wilt / At my hand its price one day! / What the price is, who can say?'

He that strove thus evil's lump with good to leaven,
Let him give his blood at last and get his heaven.

8.

All or nothing, stake it! trusts he God or no?
30   Thus far and no farther? farther? be it so.
Now, enough of your chicane of prudent pauses,
Sage provisos, sub-intents, and saving-clauses.

9.

Ah, "forgive" you bid him? While God's champion
lives,

27. *evil's lump with good to leaven*: cp. *1 Corinthians* v 6: 'Know ye not that a
little leaven leaveneth the whole lump?' A favourite tag of B.'s: cp. *Old
Pictures* 129: ''Tis a life-long toil till our lump be leaven', rhymed with
'heaven' in l. 131; the rhyme 'leaven/heaven' is also found in the revised text
of *Pippa Intro*. (see ll. 21-47n., p. 19) and in three other poems.
29. EBB. characterized duelling as a meaningless gamble with one's life: 'If it
was proposed to you to play at real dice for the ratification or non-ratification
of his calumny, the proposition would be laughed to scorn . . & yet the
chance (as chance) seems much the same' (7 Apr. 1846, *LK* 596; see also
l. 40n.). Cp. *Statue* 238-41: 'Stake your counter as boldly every whit, /
Venture as truly, use the same skill, / Do your best, whether winning or
losing it, / If you choose to play—is my principle!' See also l. 13n.
31-2. The speaker stigmatizes attempts to delay the combat, or find a way out
of it by compromise or mitigation of the original offence, as legalistic
evasions of the central moral issue. 'Chicane' is the use of legal trickery or
quibbling; cp. *Ring* iv 1092-4: 'You, a born coward, try a coward's arms, /
Trick and chicane,—and only when these fail / Does violence follow'. 'Sub-
intents' is apparently B.'s coinage: it suggests that the offensive words which
caused the quarrel might be palliated by appealing to the speaker's intention.
Cp. *George Bubb Dodington* 268-70: 'a touch / Of subintelligential nod and
wink— / Turning foes friends'.
33. *God's champion*: cp. *Count Gismond* 70-1, and *Ring* x 1155-8: 'Ay, such
championship / Of God at first blush, such prompt cheery thud / Of glove on
ground that answers ringingly / The challenge of the false knight'.
33-6. Cp. Christ's Sermon on the Mount, *Matthew* v 38ff: 'Ye have heard that
it hath been said, An eye for an eye, and a tooth for a tooth: but I say unto
you, That ye resist not evil: but whosoever shall smite thee on thy right
cheek, turn to him the other also . . . Love your enemies, bless them that
curse you, do good to them that hate you'. Cp. also the Lord's Prayer:
'Forgive us our trespasses, as we forgive those that trespass against us', cited
by the Intendant in *Pippa* iv 133 and rebutted by the Bishop. B. wrote to
EBB.: 'I can conceive of "combinations of circumstances" in which I see two
things only . . or a Third: a miscreant to be put out the world, my own arm

Wrong shall be resisted: dead, why he forgives.
35 But you must not end my friend ere you begin him;
    Evil stands not crowned on earth, while breath is in
        him.

                            10.
    Once more—Will the wronger, at this last of all,
    Dare to say "I did wrong," rising in his fall?
    No?—Let go, then—both the fighters to their places—
40 While I count three, step you back as many paces.

and best will to do it,—and, perhaps, God to excuse,—which is, approve.
My Ba, what is Evil, in its unmistakeable shape, but a thing to suppress at
any price?' (8 Apr. 1846, *LK* 604).
40. The duellists are to fire at each other from six paces, a distance which
practically ensures death. EBB. wrote to B. of 'the Englishman's six paces ..
throwing the dice for his life or another man's' (7 Apr. 1846, *LK* 596; see also
l. 29n.). In a second letter of the same date, she worried that she had made B.
angry: 'Will you challenge me to six paces at Chalk Farm[?]' (*LK* 600). In
Clive the distance (still held to be lethal) is twelve paces (l. 131).

61 After

For publication and other details, see headnote to prec. poem.

Take the cloak from his face, and at first
   Let the corpse do its worst.

How he lies in his rights of a man!
   Death has done all death can.
5 And absorbed in the new life he leads,
   He recks not, he heeds
Nor his wrong nor my vengeance—both strike
   On his senses alike,
And are lost in the solemn and strange
10   Surprise of the change.
Ha, what avails death to erase
   His offence, my disgrace?
I would we were boys as of old
   In the field, by the fold—
15 His outrage, God's patience, man's scorn
   Were so easily borne.
I stand here now, he lies in his place—
   Cover the face.

¶61.10.] there is a space after this line in *1863-88*. The line ends the page in
1855, and it is not possible to tell whether B. intended a space in this text.
13-14. Cp. *Italy* 6-11, where the speaker nostalgically evokes his boyhood
friendship with Charles, who later 'proved false' (l. 116).
15-16. B.'s long letter to EBB. of 8 Apr. 1846 defends duelling partly on the
grounds that 'man's scorn' (the social opprobrium that follows a man's
refusal to fight for his 'honour') is an intolerable burden for many men to
bear. He uses the phrase 'the poor author of the outrage' (*LK* 602), and denies
that 'wiser men might easily forego' society: '*Not so easily!* . . . if I allow a
foolish child to put the very smallest of fool's caps on my head instead of the
hat I usually wear . . . I shall be followed by an increasing crowd, say to
Charing Cross, and thence pelted, perhaps, till I reach No 50 . . . and when
Papa comes to hear how illustriously your visitor was attended thro' the
streets,—why he will specially set apart Easter Monday to testify in person
his sense of the sublime philosophy, will he not?' (*LK* 603). EBB. replied on
the same day: 'You refuse to wear a fool's cap in the street, because society
forbids you—which is well: but if, in order to avoid wearing it, you shoot the
"foolish child" who forces it upon you .. why you do *not* well, by any means'
(*LK* 607). For 'God's patience', see *Before* 15-16n.
18. DeVane (*Handbook* 249) and other commentators cite Webster, *Duchess of
Malfi* IV ii 267: 'Cover her face; mine eyes dazzle; she died young', and *King
Lear* V iii 242: 'Cover their faces' (Goneril and Regan).

Appendix A

Contents of *Dramatic Lyrics* (1842), *Dramatic Romances and Lyrics* (1845), and *Men and Women* (1855), and Browning's rearrangements in subsequent editions

Dramatic Lyrics (1842) [*DL*]
    Cavalier Tunes
        I Marching Along
        II Give a Rouse
        III My Wife Gertrude
    Italy and France
        I Italy [My Last Duchess]
        II France [Count Gismond]
    Camp and Cloister
        I Camp (*French*) [Incident of the French Camp]
        II Cloister (*Spanish*) [Soliloquy of the Spanish Cloister]
    In a Gondola
    Artemis Prologuizes
    Waring
    Queen-Worship
        I Rudel and the Lady of Tripoli [Rudel to the Lady of Tripoli]
        II Cristina
    Madhouse Cells
        I [Porphyria's Lover]
        II [Johannes Agricola in Meditation]
    Through the Metidja to Abd-el-Kadr—1842
    The Pied Piper of Hamelin

Dramatic Romances and Lyrics (1845) [*DR & L*]
    "How They Brought the Good News from Ghent to Aix"
    Pictor Ignotus
    Italy in England [The Italian in England]
    England in Italy [The Englishman in Italy]
    The Lost Leader
    The Lost Mistress
    Home-Thoughts, from Abroad

I [Home-Thoughts, from Abroad]
II ['Here's to Nelson's memory']
III [Home-Thoughts, from the Sea]
The Tomb at St. Praxed's [The Bishop Orders His Tomb at Saint
    Praxed's Church]
Garden Fancies
    I The Flower's Name
    II Sibrandus Schafnaburgensis
France and Spain
    I The Laboratory
    II Spain—The Confessional [The Confessional]
The Flight of the Duchess
Earth's Immortalities
Song
The Boy and the Angel
Night and Morning
    I Night [Meeting at Night]
    II Morning [Parting at Morning]
Claret and Tokay [Nationality in Drinks i and ii]
Saul [incomplete]
Time's Revenges
The Glove

Poems (2 vols., 1849) [*1849*]
B. reprinted the poems of *DL* and *DR & L* in the order of the
original collections, under the general title *DR & L*, omitting *Claret
and Tokay* and section ii of *Home-Thoughts, from Abroad* (*Here's to
Nelson's memory*); section iii became a separate poem, *Home-
Thoughts, from the Sea*. For other changes of title and arrangement in
1849, see headnotes to individual poems.

Men and Women (2 vols., 1855) [*M & W*]
    Volume I
    Love Among the Ruins
    A Lovers' Quarrel
    Evelyn Hope
    Up at a Villa—Down in the City
    A Woman's Last Word
    Fra Lippo Lippi
    A Toccata of Galuppi's
    By the Fire-Side
    Any Wife to Any Husband

An Epistle Containing the Strange Medical Experience of
  Karshish, the Arab Physician
Mesmerism
A Serenade at the Villa
My Star
Instans Tyrannus
A Pretty Woman
"Childe Roland to the Dark Tower Came"
Respectability
A Light Woman
The Statue and the Bust
Love in a Life
Life in a Love
How It Strikes a Contemporary
The Last Ride Together
The Patriot
Master Hugues of Saxe-Gotha
Bishop Blougram's Apology
Memorabilia

Volume II
Andrea del Sarto
Before
After
In Three Days
In a Year
Old Pictures in Florence
In a Balcony
Saul [complete]
"De Gustibus—"
Women and Roses
Protus
Holy-Cross Day
The Guardian-Angel
Cleon
The Twins
Popularity
The Heretic's Tragedy
Two in the Campagna
A Grammarian's Funeral
One Way of Love
Another Way of Love

"Transcendentalism"
Misconceptions
One Word More

Poetical Works (3 vols., 1863) [*1863*]
In *1863*, B. undertook a major rearrangement of his shorter poems.
Vol. i was titled *Lyrics, Romances, Men, and Women*. It consisted of
the poems of *DL, DR & L*, and *M & W*, with the exception of *In a
Balcony*, which became a separate piece and was included in vol. ii
with B.'s dramas. *Claret and Tokay* and *Home-Thoughts, from Abroad*
ii (*Here's to Nelson's memory*) were restored and combined as three
untitled sections of *Nationality in Drinks*. *Soliloquy of the Spanish
Cloister* was listed in the contents as a third section of *Garden Fancies,*
but appears as a separate work in the text (the contents page was
corrected in *1865*). There were three divisions: *Lyrics, Romances,* and
Men, and Women. Although the word 'Dramatic' was dropped from
the first two titles, the 'Advertisement' to the original *DL* (see
Appendix B, p.000) was reprinted as a note to *Lyrics*. Note that the
comma in *Men, and Women* (later dropped: see below) alters the sense
of the phrase.
   The order of the *1863* volume was as follows, with the original
provenance of the poems in brackets:

   Lyrics
   Cavalier Tunes (DL)
   The Lost Leader (DR & L)
   "How They Brought the Good News from Ghent to Aix"
        (DR & L)
   Through the Metidja to Abd-el-Kadr (DL)
   Nationality in Drinks (DR & L)
   Garden Fancies (DR & L)
   Soliloquy of the Spanish Cloister (DL)
   The Laboratory (DR & L)
   The Confessional (DR & L)
   Cristina (DL)
   The Lost Mistress (DR & L)
   Earth's Immortalities (DR & L)
   Meeting at Night (DR & L)
   Parting at Morning (DR & L)
   Song (DR & L)
   A Woman's Last Word (M & W)
   Evelyn Hope (M & W)

Love Among the Ruins (M & W)
A Lovers' Quarrel (M & W)
Up at a Villa—Down in the City (M & W)
A Toccata of Galuppi's (M & W)
Old Pictures in Florence (M & W)
"De Gustibus—" (M & W)
Home-Thoughts, from Abroad (DR & L)
Home-Thoughts, from the Sea (DR & L)
Saul (M & W)
My Star (M & W)
By the Fire-Side (M & W)
Any Wife to Any Husband (M & W)
Two in the Campagna (M & W)
Misconceptions (M & W)
A Serenade at the Villa (M & W)
One Way of Love (M & W)
Another Way of Love (M & W)
A Pretty Woman (M & W)
Respectability (M & W)
Love in a Life (M & W)
Life in a Love (M & W)
In Three Days (M & W)
In a Year (M & W)
Women and Roses (M & W)
Before (M & W)
After (M & W)
The Guardian-Angel (M & W)
Memorabilia (M & W)
Popularity (M & W)
Master Hugues of Saxe-Gotha (M & W)

Romances
Incident of the French Camp (DL)
The Patriot (M & W)
My Last Duchess (DL)
Count Gismond (DL)
The Boy and the Angel (DR & L)
Instans Tyrannus (M & W)
Mesmerism (M & W)
The Glove (DR & L)
Time's Revenges (DR & L)
The Italian in England (DR & L)

The Englishman in Italy (DR & L)
In a Gondola (DL)
Waring (DL)
The Twins (M & W)
A Light Woman (M & W)
The Last Ride Together (M & W)
The Pied Piper of Hamelin (DL)
The Flight of the Duchess (DR & L)
A Grammarian's Funeral (M & W)
Johannes Agricola in Meditation (DL)
The Heretic's Tragedy (M & W)
Holy-Cross Day (M & W)
Protus (M & W)
The Statue and the Bust (M & W)
Porphyria's Lover (DL)
"Childe Roland to the Dark Tower Came" (M & W)

Men, and Women
"Transcendentalism:" A Poem in Twelve Books (M & W)
How It Strikes a Contemporary (M & W)
Artemis Prologizes (DL)
An Epistle Containing the Strange Medical Experience of
        Karshish, the Arab Physician (M & W)
Pictor Ignotus (DR & L)
Fra Lippo Lippi (M & W)
Andrea del Sarto (M & W)
The Bishop Orders His Tomb at Saint Praxed's Church (DR & L)
Bishop Blougram's Apology (M & W)
Cleon (M & W)
Rudel to the Lady of Tripoli (DL)
One Word More (M & W) This poem was accompanied by a note
        explaining that the poem was 'Originally appended to the
        collection of Poems called "Men and Women," the greater
        portion of which has now been, more correctly, distributed
        under the other titles of this volume', an explanation
        required by the first line, 'There they are, my fifty men and
        women'.

Poetical Works (6 vols., 1868) [*1868*]
The three divisions appeared in separate volumes, with further
variation in the titles: *Dramatic Lyrics* in vol. iii, *Dramatic Romances* in
vol. iv, and *Men and Women* (returning to the original unpunctuated

title) in vol. v. The contents of *Dramatic Lyrics* were the same as *Lyrics* in *1863*; but *Johannes Agricola* was transferred from *Romances* to *Men and Women*, where it appeared between *An Epistle* and *Pictor Ignotus*. *Men and Women* appeared with the date 'Florence, 185—'. The note to *One Word More* was retained, with the substitution of 'edition' for 'volume'.

Poetical Works (16 vols., 1888-9) [*1888*]

The titles and contents were the same as *1868*. *Men and Women* appeared in vol. iv, *Dramatic Romances* in vol. v, and *Dramatic Lyrics* in vol. vi. *Men and Women* now had the date '184—, 185—'.

Appendix B

Note on *Bells and Pomegranates*

The idea of publishing a series of dramas in a cheap format first appears in a letter from B. to the publisher William Smith (7 April 1840; *Correspondence* iv 267):

> Sir,
>
> Mr Moxon has just published a long Poem of mine, "Sordello", meant for a limited class of readers—and I am on the point of following it up by three new Dramas, written in a more popular style, and addressed to the Public at large:—a friend has called my notice to your handsome Reprints and suggested the proposal I am about to make. Would it answer your purpose to try the experiment of coming out with a *new* work as part of your series?—As in that case I will give you the 1st. Edition for nothing—for the sake of your large circulation among a body to which my works have little access at present. Of course I mean that these Dramas should form one publication, of the same size and at the same low price as your other pamphlets.

With this letter B. enclosed a torn-off leaf from *Sordello* containing the advertisement for the 'three new Dramas' he mentions, which were announced as 'nearly ready': *Pippa Passes*, *King Victor and King Charles*, and *Mansoor the Hierophant* (later renamed *The Return of the Druses*). The implication may be that Moxon, though he had advertised the works, was having second thoughts about publishing them, and that B. was looking elsewhere. It is possible that Moxon himself recommended Smith, and this would partially confirm the traditional account of the genesis of the series, given, before B.'s letter to Smith was known, by Edmund Gosse (*Robert Browning: Personalia* [1890] 52-3, repr. Orr *Life* 112-13):

> One day, as the poet was discussing the matter with Mr. Edward Moxon, the publisher, the latter remarked that at that time he was bringing out some editions of the old Elizabethan dramatists in a comparatively cheap form, and that if Mr.

Browning would consent to print his poems as pamphlets, using this cheap type, the expense would be very inconsiderable. The poet jumped at the idea, and it was agreed that each poem should form a separate brochure of just one sheet,— sixteen pages, in double columns,—the entire cost of which should not exceed twelve or fifteen pounds. In this fashion began the celebrated series of *Bells and Pomegranates . . . Pippa Passes* led the way, and was priced first at sixpence; then, the sale being inconsiderable, at a shilling, which greatly encouraged the sale; and so, slowly, up to half a crown, at which the price of each number finally rested.

If Moxon was indeed the 'friend' to whom B. attributes the proposal in his letter to Smith, then Gosse's account (based on conversations with B. in the year before his death) may conflate the two publishers; but it should be stressed that the 'friend' may be someone else, or an imaginary figure. Whatever the sequence of events, B. eventually came to an agreement with Moxon himself similar to the one he had proposed to Smith. Moxon's list at this period includes reprints of editions of Ben Jonson (1838, price 16*s*.), Massinger and Ford (1840, 16*s*.), and Beaumont and Fletcher (2 vol*s*., 1840, 32*s*.)—large volumes, which were indeed 'comparatively cheap', all in double columns, and using the same type and layout as for the pamphlets of *B & P*. Moxon's similar edition of Samuel Rogers' popular poem *Italy*, a work comparable in length to the early numbers of *B & P*, and priced at 1*s*. 6*d*., may also have contributed to the idea. The price of the later numbers of the series went up not just for the reason Gosse gives, but because the pamphlets themselves became longer: the final number was twice the length of the first. B.'s father paid for the publication of the whole series.

In the 'Advertisement' in *Pippa Passes*, which was intended as a preface to the whole projected series, B. wrote:

Two or three years ago I wrote a Play [*Strafford*, 1837], about which the chief matter I much care to recollect at present is, that a Pit-full of goodnatured people applauded it:—ever since, I have been desirous of doing something in the same way that should better reward their attention. What follows I mean for the first of a series of Dramatical Pieces, to come out at intervals, and I amuse myself by fancying that the cheap mode in which they appear will for once help me to a sort of Pit-audience again. Of course such a work must go on no longer than it is liked; and to provide against a certain and but too possible contingency, let me hasten to say now—what, if I were sure of success, I would try to say circumstantially enough at the close—that I dedicate my best intentions most admiringly to the Author of "Ion"—most affectionately to Serjeant Talfourd.

See also headnote to *Pippa*, p. 5.
 There were eight numbers of *B & P*:

   (i) *Pippa Passes* (1841) 6d.
  (ii) *King Victor and King Charles* (1842) 1s.
 (iii) *Dramatic Lyrics* (1842) 1s.
 (iv) *The Return of the Druses* (1843) 1s.
  (v) *A Blot in the 'Scutcheon* (1843) 1s.
 (vi) *Colombe's Birthday* (1844) 1s.
(vii) *Dramatic Romances and Lyrics* (1845) 2s.
(viii) *Luria* and *A Soul's Tragedy* (1846) 2s. 6d.

After 1846 the remainder of the separate numbers were bound together and sold as a single volume.
 Apart from nos. iii and vii, which are collections of shorter poems, the series consists of plays, four of which (nos. ii, iv, v, and vi) are not included in this edition. The initial Advertisement makes it clear that B. had no definite plan for the series' length or contents. In a letter to Alfred Domett of 22 May 1842 he spoke of including a revised version of his first play, *Strafford*, published in 1837 (*Correspondence* v 357); it was Moxon who, at the same time, persuaded him to stretch the phrase 'dramatical pieces' to cover the shorter poems of *Dramatic Lyrics*. B. agreed to this 'for popularity's sake', as he told Domett (*ibid.* v 356). In a letter to EBB. of 14 June 1845 he planned to 'print this Autumn my last four "Bells," Lyrics, Romances, The Tragedy & Luria' (*LK* 95); the four numbers became the final two. In a further Advertisement in *Dramatic Lyrics*, B. wrote: 'Such Poems as the following come properly enough, I suppose, under the head of "Dramatic Pieces;" being, though for the most part Lyric in expression, always Dramatic in principle, and so many utterances of so many imaginary persons, not mine'.
 DeVane (*Handbook* 89-90) points out that all the pamphlets were published as 'By Robert Browning, Author of *Paracelsus*', and comments that 'the *Bells* show Browning beginning anew in his attempt to rebuild his literary reputation after the havoc which

Sordello had made of his old one'. However, the title of the series itself caused general bewilderment. 'Mr. Browning's conundrums begin with his very title-page', wrote the reviewer of *Pippa Passes* in the *Athenaeum* (11 Dec. 1841, p. 952; repr. *Correspondence* v 399–400): ' "Bells and Pomegranates" is the general title given (it is reasonable to suppose Mr. Browning knows why, but certainly we have not yet found out—indeed we "give it up")'. The reviewer in the *Spectator* (17 Apr. 1841, p. 349; repr. *Correspondence* v 392) assumed that *Bells and Pomegranates* was the title of a serial of which *Pippa Passes* was only the first instalment ('and that part of necessity the least stirring in its action and the least interesting from its passion'). The title derives from *Exodus* xxviii 33-5, and concerns the making of the 'ephod' (tunic) of Aaron the High Priest: 'And beneath upon the hem of it thou shalt make pomegranates of blue, and of purple, and of scarlet, round about the hem thereof; and bells of gold between them round about: a golden bell and a pomegranate, a golden bell and a pomegranate, upon the hem of the robe round about. And it shall be upon Aaron to minister: and his sound shall be heard when he goeth in unto the holy place before the Lord, and when he cometh out, that he die not'. B. wrote to EBB. on 18 Oct. 1845: 'the Rabbis make Bells & Pomegranates symbolical of Pleasure and Profit, the Gay & the Grave, the Poetry & the Prose, Singing and Sermonising—such a mixture of effects as in the original hour (that is quarter of an hour) of confidence & creation, I meant the whole should prove at last' (*LK* 241). EBB. urged him, against his inclination, to make his explanation public: 'Dearest, I persist in thinking that you ought not to be too disdainful to explain your meaning in the Pomegranates. Surely you might say in a word or two that, your title having been doubted about (to your surprise, you *might* say!), you refer the doubters to the Jewish priest's robe, & the Rabbinical gloss . . . Consider that Mr. Kenyon & I may fairly represent the average intelligence of your readers,—& that *he* was altogether in the clouds as to your meaning .. had not the most distant notion of it,—while I, taking hold of the priest's garment, missed the Rabbins & the distinctive significance, as completely as he did. Then for Vasari, it is not the handbook of the whole world . . . Now why should you be too proud to teach such persons as only desire to be taught? I persist—I shall teaze you' (24 Mar. 1846, *LK* 553). For the allusion to Giorgio Vasari's *Lives of the Most Excellent Italian Architects, Painters, and Sculptors* (1550), see below; B. presumably mentioned it to EBB. during a meeting in Wimpole Street. B. deferred to EBB. in a letter of 25 Mar. 1846: 'I will at Ba's bidding amuse and instruct the world

at large, and make them know all to be known—for my purposes—
about Bells & Pomegranates—yes, it will be better' (*LK* 558). He
placed a note between *Luria* and *A Soul's Tragedy* in the last number
of the series:

> Here ends my first series of "Bells and Pomegranates:" and I
> take the opportunity of explaining, in reply to inquiries, that I
> only meant by that title to indicate an endeavour towards
> something like an alternation, or mixture, of music with
> discoursing, sound with sense, poetry with thought; which
> looks too ambitious, thus expressed, so the symbol was
> preferred. It is little to the purpose, that such is actually one of
> the most familiar of the many Rabbinical (and Patristic)
> acceptations of the phrase; because I confess that, letting
> authority alone, I supposed the bare words, in such juxta-
> position, would sufficiently convey the desired meaning.
> "Faith and good works" is another fancy, for instance, and
> perhaps no easier to arrive at: yet Giotto placed a pomegranate
> fruit in the hand of Dante, and Raffaelle crowned his
> Theology (in the *Camera della Segnatura*) with blossoms of the
> same; as if the Bellari and Vasari would be sure to come after,
> and explain that it was merely "*simbolo delle buone opere—il
> qualo Pomo granato fu però usato nelle vesti del Pontefice appresso gli
> Ebrei.*" [a symbol of good works—for this reason the pome-
> granate was used in the vestment of the High Priest among the
> Hebrews]

DeVane (*Handbook* 89) states that the placing of this note excludes *A
Soul's Tragedy* from the series; but, though EBB. herself thought so
at first (13 Apr. 1846, *LK* 619), B. explicitly denies it (14 Apr. 1846):
'I don't consider that it excludes this last from the "Bells"—rather it
says this *is* the last, (n°· *nine* if you like,—as the title says eight *and*
last—from whence will be this advantage—that, in the case of
another edition, all the lyrics &c may go together under one
common head of Lyrics & Romances—and the "Soul's Tragedy,"—
profiting by the general move-up of the rest of the numbers, after
the fashion of hackney coaches on a stand when one is called
off,—step into the place and take the style of No. 8—and the public
not find themselves defrauded of the proper quantity!)' (*LK* 623).
However, there was no second edition of *B & P* as such, and the title
was dropped in *1849* and subsequent collected editions.

Appendix C

Essay on Chatterton

First publ., in the form of an anonymous review of a book on Tasso, in the *Foreign Quarterly Review* xxix (July 1842) 465–83; not repr. in B.'s lifetime. Repr. as *Browning's Essay on Chatterton*, ed. D. Smalley (Cambridge, Mass., 1948). Our text is *FQR*; obvious misprints have been silently corrected, with the exception of the one at l. 785. The essay was written in late May–June 1842.

Smalley was the first to notice an entry in the diary of 'Michael Field' (the joint pseudonym of the verse dramatists Katherine Bradley and Edith Cooper) for 1 June 1895 (*Works and Days: From the Journal of Michael Field*, ed. T. and D. C. Sturge Moore [1933] 208), which attributes authorship of the piece to Browning; the information apparently derived from Browning's sister Sarianna. Further, the July issue of *FQR* marked the arrival as editor of John Forster, with whom B. was at that time very friendly, and Forster is known to have solicited material from other literary friends; but even without this, the internal evidence (such as the appearance of one of B.'s favourite phrases, 'dared and done' at l. 257) would be decisive. Smalley concludes that the essay was written in the five weeks preceding its publication, after B. had obtained a copy of Willcox's edition of Chatterton (*c.* 27 May: see l. 133 and B.'s footnote). B. presented his copy of Willcox to his son in 1863 (*Collections* A627, p. 55).

The curious form of the essay (a review of a book on Tasso which becomes a free-standing essay on Chatterton) reflects the common practice in this period of using reviews as opportunities for writing substantial independent essays (e.g. Carlyle's contributions to *Fraser's Magazine*, later collected in his *Miscellanies*). But Browning's procedure is more extreme than most: rather than writing his own essay on the subject, he adopts the *method* (as he sees it) of his reviewee's work for analysis of a quite different (though to his mind analogous) subject.

Torquato Tasso (1544–95) was the author of poetry (*Rinaldo*, romance; *Gerusalemme Liberata*, epic; *Aminta*, pastoral drama) and criticism (*Discorsi dell'Arte Poetica*, *Discorsi del Poema Eroica*) which had great influence in both Italian and European literature. But Tasso's fame stemmed equally from the legend of his passion for Leonora d'Este, daughter of his patron Alfonso II, Duke of Ferrara. Tasso was imprisoned by Alfonso, 1579–86; according to legend, he feigned madness on the orders of the Duke, but the modern opinion is that he really was mad, or at least neurotic and unstable.

Thomas Chatterton (1752–70), born in Bristol, was a prolific writer from his earliest days. Educated at a charity school and apprenticed to an attorney, he began in 1767–8 to forge medieval documents such as pedigrees, which he supplied to gullible local patrons; encouraged by the success of Thomas

Percy's *Reliques of Ancient English Poetry* (1765), he turned his attention to literary manuscripts, and the poems of 'Thomas Rowley', a 15th-century monk, began to appear. Percy's publisher, Dodsley, would not however take the poems, and Chatterton tried them on Horace Walpole (1717-97), author of *The Castle of Otranto*, who was initially taken in by the material Chatterton sent to him, but later drew back. In Apr. 1770 Chatterton left Bristol for London, where he struggled to earn a living writing for various periodicals; he committed suicide on 24 Aug. 1770. The 'Rowley' poems were first published in 1777; controversy over their authenticity continued well into the 19th century, but there was widespread admiration from Romantic writers, as well as interest in Chatterton's tragic history: Coleridge (*Monody on the Death of Chatterton*), Wordsworth (*Resolution and Independence*: see below, l. 165n.), Shelley (*Adonais* 397-401, where Chatterton is among the 'inheritors of unfulfilled renown'), and Keats, who described him as 'the purest writer in the English Language', and dedicated *Endymion* to his memory. Alfred de Vigny wrote a drama on the subject (*Chatterton*, 1835). Among the finest of the 'Rowley' poems are the *Songe to Ella* and *An Excelente Balade of Charite*. The standard edition of Chatterton is the *Complete Works*, ed. D. S. Taylor and B. B. Hoover (2 vols., Oxford 1971); the standard biography is E. H. W. Meyerstein, *A Life of Thomas Chatterton* (1930). B.'s research for his 'Essay' was principally among printed sources, notably the biographies by A. Chalmers (1810), J. Dix (1837), and C. B. Willcox (1842; see above), though his interpretations are mainly his own.

A copy of the 1778 ed. of the 'Rowley' poems was in B.'s father's library, together with at least two biographies in addition to Willcox, those by John Davis (1820) and George Gregory (1789; *Collections* A626, A767, A1095, pp. 55, 67, 95). Both Gregory and Davis have extensive notes by B.'s father, suggesting that B.'s interest in Chatterton may have been stimulated by him. Among works by B.'s father in an MS music book at Wellesley College, Massachusetts (*Collections* J93, p. 533), is a version of 'Chatterton's Song'. A. Kincaid and P. Blayney, in 'A Book of Browning's and his *Essay on Chatterton*', *BSN* ii (Dec. 1972) 11-25, give an account of a copy of *Walpoliana* (ed. J. Pinkerton, 2nd ed. [1804]) which contains B.'s father's signature, a number of marginal marks and a few notes in B.'s hand. It seems probable that he used this volume during his preparation of the essay: his comments anticipate the attitude he takes there towards Walpole, whose good faith towards Chatterton he questions, and Chatterton, whom he defends. Typically, at one point where the text of *Walpoliana* speaks of 'a notorious forgery' having been perpetrated by Chatterton, B. wrote a double underline under 'notorious' and added a pencilled footnote: 'a forgery that kept the literary world in suspense 30 years c^d not be so very *notorious!*' (Kincaid and Blayney, p. 14). See also headnote to *Pied Piper* (p. 133).

B.'s essay is an attempt to rescue Chatterton's character by explaining the forgeries as the young poet's first steps in literature, which unluckily entangled him in a network of deceit from which he made unavailing attempts to escape. Smalley, comparing this account of Chatterton's career with the sources B. used, argues that the essay constitutes an exercise in creative – and unhistorical – 'special pleading' similar to that which B. had already undertaken in the case of such historical figures as Paracelsus and Sordello, and which he was later to perform in *Ring*, *Prince Hohenstiel*, and *Red Cotton*. It is true that B. frequently distorts, suppresses, and recombines historical documents and events to fit his own interpretation of Chatterton's character. Quotations from source materials are sometimes accurate, sometimes misleadingly combined, sometimes wildly wrong. But the essay is hardly, as Smalley seems to imply, an uncritical and unscholarly apologia. B. was the first to note that the knowledge of Latin apparently revealed in 'Rowley's Sermon' belonged not to Chatterton but to his unacknowledged source, Hurrion (see ll. [27-70n.]). The idea that Walpole treated Chatterton badly is at least tenable; the 'torn papers' with which Chatterton's body was found surrounded after his suicide could well have been draft poems, and were so described in more than one source; yet Smalley dismisses B.'s argument out of hand in both the last two instances, and in describing his entire case as 'strangely unhistorical', even 'an unintentional literary hoax', appears to subscribe to a naive conception both of historiography and of B.'s intentions. The essay also contains some very important aesthetic arguments, in particular the contention that all poets begin, as Chatterton did, by imitating others; in carrying imitation to the length of forgery, Chatterton achieved a supreme expression of this principle (see ll. 209-30).

B. makes only glancing refs. to Chatterton elsewhere in his work. The most important appears in *Shelley*, where B. comments that 'There is such a thing as an efficacious knowledge of and belief in the politics of Junius, or the poetry of Rowley, though a man should at the same time dispute the title of Chatterton to the one, and consider the author of the other, as Byron wittily did, "really, truly, nobody at all"' (for the parallel between the two essays, see below). 'Junius' was the pseudonym affixed to a series of celebrated satirical letters published 1769-72; there was a protracted controversy over the identity of their author, which has never been resolved. The conjunction of Junius with Chatterton may reflect the interests of B.'s father, who owned many of the pamphlets generated by the Junius controversy, and, as with his Chatterton biographies, copiously annotated them; he also drafted at least two essays of his own on the subject (*Collections* J66, J83, pp. 531-2). B. again admiringly couples Chatterton with Junius in *Waring* 193-6, and makes further reference to Chatterton in a letter to the original of Waring, Alfred Domett: 'Chatterton can only go without food a certain number of hours, so he ends it, while at that moment some benevolent man (see his name in Southey, I think) is actually started on his way to Bristol "to inquire into the circumstances of, and, if necessary, assist the author"' (20 Nov. 1845, *RB & AD* 117; one Dr Fry did make the journey B. mentions, but the source, if any, of his quotation has not been found).

The most important direct parallel, apart from the poems already mentioned, is B.'s only other work of prose criticism, *Shelley*, written ten years later, and like the 'Essay' both a statement of B.'s aesthetics and an exemplary model of their operation. Smalley suggests that its most immediate affinity is with *Return of the Druses* (1842), in which the career of Djabal closely parallels Chatterton's.

For further information, and more detailed annotation than we are able to provide here, the reader is referred to Smalley's edition, which also has three substantial essays placing the essay in B.'s poetic and intellectual development.

Art. VIII.—Conjectures and Researches concerning the Love Madness and Imprisonment of Torquato Tasso. By Richard Henry Wilde. 2 vols. New York. 1842.

> Upon the minuteness and obscurity of our attainable evidences with regard to a single important portion of a great poet's history—the Love and Madness of Tasso—great light is thrown by these clever volumes.
> 5 And further additions to a very meagre stock are not,

Review heading. Richard Henry Wilde (1789-1847) was a prominent American lawyer and senator (he was attorney-general of Georgia and served five terms in Congress) who was also a minor poet. Between 1835 and 1840 he lived in Italy; *Conjectures* is the fruit of this period. B. may have known of a literary controversy in which he was involved during the 1820s. His poem *The Lament of the Captive*, published anonymously in 1819, became the subject of a fierce debate as to whether Wilde really wrote it, or had plagiarized the work of another poet. In 1834 a hoaxer published Greek and Latin 'originals' (actually translations) of the poem, ascribing it to Alcaeus, and causing Wilde publicly to assert his authorship; the controversy continued, however, till 1871. The similarity to the debate over Chatterton's Rowley poems might have intrigued B.; he could not have known, unfortunately, of Wilde's poem *Lines Written by Thomas Chatterton*, which was unpublished. B.'s account of *Conjectures* is accurate, at least as regards Wilde's stated intentions. Wilde claims that 'truth is discovered by a close analysis of circumstantial evidence' and that the best source of such evidence is 'the authority of TORQUATO himself'; 'enough ... may be gathered from his own pen to afford grounds of satisfactory belief, or at least of plausible conjecture'. The relation between this kind of evidence and that afforded by earlier biographers is described in terms which clearly foreshadow B.'s approach: 'The object of this essay ... is not to weigh the credit of biographers, but to settle all controversy ... by the authority of the poet himself'. B.'s liberal use of quotation from Chatterton's letters reflects Wilde's extensive use of Tasso's poetry and correspondence as evidence. However, Wilde's work (again like B.'s) is as much an apologia for its subject as an objective historical account; the American *DNB* terms it 'somewhat romantic'. Wilde's title may have indirectly suggested B.'s change of subject: a celebrated account of Chatterton's life appears in Sir Herbert Croft's *Love and Madness* (1780).

it seems, to be absolutely despaired of. The Medicean
Records may be laid under more liberal contributions,
and the Archives of Este cease to remain impenetrable.
What even if a ray of light should straggle over the
10   unsunned hoards of sumless wealth in the Vatican? "If
windows were in heaven, might this thing be."
    But in our days the poorest loophole will have to be
broken, we suspect, with far different instruments
from those it is the fashion to employ just now in Italy.
15   It is enough at present if the oily instances of this or the
other Minister-Residentiary operate so happily upon
the ruffled apprehensiveness of this or the other
Chamberlain-Omnipotentiary, as to allow a minute's
glimpse of the Fortunate Isles through the incessant
20   breakers that girdle them. The rude sea now and then
grows civil, indeed; but a positive current setting
landwards is the thing wanted, and likely to remain so.
Ever and anon we seem on the point of a discovery. A
scrap of letter turns up, or a bundle of notices drop
25   out, and the Head Librarian for the time being
considers the curiosity of some Dilettante Ambassador
for the place being, and, provided the interest of the
whole civilized world is kept out of sight with
sufficient adroitness, becomes communicative.
30   "The anger of the Grand Duke arises from his being
informed that I had revealed to the Duke of Ferrara
. . . . . . ! I cannot write all freely, but this is the
gospel." So writes Tasso to "the one friend he now
believes in, Scipio Gonzaga." And "this blank,"
35   sorrowfully subjoins Mr. Wilde, "is found in the first
copy of the letter furnished for publication by the
learned and candid Muratori, then librarian to the
Duke of Modena." It contained an expression, says he,
which it would be indecorous to repeat! Thus at every
40   step, where there is the slightest prospect of a clue to
the truth, are we mortified by its destruction through
reserve or timidity. And if things were so in the green-

7-8. *The Medicean Records*: cp. *Conjectures*: 'The secret archives of the house of
ESTE are practically shut to all the world, and those of MEDICI accessible
only with great difficulty ... If the treasures of the Vatican could be exposed –
but that is hopeless' (i 140-1).
10-11. *"If windows ... this thing be."*: 2 *Kings* vii 2, an expression of
incredulity. See also *Sordello* iii 901-5.
42-3. *And if things ... Tuscany?*: *Luke* xxiii 31: 'For if they do these things in a
green tree, what shall be done in a dry?'

tree time of the Muratoris, what shall be done in the dry stump of modern Lombardy or Tuscany?

45 Of certain important manuscripts recently discovered at Rome, and now in the course of publication, we regret to learn that the authenticity is considered too questionable to allow of their being brought forward to any useful purpose: so that, for the present, 50 this result of Mr. Wilde's labour, now before us, must be regarded as conclusive: and fortunately our last, proves also our best, news. It is pleasant to find that the popular notion (we might say instinct) concerning this particular point of Tasso's career, grown up, 55 uncertain how, from biographical gleanings here and gatherings there,—somewhat shaken, as it was sure to be, by subsequent representations,—seems again confirmed by these latest discoveries.

A couplet in a canzone, a paragraph in an epistle, 60 had thus been sufficient to begin with. "Tasso was punished in a living hell by angels, because he unburthened his bosom to his lyre." "He would fain be released from this prison of Saint Anna without being troubled for those things which from frenzy he 65 has done and written in matters of love." After these, and a few other like notices, Professors might search, and Abbates research; the single Leonora become "three lady-loves at once;" and the dim torture at Ferrara a merciful effect of Duke Alfonso's consider- 70 ation for "Signor Tasso, the noted poet's, deplorable madness;"—but the world, satisfied with its own suspicion, remained deaf to it all.

"If we suppose," sums up Mr. Wilde, "that his imprisonment was occasioned by the accidental or 75 treacherous disclosure of amatory poetry suspected to be addressed to the princess, every thing becomes intelligible—his mistress's early injunctions of silence—his directions to Rondinelli—the dearer mysteries of his heart half-hinted to Gonzaga—the reference to her who 80 corresponded so little to his love—his heavy sin of temerity—Madalo's more important treasons—the attempt to extort confession—the bitter rigour and unwonted arts—the words and acts that might increase Alfonso's ire—the order to feign insanity—the sacrifice of 85 Abraham—the command that he must aspire to no fame of letters—the prohibition to write—the anger of the princesses—the allusions to his fond faults—to his Proserpine—to Ixion, and to the angels that punished

90   him. By this supposition, also, Leonora's voluntary celibacy, notwithstanding the most advantageous offers of marriage, and Tasso's constant devotion to the duke, in spite of the rigour of his chastisement, are sufficiently accounted for." *

95   How much that establishes old convictions, and how little that is even supplementary to them, have we here!

     Such as it is, however, in what Mr. Wilde has done, he has gone the right way to work and done it well. He has steadily restricted himself to the single point in

100   question. It is that point in the poet's history, indeed, from which those to whom sonnets and madrigals, the Rinaldo and Aminta, are all but unknown, will take warrant for some belief in their reported truth and beauty. It is undoubtedly that to which every student

105   of Italian verse must refer the touching glimmer, as an outbreak through prison-bars, that colours every page of the Giurusalemme. Still it is but a point; and Mr. Wilde has not perhaps done less well in leaving the rest untouched, than in accomplishing so thoroughly the

110   task he took in hand. He relies upon his subject; is sure of the service he can render by an efficacious treatment of thus much of it; nor entertains any fear lest the bringing in a Before and After, with which he has no immediate concern, should be thought necessary to

115   give interest to the At Present on which he feels he can labour to advantage. We suspect that if we would make any material progress in knowledge of this description, such works must be so undertaken. If, for example, the materials for a complete biography of Tasso are far

120   from exhausted, let some other traveller from the west be now busied in the land of Columbus and Vespucci with the investigation,—say, of the circumstances of the wondrous youth of Tasso; the orations at Naples and the Theses at Padua,—and in the end we should

125   more than probably have two spots of sunshine to find our way by, instead of one such breadth of dubious twilight, as, in a hazy book written on the old principle of doing a little for every part of a subject, and more than a little for none, rarely fails to perplex the more.

130   Thinking thus, and grieving over what must be admitted to be the scantiness of the piece of sunshine

* Vol. II., p. 166.

here, and the narrow and not very novel track it would alone serve to lead us into,—a book★ was sent to us on a subject not very different from Mr. Wilde's, but on

135 which the service he has sought to render to the memory of Tasso has not hitherto been attempted for a memory more foully outraged. We make no apology for a proposed effort to render some such service. It is no very abrupt desertion of the misfortunes of Tasso,

140 to turn to the misfortunes of Chatterton. All these disputed questions in the lives of men of genius—all these so-called calamities of authors—have a common relationship, a connexion so close and inalienable, that they seldom fail to throw important light upon each

145 other.

To the precocity of genius in the Neapolitan boy at seven years old—the verse and prose from the College of the Jesuits—no parallel can be found in modern times, till we arrive at the verses of Chatterton, to

150 whom Campbell has very properly said "Tasso alone may be compared as a juvenile prodigy." But the parallel will, in other respects, admit of application. The book before us, for example, on the love and madness of the Italian, is in itself a direct text from

155 which to speak of what concerns us most in the disputed character of our own countryman. As the whole of Mr. Wilde's argument may be said to include itself in his commentary upon the opening couplet of the first Sonnet of the Collection of *Rime*,

160   "True were the loves and transports which I sung,"

so let us say of the Englishman, that his were far from that untruth, that absence of reality, so constantly charged against them. In a word, poor Chatterton's life was not the Lie it is so universally supposed to have

165 been; nor did he "perish in the pride" of refusing to

[2]   ★ "The Poetical Works of Thomas Chatterton, with Notices of his Life, a History of the Rowley Controversy, a Selection of his Letters, and Notes Critical and Explanatory." Cambridge. 1842.

165. "perish in the pride": Wordsworth, *Resolution and Independence* 43-4: 'I thought of Chatterton, the marvellous Boy, / The sleepless Soul that perished in his pride'. For B.'s hostility to Wordsworth at this period, see headnote to *Lost Leader* (p. 176).

[2-4]. The anonymous editor of this two-volume work was C. B. Willcox. See headnote, p. 476, and *Smalley* 135-6.

surrender Falsehood and enter on the ways of Truth.
We can show, we think, and by some such process as
Mr. Wilde adopts in regard to Tasso, that he had
already entered on those ways when he was left,
170   without a helping hand, to sink and starve as he might.
And to this single point we shall as far as possible
restrict ourselves.

Mr. Wilde remarks of the great Italian, that though
there are indeed passages in Tasso's life and letters,
175   scarcely reconcilable with the strict regard for truth
which Manso, his friend and contemporary, ascribes
to him,

> "yet that to whatever dissimulation he may have been
> driven, upon some memorable occasions—by a hard and,
180   > if you will, a criminal, but still almost irresistible
> necessity—there is no reason to believe him habitually
> insincere: and that, avoiding every subtle refinement, it
> cannot be too much to assume that he was like other men,
> who in the absence of all inducement, were not supposed
185   > deliberately to utter falsehood." *

It shall be our endeavour, by extending the application
of this text from Tasso to Chatterton, to throw a new
light upon a not dissimilar portion of the latter poet's
career, and in some degree soften those imputations of
190   habitual insincerity with which the most sympathizing
of Chatterton's critics have found themselves compelled to replace the "great veracity" attributed to him
by his earliest and most partial biographer.

For Tasso, a few words will say how his first false
195   step was an indiscretion; how, having published love-
poetry under a false name and suffered himself to be
suspected its author, he, to avoid the ill-consequences,
feigned at the Duke's suggestion, Madness; and how
his protracted agony at Saint Anna was but an
200   unremitting attempt to free himself from the effect of
this false step without being compelled to reveal the
truth, and disavow his whole proceedings since the
time of that sad starting-aside from the right way. But

* Vol. I., p. 12.

---

193. earliest and most partial biographer: Chatterton's sister, who contributed a short sketch of his life to Croft's *Love and Madness* which was reprinted
in Southey and Cottle's edition.

before we speak of the corresponding passage in
205 Chatterton's story, something should be premised
respecting the characteristic shape his first error took,
as induced by the liabilities of that peculiar development of genius of which he was the subject.

Genius almost invariably begins to develop itself by
210 imitation. It has, in the short-sightedness of infancy,
faith in the world: and its object is to compete with, or
prove superior to, the world's already recognised
idols, at their own performances and by their own
methods. This done, there grows up a faith in itself:
215 and, no longer taking the performance or method of
another for granted, it supersedes these by processes of
its own. It creates, and imitates no longer. Seeing
cause for faith in something external and better, and
having attained to a moral end and aim, it next
220 discovers in itself the only remaining antagonist
worthy of its ambition, and in the subduing what at
first had seemed its most enviable powers, arrives at
the more or less complete fulfilment of its earthly
mission. This first instinct of Imitation, which with
225 the mediocre takes the corresponding mediocre form
of an implied rather than expressed appropriation of
some other man's products, assumed perforce with
Chatterton, whose capabilities were of the highest
class, a proportionably bolder and broader shape in the
230 direction his genius had chosen to take. And this
consideration should have checked the too severe
judgment of what followed. For, in simple truth, the
startling character of Chatterton's presentment, with
all its strange and elaborately got up accompaniments,
235 was in no more than strict keeping with that of the
thing he presented. For one whose boy's essay was
"Rowley" (a Man, a Time, a Language, all at once) the
simultaneous essay of inventing the details of the
muniment-room treasures and yellow-roll discoveries,
240 by no means exceeded in relative hardihood the
mildest possible annexing—whatever the modern
author's name may be—to the current poetry or prose
of the time. But, alas! for the mere complacent
forbearance of the world in the one case, must come
245 sharp and importunate questionings in the other; and,
at every advance in such a career, the impossibility of
continuing in the spirit of the outset grows more and

211-24. *Genius ... mission*: Cp. *Pauline* 383-93n. (I 49-50).

more apparent. To begin with the step of a giant is one
thing, suddenly for another's satisfaction to increase to
250   a colossal stride is a very different. To the falsehood of
the mediocre, truth may easily be superinduced, and
true works, with them, silently take the place of false
works; but before one like Chatterton could extricate
himself from the worse than St. Anna dungeon which
255   every hour was building up more surely between him
and the common earth and skies, so much was to be
dared and done! That the attempt was courageously
made in Chatterton's case, there are many reasons for
believing. But to understand his true position, we
260   must remove much of the colouring which subsequent
occurrences imparted to the dim beginnings of his
course of deception. He is to the present day viewed as
a kind of Psalmanazar or Macpherson, producing
deliberately his fabrications to the world and challeng-
265   ing its attention to them. A view far from the truth.
Poor Chatterton never had that chance. Before the
world could be appealed to, a few untoward circumstances seem to have effectually determined and given
stability to what else had not impossibly proved a
270   mere boy's fancy, destined to go as lightly as it came
and leave no trace, save in a fresh exertion of the old
means to a new and more commensurate end.
   In September, 1768, a New Bridge at Bristol was
completed, and early in the next month the principal
275   newspaper of the city contained a prose "description of
the Fryar's (Mayor's) first passing over the Old
Bridge, taken from an old manuscript." The attention

257. dared and done: from the last line of Christopher Smart's *Song to David*
(1763), a favourite poem of B.'s; he quotes versions of the line ('And now the
matchless deed's achieved, / DETERMIN'D, DAR'D, AND DONE!!!')
many times in poems and letters.

263. Psalmanazar or Macpherson: George Psalmanazar (?1679-1763), French
impostor who came to London in 1703, claiming to be a native of Formosa;
he translated the catechism into 'Formosan', a language he invented. James
Macpherson (1736-96), author of poems attributed to an ancient Gaelic bard,
'Ossian'. These became internationally famous, and their celebrity survived
the discovery of Macpherson's virtual authorship. B.'s first composition was
an imitation of 'Ossian', as he wrote to EBB. on 25 Aug. 1846, adding: 'to
this day I believe in a nucleus for all that haze, a foundation of truth to
Macpherson's fanciful superstructure' (*LK* 998-9). *Smalley* notes that the
analogy between Chatterton and both Psalmanazar and Macpherson was
drawn by Walpole.

of—what are called in the accounts we have seen—"the
literati of Bristol," was excited. Application was made
280   to the publisher for a sight of the surprising and
interesting original. No such thing was forthcoming;
but the curiosity of Literati must be appeased; and the
bearer   of   the   newspaper   marvel,   one   Thomas
Chatterton,—a youth of sixteen, educated at Colston's
285   Charity-school where reading, writing and arithmetic
only were taught, and, since, a clerk to an attorney of
the place,—was recognised on his next appearance at
the printing-office with another contribution, and
questioned whence he obtained that first-named paper.
290   He was questioned "with threatenings in the first
instance, to which he refused any answer, and next
with milder usage and promises of patronage,"—
which extorted from him at last the confession, that
the manuscript was one of many his father (parish
295   clerk, usher, or sexton) had taken from a coffer in the
church of St. Mary, Redcliff.
It was his own composition; and being the first of
what are called the Rowleian forgeries, suggests a
remark upon literary forgery in general, and that of
300   Chatterton in particular.*

[6]   * That there should have been a controversy for ten minutes about the
genuineness of any ten verses of "Rowley" is a real disgrace to the scholarship of
the age in which such a thing took place: we shall not touch on it here, certainly.
Conceive the entering on such a discussion at all, when the poor charity-boy had
already furnished samples of Rowley in the different stages of partial
completeness, from the rough draught in the English of the day, ungarnished by
a single obsolete word, to the finished piece with its strange incrustation of
antiquity! There is never theft for theft's sake with Chatterton. One short poem
only, *The Romaunt of the Cnyghte*, is in part a tacking together of old lines from
old poets, out of rhyme and time, yet at the same time not so utterly unlike an
approximation to the genuine ware. And why? Because the Mr. Burgum, to one
of whose ancestors it is attributed, and whose taste solely it was intended to suit,
happened to be *hopelessly incapable of understanding any composition of the mixed sort
which Chatterton had determined upon producing; and which, retaining what he
supposed the ancient garb should also include every modern refinement.* The expedient
which would alone serve with the good Mr. Burgum, was to ply him with
something entirely unintelligible, so begetting a reverence; and after that with

[6-8]. *That there should have been ... scholarship of the age*: cp. the note by B.'s
father in his copy of *A Supplemental Apology for the Believers in the Shakespeare-
Papers* (1799): 'Any person of ordinary ability, who is not conversant in the
language of Poetry, may detect the spuriousness of the Rowley Poems, by
merely applying his own understanding' (*Collections* A609, p. 54).

another thing perfectly comprehensible, so ministering to his pleasure. Accordingly, Chatterton, for that once, attempted to write thorough old verse, because he could, as he did, accompany it by thorough new verse too: a modern paraphrase to wit.

[27]   But though we will not touch the general and most needless question, it happens that, by a curious piece of fortune, we have been enabled, since taking up the subject of this article, to bring home to Chatterton one, and by no means the least ingenious of his "forgeries," which has hitherto escaped detection. Rowley's *Sermon on the Holy Spirit*, with its orthodoxy and scripture citations, its Latin from St. Cyprian, and its Greek from St. Gregory, is triumphantly

[33]   referred to by the learned and laborious Jacob Bryant (who wrote one folio to disprove the Tale of Troy and another to prove the Tale of Rowley), as a flight clearly above Chatterton's reach. Now this aforesaid Greek quotation was the single paragraph which struck our eye some two or three days since, in looking hastily through a series of sermons on the Nature of the Holy Spirit, by the Rev. John Hurrion, originally printed, it should seem, in 1732; on a reference to which we found Rowley's discourse to be a mere cento from their pages, artfully enough compiled. For example, thus saith ROWLEY: "Seyncte Paulle prayethe the Holye Spryte toe assyste hys flocke ynn these wordes, The Holye Spryte's communyon bee wythe you. Lette us dhere desyerr of hymm to ayde us . . . lette us saye wythe Seyncte Cyprian, '*Adesto, Sancte Spiritus, et paraclesin tuam expectantibus illabere coelitus; sanctifica templum corporis nostri et consecra inhabitaculum tuum.*' Seyncte Paulle sayethe yee are the temple of Godde; for the Spryte of Godde dwellethe ynn you. Gyff yee are the temple of Godde alleyne bie the dwellynge of the Spryte, wote yee notte that the Spryte ys Godde? . . . The Spryte or dyvyne will of Godde moovedd uponn the waterrs att the Creatyonn of the worlde; thys meaneth the Deeitie . . . Gyff the Spryte bee notte Godde, howe bee ytt the posessynge of the Spryte dothe make a manne sayedd toe be borne of Godde? Itt requyreth the powerr of Godde toe make a manne a new creatyonn, yette such doth the Spryte. Thus sayethe Seyncte Gregorie Naz. of the Spryte and hys wurchys: Γεῦται Χριστος· προτέχει. βαπτζεται· μαρτυρεῖ. Πειραζέταθ' αναγê. Δυναμεις ἐπιτελê· ξυμπαραμαρτελ. Ανέρχετα." And now let us listen to HURRION, *Serm.* 1. "As therefore the apostle prayed on the behalf of the

[27-70]. *But though ... are subjoined*: B.'s solution of this crux in the 'Rowley' controversy went unnoticed, and the source of the *Sermon* continued to puzzle Chatterton scholars until Smalley's edition appeared: see pp. 144, 177-87, and *Complete Works* i 151-2, ii 908-9. B.'s copy of Hurrion's *Works of the Holy Spirit* contains the following inscription by B.'s father: 'In Chatterton's works is a Sermon (or Homily) said to have been composed by the fictitious Poet Rowley – every sentence of which was taken from the first (& scarce) edition of these Sermons'. B. added underneath: '(This note of my Father's refers to the singular discovery I made of this fact, many years before.) RB. Jr. 1870' (*Collections* A1274, p. 109).

[33]. *Bryant*: B. refers to Bryant's *War of Troy* (1792), in which Bryant set out to expose the entire Homeric corpus as unhistorical. B.'s sketch of his interest in the Trojan story and its detractors in *Development* (1889) casts doubt on Smalley's suggestion that his sole acquaintance with this work may have derived from a citation of it in Willcox.

Is it worth while to mention, that the very notion of
obtaining a free way for impulses that can find vent in
no other channel (and consequently of a liberty
conceded to an individual, and denied to the world at
305   large), is implied in all literary production? By this fact
is explained, not only the popular reverence for, and
interest in even the personal history of, the acknowledged and indisputable possessors of this power—as
so many men who have leave to do what the rest of
310   their fellows cannot—but also the as popular jealousy
of allowing this privilege to the first claimant. And so
instinctively does the Young Poet feel that his desire
for this kind of self-enfranchisement will be resisted as
a matter of course, that we will venture to say, in nine
315   cases out of ten his first assumption of the licence will
be made in a borrowed name. The first communication, to even the family circle or the trusted associate,
is sure to be "the work of a friend;" if not "Englished
from the German." So is the way gracefully facilitated
320   for Reader and Hearer finding themselves in a new

Corinthians : . . . in these words: 'The communion of the Holy Ghost be with
you,' it is very proper to apply to him for his gracious aid and assistance. An
example of this we have in Cyprian. 'O Holy Spirit be thou present,' &c.—*Cyp.
de Spir. S.* p. 484. [quoted, no doubt, at length, like the other references, in the
first edition.] . . . . Now if he that dwells in us as his temple is God, what other
conclusion can be drawn from thence but this, that we are the temple of God?
&c. &c. [The rest of the verse, with the authority of St. Paul being the text of the
Sermon.] . . . . which is also God—as when it is said 'the Spirit of God moved
upon the waters, in the creation of the world. *Sermon* 4. Believers are born of the
Spirit . . this is a new creation, and requires the same Almighty power to effect
as the first creation did . . if the Spirit is not God by nature . . how are they said
to be born of God who are regenerated by the Spirit?' '*Christ*,' says one of the
ancients, '*is born—the Spirit is his forerunner*,' &c." And in a footnote the Greek
[70]   text and proper authority are subjoined.
It is, perhaps, worth a remark in concluding this note, that Chatterton, a
lawyer's clerk, takes care to find no law-papers in Canning's Coffer, of which
tradition had declared it to be full. That way detection was to be feared. But the
pieces on devotional subjects, to which his earlier taste inclined, came so
profusely from the "Godlie preeste Rowlie," that Chatterton thinks it advisable,
from the time of his discoveries, to forget his paraphrases of Job and Isaiah, and
to disclaim for himself a belief in Christianity on every and no occasion at all!

301-21. Is it worth while to mention ... with respect to each other: cp. *Conjectures:*
'The precaution of feigning to write for another, when, in truth, he wrote for
himself, was, in TASSO's situation, an obvious one, and had, undoubtedly,
been used by him' (i 59). Cp. B.'s explanation to W. J. Fox of his anonymous
publication of *Pauline*, his first published work: 'a loophole I have kept for
backing out of the thing if necessary' (*Correspondence* iii 74).

position with respect to each other.

Now unluckily, in Chatterton's case, this communication's whole value, in the eyes of the Bristol-
ians, consisted in its antiquity. Apart from that, there
325 was to them no picturesqueness in "Master Mayor,
mounted on a white horse, dight with sable trappings
wrought about by the nuns of St. Kenna;" no "most
goodly show in the priests and freres all in white albs."
Give that up, and all was given; and poor Chatterton
330 could not give all up. He could only determine for the
future to produce Ellas and Godwyns, and other
"beauteous pieces;" wherein "the plot should be clear,
the language spirited; and the songs interspersed in it,
flowing, poetical, and elegantly simple; the similes
335 judiciously applied; and though written in the reign of
Henry VI., not inferior to many of the present age."
Had there but been any merit of this kind, palpable
even to Bristol Literati, to fall back upon in the first
instance, if the true authorship were confessed! But
340 that was otherwise; and so the false course, as we have
said, was unforeseeingly entered upon. Yet still, from
the first, he was singularly disposed to become
communicative of his projects and contrivances for
carrying them into effect. There was, after all, no such
345 elaborate deception about any of them. Indeed, had
there only happened to be a single individual of
ordinary intelligence among his intimates, the event
must assuredly have fallen out differently. But as it
was, one companion would be present at the whole
350 process of "antiquating," as Chatterton styled it, his
productions (the pounding of ochre and crumpling of
parchments); another would hear him carelessly avow
himself master of a power "to copy, by the help of
books he could name, the style of our elder poets so
355 exactly, that they should escape the detection of Mr.
Walpole himself;"—and yet both these persons remain
utterly incapable of perceiving that such circumstances
had in the slightest degree a bearing upon after events
at Bristol! It is to be recollected, too, that really in
360 Bristol itself there was not any thing like a general
interest excited in the matter. And when at last,
yielding to the pertinacity of inquirers, these and
similar facts came lingeringly forth, as the details of so
many natural appearances with which unconscious
365 rustics might furnish the philosopher anxious to report
and reason upon them—Chatterton was dead.

Of several of his most characteristic compositions, he confessed, at various times, on the least solicitation, the authorship. He had found and versified the
370　argument of the Bristowe Tragedy—he had written the Lines on our Ladye's Church. But these confidences were only to his mother and sister. Why? Because mother and sister were all who cared for him rather than for Rowley, and would look at his
375　connection with any verses as a point in their favour. As for his two patrons, Barrett and Catcott, they took great interest in the yellow streaks, and verse written like prose without stops; less interest in the poetry; and in Chatterton least, or none at all! And a prophet's fate
380　in his own country was never more amusingly exemplified than when grave Deans and Doctors, writing to inquire after Chatterton's abilities of his old companions, got the answers on record. "Not having any taste myself for ancient poetry," writes Mr. Cary,
385　"I do not recollect Chatterton's ever having shown such writings to me, *but* he often mentioned them, *when*, great as his capacity was, I am convinced that he was incapable of writing them!" "He had intimated," remarks Mr. Smith, "very frequently both a desire to
390　learn, and a design to teach himself—Latin; but I always dissuaded him from it, *as being in itself impracticable*. But I advised him by all means *to try* at French. As to Latin, *depend upon it you will find it too hard for you*. Try at French, if you please: of *that* you
395　may acquire *some* knowledge *without much difficulty*, and it will be of real service to you." "And, sir," winds up Mr. Clayfield, "*take my word for it*, the poems were no more his composition than *mine!*" With such as these there was no fellowship possible for Chatterton.
400　We soon discover him, therefore, looking beyond. From the time of his communication of the Rowley poems, "his ambition," writes Mrs. Newton, his sister, "increased daily. When in spirits he would enjoy his rising fame; confident of advancement, he would
405　promise that my mother and I should be partakers of his success." As a transcriber, we suppose! We find Sir Herbert Croft, to whom this very letter was addressed, declaring "that he will not be sure that the writer and her mother might not have easily been made to believe
410　that injured justice demanded their lives at Tyburn, for being the relatives of him who forged the poems of Rowley." Thus only, in this sideway at the best, could the truth steal out.

415 Meanwhile the sorry reception given to the so-called falsehood produced its natural effects. On the one hand there is a kind of ambition on being introduced to Mr. Barrett and Mr. Catcott, which increases daily; but on the other we are told that his spirits became at the same time "rather uneven—sometimes so *gloomed*,★

420 that for some days together he would say very little, and that by constraint." No doubt, and no wonder! For there was the sense of his being the author of the transcendent chorus to Freedom, or the delicious roundelay in Ella; ever at fierce variance with the

425 pitiful claim he was entitled to make in the character of their mere transcriber.

We shall not pursue this painful part of the question. Day followed day, and found him only more and more deeply involved. What we have restricted our

430 inquiry to, is the justice or injustice of the common charge that henceforth the whole nature of Chatterton became no other than one headstrong spirit of False-hood, in the midst of which, and by which, he perished at the last. And we think its injustice will be

435 shown without much difficulty, in showing that he really made the most gallant and manly effort of which his circumstances allowed to break through the sorry meshes that entangled him. We purposely forbear, with any view to this, taking for granted the mere

440 instigation of that Moral Sense which it is the worst want of charity to deny to him, and with direct and strong evidences of which his earliest poetry abounded. We will simply inquire what, in the circumstances referred to, would have been the proper course to

445 pursue, had the writer of the "Bristowe Tragedy" chanced to adopt on a single occasion the practice of its

---

★ The only word in Chatterton's communication to the genuineness of which Walpole seems to have objected. "The modern gloomy," says Chatterton, in reply to some critical exception taken against poems he had sent, "seems but a refinement of the old word Glomming, in Anglo-Saxon the twilight." And in a note to a line of the Ballad of Charity, "Look in his *glommed* face," &c., he observes, "'Glommed' clouded, dejected. A person of some note in the literary world is of opinion that 'glum' and 'glom' are modern cant words, and from this circumstance doubts the authenticity of the Rowley MSS. 'Glummong,' in the Saxon signifies twilight, a dark or dubious light and the modern word gloomy is derived from the Saxon 'glum.'" It is to be added that Chatterton, throughout, only objects to men's doubting the genuineness of Rowley on the insufficient grounds they give—and is in the right there.

hero, "who summed the actions of the day each night before he slept." Confessions at the market-cross avail nothing, and most injure those to whom they are
450 unavoidably made. Should he not have resolutely left Bristol, at least? and, disengaging himself from the still increasing trammels of his daily life of enforced deceit, begun elsewhere a wiser and happier course? That he did so may in our opinion be shown. It is our firm
455 belief that on this, and no other account, he determined to go to London.

"A few months before he left Bristol," mentions his sister, "he wrote letters to several booksellers in London—I believe to learn if there was any probability
460 of his getting an employment there." He had some time previously applied to Dodsley, the noted publisher, for his assistance in printing the tragedy of *Ella*; on the strength of a submitted specimen, which the great man of the Mall did not vouchsafe, it seems,
465 to glance over. He was led, therefore, to make a final experiment on the taste and apprehensiveness of Horace Walpole: not, as in Dodsley's case, by enclosing the despised poetical samples, but by sending a piece of antiquarian ware in which his presumed
470 patron was understood to especially delight. Of nothing are we so thoroughly persuaded as that these attempts were the predetermined last acts of a course of dissimulation he would fain discard for ever—on their success. The Rowleian compositions were all he
475 could immediately refer to, as a proof of the ability he was desirous of employing in almost any other direction. He grounded no claim on his possession of these MSS.; he was not soliciting an opportunity of putting off to advantage the stock in hand, or
480 increasing; and when Walpole subsequently avowed his regret at having omitted to transcribe before returning, the manuscript thus received, what has been cited as a singular piece of unprincipled effrontery, appears to us perfectly justifiable. For even after the
485 arrival of a discouraging letter, Chatterton's words are, that "if Mr. Walpole wishes to publish them himself, they are at his service." Nay—Mr. Barrett, or

---

447-8. *"who summ'd the actions of the day each night before he slept"*: from Chatterton's *Bristowe Tragedie or the Dethe of Syr Charles Bawdin* 165-8 (*Complete Works* i 12): 'And none can saye butt all my lyfe / I have hys [God's] wordes kept / And summ'd the actyonns of the daie / Eche nyghte before I slept'.

"the Town and Country Magazine, to which copies
may be sent," or indeed "the world, which it would be
490   the greatest injustice to deprive of so invaluable a
curiosity"—may have them and welcome. And
Chatterton's anxiety to recover them afterwards is
only intelligible on the supposition that his originals
were in jeopardy. To the very conceited question
495   Walpole himself has asked—" Did Chatterton impute
to me anything but distrust of his MSS.?"—we should
answer, Every thing but that. Let the young poet's
own verses, indeed, answer.

            Walpole, I thought not I should ever see
500   So mean a heart as thine has proved to be:
            Thou, who in luxury nursed, behold'st with scorn
            The boy who friendless, fatherless, forlorn,
            Asks thy high favour. *Thou mayst call me cheat—*
            Say didst thou never practice such deceit?
505   *Who wrote Otranto?*—but I will not chide.
            Scorn I'll repay with scorn, and pride with pride.
            Had I the gifts of wealth and luxury shared—
            Not poor and mean—Walpole! thou hadst not dared
            Thus to insult. But I shall live and stand
510   By Rowley's side, when thou art dead and damned.

       In this unhappy correspondence with Walpole,—it
never seems to have been admitted, yet it cannot be
said too often,—there is no new "falsehood" discernible: there is nothing but an unavailing and most
515   affecting effort, to get somehow free from the old. He
makes no asseveration of the fact of his discoveries;
affirms nothing the denial of which hereafter would be
essentially disgraceful to him; commits himself by
only a few ambiguous words which at any time a little
520   plain speaking (and blushes, if we will) would explain
away. Let it be observed, above all, that there is no
attempt to forge, and produce, and insist on the
genuineness of the MSS.; though this was a step by
which he could have lost nothing and might have
525   gained every thing, since Walpole's recognition of
their extraordinary merit was before him. In the

505. Who wrote Otranto?: Walpole's Gothic novel *The Castle of Otranto* (1764)
first appeared pseudonymously, purporting to be a translation from an Italian
work of 1529.

course the correspondence took, alas! that very recognition was fatal. If Walpole could suspect a boy of
sixteen had written thus, and yet see nothing in a
530 scrivener's office and its duties which such an one had
any title to withdraw from, all was over with
Chatterton's hopes. At this point, accordingly, he
simply replied that, "he is not able to dispute with a
person of his literary character: he has transcribed
535 Rowley's poems from a transcript in the possession of
a gentleman who is assured of their authenticity,"
(poor Catcott!) "and he will go a little beyond
Walpole's advice, by destroying *all his useless lumber of
literature and never urging his pen again but in the law.*" Is
540 this any very close or deliberate keeping of Rowley's
secret! In a word, he felt that Walpole should have
said, "Because I firmly believe you, Chatterton, wrote
or forged these verses of Rowley, I will do what you
require."★ And so we all feel now.
545   And what was it the poor baffled youth required?
To ascertain this will in a manner satisfy our whole
inquiry—so let us try to ascertain it. His immediate

★ Walpole's share in the matter may be told in a few words. Indifferent
antiquary as he was, at best—in these matters, at worst, his ignorance was
complete. "The admirable reasoning in Bryant's work" could "stagger him," he
confesses. On receiving Chatterton's first letter and specimens, as his belief in
[94] them was implicit, so his mortification on Gray and Mason's setting him right
was proportionable. "They both pronounced the poems to be modern forgeries,
and recommended the returning them without any further notice,"—stepping a
[97] little out of their province in that, certainly; *but they might have felt Chatterton safer
at Bristol than nearer home.* Walpole himself did no more in the refusal he gave,
than avail himself of Chatterton's own statement that his communications were
"taken from a transcript in the possession of a gentleman who was assured of
their authenticity." This unknown personage had clearly the first claim to the
good things of the Clerk of the Pipe and Usher of the Receipt, and to the
unknown they were left therefore, without more heed. Who can object? Truth
[104] to say, he of Strawberry Hill was at all times less disposed to expend his doit on

[94]. *Gray and Mason's*: Thomas Gray (1716-71), poet, author of *Elegy written
in a Country Church-Yard*; William Mason (1725-97), poet and tragedian.
[97-8]. *but they might ... nearer home*: i.e. Gray and Mason felt jealous of
Chatterton as a prospective rival. There is no foundation for this innuendo.
[104-6]. *he of Strawberry Hill ... empty enough*: Strawberry Hill was Walpole's
residence in Twickenham; the allusion that follows is to Trinculo's discovery
of Caliban, *Tempest* II ii 29-35: 'Were I in England now ... there would this
monster make a man; any strange beast there makes a man. When they will
not give a doit to relieve a lame beggar, they will lay out ten to see a dead

a living beggar than on a dead Indian; and, in his way, cowls-full of Ellas and Godwyns were nothing to a spurious cardinal's hat, empty enough. Beside, what was there to him in the least pressing in the application of a mere transcriber ("who had not quitted his master, nor was necessitous, nor otherwise poorer than attorney's clerks are") to "emerge from a dull profession and obtain a place that would enable him to follow his propensities." Therefore is it more a pity that ten years after, when he had partly forgotten the matter (this must be allowed, since, with respect to two points which strengthen his case materially, he professes uncertainty), Walpole should have made, on compulsion, a statement of its main circumstances, and leisurely put himself in what he conceived the handsomest of positions,—which turns out to be not quite so handsome. Never for an instant, forsooth, was he deceived by Rowley. "Chatterton had not commenced their intercourse in a manner to dazzle his judgment, or give him a high idea of Chatterton's own." "Somebody, he at first supposed, desired to laugh at him, not very ingeniously, he thought." Little imagining all this while that his letters were in existence, and forthcoming! and that every piece of encouragement to further forgeries, by the expression of belief in those before him, which he professes would have been the height of baseness in him to make, *he had already made!* Indeed the whole statement is

[124]   modelled on Benedick's *Old Tale:* "If this were so, so were it uttered—but it is not so, nor 'twas not so—but, indeed, God forbid it should be so!" One while, "he does not believe there ever existed so masterly a genius as Chatterton." And another while, he has regard to the "sad situation of the world, if every muse-struck lad who is bound to an attorney were to have his fetters struck off." Wanting is the excellent Horace Walpole, in short, through all these unhappy

[130]   matters, in that good memory which Swift has pronounced indispensable to a certain class of statement-makers.

And here would enough seem to have been said on the subject, did not one vile paragraph in the Walpole Explanations leer at us—the news, to wit, that "all of the house of forgery are relations, and that Chatterton's ingenuity in counterfeiting styles, and it is believed, hands, might easily have led him to those more facile imitations of prose, promissory notes." House of forgery!— from one not only enabled by his first preface to Otranto to march in at its hall-door, but qualified, by a trait noted in "Walpoliana," to sneak in through the

[139]   area-wicket! *Exempli gratia.* "The compiler having learned that the celebrated

---

Indian'. 'Cowls-full' alludes to the fact that 'Rowley' was a monk; the 'spurious cardinal's hat' supposedly belonged to Cardinal Wolsey, and was included in the sale of Walpole's Strawberry Hill collections, which took place in Apr. and May 1842, shortly before B. began writing the 'Essay'. See *Smalley* 159-60. Note also the coincidence here of 'cowls' and 'cardinal's hat': see *Pippa* iv 317n.

[*124*]. *Benedick's Old Tale: Much Ado About Nothing* I i 225-8.

[*130-1*]. *that good memory … statement-makers:* 'Liars ought to have good memories': not Swift, but the republican soldier and statesman Algernon Sidney (1622-83), in *Discourses on Government* (1698) ch. ii; the idea can also be found in Montaigne, 'Of Liars' (*Essays*, bk. I, ch. ix).

[*139-46*]. *"The compiler … question:* this passage appears in *Walpoliana* (see headnote, p. 477), p. 105, in which it is circled by B.: the italics are his.

application to Walpole, on his succeeding in forcing
his notice, and seemingly engaging his interest, was
550 for some place in a government-office. Did he want to
be richer? who had from his earliest boyhood been
accustomed to live upon bread and water, and who
would refuse to partake of his mother's occasional
luxury of a hot meal,—remarking that "he was about a
555 great work, and must make himself no stupider than
God had made him." Did he want to obtain leisure,
then, for this work—in other words, for the carrying
on of his old deceptions? "He had," says his sister,
"little of his master's business to do—sometimes not
560 two hours in a day, which gave him an opportunity to
pursue his genius." Mr. Palmer states, that "Chatterton was much alone in his office, and much disliked
being disturbed in the day-time." We should like to
know what kind of government-office would have
565 allowed greater facility for the pursuit of poetical
studies and "forgeries" than he was already in possession of; since what advantages, in a literary life,
government-office-labour can have over law-business,
we are far from guessing. It may be said that the pure
570 disgust and weariness of that law business had formed
motive sufficient. But our sympathy with Chatterton's
struggles—were nothing to be escaped from worse
than this "servitude" as he styles it—would seriously
diminish, we confess. Relieve Henry Jones from the
575 bricklayer's hod, and Stephen Duck from the

epistle to Sir William Chambers was supposed to be written by Mason, very
innocently expressed to Mr. Walpole his surprise that Mason, the general
characteristic of whose poesy is feeble delicacy, but united with a pleasing
neatness, should be capable of composing so spirited a satire. Mr. Walpole, *with
an arch and peculiar smile, answered, that it would indeed be surprising.* An
instantaneous and unaccountable impression arose that he was himself the
author, but delicacy prevented the direct question," &c. &c.

574. Henry Jones: poet, b. 1721 in Ireland; apprenticed as a bricklayer (hence
B.'s allusion); patronized by Lord Chesterfield, his tragedy *The Earl of Essex*
(1753) was a success; then, in *DNB*'s phrase, 'took to irregular courses', and
died in a workhouse after an accident during a drinking bout, Apr. 1770.
575. Stephen Duck: poet, b. 1705; began his working life as a farm labourer;
patronized by Lord Macclesfield and given a pension by Queen Caroline in
1733; took Holy Orders in 1746 and became rector of Byfleet in 1752;
committed suicide in 1756. His best-known poem is *The Thresher's Labour*
(1736), hence B.'s allusion to the 'thrasher's [thresher's] flail'.

thrasher's flail, if needs must: but Chatterton, from
two hours a day's copying precedents!—Ay, but "he
was obliged to sleep in the same room as the footboy,
and take his meals with the servants—which de-
580 gradation, to one possessing such pride as Chatterton,
must have been mortifying in the highest degree!"
Now, Chatterton taking his stand on the inherent
qualities of his own mind, shall part company with an
Emperor, if he so please, and have our approbation;
585 but let him waive that prerogative, and condescend to
the little rules of little men, and we shall not
sufficiently understand this right—in a blue-coat
charity-boy, apprenticed out with ten pounds of the
school-fund, and looking for patronage to pipe-
590 makers and pewterers—to cherish this sensitiveness of
contamination. There are more degrading things than
eating with footboys, we imagine. "The desire," for
example, "of proving oneself worthy the correspondence of Mr. Stephens (leather breeches-maker of
595 Salisbury) by tracing his family from Fitz Stephen, son
of Stephen, Earl of Aumerle, in 1095, son of Od, Earl
of Bloys, and Lord of Holderness." In a word,
Chatterton was very proud, and such crotchets never
yet entered the head of a truly proud man. Another
600 motive remains. Had he any dislike to Bristol or its
inhabitants generally? "His company pleased universally," he says: "he believed he had promised to write to
some hundreds of his acquaintance." And for the place
itself,—while at London, nothing out of the Gothic
605 takes his taste, except St. Paul's and Greenwich-
hospital: he is never tired of talking in his letters about
Bristol, its Cathedral, its street improvements: he even
inserts hints to the projectors of these last, in a local
paper: nay, he will forestall his mother's intended visit
610 to him at London, and return to Bristol by Christmas:
and when somebody suggested, just before his
departure, that his professed hatred for the city was
connected with ill-treatment received there, he
returns, indignantly, "He who without a more
615 sufficient reason *than commonplace scurrility* can look
with disgust on his native place, is a villain, and a
villain not fit to live. I am obliged to you for supposing
me such a villain!" Why then, without this hatred or
disgust, does he leave Bristol? Whence arises the
620 utmost distress of mind in which the mad "Will,"
whereby he announced his intention of committing

suicide, is written? On being questioned concerning it "he acknowledged that he wanted for nothing, and denied any distress on that account." "The distress was
625 occasioned," says Dr. Gregory, "by the refusal of a gentleman whom he had complimented in his poems, to accommodate him with a supply of money." Here are his own reasons. "In regard to my motives for the supposed rashness, I shall observe that I keep no worse
630 company than myself: I never drink to excess, and have, without vanity, too much sense to be attached to the mercenary retailers of iniquity. No: it is my PRIDE, my damned, native, unconquerable pride, that plunges me into distraction. You must know that
635 nineteen-twentieth of my composition is Pride. I must either live a Slave, a Servant; to have no Will of my own, no Sentiments of my own, which I may freely declare as such; or DIE. Perplexing alternative! But it distracts me to think of it—I will endeavour to learn
640 Humility—but it cannot be HERE!"

That is, at Bristol. It is needless for us here to interpose that our whole argument goes, not upon what Chatterton said, but what he did: it is part of our proof to show that all his distress arose out of the
645 impossibility of his saying anything to the real purpose. But is there no approximation to the truth in what has just been quoted? Had he *not* reduced himself to the alternative of living, as Rowley's transcriber, "a slave, with no sentiment of his own which he might
650 freely declare as such," or "dying?" And did not the proud man—who, when he felt somewhat later that he had failed, would not bring his poverty to accept the offer of a meal to escape "dying"—solicit and receive, while earlier there was yet the hope of succeeding, his
655 old companions' "subscription of a guinea apiece," to enable himself to break through the "slavery?" This, then, is our solution. For this and no other motive—to break through his slavery—at any sacrifice to get back to truth—he came up to London.

660 It will, of course, be objected, that Chatterton gave the very reasons for his desire to obtain a release from Bristol that we have rejected. But he was forced to say something, and what came more plausibly? To Walpole the cause assigned was, "that he wished to
665 cease from being dependant on his mother;"—while, by a reference to his indenture of apprenticeship, we find him to have been supplied with "meat, drink,

clothing, and lodging" by his master. To others the
mercantile character of Bristol is made an insuperable
670   objection;—and he straightway leaves it for Holborn.
As who, to avoid the smell of hemlock, should sail to
Anticyra! It may also yet be urged—as it has been too
often—that Chatterton gave to the very last, occasional
symptoms that the fabricating, falsifying spirit was far
675   from extinct in him. "He would turn Methodist
preacher, found a new sect," &c. Now no one can
suppose, and we are far from asserting, that at word of
command Chatterton wholly put aside the old habit of
imposing upon people—if that is to be the phrase. But
680   this "imposing upon people" has not always that
basest meaning. It is old as the world itself, the
tendency of certain spirits to subdue each man by
perceiving what will master him, by straightway
supplying it from their own resources, and so obtain-
685   ing, as tokens of success, his admiration, or fear, or
wonder. It has been said even that classes of men are
immediately ruled in no other way. Poor Chatterton's
freedom from some such tendency we do not claim.
He is indeed superior to it when alone, in the lumber-
690   closet on Redcliff Hill, or the lath-walled garret at
Shoreditch; but in company with the Thistlethwaites
and Burgums, he must often have felt a certain power
he had, lying dormant there, of turning their natures
to his own account. He, "knowing that a great genius
695   can effect anything, endeavoured in the foregoing
poems to represent an Enthusiastic Methodist, and
intended to send it to Romaine, and impose it on the
infatuated world as a reality;"—but Now, no sooner is
the intellectual effort made than the moral one
700   succeeds, and destroying these poems he determined
to kill himself. Every way unsuccessful, every way
discouraged, the last scene had come. When he killed
himself, his room was found "strewn thick over with

671-2. *As who ... Anticyra*: alluding to the proverb (cited by Horace, *Satires* II
iii 166) 'Naviget Anticyram'. [Let him sail to Anticyra], i.e. 'he's insane':
Anticyra (modern Andikira), a port on the Gulf of Corinth, was famous for
its hellebore (not hemlock) an ancient remedy for madness. B.'s use of the
phrase, however, is equivalent to 'carrying coals to Newcastle'.
681-7. *It is old ... no other way*: cp. *Sordello* iv 570-94; as Smalley notes
(following DeVane *Parleyings*), this 'theory of statesmanship' also appears in
many other works by B., e.g. *Return of the Druses, Colombe, Bishop Blougram,
Mr. Sludge, Prince Hohenstiel*, and *George Bubb Dodington*.

torn papers."

705   To the Rowley forgeries he had recurred but in one
instance, the acknowledgment of which by a magazine
only appeared after his death. He had come to London
to produce works of his own; writings he had hoped to
get some hearing for. "At the Walmsleys," says Sir
710   Herbert Croft, "he used frequently to say he had many
writings by him, which would produce a great deal of
money, if they were printed. To this it was once or
twice observed, that they lay in a small compass, for
that he had not much luggage. But he said he had
715   them, nevertheless. When he talked of writing something which should procure him money to get some
clothes—to paper the room in which he lodged; and to
send some more things to his sister, mother, and
grandmother—he was aked why he did not enable
720   himself to do all this by means of these writings which
were 'worth their weight in gold.' His answer was,
that 'they were not written with a design to buy old
clothes, or to paper rooms; and that if the world did
not behave well, it should never see a line of them.'"

725   It behaves indifferently, we think, in being so sure
these were simply fresh books of the "Battle of
Hastings," or remodellings of "the Apostate." Look
back a little, and see to what drudgery he had
submitted in this London, that he could but get the
730   means at last of going on his own ground. "A History
of England"—"a voluminous history of London; to
appear in numbers the beginning of next week"—
"necessitates him to go to Oxford, Cambridge,
Lincoln, Coventry, and every collegiate church near."
735   —Any thing but Rowley! And when the hopes he had
entertained of engaging in such projects fail him, he
cheerfully betakes himself to the lowest of all literary
labour. He writes any thing and every thing for the
magazines. Projects the Moderator; supports the
740   Town and Country; "writes, for a whim, for the
Gospel Magazine;" contributes to the London,
Middlesex Freeholders', Court and City;—and
Registers and Museums get all they ask from him.
Thus, we say, with these ultimate views, was he
745   constantly at work in this London pilgrimage; at
work, heart and soul; living on a halfpenny roll, or a
penny tart, and a glass of water a day, with now and

729. *this London*: cp. *Waring* 26.

then a sheep's tongue; writing all the while brave
letters about his happiness and success to his grand-
750   mother, mother, and sister at Bristol, the only
creatures he loved as they loved him; and managing, in
as miraculous a way as any of his old exercises of
power, to buy them china, and fans, and gowns, and
so forth, out of his (we cannot calculate how few)
755   pence a day;—being, as such a genius could not but be,
the noblest-hearted of mortals. To be sure he had
better have swept a crossing in the streets than adopted
such a method of getting bread and water; but he had
tried to find another outlet till he was sick to the soul,
760   and in this he had been driven to he resolved to stay. If
he could, he would have got, for instance, his
livelihood as a surgeon. "Before he left Bristol, Mr.
Barrett," says his sister, "lent him many books on
surgery, and I believe he bought many more, as I
765   remember to have packed them up to send to him in
London;" and almost the only intelligible phrase in a
mad letter of gibberish, addressed to a friend about the
same time, is to the effect that "he is resolved to
forsake the Parnassian mount, and would advise that
770   friend to do so too, and attain the mystery of
composing *smegma*"—*ointment* we suppose. But nobody would help him, and this way he was helping
himself, though never so little.
        Sufficient for the Magazine price and Magazine
775   purpose was the piece contributed. "Maria Friendless"
and the "Hunter of Oddities" may be a medley of
Johnson and Steele;—the few shillings they brought,
fully they were worth, though only meant to give a
minute's pleasure. As well expect to find, at this time
780   of day, the sheep's tongues on which he lived
unwasted, and the halfpenny loaves no way diminished,
as find his poor "Oratorio" (the price of a gown for his
sister), or bundle of words for tunes that procured
these viands, as pleasant as ever. "Great profligacy and
785   tergiversification in his political writings!" is muttered
now, and was solemnly outspoken once, as if he were
not in some sort still a scrivener—writing out in plain

---

771. smegma" – ointment we suppose: in the original letter, this is in fact a joke
about remedies for venereal disease.
785. tergiversification: we are reluctant to emend this happy error, whether
B.'s or the compositor's.

text-hand the wants of all kinds of men of all kinds of
parties. Such sought utterance, and had a right to find
790   it—there was an end. There might be plenty of
falsehood in this new course, as he would soon have
found; but it seemed as truth itself, compared with the
old expedients he had escaped from. The point is, *No
more Rowley*. His connexion with the Magazines had
795   commenced with Rowley—they had readily inserted
portions of his poems—and we cannot conceive a
more favourable field of enterprise than London
would have afforded, had he been disposed to go on
with the fabrication. No prying intimates, nor familiar
800   townsmen, in Mrs. Angel's quiet lodging! He had the
ear, too, of many booksellers. Now would indeed
have been the white minute for discoveries and
forgeries. He was often pressed for matter; had to
solicit all his Bristol acquaintance for contributions
805   (some of such go under his own name now, possibly);
but with the one exception we have alluded to
(affecting for a passage in which his own destitute
condition is too expressly described to admit of
mistake)—the Ballad of Charity—*Rowley was done
810   with*.

    We shall go no farther—the little we proposed to
attempt, having here its completion—though the
plastic and co-ordinating spirit which distinguishes
Chatterton so remarkably, seems perhaps stronger
815   than ever in these last few days of his existence. We
must not stay to speak of it. But ever in Chatterton did
his acquisitions, varied and abundant as they were, do
duty so as to seem but a little out of more in reserve. If
only a foreign word clung to his memory, he was sure
820   to reproduce it as if a whole language lay close
behind—setting sometimes to work with the poorest

788. text-hand: 'a fine large hand in writing' (*OED*); deriving from the
practice of writing the text of ancient manuscripts in a large hand, and the
glosses in a smaller hand.
802. white minute: 'white' in this context has the rare sense of 'favourable,
auspicious' (*OED*); cp. *Sibrandus* 7: 'the white of a matin-prime'.
816-26. But ever in Chatterton ... go far indeed: cp. *Sordello* ii 215-19; also B.
to EBB. (3 Aug. 1846): 'I want to be a Poet – to read books which make wise
in their various ways, to see just so much of nature and the ways of men as
seem necessary – and having done this already in some degree, I can easily
and cheerfully afford to go without any or all of it for the future, if called
upon, – and so live on, and "use up," my past acquisitions such as they are ...

materials; like any painter a fathom below ground in the Inquisition, who in his penury of colour turns the weather-stains on his dungeon wall into effects of light 825 and shade, or outlines of objects, and makes the single sputter of red paint in his possession go far indeed! Not that we consider the mere fabrication of old poetry so difficult a matter. For what *is* poetry, whether old or new, will have its full flow in such a scheme; and any 830 difficulty or uncouthness of phrase that elsewhere would stop its course at once, here not only passes with it, but confers the advantage of authenticity on what, in other circumstances, it deforms: the uncouth-ness will be set down to our time, and whatever 835 significancy may lurk in it will expand to an original meaning of unlimited magnitude. But there is fine, the finest poetry in Chatterton. And surely, when such an Adventurer so perishes in the Desert, we do not limit his discoveries to the last authenticated spot of ground 840 he pitched tent upon, dug intrenchments round, and wrote good tidings home from—but rather give him the benefit of the very last heap of ashes we can trace him to have kindled, and call by his name the extreme point to which we can track his torn garments and 845 abandoned treasures.

Thus much has been suggested by Mr. Wilde's method with Tasso. As by balancing conflicting statements, interpreting doubtful passages, and reconciling discrepant utterances, he has examined 850 whether Tasso was true or false, loved or did not love the Princess of Este, was or was not beloved by her,—so have we sought, from similar evidences, if Chatterton was towards the end of his life hardening himself in deception or striving to cast it off. Let others 855 apply in like manner our inquiry to other great spirits partially obscured, and they will but use us—we hope more effectually—as we have used these able and interesting volumes.

---

putting, as I always have done, my whole pride, if that is the proper name, in the being able to work with the least possible materials' (*LK* 926-7).

Appendix D

Alphabetical List of Browning's Poems, Plays, and Verse Translations

Titles are those of the first published text, except those which relate to arrangements discarded in this edition, e.g. the first-edition pairing 'Camp and Cloister', which consisted of 'I.—Camp' and 'II.—Cloister': we use the titles given when the poems were separated in later eds., 'Incident of the French Camp' and 'Soliloquy of the Spanish Cloister'. We have given titles to untitled poems: in the case of published poems we use the first line; in the case of unpublished poems we give our title (marked †), followed by the first line in brackets.

Where a title was substantially revised in a later edition, we give both forms, each time followed by the alternative form in square brackets; see e.g. the entries for 'The Bishop Orders His Tomb at Saint Praxed's Church' and 'The Tomb at St. Praxed's'.

Titles of poems which are parts of a larger grouping are listed individually, along with the group title: e.g. there is an entry for 'Garden-Fancies' and for the two poems which comprise it, 'The Flower's Name' and 'Sibrandus Schafnaburgensis'. Entries for the individual poems in such groups are followed by the title, in round brackets, of the group to which they belong.

Titles of collections of shorter poems are capitalized (e.g. ASOLANDO, DRAMATIC LYRICS). Titles of single works separately published are in small capitals (e.g. FIFINE AT THE FAIR). Titles are followed by the date of publication. Single works which were first published in pairs are listed separately, with the title of the volume omitted, e.g. 'CHRISTMAS-EVE (1850)' and 'EASTER DAY (1850)'; the complete volume is also listed separately, e.g. CHRISTMAS-EVE AND EASTER DAY (1850). Shorter poems are followed by the title and date of the collection in which they were first published, e.g. 'Cleon (*Men and Women*, 1855)'. Uncollected poems are not dated.

A Bean-Stripe; Also, Apple-Eating (*Ferishtah's Fancies*, 1884)
A BLOT IN THE 'SCUTCHEON (1843)
Abt Vogler (*Dramatis Personae*, 1864)
A Camel-Driver (*Ferishtah's Fancies*, 1884)
Adam, Lilith, and Eve (*Jocoseria*, 1883)

A Death in the Desert (*Dramatis Personae*, 1864)
A Face (*Dramatis Personae*, 1864)
A Forgiveness (*Pacchiarotto*, 1876)
After (*Men and Women*, 1855)
A Grammarian's Funeral (*Men and Women*, 1855)
A Light Woman (*Men and Women*, 1855)
A Likeness (*Dramatis Personae*, 1864)
Along the Beach (James Lee iv; *Dramatis Personae*, 1864)
A Lovers' Quarrel (*Men and Women*, 1855)
Among the Rocks (James Lee vii; *Dramatis Personae*, 1864)
Amphibian (prologue to *Fifine at the Fair*, 1872)
Andrea del Sarto (*Men and Women*, 1855)
An Epistle Containing the Strange Medical Experience of Karshish,
    the Arab Physician (*Men and Women*, 1855)
Another Way of Love (*Men and Women*, 1855)
Any Wife to Any Husband (*Men and Women*, 1855)
A Pearl, A Girl (*Asolando*, 1889)
A Pillar at Sebzevar (*Ferishtah's Fancies*, 1884)
Apollo and the Fates: A Prologue (*Parleyings*, 1887)
Apparent Failure (*Dramatis Personae*, 1864)
Appearances (*Pacchiarotto*, 1876)
A Pretty Woman (*Men and Women*, 1855)
Arcades Ambo (*Asolando*, 1889)
ARISTOPHANES' APOLOGY (1875)
† A Round Robin ('Dear Hosmer; or still dearer, Hatty')
Artemis Prologuizes (*Dramatic Lyrics*, 1842)
A Serenade at the Villa (*Men and Women*, 1855)
'Ask not one least word of praise!' (*Ferishtah's Fancies*, 1884)
ASOLANDO (1889)
A SOUL'S TRAGEDY (1846)
A Toccata of Galuppi's (*Men and Women*, 1855)
At the "Mermaid" (*Pacchiarotto*, 1876)
At the Window [James Lee's Wife Speaks at the Window] (James Lee
    i; *Dramatis Personae*, 1864)
A Woman's Last Word (*Men and Women*, 1855)

Bad Dreams (*Asolando*, 1889)
BALAUSTION'S ADVENTURE (1871)
Bean-Feast, The (*Ferishtah's Fancies*, 1884)
Beatrice Signorini (*Asolando*, 1889)
Before (*Men and Women*, 1855)
Ben Karshook's Wisdom

Bernard de Mandeville, With (*Parleyings*, 1887)
Beside the Drawing-Board (James Lee viii; *Dramatis Personae*, 1864)
Bifurcation (*Pacchiarotto*, 1876)
Bishop Blougram's Apology (*Men and Women*, 1855)
Bishop Orders His Tomb at Saint Praxed's Church, The [The Tomb
    at St. Praxed's] (*Dramatic Romances and Lyrics*, 1845)
Boot and Saddle [My Wife Gertrude] (Cavalier Tunes iii; *Dramatic
    Lyrics*, 1842)
Boy and the Angel, The (*Dramatic Romances and Lyrics*, 1845)
† Burlesque on the Pronunciation of "Metamorphosis" (' 'Twas
    Goethe taught us all')
By the Fire-Side (*Men and Women*, 1855)
By the Fireside (James Lee ii; *Dramatis Personae*, 1864)

Caliban Upon Setebos (*Dramatis Personae*, 1864)
Cardinal and the Dog, The (*Asolando*, 1889)
Cavalier Tunes (*Dramatic Lyrics*, 1842)
Cenciaja (*Pacchiarotto*, 1876)
Charles Avison, With (*Parleyings*, 1887)
Cherries (*Ferishtah's Fancies*, 1884)
"Childe Roland to the Dark Tower Came" (*Men and Women*, 1855)
CHRISTMAS-EVE AND EASTER DAY (1850)
CHRISTMAS-EVE (1850)
Christopher Smart, With (*Parleyings*, 1887)
Claret and Tokay (*Dramatic Romances and Lyrics*, 1845)
Cleon (*Men and Women*, 1855)
Clive (*Dramatic Idyls, Second Series*, 1880)
Cockney Anthology—a Specimen. On Andrea del Sarto's "*Jupiter and
    Leda*"
COLOMBE'S BIRTHDAY (1844)
Confessional, The (*Dramatic Romances and Lyrics*, 1845)
Confessions (*Men and Women*, 1855)
† Conversation with the Captain ('Sipping grog one day at sea')
Count Gismond (*Dramatic Lyrics*, 1842)
Cristina (*Dramatic Lyrics*, 1842)
Cristina and Monaldeschi (*Jocoseria*, 1883)

Dance of Death, The
Daniel Bartoli, With (*Parleyings*, 1887)
Deaf and Dumb (*Dramatis Personae*, 1864)
"De Gustibus—" (*Men and Women*, 1855)
Delivery to the Secular Arm: A Scene During the Existence of the

Spanish Inquisition at Antwerp, The
Development (*Asolando*, 1889)
† Dialogue between Father and Daughter ('F. Then what do you say
   to the poem of Mizpah?')
Dictated by the Spirit of Shelley to Sophia
Dîs Aliter Visum (*Dramatis Personae*, 1864)
Doctor — (*Dramatic Idyls, Second Series*, 1880)
Dogma Triumphant, The
Donald (*Jocoseria*, 1883)
DRAMATIC IDYLS (1879)
DRAMATIC IDYLS, SECOND SERIES (1880)
DRAMATIC LYRICS (1842)
DRAMATIC ROMANCES AND LYRICS (1845)
Dubiety (*Asolando*, 1889)
Duty

Eagle, The (*Ferishtah's Fancies*, 1884)
Earth's Immortalities (*Dramatic Romances and Lyrics*, 1845)
EASTER DAY (1850)
Echetlos (*Dramatic Idyls, Second Series*, 1880)
England in Italy [The Englishman in Italy] (*Dramatic Romances and
   Lyrics*, 1845)
Englishman in Italy, The [England in Italy] (*Dramatic Romances and
   Lyrics*, 1845)
† Epigram on magistrates ('Without their ensigns, axe & fasces')
Epilogue (*Asolando*, 1889)
Epilogue (*Dramatis Personae*, 1864)
Epilogue (*Ferishtah's Fancies*, 1884)
Epilogue (*Pacchiarotto*, 1876)
† Epitaph for James Dow and his Family ('Words we might else have
   been compelled to say')
Epps
Eurydice to Orpheus (*Dramatis Personae*, 1864)
Evelyn Hope (*Men and Women*, 1855)

Fame (Earth's Immortalities i; *Dramatic Romances and Lyrics*, 1845)
Family, The (*Ferishtah's Fancies*, 1884)
Fears and Scruples (*Pacchiarotto*, 1876)
FERISHTAH'S FANCIES (1884)
FIFINE AT THE FAIR (1872)
'Fire is in the flint: true, once a spark escapes' (*Ferishtah's Fancies*,
   1884)

First-Born of Egypt, The
Filippo Baldinucci on the Privilege of Burial (*Pacchiarotto*, 1876)
Flight of the Duchess, The (*Dramatic Romances and Lyrics*, 1845)
Flower's Name, The (Garden Fancies i; *Dramatic Romances and Lyrics*, 1845)
Flute-Music, with an Accompaniment (*Asolando*, 1889)
Founder of the Feast, The
† Fragment of a Sonnet ('All we can dream of loveliness within')
Fra Lippo Lippi (*Men and Women*, 1855)
Francis Furini, With (*Parleyings*, 1887)
Fust and His Friends: An Epilogue (*Parleyings*, 1889)

Garden Fancies (*Dramatic Romances and Lyrics*, 1845)
George Bubb Dodington, With (*Parleyings*, 1887)
Gerard de Lairesse, With (*Parleyings*, 1887)
Gerousios Oinos
Give a Rouse (Cavalier Tunes ii; *Dramatic Lyrics*, 1842)
Glove, The (*Dramatic Romances and Lyrics*, 1845)
Gold Hair (*Dramatis Personae*, 1864)
Goldoni
'Good, to forgive' (prologue to *La Saisiaz*, 1878)
Guardian Angel, The (*Men and Women*, 1855)

Halbert and Hob (*Dramatic Idyls*, 1879)
Helen's Tower
† Here's to Nelson's memory! (*Dramatic Romances and Lyrics*, 1845)
Heretic's Tragedy, The (*Men and Women*, 1855)
Hervé Riel (*Pacchiarotto*, 1876)
Holy-Cross Day (*Men and Women*, 1855)
Home-Thoughts, from Abroad (*Dramatic Romances and Lyrics*, 1845)
Home-Thoughts, from the Sea ['Nobly Cape Saint Vincent'] (*Dramatic Romances and Lyrics*, 1845)
House (*Pacchiarotto*, 1876)
Householder, The (epilogue to *Fifine at the Fair*, 1872)
How It Strikes a Contemporary (*Men and Women*, 1855)
"How They Brought the Good News from Ghent to Aix" (*Dramatic Romances and Lyrics*, 1845)
Humility (*Asolando*, 1889)

"Imperante Augusto Natus Est—" (*Asolando*, 1889)
† Impromptu for Marie Bancroft ('Her advent was not hailed with shouts')

† Impromptu on a Painting ('He gazed and gazed and gazed and gazed')

† Impromptu on Burne-Jones ('Don't play with sharp tools, these are edge 'uns')

Impromptu on Hearing a Sermon by the Rev. T. R—— Pronounced "Heavy"

In a Balcony (*Men and Women*, 1855)

In a Gondola (*Dramatic Lyrics*, 1842)

Inapprehensiveness (*Asolando*, 1889)

In a Year (*Men and Women*, 1855)

Incident of the French Camp (*Dramatic Lyrics*, 1842)

INN ALBUM, THE (1875)

† Inscription on a Sketch of Himself ('Here I'm gazing, wide awake')

Instans Tyrannus (*Men and Women*, 1855)

In the Doorway (James Lee iii; *Dramatis Personae*, 1864)

In Three Days (*Men and Women*, 1855)

Isle's Enchantress, The

Italian in England, The [Italy in England] (*Dramatic Romances and Lyrics*, 1845)

Italy in England [The Italian in England] (*Dramatic Romances and Lyrics*, 1845)

Iván Ivànovitch (*Dramatic Idyls*, 1879)

Ixion (*Jocoseria*, 1883)

James Lee [James Lee's Wife] (*Dramatis Personae*, 1864)

James Lee's Wife Speaks at the Window [At the Window] (James Lee i; *Dramatis Personae*, 1864)

Jochanan Hakkadosh (*Jocoseria*, 1883)

JOCOSERIA (1883)

Johannes Agricola [Johannes Agricola in Meditation] (*Dramatic Lyrics*, 1842)

K. de K. Bronson

King, The

KING VICTOR AND KING CHARLES (1842)

Laboratory, The (*Dramatic Romances and Lyrics*, 1845)

Lady and the Painter, The (*Asolando*, 1889)

LA SAISIAZ AND THE TWO POETS OF CROISIC (1878)

LA SAISIAZ (1878)

Last Poem

Last Ride Together, The (*Men and Women*, 1855)

Life in a Love (*Men and Women*, 1855)
† Limerick for Mrs Fitzgerald ('There was a sky-painter at Folkestone')
Lines
† Lines for a Gift ('The gift is small')
† Lines for a Picture by Leighton ('Yellow and pale as ripened corn')
† Lines for Edith Longfellow ('Thus I wrote in London, musing on my betters')
† Lines for Mary FitzGerald ('Oh Love, I bring no posies')
† Lines in a Letter to Katharine Bronson ('Be the next three months a game at Tennis')
† Lines in a Letter to Katharine Bronson ('Is Loredano proved the worst of vipers')
† Lines Inscribed on the Jubilee Window ('Fifty years' flight! Wherein should he rejoice')
† Lines on Correggio ('Could I, heart-broken, reach his place of birth')
† Lines on Coventry Patmore ('A prig, sir, is Coventry Patmore!')
† Lines on Dickens ('In Dickens, sure, philosophy was lacking')
† Lines on Disraeli ('We don't want to fight')
† Lines on Publishers ('The air one breathes with Smith may be the sharper')
† Lines on Swinburne ('And now in turn see Swinburne bent')
† Lines on Wagner ('Wagner gave six concerts: five')
† Lines to a Lady ('Oh, faithless fair!')
† Lines to Helen Faucit ('There's a sisterhood in words')
† Lines to Ignaz Moscheles ('Hail to the man who upward strives')
† Lines to Isa Blagden ('Oh, my Isa! Ah, my Annette!')
† Lines to Miss Unger ('Dear Miss Unger')
† Lines Transcribed by EBB. ('How much upon a level')
Lost Leader, The (*Dramatic Romances and Lyrics*, 1845)
Lost Mistress, The (*Dramatic Romances and Lyrics*, 1845)
Love (Earth's Immortalities ii) (*Dramatic Romances and Lyrics*, 1845)
Love Among the Ruins (*Men and Women*, 1855)
Love in a Life (*Men and Women*, 1855)
LURIA AND A SOUL'S TRAGEDY (1846)
LURIA: A TRAGEDY IN FIVE ACTS (1846)

Magical Nature (*Pacchiarotto*, 1876)
'Man I am and man would be, Love—merest man and nothing more' (*Ferishtah's Fancies*, 1884)
Marching Along (Cavalier Tunes i; *Dramatic Lyrics*, 1842)

Margaret E. Keep. Magari
Martin Relph (*Dramatic Idyls*, 1879)
Master Hugues of Saxe-Gotha (*Men and Women*, 1855)
May and Death (*Dramatis Personae*, 1864)
Meeting at Night [Night] (Night and Morning i; *Dramatic Romances and Lyrics*, 1845)
Melon-Seller, The (*Ferishtah's Fancies*, 1884)
Memorabilia (*Men and Women*, 1855)
MEN AND WOMEN (1855)
Mesmerism (*Men and Women*, 1855)
† Metrical Exercise ('O the terror of the death song of Urgandea')
Mettle and Metal
Mihrab Shah (*Ferishtah's Fancies*, 1884)
Misconceptions (*Men and Women*, 1855)
Morning [Parting at Morning] (Night and Morning ii; *Dramatic Romances and Lyrics*, 1845)
"Moses" of Michael Angelo, The
Mr. Sludge, "the Medium" (*Dramatis Personae*, 1864)
Muckle-Mouth Meg (*Asolando*, 1889)
Muléykeh (*Dramatic Idyls, Second Series*, 1880)
My Last Duchess (*Dramatic Lyrics*, 1842)
My Star (*Men and Women*, 1855)

Names, The
Nationality in Drinks (combining *Claret and Tokay* with *Here's to Nelson's memory*: first published with this title, *Poetical Works*, 1863)
Natural Magic (*Pacchiarotto*, 1876)
Ned Bratts (*Dramatic Idyls*, 1879)
Never the Time and the Place (*Jocoseria*, 1883)
Night [Meeting at Night] (Night and Morning i; *Dramatic Romances and Lyrics*, 1845)
'Nobly Cape Saint Vincent' [Home-Thoughts, from the Sea] (*Dramatic Romances and Lyrics*, 1845)
'Not with my Soul, Love!—bid no Soul like mine' (*Ferishtah's Fancies*, 1884)
Now (*Asolando*, 1889)
Numpholeptos (*Pacchiarotto*, 1876)

Of Pacchiarotto, and How He Worked in Distemper (*Pacchiarotto*, 1876)
Old Pictures in Florence (*Men and Women*, 1855)

On Being Defied to Express in a Hexameter: "You Ought to Sit on
the Safety-Valve"
'Once I saw a chemist take a pinch of powder' (*Ferishtah's Fancies*,
1884)
On Deck (James Lee ix; *Dramatis Personae*, 1864)
One Way of Love (*Men and Women*, 1855)
One Word More (*Men and Women*, 1855)
On the Cliff (James Lee v; *Dramatis Personae*, 1864)
On the Deleterious Effects of Tea

PACCHIAROTTO AND HOW HE WORKED IN DISTEMPER:
WITH OTHER POEMS (1876)
Pambo (*Jocoseria*, 1883)
Pan and Luna (*Dramatic Idyls, Second Series*, 1880)
PARACELSUS (1835)

PARLEYINGS WITH CERTAIN PEOPLE OF IMPORTANCE
IN THEIR DAY (1887)
Parting at Morning [Morning] (Night and Morning ii; *Dramatic
Romances and Lyrics*, 1845)
Patriot, The (*Men and Women*, 1855)
PAULINE: A FRAGMENT OF A CONFESSION (1833)
Pheidippides (*Dramatic Idyls*, 1879)
Pictor Ignotus (*Dramatic Romances and Lyrics*, 1845)
Pied Piper of Hamelin: A Child's Story, The (*Dramatic Lyrics*, 1842)
Pietro of Abano (*Dramatic Idyls, Second Series*, 1880)
PIPPA PASSES (1841)
Pisgah Sights I (*Pacchiarotto*, 1876)
Pisgah Sights II (*Pacchiarotto*, 1876)
Plot-Culture (*Ferishtah's Fancies*, 1884)
Poetics (*Asolando*, 1889)
Ponte dell' Angelo, Venice (*Asolando*, 1889)
Pope and the Net, The (*Asolando*, 1889)
Popularity (*Men and Women*, 1855)
Porphyria [Porphyria's Lover] (*Dramatic Lyrics*, 1842)
Porphyria's Lover [Porphyria] (*Dramatic Lyrics*, 1842)
PRINCE HOHENSTIEL-SCHWANGAU, SAVIOUR OF SOCIETY (1871)
Prologue (*Asolando*, 1889)
Prologue (*Ferishtah's Fancies*, 1884)
Prologue (*Pacchiarotto*, 1876)
Prospice (*Dramatis Personae*, 1864)
Protus (*Men and Women*, 1855)

Rabbi Ben Ezra (*Dramatis Personae*, 1864)

Reading a Book, Under the Cliff [Under the Cliff] (James Lee vi; *Dramatis Personae*, 1864)

RED COTTON NIGHT-CAP COUNTRY (1873)

Rephan (*Asolando*, 1889)

Replies to Challenges to Rhyme

Respectability (*Men and Women*, 1855)

RETURN OF THE DRUSES, THE (1842)

Reverie (*Asolando*, 1889)

† Rhyming Exercise ('He a recreant; in me a true knight thou dub'st, and')

† Rhyming exercise ('He for his volume meant')

† Rhyming exercise ('Imposthume—costume—I had lost you M'M')

RING AND THE BOOK, THE (1868-9)

Rosny (*Asolando*, 1889)

'Round us the wild creatures, overhead the trees' (*Ferishtah's Fancies*, 1884)

Rudel and the Lady of Tripoli (*Dramatic Lyrics*, 1842)

Saint Martin's Summer (*Pacchiarotto*, 1876)

Saul (sections 1-9, *Dramatic Romances and Lyrics*, 1845; complete, *Men and Women*, 1855)

Shah Abbas (*Ferishtah's Fancies*, 1884)

Shop (*Pacchiarotto*, 1876)

Sibrandus Schafnaburgensis (Garden Fancies ii; *Dramatic Romances and Lyrics*, 1845)

Soliloquy of the Spanish Cloister (*Dramatic Lyrics*, 1842)

Solomon and Balkis (*Jocoseria*, 1883)

Song (*Dramatic Romances and Lyrics*, 1845)

Sonnet

† Sonnet on Rawdon Brown ('Sighed Rawdon Brown: "Yes, I'm departing, Toni!'')

SORDELLO (1840)

'So, the head aches and the limbs are faint!' (*Ferishtah's Fancies*, 1884)

Speculative (*Asolando*, 1889)

Statue and the Bust, The (*Men and Women*, 1855)

STRAFFORD (1837)

Study of a Hand, by Lionardo

'Such a starved bank of moss' (prologue to *The Two Poets of Croisic*, 1878)

Summum Bonum (*Asolando*, 1889)

Sun, The (*Ferishtah's Fancies*, 1884)

Terse Verse

Through the Metidja to Abd-el-Kadr—1842 (*Dramatic Lyrics*, 1842)

Time's Revenges (*Dramatic Romances and Lyrics*, 1845)

To Edward FitzGerald

Tomb at St. Praxed's, The [The Bishop Orders His Tomb at Saint Praxed's Church] (*Dramatic Romances and Lyrics*, 1845)

Too Late (*Dramatis Personae*, 1864)

' "Touch him ne'er so lightly, into song he broke"' (epilogue to *Dramatic Idyls, Second Series*, 1880)

"Transcendentalism: A Poem in Twelve Books" (*Men and Women*, 1855)

† Translation from the Italian ('What seems a soul where Love's outside the porch')

† Translation of Epigram by Goethe ('Be it your unerring rule')

† Translation of Lines by Apollonius ('He said—and stopped the lyre together with the heavenly voice')

† Translation of Lines by Dante ('And sinners were we to the extreme hour')

† Translation of Lines by Euripides ('Oh Love, Love, thou that from the eyes diffusest')

† Translation of Lines by Horace ('All singers, trust me, have this common vice')

† Translation of Lines by Lorenzo de' Medici ('Where's Luigi Pulci, that one don't the man see?')

† Translation of Lines by Pindar ('And to these Rhodians She, the Sharp-eyed One')

† Translation of Lines from the Anacreontea ('Horns to bulls, gave nature')

† Translation of Lines from the *Iliad* ('She, thus having spoken, departed, the swift-footed Iris')

† Translation of Poem by Wilhelime von Hillern ('The blind man to the maiden said')

† Translation of Quatrain Attributed to Pietro of Abano ('Studying my ciphers, with the compass')

Tray (*Dramatic Idyls*, 1879)

Twins, The (*Men and Women*, 1855)

Two Camels (*Ferishtah's Fancies*, 1884)

Two in the Campagna (*Men and Women*, 1855)

TWO POETS OF CROISIC, THE (1878)

Under the Cliff [Reading a Book, Under the Cliff] (James Lee vi; *Dramatis Personae*, 1864)

Up at a Villa—Down in the City (*Men and Women*, 1855)

† Variation on Lines by Landor ('An Angel from his Paradise drove Adam')
'Verse-making was least of my virtues: I viewed with despair' (*Ferishtah's Fancies*, 1884)
† Verse Telegram to George Bancroft ('Bancroft, the message-bearing wire')
Very Original Poem, Written with Even a Greater Endeavour Than Ordinary After Intelligibility, and Hitherto Only Published on the First Leaf of the Author's Son's Account-Book

Wanting Is—What? (*Jocoseria*, 1883)
Waring (*Dramatic Lyrics*, 1842)
'What a pretty tale you told me' (epilogue to *The Two Poets of Croisic*, 1878)
'When I vexed you and you chid me' (*Ferishtah's Fancies*, 1884)
Which? (*Asolando*, 1889)
White Witchcraft (*Asolando*, 1889)
' "Why from the world" Ferishtah smiled "should thanks' (*Ferishtah's Fancies*, 1884)
Why I Am a Liberal
'Wish no word unspoken, want no look away!' (*Ferishtah's Fancies*, 1884)
Women and Roses (*Men and Women*, 1855)
Worst of It, The (*Dramatis Personae*, 1864)
Written to be Inscribed on the Gravestone of Levi Thaxter

' "You are sick, that's sure"—they say' (prologue to *Dramatic Idyls, Second Series*, 1880)
'You groped your way across my room i' the dear dark dead of night' (*Ferishtah's Fancies*, 1884)
Youth and Art (*Dramatis Personae*, 1864)

Index of Titles and First Lines

This includes alternative or later titles; also the individual sections of *Claret and Tokay*, *Garden Fancies*, *Earth's Immortalities*, and *Night and Morning*, and the songs from *Pippa Passes*.